THE OBAMA ANNALS

THE OBAMA ANNALS

A Weekly Chronicle of the Obama Years

By
Andrew P. Zappia

LIBERTY HILL PUBLISHING

Liberty Hill Press
2301 Lucien Way #415
Maitland, FL 32751
407.339.4217
www.libertyhillpublishing.com

Printed in the United States of America.

Library of Congress Control Number: 2020911194

Paperback ISBN-13: 978-1-6312-9578-2
Ebook ISBN-13: 978-1-6312-9579-9

INTRODUCTION

The election of Barak Obama as President of the United States was a watershed moment for our nation. Not only was he the first African American ever elected to our highest office, but he also won in a landslide at a time of financial crisis at home, and wars and terrorist threats abroad. Mr. Obama won the presidency with a message of hope and change for America. During his eight years in office, America and Mr. Obama changed in many ways, but for millions of Americans, throughout his 8 years as President, Mr. Obama remained an emblem of a better future for America, even if at times that better future seemed remote.

This book is a chronicle of the Obama Presidency, from its first week until its last. Each week of his eight year term is recounted and analyzed, creating a clear picture of Mr. Obama the man, his goals, motivations, strategies, and his opponents. It is a contemporaneous history of his presidency, with each weekly chapter written within days of the events described. What emerges from this chronicle is a history of the man, his times, his achievements, and his failures. The chapters have neither been revised with hindsight, nor updated to reflect future events. Instead, the book is an assessment of the Obama Presidency as that presidency was unfolding, week by week. The analysis and assessments evolve during the course of the book, just as Mr. Obama himself evolved. The book ends where it began, on the West Portico of the Capitol, with one President being sworn in and his predecessor departing. It is for the reader to judge how much America changed in the interim, and how much hope endured.

Week 1

(NOT YOUR DADDY'S LIBERAL)

January 25, 2009

The first week of a Presidency sets the tone. A new president wants to convey to the country how he will govern by his words and his initial deeds. Barak Obama's first week was no different. Elected as our first African American president, Obama wanted to set a tone of change, competence, and reassurance. Obama ran on change and rode a tidal wave of discontent to victory. By both his inaugural address and his early executive orders, he signaled to the country that change has come: not just by his policies, but also by his own improbable ascendance to the presidency. Obama's executive orders closing Gitmo, limiting lobbyist access, allowing taxpayer funded international abortion counseling, and barring torture are promises kept and signposts for change.

Obama has also been very careful to show poise and confidence in his early days as president. Many Americans were not sure he was ready for the job. Projecting early competence and maturity helps calm those fears and is crucially needed in this time of economic upheaval. By surrounding himself with a diverse and impressive cabinet, Obama further instilled a sense of confidence.

Yet most telling of all was his inaugural address. Many conservatives feared Obama's leftism. Would Obama govern from the left or the center was the continual question. In his address, Obama changed the terms of the debate. He paid homage to our constitutional tradition and spoke as a patriot, but he also condemned the traditional Left/Right debate and tried to forge a new consensus. He said the issue with government is not its size, it is government's effectiveness. He said all agree the market is the engine for growth and freedom, but government as watchdog is essential. He said America must be a leader against terrorism and brutal regimes using the best of our ideals and smart power.

What does all this tell us? Obama is a progressive no doubt. But he is not an old style liberal. No, he's a Reagan Progressive. A liberal who came of age in the Reagan era. One who knows America must combat the world's evils, but wants to do so with liberal idealism as well as military might. One who believes in capitalism and free markets, but sees an essential role for government in curbing their excesses. One who respects the centrality of religious and social issues to many Americans, but strives for inclusiveness. He is the American equivalent of New Labor in Britain. He is trying to change the political debate from a traditional right/left divide, to a debate between stale ideas and a modern progressive future. The issue will be whether his departure from traditional liberalism will be as stark as Blair's break with old Labor in the U.K. Only time will tell.

1

Week 2

(STIMULATE ME BABY)

February 1, 2009

The first major legislative effort of the Obama Administration is the stimulus bill. A bill that has been touted as a program to jumpstart the U.S. economy. Its massive scope–more than $800 billion dollars–is designed to show voters that their government is focused on reviving the economy. But the bill actually says more about government as usual, rather than government as savior.

Obama ran on a slogan of "change we can believe in," but his stimulus bill is mostly about "pork we can shove in." Less than half of the spending in the stimulus bill presented this week will hit the economy in 2009, nearly all the spending is focused heavily on the public sector (rather than stimulating private section growth), and the bill includes entitlement expansions sure to lead to huge expenditures in the future.

What the Democrat Congress has done is use the current economic crisis to pursue its long term social spending goals, while dressing the bill up as stimulus. Everyone expected this from the House Democrats, but what about Obama. He ran as a post-racial post-partisan leader, but he is now the promoter of a partisan stimulus bill that failed to get even a single Republican vote in the House. In the end, the stimulus bill is a fraud, but what is the Obama role in it? Is he the mastermind of the fraud? Is he bowing to Congressional Democrats just to get any bill? Is he a true reformer who will fight to change the bill as it goes to the Senate and remake it into a true job creation bill?

We all know that the Great Depression created the opportunity for FDR to transform our system of government from a limited government of delegated powers into vast intrusive government with social engineering as its goal. Many Democrats see the current economic crisis as an opportunity to yet again transform our government into a more European style social democracy, creating a government that consumes a much greater proportion of GDP and whose appetite for tax revenue is unquenchable. This stimulus bill is the first step in their effort.

Democrats see this as their best opportunity in 60 years to reshape government. They are intent on seizing that opportunity. Whether Obama sees himself as part of that effort or a moderating influence is not clear. How he deals with the stimulus bill will help us answer that question.

Week 3

(INTERVIEWEE-IN-CHIEF)

February 8, 2009

Most believe that the office of President of the United States is the most demanding job in the world. The office combines the roles of head of state, head of government, and commander-in-chief of our armed forces. This is a full plate for anyone. This is especially true in this time of economic turmoil and international threats. Yet Obama wears of burdens of his office very lightly. Apart from his impressive intellect, the most remarkable thing about Obama is his comfort and poise in almost any situation. He has a serine self-confidence, but without obvious arrogance. He knows what he wants to do, he knows why he wants to do it, and he is confident he can accomplish it. That is leadership.

But this week, Obama seemed to forget that leadership is not just setting themes and showing poise. He seemed to confuse campaigning with governing. This week we saw Obama lose control of his message, lose control of his party, and nearly lose control of himself. The first Obama stumble came from his cabinet appointments and their tax troubles. Geitner, Daschle, and others whom the Obama team selected did not pay taxes they owed. This from an Administration that sold itself as the champion of working Americans, rather than the affluent. Hypocrisy is the bane of politicians; once you are labeled with it, credibility is quickly lost. This week Obama looked like old Washington, where wealth and access matter more than playing by the rules. This is where Obama lost his message.

Obama then lost control of his party. He made a promise to the voters that he would pass a stimulus bill. And just like his various executive orders (that kept promises even when the ultimate consequences were not thought out), Obama seemed to believe that the details of the stimulus bill matter less than just getting one through. So he allowed the appropriation barons in the House write a massive pork-filled spending spree labeled as a stimulus package. The bill was so bad, even Obama's Democrat allies in the Senate knew it had to be revamped. The bill was an embarrassment and has made Obama look weak and undermined his effort to change Washington.

Why did Obama take this approach? As a newly elected, very popular President at a time of crisis, he could have pressured Congress to pass his form of stimulus. He chose not to. He left it up to the House to craft the bill, and they did it in old Washington style. Obama had the momentum and the power to get the bill he wanted and control the process, but for some reason he chose not to. As a result, he lost credibility and lost control of his party on the stimulus bill.

Yet amidst all these problems and pressures, how did Obama spend this week: granting interviews. Obama has been on a media blitz, giving interview after interview. It seems like he would rather talk about governing than actually govern. One of the most precious things a President controls is access. Obama seems to want to give access to everyone and be on TV every night. He is starting to give the impression that he would rather interviewee-in-chief than commander-in-chief.

Week 4

(POST-PARTISAN?)

February 15, 2009

What ever happened to the post-partisan presidency? Obama was supposed to change everything, walk on water into Washington, and instantly create peace and prosperity. Well, things have not turned out that way. This week we saw Obama become what many feared he was: a partisan liberal politician. The only surprise is that it took four weeks.

Obama has made an impressive effort to change the tone in Washington. One of the frustrating things for political outsiders to observe is that our national leaders do not talk to each other. Yes, every few months there will be the photo-ops for Cabinet or Congressional leadership meetings, but those are not conversations, they are media events. Obama has made an honest effort to change that. He is gregarious enough and confident enough to invite conservatives and Republicans to the White House for meetings, lunches, dinners, and football games. He talks to them, listens, and tries to find middle ground. For this he should be applauded. But apparently, that is where it ends.

The problem for the post-partisan myth is that Obama is a liberal. Yes, he is a Reagan liberal, a modern liberal, and technocrat liberal, but a liberal nonetheless. He wants to expand government in many spheres, increase wealth redistribution, and use government to plan the private economy. That is his agenda and his supporters expect him to deliver. With that agenda, he can talk with Republicans all he wants, but he is not going to get their support or their votes. We saw that this week.

Obama's stimulus billed passed Congress. The only surprise would have been if it had not. With huge majorities and the need to get only a couple Republican votes in the Senate, there was never any doubt the bill would pass. Where the doubt lay in the kind of bill Obama would push: a true bipartisan bill or one only a liberal could love. We got the latter. The stimulus bill is not stimulus at all. It is a spending bill, setting the building blocks for Obama's plan to remake government on a European social democracy model. Most of the spending in the bill will not start until 2010, the tax cut is a mere $13 per week for most workers, the bill creates incentives to expand welfare and it bails out the overspending states.

Our economy may very well start to recover in 2009, but that recovery will have nothing to do with this stimulus bill. All this bill did was put us further in debt and further down the road to the vastly larger and more expensive government Obama hopes to create. It did not need to be this way. Obama could have taken a real step toward post-partisanship with a stimulus bill that was timely, temporary, and targeted: his own criteria for the bill. This bill is none of those things. Obama could easily have gotten Republican support if he had only added a few pro-business tax incentives to the bill, lowering the corporate tax rate for example. But he refused. Instead, he allowed the House to pass and the Senate to slightly improve a bill obviously unacceptable to any Republican. Why?

The answer is simple: Obama is deeply committed to his agenda of liberal social democracy. He is not a moderate. He is not post-partisan. He was elected to implement a liberal agenda and he is working to do it. We have a liberal president who believes there are fundamental flaws in the American way of life. Obama will use the power of his office sincerely and with the best intentions, but he wants to take our country to a place where many will not willingly go.

Week 5

(WE ARE ALL SOCIALISTS NOW)

February 22, 2009

It is well known in politics that a crisis allows leaders to do things that would not be condoned in normal times. Lincoln's repeal of habeas corpus, Roosevelt's New Deal, and Bush's Patriot Act are good examples. Now Obama's stimulus and housing plans can be added to the list. This week Obama signed his $787 billion stimulus plan and proposed a $275 billion housing bailout. Both measures are as much about Obama's political agenda as they are about the deep recession.

The stimulus plan is unprecedented for its size, but the controversy about the bill is not so much its price tag, as its priorities. As much money is spent after 2011 in this bill as is spent in 2009. That is not good stimulus by anyone's measure. The bill focuses on all kinds of Democrat priorities (like green energy, entitlement expansion, buy America provisions, and limits on executive pay) that may very well please liberals, but what do those items have to do with stimulus? The simple truth is very little and Obama knows it. These initiatives are about Obama using the current crisis as cover to achieve his agenda.

The housing proposal is a bit different. It is not just about Obama keeping political promises, it is about Obama's ideology. Ninety-two percent of American's are paying their mortgages, eight percent are not. Many of those eight percent just bought too much house or were financially irresponsible. Some were the victims of fraud or unexpected loss of income that led to default. No one knows how to separate the irresponsible borrowers from the unfortunate ones, so Obama is going to just try to bail nearly all of them out. Suddenly, Americans who were responsible and who are paying their mortgages have to pay their neighbor's mortgage as well. The responsibility society Obama purports to champion has now been exposed for what it really is: the irresponsibility society.

If you look at Obama's political agenda, his constant target for punishment are successful and responsible Americans. High income Americans must have their taxes raised, small business must be taxed to pay for healthcare, executives must not get bonuses or go to conferences, and people who pay their mortgages have to pay for other people's mortgages as well. Obama is a former law professor; he should be familiar with the idea of moral hazard. When a society rewards bad behavior, that society gets more bad behavior. When a society punishes good behavior, it gets less good behavior.

Obama's basic philosophy is that we should not have so many successful people and we should have fewer of the unsuccessful. But rather than try to expand opportunity for all people, his agenda is focused on redistribution and dependency. In his world view, the way to help the poor is to take from the responsible and successful. It is a remaking of society into a great government dependency, where government tolerates some freedom and some capitalism, but just enough so that wealth can be created, then taxed, and then redistributed by government fiat. That is social democracy and this week we see its birth.

Week 6
($4 Trillion We Can Believe In)

March 1, 2009

Obama ran on the slogan: Change We Can Believe In. Well this week, we certainly saw his vision of change, but the believing part might be hard. In his speech to a joint session of Congress and in his first budget, Obama left nothing in reserve. The plan he outlined this week for the nation is nothing short of a revolution in government on a scale similar to the New Deal. The scope and ambition is astounding. Obama proposes to create a vastly larger government that would consume some 40% of our GDP. Obama seeks to build a $1 trillion health care subsidy for the uninsured.

Obama will pursue a broad-based carbon tax that will significantly raise prices on everything from fuel, to food, to consumer goods. And how will all this be paid for: by taxing the rich of course.

Like all good liberals, Obama acts out of the self-assurance that government needs to do the thinking for the people. That is why Obama has set out a vision of fundamental change in the relationship between government and the governed. America was founded on the values of personal liberty, limited government, and free markets. Obama certainly believes in personal liberty, but he sees the ideals of limited government and free markets as relics. Obama wants an efficient and responsive government no doubt, but he also wants to government with a vastly larger social safety net and a firmer hand in the private economy. He wants government to both protect the people and guide the economy to his vision of the future. Sound familiar: it is the modern version of the same socialist agenda that swept over Europe after the crisis of World War II. Why Obama thinks it will work better this time is anyone's guess.

There is great danger in the Obama plan. America is certainly in an economic crisis, but we have been there before. But just like FDR and the New Deal, Obama has decided that our current struggle is tantamount to a guilty verdict on the traditional America system of government. Now that we have been found guilty, it is time for Obama to pass his sentence on us. Our punishment shall be government, government, and more government. The government will own your bank, pay your mortgage, give you health care, send you checks, and tell your employer to pay you more. All this sounds great, until it has to be paid for. That is where the Obama plan threatens America.

How do we pay for Obama's $4 trillion government? Well, by taxing the rich, of course. Obama is using the current crisis to make his agenda look necessary, and he is using the lie of taxing the rich to pretend we can afford it without pain. Yet Obama knows that even if you tax 100% of the income of those making more than $250,000, he still would not have enough money to pay for new his programs. Obama knows that taxes must be raised on the middle class to create his new America. Obama knows it, but he will not say it. His plan is to push his agenda through in this time of crisis and once we have our new welfare state, we will have no choice but to pay for it. Like I said, this is certainly change, but the believing part is going to be tough.

Week 7

(THE TRANSFORMATIONAL PRESIDENCY)

March 8, 2009

Most presidents are caretakers of government. Men who assume the office with modest goals fueled by political ambition. These presidents are judged by history mainly on whether they dealt competently with the challenges they faced. A few presidents take a different path. Either because of the times in which they served or their own political determination, these presidents change the terms of the debate and thereby change history. These are the transformational presidents and it is clear Barak Obama wants to be one of them.

Arguably there were only four transformational presidencies in the Twentieth Century. Theodore Roosevelt ushered in the progressive era's notion of government's responsibility to promote social good. Franklin Roosevelt created the New Deal and thus the modern regulatory state. Lyndon Johnson's Great Society brought about the beginning of the welfare state. Ronald

Reagan arrested the course of his three transformational predecessors by legitimizing a conservative alternative to activist government.

Obama's goal is to destroy the last vestiges of the Reagan Revolution and erect a government entitlement society. A society where the federal government guarantees and provides child care, welfare, education through college, health care, job training, and retirement. Our government currently does some of these things, but Obama wants to transform government programs for the needy into government entitlements and mandates for all. Obama's first budget, his pronouncements, and his messianic manner reveal his intent. He wants to transform America into a completely different society.

Obama has judged correctly that the current economic crisis creates a great opportunity for him to enact an agenda that would never pass in ordinary times. He has therefore embarked on a very dangerous game. Rather than take measures that could more effectively cure the economy (like tax cuts, tax reform, and responsible budgeting), he is using the current crisis as a rational for creating his entitlement society. Obama's gamble is that his agenda will not retard economic recovery. He thinks he can massively expand government, massively raise taxes, but nevertheless the economy will come roaring back and create the wealth needed to pay for it all. If he is correct we will survive this crisis, but we will emerge from it a different country. If he is wrong, our government will be bankrupt.

Week 8

(CLINGING TO STEM CELLS AND RELIGION)

March 15, 2009

Many people believe that Obama is a liberal elitist. His background certainly lends itself to that assessment. He attended private school in Hawaii, then went to Columbia and Harvard Law, and he taught law at Chicago while working for a politically connected law firm. Hardly a history of hardship. Yet Obama has always been skilled at projecting a common man appearance. He rarely lets his guard down enough to show how he really views the average American.

Only once during the presidential campaign did Obama have a moment of candor when he expressed his true view of middle America. During a fundraising event in California, he described middle Americans as people "clinging to guns and religion." The obvious implication of his words was that average Americans were unable to understand how to aide themselves, but instead they were deluded by Christianity and the right to bear arms. Apart from its obvious Marxist undertone, what Obama was really saying is that the average American has no idea what is good for him. That is why Obama believes government must be a social designer, forcing the average American to change habits. This is the very definition of liberal elitism, the belief that the privileged and highly educated must direct the masses to do what is good for them, because the masses are too stupid or deluded to make good choices for themselves.

Since his election, Obama has been careful not to reveal his true view of the average American. Instead, he has focused on populist rhetoric demonizing the business and the financial sectors as the authors of our current economic problems. Those private institutions have much to answer for, so not all of Obama's rhetoric is misplaced. But this week, Obama focused his first major social policy speech on a controversial issue: stem cell research. The way he framed the stem cell issue this week was a complete return to the elitism of his California speech.

In announcing his reversal of the Bush Administration's policy on stem cell research Obama described the choice before him as between science or ignorance. On the science side were medical organizations, doctors, and the pro-choice lobby, all of whom wanted stem cell restrictions lifted. On the ignorance side were those concerned about the moral implications of allowing experimentation on human embryos. By describing moral concerns about stem cell research as nothing more that the voices of ignorance, Obama was hinting at his true contempt for traditional morality.

None of the supporters of the Bush Administration policy sought to ban stem cell research. Instead, they wanted research on lines of stem cells that do not come from human embryos. Rather than address the true debate, Obama portrayed his opponents as mindless and backward. He could not resist condescending to those not enlightened enough to understand what is good for them. With his executive order on stem cell research, Obama took a swipe at every Christian who thinks our government's policies must be moral as well as practical. For that brief moment, we saw Obama's elitism in its true form.

Week 9

(POPULIST PERILS)

March 22, 2009

Presidents usually try to be a calming influence on the nation. In times of strife and stress, most presidents seek to create a sense of stability. This is a wise approach, because our democracy was structured to insulate itself from rash populist impulses. The three branches of government, the longer terms for senators, the electoral college for presidential elections, and the unelected Supreme Court were all efforts by the founders to put some breaks on populism. Our government is answerable to the people, but it also is structured with some separation of the government from the governed, so that those in power can make difficult and unpopular decisions that they believe are in the nation's best interest.

Yet when a president sees himself as the cheerleader of populists rage, rather than a moderator of it, our government can veer off course. Obama has always been adept at exploiting populism. Much of his political success has come from his ability to both identify with disgruntled groups and objectify his enemies. Lobbyists, evangelicals, "the rich," Wall Street, and bankers have all felt Obama's eloquent lash. Now it is bonuses. The recent $165 million in bonus paid by AIG are truly troubling. AIG has received hundreds of billions in government money to stay in business, so how could traders and executive merit bonuses.

To most Americans the payment of bonuses at AIG is an outrage on its face. But there are some sound reasons why AIG needed to pay at least some bonuses and Obama knows it. AIG needs to pay some bonuses to keep its best people. Some AIG units have performed well and some employees in those units disserve bonuses. AIG had contracts for certain bonuses, so not paying them could have cost AIG more money, not less. Lastly, Senator Chris Dodd and others in DC, with counsel from the Obama Administration, inserted language into legislation to allow the bonuses. All these are subtle points that have little prospect to overcoming the populist outrage, but a true leader would have the courage to tell the nation difficult truths.

Instead of seeking to modify the populist outrage, Obama has flamed it. He has stoked it. He is exploiting it. He raised the stakes so high that the House has passed a 90% tax on any bonuses paid by any company receiving government money. Sounds great until one realizes that most people in the financial sector work for bonus and this legislation will punish thousands who had no hand in AIG's troubles and who have been successful and productive. Further, this tax will weaken our financial sector, not stabilize it. Not to mention, using the tax code to punish specific groups of taxpayers is a very scary proposition.

We disserve better from government than a rash response to a difficult problem. Obama knows that, he knows the 90% tax is bad policy, and he knows the tax will hurt the economy. But will he do anything about it. Will he show leadership or will he use populist outrage to push his agenda no matter the consequence? We shall see. Yet one thing is clear, when we have a president more interested to creating populist backlash, rather than stemming it, we will have a government of very bad policies.

Week 10

(POST-PARTISAN AT THE WATER'S EDGE)

March 29, 2009

It has not been much of a post-partisan presidency so far. Yes Obama has had meetings with Republicans, he has invited them to parties, and he says he will listen to them. Yet when Obama's policies are announced and legislation is pushed, his domestic agenda is liberal to its core. No one should be surprised by this. Obama is a liberal and he was elected to pursue a specific agenda. He has every right to pursue that agenda. The problem is that he sold himself to voters as a messianic post-partisan leader who would bring the parties together and end gridlock in Washington. Only those that believed this narrative are surprised by his partisanship.

The Obama Administration has been the tale of two presidencies. On domestic issues, Obama's policies are traditional tax and spend liberalism spun with the modern themes of clean energy, education, and health care. It is the same liberal agenda, just with new poster-children. Not so on foreign policy. As liberal as Obama is on domestic issues, his approach on foreign policy has been amazingly Bush-like. Yes, Obama plans to end torture and close Gitmo, but that is political window dressing at best. His key policies on surveillance, Iraq, Afghanistan, and security generally have cheered Republicans.

Even before he was elected, Obama made clear his support for the Bush approach to domestic surveillance. In Iraq, Obama's plan is cautious. He wants combat troops out in 19 months, but he would keep 50,000 troops in Iraq for stability. It is time to get our forces out of Iraq and Obama's plan is responsible and appropriate. This week, Obama announced a new strategy on Afghanistan of more troops, more training, and more responsibility for the Afghan government. One might call the policy Afghanization. It is the only answer. America will never be able to control that country. The best we can hope for is to create a central government strong enough to keep the tribal radicals in check so that Afghanistan will not be a threat to its neighbors or a haven for terrorists. That is the focus of the Obama policy, and it is a moderate and responsible approach.

Unlike Bill Clinton, Obama is a serious and thoughtful politician. His foreign policy is not designed to please liberals. Many of them are not happy. Instead, his policies are designed to protect the nation and preserve our interests in the world. On domestic issues, Obama honestly believes that America will better prosper with a different economic model somewhere between our current system and the moderately socialist economies of Europe. He is not pursuing this agenda for some political gain, he honestly believes that is what America needs. Many will disagree on that, but at least we have a President who pursues policies because he believes they are right, rather than simply because he thinks they will be popular.

Week 11

(IT'S GOOD TO BE POPULAR)

April 5, 2009

George Bush was undoubtedly one of the most unpopular presidents ever overseas. Part of that was a result of his policies and part his demeanor. President Bush made some very tough decisions on climate change, Iraq, terrorism, and other issues that were detested in Europe and elsewhere in the world. He made those decisions based on his view of the nation's best interests, and many of them cost him at home as well as abroad. His manner also lent itself easily to the caricature of a cowboy politician.

One of Obama's campaign goals was to rebuild America's standing in the world. America's capacity for international leadership has indeed been sapped by the war in Iraq and Bush's unpopularity. That combined with the current recession, founded at least in part on Wall Street, limited America's ability to lead. Obama appears to understand that American leadership is essential to world stability and he has rightly set about reestablishing that leadership. He has been helped by Bush's changes in Iraq strategy that made victory possible and troop reductions a reality. But Obama has also been aided by the simple fact that he is both new and intriguing.

Obama traveled to Europe this week for a grand entrance on the international stage. A G20 summit in London, a NATO meeting in Strassbourg, and an EU meeting in Prague, all in the shadow of recession, war in Afghanistan, and tensions with Russia. There were riots as expected from anti-globalists, but what was most striking was Obama's tone and his popularity. Obama was frank in admitting American mistakes, but he also stood firm on the necessity of success in Afghanistan, fighting terrorism, and combating recession. He gave notice that America would be more humble and would listen, but also that America would lead. These are critical steps to reestablishing American leadership.

He may succeed in reestablishing that leadership more quickly because of his popularity. Obama is as wildly popular in Europe as Bush was unpopular. He is more popular than nearly every European leader. This acclaim can hide many sins, because underneath Obama's pleasing public persona are policies not much different from the Bush Administration. They are just package with a better tone and a new salesman. That might make all the difference, because a little popularity can go a long way.

Week 12

(THE RODNEY KING DOCTRINE)

April 12, 2009

Rodney King is an American icon for one simple statement: "Can't we just get along." Uttered in the midst of his police brutality case, this statement by King captured both a simplistic and appealing assessment of conflict. Over the decades, there have been many doctrines issued by American presidents to deal with foreign conflicts. Starting with Washington's warning on foreign entanglements, to the Monroe Doctrine, the Truman Doctrine, and the Reagan Doctrine. President Obama in his first weeks is pursuing his own foreign policy doctrine, which could be best summed up as the Rodney King Doctrine: Can't we just get along.

Obama's heart is not in foreign policy. He wants to change America more than he wants to change the world. Yet he understands that he will be judged as much by his success abroad as his achievements at home. That is because above all else the job of a president is to protect the nation from foreign threats. All other responsibilities are secondary. Obama knows that and he also knows that foreign crises can derail his domestic agenda. He wants to calm the conflicts abroad so he can concentrate on his agenda at home. His first steps in this mission have been apology and reconciliation.

Obama has reached out his hand to an aggressive and expansionist Russia, offered dialogue with Iran, sought calm with Chávez in Venezuela, and tried to appease the Europeans. He is setting a tone very different from the Bush Administration, which forcefully pursued American interests with fewer diplomatic niceties. Obama is wise to set a different tone, because America has a better chance of achieving its policy goals when it is admired. But admiration only goes so far. America needs to be respected and feared as well, and that might be where Obama's approach falls short.

Foreign policy realists understand that nations have set interests and sometimes those interests conflict. Russia is a good example. Russia seeks to challenge America's hegemony in Europe and to expel any American influence in central Asia. Both these goals are unacceptable to American interests. Russia is also governed by leaders whose aggressive and expansionist approach to foreign policy harkens back to a darker era. Will Russia see Obama's outreach as an opportunity to compromise or a sign of weakness? Many think it will be the latter.

We have seen some signs lately that a foreign policy of just trying to get along will not protect America. This week's North Korean missile launch, Iran's newest nuclear threats, rampant piracy off Somalia, and escalating violence to Pakistan are worrying signs. Obama needs to understand that we are not going to just get along with our enemies. There are forces in the world seeking to destroy our way of life. Those forces are evil and must be fought. If Obama is wise, he is seeking to reconcile with our more reasonable adversaries, so that we have more flexibility and resources to deal with our most determined foes. That approach might succeed, but if it appears that Obama will not confront any truly grave threat, then America will look weak and our enemies will be emboldened.

Week 13

(HELLO HUGO)

April 19, 2009

President Obama is on a perpetual charm offensive. His recent trip to Europe and the adoring fans he encountered appear to have convinced him that charm alone makes policy. No matter that certain nations want to harm America, as long as their leaders can be exposed to the inspiring presence of our President, that alone will dissuade our enemies from their schemes and set the world aright, or so Obama appears to believe. What else can account for the smiles and handshakes with Hugo Chávez, the dictator of Venezuela?

Chávez is a man dedicated to destroying American hegemony in this hemisphere. He has called our nation evil, he has sought to undermine his neighbors who are friendly with us, he attacks American business interests, he invites the Russian navy to joint military exercises in the Caribbean, and he has adroitly destroyed democracy in his nation. With this record, what did Obama do when Chávez approached him at this week's Americas Summit to present as a gift a book about America's rape of the hemisphere: Obama smiles, jokes with Chávez, and accepts the book.

Why would President Obama be so friendly with a sworn enemy of the United States? Put simply, he does not accept or understand that certain nations want to do us harm. Obama's world view is that in no small part the animosity toward America is warranted and as soon as our enemies know he is in charge, their anti-American agendas will go away. No doubt Bush's aggressive foreign policy and war on terror made many nations resent America. To some degree, Obama is right to strike a different tone to reassure our allies and restore our leadership. However, this approach is only wise when applied to our friends. Nations like France and Germany, that have the same basic strategic aims as the U.S. and share our basic values, were needlessly enraged by the Bush Administration. Obama's charm offensive with them is wise and might prove productive.

Yet, President Obama wants to be equally kind and friendly to our enemies. He has already begun to buckle under to the Kremlin's threats against its neighbors by weakening our alliances in Eastern Europe and slowing the missile shield. He somehow believes that the Russians will reward these friendly gestures. The current leadership in Moscow only respects strength, a fact Obama will soon learn. Likewise, President Obama thinks Chávez will change his tone if he is nice to him. All Chávez has is his anti-Americanism. He has destroyed his nation's economy and democracy. He needs to blame his nation's ills on America. By accepting Chávez's gift of a deeply anti-American book, Obama was duped into playing the exact role Chávez wanted: being an American president who legitimized Chávez's critique of America.

At some point, President Obama will realize that friendly gestures alone will not protect America. Hopefully, he will learn that lesson before it costs us too dearly.

Week 14

(INVESTIGATIONS WE CAN BELIEVE IN)

April 26, 2009

One of the most controversial policies of the Bush administration was harsh interrogation tactics, or torture to use a more pointed phrase. President Bush decided that to protect American security it was necessary to use harsher tactics to interrogate prisoners, especially Al-Qaeda prisoners. There are many good reasons to disagree with the Bush Administration's policy. Many experts say that torture yields unreliable intelligence. Also, historically we have opposed torture, so to pursue those interrogation tactics undermines our moral authority in the fight against terrorism. Finally, if we are perceived to torture, our citizens who fall into enemy hands might be more likely exposed to torture themselves.

All of these were valid bases to oppose the Bush Administration's policy. Among President Obama's first acts as President were executive orders banning harsh interrogation tactics. That order was not among Obama's more controversial ones, because even the proponents of harsh interrogation tactics had begun to recognize that the accusation that America was torturing prisoners was hurting our efforts against terrorism. The problem is that Obama's allies on the Left are not satisfied with a ban on torture; they want Bush Administration officials to be subject to criminal prosecution.

The push by liberal Democrats for a special counsel and criminal prosecutions on the issue of torture will be a true test of whether President Obama is committed to changing the tone in Washington. No one alleges that Bush Administration officials approved harsh interrogation tactics for personal gain or corrupt purposes. The tactics were approved based on the belief that harsh interrogations were necessary to get intelligence to protect America. There are plenty of reasons to disagree with that assessment, but can such a policy disagreement be a crime.

This week, Obama has played this issue very coyly. He said he does not want CIA operatives prosecuted and that he wants Congress to focus on current challenges not past errors, but he has hinted he will support investigations of Bush officials. As with so many things, Obama wants to sound moderate while encouraging the Left of his party to pursue its agenda. Yet here, Obama is playing with a fire that could easily get out of control. A special counsel investigation into torture will destroy any chance of cooperation between the parties, completely polarize the nation, and expose President Obama to a huge backlash if another terrorist attack occurs. Plus, who would the Democrats be defending in this debate, terrorists who plotted to kill Americans. Not the most appealing clients.

The torture investigation issue will reveal what kind of leader Obama truly is. Is he a pragmatist who wants to put progress over partisanship, or is he looking for political gain by trying to make policy differences criminal?

Week 15
(THE SPECTER OF CHANGE)

May 3, 2009

With the advent of the Obama Administration, partisanship was supposed to end in Washington. As it turns out, instead partisanship is reining in Washington. Just look at Obama's stimulus plan, which garnered only three Republican votes, and his budget, which got none. Many Republicans would have willingly supported those plans if they had even a hint of balance or moderation, but instead they embodied the agenda of the Democrat Left. There are plenty of accusations flying on who spoiled the predicted Obama era of good feeling, but the fact is that post-partisanship was never going to happen. This week's defection of Arlen Specter to the Democrats put the final nail in that coffin.

Specter has been a Republican Senator for 29 years. Always one of the more moderate Republicans in the Senate, Specter was never a sure vote for the Republican caucus. Despite that, on major tax, budget, foreign policy, and judicial issues Specter was a fairly steady supporter of the Republican agenda. Then came Obama. While the President has talked much about bipartisanship, behind the scenes his administration has worked relentlessly to consolidate power in Washington. The Democrats control of the House is unchallenged, but the Republicans still held on to the slimmest of influence in the Senate with 41 seats, just enough to maintain filibusters.

Of all the Republicans in the Senate, Specter was the logical target for an induced defection. His moderate voting record made a switch to the Democrats at least plausible. His recent trouble with the Republican party in Pennsylvania also made a switch expedient. Specter is up for reelection in 2010 and was facing a primary challenge that he was likely to lose. The combination of his voting record and his desire to remain in the Senate made a switch possible. All it took was some pressure and promises from President Obama and Specter took the jump.

Now with 59 seats in the Senate (and the 60th if Al Franken prevails in the election challenge in Minnesota), Obama and the Democrats will wield unchecked power in Washington. What does all this mean for the Republicans, the Democrats, and the country? For the Republicans, this year is like 1964, when they were roundly swept out of government and sent into the political wilderness. Whether they will remain there depends much on Obama's ambitious agenda. If America prospers under Obama's vision of a European-style economy, Republicans face a long exile. If Obama's agenda proves unpopular, the Republican rebound will be swift.

For the Democrats, with control comes responsibility. So far, it appears that the Democrats plan is overreach: push through the most ambitious liberal agenda possible as fast as possible. This approach, much like what the Democrats did after the 1964 election, makes a Republican rebound more likely. Lastly, for the country, we have seen historically that the nation has fared the best when no one party exerts dominate control. That is because division of power breeds moderation and practical compromise. Americans are moderate and practical by nature, so it is no surprise that divided government often suits us.

Week 16

(COURTING THE LEFT)

May 10, 2009

Few things get political partisans more excited than Supreme Court vacancies. Both the Left and the Right see the Court has an institution essential to social change. For liberals, the Court is the bulwark of personal liberties and the vehicle to enact a progressive agenda on issues like gay rights and the death penalty. Conservatives see the Court as a check on rampant federal power and hope conservative justices will reverse the very social agenda liberals admire. In presidential elections, devoted partisans often focus much of their campaigning on the impact a particular candidate will have the on ideological makeup of the federal courts, although it is unlikely the general electorate pays much attention to that. But everyone knows changes in control of the Executive Branch inevitably lead to changes in the federal courts.

The Left has very high hopes for Obama and the Courts. The first test for those hopes was the announcement this week of Justice David Souter's retirement. Although a George H. W. Bush nominee, Souter turned out to be one of the most liberal members of the Court. Thus, his departure will have little impact on the ideological balance of the Court, because it is unlikely Obama could nominate anyone more liberal than Souter. What is most interesting about the Souter retirement is what it will tell us about Obama and his plans for social change.

We know from Obama's first 15 weeks in office that he is a progressive. That is clear from his tax and spending plans, his regulatory agenda, and his new tone on foreign policy. What is not yet clear is whether Obama is a true political radical. Obama is very skilled at sounding moderate while pushing the agenda of the Left. He has been able to do this because on tax and budget issues, Obama uses the rhetoric of helping the middle class to justify every tax increases, spending program, and expansions of federal power. But with his Supreme Court nomination, Obama will have to declare whether he is a true man of the Left.

The Supreme Court tackles the most controversial issues of our time: abortion, torture, the death penalty, affirmative action, free speech, due process, and separation of church and state. These are not issues where politicians can easily hide in nuance, which is Obama's favorite home. If Obama nominates a liberal committed to judicial enactment of the Left's social agenda, he will openly declare his allegiance. Of course, his most ardent supporters hope he will do exactly that. If he instead nominates a moderate progressive, someone sympathetic to the liberal social agenda but not wholly owned by it, then Obama will signal that his objectives are less radical than many fear. There is now nowhere to hide.

Week 17

(SEEING RED)

May 17, 2009

This Spring Congress has been slowly but steadily laying out the blueprint for the Obama budget. An early insight into Obama's legislative priorities came with his stimulus bills, with their focus on expanding welfare programs, health care, and public works. Now with Obama's first budget, Democrats hope to transform federal priorities and bring into being new social contract with the electorate. Having broken for the moment the ideological equilibrium that has reigned since 1968, Democrats see their current dominance as the best chance since the 1960's to create a host of new social programs.

Obama has very detailed plans for his social spending agenda. He wants to create universal healthcare coverage, education subsidies, higher fuel efficiency and limits on greenhouse emissions. Democrats generally love all of these proposals and are happily and eagerly writing the legislation to create them. But there is one snag: how to pay for it. On that issue, there is no consensus, no clear path, and little or no enthusiasm.

We saw this week how high the hurdle will be for President Obama to pay for his massive spending programs. The Congressional Budget Office (CBO) released new estimates for both the current year and long term deficits, showing a whopping deficit of $1.9 trillion in 2010 and an ever expanding debt over the next decade. Reports were also released showing both Social Security and Medicare going into the red earlier than previously projected. What these announcements confirm is that the federal government lacks the revenues to pay for the current programs on the books, let alone pay for Obama's new social programs.

Obama knows his social programs will require massive tax increases. That is why to date he has proposed increases in income taxes, eliminating tax deductions at higher incomes, payroll taxes, creating a new carbon tax, new corporate taxes, and is reportedly exploring a Value Added Tax (VAT). If all of these proposals were enacted, the United States would quickly catch or surpass many European nations in total tax burden. Obama's proposals show that he is more than willing to take the jump to transform America into a European style social democracy. The problem is, will Congress follow.

America is still largely an anti-tax nation. That is evident from the fact that even the Democrat leadership in Congress is bucking most of Obama's tax plans. Congress supports the income tax increases, but to date has shown little support for elimination of deductions, the carbon tax, and payroll tax increases, or the VAT. The ugly truth is that President Obama pretends he can pay for his agenda by only raising taxes on the rich, but everyone knows a broad tax increase impacting every middle class family will be required to pay for Obama's social democracy. But will Congress pass the taxes, or will it just create the programs and hope.

It is a truism in politics that it is easy to create programs, but not so easy to pay for them. It is also almost always true that federal programs cost more than projected and once created can rarely never be dismantled. Obama and the Democrats are heading down the path of creating a vast new federal government that cannot be paid for. They seem willing to risk fiscal disaster in the process. If their scheme works, the programs will be created and the electorate will like them so much it will support the taxes to pay for them. But it is just as likely that the programs will be a mixed bag of successes and failures, the electorate will rebel against the taxes and regulations, and a backlash will ensue. Whichever decision the electorate makes, let's hope it is made before fiscal disaster overtakes us.

Week 18

(IT'S BAD TO BE GOOD)

May 24, 2009

President Obama likes to talk about a responsibility society where all Americans take responsibility for their own behavior and contribute to efforts to improve the behavior of others. As a political slogan, "Responsibility Society" is very appealing. Who would be opposed to our society being more responsible? But what actions has the Obama Administration actually taken to promote responsibility. This week's enactment of credit card reform is a great example of Obama's concept of responsibility: forcing those who behave well to subsidize those who do not.

Americans are debt ridden. Credit cards are a cause of the problem. People get too many cards, spend too much, cannot pay the balances, and are then subjected to high fees, penalties, and interest. Instead of reforming credit card practices to deter consumers from taking on too much debt, Obama's credit card reform law puts limitations on the ability of credit card companies to generate revenues from those who cannot pay their balances. The net result of the law will be that responsible consumers who pay their balances will be forced to pay higher fees and interest to keep their cards.

Punishing those who behave well is a central tenet of President Obama's notion of responsibility. Obama believes that Americans who follow the rules and act responsibility have a moral obligation to pay for the errors and misdeeds of their neighbors. Obama has a plan to bail out homeowners who bought too much house, paid for by those who pay their mortgages. Obama has a plan to raise taxes on small business and high earners so that their money can be transferred to lower income Americans, without any assessment of whether the beneficiaries of this wealth redistribution deserve the money. Obama is making all Americans pay for an auto industry bailout, when GM and Chrysler's mismanagement is obvious. Obama is bailing out state governments that have overspent for years, ensuring higher taxes when the federal subsidies end. None of this promotes responsibility.

The problem is, punishing good behavior, while rewarding bad actions, does not create a "Responsibility Society." But Obama seems unable to stop his pandering to those who misbehave. Indeed, all his actions to aid the irresponsible have turned the federal government into the most irresponsible actor of all: it is saddling generations with debts so huge our national capacity to pay them off is in doubt. Our government must aid those who have been victimized and it must provide a basic social safety net to all its citizens. However, when government tries to pick winners and losers in the economy, tries to decide who is allowed to be prosperous, and tries to prevent the natural consequences of bad decisions, it creates social discord, distorts the market, and undermines that very society it purports to help.

Week 19

(RACE AND THE COURT)

May 31, 2009

President Obama has been very careful in his first few months in office to avoid the culture wars. Yes, one of his first acts was to repeal a ban on taxpayer funded family planning services, but that executive order is a prerequisite for any Democrat president. Otherwise, Obama has focused almost entirely on international issues, his budget priorities, and the recession. This has been a good strategy, because on those issues Obama is very skilled at sounding moderate, while pushing an agenda that makes Bill Clinton look like a conservative. But with his nomination of Judge Sotomayor for the Supreme Court, Obama has jumped with both feet into the culture wars.

Judge Sotomayor is qualified for the Supreme Court, no doubt about that. With 17 years as a federal district and appeals court judge, she has ample experience and no one questions her intellect. But President Obama himself established that concerns about ideology trump qualifications, a fact evidenced by his votes against the confirmations of Justices Roberts and Alito. On ideology, the nomination of Judge Sotomayor confirms that President Obama is on the Left of his party on social issues and well as economic ones.

Judge Sotomayor is a culture warrior of the Left. An accomplished jurist who champions the racial spoils system, she is a judge who believes that federal courts should "make policy," and she thinks Latina women with the richness of their experiences will make better rulings from the bench than white males. She rejected without any consideration a reverse discrimination suit by white male firefighters, making clear that in her world view, white people can only perpetrate racism, they cannot be victims of it. She has equated the death penalty with racism. And while she has not ruled on a true abortion case, no one doubts her view on that issue.

With this nomination, Obama could have chosen a moderate jurist or a leading liberal thinker like Cass Susstein. Instead, he went with a political nomination. A woman to appease the feminists. A Latina to please an important and growing constituency. A liberal to cheer his base. The perfect package, or so it seems. But with this nomination, Obama has declared himself as a liberal on social policy, just as he is a liberal on economics. He has nominated a judge who will be a sure vote for abortion rights, a vote against the death penalty, a supporter of affirmative action, an opponent of religion in the public sphere, and a constant champion of federal power at the expense of the States and the people.

All these positions are core beliefs of Obama, so we should not be surprised that he nominated someone with these views. But what is shocking about Sotomayor is that her whole public career is about racial identity politics. She judges whether people should have their rights protected by what group they belong to, not whether their liberties have been infringed. This is completely against the Obama creed. He was supposed to be the post-racial president, the president who was going to solve the race problem, the president who was going to make race less important in American society. Yet for his first Supreme Court nomination, he has put forth a judge who views everything through a racial prism. Looks like the "post-racial presidency" was just a political slogan after all.

Week 20
(OM)

June 7, 2009

Despite our reputation as a free market haven, America has a long history of market intervention. The free silver movement, the New Deal, Truman's seizure of the steel industry, and the 1970s Chrysler bailout are but a few examples. The current financial crisis has witnessed an acceleration of market intervention, but most of government's intervention has been necessary and pragmatic. Not true for the GM bailout, where necessary intervention gave way to politics.

The AIG and bank bailouts were necessitated by the specter of complete financial collapse. Since the banking and financial sectors are the lifeblood of the entire economy, a reluctant political consensus was forged to take these steps. There was also an implicit understanding that the taxpayers would eventually get their money back, because there is no doubt about the basic profitability of our financial sector once the economy recovers. The AIG bailout is a perfect example. AIG got more money than GM, but most of that money went to cover debts AIG owed to other financial companies on losses from various esoteric investments. AIG has in essence been a conduit for subsidies to other financial companies and a means to stem the overall financial collapse. Further, there is little doubt about the profitability of AIG's main insurance business, so at some point the taxpayers will get at least some money back.

None of this is true for the GM bailout, which has essentially turned General Motors into Obama Motors. A collapse of the financial sector would have meant disaster for our entire economy and our financial system nearly collapsed because it was too innovative, offering overly sophisticated interlocking investment instruments. GM's failure would have been painful indeed, but it would not have hurt the entire economy. The auto industry is far less central to our economic system than the financial sector. Further, GM failed because it has too many brands, its cars are not competitive, its workers are paid too much, and its retirement and pension commitments are unsustainable. The fundamentals of our financial system are sound, while the fundamentals of GM's business are hopelessly broken.

So why did the Obama Administration use a controlled bankruptcy to stage a $70 billion government takeover of GM: politics? President Obama could not resist pressure from the unions to save their member's jobs or from the Left to use GM as a grand experiment in green technology. Obama also feared the political consequences of allowing an American icon like GM to fail under his watch. So the Obama Administration crafted a deal where the government and the unions own 80% of GM, a sure formula for failure.

So what happens now? GM will cut pay and workers, close factories, limit brands, and terminate dealers. However, the vast government subsidies flowing to GM will force GM to preserve still unsustainable compensation and pension obligations. GM will develop new products, but there will be pressure to make green cars, where there is little profit and uncertain demand. The stigma of government bailout and ownership will hurt GM's ability to compete with other car companies, a competition GM has been losing for 30 years. Even with the government takeover, GM will still likely fail, unless the government commits to further subsidies and direct invention to favor GM in the marketplace. America: welcome to socialism.

Week 21

(PAY GO AND PAY NO)

June 14, 2009

There are seemingly two contradictory sides to Barak Obama. The prudent manager who talks about an efficient government living within its means and the ambitious liberal plotting with exquisite skill to remake America into a progressive state. Not surprisingly, which Obama appears on any given day depends on who he is talking to. When addressing more conservative audiences, Obama stresses responsibility and prudence, but with liberals he is all about social justice, fairness, and expanded government. However, what appear to be contradictions are simply a distinction between means and ends.

This week, we witnessed a classic example of the difference between means and ends in Obama world. President Obama has proposed the biggest expansion of government since the New Deal, an agenda that will create trillions in debt unless taxes are increased far beyond what Obama has already proposed. Government health care, government regulation and taxation of carbon emissions, government intervention in private industry, and government expansion in education. Obama's dilemma is how to get all these new programs enacted without undermining voter support with the new taxes needed to pay for them.

Obama's answer is sly and elegant, as usual. First, he proposes vast expansions in federal spending and allows the Democrat Congress run amuck in a legislative feeding frenzy. Then he steps in, as he did this week, and pretends to try to tame the forces he has unleashed, by asserting that Congress must enact Pay Go rules for federal spending, requiring Congress to find cuts or new revenue sources for any new spending. He takes the problem he has created and purports to fix it with the even higher taxes he has always wanted. Obama's talk about fiscal prudence is just a means to achieve his ends of vastly expanded government.

However, Obama's ambitions are not limited to remaking the public sector, he wants to remake the private sector as well. We also saw that this week with Obama's proposals to limit executive compensation, another example of Obama's means being very different from his ends. Americans are outraged by high executive compensation, especially when the bad decisions of some executives led to the economic problems we now face. Obama has a government answer to the problem, as he always does, namely government limits and oversight on executive pay. Never mind that we do not regulate the millions paid to actors, athletes, or authors, when it comes to people who run corporations that employ thousands, government regulation is a must. But Obama's proposed regulation on executive pay is just a means to his larger social aim: wealth redistribution. Rather than talking about his real agenda, he is channeling the rage at executives to achieve that agenda.

Obama is a very skilled politician, who effectively uses seemingly contradictory rhetoric to achieve a fairly unified agenda. The key to understanding Obama is to ignore the means, and see clearly his ends.

Week 22
(THE DOCTOR IS IN)

June 21, 2009

There is no more central article of faith of the American Left than universal health care. The Left looks to countries around the world and envies how those countries provide "free" healthcare to their people, while America does not. For liberals, universal health care achieves two critical goals: it brings all Americans into the grasp of the welfare state and it puts government in command of our largest single industry. With these two goals achieved, the Left can then embark in its favorite pastime: social planning on a grand scale.

Barak Obama is a true believer in the Left's vision for health care reform. He wants government to control and remake health care both to ensure coverage for all Americans and to direct what kind of health care Americans get. But Obama is smart enough to understand that while liberals are now firmly in command of government, the American voters are moderate and skeptical of government schemes. So to sell socialized medicine, Obama knows he must package it in the garb of reform and efficiency.

This week we saw Obama at his best, talking to groups like the American Medical Association and trying to convince them that health care reform will be good for their industry. Obama focused his comments on out of control health care costs, the plight of the uninsured, and the evils of the insurance industry. All topics that will elicit sympathy. His prescription for these ills is required coverage for all Americans, a government health care plan to compete with private insurers, and reductions in Medicare payments to hospitals and providers. Obama says these steps are necessary because if we do not reign in health care costs, America will suffer GM's fate.

Making healthcare about cost control and reform is a shrewd strategy because it appeals to conservatives as well as liberals. All Americans recognize that health care costs are out of control and that reform is necessary. So Obama has tapped into a shared national concern. The problem is that one must suspend all disbelief to think that Obama's proposals will solve any of the problems in health care. Healthcare costs are out of control mainly because we have divorced the patient from the costs of care, our system is half government and half free market, and lawsuits force doctors to practice defensive medicine. A government run system will not solve any of these problems. We know that because Medicare is an existing government health care system and it is rife with fraud, its costs are out of control, and it is grossly inefficient. Obama wants to make all healthcare like Medicare and we already know the result.

There are ways to reform healthcare that will work, including insurance reform, tort reform, and Medicare reform. But Obama's current goal is not reform but control. He knows that once a universal health care program is established, the nation will creep towards price controls, rationing, and eventually a single payor system where everyone in the health care industry will be working for the government. Obama is no socialist. He knows socialism crushes innovation, destroys wealth, and eventually cripples the means of production. Yet when it comes to health care, liberals like Obama forget all they have learned and still think socialism is the answer, they just do not say so in public.

21

Week 23

(OBAMATHON)

June 28, 2009

Have you ever had a dream come true? It is a surreal experience, where reality and fantasy become indistinguishable. The elite media's dream has come true with Barak Obama and no matter the evidence to the contrary, they cling to the belief that he is perfection incarnate. One can hardly blame them, for decades media liberals have pined for an articulate, urbane, sophisticated liberal leader who will bridge our divisions, legislate prosperity, and bring peace through empathy and apology. Obama is all they ever hoped for and more, so they are on a mission not to report on Obama, but to promote him. Just ask ABC.

On June 24, ABC hosted an extraordinary event, a live town hall meeting with the President and selected citizens to ask questions about health care reform. The format was familiar, except that it was staged not by the Obama campaign team, but by the network bosses at ABC. Usually politicians have to pay for commercials that run on networks, but all the rules have changed with Obama. Now the networks are falling over themselves to broadcast specials with the President in an unholy alliance: the President gets free media to promote his agenda while the networks make money and see their liberal dreams fulfilled. It is like having a state media without the official censorship.

During the broadcast, Obama was cool and articulate as usual, explaining all the problems in the current health care system and why these problems need to be addressed. He answered several questions from citizens of various backgrounds and from the ABC moderators. What came out of the session was that Obama feels our pain about health care, but no cures were offered. Again and again Obama outlined the issues: out of control costs, too many specialists, too little preventive care, too many tests and unnecessary procedures. Yet no one pressed him for details on how his plans would make any of these problems better. No one noted that Medicare is a government program and it is troubled. No one asked him about confronting his trial lawyer supporters for tort reform. No one asked him why he believes government will make health care more efficient. No one pressed him on how we can afford his proposal with our massive budget deficit. One cannot expect average citizens to raise all these critiques of the Obama's program, but the moderators should have asked tough questions. Instead, they were in such agreement and awe that they decided to just let the campaign commercial play on.

The ABC event proved again that Obama has the media in his back pocket. No matter that the $787 billion stimulus package is not helping. No matter that we are sinking in debt. No matter that unemployment continues to rise. The media's attitude is we have Obama, that is all we need. We have a liberal icon, a man to remake America, so no need to nitpick him. But there is a simple truth that the elite media will not cover: Obama is far more popular than his programs. Americans are concerned about the debt, the spending, the taxes, and Obama's unending faith in government solutions for everything. The media will not cover these issues with any vigor because that would interfere with their dream. So they just let the fantasy roll on.

Week 24

(ENERGY AND SECURITY)

July 5, 2009

Energy issues are at the root of many of the challenges America faces today. We are embroiled in wars in the Middle East largely because of the importance of Persian Gulf oil. Our economy is in recession in part because of the economic shock of high and volatile energy prices. We face challenges from countries like Russia and Venezuela because energy resources have made them powerful and mischievous. And the election protests and instability in Iran demand our heightened attention because of Iran's geography and its oil.

America prospered into an economic giant in part because of our vast resources and our isolation from the arms races and wars of Europe. We emerged from World Wars I and II more wealthy and powerful than when we entered, setting the stage for an era of American hegemony. But that era is over, largely because America has lost both wealth and economic independence because of our inability to power our own economy.

Any president would have to make energy policy a central focus of governance and Barak Obama is no different. Yet Obama has made global warming, not security, the central rationale for his energy policy. President Obama hopes to spark a green energy revolution by government subsidies and incentives for new energy resources, while raising the prices of traditional fossil fuels with his cap and trade plan. Last week, the House passed this cap and trade plan, but it was riddled with pork, exceptions, and other political compromises necessary for its passage. The bill faces an uncertain future in the Senate and presents uncertain benefits for the nation.

The only sure result of the cap and trade plan is a massive tax increase on the American economy through higher energy prices. No doubt higher prices for traditional power sources will make green energy more economically viable, but no value will be added to the economy because overall energy will be more expensive, not less. As for Obama's hope that a green energy revolution will create millions of jobs, it is a central planner's dream at best. For all his intelligence and common sense, Obama is always enamored with the grand government solution. He firmly believes that government planning is often superior to entrepreneurship.

Obama seems to have learned nothing from the failure of socialism, where unwanted and warn out industries were propped up by governments to preserve production and jobs. Sooner or later, the weight of these inefficient and unviable industries becomes crippling, leading to economic crisis and collapse. With both his bailout of GM and his push to create a green energy revolution by making traditional energy more expensive, we see Obama making mistakes the same as those made by the socialist governments of Europe after World War II. The result will be industries that cannot survive without government's help and an economy that will be weaker, not stronger.

The shame is that Obama has the opportunity to achieve a grand national consensus on energy. Liberals want a new energy policy based on environmental concerns. Conservatives would support a new energy policy if it is designed to protect our security by making us energy independent. An energy policy that combines expanded oil exploration, nuclear power, and yes more green energy through incentives and additional taxation could yield political consensus. But rather than look for consensus, Obama has played partisan politics with energy, focusing his plan almost entirely on liberal's concerns, while ignoring the significant support he might get from conservatives with a balanced plan. As with so many policies, while Obama likes to talk about bipartisanship, in the end he supports the Left of his party and imperils his own objectives in the process.

Week 25

(DEBT AND DECLINE)

July 12, 2009

The greatest challenge to American power is not Al-Qaeda, or China, or the recession, it is debt. In the Twenty-First Century, power is measured more by economic might than by military strength. Those nations with stable governments and strong economic systems are best positioned to succeed in this new era. Unfortunately, America has hobbled the foundations of its economic power with the burdens of debt and shows no willingness to rebuild that foundation.

This week we witnessed the spectacle of President Obama in Europe for a Russian summit and a G8 meeting trying to convince our economic partners of the need to take bold steps to address global warming and the recession, while at home the Democrats labored furiously to cobble together a health care plan the nation cannot afford. We met failure at home and abroad, largely for the same reasons: America is weakened by debt.

Obama was unable to force any consensus at the 8G summit because American leadership is hobbled by economic weakness. America remains the world's premier military power, but that is more a liability than a strength. The cost of that military establishment has burdened our economy and our capabilities have made us the preferred provider of military services to our allies, with no compensation paid in return. America maintains the trappings of the premier power, but those trappings are paid for with money borrowed from our friends and adversaries. It is like a gambling addict mortgaging his home to get money for the next bet. Sooner or later, the bet will be lost and so will the home.

The events in Washington this week further underlined this weakness. In the midst of the global recession, our government has spent furiously to stimulate the world economy, vastly expanding our debt in the process. Other nations, like Germany, seeing that America would do the heavy lifting have sat back and waited for the free ride. The world economy will eventually recover, but the debt we have incurred will burden our ability to benefit. Far from attempting to arrest this avalanche of debt, Congress is busy trying to add to it.

Not satisfied with a nearly $2 trillion deficit this year, Obama's allies are busy crafting a health care reform plan that will cost another $1.5 trillion. Our nation is indebted, but our Congress has an awful willingness to just keep spending. What is worse, the Democrats have made pledges (like the promise not to raise taxes on the middle class) that make paying for these new programs impossible. Now we face the prospect of enactment of vast new government programs with no way to pay for them, with huge existing debts that are very hard to service, and with a diminishing ability to borrow further from China and others because the world has figured out our government is too deeply in debt. Neither Obama nor his allies seem willing to face this reality. Instead, they just keep promising a free lunch to the American people, until the bill collector arrives. One thing about a bill collector, he always arrives sooner or later, and once he does, any remaining vestige of American dominance will suffer.

Week 26
(THE 2% SOLUTION)

July 19, 2009

One of Obama's best campaign slogans is his desire to create a responsibility society. Obama wants Americans to take responsibility for their own lives, take responsibility for their children's welfare, and take responsibility for the health of the planet. The odd thing is, while Obama says he wants a society where we all take responsibility, he wants to put the burdens for creating that society on a mere two percent of the population. On program after program, from health care reform, to Social Security, to the cap and trade plan, Obama's central strategy is to promise something for nothing. The government will provide universal health care coverage, preserve Social Security, and save the planet at no cost to 98% of taxpayers. It's Obama's 2% solution.

We saw the 2% solution in action this week on health care reform. President Obama has demanded that Congress pass bills on health care reform by August, but rather than get into the details, Obama has merely set forth some general principles and then unleashed his allies to craft legislation. However, the Democrats are quickly realizing that meeting Obama's goals of providing coverage for the un-insured, reducing health care costs, and exempting 98% of taxpayers from higher taxes is basically impossible. In the House, the Democrats have now put bills together that, according to CBO, will provide coverage to many uninsured, but that contain essentially no provisions to reduce health care costs, that raise $540 billion in new taxes from the top 2%, and that will add to the deficit. The House bills are a disaster, but at least the House has made some progress. The Senate has not yet crafted any legislation.

Now that Obama has returned from the G8 summit, he is going into full campaign mode on health care reform. His first act was to praise the House bills, despite the fact that the House legislation fails to meet all but one of Obama's goals. It fails to provide coverage for all un-insured, it fails to reduce health care costs, and it adds to the deficit. The only goal it does meet is Obama's pledge to make only the top 2% pay for health care reform. Maybe Obama supports the House bills because in his mind, that is the most important goal of all.

Obama has been very clear that he wants to reduce income disparities. During the presidential campaign, he was criticized for saying he wanted to spread the wealth around. As it turns out, that is exactly what he is doing. Health care reform is a perfect example. Obama genuinely wants to provide coverage for the un-insured and reduce health care costs. He also wants to shift wealth from high earners to middle and low income families. Creating a vast new middle class entitlement through health care reform and making only the top 2% pay for it achieves both Obama goals simultaneously. The same goes for Social Security and cap and trade, where Obama wants to make only high income people bear the costs of reforms.

In the end, Obama's vision is a vast welfare state serving both the lower and middle class and paid for by the top 2%. It is not socialism, but it is as close as America will ever get to it, and just like every other socialist central planner, Obama is going against economic reality. The top 2% do not have enough wealth to pay for his programs, and his programs will destroy jobs and incentives to create wealth. It looks great on paper, but when taxes cannot be raised further on the top 2%, when the programs' costs spiral out of control, and when economic growth lags, we all will have to pay the price.

Week 27

(THE FARM TEAM)

July 26, 2009

Presidents must delegate. The job is far too big for one person, so cabinet officers and White House staff run the Executive Branch, with hopefully wise oversight from the president. So far Obama has shown himself to be a good administrator. He has chosen a skilled cabinet and White House staff and he appears comfortable as our chief executive. Obama also appears to understand that a president needs room to maneuver. He cannot get too tangled up in any particular initiative or program. That is where good executive skills come into play, because a president needs qualified and reliable people to delegate to. The problem is, Obama has decided to extend his successful approach to running the Executive Branch to Congress, making them his farm team for crafting his key programs. The problems Obama is having with his health care program demonstrate the flaws in this approach.

President Obama claims to have once been a constitutional law professor. With that experience, he should understand that our government is structured with three co-equal branches that are in natural tension with each other. Even when Congress and the executive are controlled by the same party, the agenda of congressional leaders often clashes with that of the president. That is why a president needs to forcefully push his agenda in Congress, pressuring the leadership and members to his will. So far, Obama has shown no willingness to do that. Instead, Obama seems more interested in just getting anything passed so he can claim credit. A perfect example is the Stimulus Bill, which Obama said had to be timely and targeted. Instead, we got a $787 billion bill loaded with pork and pet projects where only 11% of the spending would occur in 2009. Obama knew the economy would eventually recover, so he figured it did not really matter what was in the bill so long as it passed so he could claim credit.

The same is now true for health care. Obama's health care proposal is the most ambitious domestic policy program since the Medicare. It will impact every American, it is hugely complex and expensive, and it is fraught with political danger. But just like generals whose strategy always reflects the last war, Obama has again delegated health care to Congress with little input and no leadership. In response, Speaker Pelosi and her allies in the House saw yet another opportunity to push through a partisan bill crafted by the Democrat Left with few cost controls and loaded with spending and new taxes. But Pelosi went too far, because the House bill is so controversial that it has sparked a rebellion in the Democrat caucus. Pelosi seems to have forgotten that her majority relies on Democrats from moderate districts. In the Senate, there is so much disagreement and confusion that they do not have even an outline for any bill. All the while, President Obama sits back and watches the turmoil, preferring to give press conferences and hold campaign events rather than doing the hard work necessary to get health reform passed.

Obama has painted himself into a corner. He wants to cover the uninsured and control health care costs, while promising that it will be fully paid for with no new taxes for the bottom 98 percent of income earners. This is a very difficult agenda and only with focused presidential leadership does Obama have a chance of success. So instead, President Obama has given his farm team a free hand to craft his program. In return, the House has given him a bill that would cover many of the uninsured, but that fails to control costs, adds to the deficit, and imposes massive new taxes. The House bill might not even pass that chamber, and has no hope in the Senate. Most troubling of all, the bill cannot get a single Republican vote, turning the biggest domestic policy issue of Obama Presidency into a purely partisan affair.

Maybe this is all part of Obama's strategy. Maybe he wants Congress to exhaust itself in health policy debates and, when they reach maximum disarray and discouragement, he will swoop in with real leadership and a workable plan that has a hope of passage. Maybe, but that is a very dangerous game, because the longer and more difficult the debate gets, the more voters will become concerned and fearful about change and will opt for the status quo. In the end, Obama might get a bill, but it might be one that is entirely partisan, hugely controversial, and vastly expensive. He better hope the farm team gets it right, because it is Obama who will have to answer to the team owners, namely the voters.

Week 28

(HEALER-IN-CHIEF)

August 2, 2009

Obama views himself as a transformational leader, not just on issues like health care and the environment, but across the policy spectrum. He has such deep confidence in his own powers of persuasion that he willingly wades into almost any controversy, confident he can bridge any gap. We saw that this week when Obama injected himself into the controversy surrounding the arrest of Professor Henry Louis Gates, but rather than bringing consensus, Obama's gambit into this affair only brought more controversy.

Professor Gates is probably America's leading black scholar. That is why a media sensation arose when he was arrested for disorderly conduct during a police stop where he was questioned about his efforts to get into his own house. At first blush, there were obvious racial undertones to the case. Professor Gates lives in an affluent Cambridge neighborhood, the 911 caller and the police officer were white, and Professor Gates is black. Before all the details came out, President Obama was asked about the case at a news conference, and he commented that the police "acted stupidly." Within a few days, it became clear that the 911 caller made no comment about Professor Gates' race and that Professor Gates was abusive to the police when they arrived to investigate. The Cambridge police department protested the Presidents' comments, the 911 caller was subject to threats, and Gates stoked the racial flames.

By commenting, the President made the situation worse, not better. There is a lesson here. Presidents have huge tasks before them, so they cannot afford to get entangled in small controversies. Here, Obama injected himself into a racial feud between the Cambridge police and a black scholar before all the facts came out and without any probability of a positive effect. Obama's new conference comment might simply have been a gaff, something he should not have said. He could have ended the issue by admitting as much, but instead Obama decided to step deeper into the dispute by inviting Professor Gates and the police officer to the White House for a beer and a talk, quickly captioned as the "Beer Summit."

What we see here is that Obama did not view his comment as a gaff. Instead, he viewed it as a teaching moment. Obama wants to heal racial divisions. He sees his election as an opportunity to do that, so he willingly inserts himself into racial disputes because he has appointed himself the healer-in-chief. Obama likely recognizes that, like many Americans, he made some incorrect assumptions about what happened. Obama believes that to get beyond stereotypes and assumptions, we need to talk with each other. That is why he invited Professor Gates and the police officer to the White House. They had their talk and their beers, the guests went home, but there was no apology from either side. So in the end, no reconciliation was reached, only a president and a nation were distracted. Obama should know better. He does not have magical powers of persuasion, he cannot heal all wounds, and his efforts to do so can cause problems, not solve them. Hopefully, Obama learned a lesson.

Week 29

(OTHER PEOPLE'S CASH FOR CLUNKERS)

August 9, 2009

It was a good week for President Obama because his nominee to fill the seat of retiring Justice David Souter, Judge Sonia Sotomayor, was confirmed by the Senate. However, the talk in Washington was not about the Supreme Court, it was about Cash for Clunkers. Since the financial crisis in September 2008, the federal government has aggressively intervened in the economy. The AIG and GM bailouts, the TARP program, and Obama's Stimulus Plan are but a few examples. In the process, the federal government has amassed unprecedented debt and unprecedented power over the private economy. Arguably at least the AIG and TARP programs were necessary to stem the financial crisis, while the other interventions are more controversial and their benefits less clear. However, now that Congress has gotten a taste for economic interventionism, there will likely be no end to their tinkering, with the Cash for Clunkers program being a great example.

The Cash for Clunkers program uses taxpayer money to help people buy new cars with better gas mileage. The program is supposed to help the environment by getting gas guzzlers off the road. In reality, it is yet another taxpayer subsidy for the auto industry. By offering taxpayer funded rebates of $3500 or $4500 for new car purchases, Congress has encouraged hundreds of thousands of people to buy new cars with other people's money (namely yours). By this week, the program became so popular that the $1 billion appropriated for it ran out, so President Obama and the congressional leadership forced thought another $2 billion in deficit spending to fund it. The amazing thing is that the consensus for additional funding was near unanimous, with Republicans agreeing with Democrats that we should borrow even more money to subsidize car purchases.

The support for the Cash for Clunkers program shows that an industrial subsidy malady has overtaken Washington. Sure the Cash for Clunkers program does good things, it gets inefficient cars off the road and it helps auto dealers and auto makers. Yet the same thing can be said of almost any industrial subsidy program. Farm subsidies help farmers, green subsidies help green businesses, Cash for Clunkers helps auto makers, but do any of these programs help the public at large?

All these programs use other people's money to subsidize the businesses that lobby best before Congress. All these programs are wealth transfers from the average taxpayer to economic special interests. Inherent in the Cash for Clunkers program is a decision that taxpayers who have relatively new cars that get decent mileage have to pay not only for their own cars, but also for their neighbor's car as well. It is no different than the housing bailout, where responsible homeowners are being forced to help pay for their neighbor's homes. Most disturbing of all, with programs like Cash for Clunkers, our government has stopped acting as the referee of the private economy and has now taken sides and is deciding the winners and losers.

It is no surprise that Obama took up the cause of the Cash for Clunkers program this week, because the program furthers all his economic principles. It is a wealth transfer from the average taxpayer to less affluent people who do not have new cars. It is industrial planning, where government picks who wins (in this case the auto industry). Obama loves grand government solutions, so industrial planning is right up his alley. Lastly, it furthers Obama's vision of a green economy by getting inefficient cars off the road. The only loser in the whole scheme is the taxpayer, who yet again is being asked to pay for other peoples' pleasures.

Week 30
(TOWN BRAWLS)

August 16, 2009

Winning political parties always exaggerate their mandates. It is often hard to tell why elections are won. Sometimes it is personality, sometimes it is luck, often it is timing. Yet regardless of the uncertainties of electoral sentiments, the winners always read the results as an endorsement of their agenda, whatever it might be. Two thousand eight was a huge election win for the Democrats, and true to form they came into government convinced that the nation wanted a new type of government, a welfare state that provides subsidies and health care to all, directs industry, and taxes with reckless abandon. In the last eight months, the Democrats have run with their supposed mandate, wildly spending, taxing, and regulating. But in the process, they forgot about the voters, who struck back this week at a seemingly innocuous venue: the town hall.

The August recess is usually a quiet time in politics. Congress shuts down for the month, allowing members to go home to attend picnics, state fairs, and parades. Members also try to get out and talk to voters, with town halls the preferred format. It is not surprising that health care is the major focus of this month's town halls, but the politicians did not expect to get ambushed by voters furious with Obama's health care plans. Across the country, Democrats have faced angry crowds fearful of Obamacare. They have questioned the government's motives, how Obama's plans it will impact quality care, whether Obama's true agenda is socialized medicine, and how a bankrupt government can pay for any of it.

The Democrats and their media allies have portrayed the tough questioning as a political stunt by conservative groups, Fox News, and talk radio. Yet dismissing voter anger over Obamacare is very dangerous for the Democrats. The opposition and fears expressed at this month's town halls simply reflect the attitudes of the public at large. Polls have shown support for Obama's health plan falling for months. Voters rightfully do not trust big government plans for health care, especially because they are fatigued by this year's unprecedented government interventions and spending. The average voter does not share Obama's utopian vision of a grand welfare state, nor do they agree with a liberal faith in government solutions. The voters have tolerated a great deal of government activism over the last 9 months, but with the Democrats health care gambit, that tolerance has ended.

Obama is a great salesman and a great politician, but on health care, he may have reached the limits of his persuasiveness. Eighty-five percent of Americans have health insurance and most are happy with their care. These are the voters who elected Obama and they do not see the need for a government takeover of health care, which is Obama's ultimate objective. They also know, despite Obama's slick sales job, that when government gets involved, quality goes down, and costs go up. The Democrats have large majorities and can probably push a health bill through Congress, but this week they got a taste of the peril they face if they do.

Week 31

(NUKING THE PUBLIC OPTION)

August 23, 2009

There is really very little difference between Obamacare and Clinton's 1993 health care proposal, except that Clinton had a plan and was honest about what it contained. The collapse of Clinton's health care reform was the undoing of his first term, but Obama believes voter sentiment had changed and that the country is ready for a liberal agenda on health care. He was wrong of course, as this month's polls and towns halls have shown. Even with huge majorities in Congress, the health care planned is stalled, with no agreement even among Democrats on what the plan should contain or on how to pay for any of it.

Obama now finds himself in a difficult position. His allies on the Left are fanatically committed to providing coverage to the uninsured at any cost and a public insurance option. Moderate Democrats, many from Republican leaning districts, are stunned by Obamacare's $1 trillion plus price tag and fear that voting for the public option will expose them as liberals. And now, after being savaged at town halls across the nation, Democrats will return to Washington in September to try to salvage the situation.

Even the proposals this week on how to save health care reform ignited a further civil war among the Democrats. Obama knows his plan is in trouble, so this week he deftly floated the idea of dropping the public option. Obama knows the public insurance option is very unpopular among voters and it is the clearest evidence of his ultimate agenda: a single payor system. He figures if the public option is dropped, his plan might pass. He further understands that if the remaining elements of his plan fail to reduce costs or bankrupt the government, he can blame those failures on the absence of a public option.

Obama's liberal allies would have none of it. They went apoplectic at the very suggestion of dropping the public option and instead pushed for a nuclear option: forcing Obamacare through the Senate with only 51 votes using a reconciliation procedure usually reserved for budget bills. What Obama's liberal allies seem to forget is that it is unlikely Obamacare can even pass the House. If it did, forcing the biggest government program since Medicare through the Senate with no Republican or moderate Democrat support would turn Obamacare into a political lightning rod.

One of the reasons social security and Medicare have endured is that both Democrats and Republican share a basic belief in the need for the programs. They spar over costs and reform ideas, but no one suggests doing away with either. If Obamacare is enacted in its current liberal-only form with no consensus or bipartisanship supporting it, the program will founder. Every problem with the program will be blamed squarely on Democrats, Republicans will seek to undermine it at every turn, and any hope for cost saving in health care will be lost. Obama could have crafted a bipartisan reform plan, but instead he offered only a liberal's vision of health care reform, he subcontracted the drafting to Nancy Pelosi, and now the debate is radicalized. Moderates cannot vote for the bill, and liberals want the nuclear option to push it through.

Week 32

(INTO THE LION'S DEN)

August 30, 2009

Ted Kennedy was known as the Liberal Lion. He relished the title. During his 46 years in the United States Senate, he became the voice and conscience of American liberalism, pushing for regulations, welfare, government health care, and tough environmental laws at every turn. He was a hero to many, and loathed by equal numbers. Ted Kennedy died this week and in the reflections on his life and accomplishments there are lesson for today's liberals and their leader, Barak Obama.

Ted Kennedy was a 60s liberal. His politics came of age in an era of anti-establishment, social torment, and war. His views were shaped by this experience. Kennedy was always ready to loudly denounce the privileged, corporations, and conservatives generally. His was an in-your-face liberalism. Kennedy was also one of the first major leaders in the Democratic Party to endorse Obama, because Kennedy knew a real liberal when he saw one. One would be hard pressed to find any significant policy difference between Obama and Kennedy, but in style they are worlds apart.

Obama is a Reagan liberal. He saw in his youth the decline and malaise of the Carter Administration, and Reagan onslaught, with its agenda of lower taxes, smaller government, and anti-communism. Obama was never a convert to Reaganism, but it influenced both his style and strategy. Obama is not a child of an anti-establishment era, he spent the 1960's at a privileged private school in Hawaii. So he is little attracted in the vocal liberalism of Kennedy. Obama's goal is not to overthrow the establishment, but to become it. Having observed the conservative backlash that brought Reagan to office, Obama learned that liberalism must be pursued quietly and described in the rhetoric of the right. We have seen these lessons on display. Obama portrayed his massive bailout plan as an investment to prepare the American economy for the new century. In truth, it was a massive payout to Democrat special interests. He says his cap and trade program will both clean the environment and lay the foundation for a green economy. In truth, it is a huge energy tax and little more.

As for health care, Obama tried to sell his plan using the rhetoric of cost control and efficiency. Obama claimed that subsidizing coverage for 50 million people and giving government more control over health care would actually lower costs without any reduction in quality. It was an everything for everyone for free slogan. Yet when something sounds too good to be true, it always is. We now know that Obama's plan will not create efficiencies, it will not cover everyone, and there is no money to pay for it. In health care, we have seen the limits of trying to cloak liberalism in the rhetoric of the right.

Maybe Obama learned the wrong lesson from Kennedy and his era of liberals. Instead of rejecting their style, maybe he should have adopted their tactics. Kennedy, while combative in public, was a listener and deal maker behind closed doors. He worked closely with many Republicans and fashioned compromises that achieved his goals, boldly when he could, but gradually when necessary. Obama could have been a deal maker on health care, he could have brought Republicans into the process, sought to compromise a few points, and in the end he would have gotten a deal with most of what he wanted. Instead, he let the congressional leadership lock the Republicans out, while he tried to convince voters that his big government liberalism is something else. Now the reality of the Obama agenda has been exposed, the debate is polarized, and support for Obama's plan is declining. If Ted Kennedy were alive, he would have tried to salvage the situation by bringing in some Republicans to cut a deal. Maybe it is time for Obama to try to emulate that.

Week 33

(PULLING THE TRIGGER)

September 6, 2009

President Obama returned from vacation this week to face a daunting political reality. A majority of Americans disapprove of his handling of the economy, deficits, and most importantly health care. His personal approval ratings are now down to 50%. His Democrat allies in Congress just returned from an August recess where they were savaged by voters angry about a seemingly out of control government with an unending appetite for spending and regulating. Moderate Democrats are unwilling to support Obama's policies and liberal Democrats are threatening to revolt if Obama changes those policies. What is a transformational President to do?

Obama has never been one to run from a challenge and he has complete faith in his own persuasiveness. As he returned from vacation, the President announced that on September 9 he would address a joint session of Congress on health care. This step is a bold admission of weakness. Obama has lost control of the health care debate by having no plan and offering no leadership. Rather than presenting a specific plan, Obama opted to offer only general themes, leaving the drafting to his allies in Congress. The result was multiple competing bills, with huge price tags and no hopes of passage. By putting Congress in charge of health care, Obama also created a leadership void that was quickly filled by opponents of his health care plan.

To salvage the situation, in his address Obama needs to repent for these political errors. To start, Obama needs to offer a detailed plan. For Obama to persuade voters to support his plan, they need to know what his plan is. To date there has been no Obama plan, just his something for everyone at no cost to anyone stump speech. American voters are far too skeptical of government to be fooled by this rhetoric and they are demanding details on the plan. Obama also has to take ownership of the health care debate. The time for trying to preserve maneuverability by leaving the work to Congress is over. Obama has to go all in or he will lose. The decision to give a congressional address shows that Obama understands this reality.

But even if Obama offers a plan and commits all his political capital to it, success is still uncertain. Obama has staked the early success of his presidency on probably the toughest policy issue of all: health care. He has no choice but to give a detailed plan and commit to it, but those details might be the plan's undoing. Too many details will reveal the true scope of Obama's agenda for health care. Too many concessions to moderates might endanger his support on the Left. The details will reveal the true costs of his plan, which will be staggering and might sink the whole effort. The choices facing Obama are difficult and how he proceeds will teach us much about his judgment.

Obama is being coached by the Left to make no concessions and use parliamentary tricks in the Senate to push his plan through. Obama is being begged by moderates in his party to trim his plan and scale back his ambitions. But by far the safest course for Obama would be to let the Republicans in and craft a true bipartisan plan, possibly one with a trigger for a public option, but also one with tort reform and true cost controls. Obama's political stumbles on health care stemmed from his desire to stay away from the details to preserve his maneuverability. If he could craft a plan that could get just 10 Republican votes in the Senate, he would have all the maneuverability he needs to get most of his plan into law.

Week 34

(JOINT DISSENTION OF CONGRESS)

September 13, 2009

September 9 was supposed to mark a turning point in the health care debate for President Obama. After a grueling August when opponents of health care reform rose up and public support plummeted, Obama hoped to reignite support for his reform effort with an address to a joint session of Congress. He gave that address on September 9 with all the skill and deft we have come to expect, but what resulted was more an exposé on congressional division than a rallying of support.

In his speech, Obama tried to portray himself as the centrist amidst a shouting match between the extremes. He chided both the Left and the Right for pushing unrealistic proposals, while posturing that his approach was an achievable middle way. To appease the Left, he spoke of his support for a public insurance plan, even though he knows it will never pass. To feign common cause with the Right, he said he would start pilot programs on tort reform, knowing that neither he nor his liberal allies would ever let tort reform become law. Beyond that, his speech was a reprise of all we heard before, that his plan would cover new millions, make insurance companies to drop restrictions and pay for more care, and would reduce health care costs. Totally ignored was the colossal problem of how to pay for his reform program, especially considering that it actually increases health care costs. But such details are of little import to a great orator with a vision to reshape America.

The speech was in many respects Clinton triangulation redux, with Obama playing the role of the moderate. The problem is that Obama's world view is tilted so far Left, he is an unconvincing centrist. Obama is at home in the progressive wing of his party. His health care plan has all the marks of the liberal reform agenda, with vilification of insurance companies, personal and business mandates for coverage, greater government control, and of course huge tax increases. Obama also desperately wants a public insurance plan, knowing that such a plan will eventually swallow-up private insurers. The only faction to the Left of Obama on health care are the ultra-liberal Democrats who want to nationalize health care with a single payer system. To say Obama is a moderate on health care is akin to saying the Mensheviks were moderates compared of the Bolshevists.

All this phony moderation became too much for poor Congressman Joe Wilson of South Carolina, who after hearing one too many tall tales from the President shouted out: "You Lie." Well, of course Obama was lying, but to shout it out made for a major breach of protocol. What followed was the inevitable torrent of condemnation from the Democrats and the media, with all the usual themes of Republican intolerance. But what missed the media's attention is that Joe Wilson's outburst was a fair representation of the raw feelings and divisions in Congress. At best, one Republican might vote for health care reform, the public option is dead in the Senate while claimed to be essential to passage in the House, no one has any idea how to pay for the reform, and the Medicare cuts so often touted by Obama are political suicide. Yes, it was a great speech, but the real hurdles to health care reform and the deep dissention in Congress remain.

Week 35

(IT'S THE RACISM STUPID)

September 20, 2009

Everyone knows that President Obama is the first black President. Yet the President understands that emphasis on his race tends to hurt him with voters more than help. Obama was elected because he is an excellent politician who ran for president in a perfect political environment driven by an unpopular president, an unpopular war, and an economic crisis. Voters were willing to take a risk on him because of their desire for change and his ability to convey poise, intelligence, and moderation. Neither his election nor his presidency is about race, but did not tell that to Jimmy Carter.

The President has political problems and this week Jimmy Carter said his critics are motivated by racism. Claiming racism is a time-tested political tool. When under fire, many have escaped the consequences of improper or unwise conduct by asserting that those who criticize them are motivated by race. But it is hard to believe that a nation that elected a black president has suddenly rediscovered its inner racism. Further, by painting Obama critics as racists, Carter has both insulted and further motivated Obama's opponents. Unlike Carter, Obama is a smart politician who understands that a focus on his race will hurt his agenda, not help, so Obama was quick to disavow Carter's comments. Instead, Obama said his sudden unpopularity is driven by distrust of government, not race. A wise analysis, that Obama should heed.

Obama has run into political trouble because he has misread his mandate. He believed his election was an endorsement of liberalism and he has worked tirelessly to enact the most ambitious liberal agenda since the Great Society. However, America at its core is a free-market centrist society with a healthy contempt for government. That is why a majority of the public is now opposed to Obama's agenda. It should be no surprise to Obama that once his honeymoon faded and the tough work of policy began that the public would look at his agenda and resist. In barely eight months as President, Obama has increased the deficit by $3 trillion, proposed a huge new energy tax, pushed for costly health care reform, nationalized two automakers, and has aggressively intervened in Wall Street. The American public wanted change, but they did not want what Obama is offering. Carter may think it is racism, but actually it is simply dissatisfaction.

Week 36
(EXCEPTIONAL NO MORE)

September 27, 2009

This week President Obama made his first grand entrance on the world stage. He orchestrated a meeting between Israeli and Palestinian leaders, gave an address to the UN General Assembly, hosted the G20 Summit, and exposed a Iranian secret nuclear facility. Obama aggressively took on the mantel of world leadership, but in a way very different from his predecessors. Every American president since the dawn of the Cold War has preached the gospel of American exceptionalism. All these presidents, regardless of party, have touted America as a model for the world, with its democracy, free markets, and creed of individualism. President Obama has a very different perspective. He sees America as a great but deeply flawed nation, whose mistakes make better lessons for the world than its triumphs.

Nothing showed that more than the President's September 23 speech to the UN General Assembly. Before an audience of world leaders, nearly half of whom are dictators or tyrants, Obama offered no invitation to aspire to America's example. Instead, he pled with the world to forgive America for its errors and join us in a collective effort to control nuclear weapons, pursue peace, protect the environment, and improve the economy. Obama said these goals are the four pillars of the world's future, leaving for the end of his speech any comment on freedom or democracy.

Obama's four pillars tell us a great deal about his view of America and its role in the world. On nuclear weapons, Obama pledged to control and someday eliminate them. But nowhere did Obama reaffirm that such weapons are currently essential to the security of free nations. On peace, lost in all of Obama's rhetoric was any notion that freedom must be defended. Instead, ending conflict alone is his goal, without any recognition that wars must sometimes be waged to defend liberty. On preserving the planet, Obama said that the days of America dragging its feet on climate change are over, but ignored was the hypocrisy of nations that pledge action, but do nothing. On the global economy, Obama spoke not a word about free markets or how they further liberty. Instead, his comments were focused on regulations and government coordination. Obama's is a technocrat's agenda, politically correct, devoid of American principles, and internationalist in spirit.

It should be no surprise that Obama has no interest to touting American exceptionalism or inviting the world to aspire to our example. Obama is the product of an elite liberal establishment that is suspicious of American values, reflexively opposes American power, and has unquestioning faith in international organizations. Obama does not share all of these views, but his elitist origins influence his perspective. That is why Obama has no interest in promoting American values, and why his agenda for the world offers little to inspire.

Week 37

(THE INTERNATIONALIST)

October 4, 2009

There is no institution more central to the ethos of world government than the International Olympic Committee. The IOC does not simply manage international sporting events. The IOC is the grand dame of international organizations, independent of any government, with aspirations to lead the world to greater cooperation in every sphere. To true believers, the Olympic movement is not about sports, it is about globalism in its fullest sense. The power of the IOC was on display on October 2, when the leaders from the United States, Spain, Japan, and Brazil all travelled to Copenhagen to plead to host the 2016 Olympic games. President Obama's trip to the IOC to lobby for Chicago's bid showed both his commitment to internationalism and its shortcomings.

The central liberal criticism of the Bush foreign policy is that it was unilateralist. To these critics, America acting on its own in defense of its interests must be the last option. President Obama fully adheres to this view. During his campaign, he constantly criticized "go-it-alone" policies that Obama claimed made America weaker. To Obama, America's security is dependent on allies, the UN, and other international organizations. With this belief, it is no surprise that in his first nine months as President, Obama's central goal has been to rebuild America's relations with international organizations and revoke policies that have caused friction with allies. Today, America is no doubt more popular with the international community, but what is less clear is how American interests have benefitted.

One could say that the Bush Administration adhered too much Machiavelli's axiom that it is better to be feared than loved. In contrast, President Obama seems to believe that love alone will make America safe. Obama has courted the UN, reneged on missile defense deals with Poland and the Czech Republic, forsworn unilateral pressure on Iran, and joined all manner of international movements. But, as Obama learned at the IOC, being popular means very little in global power politics. At the IOC, Obama gave a heartfelt presentation on behalf of Chicago, but the prize still went to Brazil. Obama seemed to believe that his personal popularity and his willingness to make American interests subservient to international consensus would prompt the world to reciprocate. Instead, the IOC cheered Obama, praised him, and then promptly threw out Chicago's bid in the first round and chose Brazil.

Obama has portrayed his presidency as a redemption of America from the excesses of the Bush Administration. What Obama does not understand is that courting international organizations will not get them to support American policies if the interests of those organizations are different. The Olympics have never been in South America and the U.S. has hosted many Olympic games, so it is no surprise Brazil won. Obama thought his personal popularity could change the outcome, so he embarrassed himself by spending his personal political capital on the losing cause. This loss will do no long-term harm to Obama, but this episode reveals Obama's troubling belief that his personal popularity will further America's interests. It will not, as the IOC made clear.

Week 38
(REALITY BITES)

October 11, 2009

President Obama won the Nobel Peace Prize this week, not for actually bringing peace anywhere, but for talking about peace everywhere. The Nobel Committee lauded Obama for reengaging with international organizations and pursuing his dream of a nuclear free world. Missed in the award was any mention of any concrete Obama success in furthering international cooperation or peaceful resolutions. Apparently, the Nobel Committee thought that giving speeches for nine months about internationalism and compromise alone was enough to warrant the prize.

For Obama, winning the Nobel Peace Prize is as much a curse as a triumph. For a president who in recent months has lost popularity and whose agenda is stalled, winning the Nobel Prize seemed yet another award given too soon for doing too little. While Obama may be wildly popular overseas, he answers to American voters not European ones. When the American public voted for Obama, they voted for hope and they voted for change. Obama has offered hope by the bucketful, but it is the change part that has been lacking. Other than spending money with reckless abandon, Obama's accomplishments are modest. Conservatives are obviously unhappy with Obama's performance, but liberals are also increasingly faulting him for failing to deliver. In such a charged atmosphere, where Obama is being criticized for lack of accomplishment, winning the Nobel Peace Prize for so little only highlights Obama's shortcomings.

The Peace Prize also underscores the criticism that there is something not quite fully American about Obama. This criticism is not really about his race or background, but about his world view. America is an uncommonly patriotic and nationalistic country. Americans see their country as both different and better than any other nation and we expect our leaders, fairly or not, to be proponents of this view. But Obama is an uncomfortable patriot, more apt to see America's flaws than its virtues. As a product of an elitist liberal establishment that rarely hides its contempt for American patriotism, it is not surprising that Obama is an unconvincing nationalist. Obama also sees himself more as a global leader than an American one. The award of the Peace Prize is a recognition and reward for that view, but it is fraught with peril for Obama. Obama's exceptional popularity abroad fuels the view that Obama has divided loyalties. It also can quickly make his self-confidence look like vanity.

After nine months as President, the American voters now expect accomplishments. Rhetoric is easy, but the reality of getting results is very hard. Reality is now biting back at Obama and every time he gets honors for doing little, the expectations for results only rise.

Week 39

(SNOWE JOB)

October 18, 2009

The Obama health care plan, albeit bruised and belittled, made a small step toward passage this week when the Senate Finance Committee finally moved its version of a reform bill. The details of the bill that passed the Finance Committee are of little import, all that matters is that Olympia Snowe voted for it. To date, Snowe is the only Republican in Congress who has cast any vote for both the Obama Stimulus plan and the Obama health care plan, making her the liberal's favorite Republican. For a President who based his campaign on changing the Washington culture of partisanship, even the slightest patina of Republican support for his agenda is crucial. Snowe has been all too willing to give Obama that veneer of bipartisanship, while getting so very little in return.

In many ways, Snowe appears to have a case of Souter syndrome. When David Souter was nominated for the Supreme Court, all indications were that he was a solidly moderate Republican. Souter had no clear judicial philosophy, but he was a great stealth nominee, chosen because he would be easier to confirm. Souter's first opinions on the Supreme Court fit the moderate conservative expectation, but over time, as he lived and worked amongst the liberal legal establishment of Washington, his rulings veered Left. Without guiding principles, Souter absorbed his environment and became it. So it is for Snowe.

During the eight years of the Bush Administration, Snowe was always a moderate voice in the Republican Party, but in most respects she supported the Bush economic and foreign policy agenda. From 2001 to 2007, Washington was a Republican town and Snowe acted accordingly. Then came Obama. With a huge election win and huge majorities in Congress, it was clear that liberalism was on the march. Republican legislators had two choices in this new reality, resist or surrender to fashion. Snowe alone among Republicans in Congress has opted for the later.

Some politicians stand on principle, while others simply seek power and prominence. Snowe knows Obama needs Republican support. Snowe also knows that Obama's agenda is so liberal that few if any Republicans will join him. For a senator attracted to the orbit of power, this is an irresistible temptation. By being Obama's favorite Republican, she is courted, consulted and praised. In return, all she has to do is vote for bills at odds with most of what she has stood for in her political career. Not much to ask for a politician guided more by popularity than principle.

Prior to casting her Finance Committee vote, Snowe said the bill had many flaws, failed to do much that was necessary, and likely would not solve the health care challenge. Yet she said "when history calls" one must answer. Snowe wants to be a heroic figure answering history's call, even when the solution she is voting for is at odds with her party and what should be her principles. Snowe might be able to influence the bills she is supporting, making them slightly less liberal and less costly, but at the end, she is simply a pawn of the Obama agenda, nothing more.

Week 40

(DISENGAGEMENT)

October 25, 2009

A few weeks after the 2008 election, President Elect Obama met with a diverse group of leading Washington reporters and columnists, including the likes of George Will and Charles Krauthammer, to share his vision for change and to hear different perspectives. This week, President Obama hosted a White House meeting of liberal-only columnists to rally the troops. Such has been the change in Barak Obama. For a President who strove to end partisanship in Washington, this week witnessed the most unabashedly partisan assault on critics since the Nixon Administration. It is a decisive change in tactics by a President who likes to talk about bringing people together, but who pushes divisive policies.

Most everyone had to be impressed with President Obama's early efforts to reach out to Republicans. He kept Bush's Defense Secretary, he invited Republican leaders to the White House for the Super Bowl, and even came to Capitol Hill to address the House Republican Caucus. After his massive electoral win, Obama had such confidence in his persuasive powers that he believed dialogue and engagement alone would yield bipartisanship. Yet as early as the Stimulus Plan, we saw the limits of Obama's interest in compromise. Obama met repeatedly with Republicans on the Stimulus Plan, but he agreed to no significant modifications in the plan, instead rubber stamping the congressional leadership's bill. So it has been on every major legislative initiative, from Cap and Trade, to health care to the budget. Obama talks about bipartisanship but supports proposals so liberal all but a few Republicans must oppose.

Now President Obama has apparently abandoned any pretense of engagement or dialogue and instead is launching an all-out assault on any who dare to criticize his Administration. The insurance industry put out a report that Obama's health care plan will increase insurance costs, so Obama pushed Congress to repeal their antitrust exemption. The Chamber of Commerce criticizes Obama's environmental and health care plans, so the Administration tries to delegitimize them as an industry spokesman. Fox News offers by far the most critical coverage of the Administration, so Obama bans senior Administration personnel from the network, tries to exclude Fox from pool interviews, and sends his surrogates out to denounce Fox as a subsidiary of the Republican Party. And most telling of all, breaking all his pledges for openness, Obama is drafting his health reform bill behind closed doors, without any input from the Republican Leadership or even moderates in his own party.

All these events are evidence of a critical choice by Barak Obama. Despite his honest desire to end partisanship and forge a national consensus on key policies, he will never compromise on his liberal ideological agenda. President Obama thought he could subvert the opposition into willing pawns, but having failed, he has decided to end all pretense of engagement and has declared war on his opponents. Obama has realized that even a weak opposition can become dangerous if allowed to work unobstructed. As his popularity has ebbed and his policies have come under criticism, Obama can no longer afford to indulge his opponents. Rhetoric about bipartisanship is fine, but if it hinders Obama's dream of social democracy in American, the kind words will quickly turn into harsh reprisals. What is left of the Obama mystique, the notion that he is a different kind of politician, is fading fast.

Week 41

(WATERLOO DEUX)

November 1, 2009

Republican Senator Jim DeMint famously asserted that health care reform would be Obama's Waterloo, the epic political struggle that would shatter the President's political power. The President's pursuant of health care reform remains politically perilous, with poll after poll showing that the reform effort is unpopular, and the means to pay for it (mandates, Medicare cuts, and huge tax increases) outright detested. Yet all the political challenges posed by health care are nothing compared to the war in Afghanistan, where President Obama must decide whether to follows his generals' advice and send more troops. A misstep or failure on health care or the Afghanistan could cripple the Obama Presidency. DeMint called for a Waterloo, but Obama has gotten a Waterloo Deux. How well Obama manages through these challenges may determine the success of his presidency.

On health care, this week the debate reached a crescendo, with the House unveiling its 1990 page $1.1 trillion reform plan, while Senator Reid pushed forward a Senate plan including a public insurance option. A consensus seems to have developed among the Democrats that failing to pass health care reform poses more dangers than passing a plan unpopular with voters. As a result, they have ignored this summer's raucous town halls, polls, and political common sense to push a plan with something for everyone to hate. While the final form of the legislation remains unclear, all the pending plans include huge new Medicaid mandates on states, Medicare cuts for seniors, tax increases for businesses and individuals, and an array of new rules and regulations. Hardly an inspiring policy menu.

For his part, Obama has lavished praise on every varying proposal to come out of Congress. He praised the first House plan, with its huge costs and robust public insurance option. He praised the Senate finance bill with more cost controls and a trigger for the public option. He praised Senator Reid's plan to revive the public option and the most recent House bill, even though it blew through the President's $900 billion cost limit. It seems that Obama does not care what is in health care reform, as long as he can claim credit for achieving it. However, it is not clear what will cause more harm to Obama, getting health care reform or not. If reform in its current form passes, it will satisfy the Obama base, but seniors and independents will surely revolt against its unpopular provisions, handing the Republicans a potent political weapon. If reform fails, questions will arise on Obama's competence to govern.

Afghanistan is no better for Obama. American troops have been in Afghanistan for eight years, the costs in treasure and lives are mounting, the Afghan government is corrupt and inept, and the countryside has largely been lost to the Taliban. Obama has proclaimed Afghanistan as a war of necessity. As recently as March he sent more troops and embraced an ambitious counter-insurgency strategy. But violence has increased and now his commanders are seeking more troops. To deny their request would ensure defeat and signal weakness. To send more troops will enrage Obama's liberal base and will further commit America to a war that might not be winnable. No matter Obama's choice, a high political price will be paid. The convergence of health care reform and Afghanistan are by far the greatest tests for Obama, and no matter how he responds, he may well lose.

Week 42

(Garden State Blues)

November 8, 2009

The voters spoke this week, but no one in the Democratic Party was listening. In the first major electoral test of the Obama era, two states that went convincingly for Obama in 2008 elected Republican governors. In Virginia, Bob McDonnell trounced his Democrat opponent by more than 18 points. In New Jersey, Chris Christie beat Governor John Corzine by 4 points in that heavily Democratic state. Obama campaigned for both losing candidates, but put special effort into New Jersey, where he made three visits the week prior to the election. While the Republican victory in Virginia could be explained by a weak Democratic candidate and the history of Virginia voting against the party of the president, New Jersey was a different matter. A Republican had not won the governorship in New Jersey since 1997, the Democrats have a huge registration advantage, and Governor Corzine outspent his opponent two to one. Despite this, the Republican won by carrying independents by a large margin.

One might have expected that the Democratic leadership in Washington to have noticed the message sent by the voters. Polls during the election showed that voters rated the economy as their highest concern, and that a majority oppose the Obama health care plan and view Obama's policies as increasingly liberal. Young and minority voter participation was way down, Republican turnout was high, and independent voters swung to the right. In response, the Democrat leadership said the Republican victories in Virginia and New Jersey were mere local matters and focused instead on the election of Democrat bill Owens to Congress from Northern New York in a district that has been held by Republicans for 100 years. Never mind that Owens prevailed with less than 50% of the vote against a divided opposition led by a novice third party candidate.

The concerns and sentiments of the voters were validated on November 6, when the government reported that another 190,000 jobs were lost in October and that the unemployment rate had risen to 10.2%. Combined with the underemployed and those who have given up their job search, the true unemployment rate in now closer to 17%. At the same time, the dollar continues its precipitous fall, state and federal deficits continue to rise, and Congress continues to spend wildly, including a bloated Defense bill filled with billions in earmarks.

Yet with all alarm bells ringing, the Democrats and President Obama simply pretended not to hear. In the Senate, Barbara Boxer pushed forward with the Obama cap and trade plan for controlling carbon emissions, despite weak support and widespread industry opposition. In the House, during a special Saturday session, a $1.2 trillion health care bill was passed by a 220 to 215 vote. Despite the fact that the overall cost, public option, and new taxes in the House bill are unacceptable to many Democrats in the Senate, the House suspended all reality and passed its bill. Even with voters screaming stop, nothing will dissuade Obama and his allies from their agenda, nothing of course until the 2010 election.

Week 43

(A TERRORIST BY ANY OTHER NAME . . . .)

November 15, 2009

During the presidential campaign, Barak Obama was a vociferous critic of the Bush War on Terror, but once in office the President quietly continued many Bush intelligence and counter-terrorism policies. On his first day in office, Obama signed executive orders banning torture and calling for the closure of Gitmo, but to many these steps were mere symbolism, while Obama's continuation of other Bush policies showed that little had changed. Now with Obama's reaction to the November 5 shootings at Fort Hood, his continued delay in responding to his generals' requests for more troops in Afghanistan, and his decision to bring Khalid Sheikh Mohammed to New York City for trial, we finally see that Obama has a very different view of the terrorist threat.

Since taking office, the Obama Administration has been very careful to avoid any discussion of a War on Terror. While the President's team has certainly been attentive to the terrorist threat, they have avoided public discussion of it. Instead, the President's public acts to combat terrorism have focused on a charm offensive. He has travelled to the Middle East, given an address to the Muslim World, offered dialogue to Iran and other terror sponsors, all in an attempt to defuse the anti-Americanism that fuels terrorism. These acts in and of themselves are harmless and could even yield some benefits, as long as the President remained willing to call out and condemn terrorism when it occurred. With Fort Hood, we saw that he is not.

On November 5, Army Major Nidal Malik Hassan killed 13 and wounded 30 in a shooting rampage at Fort Hood. After, we learned that Hassan was a vocal critic of the War on Terror, that be had been e-mailing radical Muslim clerics, that he put SoA (soldier of god) on his personal business card, and that he shouted Allahu Akbar during his rampage. The evidence that Hassan is a terrorist, much of which was known by intelligence officials before the shooting, is overwhelming, but the President remains unconvinced. To date, the Obama Administration will only describe Hassan as a deranged gunman and his shootings as a tragedy. The Administration has even begun to criticism the Army, not for failing to find a terrorist in its midst, but instead for fostering an environment insufficiently accommodating to Muslims. It seems that President Obama wants Hassan's attack to be treated as simply a senseless crime. Yet this was not simply a crime, it was an act of radical Muslim ideology. The President's refusal to recognize that endangers us all.

The Administration's refusal to recognize the terrorist threat is further evidenced by the decision to bring Khalid Sheikh Mohammed to trial in New York City. Khalid Sheikh Mohammed was a key lieutenant of Osama bin Laden, killed journalist Daniel Pearl, and was the mastermind behind 9/11. For the last eight years, he has been a prisoner at Gitmo and last year he asked to plead guilty to his crimes. Instead of accepting his plea, the Obama Administration wants to bring him to New York, the scene of his greatest attack, for trial. The moment Khalid Sheikh Mohammed sets foot on American soil, he will be given all the rights of an American citizen. Thus empowered, a civilian trial will give Khalid Sheikh Mohammed a platform to attack America, could lead to damaging disclosures of American intelligence, and will give him an opportunity to put American on trial. The Administration's decision was completely unnecessary, because they could have accepted Khalid Sheikh Mohammed's offer to plead guilty or they could have tried him before a military tribunal. The decision is also dangerous. Khalid Sheikh Mohammed was captured in war, he was not read his Miranda rights, and he was subjected to harsh interrogation techniques. With all the constitutional rights of an American, these facts could allow Khalid Sheikh Mohammed to exclude much of the evidence against him and will make convicting him more difficult.

The Obama Administration's decision to put Khalid Sheikh Mohammed on trial is designed to obtain an acquittal of America, along with a conviction of him. Many in the Administration see the Bush War on Terror as the real crime against the Constitution and wanted this trial to show the world that American is a civil society of law. They also want terrorism treated just like any other crime, and a trial of Khalid Sheikh Mohammed in a civilian court is supposed to symbolize that. The Administration knows that Khalid Sheikh Mohammed will put the War on Terror on trial and they welcome that. They want the Bush Administration condemned as much as they want Khalid Sheikh Mohammed convicted. Never mind the damage a trial will have on our intelligence community and our anti-terrorism efforts, the desire to persuade our critics abroad trumps all.

Then we have Afghanistan. More than 12 weeks ago General McCrystal formally made his request for 40,000 more troops. For 12 weeks, President Obama has had meeting after meeting, requested analysis after analysis, and solicited opinion after opinion about what to do. All the while, the situation in Afghanistan continues to deteriorate and American soldiers continue to die. Obama has called Afghanistan a war of necessity, but when his generals request more troops to win the war, that necessity seems to fade. It is clear that Obama is questioning America's commitment to the war and wondering how to exit. His inability to make a decision signals weakness to our foes, just as his refusal to call Hassan a terrorist and his willingness to bring Khalid Sheikh Mohammed to America show that he discounts the terrorist threat.

Week 44
(Bow . . . Wow)

November 22, 2009

Despite being elected largely on a mandate to change domestic policy, Barak Obama has travelled abroad more in his first ten months as President than any of his predecessors. Spending so much time overseas has its perils, as this week's extended trip to Asia showed. Amidst increasing concern over his handling of the economy and growing voter discontent on unemployment and government spending, Obama travelled to Asia. Obama hoped to revive the U.S.-Japan alliance, strengthen relations with China, and achieve progress on climate change. Obama's trip achieved little, and instead will only be remembered for his humiliating bow to Emperor Akihito of Japan, fitting symbolism for a President whose policies are viewed by many as undermining American leadership in Asia or elsewhere.

President Obama's first stop was Japan, the longtime bulwark of American security in Asia. After the fifty year dominance of the Liberal Democrat Party, Japan is now being led by Prime Minister Hatoyama of the Democratic Party, whose winning platform included a promise of reassessing the alliance with the United States. Obama had hoped to use his trip to Japan to reaffirm the US-Japan alliance and send a message of resolve to those who challenge American leadership in Asia. While President Obama and Prime Minister Hatoyama mouthed all the right phrases about the U.S.-Japan alliance, the true message was continued tension. Despite the recent

U.S.-Japan treaty on American forces in Okinawa, Prime Minister Hatoyama had campaigned on revisiting the treaty. Most had expected Obama to inform the Japanese that the treaty is a closed issue. Instead, Obama bowed to pressure and agreed to reopen the treaty negotiations, a show of weakness that will be exploited not only by the Japanese, but also by others. Then in a breach of protocol, Obama bowed to Emperor Akihito during an audience, which was by far the most memorable moment of his entire trip, and one that symbolized Obama's willingness compromise American prestige.

Obama's charm offensive continued in China, where he and President Hu discussed trade, security, and climate change. Again, to accommodate his hosts, Obama made only muted comments on human rights, refused to publicly pressure China on nuclear proliferation, and acceded to the communists' demand that no questions be taken from the press. Even Obama's event with Chinese students was staged by the Communist Party, which handpicked the attendees. China is by far the greatest challenge to America in Asia, but for reasons of our own creation as much as theirs. Our dependence on Chinese imports and financing of our national debt has hobbled our ability to pressure China. With the Obama Administration's racking up the largest deficits in American history, our dependence on China has only grown, which explains why Obama struck the pose of a supplicant.

Obama's last major stop was the world climate change summit in Singapore. With the global economy in severe recession, many leaders have lost their appetite for a broad international convention on climate change. Not Obama, who continues to press the issue despite the economic hardships it will place on his own citizens. The climate change summit may have spared Obama the dangers of his climate change obsession, because Chinese, Indian, and other leaders made clear they would agree to no broad reductions in green houses gases at the upcoming talks in Copenhagen. These leaders put the health of their own economies and people first, something Obama seems unwilling to do.

During this trip, in a fit of ego, Obama also declared himself the first Pacific President. Evidently, Obama believes the accident of his birth in Hawaii is of greater historical importance than Teddy Roosevelt's building of the Panama Canal. But no amount of grand rhetoric can obscure the fact that this trip, like his prior trips to Europe and the Middle East, was an exercise moralizing and compromising on America's interests.

Week 45

(COLLAPSING THE BIG TENT)

November 29, 2009

This week there was a brief pause in President Obama's march toward health care reform as he returned from his trip to Asia and his Democrat allies in Congress used the Thanksgiving break to assess the political landscape. On November 21, the Senate mustered the minimum 60 votes necessary to begin debate on a health care reform bill. No Republican voted to start debate and several Democrats said they would allow debate, but that they could not vote for the current bill as drafted. Even with their huge majorities in the House and Senate, the health care reform debate is revealing the deep fissures within the Democratic Party. This is because, while the Democrat leadership represents the liberal wing of the party, their majorities depend on moderates elected from Republican or swing districts. The gale force winds of health care reform will severely test whether the Democrat big tent can endure.

For most of its history, the Democrat party has been an unruly alliance of conflicting interests. Southern conservatives, environmentalists, union advocates from industrial states, East and West Coast liberals, rural progressives, civil rights leaders, and many other factions. After the successive Republican victories beginning in 1994, many moderate and conservative Democrats either lost their seats or joined the Republicans, making both political parties more ideologically unified. To win back Congress in 2006, the Democrats purposefully adopted a big tent approach to win seats, courting moderate and pro-life Democrats throughout the country. The strategy was a tremendous electoral triumph, but whether it can translate into legislative successes will be tested by health care reform.

The Democrats have a 41 seat majority in the House, but they were able to pass their version of health care reform by only a five vote margin. To get liberal votes, the House bill contains public insurance option, is financed by an income tax increase on high earners, and opted not to tax expensive private insurance plans (many of which are for union members). To get moderate votes, the House leadership had to consent to the Stupak amendment, which would bar abortion coverage in any insurance plan offered by the government or in the proposed health care exchanges. The House bill was successfully calibrated to get just enough votes to pass, but many of its critical elements make getting health care reform into law more difficult.

The Democrats have 58 seats in the Senate, plus there are two independents who usually vote with the Democrats. While this is a strong majority, the Senate Democrat leadership faces the same problems as their colleagues in the House. The mandatory public insurance option so critical to passage in the House cannot overcome a filibuster in the Senate. The House's income tax increase in unacceptable to the Senate, while the Senate's tax on expensive private health insurance plans is unpopular in the House. The House bill would not have passed without the Stupak amendment on abortion, but that provision will not survive the Senate. Thus, the critical provisions necessary for passage in each chamber of Congress are unacceptable to the other chamber.

The calculation President Obama and his allies in Congress have made is that if each chamber simply passes whatever bill it can, when the bills go to conference for crafting the final legislation, the pressure to pass a bill will be so great that Democrat members will be forced to vote for it. Considering that the congressional leadership is almost entirely from the liberal wing of the party, it is safe to assume the final bill will make moderates unhappy. Thus, after inviting moderates into the Democrat big tent, with health care reform we will see if moderates will be quickly pushed to the exits.

Week 46

(OBAMASTAN)

December 6, 2009

After a two month internal debate and review, on December 1, President Obama gave an address at West Point outlining his new strategy in Afghanistan. He announced that he would send 30,000 additional troops, focus on local reforms, and push for faster training of Afghan soldiers. He described the war as vital to American security, but at the same time pledged that by June 2011 the additional troops would start coming home. To the voices on the Left calling for abandoning the war, the decision was a betrayal. The Right in contrast applauded the decision to send more troops, but they derided Obama's delay and his deadline to start withdrawing the reinforcements. But all agree that Obama's decision made the war his war, with all the dangerous consequences that entails.

When Obama first began his run for the presidency, his was an anti-war campaign. The war in Iraq was very unpopular and going badly, and Obama saw it as an opportunity to start a populist movement and differentiate himself from Hillary Clinton, his rival who voted to authorize the invasion of Iraq. Yet Obama realized that he could not win on solely an anti-war platform, so he continually stressed during the campaign his support for the war in Afghanistan. He called it a war of necessity and used his support for the war to convince voters that he would vigorously fight the War on Terror and defend the nation from threats. Two months into his presidency, he kept that pledge by sending additional troops into the war and by implementing the Bush Administration's recommendations for revamping the war strategy. Unfortunately, the situation in Afghanistan continued to deteriorate and Obama's generals asked for even more troops, which culminated in his speech at West Point and probably the most consequential decision so far in his presidency.

In 2008, few would have guessed that Iraq was the easier problem and that Obama's war of necessity in Afghanistan would prove the true challenge, but that is the reality. The Bush surge in Iraq succeeded, violence decreased, the Iraqi government grew more stable, and the US was able to begin withdrawing troops. The war Obama condemned is the war that has been largely won, while the war he praised is becoming a quagmire. For Obama, the decision to send more troops posed challenges on every level. For all his tough talk on terrorism, it is clear Obama has little stomach for war. He has preferred engagement to confrontation at every turn, from Russia, to Iran, to North Korea. But in Afghanistan, with US causalities mounting and his own statement that the war was necessary, denying reinforcements or withdrawing troops was too great a sign of weakness even for Obama. So he put off the Afghanistan decision until after key votes on health care reform to keep the liberals in line. He increased troops, but by less than his generals requested, and he pledged to start bringing them home by June of 2011 in an attempt to quell any rebellion by his allies on the Left, but each decision simply increased his peril.

By delaying so long in deciding to send more troops, he telegraphed that his heart is not in the fight and he gave vital time to our foes to Afghanistan to strengthen their hold. By deciding to send more troops, but not the number requested, he decreased the chances of success of his own gamble. By setting an arbitrary deadline to begin the withdrawal, he undermined his own comment that Afghanistan is a conflict that must be won and made our allies question whether the U.S. was committed to victory. In the end, Obama's decision was a compromise designed to be politically clever, but might prove militarily dangerous. To top it all off, in his speech at West Point, he never spoke of victory, never tried to rally the troops on the justness of our cause, and never called out our enemies on their cruelties. Instead, he gave a flat and professorial address on why he was doing what he clearly did not want to do. No matter his misgivings and doubts, Afghanistan is now Obama's war, to lose or to win, even if "win" is a word he will not say.

Week 47

(ACHIEVEMENTS SLIGHT)

December 13, 2009

Having won the Nobel Peace Prize based on expectations rather than accomplishments, President Obama faced a tricky test when he travelled to Oslo on December 10 to accept the award. Although the Nobel Committee surely believed the prize would strengthen Obama, in truth it has been a burden. For a President who has talked much, but to date achieved little, yet another unearned plaudit underscored that he is a man for whom reputation outpaces results. To defuse this in his acceptance speech, Obama started off by acknowledging that compared to the others who have won this award, his achievements have been slight. Yet after this moment of modesty, Obama launched into his finest speech so far as President. A speech that showed realism, idealism, reasonableness, and resolve. A speech that may have shown justification for the Nobel Committee's decision, but not for the reasons they expected.

President Obama's Nobel acceptance speech was much anticipated in Europe. The Europeans feel a true kinship for Obama. They see him as a sophisticate, progressive, a one-worlder, one of them. His popularity in Europe no doubt contributed to the decision to give him the prize. Yet a clear undercurrent of the award was a rebuke of America and its role in the world. This distaste for American foreign policy was personified in George W. Bush, who was not simply disliked in Europe, but actually hated. In the eyes of Europeans, Obama is the anti-Bush and awarding him the Peace Prize was a condemnation of prior presidents as much as it was an award for the current one.

Having given Obama his grand prize, many in the audience in Oslo must have expected a speech that would justify their confidence. Obama had another idea. Instead of taking the Nobel Committee's invitation to give another discourse on the shortcomings of America and the need for a new paradigm in foreign policy, Obama did the opposite. He began by putting to bed any notion that he is a pacifist. Obama devoted the first half of his speech to the concept of just war. While noting that war is a reflection of humanity's imperfections, he acknowledged that there is evil in the world and that war is sometimes necessary to confront that evil. Obama may have made these remarks rationalize the award of a peace prize to a leader who just ordered the expansion of a war in Afghanistan, but that does not dilute the essential truth of his reflections.

Next, rather than dwell on America's errors, and surely there have been many, he reminded the audience that it was the blood and treasure of America that forged the new Europe and gave it the last 64 years of peace. For a President so reluctant to talk about American exceptionalism, this was hopefully a moment of revelation for the President. Far too often European envy and distain has clouded this essential reality, and every once in a while our allies need a pointed reminder, and Obama gave them one.

Finally, Obama laid three pillars for the future avoidance of war. First, he said the world had to develop alternatives to violence that deter our foes and strengthen international unity. He noted that simply talking alternatives to war is not enough and that the international community must back up strong words with resolute actions. A subtle rebuke to those European leaders who talk about threats, but sit on their hands. Second, he said that peace alone is not enough, but instead we need to seek a peace the respects the "inherent rights and dignity" of every human being. Peace is therefore not the end, but a means to an end. Third, he asserted that peace is not just about protecting civil and political rights, but also about advancing economic rights. It is a truism that free nations that offer opportunity to their peoples rarely go to war, and Obama's comments show his appreciation of that reality.

In the end, Obama's address took the best from the foreign policy realists and the idealists and melded them into one vision for the advancement of peace. It was an address that was visionary, courageous, and thoughtful. Hopefully his policies will be as wise.

Week 48

(THE PRINCE IN DENMARK)

December 20, 2009

Other than health care, no issue is as important to President Obama as climate change. No doubt Obama believes that climate change is caused by man and that urgent action is needed. Yet the level of focus and commitment by the President to his climate change agenda far outweighs any measureable urgency. Despite dire economic conditions at home, falling public concern, and uncertain support in Congress, President Obama presses forward with his global warming crusade. So this week the President travelled to the UN Climate Change Summit in Copenhagen, to anointed himself leader of the cause. And while the summit was largely an exercise in discord, with no consensus emerging, it furthered Obama's ends, because there is far more to Obama's climate change agenda that environmentalism.

For Obama, climate change is an opportunity not only to help the planet, but also to plan a new American economy, empower Washington as its umpire, and make America subject to an international regulatory regime. Industrial planning, Washington control, and world government: the Leftist trifecta. There is nothing new in Obama's agenda, in fact what he is attempting has been done in Denmark, the host nation of the summit. Three decades ago, Denmark embarked on a national experiment to remake its economy. Through punitive taxation and regulation, the Danish government legislated fossil fuels into the economic abyss, then it instituted a complex regime of tax rebates and subsidies to force its people to stop driving, make homes energy efficient, and convert to new fuels. Those who complied with the Danish government's dictates were rewarded, those who did not were punished. The Danish energy regime has become a model for industrial and social planning, with government picking the winners and losers. That is what Obama's climate change agenda is really about.

Obama has a grand dream of creating a green economic revolution in America. He sees government as the spark for that revolution. His cap and trade bill is designed not only to decrease carbon emissions, but also to use taxation to direct resources and opportunities to those industries favored by government, while punishing those disfavored. By raising the cost of fossil fuels and by offering subsidies to favored industries, Obama hopes to erect a new green economy. But rather than trust the free markets, or innovation, or entrepreneurs, Obama's green economy is to be made by government industrial planning and a spoils system of exemptions and subsidies to those benighted companies and industries lucky enough to be given Washington's favor.

Yet the Obama agenda does not end there, because Obama not only wants to make the private sector ever more subservient to Washington, but also to make Washington subservient to international institutions. Obama seeks to bind America to an international regulatory regime on climate control, one that will make America subsidize other nations' economies and force America to comply with international dictates on climate change. It is industrial planning on an international scale.

The combination of Obama's health care and climate change agenda shows how radically Obama wants to change America's economic system. Obama is not out to end capitalism, but he wants a free market much more constrained and much more directed by Washington. To accomplish this, he seeks to create a government far larger and more powerful than we have ever known, that taxes and regulates with abandon, and whose reach will touch us all. It is nothing less than a devaluation of individual liberty and free markets to further social democracy. The crowd in Copenhagen knows this and cheered him for it, but Americans are only now starting to see the truth.

Week 49

(SENATOR SANTA CLAUS)

December 27, 2009

When the Senate passed its health care reform bill on Christmas Eve by a party-line vote, Harry Reed portrayed the victory as a Christmas present for the America people, but sadly presents were given only to a few Democrat Senators. No doubt Majority Leader Reed did a masterful job getting a bill through the Senate. With polls showing both health care reform and Democrats generally less popular with voters, it was no mean achievement to garner the 60 votes needed to close debate and pass a bill. With 58 Democrats in the Senate and two Independents, Reed needed every vote, since the 40 Republicans were unanimously opposed to closure. Reed got his 60 votes, but in a manner that will sully and possibly threaten the bill itself.

Any time every vote is needed to pass a bill, certain politicians will hold out to get goodies. In this case, Reed doled out billions in special favors to a host of Democrats to get the needed votes. The list of pork was long indeed, with hundreds of millions going to Arkansas and Louisiana to get Blanche Lincoln and Mary Landrieu's votes, expensive tax exemptions for Blue Cross in Michigan to secure UAW support, and grants for hospitals from sea to shining sea. But Senator Ben Nelson took the prize for feeding at the trough.

Probably the most conservative Democrat in the Senate, Nelson was a frequent critic of the bill. He and Senator Lieberman killed the public option and Medicare expansion, and his opposition alone forced further abortion funding restrictions. Yet what got his vote was not these principled changes, but pork. His state of Nebraska was permanently exempted from the new Medicaid burdens imposed by the bill and Nebraska insurers were likewise exempted from much of the bill's new taxes and regulations. In essence, the 49 other states now have to pay Nebraska's way. The fact that Nelson would only vote for the bill if its burdens were not placed on Nebraska highlights the problems with the bill, problems that will exact a heavy price from Democrats in the next election. Plus, these payoffs to select politicians make the process look corrupt and increase overall voter skepticism about reform.

The Senate's health care reform bill is certainly less expensive than the House version and avoids a public insurance plan, but its merits end there. The bill will place huge new Medicaid burdens on the States, makes massive cuts in Medicare, raises $500 billion in taxes that will touch every American, and will lead to higher insurance costs. Plus, all the burdens in the bill start in 2010, when most benefits do not kick in until 2014. Worst of all, between 2014 and 2024, the bill will add hundreds of billions to the deficit. No wonder upwards of 60% of Americans in most polls now oppose the bill and Democrats are falling behind Republicans in poll after poll. Reed had to play Senator Santa Claus to get a bill passed, but there will likely be no presents under the tree next year for the Democrats.

Week 50
(THE QUIET WAR)

January 3, 2010

President Obama will not utter the words "War on Terror," but he wages the war nevertheless. Unlike President Bush, who raised America's fight with Al-Qaeda constantly, President Obama fights the war covertly, while reserving his public comments mainly for liberal consumption. Obama continues the Bush surveillance policies, counter-terrorism efforts, and has expanded the war in Afghanistan, but in public he mainly touts closing Gitmo, ending torture and the nobility of Islam. It is a strategy crafted to protect the nation, while appeasing his base on the Left, which reflexively opposes aggressive efforts to fight terrorism as too Bush-like. It is Obama's quiet war.

This week, Obama realized the danger of his carefully crafted strategy. On Christmas Day, Umar Farouk Abdulmutallab, a Nigerian terrorist trained by Al-Qaeda in Yemen, boarded a Northwest flight in Amsterdam bound for Detroit with explosives in his underwear. On approach to Detroit, he tried to ignite his bomb and bring down the plane, but he was stopped by other passengers. Come to find out, his father warned American authorities about his son's intentions, which combined with his cash purchase of a one-way ticket without any baggage, should have been more than enough to put authorities on notice. Yet he slipped through, and but for luck and the vigilance of other passengers, hundreds could have died.

Sticking with his strategy, President's Obama's first inclination was to downplay the attack. While vacationing in Hawaii, Obama let three days pass before he made any public comment. He only emerged from seclusion after the furor created by Homeland Security Secretary Janet Napolitano, who said the system that allowed Abdulmutallab onto that plane worked. When he did appear before reporters, Obama showed little urgency, calling it an "alleged" attempt to attack an airliner by an "isolated" extremist. His comments were so flat and disinterested that many began to question whether the President understood the seriousness of the terrorist threat. Only after facts emerged about Abdulmutallab's training in Yemen by Al-Qaeda and the ignored warning signs did the President admit to serious flaws in security and describe the events as an attempted attack by Al-Qaeda.

A policy of publicly downplaying the importance of the War on Terror works fine when that war is well in hand. If the covert efforts to fight terrorism are working and attacks on Americans are being thwarted, Obama can have it both ways. The Left can admire him for scaling back

Bush's war, while the absence of bad consequences silences his critics on the Right. But when there is a high profile attempted attack that calls into question airline security at its core, President Obama cannot afford to make appeasement of his base his first inclination. With the Fort Hood attack, there was just enough evidence that Major Hassan was simply deranged for Obama to avoid admitting any terrorist link. But Obama tried to use the same playbook with Abdulmutallab and it did not work, because this time the terrorist link was too clear.

There is no doubt that President Obama wants to protect America, but his efforts to fight terrorism are calibrated for maximum political positioning, not maximum effort to defeat Al-Qaeda. Closing Gitmo, bringing terrorists to the U.S. for trial, investigating CIA counter-terrorism tactics, and pushing dialogue with Iran are possible for Obama only if he projects competence in protecting America. With the attempted Christmas attack, the image of competence was shaken. Worse yet, all his steps to curry favor with the Left made him look weak and out of touch to an American public that is vocal about its concerns over terrorism. Obama saw his vulnerability quickly and corrected his approach, but the fact that his first reflex was to publically downplay the terrorist threat is troubling.

Week 51
(PUBLIC TERRORIZED)

January 10, 2009

President Obama was in damage control mode this week. After trying to ignore the attempted Christmas Eve attack, then emerging from seclusion to call it an alleged attack, and only later admitting the Al-Qaeda link, Obama looked weak, irresolute, and out of touch. Obama tried to change all that this week, with dramatic speeches, a detailed outline of security failures, and stating that the buck stops with him on security. Obama even admitted that we are at war with Al-Qaeda. It was a good show, but mostly smoke and mirrors, because in the end the President is not willing to make tough and effective choices to improve security, and instead wants to put greater burdens on millions of Americans who are no threat. It seems that terrorizing the public is more palatable to President Obama than terrorizing the enemy.

The failure that led to the near disaster on Christmas Eve was not an inability to gather evidence, but a failure to connect the dots. There was plenty of evidence to indicate that Abdulmutallab was a threat. The warnings from his father, the one-way ticket with no luggage, and his trips to Yemen were clear signs. Various intelligence agencies had parts of this picture, but none had it all and no one coordinated the information. So this attack was borne of intelligence failures, but Obama refuses to take many necessary steps to address the problem. In his speech, Obama outlined plans for greater coordination between intelligence agencies, improving the terrorist watch lists, and augmenting airport security. All good steps no doubt, but pretty weak stuff for a nation at war.

A nation at war needs to treat captured enemies as combatants who can be questioned extensively on the enemy's plans. Obama gave Abdulmutallab over to civil authorities to have him treated like a common criminal, so now Abdulmutallab has all the rights of the U.S. citizen, cannot be questioned, and therefore cannot help the war effort. A nation at war needs to keep the enemies from its shores, but Obama wants to close Gitmo, bringing its prisoners into the U.S., where they will get constitutional rights, lawyers, and a pulpit to encourage further attacks on America. A nation at war focuses on the enemy not its own people, but Obama wants to place the heaviest security burdens on Americans who are not a threat. In a spasm of political correctness, Obama wants to impose even more burdensome and expensive airline security, in essence treating every American as a potential terrorist. However, our enemy in this war is radical Islam, and our airline security efforts should be focused on those mostly likely in league with them. A nation at war tries the captured enemies by military tribunal, just as we did during World War II. Although he has the statutory and constitutional authority to try captured enemies by tribunals, Obama is insisting on trials in federal courts, where constitutional protections, rules of evidence, and rights to speak in one's own defense will give aid to the enemy and its agenda.

President Obama has said that the nation is at war with Al-Qaeda, but his actions show that he still views Al-Qaeda as little more than an Islamic mafia. He will talk about security, he will spend ever more money, he'll even use the word "war," but when a President will not treat the enemy as an enemy, then that President does not really believe his nation is at war.

Week 52

(PASSION FOUND)

January 17, 2010

In recent weeks, even President Obama's allies have criticized his lack of passion. From his lackluster speech on the troop surge in Afghanistan, to his muted response to the Christmas attack on the Northwest flight to Detroit, President Obama seems unemotional and disconnected. Then a magnitude 7 earthquake hit Haiti on January 12, and Obama found his passion. He immediately addressed the nation, pledged support, dispatched the military and other aid organizations, and called on former Presidents Clinton and George W. Bush to lead relief efforts. Passion, determination, decisiveness, bipartisan: finally an impressive Obama moment.

Haiti was blighted even before the January 12 earthquake. By far the poorest nation in the hemisphere, the people of Haiti have been racked with poverty, disaster, corruption, dictatorship, and hopelessness. The world has answered the call of Haiti many times. Hundreds of millions have been spent (and wasted) on relief programs for Haiti over the decades, but the people remain impoverish and their government weak and corrupt. Few nations were less well prepared than Haiti for a great natural disaster. In the aftermath of the earthquake, tens of thousands are dead, thousands of others are trapped in the rubble, and the capital is in ruins. On the very doorstep of America a great humanitarian disaster is looming, which is why decisive action from Obama was right and necessary.

President Obama quickly understood the importance of prompt support for Haiti, but why is it that Obama has been so slow to show passion and decisiveness in other arenas. On issues of particular American interest, whether they be the deteriorating situation in Afghanistan or terror attacks on America, Obama sometimes seems passionless, unsure, and unsteady. Yet when the world calls on issues like global warming or Haiti, Obama is prompt and sure. The answer seems to be Obama's deep distain for nationalism and his deep attraction to world leadership. As a product of the American Left, Obama's first inclination is to distrust American solutions. He has been taught ever since his days at Columbia that America has done much harm in the world and that only international consensus and world cooperation can sustain progress. With this background, it is no surprise that Obama hesitates every time he is asked to lead American decisively on a controversial course. He rarely doubts himself, but he seems to always doubt his nation.

So Haiti was a perfect Obama moment. A chance to lead a great and just humanitarian cause, to rally the world, to aid the oppressed, and to try to restore social justice. Everything Obama has done for Haiti is commendable and we should all be proud of his leadership. We also should demand of him equal devotion to other challenges that more directly threaten our own people and our own interests, whether they be terrorism, or Iran, or Afghanistan. It is all well and good to play the role of leader of the world, if a President remains leader of America first. To date Obama has been at best a reluctant cheerleader for America's interests, which makes his impressive performance on Haiti both admirable and concerning.

Week 53
(MassQuake)

January 24, 2010

After the election of President Obama and the huge majorities gained by the Democrats in Congress, we heard pundit after pundit proclaim the resurgence of liberalism, the death of Republicanism, and an era of Democrat dominance. In the wake of this chorus of encouragement, the Obama Administration pursued an aggressively liberal agenda on health care, spending, taxation, and the environment. As Obama's first year continued, polls began to show increasing public unease with the Obama agenda, yet the Democrats pressed on. Despite raucous summer town halls where voters expressed deep concerns, the Democrats belittled the protests and pressed on. After Republican triumphs in off-year elections in Virginia and New Jersey, the Democrats pretended those votes did not matter and pressed on. After the public turned soundly against Obamacare in the closing weeks of 2009, the Democrats used billions to buy off senators and unions, and pressed on to Senate passage of a health care bill on Christmas Eve. Like a runaway train, the Democrats barreled down their carefully laid track, until the voters decided they could tolerate no more and threw the brakes.

On January 19, the voters used the only weapon at their disposal to stop the Democrat agenda: the ballot box. In deeply Democratic Massachusetts, the voters elected Republican Scott Brown to replace the late Ted Kennedy in the United States Senate. This was the first Republican elected to the Senate from Massachusetts since 1972 and in happened in a state that went for Obama by 26 points. Just as in Virginia and New Jersey, the independent voters who put Obama in office turned decisively against the Democrats. The Scott Brown victory not only deprived the Democrats of their 60 vote majority in the Senate, but also put fear into the hearts of scores of Democrats who have to face the voters in November. The day after the Democrat debacle, Speaker Pelosi and Leader Reid remained defiant, saying health care and the remainder of the Democrat agenda would still pass, but by week's end it became clear that the moderate Democrats would tolerate no more and that most of Obama's major legislative initiatives were on hold, if not dead.

For his part, President Obama seems to have taken the results in Massachusetts as a sign that he needs to become a more populist and aggressive proponent for change. Even before the vote in Massachusetts, Obama proposed a new tax on banks related to the financial bailout. After the election, Obama announced a new plan to heavily regulate and break-up the largest banks, leading to a 4% decline in the stock market. On a campaign trip to Ohio to close the week, Obama stuck a combative populist tone, lashing out at Wall Street and corporate interests and proclaiming 21 times that he will "fight" for average people. It appears the lesson Obama learned from Massachusetts is that he needs to be even more liberal to prevail.

When the voters gave President Clinton a setback in 1994, he pursued a strategy of triangulation and proclaimed that the era of big government was over. Clinton was able to make these adjustments because, while he believed in Democrat principles, he was no ideologue and was more interested in winning than in policy purity. Obama is now in a similar position, and how he responds will be telling. Obama might listen to the voters and moderate his policies. However, the early signs show that Obama plans to stay on the Left and push his agenda more aggressively. It is possible that Obama, a politician who has no record of bipartisanship or moderation, is simply too dedicated to his goal of social democracy to continence much compromise. The danger for Obama is that if he will not tolerate moderation, the voters are likely to refuse to tolerate him.

Week 54

(THE STATE OF THE DENIAL)

January 31, 2010

President Obama had hoped that in his first State of the Union address he could proclaim that change had come to America, by means of health care reform, a cap and trade law, and financial reform. Instead, when Obama took the podium on January 27, he addressed large but dispirited Democrat majorities with a message that he will not quit. After a year of blithely ignoring worsening poll numbers and bad election results, reality hit home for Obama and his Democrat allies with the election of Scott Brown to the Senate from Massachusetts. It was almost as if the whole Democrat apparatus was under some spell of invulnerability until Scott Brown broke the wand, leaving the party lost and confused. Obama's job in the State of the Union was to rally his troops, but he seems to have forgotten to rally the nation as well.

Political observers have known for months that public sentiment was moving against the Democrats and their marquee initiative: health care reform. Voters' primary concern was jobs and the economy, while the President spent his first year focused on health care. Despite all the storm clouds, the Democrats were so tempted by their dominate control of Congress and the White House that they dispelled all caution in pursuit of their goals. The Democrats' brief 60 vote majority in the Senate proved a curse, because they turned their focus from a bipartisan reform effort to getting their 60 votes. The process produced a wholly partisan bill filled with gimmicks and bribes for key Senators. The bill was so unpalatable to Republicans and many moderate Democrats that the addition of a single new Republican senator caused the whole legislative edifice to crumble. The failure of health care reform also endangered Obama's other coveted programs, including cap and trade, union card check, and financial reform.

Given this change in fortune, in his address Obama had two basic choices. He could acknowledge his errors and pivot to the center in an effort to seek bipartisan consensus. His other option was to dig in and encourage his troops to press on. In his speech, Obama made clear he would not compromise on his core agenda for America. He continued his bitter criticism of the Bush Administration, he chastised the Republican minority for obstructing his initiatives, he declared unwavering support for health care reform, cap and trade, more stimulus spending, and an end to the military's don't-ask-don't-tell policy on sexual orientation. Obama even used the occasion to lash out at the Supreme Court's ruling endorsing corporate and union free speech rights, to the evident distain of several justices who were sitting but a few feet from the President. Overall, it was the speech of an unrepentant progressive whose dedication to changing American society is unbowed.

Obama did strike a few notes of moderation, but all were clearly designed for political advantage, rather than policy change. After ignoring for months voter concern about jobs, Obama made this issue the primary focus of his address and proposed new tax cuts as part of a second stimulus bill. In recognition of growing public concern over the deficit, he proposed a three-year freeze on non-defense discretionary spending. A good start, until one realizes that he has presided over an 84% increase in discretionary spending and his second stimulus bill will spend much of the savings from the spending freeze. Obama said that congressional earmarks should be disclosed, completely ignoring his prior pledge to veto them. He stated support for nuclear energy and off-shore drilling, but only if combined with a comprehensive cap and trade bill. On terrorism, he touted his expansion of the war in Afghanistan, and then accused his critics of questioning his patriotism. On health care reform, he said he erred in failing to explain the reform to voters and that the process was imperfect, but on the substance he remained defiant. Each of these statements of moderation were designed to make his priorities look more attractive, while leaving the policies largely unchanged.

President Obama is a very good politician. He knows the playing field has changed. His State of the Union address shows that he wants to convince independent voters that he will focus on jobs, inspire his base with declarations of unwavering support for the progressive agenda, and co-opt a few Republicans with some moderate rhetoric. But beneath this veneer of political repositioning is a President still pressing for the same key goals declared in his Inaugural Address. The tactics have changed, but the policies are the same.

Week 55

(RED TIDE)

February 7, 2010

During his State of the Union address, President Obama spoke of the need to reduce the federal budget deficit, yet pledged continued pursuit of the policy objectives of his first year in office. Obama's rhetoric struck many as an untenable contradiction, stated for political purposes, rather than policy coherence. This became all too clear only six days later, when the President unveiled his 2011 budget plan that called for a record $3.8 trillion in spending and a $1.57 trillion deficit.

Like a magician, Obama announced his budget with the rhetoric of fiscal restraint, hoping his words would make his proposed tide of red ink disappear.

In its first year, the Obama Administration has pursued the biggest increase in federal spending since the New Deal. Obama spent heavily not only on his $787 billion stimulus plan, but also on vastly expanded government in almost every other arena, including health care, education, the environment, and defense. To get his priorities passed, he broke his pledge on earmarks and signed into law thousands of pork projects costing taxpayers billions. His 2011 blueprint follows the same path. It still contains huge increases in domestic spending and seeks yet another stimulus bill. Despite Obama's promise to review the budget with a fine-tooth comb to eliminate ineffective programs, this budget only cuts $20 billion in such programs, and most of that savings comes from cutting defense procurement. And although the budget plan seeks to freeze discretionary non-defense spending for three years, those items account for only 17% of the budget and spending levels would be frozen at the bloated amounts enacted the year before. In total, the spending freeze would save a mere $15 billion in 2011, out of the budget of $3.8 trillion.

The best proof of the Obama Administration's continued addiction to federal spending is tax policy. Obama's budget blueprint proposed $1 trillion in new taxes on high income Americans, corporations, and energy use. Even with these new taxes, his budget still yields massive deficits for a decade. Indeed, Obama's own projection is that the 2015 federal budget deficit would still be just below $800 billion or 4.5% of projected G.D.P. In essence, the Obama Administration is proposing a spending plan that ensures massive deficits for a decade. For a President who so often assails his predecessor for enacting programs without paying for them, it seems Obama plans to outdo him.

It is ironic that Obama's approach to federal spending is more a rebuke of the Clinton Administration than of George W. Bush. President Clinton ran on deficit reduction and his administration was filled with deficit hawks. The Clinton tax increases, the failure of Hillary Care, the end of the Cold War, and the spending restraint of the 1994 Republican majority all combined to create fiscal sanity. Yet the Obama Administration has no time for the deficit mindedness of centrist Democrats. Its vision is very different. The Obama Administration seeks to change the balance between the private and public sectors. The President entered office proclaiming that he would fundamentally change America and he meant it. The President and his advisors believe that government is too small, the markets are too free, and taxes are too low. They have used the opportunity offered by the recession to vastly expand government, knowing that programs or entitlements once created are very difficult to dismantle. Having created these huge deficits, Obama is betting Congress will increase the tax levy rather than reduce spending. Once these higher spending levels are retained and the tax burden increased, Obama knows subsequent administrations will be unable to reverse course.

What is most striking about the Obama budget plan is its determination. After lost elections of Virginia, New Jersey, and Massachusetts, polls showing public disgust with deficits, and the failure of health care reform, Obama offers little compromise or change in course. This shows that Obama's agenda is ideological, not political. Lost elections and public dissatisfaction mean little, achieving the Obama vision of social democracy is all that matters. That became clear on February 3 during Obama's meeting with Senate Democrats. When endangered Democrat Senator Blanche Lincoln practically begged the President to moderate his policies, Obama with no reflection or hesitation flatly refused, saying that any change or moderation would be adoption of the failed policies of the Bush Administration. With those words, Obama both sentenced to political death many in his audience and proclaimed his fealty to the red tide of debt he hopes will usher in his new America.

Week 56

(NO CHANGE TO BELIEVE IN)

February 14, 2010

Effective presidents need to know how to maneuver in changed political landscapes. The best recent example is President Clinton's declaration that "the era of big government is over" after the Republican landslide of 1994. For President Obama, faced with a nation increasingly uneasy with his policies, the moment for a course change has come. Yet what we have seen this week from the White House is the rhetoric of bipartisanship used to mask a defiant refusal to compromise. Apparently, change is not something Obama is willing to believe in.

What is emerging from the Obama Administration is an insincere campaign to divide and conquer the Republican opposition. The first salvo was the Obama 2011 budget, which touted a limited spending freeze to hide massive new spending. Next came the call for another stimulus bill (now named a Jobs Bill to make it more palatable to voters), which Obama hopes to pass by including some tax changes favored by Republicans. After that, Obama invited Republicans to a summit on February 25 to discuss how to move forward on health care reform. Yet each of these steps was designed to further the Obama agenda, not foster bipartisanship.

On the budget, Obama's 2011 spending plan maintains his vision for a vastly expanded government with greater powers over the private sector. No tough decisions were made on spending to rein in the deficits. Instead, Obama offered a minimal spending freeze simply for political cover. Obama and his allies hope Americans will excuse the deficits if they believe the government is starting to take steps to restrain spending. However, Obama's main plan for deficit reduction is taxation. His 2011 budget already has $1 trillion in new taxes, and his surrogates are actively shopping increases in social security taxes, energy taxes, and a value added tax as the most effective means to control the deficit. There is no change in the Obama budget, it is just more spending and the hope for ever more taxation.

On the stimulus bill, Democrats know they are heading for a very tough election in 2010 and want to pass a bill that will allow them to tell voters that they are fighting for jobs. When the Democrats passed their $787 billion stimulus package in 2009, they bet that the economy would recover on its own in 2010, so they crafted a bill more designed to pay off political allies rather than create jobs. The economy has not bounced back as hoped, so now the Democrats are looking to yet another stimulus bill. The problem is the government has huge deficits and the public has little appetite for more spending. President Obama could have called for re-directing the nearly $400 billion in unspent funds from the first stimulus bill to more effective uses, but that would have angered his political base. So instead he is pushing yet another budget busting stimulus bill, which includes a few Republican suggestions to attract votes. Yet even that hint of bipartisanship was too much for Senate Democrats, who immediately pledged to strip out many of the Republican proposals.

On health care reform, President Obama has invited Republicans to a summit to discuss the best ideas to move the process forward. Yet behind the scenes, the White House is still trying to push a strategy where the House with enact the bill already passed by the Senate. The President has also refused calls to start over with a new bill, a clear signal that the health care summit is designed to embarrass Republicans rather than pursue a compromise bill. Obama is hoping that the summit will allow him to look bipartisan and give him yet another chance to convince voters to support his bill.

The Obama Administration's tactical moves to look bipartisan are just that, tactics. Behind all of Obama's maneuvers is an air of contempt for a public too obtuse to recognize the benefits of the Obama agenda. That became all too clear this week when Press Secretary Robert Gibbs mocked the Conservative's Tea Party Convention and Sarah Palin's speech notes written on her hand. Gibb's distaining comments were the only honest moment by the White House all week.

Week 57

(BAYH BYE)

February 21, 2010

Yet another Democrat tried to send a message to the White House that the Obama agenda is not sitting well with the public, but again no one in the Administration appears to be listening. On February 15, 2010, two-term Indiana Democrat Evan Bayh announced that he would not seek reelection to the Senate. Despite a $12 million war chest and solid popularity, Bayh is stepping aside, giving the Republicans an excellent opportunity to pick up another seat in the Senate.

In his statement on retirement, Bayh said he was stepping down because partisanship in Washington was preventing progress on critical policy issues. However, much more was at work. Just a week earlier, former Republican Senator Dan Coats announced that he would challenge Bayh for reelection. Bayh has also been a critic of the Obama agenda, an agenda he has voted against more than any other Democrat in the Senate. Clearly, Bayh's decision was impacted by the tough political environment for Democrats and the Administration's refusal to heed his calls for a more moderate agenda. Further, he decided to retire with little notice or consultation with the White House, a clear message of frustration with the current Democrat agenda.

Bayh's announcement was met with glee by Republicans and denial by Democrats. For Republicans, Bayh's retirement offers an unexpected opportunity to pick up another Democrat seat in the Senate. With so many open Democrat seats currently leaning Republican, Bayh's retirement offers the long shot opportunity for Republicans to take control of the Senate. It will also encourage more Republicans to challenge other Democrat incumbents. Yet the huge impact of the Bayh announcement was all but ignored by the Democrat leadership in Washington.

After yet another political setback signaling trouble for the President's agenda, President Obama and his congressional allies simply press on. On cap and trade, the President reiterated his determination to pass an expansive energy tax, despite ever dimmer prospects in Congress. On health care reform, despite the February 25 bipartisan summit, the Administration is diligently planning behind the scenes to use reconciliation to force the President's bill through. HHS Secretary Sebelious even stated that the Administration plans to press once again for the public option, despite all political reality. These signals from the White House show that President Obama has no plans to moderate his agenda. Obama's ideological commitment to his agenda far outstrips any concerns he might have about voter discontent. The President's commitment to political purity might have few consequences for him, because he is not up for reelection until 2012, but his allies in Congress have no such luxury.

Week 58

(THE SUMMITEER)

February 28, 2010

When elected, President Obama promised a new kind of politics. He said he would open the windows and let the light in and that he would end partisanship in Washington. On health care specifically, he said his plan would be crafted in the open, with input from Democrats and Republicans, before the cameras of CSPAN. The truth was the opposite and the voters noticed. The health care bills passed by the House and Senate were crafted behind closed doors, by Democrats, and were filled with billions in special deals to secure votes.

To rehabilitate his image and his reform effort, on February 25, President Obama hosted a summit on health care reform, before the cameras and with Republicans in the room. The summit was advertised as an opportunity for Democrats and Republicans to get together to discuss and settle on the best ideas to reform health care. Yet, in the weeks running up to the summit, the President and his allies made clear their refusal to start over with a new bill and publicly discussed their strategy to push the current bills thought Congress using procedural maneuvers. So much for open minds and open debate.

President Obama took a huge risk scheduling this summit. While he would be the master of ceremonies and would be able to set the tone on why health care reform is needed and why his plan is the best, the summit also gave his opponents a stage to challenge the President and his plan. In the end, Obama, who never doubts his own persuasiveness, believed his superior intellect and rhetoric would win the day. As it turned out, the summit was at best a draw for the President, when he needed a clear win. The President made a strong argument for why reform was needed and why his plan was the best opportunity to fix the system. His allies chimed in with support and with various health care horror stories from across the nation. In response, the Republicans returned again and again to the bill's flaws: the dubious assertions on cost control, the special deals struck to get the bill passed, the reliance on Washington centric solutions, the refusal to pursue tort reform or interstate health insurance, and most of all, the massive cost of the bill and the nation's inability to afford it. The debate showed that Republicans had both good reasons to oppose the bills and some reasonable ideas on other approaches, which is why the summit was a failure for the President.

President Obama is committed to his vision for health care reform. He believes that cost control and expanded coverage can only be obtained through government mandates, government regulations, and huge taxation. He never planned to alter his course. Instead, the summit was designed to repent for his broken promises on openness, while at the same time embarrass the Republicans and rally his own troops. Obama bet everything on his ability to outshine everyone else in the room. The President surely performed well and was a great advocate for his agenda, but the Republicans responded in kind and were able to highlight credible principled reasons to oppose the President's plan. And after saying the summit was held to hear the best ideas and incorporate them, if the President ignores the Republicans' suggestions and presses on, all will know that he never intended to listen at all.

The Republicans were not the audience for the health care summit, and in truth neither were the voters. The Democrats have signaled for months their willingness to ignore voter sentiment on health care. No, the true audience for the summit was waiving and vulnerable Democrats, ones who voted for the House bill the first time, but now are rethinking. Obama needs to keep them in line and win some new converts, and he hoped the summit would aid that goal. But instead, the summit showed that the opposition to the bill is credible and committed. The test for the success of the summit will be whether wavering Democrats hold the line, and soon we will find out.

Week 59

(NEW YORKED)

March 7, 2010

The President entered March with a well-crafted plan to resuscitate health care reform. On February 25, he held his health care summit with Republicans to create the image of openness. On March 1, the President announced he would incorporate four Republican ideas into his health care plan to create the image of bipartisanship. After having set the stage, the President hoped to quickly rally his troops and divide the opposition by calling for a prompt vote by March 18 on health care. But the momentum was stemmed and his troops distracted, not by Republicans or their allies, but by a trio of New York Democrats who threw Congress and the President's agenda into disarray.

For the President's plan to work, he needed discipline and focus from his allies in Congress. Despite all the talk about Republican opposition to the health care bills, the simple truth is that the Democrats among themselves have enough votes to force the bills through. The President's health care summit and his incorporation of a few Republican ideas were not meant to foster bipartisanship, but rather to persuade and provide cover for wavering Democrats. Distraction and division had to be avoided for the plan to work, but three Democrats from New York had something else in mind.

Representative Charles Rangel, the powerful Chairman of the House Ways and Means Committee, has been under investigation for months on various charges of financial impropriety. This week, the House Ethics Committee reprimanded him for taking free flights from lobbyists and corporate interests, and continues to investigate him on other charges. The reprimand forced Rangel to step down from his Chairmanship. Two days later, freshman Representative Eric Massa from Upstate New York announced he would not seek reelection because of health issues, but a day later he was forced to announce his resignation because of ethics charges filed against him for harassing a male aide in his office. And then New York's Governor David Patterson became embroiled in ethics controversies for interfering in a domestic abuse investigation and taking free tickets to a Yankee's games, resulting in growing calls for his resignation. This cascade of ethics controversies left the Democrats off balance and distracted them from their goal of forcing the health care bills through.

With his recent moves on health care, the President hoped to create a narrative of an open and bipartisan effort to address critical problems in health care. Instead, the torrent of ethics problems of his Democrat allies created an image of a Congress that is both corrupt and tone deaf to voter opposition to the President's health care plan. Since the President promised his allies that the voters will support his health care reform if it is better explained to them, the President's inability to control the narrative hampered his drive to pass health care. Further, any additional weakening of the Democrats' standing with the public will make it ever more challenging to get moderate Democrats, already worried about the Fall elections, to cast another tough vote on health care. Many legislative hurdles still stand in the way of getting health care reform passed, and the Democrats increasing ethics woes only make matters worse.

Week 60
(NO MASSA)

March 14, 2010

After a two week charade of openness and bipartisanship, the Obama Administration returned to the same old tactics to pass health care reform. White House officials presided over closed-door Democrat only meetings to pressure moderate House Democrats to vote for the Senate bill and to craft a reconciliation bill to force through the Senate. In the midst of the horse trading, billions of extra dollars for health care subsidies were thrown into the bill to placate liberals, and a host of other changes are being contemplated, all without public disclosure, public debate, or public access. On the controversial issue of abortion, the White House and Democrat leaders opted to abandon the Stupak amendment and refuse any changes to the abortion language in the Senate bill, betting that they can get enough votes for passage even without the pro-life Democrats. The only open and public aspects of this final chapter on health care reform were the confident pronouncements from the reform proponents.

President Obama then took to the road campaign style to vilify the insurance companies and pharmaceutical industry and to energize his liberal base. The President also announced that he would postpone his trip to Asia for three days to work all out for passage of the Senate bill by the House. Speaker Pelosi took the podium repeatedly all week promising that the House would pass the Senate bill, but stumbled when she said that once the bills were passed, Congress and the voters would learn what is in them and would support them. Majority Leader Reid promised that the Senate would pass the reconciliation bill, despite the ruling of the Senate parliamentarian that the President must sign the Senate bill into law before the reconciliation bill can be considered. Many wonder with a Senate bill already signed into law, what incentive would the Senate have to pass the reconciliation bill, especially considering the procedural hurdles that could extend the health care debate for many more months.

Throughout all of these maneuvers, Republicans kept up their criticism of the bills and repeated their efforts to redirect the debate to a bipartisan approach. Senator McCain tried to resurrect the Gang of 14, a group of moderate Democrats and Republicans created to address an impasse on judicial nominations during the George W. Bush Administration, to forge a new health care bill, but he was quickly rebuffed by Democrats who have no intention of considering any new approach to health care reform. With little else at their disposal, Republicans were relegated to trying to sow distrust between the Senate and House, trying to make moderate Democrats suspicious of whether the Senate would ever pass the reconciliation bill.

And thrown into it all was Eric Massa, the Upstate New York Democrat who resigned on March 8 due to harassment charges filed by a male staffer. Massa gave a radio interview before his resignation asserting that the Democrats forced him to resign because he had voted against the House's prior health care bill. What followed was a torrent of criticism by Massa of both the House leadership and the White House for hardball tactics on health care. As the week continued, it became increasingly clear that Massa was more unbalanced than credible, but his criticisms of White House tactics only reinforced the view that nothing has changed about the Administration. It is still determined to pass a partisan health care bill, with no Republican support, using procedural maneuvers, and despite the strong opposition of the American public.

Week 61

(YOU BREAK IT, YOU OWN IT)

March 21, 2010

During the first Gulf War, General Colin Powell dissuaded President George H. W. Bush from marching on Bagdad with the simple aphorism: you break it, you own it. The same now applies to health care in America. On March 21, after a week of secret negotiations, payoffs, and presidential pressure, the House passed the Senate's health care reform bill by a vote of 219 to 212. Thirty-four Democrats, along with every Republican, voted against the measure. Next, the House quickly approved a reconciliation bill to change certain unpopular provisions in the Senate bill. That Reconciliation measure will now go to the Senate, where the Democrats hope to quickly push it through on a simple majority vote. If the strategy works, and at this point there is every reason to believe it will, the Democrats will have achieved a goal they have coveted since Harry Truman: universal health care coverage by government fiat. A grand achievement indeed, but at what cost.

Never before in American history has major social reform legislation been passed on a purely partisan vote and despite broad popular opposition. Social Security and Medicare were both very controversial, yet both ultimately garnered significant Republican support and strong poplar acceptance. That model was discarded for President Obama's health care reform effort. Instead, emboldened by the huge Democrat majorities in Congress, President Obama pursued a model for health care reform that no Republicans could support. His strategy almost proved disastrous when the Democrats lost their 60 vote majority in the Senate, but President Obama would not be denied. Disregarding the message from the voters, he pressed on for enactment of his vision for health care reform, pushing the Senate bill through the House with brute force and supporting a reconciliation bill to prevent a filibuster in the Senate. President Obama tried to soften the partisan edge of his agenda with his health care summit and willingness to include a couple minor Republican proposals in his plan, but ultimately his strategy was pure power partisanship.

The result is the enactment of health care reform, an achievement surely to be praised by the President's liberal allies. Yet in reaching their goal, the President and his allies have now made health care the ultimate partisan issue. They hope their reform will fix the problems in health care, but if premiums continue to rise, if cost estimates sore, if hospitals close, if care gets rationed, the Democrats and the Democrats alone will own the problem. They broke any bipartisan consensus on health care, so they now own all the problems in health care. This will be a daunting challenge for the Democrats. The version of health care reform they enacted provides impressive new benefits and coverage, but few mechanisms to reign in premiums. The bill might be rated by the CBO has deficit reducing, but that result was achieved by front loading the taxes, double counting the savings from Medicare cuts, and excluding from the bill a fix to doctor reimbursements that will costs hundreds of billions. Like Medicare and Medicaid, this new entitlement will far exceed the cost estimates and will put ever more pressure on the budget. And ultimately, when premiums and deficits soar and a budget crisis looms, rationing and further nationalization of care will result, along with ever increasing taxation. It is a disturbing prospect, but the collapse is likely a decade away, long after Obama and most of his allies have departed from the political scene. Others will suffer the reckoning.

The passage of health care reform will also fundamentally alter the relationship between the governed and their government. Our system of limited government, individual liberty, and free enterprise will survive, but in a weakened and altered state. Now the government will control and aggressively direct another 20% of the economy. Free choices will dwindle, government mandates will multiply, and options in health care will be restricted. More will gain coverage, but for the 85% who have it now, the system will be no better, and probably will be appreciably worse. Obama will achieve a great leveling, diminishing quality, but forcing more equality. President Obama and his Democrat allies have also bet that American economic dynamism will endure despite yet another grand government incursion into the private sector, but even American ingenuity and innovation can fail when our government neither knows nor recognizes any limits on itself.

Week 62

(MOST-PARTISANSHIP)

March 28, 2010

This week, President Obama signed health care reform into law, at a ceremony exclusively attended by Democrats who applauded a bill no Republican supported. In his remarks, the President gave no ground and offered few healing words for a nation ripped apart by the rancorous debate. Instead, he continued to lash out at his enemies, condemned insurance companies and health care providers, and promised to press on with ever more reforms. After forcing through an unpopular bill using unseemly tactics, the President showed no regrets.

One of the winning themes of the Obama presidential campaign was post-partisanship. President Obama portrayed himself as a new kind of leader who would bring the factions together and create a bipartisan consensus on the issues of the day. No doubt Obama believed his own rhetoric and wanted to reduce partisan rancor, but this week's final chapter in the health care debate showed that when faced with a choice between liberalism and compromise, Obama will choose liberalism every time. Most politicians, when faced with election defeats and popular opposition tend to trim their sails and seek compromise. However, ideologues pay little attention to such things. For them, all that matters is their goals, how those goals are achieved and what the people think mean little. So it has been with health care.

President Obama had a vision of health care reform that allowed little compromise. He wanted a system the extended coverage to the uninsured, limited perceived insurance company abuses, and enhanced government regulation and control. Some aspects of his plan, like the public insurance option, had to be discarded for expediency, but the President understood that highly regulated private insurers would be the same as a public option. The President also wanted to use health care reform to "spread the wealth around" by paying for reform with taxes on high earners. All these goals were achieved by the plan he signed into law, but something essential was lost in the process: any notion that President Obama is a new kind of politician who is less interested in partisanship and ideology. Indeed, the health care reform debate showed that President Obama is likely the most ideological and partisan President in generations.

There were so many opportunities to forge a bipartisan consensus on health care. The Republicans were weak and divided and resigned that reform would pass. Some minor tort reform, allowing health insurance to be sold across state lines, and a few tax credits for health care purchases would have yielded Republican support. But the President and his allies would have none of it. Their vision for health care reform was Medicare light: a system of government regulation and control modeled on Medicare but achieved through regulation rather that direct nationalization of health care. Tort reform, tax credits, or market-based reforms had no place in their vision, so those ideas were excluded.

Having chosen ideological purity, the Democrats pressed on with no regard to political or fiscal consequences. In the end, their dominant power in Washington won the day, but in the process they divided the nation and set the stage for an ideological battle that will last years, if not decades. The Democrats have now proudly proclaimed themselves the party of government activism and high taxation. The Republicans are again clearly the party of limited government and free enterprise. Between now and 2012, these opposing forces will do battle and the voters will decide, but one thing is certain, there will be no more talk of post-partisanship.

Week 63

(THE HANGOVER)

April 4, 2010

For the last two weeks, the President Obama and his Democrat allies have been celebrating their triumph on health care reform. No doubt the achievement of health care reform was a huge victory for the President and his party, but it was an ugly victory. The President prevailed by getting the House to enact the bill passed by the Senate, and then by getting both the House and the Senate to pass reconciliation bills to change the original legislation passed by the Senate. The strategy was a triumph, but the question is will the politics be a victory as well. The Democrats convinced themselves that if they got health care reform signed into law, the voters would support the legislation and reward the Democrats for the accomplishment. For a few brief moments, that appeared to be the case. Early polls showed increased support for the new law and President Obama saw an increase in his approval ratings. Yet, within a mere two weeks, those hopeful signs have passed, and now polls again show stiff resistance and opposition to the new law, and President Obama's approval ratings have sunk to 44%. After the Democrats big party, the hangover has set in.

The reaction of the public to health care reform should be no surprise to the President or his allies. Long ago, the public passed its verdict on President Obama's plan, deciding that his version of health care reform would make health care more expensive for those who have it, reduce the quality of health care those who get it, and would vastly increase government spending and deficits for a nation that cannot afford it. The Democrats convinced themselves that all this would change once reform was a reality. Instead, attitudes have hardened and the consequences for the President and his party are now becoming clear.

Faced with the public's reaction, the President and his allies have pursued a two part strategy. First, they continue to extol the virtues of the law they forced through. Second, they are trying to change the topic. This week, the Democrats began their push for financial and immigration reform and the President turned his focus to foreign policy, with a meeting with the Israeli Prime Minister and a surprise visit to Afghanistan. The problem is, after more than a year devoted to health care reform, it is not so easy to change the topic, especially when a majority of the public and a unified Republican Party opposed the law. No doubt, as time passes the public will turn its immediate attention to other issues, but health care reform will neither be forgotten nor be forgiven.

This is all too true because of the other big news this week. The CBO came out with projections that the federal deficit will be larger than predicted, adding fuel to the public's concern over federal spending, including health care. Also, the March unemployment report showed that even with 44,000 new federal jobs for the census, the unemployment rate stayed at 9.7% and the private economy only created 120,000 jobs. For employment to recover to pre-recession levels, the economy must create 300,000 jobs a month for the next five years, something few predict will happen, especially with the policies coming out of Washington. So with the jobs picture remaining weak, and federal spending and deficits soaring, there will be ample reminders to the opponents of health care reform of why they opposed the law. So the President and his allies certainly had a right to celebrate, but the hangover is coming.

Week 64

(Arms are for Hugging)

April 11, 2010

President Obama's agenda for change is not limited to domestic policy. After his fourteen month push to vastly increase the size, scope, and expense of the federal government's domestic programs, this week President Obama pursued his vision for change in America's defense posture. To many on the Left, one of the few disappointments of the Obama Administration has been the President's perceived hawkishness on foreign policy. He resisted calls for an expedited withdrawal from Iraq, he has expanded the war in Afghanistan, and has quietly kept in place many Bush-era counter-terrorism policies. Indeed, most of his reforms have been symbolic, like his unfulfilled pledge to close Gitmo and his Administration's transition away from terms like "War on Terror" and "Islamic Extremist." But on nuclear issues, the President's agenda is anything but symbolic.

Since 1945, nuclear weapons have been the foundation of America's defense. In the Cold War, each side's nuclear weapons were credited with preventing open conflict and were deployed heavily in Europe to counterbalance Soviet conventional superiority. With the end of the Cold War, former Cold War adversaries have found themselves with unnecessarily vast inventories of nuclear weapons. In response, Russia and the United States have worked to reduce nuclear stockpiles and ensure the security of nuclear materials. All this has been done in the shadow of nuclear threats from rogue states and terrorists who hope to acquire such weapons to blackmail and murder.

In this era of new threats, President Obama sees a diminished role for nuclear weapons. The President talks openly about his desire to eliminate all such weapons, while recognizing that while nuclear threats remain, so must our deterrent. In accord with this view, the Obama Administration's April 6, 2010 Nuclear Posture Review did not proclaim unilateral disarmament, instead it greatly reduced the important of nuclear weapons in our defense strategy. The Nuclear Policy Review for the first time stated that nuclear weapons would only be used against nuclear-armed opponents or violators of the Nuclear Non-Proliferation Treaty, and said the United States would stop all development of new nuclear arms and stop nuclear testing. The Nuclear Policy Review did not forswear the first nuclear strike option, but did pledge a reduced role for nuclear arms in America's defense infrastructure.

After proclaiming these significant changes in America's nuclear deterrent, the President flew to Prague to sign a new START Treaty with President Medvedev of Russia. The Treaty signed on April 8, would reduce strategic nuclear arms by about a third and expand systems for control and verification of nuclear arsenals. Although not part of the current Treaty, the President proclaimed his desire to expand nuclear arms reduction efforts to tactical and non-deployed nuclear warheads. So in the same week, the President downgraded the role of nuclear arms in America's defense and took significant steps to eliminate excess nuclear stockpiles.

It is important to remember that many American Presidents, including Ronald Reagan, have talked about the desire to eliminate nuclear weapons. Weapons that have the potential to kill billions are inherently dangerous and troubling. But it is equally important to remember that in the 25 years before the nuclear era began in 1945, there were two world wars, while in the 65 years since, there has been no world war. No doubt, the existence of nuclear arms has given pause to many would-be belligerents. Nuclear arms are also relatively cheap, allowing us to save money by limiting our conventional arms infrastructure.

With the Cold War at an end, many like Obama see a reduced role for such arms. These observers see different threats, threats from extremists and rogue states, not threats from nuclear armed nation states. That is why Obama is willing to cut nuclear arms, stop development of new weapons, and stop testing. But all too often, governments plan to fight the last war, rather than seeing the true future threat. Our last (and continuing) war has been against terrorist threats and states, so the Obama Administration's approach to nuclear arms assumes that will be the threat of the future. The Administration's nuclear policy fails to perceive that nuclear states like China and evenly possibly a future Russia could pose a significant threat to the United States. Rather than maintain a robust capability to confront these potential threats, President Obama instead assumes that sophisticated nation states will no longer war against each other, so new nuclear arms and testing will play a diminishing role in our defense future. Everything in history teaches against that assumption, but for a progressive like Obama, who believes in his vision of the future above all else, history is something to remake, not respect.

Week 65
(THE VISIBLE HAND)

April 18, 2010

It was a busy week for President Obama. A vacancy to fill on the Supreme Court, a Nuclear Security Summit, and the usual rush of good and bad economic data to digest. With so much swirling activity in Washington, most failed to notice the most significant event of the week, which was President Obama's issuance of an executive memorandum requiring hospitals that accept Medicare or Medicaid to provide equal access to same sex partners. Many might say such an order matters little compared to the Supreme Court or nuclear security, but for an Administration whose goal is increased government influence in every sphere, the President's memorandum is a troubling sign of things to come.

When Justice John Paul Stevens announced his retirement, the media and political establishment in Washington went into a frenzy of speculation on the next Supreme Court nominee. Since Stevens is the Court's leading liberal, few expect the impending nomination to have any impact on the Supreme Court's ideological balance. Nonetheless, each side is set for a battle. Liberals hope to use the nomination to put in place a young, smart, and activist judge who will help lead the Court to a future liberal majority. For conservatives, the nomination offers the opportunity to highlight social issues and pick a fight with the President. With an election less than seven months away, each side hopes to use the nomination to energize its base.

Amidst all the Supreme Court speculation, the President also invited to Washington a host of world leaders for a Nuclear Security Summit. Quick on the heels of his Nuclear Posture Review and the signing ceremony for the new START Treaty with Russia, the Nuclear Security Summit is the latest effort by the President to revamp the whole dialogue on nuclear weapons, going from development, defense, and security, to dismantlement and non-proliferation. As with most summits, the rhetoric far outpaced results, but the event certainly put increased focus on the threat from the spread of nuclear arms to terrorists and rogue states, even though that terminology is no longer used by the President.

With Supreme Court nominees dancing in people's heads and world leaders rushing around Washington, it was easy to discount a memorandum issued by the President on the evening of April 15 requiring hospitals to give equal access to same sex partners. On its merits, most Americas agree that the same-sex partners of those who are sick or dying should have equal access. Most hospitals grant such access or it can be guaranteed by the patients themselves through various legal mechanisms. In that respect, the President's memorandum might be seen as simply filling a gap in the law or addressing a few outlier institutions. It was also the latest step by the President to quietly and carefully fulfill his promises to gay rights activists, who were ardent supporters of his campaign. However, it is not the merits of what was done that is troubling, it is the precedent.

President Obama believes to his core in the potential for government to better lives and to wisely direct the populace. His Administration has embarked on bold efforts to widen the scope of government activity, not just in health care, but also through bailouts, takeovers, regulation and subsidies to private industries. President Obama is extending the visible hand of government and its purse into ever more corners of national activity. No doubt some of these steps were born of necessity, like the GM takeover, but they are also part of the President's philosophy of a partnership between government and the private sector to achieve a re-making of our economy and society.

Seen in this context, the President's memorandum on hospital access should be a sobering sign for us all. With that memorandum, the Obama Administration made clear that those who accept government money must adhere to the government moral code on issues such as gay rights. With government intervening in ever more private spheres, and with government using its purse and its power to influence ever more business endeavors, there will be more dictates from government, not only on gays rights, but also on abortion, euthanasia, child care, marriage, wages, the list is endless. Soon the invisible hand of liberty and the market will be firmly clinched by the visible hand of government.

Week 66

(AGAINST THE WALL)

April 25, 2010

After his triumph on health care, President Obama had a choice to make. Would he seek reconciliation with political opponents after rancorous debate, or would go all out to enact his agenda while his large congressional majority is still intact. His decision is clear now, with his determination to push through Wall Street reform, an immigration bill, and a climate bill all before the Fall election. The first target on the Obama hit list is Wall Street, surely chosen because it appears to be the most vulnerable opponent. There is deep anger at the financial sector for the banking meltdown that led to the current recession. Obama is hoping that he can utilize that anger to fuel populist support and to intimidate Republicans to back the bill. Obama believes he has the financial sector against the Wall, and he is probably right.

President Obama loves to talk about his support for free markets every time he is about to propose yet another government program to control them. He sold his stimulus plan as a program to create private sector jobs, while the bill was mostly government spending and subsidies to favored industries that Obama believes should be ordained by the government as the job creators of the future. The TARP program has been used to bailout GM, at the behest of unions and to the detriment of bondholders and competitors who do not have the benefit of unlimited federal dollars. Obama's health care reform was sold as a program of free choice in health care, when in reality the reform law is designed to turn health insurance companies into public utilities with the government deciding the coverage they can offer.

With this pedigree, it is no surprise that when President Obama travelled to the Cooper Union this week to sell his Wall Street reform bill, he started with the obligatory statement that he believes in free markets. Perfectly on cue, he then launched into a defense of a host of regulations to limit market freedom. First, the President's bill would limit the size of banks and give the government the power to break up banks that become too large or appear about to fail. Second, the bill seeks to regulate the derivative market. Third, the Administration wants to change the rules for executive pay, giving shareholders greater control over compensation determinations. Fourth, the bill seeks to create a federal office of consumer protection. In its initial form, the bill also included a 50 billion dollar fund to pay for future bailouts, but most believe that provision will be dropped because of the public's concern it will lead to more bailouts in the future.

There is Republican support for some aspects of this agenda, including certain regulation of derivatives and enhanced powers to address failing banks. But bipartisanship is not the Obama Administration's style. The bill was pushed through the banking committee over Republican objections and without Republican support. All 41 Republicans signed a letter stating that they could not support the bill in its current form, but rather than engage Republicans on the issues, the President and his allies went straight to intimidation tactics, calling the Republicans friends of bankers. The strategy seems to be working, because by week's end Republican opposition seemed to be ebbing and there was talk of compromise. The President certainly hopes that this will be a repeat of health care, where power politics will overcome the opposition and force his agenda through.

Less interesting than whether the President wins is what this debate says about his philosophy. President Obama sees himself as creating a New Deal for the 21st Century. Universal health care, a government mandated green economy, controls on free markets, and a massive expansion of federal power and influence. Obama believes he knows what the future must look like, and he is doing his utmost to achieve it. But his future is what Europe has been doing for 50 years. He is not creating some dynamic new economy; he is trying to make America into what we already see in Europe. A free market, but also a high tax, high regulation, welfare state society. For some reason, President Obama seems to think he can do the same things socialists did in Europe 50 years ago, but the results will somehow be different.

Week 67

(GOING SOUTH)

May 2, 2010

In a week when most in Washington thought the focus would be on financial reform, two very different threats to our Southern border dominated the political debate. One threat holds great promise for President Obama, while the other great peril. The first threat comes from illegal immigration, a hot button issue in border states, which are being overrun by illegals and are being ever more impacted by the rampant drug wars in Mexico. On April 24, Arizona Governor Brewer signed a new law designed to counter that threat, by giving police more discretion to ask for immigration papers and toughening the penalties for illegals. The law has outraged immigration advocates and has emboldened President Obama's push for immigration reform. The other threat is a massive oil slick heading for the Gulf Coast created by the April 20 explosion of a British Petroleum (BP) offshore oil rig. The impending environmental disaster and the slow federal response have called into question both the Administration's competence and its energy policies. What's going on down South could have a huge impact on two of President Obama's key policy objectives.

For many years, Washington has tried to grapple with immigration reform. With millions living in the United States illegally and the border states being overrun, everyone recognizes that America must deal with both immigration policy and border control. President George W. Bush tried to enact immigration reform, but was thwarted by his own party, which saw the reform effort as too pro-immigrant. President Obama sees immigration reform as a policy and political opportunity for his Administration. The President wants to deal with illegals and border issues in a way that will win him even stronger support from Hispanic voters. In recent weeks, the President's allies in Congress have accelerated their push for immigration reform, attempting to put it on a fast track ahead of an energy bill. Most recognize the Democrats' focus on immigration reform now as political opportunism. Immigration reform is popular with both the Democrats' liberal base and the Hispanic community, a key constituency for the Democrats.

The Democrats' fast track strategy for immigration reform hit a roadblock when Republican Senator Lindsey Graham said he would withdraw his support of a potential bipartisan deal on an energy bill if the Democrats did not stop playing politics on immigration. However, immigration issues got more political with the enactment of Arizona's new immigration law. Arizona has been particularly hard hit by illegal immigration. The recent murder of a rancher by smugglers has only heightened public outrage at the immigration crisis. In response, Arizona's new law tries to crack down on illegals by giving increased powers to police to ask for papers, jail illegals, and deport them. While popular among some in border states, the new law has been portrayed by the media and liberal groups as authorization for racial profiling and discrimination. The President has criticized the bill and liberal groups are planning lawsuits and legislative initiatives to overturn it. The Arizona law has energized the immigration lobby and increased the political pressure to push through immigration reform this year.

For the President, the other Southern threat is far less attractive. When a BP oil rig in the Gulf of Mexico exploded on April 20, initial reports were that the resulting oil spill would be contained. As a result, federal authorities were slow to take steps to contain the threat. As the days wore on and the oil slick grew and grew, there was increasing alarm that a massive environmental disaster was looming. With beaches, habitats and fisheries threatened, by week's end the President took ownership of the crisis, putting Coast Guard Admiral Allen in charge of the response team and pledged full federal support. It does not help that the oil slick is south of Louisiana, invoking our national memory of the Katrina disaster.

While the timing of the Arizona immigration controversy is perfect for the President, the oil slick comes at a very bad moment. To date, President Obama's efforts at energy reform have hit a roadblock. The President succeeded in putting billions into the Stimulus Bill for green energy, but his cap and trade bill is languishing in the Senate. To try to build support, the President made a symbolic gesture to lift the federal ban on certain offshore drilling. This step enraged environmental advocates and underwhelmed conservatives. Now with the explosion of the BP oil rig, the President's stance on offshore drilling will be more untenable. Also, for a President who has sought to portray an image of cool competence, the lackluster federal response to the cleanup effort opens the Administration up for criticism. On top of it all, there is no easy solution to stopping the oil leak or containing the slick, which makes the President's pledge to address the crisis even more problematic. So the twin threats of illegals and the oil slick on the Southern border are each very different game changers for the President's policies.

Week 68

(BOMBS & BEARS)

May 9, 2010

A key message for the Obama Administration is that the President is ushering in a new era of reduced threats, both at home and abroad. The Administration has made the fight against terrorism the quiet war that is rarely spoken of, just as it has made economic recovery its constant narrative. But this week, the quiet war got very loud with the May 1, 2010 bomb plot in Times Square and the talk of economic recovery seemed hollow with a world financial panic driven by the sovereign debt crisis in Europe. These events gave a clear reminder that little has changed other than the rhetoric from the White House.

Faisal Shahzad is a Pakistani-American. Like so many terrorists, he came from a prosperous and privileged background, but got swept up into terrorism sponsored by the Pakistani Taliban. After receiving terrorist training, he packed a car with crude explosives and on May 1, attempted to set off his bomb in Times Square. The bomb ignited, but did not explode and was quickly discovered and defused. The attempted bombing set off a panic in New York and led to an intense manhunt to catch the bomber. Shahzad was caught attempting to get on a flight to Dubai. Two other plotters were also captured.

For an Administration that usually refuses to use the word terrorism, the Times Square bomb plot was an unwelcome reminder that the terrorist threat can be downplayed, but not ignored. For the most part, the Obama Administration has maintained a determined fight against terrorism, with the main difference between Obama and Bush being messaging. President Bush believed that the nation and our enemies needed constant reminders of the threat and of our determination to combat it. In contrast, the Obama Administration believes the best way to defeat terrorism is to take a public posture of assurance and reconciliation, while fighting the war behind the scenes. Both are respectable strategies, but the Obama approach only works if the terrorists do not attack. A President who seldom talks about the threat and looks like he is not focused on terrorism can be perceived as not protecting the nation. An unfair charge against the President, but a charge to which he is vulnerable because of his reticence to lead a public war on terror.

President Obama has no reticence when it comes to talking about economic recovery. The 2008 financial panic in the United States was the biggest factor in Obama's convincing victory in the election and his promise to fix the economy is his biggest commitment to the public. He pushed through a huge a stimulus plan and other huge increases in public spending claiming those measures would create jobs and foster new industries. Most polls show the public sees this spending as wasteful and doubts claims of job creation. Economic growth has returned, but not jobs. The May 7 jobs report underlined that, with the economy producing 290,000 new jobs, with 60,000 temporary census positions. Sounds like a lot, but our economy needs to produce at least 300,000 jobs per month to put a dent in the unemployment rate, which increased to 9.9% with the recent jobs report.

One valid claim of success for the Obama Administration is stabilization of the financial sector. Eighteen months after the mortgage panic, most banks are now well-capitalized and almost all the TARP money given to the financial sector has been repaid. As a result, until this week world stock markets have shown a resurgence, recouping much of the value lost in 2008. Yet lurking behind this good financial news is an ugly truth: much of the economic recovery has been bought with borrowing and spending by central governments (ours included). Even governments must pay their debts, and when Greece was on the verge of defaulting on its public debt this week, requiring a European bailout plan, faith in the stability of the recovery was again shaken.

Rating agencies downgraded Geek debt to junk bond status, concerns were raised on the high debt levels in Spain and Portugal, and there was a run on the Euro and the Pound. Stock markets around the world fell, with the Dow losing more than 700 points. The debt concerns are not limited to Europe. There even have been whispers about the ability of the United States to pay its debts, especially considering the massive spending proposed by the Obama Administration and the huge financial commitments in the recently passed health care reform law. For a President who touts economic recovery and increased federal spending, a sovereign debt crisis undermines both his achievements and his economic philosophy. As we have seen this week, if the economy falters because governments are borrowing too much and terrorist are attacking when our government seems uninterested in the threat, much of the Obama narrative of success on those fronts evaporates.

Week 69

(Not to Judge)

May 16, 2010

Only sixteen months into his tenure, President Obama has a chance to name his second Justice to the Supreme Court. Although appointed by President Ford, Justice John Paul Stevens thirty-four years on the bench were marked by a steady march to the Left on most judicial issues. By the end of his tenure, Justice Steven was the leader of the four-Justice liberal wing of the Court and he issued increasingly bitter dissenting opinions on the Court's rulings on federal power, second amendment rights, and political speech. With the election of President Obama, most expected Justice Stevens to retire, given the ideological alliance between the aged Justice and the new President. When the opportunity came this week, President Obama responded with the nomination of Elena Kagan, who has never served as a judge and never even argued a case until she became Obama's Solicitor General last year. But Kagan's lack of judicial experience matters little, because Obama wants a disciple of the Left on the Court, not a judge, and Obama thinks he has just that with Elena Kagan.

The Obama Administration can only succeed on its agenda to vastly increase the size and scope of the federal government if the courts concur. With his huge majorities in Congress, President Obama has pushed through health care reform and massive new federal spending, and he is working fervently to enact the remainder of his key agenda (financial reform, immigration reform, and cap and trade). At the same time, administrative agencies now led by Obama appointees are rapidly issuing new rules and regulations in nearly every sphere. Indeed, this week the EPA announced that in July 2011 its new regulations on carbon emissions will go into effect, forcing every private sector entity that emits 75,000 tons of carbon dioxide per year to buys permits to operate. The new legislation and regulation coming out of Washington is aimed at transforming America into a much more regulated and controlled society, where the private sector is ever more subservient to federal power and where Washington directs both government and private activity. Yet hanging over all that Obama has done is a serious question: it is constitutional.

President Obama seeks to create a European-style welfare state and regulated economy. However, he is the Chief Executive of a constitutional government of delegated powers. For a man who wants to transform American society, he needs a federal government of unchecked and unlimited power to achieve his ends. Increasingly, the Obama Administration is concerned that its legislative victories will be defeated in the courts. Ever more states are joining constitutional challenges to the health care law and the Administration's new rule making is under judicial attack as well. Much of Obama's agenda will ultimately be decided in the Supreme Court, with its current conservative majority and its penchant in recent years to limit federal power. President Obama does not want the Supreme Court to be the graveyard for his agenda. That's where Elena Kagen comes in.

Kagan is an intellectual who comes from elite liberal society. She is a student of the law, but has no experience practicing it or judging it. Instead, her great asset to President Obama is her ideology and her personality. President Obama does not want a new justice on the Court, he wants an advocate for his vision of the constitution and society. He also wants a consensus builder, who can persuade the other Justices and build majorities. Elena Kagan was nominated not to judge, but to advocate for President Obama's vision of the future, to which Kagan surely adheres. While the nomination debate will surely focus on the usual topics of abortion, the death penalty, and the rights of terrorists, the more pertinent and important issue will be Kagan's views on federal power. President Obama wants a pro-choice, separation of religion, criminal rights justice, but he absolutely needs an adherent to unlimited federal power on the bench. All depends on that. President Obama nominated Kagan because President Obama surely believes she will uphold the constitutionality of the vast new government the President seeks to erect. Once that is achieved, little else will matter.

Week 70

(TEA LEAVES)

May 23, 2010

With deficits soaring, stocks falling, and unemployment rising, it is no surprise that incumbents fared poorly in the May 18 party primaries. Arlen Spector, who switched from a Republican to a Democrat in a vain effort to keep his Senate seat, went down to Congressman Sestak in Pennsylvania and Democrat Blanche Lincoln failed to garner enough support to avoid a run-off in the Democrat Primary in Arkansas. At the same, Tea Party Insurgent Rand Paul won the Republican senate nomination in Kentucky over the party establishment candidate Ted Grayson. It seems a jittery nation that is unsure about the future is lurching to extremes, throwing out moderate veterans like Spector, Lincoln, and Grayson in favor of more ideological outsiders. It is part of a trend in our current politics driven by the President's agenda, which instead of creating post-partisanship is further polarizing our politics.

In the last four months, we have seen the fruits of President Obama's agenda. After stinging rebukes by voters in Virginia, New Jersey, and Massachusetts, the President and his party, rather than moderating and seeking consensus, instead marched ahead with their huge majorities to force their agenda through. Health care reform was passed without a single Republican vote, and this week a Wall Street financial reform bill was pushed through with only four Republican supporters. It should be no surprise that the Democrats can enact their agenda. With 59 votes in the Senate and a 40 seat majority in the House, the votes are there for nearly any Democrat bill. What is surprising is that the Democrats are pushing ahead in the face of such clear public concern.

The public is concerned about jobs, the economy, the deficit, and the size of government. In response, President Obama and his allies have pushed through bills that expand government power and spending, will increase the deficit, and that will do little to spur economic growth or job creation. It seems the President and his Democrats are so sure that their vision of a social democratic future is correct that they are willing to risk voter backlash. Through it all, the President has shown himself to be a very amenable ideologue. President Obama is more than willing to sit down and talk with Republicans, he just refuses to compromise or moderate his views. He is committed to his vision of the future and is willing to use unfettered federal power to force it on the nation.

The voters have a say in all this, and they have been talking very loudly. Democrat incumbents have been retiring rather than face angry voters, incumbents have been defeated in primaries, every off-year senate or gubernatorial candidate the President has campaigned for has lost, and Republicans have won every statewide race since the 2008 election. This would give any cautious politician pause, but President Obama is not a cautious politician. Obama believes he was elected to complete the work of Franklin Roosevelt. FDR created the modern administrative state and welfare system, but World War II halted the march toward a full welfare state with nationalized health care and government guarantees of income, housing, education, full retirement. President Johnson's Great Society re-started that march but then Vietnam got in the way. Now, Obama seeks to finish what FDR and LBJ began.

Obama's agenda seeks ambitious change and it is not necessary to read tea leaves to figure out that voters are concerned. Indeed, the rise of the Tea Party itself shows the depths of voter discontent. Through it all, the President and his allies march forward, undeterred by all they see around them. One must admire their commitment, but question their wisdom.

Week 71

(BLACK TIDINGS)

May 30, 2010

Events finally caught up with the Obama Administration this week. After weeks of halting focus on the spreading oil slick in the Gulf of Mexico, the President finally returned to the Gulf and pledged full federal support, but only after stinging criticism of his Administration's perceived ineptitude and unconcern. Then, after months of dodging questions about whether the White House tried to bribe Congressman Sestak to drop his Pennsylvania primary challenge against Senator Arlen Spector, a rising political firestorm forced the White House to admit that it deployed former President Clinton to make the offer to Sestak. Indeed, the rising chorus of criticism from these two events has become so serious that the President was forced to do something he has not done for ten months, hold a press conference and answer questions. It is ironic that both of this week's major events harkened back to the Clinton Administration. The BP oil rig explosion and the ever expanding oil slick has been a looming environmental disaster for weeks, but the potential for a political backlash only became clear when Clinton Administration stalwart James Carville blasted Obama for being lackadaisical on the problem. At the same time, the Sestak bribery scandal took a new turn when the White House was finally forced to admit that Carville's former boss Bill Clinton was the one who offered a federal job to Sestak. For a President who has tried mightily to differentiate himself from the last Democrat president in both policy and rhetoric, it seems he forgot to keep the Clintonites at a distance.

Now the ever expanding oil slick is symbolic of a black tide of political troubles for the President. It is unfair to blame Obama for the oil rig explosion itself. Years of bad management by BP and the regulators led to the disaster. Obama's failure was inattentiveness. As is the case for many disasters, both manmade and natural, the ability of leaders or governments to halt them is often limited. What leaders and governments can do is show focus and concern and try to address the effects. Hurricane Katrina was such a disaster for the Bush Administration not because anyone thought Bush caused the levies to break, but because Bush was perceived as incompetent and unconcerned in the early days of the disaster. Obama should have learned that lesson well, but it appears he did not. Surely his Administration was taking steps to address the oil slick, but the President refused until this week to take charge and focus the nation. Likely Obama understood that the technical obstacles to stopping the oil slick are huge and uncertain, so he opted to condemn BP rather than personally take charge of the response. He hoped the public would blame the oil companies and absolve him. What Obama failed to understand is that as President, even problems he did not cause and cannot solve require his leadership and focus. Obama has now figured out he cannot demagogue his way out of this problem, he has to show leadership and try to fix it.

This week's political scandal also showed a lack of political judgment. Most Americans likely think it is common to offer a politician a job to get him to drop a bid for office. The problem is, such offers can constitute bribery. Arlen Spector joined the Democrats in return for the President's pledge of support to get him the Democratic nomination in Pennsylvania. When Congressman Sestak rose to make a challenge, the White House sent Bill Clinton to offer him a job to drop out. Sestak told the press about the job offer months ago and for months the White House has dodged the questions, hoping the press' general sympathy for the President would get them to drop the story. But when Sestak won the primary, the story took on more importance and the White House was forced to take the first small steps toward coming clean. The story is dangerous for the President because Obama claimed he would usher in a new politics and openness, so now he and his Administration look like hypocrites. Obama forgot that no matter how much the press sympathizes with his agenda, they will not ignore a political scandal. So now Obama is challenged with a black tide in the Gulf and a rising tide of scandal in Washington, both of which are problems of his own creation.

Week 72

(COUNTING JOBS)

June 6, 1010

With oil continuing to gush into the Gulf of Mexico and the bribery scandal continuing to simmer in Washington, the Obama Administration hoped it could temper the torrent of bad news with a positive May unemployment report. Those hopes were dashed. The June 4 jobs report showed that while we have some economic growth, we have very little job creation, and those jobs that are being created are mostly in the public sector. At first blush, the jobs report looked positive, with 441,000 new jobs created in May and the unemployment rating dropping to 9.7%. However, 411,000 of the new jobs were government counting jobs for the census and the unemployment rate only dropped because 332,000 people gave up looking for work. The private sector only created 41,000 jobs in May and total unemployment and underemployment actually stands at more than 17%.

The economy needs to created 100,000 jobs per month just to keep up with new entrants into the job market and job growth of 300,000 per month is needed to make any significant dent in the unemployment rate. As much as the President likes to tout the economic recovery, for the average American little has changed. Jobs remain scarce, college expensive, taxes high, and wages stagnant. For a President who has claimed he measures economic progress by job creation and helping "middle class" families, there is precious little in current economic data suggesting that his agenda is working. More troubling, most of the economic recovery to date has been paid for by huge deficit spending at the federal level, and despite nearly two trillion dollars spent on new programs, tax rebates, and bailouts, the private sector recovery remains weak. With poll after poll showing that the massive federal deficit is the number one public concern, President Obama risks a huge political backlash if he tries to fuel further economic recovery with even more deficit spending.

The Administration has put itself into an economic box that will be hard to escape. The guiding principle of the Obama Administration is that a larger and more activist federal government will better of the lives of average Americans. To date, the more activist federal government has only created deficits and distrust, and paying for that activist government is growing more problematic. President Obama promised he would not raise taxes on those earning less than $250,000, but even if high earners are taxed at a rate of 100%, the federal government would fail to raise enough money to pay for current programs, let alone reduce the debt. So the Obama Administration has promised big government as the cure, but its pledges on taxes make big government impossible to pay for. The only way out for the Obama Administration is vigorous private economy growth, which will reduce the cost of social welfare programs and increase tax revenues. Unfortunately, that seems to be the one part of the economic equation Obama has ignored.

Since 1940, the United States has had a consistently productive, dynamic, and innovative economy. Although beset by occasional recessions, our economy has consistently recovered and thrived. Fueled by flexible labor laws, fewer regulations, and lower taxes than most of our competitors, our economy has produced better growth and job production, albeit with greater income disparity. Liberals like Obama simply assume our free market economy will continue to thrive no matter the stresses put on it by regulations, taxation, and deficit spending. Only that can explain the Administration's economic policies, which have been to combat the recession with staggering government spending and interference in industry, an avalanche of new regulations, and huge tax increases on both individuals and businesses. The White House appears to have foresworn any effort to try to overcome the recession by creating an environment where investment and risk taking are rewarded.

In the end, the Obama Administration is being undermined by its own redistributionist ethos. Obama truly believes that we can create economic prosperity by spreading current wealth around. His Administration seems obsessed with maximizing taxation of the top 2% of Americans, with little concern that those citizens are the risk takers and job creators who fuel a recovery. Rather than taking a balanced approach that seeks to reward the job creators while at the same time asking them to contribute more to the tax coffers, the Administration has rejected any policy that might lead to an economic benefit to high income earners. The result is an investor and corporate class now focused on increasing efficiency, cost cutting, and amassing cash reserves, rather than investment and job expansion. Nothing shows that more than our 100 million strong labor market creating only 41,000 jobs in May, a sure sign that government policy and deficits are retarding the economic recovery.

Week 73

(ASS KICKER)

June 13, 2010

Bruised by continuing criticism of his lack of leadership on the BP oil spill, President Obama set out this week to show engagement and outrage. He took the opportunity during a Today Show interview with Matt Lauer to say that he does not approach the presidency like a faculty debating club, but instead he meets with experts to figure out "whose ass to kick." For a President whose "cool" now seems like coldness, the President's use of profanity is a sign of both condescension and desperation. President Obama has implied again and again that he sees average Americans as ignorant and unthinking, so he is now trying to appeal to them by showing his crude side. What the President fails to understand is that while average Americans might lack his education and sophisticated perspective, they have deep common sense and good judgment, and can tell when their leaders are failing them.

One of the reasons the liberal elites love President Obama is because he so perfectly fits their vision of the ideal leader. Liberals believe the best leader is the detached well-educated technocrat with sophisticated globalist views, who is prepared to use government for farsighted social engineering, i.e. making Americans do what the government thinks is good for them. To date, that is exactly the type of leader Obama has been. He has unabashedly advocated for bigger and more intrusive government, has pushed through policies like health care reform regardless of voter opposition, and has toured the world apologizing for the policies of the Bush Administration. Yet Obama has been too much the detached technocrat.

Bill Clinton always understood that Americans want their Presidents to feel their pain. All our great leaders have been able to recognize and tap into popular concern and anxiety. Obama showed his mastery of this skill during his campaign, where he crafted a message perfectly fit for the times. However, once in office, the President has simply stopped listening to the people. For the last year, voters have been telling the Administration that they oppose health care reform and the cap and trade tax, are concerned about deficits, and think the government is getting too big and doing too much. Rather than addressing these concerns, the President simply ignores them by quipping that if his critics only understood his policies, then they would thank him. One can almost hear the echo of his "clinging to guns and religion" line during the campaign.

Having had some success for sixteen months ignoring voters, it is no surprise that when BP's offshore oil platform exploded and oil began gushing into the Gulf of Mexico the President thought it of little consequences. Instead, he focused his efforts on the cap and trade tax, and financial and immigration reform. When the public started showing its heightened concern, the President went to his automatic default response, condemnation of the oil industry, greedy executives, and Bush policies. After a few weeks of that, with no visible evidence of any concerted effort to address the spill, the voters and the media started to realize that the President was not doing his job. With a great environmental disaster in the making, Obama was more concerned with his campaign agenda than helping suffering Americans. Then came the "ass kicker."

With the evidence mounting of public disenchantment with his oil spill response, Obama finally went into crisis management mode, dispatching his Cabinet, touring the Gulf region, and talking to the press about the response. Despite all these efforts, what clearly lies underneath is the President's annoyance that the oil spill has delayed or derailed his agenda in Washington. So when the people want a fixer, Obama still wants to be the blamer, kicking the ass of those who upset his apple cart. At some point, maybe the President will realize that it is not all about him and his grand designs, and sometimes the needs of the American people come first.

Week 74

(BEING PRESIDENT)

June 20, 2010

After sixteen months of playing the role of visionary leader, forger of the future, tormentor of the privileged, and champion of world peace, this week Barak Obama had to try his hand at being President. The BP oil spill and the national outcry over the lackluster federal responses called for presidential leadership, and this week we got a taste of that leadership Obama-style. With a June 15 Oval office address and a meeting with BP executives the next day, Obama made clear that his plan to address the oil spill would be an exploitation and shake-down two step. Exploiting the spill to try to get his cap and trade tax passed and holding up BP and the oil industry for cash. Unfortunately for the President, the public does not feel like dancing this time.

The one point of consensus among the political class is that the President's Oval Office address was underwhelming. Liberals and conservatives alike were looking for a specific plan and vision to address the two most pressing concerns: stopping the oil leak and cleaning up the mess. Instead, what Obama gave us was bland statistics on the spill response and an emphatic but empty show of presidential resolve. Viewers were left with the no doubt accurate impression that Obama is mad, but has no plan, at least no plan for plugging the leak and cleaning up the spill. After his forced march through the mundane task of addressing the people's concerns, Obama was finally able to turn to what he really cares about: the cap and trade tax and attacking oil companies.

The President began by stating that the oil spill shows why it is so important to make America a leader in the green economy, so we can end our dependence on oil. He then touted his cap and trade bill, which would function as a huge carbon tax. Clearly, the President hopes to use the oil spill for political advantage by arguing that it shows why it is so crucial to pass his energy agenda. However, most anyone can see there is little connection between the carbon tax and the oil spill. Even with the carbon tax, the United States will continue to use oil in huge quantities for decades and there will still be offshore drilling. At best, the carbon tax is a promise that if we raise the expense of carbon-based energy now, we might create an environment that will lead to other cleaner fuel sources in the future, after we all pay hundreds of billions in new taxes for the privilege. Clearly, the President's focus on the carbon tax was an effort to dodge the real issues on the oil spill: negligence by BP, poor oversight by the government, and a horrible federal response to date. The carbon tax addresses none of these concerns, and Obama undermined his credibility by pretending it is the solution to the mess.

While pushing his carbon tax, the President did not forget his other favorite pastime: singling out a sector in the private economy and lambasting it. After hitting banks, Wall Street, insurance companies, and the oil industry since his inauguration, the President has now zeroed in on BP as his current favorite example of private sector malfeasance. BP is a proper target for government scrutiny. The evidence increasingly shows that it did not follow best practices in drilling safety, and its response to the spill has been misleading, halting, and inadequate. Everyone agrees that BP must be held to account for its misdeeds, which should include vigorous regulatory scrutiny, fines, and even potential criminal charges. But that was not enough for President Obama, who also wants to lead a White House shake down of BP. In his speech, he demanded that BP set up a fund to compensate victims and threatened BP if it did not. The next day, during his meeting with Tony Hayward, BP's president, Obama again pressed for the fund. The President got his money, when BP announced the creation of a $20 billion victim fund. The result may be admirable, but the precedent is troubling. There was little legal authority for the President's demand, and there was something very unseemly about a President ignoring due process and demanding cash.

President Obama clearly thinks he can get through this crisis by distraction and scapegoating. He hopes to distract the public by focusing on his energy agenda and he plans to use the oil industry in general and BP in particular as his scapegoat. The problem is, these are not the solutions the public is demanding. The public wants a federal plan to plug the leak. The public also wants a competent response at the federal level to clean up the mess. To date, Obama has not met either expectation, so touting a new energy tax and demonizing BP simply are not going to solve his problem.

Week 75

(THE CRACK-UP CRACK DOWN)

June 27, 2010

This was the week President Obama got tough. After hemorrhaging political support for months over the weak economy, the weak response to the oil spill, and the weak state of the war in Afghanistan, the President took some muscular shots at his critics. The White House put in all-nighters to forge a compromise on its financial reform bill, put the finishing touches on the BP escrow fund to compensate those hurt by the spill, and fired the commanding general in Afghanistan after he and his staff made unflattering comments about the Administration. To the President's supporters, these moves showed that Obama is in charge and is taking the initiative, but the Administration's crackdown on Wall Street, BP, and the military is more a sign of a crack-up than strength.

The President is facing a series of intractable problems, some of which are of his own making. On the economy, the President promised that a trillion dollars in stimulus spending would yield an explosion of jobs. Sixteen months later, the economy is again slowly growing, but unemployment still hovers near 10% and the financial markets remain shaky. On foreign affairs, the President said the war in Afghanistan must be won, yet he dithered for four months before he answered his generals' call for more troops, and then gave them less than they asked for. Those troops are now engaged in a very difficult fight, with an uncertain partner in the Afghan government, with no clear path to victory. Then came the oil spill, which exposed the White House as obdurate to the problem and incompetent in the response.

With all these challenges understandably putting the President on the defensive, it was necessary for the Administration to go on the offensive and exert its authority. The problem is, the President's answer for the weak economy and the weak state of the Afghan war is to crack down on the private sector and the military, an approach that will only make the problems worse. The nation is saddled with a weak economy, weak private sector investment, and weak job growth. A natural solution for this state of affairs would be for the government to try to take steps to encourage investment and hiring. Instead, the Administration likes to talk about the importance of job creation and economic growth, while pursuing policies that will retard both. To date, the Administration's answer to the weak economy has been massive increases in public sector spending and hiring, tax increases, and mountains of new regulations on the private sector. The government is increasing the cost of doing business, yet for some reason is surprised that the result is businesses doing less. The President's show of strength this week on financial sector reform is a telling example. With credit still tight and investors uncertain, the White House's solution is more regulation and taxation of the financial sector, more government oversight, and more limitations of capital flow. In an environment where corporations and individuals are hoarding cash, instead of giving incentives to invest and loan, the Administration is encouraging less investment by raising the costs and risks. And when corporations do injury, like BP has, the Administration has made clear they will be vilified, prosecuted, and looted for cash. The President might be very good at being tough on Wall Street and big corporations, but how that will create jobs or encourage investment is unclear.

The President also likes to talk tough on Afghanistan, but to date his steps have been tentative and inconsistent. President Obama says the war must be won, but he gave his generals fewer troops than they asked for, months late, and with rules of engagement that make effective operations more difficult. His halting steps to win the war have engendered distain from his commanders, including General McCrystal, whose staff made critical comments about the Administration to a *Rolling Stone* reporter. General McCrystal was promptly called to the White House woodshed and fired. This step might have cured a symptom of the criticism, but did nothing to address the disease, which is a lack of confidence in the President's commitment to the mission. Switching generals will not win the war, only a national commitment from the Commander-in-Chief can achieve that. So the President got tough this week, but nothing he did will improve the economy or the prospects for the war, and in many ways his actions make a crack-up on both more likely.

Week 76
(BASE MOTIVATIONS)

July 4, 2010

The torrent of bad news continued for the Administration this week. The jobs report showed only 83,000 new private sectors jobs created in June, and an overall loss of 125,000 jobs due to census layoffs. The stock market continued its drop, oil continued spewing into the Gulf, Americans continued dying in Afghanistan, and not surprisingly the President's approval ratings continued to drop. Now with only four months until the midterm elections, the Democrats have begun to realize that they are facing a potential electoral rout. This week, the White House tried to calm its wavering troops with a preview of the President's strategy to avert disaster in the Fall: motivate the base by blaming Republicans.

President Obama is unusually dependent on having a huge majority in Congress. This is because the President's major policy priorities are left of center and unacceptable to even a majority of moderate Democrats. From Obamacare, to the carbon tax, to bailouts, to immigration reform, the President can only pass his legislation if his majorities are large enough to overcome unanimous Republican opposition and substantial moderate Democrat defections. Indeed, the President has yet to support any major bipartisan legislation. Every significant bill the President has championed has been calibrated to be as left of center as possible while still being capable of garnering the minimum votes required for passage. The strategy worked for health care reform and will likely soon work on financial reform, but his huge majorities are at risk, and so the President is now launching his counteroffensive.

The great paradox of the Obama Administration is that he won election promising a new politics and an end to partisanship, but he has governed as an orthodox liberal who has consistently rejected bipartisan compromise. For much of his first 18 months in office, Obama effectively used his rhetorical skills to maintain the image of moderation, while pushing legislation whose only bipartisan aspect was the opposition to it. However, polls now show that the President's strategy of feigning moderation while pursuing partisan liberalism is no longer working, so this week Obama showed his partisan side. During a town hall in Wisconsin, the President gave a test flight to his newest narrative: Republicans are the problem. He blamed them for the economy, the problems with the war on terror, and said all they care about is cutting taxes for rich people and letting the private sector run rampant. In another speech, he blamed Republicans for holding up immigration reform, implying intolerance if not racism. He also lit into Republicans in Congress for opposition to the financial reform bill, painting them as champions of Wall Street rather than ordinary Americans. At the same time, the President is pushing the Democrat leadership in Congress to move on bills like immigration reform and the carbon tax to highlight Republican opposition and create a convenient foil for the President to rail against.

The goal of these speeches and legislative maneuvers is to motivate the base. For the Democrats to avoid huge losses in the Fall, the young and minority voters who turned out in the 2008 presidential elections have to turn out in 2010 to help Democrats keep their seats in Congress. Poll after poll has shown that Republicans are much more motivated to vote this year than Democrats. That combined with the poor state of affairs in the country could lead to an electoral catastrophe for the President. The economy is not going to magically recover in the next four months, oil will still be washing up on the shores of the Gulf in November, and Americans will still be dying in Afghanistan, so the President cannot afford to hope for better news, instead, he needs to concentrate on getting his troops to the polls. To do that, he has to motivate his progressive allies, by vilifying Republicans and pursuing partisan liberal legislation, even if he understands it cannot get enacted. This is the Obama strategy that was put on display this week.

Everyone understands that Republicans are going to do well in the election. The question is will they gain 25 seats in the House or 45. That is the battlefield. To win that battle, the President's focus is now base motivation. But whatever the outcome, what will this strategy mean for the remainder of the President's term. If the Republicans fail to capture any majority, the Democrats will still have far fewer seats, so to pass legislation, Obama must actually show some bipartisanship, something he has flatly refused to do so far. If Republican manage to take one of the chambers of Congress, this week's rhetoric is likely a preview of what we will see until 2012: a partisan President attacking Republicans to push his progressive agenda. Either way, it does no auger well for Americans hoping that their leaders will stop bickering and work together to address the nation's problems.

Week 77

(COURT CAMPAIGN)

July 11, 2010

This week the President continued his campaigning crusade against Republicans, with more speeches, rallies in battleground states, and fundraisers in Missouri and Nevada. At these events, he continued his efforts to convince voters, against all evidence, that the economy is good. He also continued to avoid the topics of the oil spill and Afghanistan, because even President Obama recognizes that spinning those challenges to a positive is beyond his powers. The President likewise continued to paint Republicans as extremists, most notably with his description of Sharon Angle, who is challenging Harry Reid in Nevada, as "even more extreme than the Republicans in Washington." But the President is not satisfied using speeches and rallies as campaign tools, it is now clear he plans to use the courts to campaign for votes.

This week the Department of Justice sued the State of Arizona over its immigration law, which among other things allows law enforcement to question those suspected of being illegal immigrants. For weeks, the Administration has been using the Arizona law as a rallying cry to motivate Hispanic voters to get to the polls this Fall to save Democrat seats. The President has attacked Arizona's governor, criticized Arizona during a meeting with the President of Mexico, tacitly given encouragement to the boycott movements, and used the law as his theme for Republican intolerance. But not satisfied with these pedestrian political tools, this week the Administration filed suit to have the Arizona law ruled invalid as preempted by federal immigration law.

The rhetoric against the Arizona law has been that the law is racist and unconstitutional because it encourages profiling of suspected illegal immigrants. However, the law simply implements enforcement of federal statutes dealing with illegal immigration. To mount a constitutional challenge based on impermissible profiling, there would need to be evidence of unconstitutional and disparate enforcement of the Arizona law. It takes time for that sort of evidence to develop, and the Administration has a campaign clock to keep, so the suit filed this week argues federal preemption, not due process violations. The fact that the Administration has relied on preemption for its lawsuit reveals both the hypocrisy and true motivation for the litigation.

For years, the federal government has allowed state and local government to pass legislation that conflicts with federal immigration laws. The best examples are sanctuary cities. Cities like San Francisco have passed local ordinances that illegals will not be automatically turned over to immigration officials or deported. These ordinances flatly contradict federal immigration laws and have been on the books for years, yet the Administration has done nothing. In contrast, the Arizona law may overlap with federal statutes, but it seeks to enforce them at the state level. The fact that the Administration has chosen to challenge a law whose goal is enforcement of federal statutes, while it ignores and refuses to challenge ordinances to seek to nullify federal law, shows the deep hypocrisy in the Administration's lawsuit.

The true motivation of the lawsuit is to get Hispanics to the polls to vote for Democrats. Even though polls show a majority of Americans support the Arizona law, the White House is no longer focused on what the majority of voters want. Instead, the entire focus of the Administration is constituency politics. With 90% of Republicans, 60% of Independents, and even 20% of Democrats disapproving of the President's performance, the White House does not have the luxury of focusing on the interests of the majority. Government workers, unions, minority activists, and feminists are all the White House can rely on to prevent an electoral disaster, and the President is going to use every tool, including the courts, in his campaign to keep majorities in Congress. So too bad for Arizona, where Mexican drug wars are raging, illegals are killing and stealing, and the border is unprotected, the President has an election to salvage.

Week 78

(PLUGGING LEAKS)

July 18, 2010

This was a week of fixes for the Obama Administration. The President praised the Senate's passage of financial reform, saying it would fix the problems that led to the mortgage crisis in 2008. The Administration touted BP's new cap on its leaking oil well, which for the moment has stopped the flow of oil into the Gulf. President Obama made a recess appointment of Dr. Bertwick to run the Medicare and Medicaid systems, saying he would start the process of fixing the problems with health care using the broad authority granted to him under the health care reform legislation. And the President continued his tour around the country handing out billons stimulus money to fix the ailing economy. The question is whether any of these fixes will help plug the President's leaking support.

The financial reform bill that passed the Senate was praised by the Administration as the most significant financial reform since the Great Depression, but it is far from clear it will fix the key problems that led to the mortgage crisis or improve the flow of credit. The new law gives the government more powers to seize and break-up failing institutions, compels greater transparency in financial transactions, places new controls and requirements on banks, and requires more separation between commercial and investment banking. But forgotten in the legislation was any significant reform of mortgage giants Freddie Mac and Fannie Mae, whose policies helped foster the mortgage crisis. Also, the bill's limitations on derivative trading will lead to much of that investment business going overseas and will make it harder for many industries (including agriculture), to hedge its risks. Also, ironically, the new legislation will hit small community banks the hardest with a host of new regulatory burdens, while the big banks feel they dodged a bullet. So the legislation certainly increases government power and controls over the financial sector, but how it will increase credit or avoid another mortgage crisis is unclear.

Like the financial reform legislation, it is also unclear how the new cap on the BP oil well will address the President's political problems arising from the Gulf Oil leak. After vilifying BP for weeks, it was BP technology and effort that got the new cap on the well, with the federal government largely sitting by as a spectator. If the cap holds, no new oil will flow into the Gulf, but the oil that has already leaked will continue to wash ashore for months, hurting tourism and fishing. Even more damaging is the Obama Administration's determination to maintain a moratorium on deep water drilling. After being twice rebuffed by the courts, the Administration has re-written the moratorium yet again to pass judicial scrutiny. The moratorium might please certain allies of the President, but it further injures the Gulf economy, which is heavily invested in the oil industry. BP certainly helped the President by capping the well, but the public's concern over the weak federal response remains.

The public also remains deeply skeptical of health care reform, with polls showing it remains the key issue along with the economy hurting Democrats this year. After forcing the legislation through despite public opposition, the President has continued to try to sell his reform plan. This week, the Administration announced a list of treatments that health insurance companies will now be required to offer without additional charge, but how these mandates will impact premiums was not addressed. With the estimates for the cost of health care reform and its effect on premiums continuing to rise, the President was eager to avoid further debates on health care. So when his nominee for running Medicare and Medicaid, Dr. Bertwick, was meeting opposition in the Senate for his past statements praising health care rationing and single payor systems, the President simply waited for Congress to recess and appointed him. The President hoped this tactic would avoid further debate on his reform, but instead his move simply underlines that health care is now a deeply partisan and politicized issue.

Of all the fixes the President pursued this week, none was more important than the economy. The fortunes of the Democrats and the remainder of the President's agenda depend largely on public perception of the economy between now and November. Polls show the vast majority of American's believe President's Obama's stimulus bill created no jobs and was a waste of money. To dispel this view, Obama has declared the summer of recovery and is travelling the country like a salesman handing out money and promising better days ahead. The problem is that the voters do not want the federal government borrowing billions to give handouts to political favorites. The public thinks the government is doing too much, spending too much, and borrowing too much. That combined with weak job growth makes the President seem out of sync with voters. So the President touted many fixes this week, but most do not address the problems, are what created the problems in the first place, or were done by others despite the federal government. That is not a recipe for effective leadership.

Week 79
(THE DOLE COMETH)

July 25, 2010

One of the hallmarks of the Obama Administration has been the creed that America must change its way of doing business. The President and his allies believe that America is falling behind because its markets are too uncontrolled, its income disparities too wide, its taxes too low, and its government too reluctant to interfere in the private sector. The model for the Obama Administration is Western Europe, with its more regulated free market, its generous welfare state, and its much higher levels of taxation. It is also no coincidence that in his first 18 months in office, the President's focus has been transforming America into a European style economy, based on capitalism certainly, but a much more regulated and redistributionist form of capitalism. What the President has ignored is that at the very moment he pines for European social democracy, Europe is dismantling the very structures the President is working to erect here.

This reality hit home this week when David Cameron, Britain's new Conservative Prime Minister, came to the White House on July 20. After 13 years of Labor Party rule, Cameron's Conservatives now govern Britain in a coalition government with the Liberal Democrats. Given the deep ideological differences between the Conservatives and the Liberal Democrats, many expected cautious moderation from Cameron's government. Instead, Cameron has set a bold agenda for transforming Britain in a direction nearly opposite from the course charted by President Obama. Under Labor, government spending, the government workforce, and taxation rose to nearly 50% of Britain's GDP. After the 2008 financial crisis, Britain found itself deep in debt and unable to pay for the vast welfare state and expensive National Health System augmented by the Labor Party. In response, Britain's collation government has proposed shrinking the size of government, a 25% reduction in government spending, and de-centralization of the National Health System. The goal is to balance Britain's budget, reduce state spending, and introduce more competitions and private incentives. It would be a radical agenda for a Conservative-only government, but the fact that it has been proposed by this collation government emphasizes the consensus that is rising throughout Europe that the social democracy model is too expensive and stifles growth and innovation.

The contrast with the Obama agenda could not be more startling, as events this week demonstrated. Unlike Britain's plan to control deficits and spending, this week the President vilified Republicans for insisting that any further extension of unemployment benefits be paid for by spending cuts elsewhere in the budget. Using his huge majorities in Congress, President Obama forced through his expansion of unemployment payments to a total of 99 weeks, adding $34 billion to the deficit with no plan to pay for the program going forward. Instead of promoting deficit reduction, spending control, and cuts to the welfare state, the Administration is pursuing programs in every sphere to expand the social safety net, government spending, and deficits. The President defended his effort stating that people need help and government must provide their income. A defense eerily similar to that made by the defenders of the dole, the need for government subsistence programs in Britain.

The week ended with a punctuation on the consequences of the Administration's policies, with reports that this year's federal deficit will be $1.47 trillion, that trillion dollar deficits will continue for years to come, and that President Obama's health care reform will add to the deficit, not reduce it. So when Britain and other nations across Europe are reigning in their welfare states and reducing government spending, President Obama is doing the opposite. It seems that nothing can shake the President's love for European-style social democracy, even though the Europeans themselves don't love it anymore.

Week 80

(OBAMA'S VIEW)

August 1, 2010

Several months ago, President Obama commented that 2010 would not be another 1994 (when Republicans took Congress) because this time the Democrats have "him." This comment reveals both the President's deep narcissism and his actual strategy. After forcing through program after program unpopular with the public, the President believes he can reignite their love affair with him by travelling the country, handing out cash, and re-connecting with voters. This week, the President put that strategy on national display with his appearance on ABC's daytime talk show, *The View*. Sitting on a long yellow couch with the five women hosts of the program (including the likes of Whoopi Goldberg and Barbara Walters), the President extolled American grit, optimism, and ingenuity, talked about his kids and family, and took subtle swipes at his opponents. But when asked about the lack of robust job growth and his biggest "thorn" over the last month, he dodged and evaded, and there lies the problem.

Obama's visit to *The View* was the first time a sitting President has ever appeared on a daytime talk show. For that reason, the hosts of *The View* were understandably ecstatic about the President's appearance. However, the President's advisors should have been less so. President Obama has an affection for populism, the us vs. them creed, that so easily allows him to paint his critics as retrograde oppressors of average Americans. He uses of populism are not simply rhetorical, he also practices it in selecting appearances. While the President assiduously avoids formal press conferences (with all the regalia of the Presidency and the tough questions from the White House press corps), he loves the one-on-one interview, with friendly hosts, where he thinks he personal charms will dominate. He loves this format so much, he does these types of interviews constantly. Only when his Administration is under critical fire, as with the BP oil spill, will he take the podium at a formal press conference. The President believes with this strategy he can freeze out the press corps, avoid tough questions, and control the message.

The appearance on *The View* was simply a ratcheting up of the same strategy. If you do a one-on-one interview for a news program, why not appear on a daytime talk show whose hosts are mostly from the entertainment industry and whose focus is popular culture, not politics. For a President who hates tough questions, it looked like a good choice. The New York City television audience was very supportive and four of the five hosts unapologetic liberals. Not surprisingly, the questions were easy, the answers smooth, and the problems facing the country were papered over with vague comments about American optimism. But what is not clear is how appearances like this one will help the President or his allies in Congress.

One of the problems the President is facing is the impression that he is disengaged, lazy, and more interested in public acclaim than hard policy work. The more he golfs, hangs out with the liberal elites, and overexposes himself with constant speeches and one-on-one interviews, the more the public can conclude that what he loves about the job is applause and praise, not policy. Likewise, the more he translates his populist creed into actions, by appearing on television shows that were previously viewed as beneath the presidency, he risks weakening himself and his Administration. The voters want a decisive leader with good judgment, not a best friend and convivial conversation companion.

Appearing on shows like *The View* also will likely do little to address voter concerns. Voters are worried about the economy, the deficit, and government getting too big and intrusive. Talking to four liberal hosts, before a liberal audience in New York City, without ever addressing the issues, will do little to allay those fears. The President said nothing about the deficit and the rampant expansion of government. Instead, he talked about the confidence and resilience of the American people. The President thinks if he positions himself as the defender of the people, the people will ignore his unpopular policies. But the people are smarter than the President gives them credit, and a fawning appearance on a daytime talk show, with few hard questions, and no real answers, will only reaffirm the view of many that the President does not get it.

Week 81

(UPS AND DOWNS)

August 8, 2010

After so many tough weeks, the President deserved a week of good news, and he got it. BP confirmed the successful temporary plugging of its well in the Gulf, Elena Kagan was confirmed by a vote to 63-37 to the Supreme Court, Democrats forced through a $26 billion bailout of states' and public employees' unions, and a federal judge found California's gay marriage ban unconstitutional. These amounted to wins on environmental, legal, budgetary, and social policy. But for all these achievements, there was some troubling news. A federal judge in Virginia allowed that state's legal challenge to the health care law to proceed and the August 6 jobs reported showed only 71,000 private sector jobs created and an overall job loss of 131,000. For every up there is a down, and this week the downs were less prominent, but more ominous.

The President's policies have created a highly charged political environment because every one of his major achievements has been a partisan affair. The stimulus bill, health care, financial reform, and the various bailouts all stemmed from laws written for and passed by Democrats. So every piece of good news for the President's allies engenders an equally strong backlash from his opponents. Clearly, both the President and the public benefit from BP's success plugging the oil leak in the Gulf. That coupled with this week's reports that most of the oil already leaked has largely dissipated has calmed fears on the scope of the environmental disaster. Yet the concerns over the weak federal response linger and now the President must face a tough choice on his offshore drilling moratorium, which he has re-written and re-written at the behest of the environmental lobby to keep the rigs closed. Plugging the leak could make the moratorium the big issue, because the economic harm caused by a prolonged moratorium could outweigh the damage from the spill itself.

Unlike the events in the Gulf, the confirmation of Elena Kagan and the passage of another $26 billion in bailouts for states and public employees unions pose no immediate tough choices for the President. Kagan is a liberal replacing a liberal, so her confirmation will not change the ideological balance on the court. That combined with her intelligence and political skills led to an easy confirmation. President Obama hopes Kagan will render rulings like the one in California this week, which overturned an initiative passed by voters and resurrected California's legalization of gay marriage. There was some controversy over the $26 billion bailout passed this week. The bill was written by the public employee unions and designed to exempt them from the consequences of overspending at the state level. Regardless, both the confirmation and the latest bailouts were hailed by the President's allies and inspired indignation from the President's opponents. The consequences of both decisions will be significant, but delayed. The President's desire for a liberal Supreme Court and an ever expanding government (which the bailouts help preserve), will create a backlash, with taxes, deficits, and legal rulings that will divide and upset the voters.

In this torrent of good news, the President's allies probably hardly noticed that a constitutional challenge to the health care law was allowed to proceed in Virginia and a jobs report came out on Friday showing slow job growth and a weakening recovery. Unlike the President's victories this week, neither of these pieces of bad news gained much attention. It will take many months (if not years) for the challenges to the health care law to make it to the Supreme Court. The impact of the weak economy will be felt in the November election, but for now, the President can avoid the consequences. Despite his short term victories this week, if his signature achievement falls to a constitutional challenge and the economy does not robustly recover, all the President's little ups will do little to stop a very bad down in 2012.

Week 82

(MOSQUE MIRE)

August 15, 2010

One of the lessons President Obama has learned very well is that engaging in the culture wars will do little to advance his larger agenda. For this reason, the President has tried hard to avoid the hot button cultural controversies of the day. While ardently pro-abortion, he rarely addresses the question. While taking a formal position against gay marriage, his Administration praises every legal win by the gay rights lobby, including last week's ruling resurrecting legal gay marriage in California. On issues of race, he recognizes that using the race card poses as many dangers as benefits, so he keeps it in his deck. But this week, the President forgot the lessons he had learned so well, when he waded into a controversy over a proposed Islamic Center near Ground Zero.

For many months, a dispute has been raging in New York City over a planned Islamic Center, which will include a mosque, a few blocks from Ground Zero. The project has been vigorously opposed by 9/11 families and conservatives, while it has been championed by Mayor Bloomberg and liberal groups, who see approval of the Center as a sign of tolerance and reconciliation. At a Ramadan dinner on August 13, the President publicly addressed the issue, stating that our nation is founded on freedom of conscience and as a nation we must be tolerant, respect all faiths, and support the free exercise of religion. With this as his premise, President Obama commented directly on the Islamic Center, implying that building it near Ground Zero will re-affirm American values.

The reaction to the President's comments was swift and furious. Jewish conservatives, 9/11 families, and some local politicians turned the President's words against him, noting that the location of the Center shows little tolerance or respect for the nearly 2800 people who were murdered by Islamic terrorists on 9/11. The President's critics saw these latest comments as another sign that the President's central strategy to defeat terrorism is appeasement of Islam. They also saw the comments as disrespectful of the pain the Center will cause to the families of those who died at Ground Zero. Immediately recognizing his error, on Saturday morning the Administration clarified that the President was only discussing general principles and that he was not endorsing actually building the Islamic Center near Ground Zero. However, this spinning came too late, because in a rare moment of candor, the President revealed his true perspective.

One of the reasons the President carefully avoids cultural issues is that his views are not supported by a majority of Americans. President Obama is firmly on the Left of his party on every social issue, from abortion, to gay marriage, to the racial spoils system. As an astute politician, President Obama knows he can further his cultural agenda better by talking like a moderate, while acting behind the scenes to advance his agenda. This very strategy could have worked with the Islamic Center as well, which had overcome most hurdles to its construction. However, the President got tripped up because at his Ramadan dinner, he could not avoid the temptation to lecture Americans on tolerance. He felt the need to remind the country that if we really believe in religious freedom, we should support this Islamic Center regardless of its proximity to Ground Zero. President Obama loves displays of moral superiority, which made the Islamic Center so tempting a topic for sermonizing on tolerance and moral superiority.

Forgotten in the President's hasty analysis at that Ramadan dinner was the reality of 2800 lives lost at Ground Zero and the pain and provocation inherent in building an Islamic Center so close to that site. Surely, in the faculty lounge, the idea of a center promoting Islam so close to Ground Zero would seem a wonderfully appealing monument to multiculturalism. But to the families of victims, where is the tolerance and respect for them. President Obama forgot that part.

Week 83

(BLAGO'ED)

August 22, 2010

With his Summer of Recovery tour going bust with the latest report of 500,000 new jobless claims on August 20, the President circled his wagons even tighter this week, sharpening his already tough rhetoric against Republicans, touring Hollywood to raise millions for Democrats, and using his weekly webcast to accuse corporations of attempting to hijack our democracy. But it is hard to get traction with accusations of corrupt Republican motives, when so many Democrats are under prosecution for corrupt actions. For weeks, there have been headlines about the ethics investigations against Charlie Rangel and Maxine Waters, two prominent members of the Congressional Black Caucus, who have been charged with ethical violations. This week, a jury in the trial of former Illinois Governor Rod Blagovevich returned one conviction on lying to federal officials and hung verdicts on all the other corruption charges levied against him. This victory for Blagovevich was a loss for Obama and the Democrats, because they now face the prospect of three ethics trials against three high-profile Democrats in the middle of the Midterm election season. No wonder the President was so excited to fly off to Martha's Vineyard for vacation.

The last thing the Democrats need are ethical controversies to compound their other problems. Their hope that the public would suddenly take a shine to bailouts, health care reform, and deficit spending is now clearly dashed. The recovery they prematurely heralded is losing steam. The President, who had been praised for his skills at touching the hearts of average Americans, is now seen by many as out of touch and too liberal. In fact 18% of Americans now think he is a Muslim in the wake of his comments in favor of building a mosque near Ground Zero. Adding the label of "crooked" to the Democrats is the last thing the President needs.

It does not help matters that the accused Democrats are utterly defiant and unrepentant. Charlie Rangel is charged with a host of violations, including lying on financial forms, failing to pay taxes on his home in the Caribbean, and misleading tax authorities over his rent controlled apartments in New York City. Maxine Waters is charged with improper use of her staff and pressuring federal regulators to bailout a California bank where her husband was on the Board. And of course, Rod Blagovevich is charged with a long list of public corruptions, including trying to sell Barak Obama's Senate seat. None of them have admitted any wrong-doing, none apologizes for anything, and all of them will be under active prosecution during the Fall campaign.

President Obama promised clean and transparent government, but his Administration has been utterly silent on the charges levied against these Democrats. Since the President is politically weakened, he dares not speak out against any liberal supporter, no matter his or her wrongdoing. The Administration's entire focus is on rallying the base and fear mongering over Republicans, so all of the President's good government rhetoric has been discarded. It has been replaced with misdirection on the economy, and cutting comments about any who oppose his agenda. This week's presidential webcast, with its ominous warnings about a corporate coup d'état, were an effort to change the topic and energize his base. But abstract allusions to corrupt and evil opponents will not steal the limelight from the real life ethics trials of three well-known Democrats.

Week 84

(LOBSTER TRAP)

August 29, 2010

Five years ago, Hurricane Katrina hit New Orleans while President Bush was on vacation in Crawford, Texas. As the levies broke and the city was flooded, President Bush was roundly criticized for being too slow to leave his vacation and out of touch on the disarray of the federal response. President Obama seems to have ignored that lesson when he left for his 10 day vacation to Martha's Vineyard. Unlike 2005, today the nation is not grappling with a stark disaster like Katrina, but instead a slowing of the economy, rising unemployment, and unprecedented government deficits. While this state of affairs continued to fuel a storm of public outrage this week, the President relaxed at his rented mansion, played five rounds of golf, and repeatedly enjoyed lobster diners with well-to-do friends.

Presidents always take criticism for their vacations. The burdens of the presidency are heavy, so the public does not begrudge its Chief Executive a well-earned rest. However, Presidents need to be careful that their private amusements do not create the impression of an out of touch leader. The President's vacation this week did just that. President Obama is the king of cool. Even in a tense environment, his supreme self-confidence and serene demeanor show through. This attribute is one of his greatest strengths, but it also exposes a great weakness, namely, his arrogance. The President honestly believes that he saved the nation from a depression and that the vast expansion of government power and spending will revive the nation and remake the economy. He also believes that he can single-handedly turn the tide in the Fall election with his powers of persuasion. With so much confidence, it does not surprise that he saw no risk in taking a 10-day vacation to an island playground of the rich and privileged.

The problem is that the President is not the leader he was in 2008, but he has not figured that out yet. He still sees himself as the great unifier, the great reformer, and the leader who will fundamentally change America. Yet his promises during 2008 and his rhetoric do not match his deeds. He promised to change our politics, but instead has ruled through secrecy, deal-making, and hard partnership. He ignored public sentiment, pushed through unpopular programs, and has vilified any who oppose him. All of this would have been okay if he had achieved his one central promise to right the economy, but he has not. Again this week projections for economic growth continued to fall, while fears of deflation and a new recession rose. And abroad, the troubled war in Afghanistan continued, with this month's death toll reaching 47. No matter, the President swam, and golfed, and hobnobbed with the elites.

In the wake of the President's unwise comments praising a mosque near Ground Zero, the worst thing for the Administration was more imagery of an out of touch leader. The public is worried about the economy, the war, the deficit, the size of government, and power grabs by Washington. Independent voters are abandoning the Democrats and the election environment continues to worsen for them. No Democrat any longer harbors a hope that a strong economy will turn the tide. No matter, the President would have none of it interfere with his fun. In doing so, the President made himself look even more out of touch and even less of the leader we need in these difficult times. Obama put himself in a lobster trap of his own making.

Week 85

(CATEROLOGY)

September 5, 2010

A weak economy, troubling challenges in the Middle East, high energy prices, America off balance in foreign affairs, and a besieged Democrat in the White House. 2010 is sounding a lot like 1978. For Democrats hoping the responses to these challenges would be different from the ones employed by President Carter, there was little solace this week. After returning from a 10-day vacation, President Obama's focus was not on the troubling economy, but rather on issues of war and peace in the Middle East. By declaring withdrawal but not victory in Iraq and sponsoring a summit to re-start Israeli Palestinian peace talks, President Obama turned to foreign policy when domestic issues are paramount to the public. Foreign policy success did not save President Carter, and it is not likely to help President Obama either.

During the campaign, President Obama pledged to end the war in Iraq and criticized the troop surge as a futile effort to turn the tide. By the time of the election, it was becoming clear that the surge had in fact stabilized Iraq and restored a sufficient modicum of security to allow the pullout that Obama had promised. In August 2010, the last combat brigade left Iraq and on August 31 the President addressed the nation to declare the end of combat operations. All recognize that the current stability in Iraq is fragile, so the President wisely avoided any declaration of victory in his address. But in heralding the end of combat operations, the President missed an opportunity to recognize America's significant achievements in Iraq.

Barely three years ago, the consensus was that America would be defeated in Iraq. The troop surge and other policy changes put in place by President Bush in 2007 salvaged the situation and restored enough stability to allow U.S. forces to turn over security duties to the Iraqi military. It is too soon to call this victory, but it is success. The President made no effort in his address to recognize the significance of this achievement, instead he praised the troops and reminded viewers that he is keeping his promise to end the war. Rather than inspire the nation by praising the surge or recognizing success, the President kept his anti-war tone, no doubt to placate his liberal base, which wants no talk of victory in Iraq. By taking this tact, he turned his address into another exercise in self-promotion.

The President's speech also addressed the war in Afghanistan. It is ironic that during the campaign the President declared as all but lost a war in Iraq that could be won, while claimed as essential a war in Afghanistan that is a much tougher challenge. The President and his Administration continue to refuse to credit the surge in Iraq, while at the same time they are now employing the same strategy in Afghanistan, with one key difference. President Bush always stated that America would stay and fight in Iraq until victory was won, but President Obama has pledged that America will start withdrawing from Afghanistan next year. He made that pledge again in his speech this week. This sent a message to our enemies that President Obama is a half-hearted warrior, who is not in the fight to win. A few generals said this week that the President's withdraw pledge is giving succor to our enemies, but no matter, because like Iraq, the President wants out of Afghanistan, whether we have success there or not.

Not yet having his fill of Middle East matters, the President next turned to the peace process with Israel. The President hosted a summit with Prime Minister Netanyahu and Palestinian President Abas and declared a one year process to seek a two state solution for the Israeli Palestinian conflict. No one can criticize the President for political motives in re-starting a new peace process that has so little chance of success, considering the challenges and all those who have failed at it in the past. But like President Carter, it seems President Obama craves the mantel of peace-maker as much as he hates the role of war leader.

The President's foreign policy week ended with a hint of domestic reality with yet another jobs report showing 54,000 jobs lost in August 2010 and an unemployment rate of 9.6%. The President stood in the Rose Garden and haltingly and unconvincingly praised the report as showing things are moving in the right direction. And after a week where his focus seemed to be on everything but the state of the economy, the President pledged yet again to make job creation his number one priority. He then left for Camp David and another three day vacation.

Week 86

(STIMULATING THE GUARANTEE SOCIETY)

September 12, 2010

Labor Day traditionally kicks off the campaign season in election years, and this year was no different. With his party down in the polls and the economy in the dumps, the President launched a multipronged offensive to avert an electoral disaster. With a fiery speech before a union crowd in Wisconsin, proposals for a new stimulus bill, and a rare press conference, the President tried to inspire confidence in his allies and put pressure on the Republicans. But by calling for a guarantee society in Wisconsin, coupled with proposals for more unpopular stimulus spending, the President provided ample ammunition for his opponents.

With polls showing Republican voters far more enthusiastic than Democrats, the President's central goal in the Fall campaign is to get out Democrat voters. We saw that strategy in action in the President's Labor Day speech in Wisconsin to a union crowd. The speech was filled with the usual praise for government initiatives and shots at Republicans, but what was most striking was the portrait the President painted of the type of society he craves. The President spoke of erecting a society that guarantees to every American an education, health care, employment, a good salary, and a secure retirement. The President did not speak about opportunity, but entitlement. The union crowd loved it, but by stating so clearly his desire to create a cradle to grave entitlement society, the President made evident his vision to transform America into a true social democracy. It is this very agenda that is motivating his opponents, and by trumpeting it to his allies, he only further emboldens his foes.

The President also offered a prescription for the ailing economy: more stimulus. Recognizing the public has rendered its verdict that the first stimulus was a failure, the Administration avoids the word "stimulus," but proposes more of it nevertheless. The President proposed another $50 billion in infrastructure spending (even though none of the projects could begin until next year) and $300 billion in temporary business tax cuts (paid for with an equal amount of business tax increases). The President knows neither proposal has any chance of passage. Immediately after the infrastructure proposal was made, four Democrat Senators issued a statement that they would not support it. As for the tax cuts, they are coupled with so many tax increases that it is unlikely any consensus bill could be passed during the very short legislative session prior to the election. Further, any chance for progress on taxes was undermined when the President made clear that he would support the extension of only some of the Bush tax cuts, creating tension with not only Republicans, but also a growing chorus of Democrats who want all the tax cuts extended. In the end, the President's proposals are not about economics, but rather politics. He proposed the infrastructure spending as red meat to unions and liberals. He proposed tax cuts (coupled with tax increases) to create a campaign issue.

We saw the President try to use this tax issue during his press conference on September 10. During an unusually long session with reporters, the President hit again and again on his campaign theme that the Republicans are holding the economy hostage by opposing pro-business measures designed to jump-start growth. The President ignored the adverse economic impact of huge deficits, expansive new regulations, and the uncertainties created by his health care and energy policies, and instead argued that Republicans' opposition to a $30 billion small business loan program was the reason for the economy's problems. The argument is absurd on its face, but no matter, since all the President is trying to do is fire up his troops. But talking about a guarantee society and more stimulus is just as likely to fire up his opponents.

Week 87

(PARTY CRASHERS)

September 19, 2010

The President often touts the fact that the Democrats will avoid an electoral debacle in the Fall because of him. He believes his rhetorical skills, connection with voters, deep pockets, and army of activist and union supporters will turn the tide for the Democrats. The President has donated millions to fellow Democrats from his personal campaign coffers, and revived his entire presidential campaign network to get his supporters to the polls. The unions have done the same, spending millions and working to fire up their membership. While the President, through edict and rhetoric, tries to recreate the populist movement that carried him to office, he ignores and reticules an authentic and massive populist movement rising across country, in the form of the Tea Party. The Tea Party this week definitively crashed into the Republican Party, and is planning to crash directly into the Democrats in the Fall with even greater fury.

The Democrats and the elite media first saw the Tea Party as a curiosity, then as a fringe right-wing movement, and now as a disturbance and civil war in the Republican Party. To date, most Democrats have enjoyed watching the victories of the Tea Party. With no national or governing apparatus, the Tea Party has organized itself in most of the 50 states as a movement for smaller government and lower taxes. It is a direct reaction against Washington's deficits and spending, and what the Tea Party perceives as the socialist agenda of the Obama Administration. But rather than starting a true third party, which would have divided the opposition to the President and made his agenda easier to enact, the Tea Party charted a different course. First, they are seeking to cleanse the Republican Party, and then they plan to clean the clocks of the Democrats. Across the county, Tea Party candidates have defeated establishment Republicans in primaries. The movement has been most notable in Senate races, where Marco Rubio in Florida, Sharon Angle in Nevada, Joe Miller in Alaska, Pat Toomey in Pennsylvania, and Rand Paul in Kentucky all rode the Tea Party mantle in victory.

This week, the greatest Tea Party shock wave hit when Christine O'Donnell defeated moderate and highly popular Mike Castle for the Republican Senate nomination in Delaware. Liberals happily cheered this result, because it took Castle, a sure winner in November, and replaced him with a controversial and unknown conservative. This result might in the short term cost Republicans a Senate seat, but Democrats should be wary of too much celebration. The fact that moderate Delaware Republicans favored a little known O'Donnell over a 30 year and popular incumbent shows the deep dissatisfaction among voters. O'Donnell's victory has also energized the Tea Party even more and may create a false sense of security among Democrats. It's easy for Democrats to enjoy the Tea Party wave as it crashes into Republicans, but what they are forgetting is this is just the preview for the true tsunami that the Tea Party plans for the Democrats.

For his part, President Obama seems to pretend the Tea Party does not exist. The President's entire focus is on motivating liberals to vote. On the campaign trail, he continues to extol health care reform, financial reform, stimulus spending, and an activist federal government. This week, he again rejected calls from within his own party for extending all the Bush tax cuts, and continued the fight for more taxes and spending. Nearly forgotten in the President's rhetoric are the deficit and the unprecedented levels of federal spending, because his liberal base does not want to hear about such things. Poll after poll show that after the economy, those issues are the key concerns of independent voters, but the President ignores them. Likely the President intends to change his tune and address these issues after the election. Yet it is puzzling that the President believes he will avert disaster in the Fall by ignoring the messages the voters are sending him. The rise of the Tea Party should be a wakeup call for Democrats, but instead it is making them think they have nothing to worry about.

Week 88

(VELMAFICATION)

September 26, 2010

With the campaign season on, President Obama is working feverishly to try to recreate the magic of the 2008 campaign. One of the hallmarks of that campaign was dozens of town hall meetings, where the President fielded questions from voters. After 18 months of carefully trying to avoid unscripted events, on Monday, September 21, the President returned to his favorite format with a town hall meeting sponsored by CNBC. The President wanted to use the event to reconnect with voters, but even with a largely friendly crowd and a favorable format, he got mugged by the most unlikely of assailants, Velma Hart.

Velma Hart is African American, a CFO of a non-profit, a self-professed middle class voter, and an Obama supporter, so when she stood up Obama surely felt a softball coming. Instead he got beaned in the head with a 90 mile-an-hour fast ball. After a brief introduction, Ms. Hart said: "I'm exhausted. I'm exhausted of defending you. I'm exhausted of defending your Administration. I'm exhausted of defending the mantle of change I voted for, and I'm deeply disappointed with where we are right now." Obama laughed on the outside, but was crying on the inside. The media played and re-played Ms. Hart's comments all week, using them as a symbol of middle class angst and a portrait of the President's political problems. But Ms. Hart's comments are far more troubling than the mainstream media realizes.

President Obama won the 2008 campaign by portraying himself as a messianic figure who would solve all of the country's problems and change our politics forever. Obama's message was perfect for that political moment, but it was also brazenly irresponsible, because while Obama knew it was just campaign rhetoric, his supporters actually believed it. Millions went to the polls convinced that a President Obama would cure the economy, protect the middle class, give free education and health care to all, ends the wars, and balance the budget in the process. With expectations so high, disappointment was inevitable, but the President did far more than simply disappoint, he was disingenuous. After campaigning as a moderate, he put all his focus and energy on passing legislation (stimulus, health care, and financial environmental reform) written for the maximum liberalism that could still garner a bare majority of votes in the Democrat dominated Congress. He played partisan, hardball politics, was secretive, and seemed a detached elitist. His supporters might have forgiven it all if the economy had recovered as he promised, but it has not. And now not only are his supporters' dreams dashed, but the reality that it was all empty rhetoric has finally set in.

So the Velma Harts of America are now asking why hasn't the President solved all their problems. Obama said he would, he said he was the transformative savior of the nation, so why do we have an economy stalled, a deficit soaring, 10% unemployment, and a lingering and difficult war in Afghanistan. Voters like Ms. Hart were actually counting on the government to make their lives easier, since that is exactly what Obama promised. Now that they realize that they have to look to themselves, not the government, for salvation, they are lost and bewildered. To people like Ms. Hart, Obama has not done enough, not fought enough, not changed enough, so supporters like her are exhausted of defending him. These supporters are disenchanted, discouraged, and very likely disinclined to rush to the polls in November.

But what the media missed is that Ms. Hart was not the true voice of the middle class. Her criticism of the President centered on his failure to change things more radically, where most independent voters think the President has changed too much. Even after the town hall, Ms. Hart said she still supported the President, while polls show 60 percent of independents now oppose the Administration. While Ms. Hart is disappointed that the government has not made her life easier, most independent voters now think that government spending and interventions are the problem. So to please his based supporters like Ms. Hart, the President has to be more radical, while being more radical will surely lose him more independent votes. Obama is realizing it's not easy being the messiah.

Week 89

(DOWN AND OUT)

October 3, 2010

When Congress returned from summer recess, there was plenty of talk about how much would get done before the November election. The President touted a second stimulus bill of tax incentives and $50 billion in additional infrastructure spending, Majority Leader Harry Reid promised a comprehensive tax bill to address the expiring Bush tax cuts, immigration reform was set for a vote, and even the cap and trade bill was on the agenda. Not only did Congress fail to pass any of these bills, it did not even attempt a vote on them or even a single appropriations bill for the 2010 fiscal year (which is half over). With the President and his allies down in the polls, they decided to just get out of town.

It is not surprising that Congress failed to pass any significant bills during its abbreviated session (beyond a $30 billion small business lending bill), since an election season is a notoriously difficult time to enact legislation. The difference this time is that the Democrats' plan was to push through some landmark legislation to set the stage for a comeback in the final weeks before election day. But when they got back to Washington, they found their members both terrified and mutinous. Dozens of moderate Democrats, who are fighting for their political lives, did not quietly tell the leadership that they would not support these measures, they signed pledges proclaiming their opposition. Several Democrat congressman even said they would not support

Nancy Pelosi for speaker in the next Congress, and one several weeks ago hypothesized about her death. Things are little better in the Senate, where half a dozen Democrat incumbents are endangered and the hangover from all the spending they forced through is finally making a large cadre of Democrats find their inner fiscal conservative.

Amidst all the talk of a civil war within the Republican Party, a true civil war is now being fought among the Democrats. The conflict arises from a basic disconnect between the members and their leadership. The Democrats' majority was built on members elected from Republican-leaning states and districts, who got into office during the highly favorable political environments of 2006 and 2008. Their leaders, especially in the House, are the establishment liberals who have been running the party for decades. These leaders convinced their moderate members that there would be no adverse consequences if they voted for bailouts, bloated stimulus bills, and health care reform. They were promised that the voters would reward them for their courage and fore-sight. Every promise made by the leadership was wrong, and the moderate Democrats now know it, and that's why they are in full revolt and full retreat.

For his part, the President is powerless to help his moderate allies, because he has lost sup-port from the vast majority of moderate and independent voters who elected them. So all of the President's attention is now focused on the liberal base of the party. On September 28, he gave an interview to *Rolling Stone* touting his long list of progressive accomplishments, avoiding any comment on the deficit, and saying his critics were motived by dark forces. That same day, he headlined a rally in reliably liberal Madison Wisconsin, where he excoriated Wall Street, the rich, and the Tea Party. Embattled Wisconsin Senator Russ Feingold skipped the event, because even in Wisconsin, being seen with the President is a political hazard. So we now have the Democrats in Congress in open revolt and a President who dares not show his face in most of the nation and acts more like chief of the liberal wing of his party, rather than chief of state. No wonder Democrats are down and out.

Week 90

(GAS ON THE FIRE)

October 10, 2010

For the last two weeks, there has been much talk about the comeback of the Democrats. With improving poll numbers in a few races (notably California and Washington State), liberal com-mentators proclaimed that the Republicans had peaked and that the election would not be a disaster after all. That perspective held sway for about ten days, then reality started to set in, with the last jobs report before the election. On October 7, the Labor Department reported that the economy lost 95,000 jobs in September, led by the loss of 159,000 public sector jobs, with only a feeble 64,000 jobs created in the private sector. The unemployment rate held steady at 9.6 percent, but under underemployment rate jumped to over 17 percent. The bleak picture was not limited to jobs. The weak dollar continued its slow collapse, as investors rushed to safe havens like gold. The continued devaluation of the dollar contributed to a strong rally in oil, pushing prices at the pump ever higher, and threatening $3.00 per gallon by election day. Throwing gas on a brewing political fire storm is the last thing the Democrats need.

The President's response to the Labor Department report was to take refuge in rhetoric. He simply repeated the mantra he has been offering for months after each set of bleak employment data: we are moving in the right direction, but not fast enough. The President then took his usual pivot, blaming Republicans for not passing small business legislation and asking Congress to pass even more stimulus spending. It is not clear who would pass the new stimulus spending, since Congress left town last week, without even passing a budget or setting the tax rates starting January 1, 2011. Even the President now realizes that there will be no economic salvation for the Democrats this year. It seems the Summer of Recovery has given way to the Fall of Stagnation, with a soon to follow the election of consequences.

The President's message was also hampered by the perception that his closest aides are fleeing the ship. This week, Rahm Emmanel resigned as Chief of Staff, to pursue a campaign for Mayor of Chicago, and National Security Advisor George Jones announced his departure as well. This comes on top of the resignations of economic advisors Lawrence Summers and Christine Roemer. There were even reports this week that the President plans to dump Vice President Biden in favor of a stronger running mate, possibly Hillary Clinton. To cap it all, Clinton supporters publicly touted this year's election as a referendum on Barak Obama, barely hiding their joy at the President's troubles. A recent poll showing the President's approval rating at 38% has no doubt emboldened Clinton supporters, who have never reconciled with the Obama team since their defeat in the 2008 Democrat primaries.

The best evidence of reality hitting home were comments this week by David Plouffe, the President's political guru. Speaking to the Democratic National Committee, he said it would be a disgrace for the Republicans if they did not sweep the Fall elections given the favorable political climate. When professional political operatives start spinning the election outcomes more than three weeks before the vote, you know a disaster is coming. As for the President, he headlined more rallies and fundraisers this week, in those few districts where he dares to appear in person. He also continued his criticism of the business community, this time attacking the Chamber of Commerce, declaring that they were using foreign funds to support Republican candidates and vowing a federal investigation. But the President's blame game is getting increasingly stale, just as the election is continuing to look increasingly bleak.

And then we have those gas prices. All the weakness in the U.S. economy has led to a run on the dollar and a resulting rally for oil. Fluctuations in gas prices are typical, but if the price rises to near $3.00 per gallon now, the timing could not be worse for the Democrats. Every gas station would become an advertisement for the sad state of the economy, and the voters have already decided pretty well who should take the blame.

Week 91

(GONE AWAY YOUNG MAN)

October 17, 2010

One of the constituencies that propelled Barak Obama to the White House was the youth vote. The President won younger voters by a wide margin, with his promises of hope and change. Now, in the middle of a difficult midterm election fight, youth voters are yet another group where the

President is trying to recreate the magic of 2008. To that end, this week he hosted a Youth Town Hall sponsored by MTV. In 2008, youth voters were like entranced worshipers, bowing at the President's every word, but the MTV town hall showed how starkly the tone has changed. Where once there was devotion, now there is skepticism. Where once there was fawning acclaim, now there are tough questions.

One of the great ironies of the Obama Presidency at the midpoint of its first term is that the President's most ardent supporters — the youth voters — are the ones suffering most from his policies. Unemployment among workers ages 18 to 26 is well above the national average, college costs continue to soar, the stimulus spending has helped unions and public employees far more than the young, and massive deficits spending will have dire financial consequences for the same young voters who put the President in office. Added to this is the disappointment of young voters, who believed Barak Obama was a new kind of politician, more modern and post-partisan, but who now realize that he is not much of a departure from what they have known.

Given all this, the President's effort to create anew his magic with young voters is admirable, but perhaps futile. It will be very hard to motivate masses of young voters to march to the polls when they have no jobs, their parents are under financial stress, and the federal government seems incompetent at best. This reality came to light very quickly at the MTV event, when the President was asked about the poor state of the economy, partisanship in Washington, the insolvency of Social Security, illegal immigration, and the rise of the Tea Party. The President fielded all of these unusually tough questions well, as usual blaming President Bush and the Republicans for the poor economy, saying the economy was moving in the right direction, and indicating that increasing payroll taxes was the key to saving Social Security.

The substance of the questions and answers was not the telling feature of the event, it was the tone. Gone is the automatic support and adulation for the President. It has been replaced with respectful skepticism and a growing disillusionment. Youth voters still want to believe in and support President Obama, but everything they see around them is making them question whether his campaign of hope and change was empty rhetoric. If the economy improves, there is still a good chance these youth voters will return to the fold and support the President in 2012, but what about 2010. With all the questions and concerns swirling around the President's policies, it is hard to see how these youth voters will be motivated to save the President from defeat in the election just two weeks off. No matter, the President still thinks he has the same magic with the young who put him in office 2 years ago. Soon we will find out if that is true.

Week 92

(THINKING CLEARLY)

October 24, 2010

As the President continues to dash desperately across the country campaigning for embattled Democrats, his true views on why his party is facing broad election losses is coming through, slowly but perceptibly. On the stump, the President is all fire and indignation, claiming Republicans are selling snake oil and pleadings with voters not to return the keys to the people who drove us into the economic ditch. He trumpets his spending, and health care and financial reforms, as pillars of the more equitable future he seeks to create. Most of all, he vilifies his political opponents and deflects any blame for the sad state of the economy. These are the President's rousing public pronouncements and his election appeal, but they do not reflect his true views on why he and his party are in trouble. His true views come through when he speaks in small friendly forums, where he is more at ease and where he sometimes allows himself, for brief moments, to say what he really thinks. And what the President really thinks is that his critics are misguided, ignorant bigots too stupid to know what is good for them.

During his 2008 campaign, at California fundraiser then-candidate Obama said that rural American are fearful and compensate by clinging to guns and religion. These comments revealed Obama's elitist tendencies and his contempt for average Americas. This statement was damaging to the President, but the favorable political climate of 2008 allowed him to survive these comments and ride on to victory. He tried to explain them away, by touting his support for gun ownership and claiming his own deep religious faith. That was enough in those times, but many who heard these words wondered if that is how the President really views average Americans.

After his election, the President mastered the proper political tone and avoided further comments demeaning to average Americans. Instead, he focused on vastly expanding the power, scope, and spending of the federal government, all in the name of helping the middle class. He championed unions, attacked industry after industry, and on those rare occasions when he tried to pay for the costs of all his new spending programs, he insisted that new taxes only be levied on the highest earners. Now, two years into his Presidency, he looks back on his accomplishments and sees great gains enacted for average Americans, with the costs placed solely on the "rich." With this perspective, it is not surprising that the President is befuddled about the rise of the Tea Party and his collapsing support among independents. President Obama has often said the Tea Partiers should be thanking him, and he really believes it.

President Obama is an economic determinist. He believes if his programs give economic benefits to certain constituencies, like the middle class for example, those constituencies, if thinking rationally, will support him. This is close to a Marxist perspective, and one that borrows heavily from Leftist ideology that economic circumstance should determine political judgment. The President sees himself as giving huge benefits to middle class people, including tax cuts, health care and financial reform, cheaper student loans, and attempts at better employment protections. With this record, the President believes that any middle class person who is opposing him is irrational.

With the mounting political pressure of the Fall campaign, the President has not been able to hide what he really thinks. During his *Rolling Stone* interview, he said the Tea Party was motivated in part by "dark forces." During his MTV Town Hall, he said the difficult economic times were making people act in a "tribal" fashion. Most recently, at an exclusive Democratic fundraiser in New York City, he said humans under stress are hard wired to "not think clearly." These comments are the true Obama. The President believes he has heaped great economic benefits on lower and middle class Americans and their waning support for him must be explained by tribalism, dark forces, or incoherence thought. With these views, it is unlikely the President intends to listen to the voters if they hand him a defeat in November. When the President likens the voters' concerns to mental illness, it is clear he intends not to listen.

What President Obama does not understand is that people's political views are not governed solely by their sense of economic self-interest. Many Americans simply believe in smaller government, less federal power, and balanced budgets regardless of whether they will personally benefit from such policies. These views are driven by political principles, not economic self-interest.

The President's philosophy of economic determinism makes it impossible for him to comprehend or respect the views of these voters, which is why, when he lets his guard down, he insults them.

Week 93

(THE NIXONIAN)

October 31, 2010

There is no recent politician more vilified by Democrats than Richard M. Nixon. To them, he is the epitome of corruption, a politician who used the levers of federal power to attack his opponents, who broke the law, and who undermined the democratic system. This critique has force because most of it is perfectly justified. But there is risk in the constant references to the abuses of Nixon, because it makes today's politicians particularly vulnerable to attack when they start acting Nixonian. That is exactly what Barak Obama started doing this week, and there will likely be bad consequences if the election goes poorly for the Democrats.

At yet another Democrat fundraiser, President Obama said Republicans could come along for the ride as he drives America toward his vision of the future, but they had to get in the back of the bus. During an interview with Univision, President Obama said: "We're gonna punish our enemies and we're gonna reward our friends who stand with us on issues that are important to us." Then, during an appearance with John Stewart on the Daily Show, Obama pointed his finger at the liberal host and the overwhelmingly liberal audience, explaining why they should be grateful, not critical. Obama has been remarkably divisive for many months, but these types of comments have started to raise questions on whether the President is coming unhinged.

It has been clear for several months that the Democrats were not going to be able to rely on a strong economic recovery or the popularity of their programs to win elections this year, since the economy is not strong and their policies are not popular. With this reality facing them, the Democrats decided that their salvation was in attacking their opponents and motivating their base. So in a political climate dominated by a conservative reaction against the Democrat's agenda, the Democrats decided they could save themselves only by being even more stridently liberal. There is nothing new in this strategy, what's new is that the President decided that he, not a cadre of surrogates, would lead the charge.

Our Presidents are both head of state and head of government, a constitutional officer who is the leader of the nation as a whole. These obligations require a certain dignity and restraint in the use of the office, which is often in conflict with the fact that Presidents are also politicians and the leaders of their party. Most Presidents deal with this conflict by delving into highly partisan rhetoric sparingly, instead relying on others to do the dirty work. This tradition goes back to the 19th century, when Presidents did not campaign for election, but instead relied on others to represent them. This seems to be yet another aspect of American tradition that President Obama seeks to transform. Gone is dignity and restraint in the office. It has been replaced with a President who goes on MTV and comedy shows to push his agenda and by a President who calls Republicans enemies who need to get on the back of the bus. The great post-partisan unifier has transformed himself from the leader of the nation into solely the leader of his party, using the most divisive rhetoric he can conjure to rally his troops.

President Obama may believe that this rhetoric is necessary to get out his vote, and he might be correct. And in his mind, it might just be rhetoric, designed only to motivate the most partisan liberals to vote. But what he has forgotten is that he is head of state, and that the Republicans are the loyal opposition, not enemies of the state. After the election, he needs to lead the nation as a whole, in concert with a Congress that will be much more Republican, in service of a populace who is sending a message that they are unhappy with his policies. His ability to do the work of the American people over the next two years may be undermined by the rhetoric he is using now. After creating a great partisan rift during the election, the President may believe that he can heal the wounds and return dignity to his office. Nixon tried that before and failed, but in this task, Obama thinks: yes he can.

Week 94

(SHELLACKING)

November 7, 2010

Since his election in 2008, President Obama has predicted that there would be no debacle for Democrats in the 2010 midterm election. He simply stated things would be different this time because of him. Throughout his first two years in office, the President persisted in his belief that he maintained a magical hold over the American people and no matter what the polls might show, the voters would never punish him or his party. Armed with this belief, for more than two months, the President focused almost entirely on fundraising and campaigning for Democrats to prove himself correct. He raced from state to state, raised tens of millions for Democrats, called Republicans enemies who had to get on the back of the bus, and told the voters they were not thinking clearly. All to no avail. As Obama himself stated at his November 3 news conference, he and his party took a "shellacking" in the election.

The numbers tell the story. In the House of Representatives, the Republicans gained more than 60 seats, defeating 53 Democrat incumbents and building a majority of some 240 seats, their biggest majority since 1948. In the Senate, the Republicans gained 6 seats, increasing their strength to 47, more than enough to give them significant leverage over the Democrat majority. But the worst results for the Democrats were at the state level. Republicans finished election night controlling 29 of the nation's 50 governorships, picked up more than 675 state legislative seats, and took control of at least 19 state legislative chambers. These victories will give the Republicans a huge advantage in the 2011 redistricting process, which will help them maintain and build upon their majority in the House of Representatives. Most disturbing for President Obama, the Democrats suffered a complete collapse in Ohio, Michigan, Wisconsin, Pennsylvania, Indiana, and Virginia, many states he carried in the 2008 election. These results came from independents, white voters, women, and college educated voters (except on the West coast), all flocking to the Republicans.

Up to the final hours before the election, the Democrats continued to proclaim that there was no chance they would suffer another defeat like the 1994 midterm, where the Republicans took both houses of Congress. They avoided another 1994 in the Senate, because the Republicans failed to take control and lost several key races (including Colorado, Nevada, and Washington State) because of weak candidates. But the Democrats would be wise not to take too much solace from this result. The Republicans held every one of their open seats, and had a huge hill to climb to take back the Senate, because many of the seats they needed to win were in heavily Democratic states, like West Virginia, Washington, and California. The Republicans needed to run the table to get a majority in the Senate, and they fell well short. The story will likely be very different in 2012, when Democrats (and their independent allies) will have 23 seats to defend, as compared to 10 for the Republicans.

In every other respect, the Democrat defeat in 2010 was far worse than 1994. In the first place, in 1994 the Democrats were complacent and caught off guard. This time, every Democrat operative and candidate was focused on stopping a Republican wave, but they still could not do it. The Republican victory in the House was bigger than 1994 and at the state level the Republicans wiped out an entire generation of Democrat politicians. And unlike 1994, the 2010 election has huge implication for redistricting. So Democrats who focus on their victories in Senate contests are missing the key fact of the 2010 elections, which was that the Republicans achieved a huge victory at every level of government.

At his post-election news conference, the President acknowledged the scope of the defeat, but remained defiant on the correctness of his policies. While striking a tone of compromise and conciliation, the President refused to recognize that the unpopularity of his policies contributed to the defeat. Instead, he blamed the economy and his failure to better communicate with the voters. Rather than appearing chastened, the President seemed shocked that the voters failed to appreciate how great his policies are. He showed no sign of a willingness to change course and made little reference to voters' concerns about rampant spending and deficits. The President then left for the 10 day foreign trip, which will cost the taxpayers tens of millions.

Week 95

(FOREIGN FLAILING)

November 14, 2010

Before the midterm election, there was a great deal of commentary on how the President was scheduled to leave on his longest foreign trip just two days after the election. Just as Bill Clinton did in 1994, the Obama Administration appeared to want to get the President out of town to change the subject if the election results were bad. They were very bad indeed, but things only got worse for the President once he arrived on foreign soil. After the Democrats suffered a historic defeat at the polls on November 3, in part because of the poor economy, the President quickly tried to recast his foreign trip as a jobs mission. He also hoped to rekindle the adulation that so often greets him overseas. But instead of demonstrating leadership, accomplishment, and acclaim, the President was rebuked on every front on his Asia trip, only leaving him to limp home after flailing abroad.

Over the last two years, poll after poll has shown that the American public fears that our nation is in decline. The ravages of the financial crisis and recession certainly contribute to that sentiment, but it runs deeper than that. The economy has yet to begin a strong recovery from the recession, federal, state, and local governments are in dire budgetary circumstances, and many perceive the federal government as impotent, misguided, and wasteful. The public blamed this state of affairs on the Democrats and punished them accordingly in the midterm elections, but what is more worrying is that President Obama's foreign trip actually confirmed America's current state of decline. The President failed to get a trade deal with South Korea, failed to get our trading partners to deal with trade imbalances, and failed to get China to stop its currency manipulations. The President was also rebuked on his calls for more stimulus spending, criticized for America's irresponsible budget deficits, and accused of hypocrisy on currency manipulation because of the Federal Reserve's recent $600 billion quantitative easing program, which results in further deflation of the dollar. President hoped to lead the world toward his economic vision, but instead he was the one told to get in line.

President Obama hoped to change the story from the election defeat to economic accomplishments abroad, but instead he returns weakened. America is used to being the leader on the foreign stage and the agenda setter on economic issues. Obama tried to play that tune again, but no one would listen because his economic policies are as unpopular abroad as they are at home. Nation after nation abroad has turned to tight fiscal management and deficit reduction to restore confidence, while President Obama continues to preach stimulus and deficits. Nation after nation abroad is seeking to control their welfare states and free up their economies, while President Obama pursues entitlement expansion and vigorous regulation. The President showed himself to be just as out of step overseas as he is at home.

After accomplishing essentially nothing on the economic front after his 10-day trip, the President returns home to face a lame duck session of a defeated Democrat Congress that has yet to set tax rates or for 2011 or pass a budget. Added to that heavy load of work will be the Deficit Commission's report in early December. President Obama faces tough choices on all these issues. The Republicans want spending cut and all current tax rates extended. In his absence, the President's operatives have responded with the rhetoric of both compromise and defiance. After his defeats abroad, the President will have a stark choice of fighting the Republicans to appear strong, or compromising, which his allies will see as an admission of defeat. Neither choice is a good one.

Week 96

(Stop START)

November 21, 2010

After returning from his 10-day trip to Asia, President Obama hoped to make progress on two major issues, one foreign and one domestic, during the lame duck session of Congress. The President hoped to get the Senate to ratify the START II treaty with Russia and to reach a consensus on at least a partial extension of the Bush Tax Cuts, set to expire on January 1, 2011. After taking a beating in the midterm election, the President hoped to use ratification of the START II treaty to show his effectiveness, while reaching a compromise on tax cuts would demonstrate bipartisanship. To achieve either goal, the President needed to do something he has never done since his election to the White House, seek agreement from the Republican leadership. But just as he was trying to woo Republican Senators on the treaty, the newly re-elected Democrat leader in the House Nancy Pelosi pledged to force through the lame duck Congress only a partial extension of the tax cuts. The President could have rebuked Ms. Pelosi and called for negotiation, but he remained silent. So the Republicans responded in kind, making clear they would stop START, at least for now.

The President's focus this week was the START II treaty he signed in April of 2010. The treaty seeks to build on the START I treaty signed by President George H. W. Bush, which established a regime for the reduction of nuclear weapons and verification. START II takes the place of that expiring treaty and adds modest additional reductions in deployed nuclear warheads and imposes a new, but less robust, verification regime. The first START treaty was easily ratified with broad bipartisan support, but it is a testament to how deeply the President has poisoned the well that Republicans are now seeking to delay ratification. When the chief Republican negotiator, Senator John Kyle, announced this week that he would not support ratification during the lame duck session, he had two principal reasons. First, he said the newly elected Senate should review the treaty in 2011. He also said the Administration had yet to commit sufficient resources to nuclear modernization, which Republicans view as essential to maintain America's nuclear deterrent. Senator Kyle said these goals were incompatible with forcing the treaty through a lame duck Senate, but the real reason for the Republicans' decision to stop START runs deeper.

President Obama has not limited his rhetoric on transforming America in the domestic sphere. The President has made clear that he also wants to re-make America's image in the world and change our international security posture. His efforts to reach out to the Muslim world and seek more consensus from allies are just part of his agenda. He has also made clear that he would like all nuclear weapons eliminated, and that is what is really fueling Republican concerns about START II. Ronald Reagan also talked about a world without nuclear weapons, but that was akin to Nixon going to China. Reagan was a cold warrior, an ardent anti-communist, and made clear he would meet force with force. With this record, Reagan could talk about the goal of a nuclear free world without prompting undo concern. President Obama is in an entirely different position. During the campaign, President Obama refused to credit the surge or talk about victory in Iraq. After his election, he reluctantly ordered more troops to Afghanistan and pledged a tight timetable to starting a draw-down. He talks far more about outreach and bilateralism than the use of force. When Reagan talked about nuclear disarmament it sounded aspirational, but Obama's record makes his similar comments look naive if not dangerous.

The Republican distrust of the President's commitment to the nuclear deterrent was not the only issue causing problems. The President's continuing refusal to listen and consult with Republicans is also creating a roadblock. After the midterms, the President proclaimed that the voters want the parties to work together, but since November 3, there is little if any evidence that the President is committed to that path. President Obama did schedule a meeting with Republicans for November 18, but failed to consult with them on their schedules or event make clear the White House's position on key issues like the tax cuts or spending. Sensing a set-up, the Republicans cancelled the meeting. The Administration talks both compromise and confrontation with Republicans on every issue, clearly trying to calibrate its message to placate the Left while looking bipartisan. And the President continues to refuse to admit any shortcomings of his policies.

With the backdrop of a partisan and unrepentant President, viewed by many Republicans as a radical, who is clearly scheming to outmaneuver them, is it any surprise the Republicans put an end to START in the lame duck. To date the President has not reached out his hand in compromise on any domestic issue, yet wants Republicans to line up behind him on START II. Politics is a game of give and take, but the President remains in take-only mode. Maybe the Republicans' decision to stop START will wake the President up to his new reality.

Week 97

(TAKING FIRE)

November 28, 2010

After a long foreign trip, President Obama was likely looking forward to a quiet Thanksgiving week before grappling with the expiring Bush tax cuts, the deficit commission report, and the START II treaty in the lame duck Congress. No such luck. On November 23, North Korea unleashed an artillery barrage on the South Korean Island of Yeonpyeong, killing two civilians and two South Korean marines. The attack sent South Korean President Lee Myung-bak into crisis meetings with his military advisors and led to immediate mobilization of the United States' 28,000 troops in South Korea. The North said the attack was in response to provocations from the South, but was more likely an attempt by Kim Jong-Un to curry favor with the military, to solidify his position to succeed his father Kim Jong-Il as President. After this military attack, the Obama Administration also suffered a cyber assault, when on November 28 Wikileaks released a trove of top secret cables, including top secret U.S. communications with its allies and diplomats abroad. So, instead of a restful Thanksgiving, the President took fire on two fronts.

The Obama Administration's response to these attacks was swift. In an interview with ABC News, President Obama reaffirmed America's commitment to defend South Korea, ordered the U.S. Commander in South Korea, General Walter Sharp, to make a high profile inspection of the damage on Yeonpyeong Island, and sent the Nuclear Aircraft Carrier George Washington to the Yellow Sea for joint naval exercises with South Korea. The message was simple, the United States would honor its treaty with South Korea and will defend the South if North Korea moves to open hostilities for the first time since the 1953 armistice was signed ending the Korean War. Defiant proclamations continue to issue from the North, but to date North Korea has not launched a further attack.

More disturbing than even the North Korean attack was the silence from China. China is the North's only significant ally, providing fuel and food to sustain Kim Jong-Il's totalitarian state. As a result, China is one of the few nations that can put pressure on North Korea to change course. After the attack, the United States called on China to condemn the assault. To date, China has made no public condemnations. This underlined the relative weakness of the United States in its dealings with China. China's growing economic strength and America's dependence on Chinese financing for its debt has made the task of getting China to act responsibly in its dealings the North ever more difficult. For President Obama, this poses both an international and a domestic challenge, requiring the President to deal with economic challenges at home to allow America to regain influence abroad.

While North Korea's attack is causing great international tension, at least it was a familiar type of attack by a known rogue state. The cyberattack by Wikileaks is in many ways more troubling. The attack was launched not by guns but by the worldwide web, by no state but by a new breed of cyber anarchists. The release included reams of top secret documents dealing with issues like Pakistan's security services, Iran's nuclear programs, and attempts by China to infiltrate and disrupt computer systems in the United States. For Wikileaks, these releases are done in the name of openness and a dogma of distrust of government. A consequence is that governments are paralyzed because they fear they can no longer confidentially communicate with their diplomats, allies, or adversaries. As governments see their highly guarded secrets revealed, they fear for their officials and military personnel abroad. There is no good response for President Obama to an informational cyber attack by a state-less foe who appears to have equal distain for all governments of the world.

So a week that should have been quiet turned out to be quite the opposite and was a reminder of the challenges facing the President. With a new and more Republican Congress, budget woes, expiring tax cuts, and a START Treaty languishing, the President certainly did not need to be under attack internationally by foes against whom there can be little effective response. Whether the President emerges strengthened or weakened by these challenges will depend on whether he can succeed in dealing with any of them.

Week 98
(9.8)

December 5, 2010

The overriding threat to the success of the Obama Administration is high unemployment. When the President was elected, the economy was in free fall with hundreds of thousands of jobs being lost each month. The President promised that stimulus spending, health care reform, and vigorous regulation would retool the economy, make business more competitive, and lead to a flourishing job market. But for cap and trade carbon tax, the President succeeded in forcing most of that agenda through, but the result has been mounting debt and no significant job creation. A stark reminder of that came this week, when the Labor Department reported that despite modest economic growth, the economy produced only 39,000 new jobs in November, making the unemployment rate shoot up to 9.8%. The longer unemployment stays high, the weaker the President will become, as we began to see all too clearly this week.

There were many factors that led to the Republican landslide in November 2010, but first among them was high unemployment. As Bill Clinton best exemplified, the voters will forgive many sins if a President appears to be a good steward of the economy. Conversely, even the best conceived policies will get little acclaim in a sputtering economy. President Obama told the voters that federal spending and intervention in the economy would result in job creation, but voters do not see the jobs, so they punished his Democrat allies in the election. Now the President must grapple with high unemployment, huge deficits, and a Republican Party determined to change economic course from government spending and regulation to budget cutting and free markets. Ordinarily, President Obama and his liberal allies would welcome this debate, since it gives them the opportunity to argue that Republicans want to return to the policies that created the problems, but the high unemployment rate has weakened their resolve.

This was best seen this week in the maneuverings on tax policy. The central rhetorical refrain of the Democrats is that Republican policies favor that rich at the expense of the middle class. That is why President Obama pledged to keep the Bush tax cuts only for those who earn less than $250,000. The Democrats purposefully delayed voting on this tax policy until the Fall of 2010 because they thought the issue would create a perfect electoral theme. But the high unemployment rate made many Democrats question whether raising taxes (even if only for high earners) would leave them vulnerable to allegations of damaging the economy. Spooked, the Democrats postponed addressing the Bush tax cuts until after the election.

With the tax cuts set to expire on January 1, 2011 and Republicans sweeping to victory in the midterms, the President had a choice between compromise and confrontation with Republicans on this central dispute between the parties. Liberal groups and prominent media outlets like the New York Times demanded that the President pick a tax fight with Republicans. When President Obama met with congressional leaders on November 30, tax policy was high on the agenda and each side refused to admit any compromise. Then all 42 Republicans in the Senate signed a pledge to stop all action in that body until tax policy was addressed. The lame duck Democrat majorities in Congress held symbolic but meaningless votes to extend only the tax cuts for lower earners, knowing the Republicans had them beat. Then, with Friday's disappointing jobs report, it became readily apparent that the Administration had no stomach for a fight, so reports were quickly leaked of an agreement to temporarily extend all the Bush tax cut in return for a further extension of unemployment benefits.

With high unemployment, the President could not risk expiration of the Bush tax cuts in January, so he lost his leverage and had to compromise. This was just a precursor to the budget battle looming in 2011, where Republicans are seeking deep cuts in spending to address the deficit. The President will again have to decide whether he can risk confrontation by vetoing budget bills if unemployment remains high. So of all the developments this week, the simple number 9.8% is the best indicator of the changing fortunes and narrowed options facing President Obama.

Week 99

(TAXING THE LEFT)

December 12, 2010

For the last two years, the American Left has seen the Obama Administration as a half-hearted proponent of the progressive agenda. They saw the bailout programs as too generous to Wall Street, Obama as an ineffective advocate for a public health insurance option, the financial reform bill as a half measure, and Obama's support for cap and trade and union card check mere rhetoric. With these critiques, the Left has mostly broken with Obama because his liberal accomplishments were not Leftist enough for their tastes. This week, those restrained criticisms turned into outright rebellion when Obama announced the first true bipartisan compromise of his Presidency, which came in the form of a deal with Republicans on taxes. The President and congressional Republicans agreed to maintain current tax rates, cut the payroll tax, and extend unemployment benefits for 13 months. With this deal, liberal disappointment has turned to contempt, taxing the Left's support for the President.

The tax deal announced by the President during a December 7 White House press conference was the result of miscalculations by the Democrats. A series of political misjudgments left a lame duck Congress with a mere seven weeks to pass a tax bill to prevent a massive tax increase in the midst of a fragile economic recovery. The pressing need to pass a tax bill combined with the drubbing taken by Democrats in the midterms left Republicans with the upper hand in the tax debate. The Republicans flexed their new muscle by making clear they would not budge and wanted all the Bush tax cuts extended. With the deck stacked against him, the President decided to make a deal.

Having put himself in this bind, President Obama could have tried to rally his party to use the last fleeting moments of their dominance in Washington to force Republicans to accept only a partial extension of the Bush tax cuts or risk a massive tax increase. The Democrats and the President toyed with this strategy until the Republicans called their bluff when all 42 Senate Republicans signed a pledge that no bills would proceed until an agreement was reached to renew the Bush tax cuts. The Left wanted Obama to push the issue even further and force expiration of all the tax cuts, but Obama opted to compromise instead. The agreement the President reached with Republicans extended all the Bush tax cuts for 2 years and reduced the estate tax, but also met Obama priorities by extending unemployment benefits for 13 months and funding green initiatives. The agreement also called for a 2% reduction in the payroll tax, viewed by many as the most effective means to stimulate consumer spending. The proposed bill would cost $900 billion over two years, making it even bigger than the much maligned Obama stimulus bill passed in 2009.

One might have thought that liberals, many of whom have been pushing for more stimulus, would have applauded Obama's compromise because it would pump hundreds of billions into the economy to spur economic activity. Yet President Obama's compromise was met with hostility from his own party. Moderate Democrats said the bill raised the deficit too much, while liberals said the program was too generous to the affluent, with its extension of current upper income tax brackets and the restructuring of the estate tax. But in the end, for Democrats the desire for more stimulus was outweighed by their commitment to the mantra of soak the rich.

In the House, the Democrat caucus voted down the Obama proposal and took to the airwaves to attack the President as selling out the liberal cause. The rebellion grew so strong that the President was forced to do a press conference with Bill Clinton, in the hope that Clinton could sell the compromise better than he could. Clinton did exactly that, explaining briefly and in understandable terms why the deal was necessary, as Obama watched in admiration. The tactic seemed to work, because as the week closed, opposition to the compromise seemed to ebb, but at what cost. The President cut a deal that should help the economy, and in the process his reelection effort, but the Left now distrusts him and he needed Clinton to bail him out. The President emerged from this deal less popular with his party, but if the economy recovers and unemployment falls, none of that will matter.

Week 100

(OMNIBUST)

December 19, 2010

The new Washington reality struck like a thunderbolt this week, even before the new Congress convenes in January. The Democrats had hoped to use the lame duck session to push through some cherished pieces of legislation and set up a narrative for the 2012 campaign before a new wave of Republicans came to town. Their legislative agenda included repeal of the Bush tax cuts for the affluent, the Dream Act for children of illegal immigrants, a repeal of the Don't Ask Don't Tell policy for gays in the military, an omnibus 1.1 trillion spending bill packed with pork, and ratification of the START II arms reduction treaty with Russia. Other than the repeal of Don't Ask Don't Tell and START ratification, the Democrats, despite their huge majorities in Congress were thwarted on every front. President Obama undercut the Democrat congressional leadership by making a deal with Republicans on taxes and unemployment benefits, which ultimately passed by comfortable majorities. The Dream Act for illegal immigrants died in a filibuster. As of week's end, ratification of START II was unclear, as key Republicans came out against immediate ratification. And most worrisome of all for the Democrats, their $1.1 trillion omnibus spending bill to fund the government through October 2011 became an omnibust, when it was pulled from consideration in the Senate.

Many of the legislative initiatives pushed by the Democrats during the lame duck session could have gained bipartisanship support if considered in normal session. There was consensus in Congress to extend most of the Bush tax cuts for the middle class. Many Republicans support a path to citizenship for illegal immigrants, although they are careful to disguise their views. The START II treaty is supported by many Republicans. Even the repeal of Don't Ask Don't Tell was quietly popular with some GOP members. The failure of most of this legislation in the lame duck was more a result of Republicans resisting giving the Democrats victories during their last few weeks of dominance, rather than ideological opposition. But the omnibus spending bill was a different matter.

The 111th Congress never passed a budget for the 2009-2010 fiscal year. Instead, the Democrats were focused on passing health care reform. Since October, the federal government has been running on continuing resolutions, which are short term spending bills to keep the government open. Like the tax issue, the Democrats hoped to use the lame duck session to cement their priorities by forcing through a spending plan for the 2010-2011 fiscal year that would guaranty their spending priorities, fund implementation of health care and financial reform, and spread pork to key Democrat constituencies. The omnibus bill purported to keep spending at the 2009-2010 spending levels, but that budget was so hugely inflated that in reality the Democrats were trying to lock in big increases in federal spending. The Democrats also loaded the bill with earmarks, including packing the legislation with earmarks requested by Republicans, even though many of those requests were old and had been disavowed by their original sponsors. Including those Republican earmarks had two purposes, enticing GOP members to vote for the bill, and hopefully exposing Republicans as hypocrites on the issue of fiscal restraint.

The omnibus bill was crafted behind closed doors and revealed just days before the end of the lame duck session, with the plan to force a vote on it before members could read it or the media could dissect it. The plan seemed to be working. Forcing the bill through the House would be easy with the huge Democrat majority. In the Senate, the Democrats only needed to garner two Republicans supporters and then they could break a filibuster and get the bill to passage. All those earmarks for Republicans were supposed to get those votes, but in all their scheming, the Democrats missed a sea change in the public's attitude. It used to be the case that bringing pork to your district was the highest achievement for a politician, but now being a big spender is as much a vulnerability as an asset. The public is concerned that America is in decline, the government is overreaching and bankrupt, and that Washington is broken. The spending bill re-enforced all of these perceptions, by putting on display a government spending money it does not have, buying influence, and using tricks to force through unpopular policies. The public figured out what the omnibus bill was all about, wanted none of it, and made clear to GOP members that a yes vote would come with bad consequences.

It took a few days for this new reality to set in even with GOP members. It was not until the end of the week that it became clear that no Republicans would support the bill, forcing Majority Leader Reid to pull it from consideration. Instead of cementing Democrat spending priorities until October 2011, now the Democrats could only pass a short-term continuing resolution to fund the government until March 4. This means the new Congress, with the GOP House majority, now gets to control the budget for the remainder of this fiscal year, as well as the next. The failure of the omnibus bill also deprived Democrats of the chance to call Republicans hypocrites on earmarks. It also stopped funding for implementation of health care and financial reform.

Now the narrative is that Republicans stood up against a budget busting bill. Combined with the tax cut deal with President Obama, the failure of the omnibus spending bill sets the stage for an ideological confrontation on the size and scope of government. The GOP has promised to reduce non-military discretionary spending to 2008 levels. The President says spending must be controlled, but wants new taxes as well. The battle will be joined in January, with the need to pass a budget for this fiscal year by March 4. The question is who will blink first.

Week 101
(GETTING **START**ED)

December 26, 2010

After the midterm election, a popular narrative among the chartering classes was that President Obama was fatally weakened. His signature policies, like health care reform and stimulus, were unpopular. The voters threw his Democrat allies in Congress out in droves. Even the President's personal popularity rating was dropping below 45%. With all these headwinds, many thought President Obama would be at least temporarily powerless to set the agenda. They were wrong. The President had a long list of agenda items for the lame duck session of Congress, and it would be a tall order to get most of those bills passed in the wake of the midterm election results. So the President focused on battles he could win, and he won just enough of them to claim success, allowing him to start 2011 with some modicum of momentum.

There is no doubt that the President and his party lost the most important battles in the lame duck session. The President going all the way back to the 2008 campaign had promised to repeal the Bush tax cuts for the affluent. Due to the bad economy, he allowed those tax rates to stay in place during his first two years in office, but promised that they would not be extended into 2011. But after the Democrats allowed the tax cut extension to languish until the lame duck session, and with the huge Republican victories in the midterms, the President had little room to maneuver and had to cut a deal. The liberals in his party howled, but the public approved, the bill passed by wide margins, and Obama put got enough new stimulus to possibly help the economic recovery. Unlike the tax cut bill, the President and his party got nothing on the Dream Act or the Omnibus spending bill, both of which failed. The Dream Act died in a filibuster, while the Democrats had to retreat on the Omnibus spending bill, handing power to the Republicans in Congress to set the spending priorities for the 2010-2011 fiscal year.

These were the most important pieces of legislation under consideration in the lame duck session, and Republicans got the better of the Democrats on them. But the President picked his battles wisely and won some. The repeal of Don't Ask Don't Tell was unexpected, and won the President some praise from the same progressive circles that had bitterly criticized his tax cut deal. President Obama got the repeal enacted despite opposition from the Republican leadership, and in so doing showed that he was willing to take political risks to champion an issue of principle. So the President managed to leverage a minor piece of legislation into a major political victory.

The President built upon that success by getting the START II treaty ratified. While Don't Ask Don't Tell was all about principle, START II was all about politics. The treaty had fairly broad bipartisan support and would have been ratified in 2011 anyways, but the President pushed for ratification during the lame duck despite opposition from the Republican leadership. Most Republican supported the treaty, but wanted it considered next year in the new Congress, when there would be more time for deliberation and debate. The President wanted the treaty ratified immediately to send a strong message to Russia and our allies on America's commitment to arms control. The Republicans leadership tried to stop ratification, but failed when 13 Republicans voted for the treaty. Ratification was more of a political victory for the President than a policy achievement. The treaty was destined for ratification, but the President showed he could best the Republican leadership and achieve a bipartisan win.

With these successes, President Obama heads into 2011 with some momentum, but it must be remembered that the few hard fought wins gained by the President still came from the 111th Congress and its huge Democrat majorities. In January, all that will change. The Republicans will have a huge majority in the House and 47 seats in the Senate. The power dynamic will be different, and the President will no longer be able to pick off a few Republicans to get bills passed. If the President's lame duck successes are a sign that he is learning the art of bipartisanship, then the prospects for progress in January are good. But good politics and good policy are often at odds, and whether the President plans compromise or confrontation is yet to be seen.

Week 102

(GOING DARK)

January 2, 2011

After winning a few hard fought victories in the lame duck session, just before Christmas President Obama gave a celebratory press conference and then jetted off to Hawaii for an eleven-day vacation. Since arriving in Hawaii, the public has barely seen or heard from the President. The White House has released two very brief weekly addresses and nearly every day there has been a quick photo op of the President relaxing or golfing, but otherwise the White House has gone dark. The President made little comment on the huge storms that pummeled the East and West coasts, the White House was largely silent on some recent encouraging economic data, and the Administration avoided the usual prominent Holiday terrorism warnings. Instead, the President and his family decided to vacation like ordinary Americans and literally get away from it all.

It's hard to criticize that approach. After such a tumultuous political year, the public and the President were both ready for a break from the back and forth of politics. It is understandable that the President decided to pause and disconnect from politics for a few days to recharge and reassess before reentering the fray. The Christmas break was a natural opportunity for this because the end of the lame duck session was not just the end of a political year, but also an end to a very brief era of complete political dominance for the Democrats. In their two years of control of the elected levers of power in Washington, the Democrats achieved much of their agenda on spending, regulation, and health care. They paid a terrible price at the voting booth, but most Democrat leaders believe that the losses sustained are more than outweighed by the legislative accomplishments, which they hope will help cement a significant expansion in federal power and control over every facet of American life.

Entering into January, the President and his party face a new daunting reality. There is no federal budget for the current fiscal year and the government will shut down March 4 unless a budget is adopted. The federal government is about to hit its debt limit, and without extension of that debt limit, the nation will default on its debts, causing a potential economic cataclysm. Unemployment is at 9.8%, and while job creation is accelerating, it is not growing fast enough to dent unemployment. Foreclosures are on the rise again, and a recovery in housing prices has stalled. A host of Democrat-controlled and union dominated states (like California, Illinois, and New York) cannot pay their bills and are on the verge of bankruptcy. Nearly thirty states are seeking to overturn the Obama health care law as unconstitutional, and some lower courts have agreed with them. And without authorization or legislation from Congress, the EPA is about to force carbon emission controls on the private sector, which will unleash a significant backlash.

It is not a pretty picture for the President. These challenges would have been hard enough to deal with even if his party still controlled Congress, but with Republicans in outright control of the House and with enough seats to deny Democrats effective control of the Senate, the task facing the President is even more daunting. So the President is smart to saver his victories from last year and take a break to retool, because if he thinks his first two years were tough, he has a whole new set of challenges to face over the next two.

Week 103

(TRANSITIONS)

January 9, 2011

This week was marked by transitions in Washington, on both ends of Pennsylvania Avenue. On January 5, the 112th Congress was seated, while at the same time the White House set about reshuffling President Obama's senior staff to gird itself for what is sure to be a challenging year. For the Republicans, their new power in Congress offers an opportunity for redemption. The Republicans lost their majorities four years ago because all voting constituencies — liberals, independents, and conservatives alike — lost faith in them. Now, powered by the Tea Party movement, they have the chance to make amends and lead in accord with their conservative rhetoric. For President Obama, the transitions in the White House are more about reelection than redemption. The President believes his spending, legislative, and regulatory achievements in the first two years were exactly what the nation needed, but the voters do not agree. So with reelection on the horizon, the President is transitioning his team to old hands from the Clinton Administration, hoping to recreate that Clinton magic with voters.

For conservatives, the seating of the 112th Congress was the culmination of nearly two years of soul searching, retrenchment, and counterattack. After the 2008 election, both the Republican Party and the conservative movement were in tatters. The Iraq and Afghanistan Wars, the financial crisis, and perceptions of corruption and incompetence left them besieged on all sides. The conservative movement was in such a sorry state that early in 2009 there were predictions of the demise of the Republican Party and the advent of at least 40 years of progressive dominance. Lopsided elections usually inspire such predictions, even though they are nearly always wrong. So too this time. The voters certainly threw the Republicans out, but they did not intend to endorse any sharp turn to progressive politics. President Obama won election due to great timing, great rhetoric, and great campaign skills. He successfully convinced the voters that he was a moderate and safe choice, and by so doing got himself elected. But once elected, he and his allies over-read their mandate, as winning parties usually do. They spent too much, regulated too much, pushed unpopular programs like bailouts and health care reform, and were punished for it. The conservative movement benefitted from the backlash, not so much because the voters had forgiven them, but more because they were the only refuge for those who became increasingly uncomfortable with the President's policies.

This reaction against the President is what put the Republicans back in the majority in the House and increased their strength in the Senate and in the States. Republicans won elections by promising to reduce federal spending and intervention and repeal health care and financial reform. Yet as Republicans moved into their new majority in the House, they were mindful of what happened to another newly elected Republican majority back in 1995. Then, under the leadership of Speaker Gingrich, the Republican House passed a barrage of bills in the first 100 days, most of which died in the Senate. That same majority then lost a budget confrontation with President Clinton after the public recoiled at government shutdowns. In the process, Speaker Gingrich was successfully demonized by the Democrats, never fully recovering. The lessons learned from that defeat were evident in Speaker Boehner's acceptance speech on January 5. He emphasized his humble origins in Ohio, noted the great challenges facing the nation, and said the 112th Congress could not "kick the can down the road" but instead had to confront the nation's pressing problems. The speech was not eloquent, but humble, was not ideological, but practical.

Speaker Boehner will be harder to demonize that Speaker Gingrich, but the Democrats will try nonetheless. The Democrats also hope that this new Republican majority will overreach on the budget, just as the Republicans did in 1995. However, circumstances might favor the Republicans more this time. Their first major vote will be repeal of health care reform, which both keeps a promise and forces Democrats to again endorse a law deeply unpopular with voters. On the budget, there is greater public concern over spending and government overreach now than in 1995, and more Democrats, especially in the Senate, might be inclined to support retrenchment in public spending. The Republicans have also positioned themselves better by pledging to reduce all non-defense discretionary spending to 2008 levels, while avoiding for now the issue of entitlement spending. And since no spending can be passed without endorsement of the House, the Republicans have huge leverage to force spending reductions. Despite all this, a pitched battle is looming on the budget, which is why the President is building a team ready for battle.

It is typical for Presidents to reshuffle senior advisors after their first two years, especially after election defeats. What is interesting is not that President Obama is changing his inner circle, but who he is putting on his team. This week the President announced that two Clinton Administration veterans would step into key White House position. Bill Daley, seen as a moderate and pro-business Democrat has been tapped for Chief of Staff, while Gene Sperling, will reprise his role from the Clinton Administration, as a senior economic advisor. Both these picks signal the President's strategy for reelection. First, the President wants seasoned hands who might be able to cut deals with Republicans to help him manage the new Republican strength in Congress. Second, he wants to recast himself in a more moderate mold, so he has picked new advisors who are seen as more pro-business. The President has made clear that he believes he achieved his key progressive goals in his first two years, so the next two will be about looking moderate, focusing on jobs, and working for reelection. What is more unclear is whether the President's transition in personnel will result in any real change in his policies.

Week 104
(Shooting Right)

January 16, 2011

For weeks, Republicans and Democrats have been positioning for the ideological struggle to come. Republicans were preparing votes to repeal health care reform and force budget cuts in return for raising the debt limit. Democrats were poised to caste themselves as fiscally responsible defenders of the social safety net. However, this carefully set struggle was shattered by shots that rang out from a strip mall in Tuscon, Arizona. On January 8, Democrat Congresswoman Gabrielle Giffords was holding a Congress on Your Corner meeting in front of a SafeWay supermarket in Tucson. In attendance were supporters and onlookers, including nine- year-old Christina Green and Federal District Judge John Roll, who stopped by to say hello to the Congresswoman. This ordinary political event was transformed into a scene of murder and mayhem when Jared Lee Laughner approached the crowd with a semi-automatic handgun and shot Congresswoman Giffords and killed six others.

Congresswoman Giffords suffered a gunshot to the head, and was rushed to the hospital in critical condition. Not so fortunate was Judge Roll, who was killed. Others killed included constituents Dorothy Morris, Phyllis Schneck, Dorwin Stoddard, and Gabe Zimmerman, an aide to the Congresswoman. Most disturbing of all was the death of Christina Green, who was born on September 11, 2001 and attended the event because of a budding interest in politics. She was shot in the back and died at the scene. Numerous others were wounded. As for Laughner, he was tackled by members of the crowd as he struggled to reload his pistol. For her part, Mrs. Giffords survived the shooting and continues what will be a slow and difficult recovery.

The crime was heinous, but the immediate political backlash from it was even more disturbing. Congresswoman Giffords is a Democrat who barely won reelection over a Tea Party challenger. She represents a swing district that is ground zero for the immigration and border control crisis gripping the Southwest. Though often a critic of the Obama Administration and its policies, Congresswoman Giffords was a prime target for the Tea Party in the last election. In fact, she was one of the representatives who had a crosshairs placed on her district in a campaign map distributed by Sarah Palin and her supporters. As soon as the shooting became known, liberal groups blamed Republicans, the Tea Party and Sarah Palin for inspiring Laughner to violence. The media quickly joined suit, attributing the shooting to heated political rhetoric, anti-government sentiment, and a climate of hate. It seems everyone assumed this was a rightwing political crime, much like the Oklahoma City bombing. The problem was, there was no evidence to support the media's chosen narrative.

As the facts slowly came out this week, it became clear that Jared Laughner was not a political crusader, but instead a deeply disturbed young man. It seems he took offense at how Congresswoman Giffords answered a question at a town hall meeting in 2007, before the advent of Sarah Palin or the Tea Party. He was declined entry into the military and kicked out of Pima Community College for erratic behavior, intimidation of other students, and making a video accusing the college of perpetrating genocide. His internet postings paint a picture of delusion and paranoia, including a belief that the government of monitoring his thoughts. No evidence has been uncovered of any political motivation, connection to the Tea Party, or interest in conservative causes. The Left and the media decided that heated political rhetoric caused this carnage without any evidence whatsoever.

Once the Left unleashed its accusations, the horrible crime became a political firestorm. Conservative commentators fired back that the Democrats for trying to obtain political gains from murder. Sarah Palin released a video accusing her critics of committing "blood libel" by blaming her and her movement of murders that had no connection to them. Then, use of the term "blood libel" unleashed more fury, because the term is usually applied to false accusations against Jews, and Congresswoman Giffords is Jewish. A crime allegedly caused by heated rhetoric was causing even more of it. In the midst of this controversy, President Obama saw an opportunity to strike a note for calm. After holding a moment of silence for the victims on January 10 in Washington, the President flew to Tucson for a memorial service on January 12. In his speech, after paying respect to the victims, praising the bystanders who stopped the killing, thanking the first responders who saved lives, the President addressed the issue of our national discourse. The President made clear that he believed this crime was not caused by political rhetoric, but said the sad events at Tucson should nevertheless inspire all political leaders to "use words that heal, not words that wound." He called on all Americans to be more civil with each other and remember that more unites us than divides us. While at times the speech was too much of a political rally than a memorial, the President struck a needed moderate and calming tone, while avoiding any accusation or blame.

Whether the events in Tucson will make any lasting change in political discourse is doubtful. Political rhetoric had nothing to do with the shooting, and the rhetoric has been just a scathing on the Left as on the Right. The issues that divide the parties are stark and the challenges formidable. Not a likely recipe of restraint. But if the President lives by the fine words in his speech, if he uses calm rhetoric, if he reaches out for compromise, consensus, and understanding, then there is a glimmer of hope that our politics will improve.

Week 105

(VERY REPEALING)

January 23, 2011

This week Washington slowly returned to normal after the trauma of the Tucson shooting. But the effort by the President and both political parties to avoid strident rhetoric was in tension with the Republicans' major agenda item for the week: the repeal of health care reform. Health care reform was by far the most controversial and consequential issue during the first two years of the Obama Administration and it galvanized much of the opposition to the President. That is because to the President's opponents, health care reform provided perfect symbolism for the Obama political philosophy. The new law, with its federal mandates, more than a hundred new government agencies, new entitlements, trillions in spending, and massive tax increases, was seen as encapsulating the President's progressive governing philosophy. The controversial nature of the bill itself, combined with the procedural tricks and purely partisan support used to get it enacted, made it the perfect target for the Republicans.

A repeal vote was promised by the Republicans in their Pledge to America offered during the 2010 campaign. After winning the House, the Republicans scheduled the repeal as their first significant vote in the new Congress. When the votes were counted on January 19, the repeal passed by a margin of 245 to 189, with only four Democrats supporting the bill. It was a significant victory for the new law's opponents, but not likely to be a substantive one. Senator Harry Reid has made clear that his Senate Democrat majority would not even take up the repeal, and even if the bill passed both houses of Congress, President Obama surely would veto the measure. The House Republican majority proceeded nevertheless, stating that a promise made must be kept and that health care reform has to be repealed because its provisions would ruin the health care system, destroy jobs, and bankrupt the federal government.

By voting on the repeal, the House Republicans were also sending a signal to the President that they will do whatever it takes to undermine his signature legislative achievement. Beyond the repeal vote, the House majority has made clear that it will attempt to obstruct implementation of the new law by depriving funding, opposing regulations, and encouraging more and more states to join the lawsuits seeking to overturn the new law. The Republicans have the most leverage on funding for implementation, since all new spending must be approved by the House. However, the only real opportunity to stop the law resides in either electing a Republican President in 2012 or persuading the Supreme Court to overturn it.

President Obama made clear his opposition to repeal, but avoided an all-out confrontation with the Republicans. After the Tucson shooting, the President has seen a jump in his public approval by casting himself as a moderate and a unifier. Thus, the President largely left it to his allies in Congress to denounce the repeal effort. He was aided by the State Visit of President Hu from China, which gave him plenty a cover to avoid getting dragged into the debate on the repeal. Considering the stark differences between Republicans and Democrats on the health reform law, the President will not be able to stay above the fray for long. As the Republicans push forward with their pledge to reduce non-military discretionary spending to 2008 levels, surely they will find little if any money to spend on implementing health care reform. So the budget battles to come will likely be more important to the health care debate than the repeal vote itself.

Week 106

(MARSHALLING THE FUTURE)

January 30, 2011

On January 26, President Obama strode into the House chamber to give his State of the Union address facing a stark change in political reality. For his first two years in office, his party enjoyed massive majorities in the House and the Senate, allowing them to pass nearly any legislation with little if any Republican support. Their dominance was productive, but temporary. The Democrats pursued expansions of spending, regulation, taxation, and entitlements with abandon that proved to be reckless when the voters turned them out in the 2010 election. So instead of addressing a Congress of allies, he President stood before a Congress divided, with the largest Republican majority in the House in half a century, and Democrats clinging onto a slim majority in the Senate. After his rebuke at the polls, the President could have opted to change course and address voter concerns about government overreach, but Mr. Obama would have none of it. Instead, the President revealed yet again his deep devotion to progressive politics. He laid out a vision for a new Marshall Plan for American, where government would forge the future. The applause was polite, but the skepticism palpable.

In many ways, President Obama described the exact same agenda he has been pursuing for the last two years, simply clothed in new rhetoric. In his first year in office, he defended massive expansion in government because of the urgency of the financial crisis. In his second year, he defended massive expansion in government to reign in greedy corporations and provide health care for all. Now in his third State of the Union, he called for further expansion of government, but this time in the name of competitiveness. The President understands that the greatest threat to his reelection is unemployment. Despite economic growth and a recovering stock market, to date job growth has remained tepid at best. After having achieved most of his key policy objectives in his first two years, the President's remaining goal is simply staying President, so the State of the Union was not a policy address, it was a campaign rally.

The President's true goal became clear in the lame duck session on this issue of taxes. The liberals in his party were encouraging him to fight the extension of the Bush tax cuts to draw an ideological line in the sand. Instead, President Obama struck a deal with Republicans to extend all the tax cuts for two years in return for extension of unemployment benefits. Thereby, the President extended tax cuts he has been condemning from the day they were passed. Why? Reelection. Obama knows that if nothing else, the extension of the tax cuts will help stimulate the economy, so he took the deal because anything that will help him stay in office will get his support.

The President's State of the Union was simply an extension of this strategy. Knowing the voters hate bailouts and stimulus, distrust government, and want jobs, the entire first half of the President's address was devoted to an agenda of competitiveness led by government. A focus on competitiveness allows President Obama to use positive and pro-market rhetoric to talk about job creation and bigger government at the same time. The President set the stage by arguing that government has been the foundation of our past economic prosperity and that government can do the same again. He argued for increased "investments" in clean energy, schools and infrastructure, all with the objective of being more competitive and creating good jobs. The President's vision amounted to a kind of Marshall Plan for America's economic future. But stimulus by any other name still costs the same, and that is the challenge for the President.

Our nation faces not only a jobs deficit, but also a huge financial one. The President wants investments to lead competiveness, but what about the debt. The President gave little time to that issue in his Address. He offered to freeze discretionary spending at the current inflated levels for five years and vaguely suggested a dialogue on taxes and entitlements, but said little else. The President's focus on competitiveness and relative disregard for reducing the deficit is revealing. The President has made a political calculation that if he can get jobs for the voters they will reelect him despite the deficit. So his agenda is more stimulus for jobs to get reelected, and confrontation with the Republicans on deficit reduction to please the Left and show that Republicans are against competitiveness. The Obama agenda remains the same, only the rhetoric has changed.

Week 107

(ROCK'IN THE CASBAH)

February 6, 2011

The Middle East was always going to be the major foreign policy challenge in the first few years of the Obama Administration. The wars in Iraq and Afghanistan, terrorism, the Arab-Israeli conflict are all difficult, but known challenges for the President. But what erupted in Cairo's Tahrir Square this week caught the Administration and the world by surprise. A revolt in Tunisia, fueled by economic discontent, unemployment, and the power of social media, spread like wildfire across the desert into Egypt, leading first thousands, then tens of thousands, then millions into the streets of Cairo. At first the crowds protested for economic opportunity, then demanded more freedoms, and then as their numbers swelled, regime change was the rally cry. The Egyptian Army took to the streets but would not stop the protesters. The city ground to a halt, foreigners and tourists fled, and the world watched in awe and apprehension of what might come next. Hanging over it all was the realization that if this could happen so quickly in Egypt, it could happen everywhere in the Middle East.

For the past thirty years, Egypt has been America's staunchest Arab ally. Under the leadership of Hosni Mubarak, who took power after the assassination of President Anwar el-Sadat, Egypt sought to crush its indigenous Islamic radicals, kept peace with Israel, joined the first Gulf War, and promoted stability in the region. Its pro-American stance came at heavy cost to the Egyptian people. Mubarak has ruled as a near dictator, using a 1981 emergency law to crush and jail political opponents, outlaw rival political parties, control the press, and execute thousands. Much of his wrath has been focused on the Muslim Brotherhood, an Islamic fundamentalist group that has been outlawed and brutally suppressed, but that has nevertheless endured as by far the largest and most potent opponent to Mubarak's rule. Just weeks ago, Mubarak seemed in firm control of the country and was widely expected to run for yet another six-year term in the September 2011 Egyptian elections, but that was before Tahrir Square.

By early last week, it became clear that the protests were more than an expression of temporary frustration with the Mubarak regime. The protests took on the aura of a true revolution, seeking to change Egyptian political culture and the Egyptian government. For the Obama Administration, a devotion to American interests slowly gave way to the necessity of championing American ideals. Early in the crisis, the Administration stressed the need for stability in Egypt and support for the Mubarak government as it worked to address the legitimate demands of the protesters. But by Tuesday, events had progressed so far that the Administration risked looking like an opponent of the protesters. So the President publicly demanded a transition to a new political order in Egypt, which the President said must be substantial, peaceful, and had to begin now. Since then, President Obama has stated repeatedly that President Mubarak must step down, but has stopped short of demanding an immediate change in regime. The President was wise to do so, because if the Mubarak government collapsed too quickly, the Muslim Brotherhood was best positioned to fill the void.

By week's end, the fear of an Islamist government quickly taking power in Egypt began to fade. After years of demands that he appoint a vice president, Mubarak named Omar Suleiman to that post. The government also agreed to rescind the 1981 emergency law, restore some press freedom, and allow more political rights. The protesters were not satisfied, so President Mubarak pledged to not run for reelection and gave more power to his new vice president. On February 6, Vice President Suleiman then held a conference with political opponents, including the Muslim Brotherhood, to begin planning for free elections and a new government. While the hardcore protesters said this still was not enough, the crowds now began to shrink and the city slowly started to function again.

The challenge for the Administration is now three-fold. To try to manage a transition in Egypt that will bring a democratic government that will also be a friend of the United States and will keep the peace with Israel. The United States also needs to try to stop the spread of the destabilizing revolution across the region. The hard truth is that in many Arab countries, democracy may mean the triumph of Islamic radicalism, something America can ill afford. So now the transformational presidency has an opportunity to live up to its self-anointed title, at least in the Middle East.

Week 108

(GOOGLUTION)

February 13, 2011

On February 7, the release of an obscure Google executive Wael Ghomin from detention in Egypt toppled a government. After ten days of destabilizing protests starting in Tahrir Square and spreading across Egypt, the movement began to lose momentum after a number of gestures by the Mubarak regime to quell the demonstrations. The appointment of Vice President Suleiman, the pledge to repeal the 1981 Emergency Law, the promise of press freedoms, and the February 6 meeting between Suleiman and opposition leaders all started to sap the strength of the protest movement. The crowds were shrinking, moderates were calling for a pause, and streets and shops started to reopen. Then Ghomin was released by the Egyptian security service and everything changed.

Wael Ghomin is an Egyptian marketing executive for Google, who has recently spent most of his time in Dubai. As a reform activist, he was one of hundreds of young people who helped organize the early protests in Tahrir square. As the demonstrations grew and began to threaten the Mubarak regime, on January 28, he was arrested by Egyptian security forces. His arrest was yet another reminder of the oppression of the Mubarak government. Even without Ghomin's leadership, the protest movement continued to grow, forcing the government to make a host of concessions to quell the movement. A modicum of stability had returned by February 6, so in one of many steps taken by the government to show moderation, Ghomin was released. Little did they know that act would reignite the protest movement. Ghomin headed directly for Tahrir Square and addressed a diminished crowd of protesters, using both his words and his experience to highlight once again the true nature of the Mubarak regime. His words re-inspired the nation.

What followed after Ghomin's release was nothing short than an awe inspiring example of the power of mass peaceful resistance. Starting of February 8, huge crowds again began to rush into Cairo, demanding more than the half measures offered to date of the government. The military continued its policy of restraint and did not act to try to stop the demonstrations. Pressure grew on the Mubarak government, and his power base in the military began to crumble. The military pressed him to step down immediately from the presidency, and he privately pledged to do so. On February 10, rumors spread that Mubarak would resign in a speech that evening, but when the speech came there was no resignation, just a statement that certain executive powers would be transferred to Vice President Suleiman. The protesters and the military had been duped. The very next day Mubarak lost his last remaining support in the military, he left Cairo for his home on the Red Sea, and Vice President Suleiman addressed the nation to confirm that Mubarak was no longer President.

The Tahrir Square protests toppled the staunchest American ally in the Middle East in just 18 days. The challenge for the Administration is what comes next, both in Egypt and across the region. With the military now in control of the Egyptian government and promising elections, for now there is some stability, but also a threat that with those elections a more radical and Islamic government might take control. Also the success of the protests in Egypt has inspired similar movements elsewhere, with new protests beginning in Algeria, Yemen, Libya Jordan, and Iran. The Egyptian revolution could lead to a transformed Middle East, but not necessarily one that will be a friend to America.

Throughout the demonstrations, President Obama seemed inclined to support the youthful protest movement, while the State Department struggled to maintain stability and repeatedly flirted with continued support for the Mubarak regime. At times it seemed the President was not in full control of his government as he worked to respond to the quickly changing events in Egypt. No matter, the protesters were not to be stopped and the Mubarak government could not be saved. Now, the Administration needs to manage the transition to a democratic government in Egypt that will also be a friend to America and Israel, and prevent instability in the whole region. A big job, in large part put in the President's lap by a Google marketing executive named Wael Ghomin.

Week 109

(UNBALANCED)

February 20, 2011

While the focus of much of the nation was on the protest movements spreading across the Middle East, a battle was brewing in Washington that will not topple a government, but might shut one down. This week, while the House held four days of open debate on a bill to fund the federal government through October, the President proposed his budget for 2012 and beyond. The contrast between these two budget proposals could not be more stark. Fueled by their pledge to restrain federal overreach by cutting government spending, the Republican majority in the House pledged to cut $61 billion in non-defense discretionary spending for the remaining seven months of the fiscal year. In contrast, President Obama proposed a $3.7 trillion budget for 2012 that contained more new taxes and spending and no real cuts. With the federal government set to run out of money by March 4, with the debt limit to be exceeded by April, and with Republicans and Democrats on a collision course, the prospects for compromise look bleak.

The most surprising aspect of the impending budget impasse is the President's determination to play politics. Even before the 2010 election, the President began to realize the public's growing concern about the deficit and the debt. In response, he began to pivot his rhetoric towards fiscal responsibility and debt reduction. During the midterm election campaign, again and again he championed his fiscal responsibility commission as the key to putting Washington back on a sound fiscal path. After the election, many saw President Obama's tax deal with the Republicans as a sign that he was ready for a serious bipartisan deal on the budget. The President's 2012 budget proposal ended that speculation. Rather than deal with entitlement spending, the President's budget ignores the issue entirely. Rather than attempting to cut spending, the President merely proposed to freeze discretionary spending 2010 levels (representing a 24% increase since his election). Rather than proposing any meaningful spending restraint, the President relies rosy economic projections and fictitious savings from the wars in Iraq and Afghanistan to claim deficit reduction. On top of it all, the President proposed more than $1.6 trillion in new taxes on businesses and high earners. Yet, even under the President's proposal, the deficit in 2012 would be $1.6 trillion and over the next 10 years the federal government would pile on more than $7 trillion in additional debt. The gimmicks and duplicity was too much for even the *Washington Post*, which proclaimed his budget proposal a timid failure.

There could not be a greater disconnect between Congress and the White House on the budget, with the House holding an open debate on cutting spending, while the President proposes maintaining spending levels and raising taxes. The disconnect is the product of the President's raw political calculation. The President and his allies believe that voters care about jobs, not deficits. They also believe that the best way to defeat the Republicans is to portray them as anti-government reactionaries who seek to deprive the populace of basic government services. The President also wants to provoke the Republicans into a government shutdown by refusing to agree to budget cuts. The Administration hopes for a replay of 1995 and 1996, when federal government shutdowns over a budget impasse destroyed the momentum of that Republican Congress, helping Bill Clinton win reelection.

President Obama wants history to repeat itself, so he has decided to ignore the serious threat posed to the economy by the deficit in favor of political gimmicks. The likelihood of Republican overreach is great, and the President could benefit at the polls as a result. But what will be lost is the opportunity to make true progress putting the federal government back on a sustainable fiscal path. The President talks about the need for deficit reduction. The Republicans won election on the same theme. Honest engagement on both sides could produce real progress. However, if the President continues to make political gain his primary objective, we are much less likely to avoid the looming debt crisis.

Week 110

(UNCIVIL DISOBEDIENCE)

February 27, 2011

This week the agenda in Washington was driven by the power of protests. In Libya, a popular revolt threatened the rule of Muammar Qaddafi and sent oil prices to near $100 a barrel, while in Wisconsin union activists continued their protests to stop a bill that seeks to curtail collective bargaining rights on benefits. While the nature of these two sets of protests is quite different, both pose a dire threat to the Obama Administration. The protests in Libya represent an uprising of a beleaguered populace against a brutal dictator, but threaten continued instability in the Middle East, which has security and economic consequences for the United States. In Wisconsin, Governor Scott Walker and the Republican legislature faced with a huge budget deficit have taken aim at public employee unions, the very backbone of the Democrat electoral machine. Whether President Obama can get reelected will turn heavily on whether he can maintain stability in the Middle East and maintain the power of his union allies, so he surely watched both developments with interest.

Coming on the heels of the successful protest movement in Egypt, the sudden eruption of protests in Libya has reminded all that even the most entrenched dictators are vulnerable to popular revolt. Muammar Qaddafi has ruled Libya since 1969. He has support terrorism, then disowned it, pursued weapons of mass destruction, then abandoned them, but one constant has been his eccentricity and ruthlessness. As revolutions have swept through Tunisia and Egypt, Qaddafi despite his best efforts was unable to quell his populace. Protesters took to the streets in Tripoli, and revolts erupted in Benghazi and the Eastern portions of the country. Not one to step aside quietly, Qaddafi unleashed his military on the protesters, reportedly killing thousands. But his repression backfired. The protesters took control of the Eastern part of the country, Libya's UN ambassador defected, and more and more military units joined the revolutionaries. By week's end Qaddafi was relegated to calling in African mercenaries to kill the protesters and he was losing control of the capital.

In Washington, the events in Libya were as much a cause of alarm as celebration. The United States is no friend of Qaddafi and is happy to see his regime undermined. But the forces at work in Libya have the potential to upend of entire political order in the Middle East. Governments in Egypt and Tunisia have already fallen. Yemen and Bahrain are facing uprisings. Algeria and Jordan are dealing with growing dissent. Many worry that Saudi Arabia will be next. Already the instability in the Middle East has caused a huge run up in oil prices, threatening the economic recovery in the United States. If the revolutionary movement spreads to Saudi Arabia, oil prices could reach unprecedented levels, possibly causing dire economic dislocation. In truth, the forces at work in the Middle East are far beyond the control of the President, but how he manages through the crisis will be critical to his political survival. Many of the threatened governments are friends of the United States, and democracy in the Middle East could lead to more Islamic governments, hardly what Washington wants. So the President is forced to support democratic uprisings that might in the end threaten American interests. The trick will be whether the President can be sufficiently supportive of the revolts to maintain credibility with the new political order while not undermining friendly regimes in the process.

President Obama has no such political tightrope to walk in Wisconsin. The union protests there are simply the result of a direct assault on the powerbase of the Democrat party. Unions are the foundation of Democrat political power. Unions spend hundreds of millions to elect Democrats each election cycle. While union membership in the private sector is withering, it is growing in the public sector, whose unions are the most loyal supporters of the Democrat agenda. For years these unions have used their political power to extract lucrative wages and benefits from state governments in return for political support for the elected politicians with whom they are negotiating. While times were good and revenues were rising, state government could afford to pay into this scheme, but the time of reckoning has come. The recession combined with the end of free stimulus money has left many states with huge deficits, huge union wage and pension obligations, and no way to pay for it all. When a host of Republican governors swept into office in 2010, they pledged to reform the system. Their leader is Wisconsin Governor Scott Walker, who has pledged to not only extract increased contributors from union members for benefits and pensions, but also to end collective bargaining for those items. In response, 14 Democrat state senators have fled the jurisdiction to deny a quorum in the state senate, while thousands of union protesters (many from out of state) have flooded the capital demanding that the collective bargaining rights be maintained. President Obama condemned Governor Walker's plan as union busting and unleashed his political machine to support the protesters, while Republican governors in Indian, Michigan, and New Jersey pledged to get tough on public sector unions as well.

What is at stake in Wisconsin and across the country in nothing less than a political Waterloo for state governments that have lived beyond their means for years and now must face the consequences. For Republican governors, that means drastic budget cutting and confrontations with unions. For the Administration, it means defending union rights even if it will bankrupt state and local governments. President Obama will be forced to fight all out to save the public sector unions, because their financial support is critical to his success and the success of his party.

Week 111

(8.9)

March 6, 2011

Starting with his State of the Union address, President Obama made the new theme of his Administration "Winning the Future." Armed with better education, better infrastructure, and better government incentives for select industries, the President told the nation that America can retake global leadership. It was a bold vision based on his faith in the skill of government to forge a better future of America. However, President will not have the ability to win the future if he cannot create jobs today, because high unemployment is the biggest threat to his reelection. That is why this week's jobs report, showing 192,000 jobs created and an 8.9% unemployment rate cheered the President's supporters. The question is whether this seemingly good news for the economy is only masking much more troubling trends.

The American economy has been growing for 18 months, the stock market has recovered, and corporate profits are strong. The problem is that jobs have not returned at a normal pace for economic recoveries. There has been job growth for 12 consecutive months, but at a very slow rate. That is why the February jobs report was so welcome. It showed that the private economy created 211,000 jobs, which combined with job cuts in the public sector yielded net job growth of 192,000. It was the best jobs report since the recovery began and helped the unemployment rate drop to 8.9%. The President quickly took to the airwaves to tout the report as evidence that his policies are working. The report certainly made for good politics, but it is less clear whether it proves good economics.

The private economy needs to create 300,000 jobs per month to cover new entrants into the job market and to make any serious dent in unemployment. Even the February report, good as it was, showed nowhere near the job creation needed to bring the nation back to a state of full employment. The unemployment rate dropped to 8.9%, but that was largely because millions have dropped out of the job market altogether. The underemployment rate (which looks at the unemployed, the partially employed, and job market dropouts) is closer to 17%. Modest job creation numbers and drops in the unemployment rate make good news, but give little comfort to the millions out of work and unlikely to find good jobs in the future.

More troubling, Labor Department data shows that those jobs that are being created are lower level and lower pay than the millions of jobs lost in the recession. So the economy is creating jobs, but not particularly good ones and not particularly quickly. There is also increasing evidence that the economy is changing and that many of the lost jobs are not coming back. Corporations are making more money with fewer people, producing overseas at lower cost, and using technology and innovation to cut employees. The President has made job creation the measuring post of his economic policies, but macroeconomic trends are working against the very job creation he seeks.

The President's policies are likewise retarding job growth. The Administration's aggressive regulation, pro-union bias, and reluctance to reign in deficits have made businesses cautious and unwilling to take risks. More troubling, the President's energy agenda combined with turmoil in the Middle East are putting huge new burdens on the economy. As unrest spreads in key oil producing countries, gas prices continue to rise, now exceeding $100 a barrel. All the while, the Administration continues to limit deep water drilling, has rescinded its initial plan to expand offshore oil exploration, and will do nothing to encourage increased domestic oil production. Instead, the President keeps talking of green energy and green jobs, neither of which have materialized.

So while 8.9% unemployment might seem like a good sign for the President, there is a more troubling story underneath of an economy that cannot produce the jobs of old and an energy policy that seems to ignore the impact of high oil prices on the economy. The simple truth is that public perception of the job market is divorced from Labor Department statics. Confidence in the job market grows when we see our friends and neighbors getting good jobs. Job growth occurs when businesses have the confidence to invest. There are steps the government can take to address these concerns, including getting the deficit under control, pursuing pro-business policies, and encouraging domestic energy production, but each of these steps requires President Obama to believe in the private sector more than he believes in government. So far, there is no sign he is willing to do that. Instead, he just wants to talk about the number 8.9.

Week 112

(THE PRETENSION DOCTRINE)

March 13, 2011

President George W. Bush came under much criticism for his Preemption Doctrine, which held that America should strike first at growing threats before those threats could injure America. President Obama was a leading critic of this policy, using it to fuel the antiwar movement that led to his early victories in Democrat primaries. Now as President, he has taken his critique of the Bush Administration to a new level, by replacing the Preemption Doctrine with a Pretension Doctrine, where the President lectures with moral platitudes on the pressing issues of the day, and then does nothing about them. This week, we saw the Pretension Doctrine on full display, as the President talked about the need to overthrow Qaddafi while doing nothing, spoke about the threat from soaring deficits while doing nothing, and warned about the challenges of rising energy prices while doing nothing.

It is clear that the part of the Presidency that Obama loves most is the speechmaking. The President is in his element when he is standing on a stage, offering soaring rhetoric to adoring crowds. It allows him to tout his genius for language and argument. Obama seems to abhor or avoid the more mundane aspects of the presidency. We saw him vacillate for weeks over expanding the war in Afghanistan, outsource to Democrats in Congress the stimulus, health care, and financial reform bills, and for weeks ignore the Gulf oil spill. It seems President Obama finds the hard work of the presidency much less appealing than his role at lecturer-in-chief.

During untroubled times, the nation can afford a President who prefers glamour over the gritty details of leadership, but challenging times require more from our leader. On Libya, as the protest movements grew and Qaddafi opponents were taking control of more and more of the country, Obama spoke of the need to end the Qaddafi regime. But when the protesters asked for guns, for a no-fly-zone, and for other material support, the President did nothing. He gave great speeches, then sent his Defense Secretary to Congress to explain why America could not actively oppose the regime and why the Europeans should take the lead. Now, after two weeks of bombing and murder by Qaddafi, the regime is beating back its opponents and reclaiming control of the country. The Europeans and the UN have imposed sanctions and an arms embargo, but done nothing else to stop Qaddafi, and now momentum has been lost. The President gave great speeches on freedom in Libya, but it was pretension because he was willing to do little to achieve it.

Since the Fall, the President has been talking about the need to get the nation's fiscal house in order, but his 2012 budget proposal expanded spending, raised taxes, and still projected a $1.6 trillion deficit. Now, as Congress has been struggling to reach agreement on a bill to fund the government for the remainder of 2011, the President has refused to engage or lead. Out of a $3.7 trillion budget, he proposed a mere $6 billion in cuts and has refused to even discuss entitlement reform. Instead, the President is sitting back, awaiting the opportunity to demagogue the Republicans as soon as they make any proposal that might meaningfully address the nation's impending debt crisis. It is fun to give high-minded speeches on fiscal restraint, but it is mere pretension when the President refuses to do anything to address the problem.

Likewise, the President loves to talk about ending the nation's dependence on foreign oil. He has used the mantra of green energy as an excuse for billions of dollars in stimulus funds for his favorite pet projects. All the while, he used the Gulf Oil Spill and federal regulatory apparatus to try to limit domestic oil production, only increasing our dependence on foreign oil. Now, with revolutions spreading across the Middle East and uncertainty stemming from a severe earthquake in Japan, oil prices have skyrocketed, threatening the economic recovery. As usual, the President is everywhere talking about domestic energy production, while behind the scenes his Administration continues to stall on drilling permits, limit its support for nuclear energy, and pursues carbon limiting regulations. With this energy agenda, the President's talk of energy independence is simply pretension.

So today we are failing to support freedom abroad, sinking in debt at home, and sending billions overseas for energy, while our President sits passively in the White House offering pronouncements without actions. The Pretension Doctrine is clearly firing on all cylinders.

Week 113

(ABDICATION)

March 20, 2011

There was a time when American leadership was essential to protect the interests of the Free World. Since the Second World War, American Presidents have accepted their responsibility to lead, recognizing that America was the indispensable champion of Western values. President Obama has always been at best a reluctant adherent to this doctrine, and with the conflict in Libya he has found the perfect opportunity to abdicate America's traditional leadership role and test his vision for multi-lateralist foreign policy. So America has allowed France and Britain to lead the charge on Libya, sat idly by as the United Nations debated and debated, and only as Qaddafi was on the verge of victory, joined a limited military effort to halt his advance.

The contradictions in President Obama's policy on Libya are striking. The President has stated repeatedly that Qaddafi has to be removed as the leader of Libya, but he refused for weeks to take the initiative to strike at his regime or aide the Libyan rebels. He has said that vital American interests are served by a new government in Libya, but he has expressly ceded leadership on the issue to the French and the British. He has said that American military force should only be deployed with clear objectives and the means to achieve those objectives, but has embarked on a limited airstrike campaign against Qaddafi at the behest of a UN Resolution that cannot alone achieve his own stated goal. He has said that success against Qaddafi is essential, but the airstrikes had barely begun when the President stated that no U.S. ground forces would be deployed in Libya. He claims to be actively focused on the military campaign, but promptly after it began he flew with his family on a Spring Break trade mission to South America. President Obama's rhetoric on Libya is starkly mismatched with his actions.

There is a great deal of debate in foreign policy circles on the wisdom of military action in Libya. On the interventionist side we have the idealists, who assert that America must stop a genocide in the making and send a signal that we will support revolutionary movements in the Middle East that seek to topple oppressive regimes. Foreign policy realists say that America cannot rid the world of every tyrant and intervention in a Libyan civil war will likely prolong the conflict and lead to greater American commitment, which we can ill afford. It is a worthy debate and the proponents on each side have valid points. The problem is the President has sought to straddle the fence between these two warring camps. By trying to limit his military commitment in Libya, the President seeks to satisfy the realists. By rhetorically condemning Qaddafi and joining the UN and NATO effort to establish a no-fly zone and repel Qaddafi's forces, he seeks to satisfy the idealists.

As leader of the Western powers, the President could have said Qaddafi must go and forced quicker military action to oust the regime. This type of assertive leadership could have led to earlier airstrikes before the tide had turned in Qaddafi's favor. There was a moment of great vulnerability for the Qaddafi regime, and if the President really believed American interests were served by Qaddafi's removal, that was on opportunity to strike. Instead, the President used strong words and no action. In contrast, if the President was truly concerned that we should not get embroiled in the Libyan civil war, he could have quietly tried to persuade the allies to step back, and if they realized American support would not come, they likely would have avoided military action. Instead, the President offered to join an effort only if it garnered UN approval, which came so late that the military task became much more daunting.

So now we have a military intervention in Libya that is too late and too timid to achieve the quick ouster of the Qaddafi regime. As a result, we are more likely to prolong the conflict and have set the stage for an ever deeper entanglement in Libya. We got to this state of affairs because the one man who could have rallied the world to either intervene or forebear chose not to lead, and instead abdicate.

Week 114

(SPEAK NO EVIL)

March 27, 2011

President Obama has ushered in a new term in warfare. For years we have been accustomed to hot wars, cold wars, and covert wars, but the President now has brought us our first quiet war. Faced with a supposed genocide in the making in Libya, and at the behest of the UN, the President authorized American air and naval forces to join a coalition effort to attack Libya and prevent a rout of rebel forces challenging the Qaddafi regime. Before the shooting started, the President spoke forcefully and repeatedly about the evils of Qaddafi and why he must go, but allowed others to challenge the dictator. As the rebels advanced and Qaddafi began to teeter, the United States and its allies only observed. Only as the regime rebounded and drove the rebels back did Britain, France and other allies push the UN to take action. All the while, the President spoke loudly, but refused to carry any stick. Then war came and the President went silent.

No doubt the President's heart is not in the mission in Libya. He did not take the lead in challenging Qaddafi, and he joined the coalition air campaign only on the conditions that it would be limited, led by others, and that no ground forces would be deployed. However, in warfare it is usually best to intimidate your adversaries, not tell them all the things you will not do to defeat them. The President could have used his rhetorical powers to threaten Qaddafi with the full force of American power, while quietly making clear to our allies the limitations of America's commitment. Instead, the President launched a limited war with express conditions and then went quiet, leaving the country for a trip to South America, avoiding public pronouncements, and not even informing Congress before military action commenced.

This week, upon his return from South America, the President tried to continue his quiet war. He spoke about the conflict and the bravery of U.S. forces, but his public appearances were mostly devoted to more mundane domestic issues. But the pressure grew on the President to explain his actions to the American people. A diverse group of liberals and conservatives increasingly criticized the military campaign. All questioned the cost, the commitment, whether vital U.S. interests were at stake, what would happen if Qaddafi endured, and what would come next if he did not. By embarking on a half policy by using half measures, with at best half support from half of each political party, the President left himself isolated and vulnerable.

The President so far has been able to weather the criticism because the air campaign has not yet claimed any U.S. lives and rebel forces have at least temporarily rebounded and recaptured lost territory. But his quiet war strategy, where we attack a nation but pretend we are no doing so, is not working. His policy in Libya is too controversial and too contradictory for the President to just ignore the issue. The White House came to that realization by the end of the week, when it scheduled a speech to the nation for March 28. It appears the quiet war may be at an end, but the question is when will the actual one start.

Week 115

(DESERT OUTFOXED)

April 3, 2011

Anyone who has taken the time to study the history of the North African campaigns during World War II knows that in the seesaw battles between the British and the Germans, supply lines and flanking movements governed the day. The Germans under Field Marshall Rommel, the Desert Fox, would advance, outrun their supply lines, and would have to retreat after the British outflanked them. Then the Germans would push back the British in the same way. Only when the British assembled a hugely superior force near their base in Egypt were they able to win a decisive victory at El Alamein. So early this week, as the rebels in Libya were pushing Qaddafi's forces backs towards Tripoli, it would have been wise to remember the lessons of history. Instead, the White House started to celebrate its victory, only to watch as the rebels outran their supply lines, got outflanked, and were pushed back most of the way to Benghazi. There were certainly are not any military historians in the White House, because instead of remembering the Desert Fox, they got desert outfoxed themselves.

President Obama's half war by half measures got twice as complicated this week as the rebels faltered, the allies bickered, and the President dithered. The President tried to ignore the war for its first two weeks, but with progress uneven and the public uncertain, he was forced on March 28 to address the nation on why military action was needed in Libya. He gave a good speech, making the humanitarian and strategic argument that we had to step in the save lives and show support for the reform movements in the Middle East. What was not very convincing was the meager tools the President decided to employ to support what he claimed were worthy goals. The President said America had to act to stop Qaddafi and support our allies, but that America at best would only play a supporting role. Those statements were backed up this week when U.S. forces formally handed control of the Libyan operation to NATO. But having started a war, it is not so easy to contain ones participation, as the President is now learning.

The President had hoped that a short but aggressive air campaign would oust Qaddafi. Shock and Awe did not work in Iraq, and so far it is not working in Libya either. Allied aircraft attacked Qaddafi installations and destroyed armored columns, but with no forces on the ground Qaddafi's troops were able to quickly change tactics. They left their tanks behind and switched to jeeps, like those used by the rebels. They left the main highways, and instead attacked the rebels from the desert. They took off their uniforms and instead mixed in with the populace. These tactics, combined with an incompetent and leaderless rebel army, led to a defeat of the rebel forces. With a quick military victory unlikely, the issue of arming and training the rebels is at hand. But here again the President is uncertain. In an interview, he said the rebel forces were mostly composed of professionals and secularist, but in secret President Obama has deployed CIA operatives in Libya to ascertain the true composition of the rebel forces. By late in the week, there were reports of connections between the rebels and Al-Qaeda. So now we have a war we will not fight and rebels we probably will not dare to train or arm.

Matters got worse over the weekend when NATO asked the U.S. to continue bombing campaigns because allied forces could not complete missions due to bad weather. This episode reminded all that the U.S. might say it is stepping back from the operation, but the realities of capabilities and logistics will dictate a continued U.S. role. By the end of the week, the White House was clinging to defections from the Qaddafi regime to claim his government was crumbling, but there was no evidence of that on the ground. Instead, the battle in Libya is at a stalemate, with neither side strong enough to beat the other and the U.S. and its allies unwilling to take steps to force a resolution. So now instead of the Powell Doctrine (clear objectives, overwhelming force, planned exit strategy) we have the no doctrine (good intentions, half measures, and no way out). No doubt the President is now looking for any excuse to stop talking about Libya, because Qaddafi has so far outfoxed him.

Week 116

(SHUTDOWN SHOWDOWN)

April 10, 2011

If there was one cry that rallied Republicans to victory in the 2010 midterm elections, it was "Cut Spending." The Republicans were elected to the majority in the House on a platform of rolling back federal spending. This week, the first skirmish in that battle was fought and won by the Republicans, when Speaker Boehner went to the brink of a federal government shutdown to force the President and the Democrat majority in the Senate to agree to a $38.5 billion spending cut. Not only did the President and the Democrats agree to this cut, they actually took to the airwaves to praise it. The President then announced that he would offer a new plan to reign in the deficit on April 13, a plan that would address both revenues and entitlement spending. So completely have the Republicans taken over the terms of the debate that everyone in Washington is now talking about reducing the size of government. Clearly, the era of stimulus is over.

Neither the President nor the Democrats planned it this way. When the President proposed his spending plan for 2010-2011, he called for a $30 billion increase in non-defense discretionary spending, not a cut. But the Democrats never passed that budget because they were focused on other priorities and on the 2010 election. Then, after losing the midterm election, the Democrats tried in the lame duck session to force through these elevated spending levels by loading a bill with earmarks to try to entice some Republicans support. No Republicans took the bait, so the bill was dropped and the issue of the 2010-2011 budget was left to the new Congress with its swelled Republican ranks.

The Democrats then hoped that the Republicans would make the same mistake made in 1995 when the House shutdown the government and paid the price. To try to force a shutdown, neither the President or the congressional Democrats offered any plan to cut any federal spending. The House leadership ignored the Democrats and first suggested $31 billion in cuts, but the Tea Party pushed for more and eventually the House passed a bill cutting $61 billion compared to 2009-2010 spending levels. Senate Democrats offered no cuts in response, decried the cuts as cruel, and called the Republicans extreme and aiming to shut down the government.

But a funny thing happened to the Democrats' 1995 playbook that they reopened for 2011: the public was not buying it. Poll after poll showed that voters wanted spending cut and would blame Democrats and Republican equally for a shutdown. Speaker Boehner then artfully got the Democrats to agree to two short term spending bills that locked in $10 billion in cuts, while continuing to build the pressure for more cuts. The second of those temporary spending bills was set to expire on April 8. As the date approached, the Democrats slowly and consistently upped their offered cuts, from $6 billion, to $20 Billion, and ultimately to $33 billion. Speaker Boehner watched as the Democrats moved step-by-step closer to the Republican position, but refused to commit to any early deal. Instead, he continued to resist a deal right up until 10:45 p.m. on April 8, and mere 90 minutes before the shutdown deadline. He also used policy riders in the House's budget bill (on issues like defunding Planned Parenthood and blocking EPA regulations on carbon emissions) as useful bargaining chips. Increasingly, the Democrats were reluctant to criticize cuts (because they are politically popular) so they took aim at those riders. In the end, Boehner was able to compromise on those policy riders, in return for even more spending cuts, upping the total to $38.5 billion.

The President's role in all of this was circumspect as usual. The President largely avoided the spending debate until the final week, refusing to take a position or make a compromise proposal. Clearly, President Obama was holding back to see where public sentiment was heading. As it became increasingly clear that the public wanted cuts and that a shutdown was as dangerous for him as it was for the Republicans, he finally joined the debate. He called in congressional leaders and held late night sessions. In the end, the President got a deal, but on Speaker Boehner's terms. Nothing made that more evident than the President's remarks Friday night touting the agreement as the largest spending cut in history and his commitment to make proposals the following week to address the long term deficit, something he made no attempt to do in his first budget proposal. So now the issue is not will federal spending be cut, but rather where and by how much. The shutdown showdown was a watershed moment for the Republican agenda.

Week 117

(HE'S ENTITLED)

April 17, 2011

After touting spending cuts in his April 8 speech on the 2011 budget deal with Republicans, many expected the President's April 13 address on the nation's deficit to be a call for unison in the face of a mounting fiscal crisis. Hardly. In his address, rather than attempting to unify the nation on a mission to pursue fiscal discipline, President Obama instead launched a full throated defense of the entitlement state, while excoriating Republicans for trying to repeal America's basic social compact. The address shows that President Obama is both unserious and narcissistic when it comes to the debt crisis. The President is unserious because his defense of the very entitlement programs that are driving the debt shows a basic dishonesty about the scope of the debt threat. He is narcissistic because he is mainly interested in using the debt crisis to further his reelection. It seems Obama believes his defense of the entitlement state will entitle him to reelection,

Poll after poll shows unprecedented public concern over the deficit. That, combined with the weak recovery, has contributed to President Obama's slide in the polls and his willingness to cut deals on taxes and spending with Republicans. It even led the President to praise the $38.5 billion in spending cuts in the April 8 deal with the GOP, when the President's original budget actually sought more spending. Some took this as a sign of seriousness, that the President might put politics aside and strive for a bipartisan deal to address our long-term deficit. Such an approach would have taken perfect advantage of the impending need to raise the debt limit to force all factions in Congress into serious discussions on reforming spending and taxes. However, the temptation of demagoguery and self-advantage proved too much for President Obama to resist.

The President began his address by praising American's natural distrust of government, a sure sign that the President would then proceed to explain why we need more of it. He said that the deficit was a serious threat to our economy and our world leadership, but then he embarked on a lecture on the virtues of government. He talked about how government has led us to innovation and prosperity, how government created the conditions for progress, and how we would not be a great nation without the entitlement state. After extolling government, the President took aim at Republicans, accusing them of a mean-hearted scheme to dismantle the social safety net, privatize Medicare, cut social security, and create a state that serves only the rich. His favorite target was the plan put forward by House Budget Committee Chairman Paul Ryan, which calls for $5.8 trillion in deficit reduction over 10 years by reforming social security, Medicare, the tax code, and the federal government's discretionary spending habits. The President attacked every aspect of Ryan's plan, from its failure to include tax increases, to its plan to reform Medicare based on the private insurance mechanisms used by Medicare Part D, to its supposedly draconian cuts to education, health, and environmental programs.

While the President offered many details on why government is good and Republicans are bad, when it came to his plan to address the debt, he seemed to lose interest in specificity. In the speech he claimed to offer a plan for $4 trillion in deficit reduction over 12 years. Nearly a trillion of that reduction comes from savings on inflated estimates for the costs of the wars in Iraq and Afghanistan over the next ten years. Hundreds of billions more come from rosy projections of economic growth, and the rising tax revenues that come with it. As for spending cuts, the President said discretionary spending must be controlled, but offered no plan how, said defense savings could be made, but offered none, and said the growth curve in Medicare expenditures must be trimmed, but beyond calling for further powers for a government board to find waste and control prices, offered no plan to reform that program. As for social security, the President simply punted, saying it is a problem that should be examined. All in all, on the spending side the President wants to look like a fiscal conservative, without doing anything to act like one.

But the most interesting part of the President's speech addressed taxes. President Obama again called for raising taxes on anyone who makes $200,000 or more, saying Republicans want to deprive seniors of health care to give money to millionaires and billionaires. Then the President said he wants to limit "expenditures in the tax code." By this he meant raising taxes by limiting deductions and tax benefits for businesses and the wealthy. Apparently, President Obama believes that every dollar earned by every American starts off as property of the government and any tax rule that allows a private citizen to keep any of his or her money is an expenditure by the government. In essence, President sees himself as not only the defender of the entitlement state, but also entitled to every dollar every citizen earns.

After praising government, demonizing Republicans, and pretending to offer something other than more taxes to reduce our debt, the President closed his address by calling for joint efforts to solve the debt crisis. In essence, he poisoned the well and then asked Republicans to drink from it. It is clear the President thinks the Republican's plan to reduce the deficit is his best wedge issue to win reelection. So he used this address not to do the nation's business, but to help himself. He then took his reelection show on the road, touring the country to attack the GOP and defend the status quo. A risky tactic, because with the nation reaching its debt limit in May, he will need Republican support to avert a default. Whether his strategy will be good politics this time around, with the public so concerned and the threat so severe, will have to be seen, but he is certainly entitled to give it a try.

Week 118

(BY ANY STANDARD WE'RE POOR)

April 24, 2011

The keen political minds in the Obama White House were so sure the stage was perfectly set for the President's reelection campaign. They had a Republican Congress to vilify, the Paul Ryan deficit reduction plan demonize, and a strengthening economy to highlight. So sure were they that rather than seize the opportunity of the debt limit vote to build a bipartisan consensus for deficit reduction, they decided to declare war on Republicans and defend big government instead. The Democrat scare tactic playbook was dusted off, burnished with new attacks and taken on the road. The President loved it, as he toured liberal bastions on the coasts, collecting millions for himself and proclaiming Republican plans to rein in spending as un-American and cowardly. Then reality struck like a thunderbolt, when Standard & Poor's issued a warning on April 18 that the dimming prospects for a bipartisan deficit reduction plan might result in a downgrade of U.S. government debt in 2012. That, combined with ever rising oil prices, caste a long shadow on the President's strategy and called into question whether playing politics with deficit reduction is wise.

For the last 60 years, America has become accustomed to setting the world's political and economic agenda. With the largest and strongest economy, the most powerful military, and a competitive and technological edge over its peers, America stood unchallenged. However, the strain of the War on Terror and the massive expenditures it has required, along with the rise of China and the loss of industrial capacity has changed the economic and political balance of power. Rising oil prices have further accelerated the American's growing sense of dependency. America's inability to supply the energy to fuel its own economy is both bleeding the nation of resources and enriching foreign regimes that might challenge us. Slowly, Washington is beginning to realize that it is no longer the sole master of its own fate. So when President Obama decided to get political on the deficit, there was a counterattack not from Republicans, but from the bond market, the essential mechanism for financing America's massive budget deficits. When Standard & Poor's warned this week that U.S. government debt might lose its AAA rating, it sent a shock through the political class. A downgrade would not only increase the government's borrowing costs (and thus the deficit), but also could make it much harder for the U.S. to finance its debt. The international bond and oil markets are also beyond the control of any government, and their negative verdict on the nation's economic health cannot be ignored.

President Obama's basic strategy since taking office has been to use the rhetoric of fiscal restraint, while pursuing a massive expansion in federal spending and power. The President seemed to believe no one would notice as the nation's debts mounted and mounted. He and the Democrats ignored the growing backlash against their spending and regulatory agenda, and even well into the Fall of 2010 believed the Tea Party and Republicans would not make midterm election gains. When those gains were made, the President seemed for a time to understand that the political landscape had shifted. He cut deals on taxes and spending and talked more about deficit reduction. Yet it was all just a political game, because as soon as the Republicans announced a detailed plan to attack the deficit, President Obama took on the mantle of the defender of the State. But clever rhetoric cannot fool the bond and oil markets, as the President is starting to learn. The President can attack Republicans as mean-spirited all he wants, but the simple truth is that America cannot afford the expense of its government, and is getting poorer as a result.

In May of 2011, the United States will hit its debt limit, and without an extension of borrowing authority, the U.S. could default on its debt by July. The U.S. economy is slowly starting to grow and create a modest number of jobs, but all that is threatened by rocketing oil prices. And while corporate profits are strong, the dark underside of that story is that the private sector has learned how to make more with fewer employees, creating the prospect that job growth simply will not recover to pre-recession levels. Against this backdrop, it is not surprising that the President's poll numbers are the worst of his presidency. In the face of impending debt limit default, the President has a choice. He can play politics with these crises or try to avert them. Which course he chooses will reveal the true character of the man the American people elected.

Week 119

(CERTIFIED)

May 1, 2011

Ever since the issue was introduced by operatives of Hillary Clinton, there has been a growing movement of conspiracy theorists who have questioned whether Barak Obama was born in the United States. The question is of critical significance because there is a constitutional requirement that the president must be natural born American citizen. If it were proven that Obama was born outside the United States, he would be forced to resign as President because the Constitution would bar him from holding the office. The President's African name, the fact that his father was a Kenyan, and rumors of his birth in Kenya or Indonesia, all have fueled what has become known as the birther movement. Relegated to the fringes for most of the last three years, in recent months polls have shown an increasing number of voters questioning the President's place of birth. Then presidential aspirant Donald Trump played up the issue in interview after interview. Finally, this week the President released his long form birth certificate to show he is a certified natural born citizen to end the controversy.

There was never much evidence to support the birther argument beyond rumors from Kenya and Indonesia. In contrast, the President's certificate of live birth and newspaper announcements at the time of his birth seemed to show that Barak Obama was born in Hawaii. However, for years the President refused to release his long-form birth certificate. This fueled the conspiracy theories and implied that the President has something to hide. When the long-form birth certificate was released this week, it clearly showed that Barak Hussein Obama was born on August 4, 1961 at 7:24 p.m. at Kapiokaui Maternity & Gynecological Hospital in Honolulu. Accept for the most devoted birthers, this settled the issue.

The interesting question is not whether the President was born in the United States, but why he hid his birth certificate for so long and allowed the controversy to swell and swell. One school of thought is that the President saw the birther movement as a convenient way to caricature his opponents as mindless reactionaries and racists, so he allowed the movement to persist. If that was his strategy, it backfired, because as the President started losing more and more support because of the economy and the deficit, the birther movement actually started growing, despite the fact that no true evidence developed to support it.

More likely, it was the President's ego that prevented him from dealing with the issue earlier. Whether one supports his policies or not, one must admit President Obama is an intelligent, accomplished, and impressive leader, who is as American as anyone else. The birther movement surely had its genesis among those who disliked not only the President's politics, but who also believe there was something alien about him. This perception was not simply about his race, but was also influenced by his name, his background, and his liberal internationalist perspective. The President understandably resented any implication that he was not a true American, so he refused to dignify the birther attacks by disproving them.

The fact that the President had to change his strategy and release his long-form birth certificate shows how much his political base has deteriorated. With falling poll numbers, Americans upset about the lack of jobs and mounting debts, even the most outlandish attacks on the President were gaining traction. So the President had to humble himself and act to end the controversy. By releasing his long-form birth certificate, the President showed that he is a natural born citizen, but he also showed that he is an endangered politician.

Week 120

(GOT'EM)

May 8, 2011

Like many successful politicians, President Obama has often been the beneficiary of great timing. His speech at the 2004 Democratic convention, his change message for the 2008 campaign, and the financial crisis that sealed his victory all were perfectly timed to benefit the President. So at a moment when the President was falling in the polls, his leadership was being questioned on the Right and the Left, and his grip on the affection of the American people was starting to loosen, the timing could not have been better for the raid that killed Osama bin Laden. For nearly a decade, the United States has been searching for bin Laden. His escaped U.S. forces in the Tora Bora mountains of Afghanistan, and his subsequent videos attacking the United States and urging others to take up the Jihad were frequent reminders of America's all too limited success in the War on Terror. But as we are now learning, behind the scenes the noose was slowly tightening around bin Laden. We learned the code name for his courier, after years of effort we identified the courier, then we tied the courier to a compound in Abbottabad, Pakistan. The CIA set up a safe house to monitor the compound, and then, when we confirmed as best we could that bin Laden was there, we attacked and killed him.

It is the last part of this narrative where the President rightly deserves credit. The groundwork for the raid on Bin Linden was being laid for years with the efforts of hundreds if not thousands of intelligence and military personnel. Yet in the end, it was the President's call whether the intelligence was sufficient, and the opportunity was right to move on the compound in an effort to get bin Laden. The President made the call and ordered the attack. We now know that on May 1, Seal Team Six , the most elite of U.S. Special Forces, raided the compound using stealth helicopters. We know the plan went awry when one of the helicopters had engine problems and had to do a hard landing near the compound. Nevertheless, Seal Team Six moved in, killed a few guards and couriers in the compound, and then cornered bin Laden in his bedroom. After wounding bin Laden's favorite and most loyal wife in the leg, the Special Forces state that bin Laden showed signs of resistance, so he was shot dead in the chest and head. The body was taken, buried at sea so there could be no shrine, and the President made clear no photos of the dead bin Laden would be released. President Obama made the call with a smart plan, and the raid was a tremendous success.

The killing of bin Laden was the headline on the success of the raid, but its accomplishments go much deeper. Although the raid was planned to only last 10 minutes, Seal Team Six subdued the compound so quickly that they were able to spend 40 minutes there, gathering documents, computers, videos, and other evidence on Al-Qaeda and its plans. This treasure trove of evidence will no doubt be used for yet more raids (both overt and covert) to degrade Al-Qaeda's capabilities. From the little evidence released so far, we have learned that bin Laden was not so isolated as we may have thought. For years, the assumption had been that bin Laden was hiding in a cave in remote regions of Pakistan's tribal areas, cutoff from his Al-Qaeda's operatives and at best only a symbolic leader. We now know he was living very comfortably in an affluent Pakistani town, near a prestigious Pakistani military academy, and that we was in contact with his operatives and was trying to plan ever more attacks. So the raid did far more than kill a symbol and write a wrong, it damaged Al-Qaeda deeply and scored an important victory in the War on Terror.

For the President, the raid was a triumph. On the evening of Sunday, May 1, he announced to the nation that bin Laden had been killed. Then on May 4, he visited Ground Zero to pay homage to the killed, reflect on the accomplishment, and ask the nation to unify to address the challenges that face us today, just as we unified after 9/11. Then on Thursday, he visited the base for Seal Team Six to congratulate U.S. forces for a job well done. No doubt the President is making the most of his achievement, and using it to try to change the narrative about his Presidency. He wants to be seen as a strong, decisive leader who makes tough calls and does big things. He hopes to use the killing of bin Laden to arrest his decline in the polls and position himself for reelection. Conservatives have started to criticize the President for milking his success too much and using it too politically, but that is mostly sour grapes. The President made the call, got his guy, and did it in a smart and dignified way.

The President and his supporters are rightly on a high, and deservedly so, but politicians who rise too high often fall too hard. Just ask President George H. W. Bush, who won the first Iraq War, was proclaimed unbeatable, but then lost reelection to Bill Clinton. So too, President Obama and his allies must not read too much from this victory. Indeed, the victory itself has created a major problem for the Administration in Pakistan. Bin Laden was living openly, in an affluent town, near a Pakistani military base for five years. There is no doubt he was being protected and supported by members of the Pakistani security forces. President Obama needs to balance chastisement of Pakistan with maintenance of the U.S.'s alliance with them, because Pakistan is critical to the War in Afghanistan and its nuclear weapons must not fall into the hands of Islamic radicals.

On the home front, no matter how great the achievement of killing bin Laden, domestic issues, not foreign policy, will most likely determine who will win the 2012 election. On May 6, the unemployment rate rose to 9% despite the creation of 244,000 new jobs in April, U.S. productively is falling, energy prices are high, economic growth is slowing, the federal debt remains huge, and the public still sees the country on the wrong track. These issues can still be the undoing of the President. So the key for his political success is not basking in the glory of the bin Laden raid, but instead using his new political capital to address domestic challenges. That is how President Obama wins reelection.

Week 121
(UNIFY ME)

May 15, 2011

President Obama's theme from the bin Laden raid is that America can do big things when we unify. He struck that tone in his speech on May 1 announcing the killing of bin Laden, and he continues to pursue it. The President sees the unity theme as a means to re-create the "Change we can believe in" mantra that propelled his victory in 2008. It is all part of a plan by the President to leverage the bin Laden success into his personal success. This week, he plied his new favorite theme in every forum, and on every issue he could think of, to try to create a sense of momentum.

The President is desperate to push this unity theme because of his political vulnerability. The bin Laden killing has given him a modest bump in the polls, but in key battleground states and in early polls on the presidential campaign, there remain warning signs. Obama is running behind in a host of states in carried in 2008, and polls this week show him leading a hypothetical Republican presidential candidate by 43 to 40 percent. What this shows is that the public credits the President for his success on bin Laden, but they are not going to judge the success of his presidency by the same measure. So Obama is trying to leverage his temporary renewed strength to make progress on immigration, the debt, and energy policy to strengthen his position for reelection.

On immigration, this week the President travelled to Texas to again push for immigration reform. The White House unconvincingly tried to tie bin Laden to immigration reform, saying that the unity that led to the killing of bin Laden should likewise unify us to address immigration issues. The connection between the two is far from obvious, unlike the White House's political agenda, which is clear. The President is pushing immigration reform in an effort to maximize Latino turnout in 2012. The President travelled to Texas because Democrats are trying to put Texas in play for the election, not because they expect to win the state, but because they want to force Republicans to spend money there. And the President likes the immigration issue, because it allows him to play the unifier.

On the budget, the President again played the unifier role, by inviting the Republican caucus from the Senate to the White House to discuss raising the debt ceiling and addressing the debt. For the President, the meeting was part politics and part necessity. The huge debt has become a huge political liability for the President, so holding high profile meetings with Republicans to discuss the issue makes him look reasonable, centrist, and engaged. Yet in many ways, the necessity far outstrips the politics. The Treasury Department now says that the nation will default on its debt if the debt ceiling is not raised by August. To raise it, the President must get the Republicans on board and the Republicans have most of the leverage. While the public hates government shut-downs, it equally hates increases in the debt limit, and polls show huge majorities oppose any increase. So the GOP sees little danger in opposing the President. The GOP has been clear that spending cuts will be the price for their support, and this week minority leader McConnell said that a comprehensive deficit deal is what is needed to get the debt limit raised. The President held his meeting with the GOP to look the unifier and set the stage for what will certainly be very difficult negotiations.

On energy, the President played the unifier theme by a policy pronouncement that finally bought him to the center on the energy debate. The truth is the President wants high oil prices because they force fuel economy and make alternative energy sources more competitive. For that reason, after the Gulf oil spill, the Administration maintained the drilling ban beyond all reason and has been delaying new drilling permits as much as possible. No matter how much the President likes high oil prices, he likes the idea of reelection even more, so this week he announced that the Administration would speed drilling permits and open some areas for more drilling. None of these steps will address the current high oil prices because of the lag between permitting and production, but with these executive orders the President is trying to insulate himself from accusations that he is contributing to high oil prices. A more centrists and unifying position on energy production is designed to further the President's political standing. So on a host of domestic issues the President is using the unity theme to further his agenda, and more importantly try to get himself reelected.

Week 122

(Borderline)

May 22, 2011

Propelled by the successful killing of Osama bin Laden, this week President Obama sought to leverage that victory to change the terms of the Middle East debate by calling for a resolution of the Arab-Israeli conflict based on the 1967 borders. For the United States, there has always been a conflict between idealism and national interests when it comes to Middle East policy, and the President's comments on the 1967 borderlines were designed to both catch attention and signal a shift to a more idealist approach. America has been a critic of the dictatorial regimes and limits on women's rights in the Middle East. However, national interests deeply intertwined with America's energy needs has led the United States to bolster regimes and policies that would garner condemnation in almost any other region of the world. The consequences of these contradictions include the attacks of September 11 which were motivated in part by American support of Israel, and American forces stationed in Saudi Arabia to support America's allies of the Gulf. With his speech this week, President Obama, hoping the time is right to change the terms of the debate, tried to tilt the scale in favor of more idealism in American policy in the Middle East,

In two speeches on Middle East policy, President Obama addressed the war on terror, the Arab Israeli conflict, and the consequences of the Arab Spring. He said that the world must embrace the uprisings of the Arab Spring and support the rise of democracy. He said brutal leaders like Assad in Syria must heed their people's calls for reform or leave power, and he said that the Palestinians must have their own contiguous state. Most controversial of all, the President said that the borders of a new Palestinian state must be based on the lines in place before the 1967 war. He built upon these themes at a second speech before AIPAC, where he both emphasized America's unyielding support for Israel and our obligation as a friend to coax Israel into a workable compromise with the Palestinians. With these speeches, the President hopes to recast America as an ally of democracy and an honest broker in the Arab-Israeli conflict.

The central theory behind the President's speeches is that America can no longer afford a purely realist approach to Middle East policy, where we simply support regimes and policies that further the security and energy interests of the United States. That was approach of American policymakers for most of the period from the founding if Israel in 1948 until September 11, with some very negative consequences. America's often unreserved support Israel and alliances with brutal regimes made it easy for our opponents to label us the Great Satan. Al-Qaeda and other terrorist movements have their origin in the backlash against American Middle East policy. With democracy starting to sweep over the Middle East, the President wisely sees that America must shed its image as a constant supporter of Israel and authoritarian Arab regimes. America must also attempt to force a sustainable long-term resolution of the Arab-Israeli conflict, because the longer that conflict lingers, the more entrenched the resentments and terrorism it fosters will become.

Ironically, President Obama entered office with a bias against an idealist approach to Middle East policy. He was a harsh critic of President George W. Bush's policy of fostering democracy in the Middle East. Much of that opposition likely sprung from the Iraq War, where the Bush Administration used military force to oust a dictator and replace him with a democratic government. The Bush Administration hoped success in Iraq would further American security interests by removing an opponent, creating a hedge against Iran, and starting a process of democratization that would sap the strength of terrorist movements. However, the drawn-out campaign in Iraq helped fuel terrorist groups and the at best sputtering success of Iraqi democracy has not exactly inspired others to emulation. President Obama saw the Bush Administration policy as wasteful of American resources and counterproductive to its interests.

The President's realist approach was still on display as recently as last year, with his muted reaction to protests in Iran, when thousands marched for reform and democracy and were brutally suppressed. The Administration's weak response to the crackdown in Iran showed how little appetite the Administration had for inspiring populist movements. But all that changed with the Arab Spring. The President now realizes that democracy is on the march in the Middle East and America risks being left behind if it does not rally to support it. The President also realizes that America can never have credibility with populist movements in the Middle East while the Arab-Israeli conflict continues. That is exactly why the Administration has started a push to force a final resolution.

The President used his speech and his meeting with Prime Minister Netanyahu a few days later to press home that message. Unfortunately, Prime Minister Netanyahu made clear during a photo op that he would never accept the 1967 borders or any Palestinian right to return into Israel proper. So the President's effort to curry favor with Arabs has already engendered a backlash from Israel. However, in the President's view, we must embrace popular movements, support democracy, and temper our unquestioning support of Israel, or risk being left behind.

Week 123

(WARNING SIGNS)

May 29, 2011

After several weeks dominated by Middle East policy, with the killing of bin Laden and major policy speeches on the peace process, the President continued his foreign focus with a trip to Europe to visit Ireland, the homeland of his maternal grandmother, a visit with Queen Elizabeth, and a trip to Poland. But while the President continued his focus abroad, warning signs were growing for both the Republicans and the Democrats at home. The President has an understandable interest in promoting his success with bin Laden and his renewed effort to solve the Arab-Israeli conflict, but in the end it is the battles at home, not the battles abroad, that will decide his electoral fate.

At first blush, the political news for the President was very good. Ever since the Republican majority in the House put forward its 2012 budget plan, with substantial changes to Medicare, Democrats have been salivating at the opportunity to exploit the issue and accuse Republicans of attacking health care for seniors. They got their first chance with a special election in the 26th congressional district in Upstate New York. Republican Chris Lee represented this solidly Republican district until shirtless photos of him soliciting women surfaced on the internet. Lee's resignation led to a special election with a three-way race between the GOP's Jane Corwin, Jack Davis a perennial candidate this time running as a Tea Party candidate, and Kathy Hochul, the Democrat clerk for Erie County. Party and outside money flooded the race, with Republicans attacking Hochul as a tax-raiser and Democrats portraying Corwin as trying to repeal Medicare.

Hochul won the three-way race, giving hope to Democrats that the Medicare issue could win the House back for them in 2012.

Building on the same there, the Senate this week voted on the Ryan budget plan, with its Medicare reforms. The budget failed, as expected, with 42 of the 47 Senate Republicans voting to support those Medicare reforms. Democrats welcomed the vote as an opportunity to get Senate Republicans on the record as supporting changes to Medicare that Democrats hope to exploit in the 2012 election. The special election loss in New York and the defeat of the Ryan plan in the Senate led many Democrats to paint a bright picture of their prospects next year. But these tactical victories were far overshadowed by the impending debt limit crisis.

The federal government has already surpassed the debt limit, meaning new borrowing power of the government has been halted. For now, the Treasury Department has devised means to borrow from pensions and other funds to pay government bond holders, but those temporary measures will run out by early August. If no deal is reached to raise the debt limit by then, Democrats universally predict disaster as the government defaults on its debt, leading to a shock to the economy that might trigger another recession. For their part, Republicans say default is unacceptable, but that it is more important to reach a deal to reduce the debt than it is to raise the debt limit. It is the ultimate great game of chicken, but one where the Republicans have most of the leverage.

The American public is disgusted with the federal government's big deficits and oppose raising the debt limit. Given this, Republicans see little political risk in forcing deficit reduction as the price for raising the debt limit. Republican leaders also see the debt limit issue as the means to neutralize the Medicare issue by forcing the Democrats to agree to a Medicare reform deal as the price for increased borrowing authority. The Republican reasoning is that President Obama and his allies will not be able to demagogue the Medicare issue if they themselves sign on to a reform package. As a result, it is clear that Republicans plan to push for comprehensive budget and entitlement reform before they will raise the debt limit.

The Republicans are so sure of their strength that next week the House plans to accede to the President's demand to allow a vote to raise the debt limit without any requirements to cut the deficit. The Republicans know the vote will fail and also know that large numbers of Democrats will be forced to vote against raising the debt limit because of opposition from their home districts. So this week's warning signs for Republicans masked dangerous tremors for Democrats, because Republicans have the upper hand in the budget debate, and plan to use that leverage to deprive Democrats of a weapon to use in the next election.

Week 124

(HELP WANTED)

June 5, 2011

Certain unpleasant realities started coming home to roust for President Obama this week. Nearly a year after he proclaimed the Summer of Recovery, the markets were battered with a torrent of bad economic news, from falling home prices, to weakening manufacturing, to rising unemployment. This news forced the stock market into its fifth straight losing week and economists quickly downgraded their economic growth forecasts for the remainder of the year. While the economy is slowing, the debt continues to go gangbusters. The Administration has been asking for months for a clean vote from the House to raise the debt ceiling, and this week they got it, with an unpleasant result. The bill failed 97 to 318, with all Republicans and nearly half of the Democrats in the House voting against an increased debt ceiling. Already, the President's brief bump in the polls from the bin Laden killing is melting away, replaced by pessimism on the economy and the debt. It might be time for the White House to put a help wanted sign on 1600 Pennsylvania Avenue.

The President was hoping to set a good economic theme this week with a trip to Ohio to visit a Chrysler plant to tout the success of his auto bailout. He timed the trip to coincide with the May unemployment report, hoping to talk about how his policies are bringing needed jobs. Instead, when the Labor Department reported that the economy only added 54,000 jobs in May and that the unemployment rate rose to 9.1%, the President decided to make no comment whatsoever on the report, and even dodged questions from reporters on this issue. The President tried to change the subject by talking about the success of the auto bailout, but he got a bit over excited and said Chrysler had repaid all federal money, when in fact they still owed more than $7 billion. This exaggeration only highlighted a President desperate to try to find something positive to talk about on the economy.

For nearly 18 months, the United States has had solid, albeit somewhat tepid, growth, with the assumption that the recovery would keep gaining steam, ultimately leading to accelerated job creation. It simply has not happened. Corporate profits are still solid, but growth has slowed, and housing remains stubbornly in the dumps. This landscape poses a challenge for an activist progressive President. Not comfortable with unshackling the private sector with decreased regulations or lower taxes, the President would prefer more public spending. He got some of that spending in the tax cut deal with Republicans in December 2010, but now the till is empty. His only option is to compromise with Republicans, not a favorite approach for the President.

It was almost like rubbing salt in a wound when the Republicans did exactly what the President asked and held an open vote to raise the debt ceiling. The bill only got 97 yes votes, showing once and for all that the Administration has little support for raising the debt ceiling without spending restraints. The Democrat majority in the Senate refuses to even schedule a clean vote to raise the borrowing authority because they know it would fail just as badly. So all the Administration's accusations against Republicans on the debt ceiling have been shown to be empty rhetoric because the President cannot even get Democrats to support more borrowing.

The entire theme of the Obama Administration is that they inherited a mess and are cleaning it up. The problem is there is increasing evidence that they have only made matters worse. They have spent trillions to spur economic growth, with little result other than an indebted federal government that could soon default. The President seems to think that with a bit more rhetorical flourish he can change the narrative, but already the mantra of "change you can believe in" has been replaced by "Help Wanted," and the person in Washington, DC who needs the most help is the President himself.

Week 125

(WE HAVE A WEINER)

June 12, 2011

Sometimes our nation's politics gets distracted by the salacious. At a time when Congress is facing the looming debt crisis, the last thing needed was a sex scandal to distract lawmakers from an urgent task. But then came Weiner gate. Anthony Weiner, a six-term Democrat from Queens was viewed by many as a rising star among Democrats. His witty quips, open access to the press, and unabashed liberalism made him a favorite in Democrat circles. Wiener's ultimate goal is the Mayoralty of New York City, and he made no secret of the fact that he intended to seek that office at the end of Mayor Bloomberg's current term. But two weeks ago a mysterious photo of a man's crotch clothed in white underwear appeared on Weiner's Twitter page. Weiner spent a week claiming he was hacked, punked, and tricked. He even lashed out at the conservative blogger who broke the story, claiming his variant of a great rightwing conspiracy. But when asked directly whether the photo was of him, his equivocal answers created suspicion. Then, on June 7, he admitted his whole story was a lie, it was him, after all.

What has come to light since Weiner's admission is a long string of lude photographs sent to an equally long list of women, including some girls as young as 17. Shirtless pictures, nude pictures, and simply bizarre pictures, all sent to women Weiner claims he knows only on the internet. Weiner claims he has never had physical relations with any of these women and so far that part of his story is holding up, but not much else. At first, the Democrat leadership was silent on the scandal, hoping it would go away quickly. But as the story grew and grew, the bad political consequences for Democrats became more clear. By the end of the week, Minority Leader Pelosi and most of her team were calling for Weiner to resign.

Unfortunately, Weiner is not making it easy for his Democrat colleagues. Weiner is in love with politics and the political fray. He wants to keep his seat no matter what. In the very same press conference where he admitted this lies about being punked, he was emphatic that he would not resign. He stuck to that position for most of the week, As the chorus for resignation grew louder, Weiner decided to try the Tiger Woods strategy, putting himself in treatment to try to heal himself. Few believe that is his real motivation. His true goal is to quell the story and hope the press gets distracted and moves on to other prey. Weiner sees time as his friend, and the longer he can hold on, the better the chance he can keep his seat. The question is how much damage is he willing to do in the interim.

President Obama has wisely stayed away from the Weiner controversy, but it impacts him as well. He and his party are bracing for what will likely be the defining policy struggle of the remainder of his terms, namely the debt crisis. With each week the economic news for the White House gets worse. With the stock marketing falling for a sixth straight week and unemployment claims again rising, the President is approaching the endgame with Republicans on the debt in a weakened position. The last thing he needs is a scandal to sully the image of his party and distract the troops. That is exactly what Weiner's obstinacy is doing.

It does not help that Weiner is a true man of the Left, an open supporter of single payor health care, expanded government, and higher taxes. He has often advocated for these positions based on the fundamental moral need for the nation to take care of its most needy citizens. Now those high moral tones look like bad parody, with Weiner revealed as a narcissistic pervert. President

Obama bears no responsibility for Weiner or his actions, but he will be impacted by them nonetheless, because it weakens his party at time when the challenges are great. So while the Weiner story is all the rage, it will soon pass into the long annals of Washington sex scandals, only to be mentioned in the occasional joke and gossip tidbit. However, the timing of the story and how it is distracting the Democrats and weakening the President could have a more lasting impact, because the next few weeks will decide the size and scope of government for years to come. The President cannot afford distraction.

Week 126

(DEBATING THE FIELD)

June 19, 2011

The conventional wisdom on the 2012 presidential election has been that an improving economy and a weak Republicans field will mean a comfortable Obama reelection. The recent spat of bad economic news has called the former assumption into question, while this week's Republican debate showed that the later theory may be unfounded as well. The media is replete with reports on dissatisfaction with the Republican candidates, but it was not until June 13 that the current Republican field took to a stage for a debate. What ensued was a serious and spirited discussion on the failings of the Obama Administration by a diverse group of candidates. The Republicans focused their fire almost entirely on President Obama, attacking him on spending, Obamacare, anti-business policies, the stimulus, bailouts, and weakness abroad. The critiques were partisan to be sure, but they also closely track much of the dialogue in the country about the performance of the Administration.

President Obama and his allies have tried to craft an aura of invincibility around the 2012 campaign. The President is re-engaging his massive fundraising network, re-starting his grass roots campaign, and using every opportunity to try to frame issues for the upcoming election. However, the President has been hobbled by the unpopularity of many of his domestic programs and the weak economy. He cannot tout strong growth, or falling unemployment, and sound federal finances, because his record is weak on them all. So instead, the President blames Republicans for the country's ills, and portrays his opposition as reactionaries who will destroy the social safety net. Instead of campaigning on "Change You Can Believe," the President's new theme is "Not as Bad or Scary As Republicans." That approach might work if the Republican field were made up of rightwing evangelicals and kooky candidates, but despite all the griping about the Republican candidates, they are actually an impressive group.

Looking at the field, one sees depth and diversity. The candidates include former governors Mitt Romney and Tim Pawlenty, current Congressmen Ron Paul and Michelle Bachmann, former senator Rick Santorum, former speaker Newt Gringirch, and businessman Herman Cain. Plenty of experience in the federal government, state government, and in business. Also, the candidates most likely to look like fringe players have not run, including Sarah Palin and Mike Huckabee. Indeed, the Republican field looks to get even more depth as Jon Huntsman, former governor of Utah and Obama ambassador to China, joins the race, along with Texas Governor Rick Perry, who is showing every sign of a run. Not only are the credentials strong, but the message is as well. The

June 13 debate was nothing if not a stinging attack on the record of the Obama Administration on spending, debt, and the role of government. From that debate, it is clear the Republicans hope to make 2012 not only a referendum on Obama, but also a referendum on the size and scope of government.

That type of debate puts Obama in a difficult position. Most of his big government programs, like the stimulus, bailouts, and Obamacare are unpopular, so the President's ability to use those accomplishments to get independent votes is limited. Also, it is rarely good politics to stand up as the defender and champion of government. No matter how much Obama believes in the central role of government to forge America's future, he dares not take that line too far. So he is forced to use the rhetoric of limited government to defend and promote his policies of expanded government. If the economy were strong, it might be an easy sell for the President because voters would give him the benefit of the doubt, but that is not the case. So it should be no surprise that polls this week showed Obama losing by 5 points to a generic Republican and Obama leading Romney only slightly and with support well under 50%, bad news for any incumbent.

A great deal can change before the 2012 election. The economy could improve, Obama could win key victories on the budget or taxes, or he could have foreign policy successes that help propel his reelection. But the Administration cannot pin their hopes on any of those things happening. It also became increasingly clear this week that President Obama also cannot assume he will face a weak opponent, because as his standing continues to erode, the opposing field continues to strengthen. So political reality should now be hitting home for the President, making the stakes for him very high in the impending debt ceiling and deficit debate. How he handles those issues might determine his fate.

Week 127

(HALF MEASURES)

June 26, 2011

President Obama prides himself on being the adult in the room. He always likes to strike the pose of the practical moderate seeking the reasonable solution between the extremes. That image is all the more important to him in recent months, as his approval among independents has plummeted, threatening his chances for reelection. Faced with weakening support, the President hopes to reconnect with independent voters by portraying both the Left and the Right as too rigidly ideological, while he in contrast seeks the middle ground. Yet the President's addiction to seeming moderation carries the risk of pleasing no one. That reality was on display this week, when the President proposed half measures on the War in Afghanistan and on energy policy that pleased no one, and infuriated many, leaving him looking indecisive rather than moderate. The War in Afghanistan has always posed the biggest challenge for the President's desire to look the moderate. When running for President, he used that war to temper any implication he was a pacifist by saying Afghanistan was the right war that must be won, while Iraq was a wrongheaded war of choice. Once elected, the President had to deal with the fallout of his rhetoric, because Iraq proved the easier war to end, while Afghanistan proved the harder war to win. After delaying for months, he ultimately decided to add combat forces to Afghanistan to turn the tide, but promised to bring them home within a year. On June 20, the President gave his long awaited speech on that troop withdrawal. Since the surge began, the war has only gotten less popular, so the Left of his party wanted the speech to outline a rapid withdrawal of U.S. forces. In contrast, much (but not all) of conservatives worried that recent progress in Afghanistan would be threatened by an early removal of troops.

In typical form, the President offered a plan pleasing to no one. The President outlined a plan to remove 10,000 troops this year, and another 23,000 in 2012 to keep his promise to end the Afghan surge. He talked about the successes in the war and the need to achieve our objectives, but also spoke of the need to do "nation building at home" and how America cannot fight every foe. He honored the service of the troops, but did not speak of victory, but rather of bringing the conflict to an honorable end. He was neither war ender nor war winner, but instead simply a war prolonger. Liberals were the most critical of the speech, because they are the most committed to ending the war and the President's speech made clear that the conflict would continue for many more years. But conservatives also took shots at the President's plan as being more calibrated to help his reelection than designed to achieve the objectives of the war. Just like his announcement of the surge, this speech showed a reluctant warrior interested more in his public image than prevailing against America's foes.

The President's speech on Afghanistan was not his only half measure of the week. He had one on energy policy as well. Until recent weeks ever rising gas prices have put yet another burden on the weak recovery, helping to stall job growth. For most of his first two years, the President's energy policy has been based on a carbon tax, billions in subsidies for green energy, and bashing oil companies. It was a strategy pleasing to the liberal base, but one that did little to ease energy prices for consumers. After the Gulf Oil Spill, the President added a moratorium for drilling permits to his energy agenda, further dampening energy production. The President could get away with all of this if gas prices had remained in the $2-3 dollar range, but as prices rose to the $4 range, his hostility to energy producers began to exact a political price. In response, the Administration has increased drilling permit approvals, but only slightly for fear of enraging the environmental lobby. So instead, this week the President announced the release of 30 million barrels of oil from the nation's strategic reserve to ease oil prices.

As expected, the release did drop the price of oil by nearly $5 per barrel, but it did nothing to address the basic market dynamics pushing oil prices higher. The ill-fated war in Libya, growing demand in Asia, and the Arab Spring will push prices higher again, and soon. The oil release was public relations done at public expense, and will have no long term impact on the price of oil. Oil executives said the release was the best evidence of the failure of the President's energy policy, while environmentalist used the released as yet another excuse to bash oil producers. The President could have made a long-term impact on oil pricing by announcing support for expanded domestic production, but that would have made liberals unhappy. He could have said high prices are painful, but necessary to push the nation toward green sources of energy, but that would have risked a consumer backlash. So instead he spent taxpayer dollars releasing emergency fuel reserves to look like he was doing something about rising prices. A half measure that pleased no one.

President Obama certainly knows it is not easy playing the role of the adult in the room, but he might find that role easier if he grapples with the notion that adults are supposed to make decisions and live with the consequences, not adopt policies mainly designed to make themselves look good.

Week 128

(SHOWING UP)

July 3, 2011

Much of the news this week was taken up with budget battles in Washington and in the States. In California, Governor Jerry Brown vetoed the budget passed by his Democrat allies because it was full of gimmicks that failed to address the State's deep fiscal crisis. Minnesota's government shut down when the Republican legislature refused to accept Democrat Governor's Doyle's proposal for higher income taxes, while Chris Christie pushed through yet more budget reforms in New Jersey with limits on union collective bargaining rights. Chris Christie was asked about his successes and how he worked with Democrats to push his agenda, and he said the first step is showing up. It seems President Obama was listening, because this week he decided to finally show up to address the impending federal budget crisis, but it appears that the President did not like what he heard, because after only a single day of meetings be bowed out of the process yet again, preferring to ridicule his opponents rather than work to forge a compromise.

The level of concern among the chattering classes in DC that the politicians will fail to overcome the budget impasse that is threatening a default on the United States' debt obligations by August 2 is increasing, with good reason. For more than a month, Vice President Biden has been holding talks with congressional leaders on the budget, trying to work a compromise to allow for an increase in the debt ceiling. But with Democrats pushing for higher taxes and Republicans resisting, the Republican leaders pulled out of the talks, stating that a deal can only be made if the President gets involved in the process. Heretofore, President Obama has played little public role in the budget debate. In February, he proposed a budget that called for higher spending and higher taxes without addressing entitlements or the long-term debt. The Administration's budget blueprint was roundly criticized by all factions and was promptly withdrawn. After reaching a deal with Republicans for the 2010-2011 budget, the President then gave his April speech at Georgetown, not to create a consensus for moving forwarded, but to vilify his opponents as friends of the rich, enemies of the middle class, and scheming to destroy the social safety net. Other than some generalities offered in the April speech, neither the Administration nor the majority Senate Democrats have offered any budget plan, opting instead to take pot shots at the budget passed by the House Republicans.

Many assumed that the Administration's tactics are just political posturing and that the President would eventually be prepared to engage on the issue. So after waiting weeks for President Obama to get involved, the Republicans forced his hand by pulling out of the Biden budget meetings. So on June 27, the President finally held a single meeting with Senate Minority Leader Mitch McConnell, along with Democrat Leader Harry Reid. The meeting apparently did not go well, because the President rejected a request to meet with House Republicans and then took the podium for a new conference on June 29 for his most petulant performance as President. He said the Republicans were willing to put the nation in default to protect millionaires, billionaires, private jet owners, and oil companies. After failing put to forth any detailed plan to address the debt, he accused Republicans of not doing their jobs, taking too many recesses, and said when there is a job to do, they should just get it done. He then left town to take his attack on the road, repeating and repeating what were clearly focus group tested attacks on the Republicans.

The President's approach on the budget is nothing new, he has done the same thing on every major piece of legislation since his election. He gives speeches and outlines his principles, but he does not want to get his hands dirty doing any actual work of governing. He expects Congress to do his work for him. He outsourced the stimulus bill, health care reform, and financial reform to Congress, and he basically signed what Congress gave him. His press conference showed he wants the same thing to happen on the budget. He expects Congress to fix the problem for him, while he travels the country attacking the Republicans. But there is a big difference this time, because his party no longer runs the House, and the Republicans are much stronger in the Senate. This divided government would seemingly call for the President to engage and force a compromise, but President Obama signaled on June 29 that he prefers political gamesmanship to solutions.

After adding nearly 4 trillion to the national debt in barely 2 ½ years, the President is desperate to find a way to blame Republicans for the problem he created. Betting that Republicans will blink before he will, he is trying to change the narrative from out of control federal spending to Republicans' willingness to create a international financial crisis to protect the rich. President Obama believes he can get political advantage from this line of attack, he appears not to care whether the collateral damage includes a default on the national debt. What all this reveals is that our President less interested in showing up and reaching deals to get the nation's business done, as he is in himself, his interests, and above all his own reelection. The President is betting he can persuade the nation to blame Republicans for a default, but what he forgets is that the buck stops with him, and to date he refuses to play any productive role in the budget debate.

Week 129

(RUNNING ON EMPTY)

July 10, 2011

After thrashing Republicans last week for taking too many vacations, favoring too many private jet owners, and taking too long to raise the debt ceiling, this week President Obama took on a new role as conciliator-in-chief. Gone were petulant attacks on Republicans, replaced with calls for unity, reasonableness, and compromise. It seems President Obama offered last week's attacks on the Republicans solely to satisfy his base, only to quickly pivot to deal maker role on the budget and debt ceiling. The wisdom for this change in strategy is clear. The President is already receiving very poor marks from voters on his handling of the economy, and can ill afford a budget and debt meltdown that sinks the economy. A point that struck home like a thunderbolt with the July 8 jobs report showing that the U.S. produced only 18,000 jobs in June (less than Canada which has a tenth our population). If a deal on the budget was necessary for the President before that report, it became critical after it.

Throughout his presidency, Mr. Obama has often been inconsistent. He likes to lurch from fiery populist and thoughtful moderate, not quite sure which person he should be at what moment. He also likes to test drive his various persona's, with press conferences, speeches, and road trips designed to gauge the reaction to his latest rhetorical inventions. During the 2010 election, the President tried out nearly a dozen different lines of attack on Republicans, with no avail because his party got trounced in any event. Now with the budget battle underway, the President tried the same playbook. After largely ignoring the debt ceiling issue and outsourcing it to Vice President Biden, after one meeting with Senate Republicans he took to the podium to attack both the Republican's plan and their motives. But that changed when the President realized that attacks on Republicans might fire up his base, but did nothing to help get a deal on the debt ceiling, and a deal is what the President desperately needs.

So this week, the President held a secret meeting with Speaker Boehner on July 3 to discuss a major deal on the budget to reduce the deficits by more than $4 trillion, including entitlement reforms and new revenues. Then the President gave another press conference, but this time he talked about Republicans as partners, not enemies. He then called the congressional leadership back to the White House on Thursday for another session, cajoling them to do a big deal on the deficit, and asking them to come back again on Sunday, July 10 with their bottom line proposals for a deal. After months of inaction, the President has now struck a tone of urgency, and there is no need to look beyond the July 8 jobs report to understand why.

President Obama has the most to lose from the bad economy. He advocated for the stimulus bill, Obamacare, and other government interventions on the theory that they would improve the economy. While there is room for debate on the impact of those programs, it is clear the voters' verdict is negative to date. President Obama himself made job creation the measure of the success of his program, and by that measure he is getting an "F." The July 8 jobs report showed unemployment rising to 9.2%, and combined with under employment, the rate was 15.8%. Job growth in prior months was also revised down, and it became clear the public sector job cuts would continue to drag employment numbers down, as states and the federal government finally start to adjust their workforces to address a recession that started three years ago. When the President gave a statement on the jobs report, he did everything he could to try to ignore its import, focusing on the total jobs produced in the last two years rather than the current weakness in the job market. He also struggled to offer any solutions, other than more stimulus spending, free trade deals he put on the slow track for a year to please unions, and of all things patent reform. It was a weak performance for an Administration that has run out of answers.

That is why the President needs a budget deal. The problem is, after vilifying Republicans at every turn, it is hard to do a deal with them when you need their help. This is especially the case when your offer requires Republicans to raise taxes, something they will not do. The President believes that by playing the reasonable centrist pushing for a deal he can win no matter what. If a deal is made, he will get the credit. If a deal founders and the debt ceiling is not raised, others will get the blame. In the end, the President needs a debt ceiling increase more than anyone else. That is why Speaker Boehner called the President's bluff on July 9 and said Republicans would not agree to a tax increase. The simple truth is that the Administration is running on empty now, and the Republicans are going to exact a big price before they help push them to a gas station.

Week 130

(THE NO LOSE SCENARIO)

July 17, 2011

President Obama entered the debt limit negotiations in a weakened position, because of the sluggish U.S. economy, but seems to have found a strategy to turn the tide. After months of ignoring the debt limit increase issue, the President has divined that he can use that debate to recast himself as a moderate and win back support of independents. So this week he used tactical leaks, marathon meetings, and frequent press conferences to portray himself as the moderate problem solver, trying to achieve a big and balanced solution to the federal debt issue, only to be opposed by fanatical Republicans who care more about protecting the rich than preventing default. For a President whose own budget proposal in February increased spending and expanded the debt, his new mantra was audacious, but effective. No matter the outcome, the President hopes to be the winner. If he gets a deal, he will be the effective centrist. If he fails, he can call Republicans extremists. A No Lose Scenario.

In many ways, the bleak jobs data has propelled the President into his current strategy. It had been the assumption of Democrat strategists for many months that a strong and recovering economy would ensure President's Obama's reelection and eclipse his unpopular policies like health care and the stimulus. Yet with all indicators showing a weakening recovery and a sovereign debt crisis continuing to roil Europe, a grudging consensus has taken hold in the Administration that the President is going to have to win reelection in the midst of a weak economy, not a strong one. So the President has used the debt limit debate to recast himself with independents as the only centrist option to get things done. So this week's meetings and debates on federal spending are really more the opening act of the 2012 election than a policy debate.

To pursue his strategy, the President has been forced to cede considerable ground to the GOP. He has proposed a deficit reduction approach heavily weighted towards spending cuts, offered to increase the Medicare eligibility age to 67, and in so doing, has turned his focus from activist government to spending restraint. Liberals are crying foul, but the President bets that the Left will support him no matter what. The President hopes that his tactical retreat on substance will achieve a victory in public relations. Yet while he has moved toward to GOP on spending, he has included in his proposals a poison pill he hopes will help him in 2012. The President has stated that he wants a big deficit reduction deal ($4 trillion or more over 10 years), but his price is tax increases for the affluent and corporations. Using the anti-tax creed of the Republicans against them, the President hopes to either force the GOP to accept a tax increase, or blame them for cratering a deficit reduction deal over their anti-tax obsession.

There is no doubt that the President's new strategy has knocked the GOP off its game. The President is talking about spending cuts and a big deficit reduction deal (just like them), but with some strings attached in the form of taxes that make the deal unpalatable for many in the GOP. The President's strategy has caused a rift among Republicans, pitting the deal makers who want to take this opportunity to put the nation's fiscal house in order, against its more doctrinaire members, who will not accept any tax increase. Indeed, the President and his party are seeking to divide the GOP exactly along these lines in the hope of breaking their resistance.

As the talks continued this week, many grew pessimistic that the impasse could be overcome. The President continued to push for his vision, the GOP continued to resist new taxes. Senator

McConnell, who has very publicly stated that the deficit problem can be solved only by ousting the President, offered a backup plan if no new deal could be reached in the form of a bill that would allow the President to raise the debt limit 3 times between August and the end of 2012, putting the burden of increasing the debt limit on the White House, not Congress. The Democrats reacted cautiously to the idea, seeing it as both a way out and a clever effort to turn the debate against the Democrats. But even this proposal is unlikely to pass the House without spending cuts attached, so negotiations began in the Senate to add spending cuts to the McConnell proposal. The week ended with reports of a glimmer of hope, with discussions restarting between the GOP and Democrats on a bigger deficit reduction deal more in line with President Obama's proposals, possibly using a special committee of Congress and a fast track approval process.

At the end of the week, despite the hot political rhetoric, there seemed to be an undercurrent of progress. The McConnell proposal appears to have opened a new path for negotiations, and possibly some solutions. For the President, the debate has been an useful opportunity to try to burnish his credentials as a centrist and bash the GOP as extreme. Clearly, the Administration sees this debate as a winner for them no matter the outcome. Yet the White House should be careful not to over read their success. For starters, most voters are not paying close attention, so scoring debating points now is not likely to help much in 2012. Further, if no deal is made, there will be plenty of blame to spread around and it is far from assured that Obama will come out the better. If a debt limit increase is passed as part of an overall deficit reduction plan, Obama will have won a victory, but only by giving in to the GOP mandate for spending cuts. Obama will have shown himself effective, but with 9.2% unemployment and other unpopular policies, his no lose scenario is not assured.

Week 131
(MR. HOLLYWOOD)

July 24, 2011

President Obama's critics often say he likes the role of President more than the duties of the job. The grand spectacle, speeches, and events fuel Obama's self-image as a transformational leader. However, greatness in a president is defined by accomplishments that meet the challenges of the day. So far, on that scale, President Obama has fared badly, by pushing unpopular policies and failing to foster a strong economic recovery. President Obama had a chance to change this dynamic in the debt limit debate, but yet again the lure of podium and the television screen has gotten the better of him. He started the week working quietly to obtain a historic compromise on the budget, but ended with partisan maneuvers and public spectacles. Mr. Policy morphed into Mr. Hollywood yet again.

Last week ended with deep pessimism on the budget. Despite marathon meetings at the White House, no deal was emerging that could get through Congress, and increasingly the focus turned to escape hatch plans, like the one offered by Senator McConnell to place on burden on the President to raise the debt limit. But no sooner had despondency reached its greatest depths than hope started to emerge on two fronts. First came a plan from the Gang of Six, three Democrats and three Republicans Senators, that sought to cut the deficit by $3.7 trillion with a combination of spending cuts and tax reforms designed to increase revenue. The memo outlining the plan was presented to 50 Senators on July 19, initially garnering considerable support. Then, word leaked out that President Obama and Speaker Boehner had again begun secret negotiations on a grand bargain to cut more than $4 trillion in debt, initially with spending cuts and then tax reform that would yield additional revenue in the range of $800 billion. On paper, both plans looked like plausible solutions, then leadership failed.

Despite an endorsement from the President, the Gang of Six plan lost steam on the Republican side because some Senators and a large number of Republicans in the House would not accept the tax increases, and doubted the amount of the spending cuts. For liberal Democrats, the cuts to entitlements and other spending programs were too much to take. Likewise, the plan being secretly negotiated by the President and Speaker Boehner fell apart because a Democrat revolt against too much emphasis on spending cuts, leading to the President's July 22 demand for $400 billion more in revenue increases, leading to Speaker Boehner withdrawing from the talks on July 23. With only 11 days until hitting the debt limit, the federal government seemed paralyzed.

It is in moments such as these that Presidents are supposed to lead and force consensus, but Mr. Obama did neither. On Thursday, while making his demand for more tax increases, he took to the road for campaign-style town hall meetings, rather than hunkering down in the White House to forge a deal. Then, when Speaker Boehner pulls out of talks with the Administration, rather than trying to calm nerves he gave a Friday evening press conference attacking Republicans and trying to position himself for reelection. He then ordered House and Senate leaders to an 11:00 am meeting at the White House Saturday morning, for the obligatory photo shoot to show just how engaged and hardworking he is, while all opportunity for compromise melted away. In this time of potential crisis, the job of the President is to lead, but Mr. Obama opted for theatrics instead.

In many ways, President Obama is the victim of his own bad reputation among Republicans. Since being elected, nearly every decision he has made has been carefully calibrated to further his political standing. He forced through a stimulus bill with no bipartisan support to pay debts to his liberal base, employed procedural tricks to pass Obamacare despite unified Republican and substantial popular opposition, and used divisive political rhetoric during the 2010 campaign. As a result, few Republicans dare to work with him, and fewer still trust him. He could have overcome all this by working in good faith for a debt reduction deal, but he opted instead to use the present debt crisis as the kick-off for his 2012 presidential campaign, devoting more time to public relations than actual negotiation. So we have an abundance of speeches, photo ops, and press conferences on the debt crisis, but no plan from the White House and no compromise with Republicans. The power of the bully pulpit is great and his maneuvers might yield electoral gold, but Mr. Obama has failed in his first responsibility, which is to lead.

Week 132

(DESPERATION AND DESPAIR)

July 31, 2011

President Obama had hoped to use the debate over the debt limit increase to rebrand himself as a political moderate and good steward of public finances. He approached the whole issue more as a political campaign than a negotiation. He spent as much time giving press conferences, speeches, and doing campaign events, as he did negotiating. It was a good plan, talk about a balanced approach, reach out to moderates, and force a consensus. The President and his advisors probably had dreams of cheering independents dancing in their heads. But they forgot one critical item, first and foremost, voters want their President to be effective, and in this debate, effectiveness required a deal. That did not happen this week, with potentially dire consequences for everyone in Washington, including the President.

As last week was coming to a close, it looked like the President was close to achieving his goal of a big deal. After his highly publicized meetings with congressional leaders broke down, his secret talks with Speaker Boehner seemed near a comprehensive deal that would cut $4 trillion from future deficits with spending reductions and $800 billion in new revenues. But when liberals started hearing the details and demanded more revenues in the deal, the President had a choice. Do a deal or cater to his base. He went with his base, demanded $400 billion more in tax revenues, the deal fell apart, and Washington spun out of control. It seems the President was willing to play the effective moderate for the cameras and the campaign trail, but when it came time to make his choice, he chose his liberal base, and lost his advantage. What ensued was chaos, and chaos is never good for the chief executive. Speaker Boehner began working with his fractious caucus to craft a plan, while Senate Majority Leader Reid did the same in his chamber. All the while, the White House sat on the sidelines, watching the carnage. The first action came in the House, where Speaker Boehner put forth a plan calling for roughly $1 trillion in cuts for a corresponding increasing in the debt ceiling, requiring the President to come back to the Congress for yet another debt limit increase in early 2012. Boehner's plan was crafted to put maximum pressure on the President, while keeping his pledge to match any debt limit increase with spending cuts. He had hoped to pass the plan on July 27, but he had to pull the bill because Tea Party conservatives rebelled and demanded more cuts, especially after the CBO scored the bill as cutting less spending than the Speaker claimed.

In the Senate, Majority Leader Reid looked on with delight at Boehner's troubles. Reid had crafted a plan to raise the debt limit through 2012 using about $1 trillion in spending cuts and various budget gimmicks (including saving from wars already scheduled to end, changes in baselines, and interest savings) to claim cuts greater than the debt limit increase. Senator Reid used Boehner's problems in the House to obscure the simple reality that his plan could not pass the Senate. As July 29 started, it looked like there was no plan that could pass either chamber, and a default was starting to look like a real possibility. Then Boehner reached a deal with the Tea Party by adding to his bill a requirement for passage of a balanced budget amendment, and by that evening he got his bill through the House. Barely two hours later, the Senate killed the House bill, with a combination of votes from all the Democrats and seven conservative senators who objected to the absence of deeper spending cuts. Then on Saturday July 30, the House cast a symbolic vote rejecting the Reid plan by a wide margin.

As the week ended, the Senate had not yet even attempted to pass its own debt limit increase bill, and each chamber had rejected the proposal of the other. Rarely has Washington descended into such chaos on an issue of such national imperative. There was no leadership, just feuding factions and political posturing. Early in the debt limit debate, the perception was that President Obama had the better of the narrative as he spoke about a balanced approach to deficit reduction, but when his talks collapsed and events spun out of control, the Washington he presides over looked more dysfunctional than ever. Each faction entered the debt limit fight with its own agenda, Obama to look a moderate, the Tea Party to reduce government and break Obama, and the Democrats to raise taxes and protect entitlements. The problem is that voters see these agendas taking precedence over the national interest. So it is not surprising that polls throughout the process show falling voter approval for all involved, including the President, whose approval rating dropped to a new low of 40% in a Gallup poll at the end of the week.

With the debt limit deadline only three days off and Washington in a state of paralysis, President Obama's scheme to use this debate as a grand kick-off of his reelection campaign stood in ruins. It is clear that he will be injured by this debate, as will all others involved. With the opportunity for advantage gone, by late on July 30, there were whispers of new talks at the White House and progress on a compromise deal. In fact, prospects for a deal prompted Senator Reid to delay a planned July 31 vote on his plan. Even if a deal is reached, it will be too late and too compromised for anyone to be able to claim any great victory.

Week 133

(DEBT'ACHE)

August 7, 2011

Debt again dominated the week in Washington; debt deals, debt votes, debt downgrades and debt fallout. Rarely has the issue of government spending and government debt been more at the center of the public debate. Maybe that is a testament to the success of the Tea Party, or maybe it is simply the inevitable result of years of Washington mismanagement. Either way, government spending is the topic of the day, much to the chagrin and disadvantage of President Obama. Despite a debt deal that prevented default, the President was criticized from every corner, the stock market crashed, and by August 5, U.S. government debt lost its AAA rating for the first time in history. No doubt the President now has the mother of all debt aches.

The week began with the continued debate over raising the nation's debt limit. After a chaotic week of competing plans and votes rejecting each side's proposals, on July 31 a deal was finally struck. The ultimate compromise was a result of a melding of Senator Reid's plan calling for a debt limit increase sufficient to get through the 2012 election, and Republican demands for deeper cuts and an enforcement mechanism. The parties agreed to $900 billion in immediate cuts to support a commensurate increase in the debt limit, followed by a further $1.4 trillion increase in the debt limit balanced by a requirement of equal automatic spending cuts if a super committee fails to reach agreement on a plan for deficit reduction by the end of the year. The plan passed the House in a bipartisan vote on August 1 (with only the most liberal and conservative members voting no), and passed by an overwhelming margin in the Senate. The President signed the bill into law on August 2, thus avoiding a default.

Some in Washington may have thought that after the debt limit deal, Washington would have a moment to take its breadth and prepare for the next spending battles, namely the work of the super committee and the 2012 federal budget. Instead, the bottom fell out of the markets. After a mixed day on August 3, on August 4, the Dow Jones Industrial average lost 500 points due to fears over the U.S. economy and a growing debt crisis in Europe, with Italy and Spain increasingly at risk. Then, after a brief and modest recovery on August 5, the hammer blow struck when Standards & Poors downgraded U.S. debt, depriving U.S. bonds of their coveted AAA rating for the first time ever. Then, to make matters even worse for the President, on August 6, 31 U.S. soldiers were killed in Afghanistan (including many members of Seal Team 6 who helped kill bin Laden), when their helicopter was shot down by the Taliban.

It's hard to exaggerate the difficulty of the challenge now facing the President. He had hoped to use the debt debate to gain an advantage over his opponents, instead he has suffered a staggering blow. He seemed weak and irrelevant in the debt debate, unable to rein in the chaos, and now appears to be presiding over an economy on the brink of a double dip recession and possibly another financial crisis. The constant focus on government debt only highlights the public perception that the President is a big spender whose policies have put the nation in this plight. President Carter was ultimately viewed as a weak and irresolute leader who could not manage foreign or economic challenges, and President Obama is increasingly looking similar.

Last summer, the President declared the Summer of Recovery, only to see his economic hopes and midterm electoral goals dashed. He made no such rhetorical error this summer, he made a much more fundamental one. He pushed a debt confrontation with no plan, trusting entirely on his powers of persuasion. His tactics failed, Washington looked dysfunctional, and when a deal was finally reached, it was too late to restore confidence. The issue will now be whether he can reassert himself, calm the markets, and build a consensus to address the debt, jobs, and economic growth. If he cannot, his debt'ache will become incurable.

Week 134

(VOLATILE)

August 14, 2011

The private sector struck back this week against policymakers in Washington who have, from the market's perspective, mismanaged the public purse. After the downgrade of US debt after trading hours on Friday, on August 5, most expected a wild ride on Wall Street, and they got it. On Monday, the Dow Jones Industrial Average dropped more than 600 points, gained some 435 back on Tuesday, lost another 500 on Wednesday, and then posted gains on Thursday and Friday, resulting in only modest losses for the week. While the point loss turned out to be less troubling than many had feared, the huge volatility and trading volume reflected a panicky and nervous market, swinging wildly from losses to gains at the slightest provocation. All the while, policymakers could only watch as the markets drove the debate, making all look powerless, especially the President.

Clearly, the weak economy is a major threat to President Obama's reelection. In the prior week, the stock markets suffered substantial losses from bad economic data despite the deal on the debt limit. The decision by Standard & Poor's to downgrade federal debt gave yet another reason for pessimism in the markets. All the while, the Obama Administration stood seemingly powerless to bring any calm. As the markets tumbled on Monday, August 8, the White House said that the President would address the nation at 1:00 p.m., then moved the time to 1:30, with the President not appearing at the podium until nearly 2:00 p.m. When he did appear, he spoke haltingly and without conviction on the state of the economy, offering comments designed to deflect blame and gain political advantage. The President started by squarely blaming Republicans for the market's slide. The President then offered the same stump speech on the need for balanced policies to address the federal deficit and the economy, meaning higher taxes and more spending. The President took his usual shots at corporations and the wealthy, only tempering his rhetoric slightly by talking of those "most able to pay" rather than his usual attack line against oil companies and billionaires. As for specifics to improve the economy, the President had nothing to offer other than a request for more stimulus spending, extending unemployment payments and payroll tax cuts, and references to free trade deals that his Administration has slow-tracked at the behest of his union allies.

The President has been put in a very tight spot by the unexpectedly sputtering economy. He made jobs the measure of his own success, but he allowed his allies in Congress to pass a stimulus bill more designed to pay off Democrat allies that spur economic growth. He also pursued unpopular policies like health care reform that many believe have deterred hiring rather than improved it. It seems the President assumed that the economy would recover regardless of the policies coming out of Washington, so his Administration focused on Democrat legislative and regulatory priorities rather than job growth. The President assumed that by the Fall of 2010, and certainly by 2011, the economy would be back in high gear, ensuring good prospects for Democrats at the voting booths. But a funny thing happened on the way to the Democrats dreamed-of victories, they realized their policies impact the economy. This was an unhappy realization by the party of bigger and more activist government. For so long the Democrats just assumed that America's private sector would produce jobs and wealth, so their entire focus has been on how to take and redistribute that wealth. Having done so with reckless abandon during their 2 years of unhindered control in Washington, they have found that the wealth they so eagerly planned to take has been dissipated by those very policies.

It would be an overstatement to say that the Administration has killed the golden goose, but it has certainly broken one of its wings. Now, faced with a weak economy and high unemployment, politicians like President Obama, so used to using corporate America as a target, must try to make it an ally instead. The problem, which shown through in the President's speech on August 8, is that President Obama does not know how to be a cheerleader for the private sector. In fact, he is uncomfortable in that role. President Obama is a man who has always seen government as the source of solutions, but with the federal purse empty and skepticism of government at a high ebb, the President has few tools he can use to encourage economic and job growth. So he blames, attacks, offers the same old solutions, and evades any responsibility for himself.

The President's greatest advantage is the very resilience of the U.S. economy that his policies have done so much to test. Even with the week's volatile trading, there was some good news on spending and unemployment claims that gave hope that the economy is not so weak as was supposed. It is entirely possible that the economy will regain strength in the next 12 months, but that recovery will be despite, not because of, his Administration's policies. Nevertheless, the credit will go to the President, as will the blame if economy does not recover. It is all in the hands of the private sector now, with the President just a spectator, hoping for the best.

Week 135

(Getting Harry)

August 21, 2011

After a bruising debt ceiling battle and near panic selling on Wall Street, President Obama was likely eager to get out of Washington and start his three day bus tour of the Heartland. Starting in Minnesota, the President in his newly minted and armored black RV would travel through the Midwest, meet common folk, and show his concern for the average American. But what emerged was more an education on President Obama's plan for reelection that a true listening tour. With the economy rocky and his hold on voters ever weakening, it became clear the President was using this bus tour to test his newest campaign theme: better me than a do nothing Congress. It worked for Harry Truman, and Obama hopes it will work for him.

The White House's plan is simple: try to figure out a way to blame someone else for the poor state of the economy. The President had hoped to campaign on successful stimulus, health care reform, and jobs, but all three are a minefield of unpopularity. So in an ironic twist on Harry Truman, who famously said "The Buck Stops with Me," the President's new theme is "The fault lies with Them." Again and again on his bus tour, the President attacked Republicans and Congress in general for taking actions that have worsened the economy. He blamed the Republicans for putting party over country and tried to pin every lost job and every stock market drop on them. After erecting the premise that others are to blame, the President then announced that after Labor Day he would unveil a specific plan to grow the economy, create jobs, and reduce the deficit and challenged Congress to "Get it Done." The strategy of the Administration is simple, propose a plan that sounds good but cannot pass, and then use Congress's failure to act as the central plank in a campaign for reelection.

Harry Truman was very successful in 1948 running against a Republican Congress he accused on doing nothing to address the nation's needs. However, Truman ran for reelection soon after the Depression and the Second World War, when voters credited the federal government in general, and Democrats in particular, for navigating those very difficult times. In 2012, it is far from clear that Obama's blame Congress strategy can turn the tide in his favor. Most importantly, the President pushed through unpopular programs by overpromising the benefits. He said health care reform would create jobs, something no one thinks has happened. He said the stimulus bill would prevent unemployment from rising above 8%, but it currently stands at 9.1%. He promised that activist government would better peoples' lives, but instead distrust in government is at an all-time high. After promising so much, and delivering little, will voters really be so quick to just blame the other guy.

The Obama strategy seems to come down once again to his never failing belief in his own rhetorical skills. The President seems to think the voters will reelect him, even if his policies are unpopular, if he can paint his opponents as extremists responsible for the problem. Yet his own bus tour showed the vulnerabilities in that strategy. He said he would offer a plan to address the faltering economy in three weeks, as the stock market dropped 4% the week of his bus tour. He tried to portray himself as a man of the people, while traveling in an intimidating armored black RV. He said he would connect with normal folks, but his events were filled with hand-picked supporters, and even with that he got plenty of tough questions about his policies. And worst of all, while the nation was dealing with deep economic anxiety, the President was preparing for a 10-day vacation on the elitist bastion of Martha's Vineyard.

The President's performance on his bus tour was reminiscent of his campaign trips before the 2010 election, where he took to the road over and over again to test multiple varying ways to bash Republicans. Try as he might, he could never quite come up with the perfect rhetoric that could turn the tide in 2010. The same fate is before him in 2012. He cannot run on his record, because it is unpopular. He cannot run on the economy, because it is weak. So it seems his plan is to run against do-nothing Republicans, in the best tradition of Harry Truman. That strategy worked for that president, but whether voters will be so quick to blame the other guy this time is less clear.

Week 136

(States of Emergency)

August 28, 2011

Even the strongest critics of the President would admit that the last few weeks have been intense and difficult times for all the leaders in Washington. So while many criticized the length of the President's vacation (10 days) and its location (Martha's Vineyard), no one could begrudge him a bit of rest, no one except Mother Nature it seems. While the President was in Martha's Vineyard on August 23, a 5.8 strength earthquake struck central Virginia, doing little damage, but rattling residents of the East Coast, who are not used to seismic events. No sooner than the East Coast regained its footing after the earthquake, on August 27, Hurricane Irene struck all the states from North Carolina through New England with high winds, storm surges, and torrential rain. After being battered by Republicans, by the voters, and by commentators for his vacation choice, it seemed nature itself was taking a shot at the President.

We know from President Bush's experience from Hurricane Katrina that a bad federal response to a natural disaster can cause grievous political damage. President Obama himself suffered the same fate on a smaller scale with the Gulf Oil Spill, where a poor federal cleanup effort only highlighted the inadequacies in the federal emergency response system. There was little the federal government could have done about this week's earthquake, since it was wholly unexpected, and caused little damage in any event. But Hurricane Irene was a wholly different matter. The storm was being tracked for more than a week, as it gained strength and battered the Bahamas. When it became clear the storm would hit the East Coast, the President began giving press conferences from his vacation house on government preparations and eventually returned to Washington early from his vacation on August 26. President Obama was not going to look unprepared and uninterested as this hurricane hit the most heavily populated section of the United States.

In the end, the storm itself turned out to be more hype that true trouble. Hurricane Irene weakened to a category 1 storm by the time it made landfall, and its winds, while strong, did no damage on the scale feared. The storm's pounding rains turned out to be the worst aftermath of the hurricane, causing more flooding to an already rain-soaked region. Most concur the federal response was adequate, if not a bit overblown. However, President Obama could not afford to have taken the storm less seriously. No longer popular with voters, it is ever more important for the President to seem an effective leader. Also, since he is an advocate for the effectiveness of government, it was critical that in this instance government did its job well. The President even saw an opportunity to make a small political point about the storm, commenting on August 28, after the worst of the winds had pasted, that the federal response was an example of how good government can improve the lives of the people. The President was careful not to take that political point too far, but simply making it showed how his obsession with reelection is coloring everything he does. He survived this week's emergency unscathed, now he must turn from combating nature to overcoming political headwinds.

Week 137

(0-BAMA)

September 4, 2011

There was no pause for President Obama after his early return from his Martha's Vineyard vacation to deal with Hurricane Irene. The storm's heavy rains caused flooding throughout the Mid-Atlantic and Northeast, with New Jersey, New York, and Vermont particularly hard hit. The President put his focus on the emergency response, and took time out to tour the damage in New Jersey, but clearly his mind was on other matters, namely reelection. Several weeks during his Midwest bus tour, the President announced that after Labor Day he would present a new jobs plan to Congress. This week, the President planned to build expectations for his plan by selectively leaking portions of it and announcing that he would present it to a joint session of Congress. After a dispute with Speaker Boehner on the timing of the speech and a devastating jobs report on September 2 showing zero jobs created in August (and downgrading the job creation numbers for prior months), the President was on his heals yet again.

The United States is facing some of the worst persistent long-term unemployment since the Great Depression. Most agree that fixing the unemployment crisis will take many years and will be heavily impacted by international economic circumstances over which the federal government has little control. Given this, it is curious that President Obama has pinned his hopes of rebuilding his political standing on a new jobs plan. It is very unlikely that any plan can quickly cure the unemployment problem, and equally unlikely that the President's preferred solutions (most of which will come in the form of more stimulus spending) can pass Congress. Nevertheless, the President worked all week to build expectations for his speech, almost ensuring he will never be able to equal the hype. It seems President Obama is making the same mistake President George H. W. Bush made in 1991 and 1992, when facing a similar time of economic distress, he stoked expectations for his 1992 State of the Union address, only to find his plan deemed disappointing. President Obama is making the exact same mistake.

The White House will say they are not making any mistake, they are making a political calculation. The Administrations knows the economy is weak and the job market is stagnant, and it is unlikely that these circumstances will change sufficiently over the next 14 months to improve the perception of the President's performance on economic issues. So the White House's jobs plan is not about jobs at all, it is about blame. The President wants to make a speech setting forth a jobs plan that can never pass, and then when it does not pass and the economy stays weak, he can blame Republicans for the poor economy. The White House's strategy is insincere, calculated, and totally cynical.

The reality that politics is driving the President's jobs plan became evident this week when the White House announced that the plan would be presented to a joint session of Congress. Clearly, the President wants a political stage to make a campaign speech and attack the Republicans. But the Administration miscalculated when it tried to cleverly schedule the speech for September 7 to coincide with a long-scheduled Republican Presidential debate. The President's political advisors loved the imagery of the President being Presidential contrasted with bickering and debating Republicans. Speaker Boehner quickly saw the raw politics in the President's maneuver, and seized upon the White House's failure to clear the date for the speech to force the President to move his address to September 8. Instead of looking like a strong leader, President Obama was forced to yet again give in to Republicans and move the speech.

If the President truly wanted a bipartisan jobs bill, he would quietly engage Republicans to try to reach agreement on an approach to job creation. Rather than talk with Republicans, the President has already started to vilify them for opposing his jobs plan before he has even proposed it. Worse still, President Obama's new favorite attack line in his speeches is that Republicans need to put country ahead of party. Accusing the opposition of being unpatriotic if they do not agree with you is not an effective means to build a consensus. But in the end, President Obama is not looking for consensus, he is looking for a fight, and the Administration is doing everything they can to provoke one. Given this mentality, it is likely many in the Administration saw the "0" job growth report for August as an opportunity. The worse the job growth, the easier it is to blame Republicans when they do not enact the President's plan. Of course all this assumes that voters will exempt the President from responsibility for the poor economy, a risky assumption the White House appears ready to make.

Week 138

(THE STRAW MAN COMETH)

September 11, 2011

This week marked the formal opening of President Obama's re-rebranding and reelection campaign. Battered by a poor economy, falling support, and even rising criticism from the liberal wing of the Democratic Party, the Administration used an address to a joint session of Congress on September 8 to try to reframe the issues for the 2012 campaign, with President Obama playing the role of the crusader for jobs fighting a do-nothing Republican Congress. The plan unveiled in the President's address was impressive for its size and its audacity. A second massive stimulus bill costing $447 billion in the form of $250 billion in payroll tax cuts and hiring incentives, $100 billion in infrastructure projects, and nearly another $100 billion in bailouts for states and an extension in unemployment benefits. The President said the choice was between those who say government has no role in fixing the people's lives, and those like himself who want to aid the unemployed. Having built his straw man, and President gave a combative speech not designed to win support, but instead to provoke opposition. But the question arose, who is the straw man, the President's caricature of his opponents, or the President himself, who had to mount this audacious attack to reestablish his relevance.

Despite the strong public perception that the 2009 stimulus bill was a failure and that government spending is out of control, the President has gone to the stimulus well yet again. The White House assiduously avoided the word stimulus, but a big spending bill by any other name, is still the same. The President crafted his bill along the same lines as the 2009 stimulus, temporary tax cuts, bailouts for states and localities, and construction spending. Unlike 2009, the balance in this new stimulus bill slightly favors tax cuts, but the strategy and the tools are largely a repeat. In his speech, the President said every aspect of his bill had garnered bipartisan support before, and he repeatedly demanded the Congress pass his bill now, despite the fact that the Administration does not plan to even present a bill until the following week. He directly attacked his Republican critics by saying that they favor millionaires and billionaires, and want to dismantle basic protections for clean water and safe food. He did everything he could to start a fight, the problem was the Republicans were not biting this time.

The Republican leadership is on to the Administration's strategy of proposing a bill that will not pass, to only then blame Republicans for the sad state of the economy. They had hoped Republicans would come out swinging against the plan, allowing the President to bolster his caricature of them. But Speaker Boehner took a different tact. He offered no rebuttal to the President's speech, said the President's ideas merit consideration, and asked the White House to present a detailed plan that can be reviewed by the Congressional Budget Office. The muted response was by designed, because it will be harder for the President to demagogue Republicans if Republicans appear willing to consider the President's plan. The President wants a fight, and the Republicans are going to do their best not to give him one.

The President is always looking for the win-win scenario, and this most recent stimulus plan is no different. On the debt limit increase, the President's win-win was pushing for tax increases at the risk of default. If he got them, he would have created a civil war in the Republican Party. If he failed and default ensured, he could blame the Republicans for the economic fallout. But his game failed when it became clear the voters were blaming him as well for the debt limit stalemate, and in the end the President was not willing to risk a default. Republicans are hoping the same dynamic will play out this time. The President says he wants a jobs bill. The Republicans are betting they can craft a bill to their liking, without the spending and with measures that will improve business confidence, and force the President or his allies in the Senate to be the ones to kill it. The Republicans might even include a significant portion of the President's spending proposal, but link it to spending cuts or regulatory changes the White House will oppose. They are betting that they can outwit the President again by appearing cooperative.

As for President Obama, the September 8 job bill speech was another gambit to strengthen his reelection campaign. The economy could recover on its own before the 2012 election helping to ensure another 4 years, but the Administration is no longer willing to assume that. So instead, they have decided to provoke an ideological battle, creating a Republican straw man who wants to starve seniors, poison children, and enslave women, opposed to a benighted progressive leader who can bring us together under the mantel of shared sacrifice. To follow this plan, the President needs the Republicans to be radical, while he must risk being openly liberal, casting away on veneer of his supposed moderation. It is a play to his base, and a pitch to independents to reject mean-spirited conservatives. The man who ran on a platform to bring us together has decided a great ideological war, where he demonizes his opponents, is his best route to victory. And so it begins.

Week 139

(PANIC)

September 18, 2011

This week began with a solemn commemoration of the 10th anniversary of the September 11 attacks, and ended with a panic attack at the White House. The President had hoped to use this week to make the next key move in his reelection campaign. After unveiling his American Jobs Act to a joint session of Congress on September 8, on September 12, the President planned to explain how he would to pay for his latest stimulus bill. For those who still had a lingering hope that the President would try for a compromise to address high unemployment, it was dashed when the President proposed to pay for his plan entirely with new tax on high earners, including many tax proposals that were rejected by the Democrat Congress before the 2010 election. With this proposal, it became clear the President wants a campaign issue, not a jobs bill. But the President's planned narrative of a do nothing Congress got knocked off course by a series of blows that incited a near panic in the Democrat ranks.

The trouble started on Tuesday, September 13 with two special elections for vacant house seats, one in New York's Ninth District, a seat that has been Democratic since 1923, and another in Nevada's Sixth District, which leans Republican. Democrats assumed they would hold the New York seat, and saw the Nevada seat as an opportunity for an upset. Instead, Republicans won both seats, sending two very chilling messages to the Democrats. The Republican victory in New York showed that President Obama has become so unpopular with white blue collar Democrats that even a seat with a three to one Democrat voter registration edge is vulnerable. As for Nevada, the close race Democrats hoped for turned into a rout, with the Republican winning by 22 points. These victories showed weakness in safe Democrat districts and evaporating support for the Democrats in a swing state like Nevada. Although the Democrats tried to put on a brave face, calling these local elections driven by local issues, everyone knew the truth: the party had been dealt a shocking blow to its confidence.

Then scandal erupted in the halls of Congress and on the front pages of the national press concerning nearly $535 million taxpayer dollars lost in a failed stimulus loan to the now bankrupt solar panel company Solyndra. Emails were uncover showing that the White House pressed for approval of the loan despite warnings that the deal "was not ready for prime time" and that Solyndra would run out of cash by "September 2011." Nevertheless, the Administration twice pushed through the loan guaranties, resulting in a massive loss of taxpayer dollars that proved the warnings correct. Then, it was revealed that two major Obama donors were principal investors in Solyndra, raising the specter of a dirty political payout as the motivation for ill-conceived loans. With Americans already skeptical of the merits of the Administration's 2009 stimulus bill, the Solyndra controversy provided further ammunition to the opponents of continued federal stimulus.

Then at the end of the week, further bad economic news dominated the headlines, with reports that Bank of America and other financial institutions planned layoffs exceeding 60,000 people. This combined with further financial problems in Europe driven by the Greek debt crisis led to a growing consensus that the United States is increasingly likely to experience a double dip recession. While all this news was certainly bad for the President's political standing, no doubt some in the White House believe they can neutralize the economic issue if they can only succeed in blaming Republicans for failing to address the jobs crisis. But the events of the week knocked the Administration's plan off course, leading Democrat strategist James Carville to write an op-ed that it is time for the White House to panic, fire the incompetent political team, and prepare itself for a very tough reelection fight.

The White House's strategy was simple, propose yet another stimulus to bailout states, unions, and political supporters, claim it would create millions of jobs, and then blame Republicans when it does not pass. It sounds great on paper, but it assumes the public will be quick to exempt the President for responsibility for the bad economy. We saw from the debt limit debate that even though Republicans were blamed more for the impasse, the President was hurt as well because the voters expect presidents to rise above the fray and get things done. When Washington fails, presidents always get some of the blame. President Obama hoped to change this dynamic by proposing a plan that sounds good but cannot pass, and then persuading the public that Republicans are so radical, unreasonable, and devoted to protecting the rich that they cannot be trusted in the White House, no matter how unhappy voters are with the Administration's performance. The sad part of this strategy is its cynicism. Rather than trying to reach a deal to improve the economy, the President is willing to risk higher unemployment and a worse economy just to trap the Republicans. In essence, the President is putting his personal political interests ahead of the national interest, but that plan can only work if he can keep his troops in line before panic sets in.

Week 140
(CAMPAIGNING WHILE ROME BURNS)

September 25, 2011

While the nation faced increasing problems at home and abroad, the President spent his week campaigning, seemingly oblivious to the mounting threats around him. The President started the week with the next move in his carefully crafted chess game to win reelection. After proposing his jobs bill and a massive tax increase to pay for it, on September 19, the President announced his plan for long-term deficit reduction. Then, after a speech at the UN General Assembly, the President was scheduled to travel to a decaying bridge between Kentucky and Ohio (with the White House claiming it was only a coincidence that these are the home states of the Republican leaders of the House and Senate) to highlight the need for more infrastructure stimulus, only then to head out West for no less than 7 fundraisers. A very busy political schedule for a President who apparently has no actual governing to do.

For a White House focused on politics, it was no surprise that the week began with another politically motivated policy proposal. Like his budget offered in April 2011, the President's deficit reduction plan offered on September 19 was a political document, not a plan to address the debt crisis. Relying on yet more tax increases not supported by many Democrats, gimmicks (like counting saving from wars already scheduled to end), and double counting the deficit reductions to be addressed by the Congressional Super Committee, the President claimed his plan would cut the deficit by nearly $4 trillion. In fact, the plan contained less than $400 billion in cuts over ten years, avoided structural changes to Medicare or Social Security, and called for spending to remain at nearly 25% of GDP for the foreseeable future. The plan was so bad that most of the major print media, except for the *New York Times*, panned it. No matter, the only purpose of the plan was to give the President another chance to bash the rich and Republicans, and further the fiction that the deficit problem can be solved without reforming entitlements or significantly reducing spending. Then the President hit the road to continue the reelection effort.

His first stop was New York City, to shore up support from Jewish voters by playing the role of the steadfast supporter of Israel, despite nearly three years of asserting moral equivalency between Israel and the terrorists who attack it. Ironically, the President was forced to defend Israel vigorously this week, because his prior lukewarm support had encouraged the Palestinian Authority to seek formal recognition as a State from the UN. Knowing he would further threaten his Jewish support if he did not stand up for Israel this time, the President offered an impassioned defense of Israel, but it was too late, because the Palestinian Authority asked for statehood recognition anyways, meaning the US will likely have to veto the resolution if it passes.

After this brief policy foray, the rest of the week was all politics, all the time. The Administration's entire focus was on speeches bashing Republicans, photo-ops pushing for more stimulus, and fundraisers to fill his war chest. All to further the campaign strategy of blaming Republicans for the economy and painting them as too radical to be trusted. Yet while the President was focused on his personal political fortunes, America saw yet more threats. Abroad, the US embassy in Pakistan was attacked, apparently with the support of the Pakistani intelligence service. At home, the stock market had its worst losses in three years, fueled by gloomy statements from the IMF and the Federal Reserve, a Census Bureau report on falling household incomes and rising poverty, and further fears of a Greek debt default. The stock market lost more than $1 trillion in value.

The President made few comments on these events, and certainly took no bold action to address them. Instead, he stuck to his plan of proposing things that please his base, even if they cannot pass and will not create jobs or aid the economy. The week ended with yet another impasse between the House and Senate on a spending bill to keep the government open through November 30, but again the President made no effort to effect a compromise. In the end, it seems the President has written off the economy, compromise, even dialogue with Republicans. He has replaced those things with obvious political calculations and shrill speeches. In these tough times, the nation needs a President, but unfortunately all it has is a campaigner.

Week 141

(SUPREME RISK)

October 2, 2011

As the President continued his political barnstorming campaign doubling down on populist liberal rhetoric as the salvation of his political fortunes, his Administration made a curious decision this week that will inject a huge and unpredictable issue into the 2012 campaign, namely health care reform. Lawsuits have been filed across the nation challenging health care reform, with the Administration prevailing in the Sixth Circuit, getting a favorable ruling finding the challengers lack standing in the Fourth Circuit, and losing an appeal brought by 26 states in the Eleventh Circuit. The only case that could have been heard by the Supreme Court in time before the 2012 election was the Eleventh Circuit case, but the Obama Administration could have delayed that appeal by seeking full court, or en banc, review of that decision. However, the White House took no such appeal and instead quickly asked the Supreme Court to review the constitutionality of health care reform, thus almost ensuring a ruling before the election.

The reason this decision is so curious is because for the last two months every decision by the White House on major policy issues has been solely and completely focused on electoral advantage for 2012. The second stimulus bill, the President's budget proposal, the speech to a joint session of Congress, and the President's call for $2 trillion in new taxes have all been calibrated to further the President's campaign objectives. The President wants to blame the Republicans for the bad economy and re-energize his base, so he has put forth an unabashedly liberal policy agenda that cannot pass. Merely making the proposals pleases liberals, while their failure gives the President the opportunity to blame Republicans. It is the very predictable Obama win-win strategy.

Given this track record, one must assume the White House sees some kind of win-win scenario for the health care reform appeal. It is hard to believe that the Administration allowed the appeal to proceed because they thought it was the right thing to do when everything they have done of late has been politically motivated. So where is the political advantage for the President in pushing forward a Supreme Court's ruling on the constitutionality of health care reform. No doubt the White House believes if the law is upheld it will enhance the President's stature as an effective leader, while if it is overturned, it will outrage liberals and bring them to the polls to support the President. A clever strategy except for the fact that it bears no relation to reality.

The health care reform law is deeply unpopular with voters, with strong majorities opposing the law and a plurality of voters hoping it will be overturned. Given that the law is unpopular, there can be no upside for the President in a Supreme Court decision, no matter how it turns out. If the law is overturned, it will show Obama as an ineffective and incompetent leader who spent much of his presidency pushing for a law that was unconstitutional when he should have been focused on the economy. If the law is upheld, a majority of voters will be unhappy and electing a Republican will be the only hope of stopping Obamacare. Either result will help the President's opponent more than it will help him.

The decision to allow the appeal to proceed reveals an unwillingness by the President to accept that the voters have rendered their verdict on Obamacare: they oppose it. The President seems to believe that when faced with the prospect of losing the reform, the voters, or at least his liberal base, will rally to him. It is a strategy founded in Obama's supreme self-confidence and stubborn adherence to ideology. However, the Administration has taken a supreme risk in allowing the highest court to rule on the law before the election, and may end up paying the supreme price at the ballot box.

Week 142

(PRE-OCCUPIED WITH WALL STREET)

October 9, 2011

The President continued his campaign attacks on Republicans this week in an effort to redirect the blame for the faltering economy, but it was a protest movement that started in New York City, not the President's fiery speeches, that caught the nation's attention. For the last 23 days, a leaderless and initially spontaneous protest movement that started in lower Manhattan under the name Occupy Wall Street has gone national, with protests springing up in major cities across the nation. The movement has no central theme or agenda beyond a vague notion that the current economic system in the United States is unfair. That premise alone has been enough to galvanize a growing army of adherents. Initially attracting students and the twenty-something unemployed, the movement has now grown to include an array of progressive constituencies. While it is true that the President has been preoccupied with attacking the affluent (for which Wall Street is a powerful symbol), the White House is not behind the Occupy Wall Street movement. Nevertheless, the Administration is desperately trying to decide if the movement is an ally or a threat. However, that will turn on the course of the movement, not the choice of the White House.

President Obama has repeatedly taken a populist tone during his Presidency, especially when he has been under political threat. During the health care debate and in the 2010 election, the President ramped up his rhetoric to try to fire up his base and defeat his opponents. He succeeded in health care by pushing his bill through at a terrible political cost, but failed in the 2010 midterm, where his party was soundly defeated. Now with his own reelection looming and after being badly damaged in his deficit fights with Republicans, the President has gone to the populist well again, using denunciations of millionaires, billionaires, private jet owners, oil companies, and Wall Street risk takers. The irony is that many of those under attack are the same people the President is asking to create new jobs. No matter, the President is pursuing his own "the people against the powerful" theme no matter the cost.

We had yet another display of the President's strategy with an October 6 press conference from the East Room at the White House, where the President repeated all his favorite attack lines and threatened Republicans with political retribution if they did not vote of his jobs bill. The President's press conference was just more political theater, but it took on a different importance with the rise of the Occupy Wall Street movement. Leaders who delve into populism always risk that their rhetoric might overheat the populace, leading to civil unrest and possibly violence. In this respect, it is an unhappy coincidence for the Administration that the Occupy Wall Street movement has taken on national prominence just as the President's rhetoric has gotten most heated. If the protests lead to property destruction, rioting, or other violence, the White House will be exposed to potential blame because of the President's attacks on business interests. However serious the risk, the opportunity is equally significant. Republican victories in 2010 were powered by the Tea Party. With sagging popularity and a bad economy, the White House was facing a difficult task getting the enthusiasm of the President's supporters to match that of his opponents. If the Occupy Wall Street movement continues to grow, it offers the chance for the President to harness its enthusiasm for his advantage, but to do so the President must embrace the protests and become their political outlet.

For a President always looking for the win-win scenario, the Occupy Wall Street movement is an unwelcome risk/reward moment. Yet if the economy remains bad and his popularity does not recover, he may have to risk endorsing the movement, or he might have to forgo the reward of reelection.

Week 143

(RAISING CAIN)

October 16, 2011

Currently, the two most prominent black politicians in the United States are a study in contrasts. The first is President Obama, raised by white grandparents, a product of private schools and elite universities, a community organizer, a career servant of government, and an unabashed believer in the state's ability to improve people's lives. The other is Herman Cain, who grew up poor, worked his way up in the private sector to become CEO of Godfather's Pizza, a devout Christian and part-time minister, and a true skeptic of the curative powers of government. With Obama, we have a politician who reached his zenith in the perfect moment of the 2008 election, and since taking office has seen his popularity decay as his big government philosophy failed to reignite the economy. With Cain, who is running for president despite never having held political office, we have a rising star with a message nearly opposite that of the President. Which man's philosophy captures the hearts of the voters will determine the future course of the nation.

The scope of the clash of philosophies between Obama and Cain was on full display on October 11. On that day, the Senate defeated the President's spending and tax laden jobs plan, while Cain the same day promoted a radical restructure of the tax code during a Republican presidential debate. For the President, the defeat of his jobs bill was just another step in his campaign to blame Republicans for the bad economy. With nearly half a billion in temporary tax cuts and spending, balanced with an equal amount of permanent tax increases, the bill was designed to cast government as the economic savior, while showing Republicans as heartless protectors of the rich. The plan made for great populist rhetoric, but very poor legislating. Even the Democrats in the Senate majority lacked the votes to pass it, and had to revamp the tax increases by adding a 5.6% surtax on incomes over $1 million to get support in their caucus. Even with that change, the Senate voted only 50-49 to advance the bill, 10 votes short of the 60 required, and even then three of the yes votes (Webb, Manchin, and Lieberman) said they would oppose the final bill. Indeed, to even get to a vote, Majority Leader Reid had to employ the so-called nuclear option, using a procedural trick to deny Republicans the opportunity to offer an amendment that would have forced the Democrats to vote on the President's bill. The President's bill had so little support, Senator Reid was willing risk infuriating the minority Republicans just to avoid a vote on it. So legislation that was never designed to pass did exactly what it was supposed to do: fail.

Armed with the failure of his own legislation, the President now had yet another pretext to ramp up his demagoguery, campaigning, and fundraising. He hoped the heartless Republicans would be the story of the week, but instead the attention was on a different black politician. Herman Cain has long been viewed as an interesting and affable fringe candidate in the Republican field. A great speaker with a great story and a clear policy view, most believed his lack of experience and money would keep him in the second tier. Yet, when Texas Governor Rick Perry faltered in the debates, conservative and Tea Party voters starting looking for alternatives, and Cain has been the beneficiary. He won a straw poll in Florida, has replaced Perry in second place in the polls after former Massachusetts Governor Mitt Romney, and has now changed the Republican contest to a three man race. While the President has been touring the country calling for ever bigger government and ever higher taxes, Cain's campaign has caught fire with his 9-9-9 plan, which calls for cutting personal and corporate tax rates to 9 percent while instituting a 9% national sales tax. Cain says his plan would save the nation half a trillion dollar in tax compliance costs, restore economic growth, and make America competitive. The exact same agenda espoused by President Obama, but pursued with nearly opposite policies.

There are many ways to read the Cain phenomenon. Some say it is just a sign of instability in the Republican field, with conservatives lurching to any alternative in an endless quest for the perfect anti-Obama. Others say it is sign of Romney's weakness. Still others claim it is just an effort by the Tea Party to show they are not racist. There may be some truth in these theories, but the true source of Cain's growing strength is something deeper, a thorough skepticism of government and politicians that makes a no nonsense political outsider and businessman an appealing candidate. The fact that he is black only makes Cain more enticing, because he is an even more stark contrast with the President. It is too early to tell if the rise of Cain will have a lasting impact, but it certainly demonstrates again that the 2012 election will be a battle of different philosophies about government, which is what elections should be about.

Week 144

(REJOICING RETREAT)

October 23, 2011

One of the consequences of America's economic decline is our increasing difficulty projecting power. Economic power translates into political and military power, and with the United States' economy weak for a third consecutive year, the nation's ability to maintain its global influence in waning. This fact is most evident by observing China, which is openly flaunting its power and taking provocative steps to annoy Washington. But this week, we saw evidence of declining American power in the Middle East, with America celebrating the ousting of Qaddafi in Libya by a NATO effort and touting the withdraw of all United States forces from Iraq, a move that will weaken the Iraqi democracy and increase the influence of Iran. So the week saw America in retreat in the Middle East, which could be just the beginning of the decline of the United States' global influence overall.

It is no coincidence that the Middle East has often been the graveyard of empires. The region has always been a strategic crossroads, and with the increasing importance of oil, it has become the center of international power politics. For more than 100 years, Britain was the lead power in the Middle East, holding sway over Egypt, Mesopotamia, and the Arabian Peninsula. After two world wars, Britain tried to maintain its influence in the Middle East, but after the 1956 Suez crisis and the high cost of maintaining bases in the region, Britain ceded its position to the United States. This was an admission that Britain was no longer a first rank global power. The United States has not yet reached that point, but troubling signs are emerging that we are on the same course as Britain.

In Libya, the United States took the position that Qaddafi was a danger to the region and his people and had to be removed from power. However, when it came time for action, the United States refused to lead the effort, instead deferring to Britain and France, which were leading the charge for military intervention in Libya. The result was a NATO air campaign supported by the United States, where America provided logistical support and limited number of initial combat stories, but where the heavy lifting was done by our allies. This result was a sputtering campaign that dragged on for many months and likely led to far more loss of life and property than would have occurred if the United States had directly intervened. Ultimately, Tripoli was taken and Qaddafi was ousted, and finally on October 20, his last stronghold of Surte was taken and Qaddafi was killed. No doubt the mission was a success, but it was equally clear that the United States did not take its usual leadership role because of the cost of the effort and domestic resistance to yet another foreign intervention. The President praised the success in Libya, but ignored the clear implication that a powerful and prosperous United States would never have tolerated such a ragtag effort.

If Libya was a troubling sign, Iraq was a gaping admission of declining American influence in the Middle East. The United States launched the Iraq invasion in 2003 and after nearly a trillion spent and more than 4000 lives lost we were ready to enter a new phase as the guardian of the fragile Iraqi democracy. While President George W. Bush signed the treaty calling for the withdrawal of all United States troops from Iraq by the end of 2011, everyone expected that a small American force would remain to train Iraqi troops and deter Iran from trying to increase its already substantial influence. The Obama Administration never supported the war effort, but acted responsibly in conducting the withdrawal. However, the White House dragged its feet on starting final negotiations on a residual force to remain in Iraq, leaving insufficient time to reach a deal to allow some forces to stay. With time running out and negotiations at an impasse, the President announced a complete withdrawal on October 21.

The President tried to portray the withdrawal as a campaign promise kept and a victory, but the truth was obvious to most observers. With no America forces in Iraq, its government would be more vulnerable and Iran would have a clear opening to increase its influence. The fact that President Obama described this result as a "success" showed how far America has declined as a power in the region. As in Libya, the United States now seems more concerned with removing its forces and conserving resources than in protecting its vital interests. This is the hallmark of a declining power. With a weak economy, massive deficits, and a President unwilling to project power, it is no surprises we are reduced to praising retreat.

Week 145

(HE CAN'T WAIT)

October 30, 2011

It is a curious thing to observe a White House entirely devoted to campaigning rather than governing. Ever since the failure of President Obama's debt ceiling talks over the summer, it appears the Administration has decided that campaigning is its only option. The strategy started with the President's jobs plan, where he refused to meet with the Republicans, offered a plan that mirrored his 2009 stimulus bill, and then proposed to pay for it entirely with new taxes. It was a strategy designed for failure to fuel campaign slogans. Now the Administration has entered phase two of its reelection strategy. After trying to establish the premise that do nothing Republicans in Congress will not act to aid the economy, the President is now stepping in to save the day. The President is touting his new strategy under the slogan "We Can't Wait."

The President began his "We Can't Wait" campaign earlier this month by granting states waivers to the No Child Left Behind education law, allowing states to opt out of portions of the law. This was sold by the White House as an education reform that will help train our kids for the economy of the future, when in reality it was the result of a failure to pass comprehensive education reform. Now this week, the President took his campaign to Nevada and Colorado. It is no coincidence that the White House chose two swing states to unveil its latest initiatives. With many political observers concluding that southern states like Florida and North Carolina might be out of reach for the President in 2012, the White House is looking to western states for the margin of victory.

Las Vegas was the first stop, where the President announced his latest program to help struggling homeowners. Nevada is ground zero for the housing crisis, with some of the highest unemployment and foreclosure rates in the country. In 2009 the Administration launched its first program to help homeowners, but it has done little to assist the millions who are unable to pay for their homes. The same is true for the program announced on October 24, although it was unveiled as a dramatic initiative. The President's latest program, done by executive order, allows homeowners to refinance even if their mortgages are 25% more than their home values, lowers closing costs, and provides more options to shop for lower rates. The problem is, these proposals only apply to those holding mortgages backed by Fannie Mae or Freddie Mac, only about 10% of outstanding mortgages. So out of the approximately 11 million troubled mortgages, only about 1 million would benefit. So like his 2009 mortgage initiative, this program will have a limited economic impact, but that does not matter since it is the political impact that the President cares about.

The next stop on the We Can't Wait tour was another swing state, Colorado, where on October 26, the President announced an initiative on student loan repayment. Clearly, the White House was responding to the Occupy Wall Street movement, since the burden of student debt is one of the protestors' major complaints. The President announced that by executive order he would speed student loan reforms passed in 2010. First, starting in 2012 students would only have to devote 10% of their incomes to repayment of student loans. Second, loan forgiveness would be triggered after 20 years (not the 25 under current law). These steps will have a marginal impact on the burden of student loans since they only impact federal (not private) student loans and represent only incremental charges over current law. No matter, since the objective of the proposal is political. This was clear from the President's speech, where he pivoted between his proposals and calls for students to support his campaign. With youth voters suffering the worst from the economy, the White House needs ways to motivate them to vote for Obama, and this was the first foray in that effort.

No doubt, the "We Can't Wait" campaign, with its clever play on the "Yes We Can" theme from the 2008 campaign, is an artful political maneuver. President these days is all about artful politics, not policy. It appears the White House has given up on actual legislation, and instead just wants to raise money and campaign. That means that the next 12 months will be about politics, and portends a poisoned political environment even if the President is reelected.

Week 146
(GREEK-20)

November 6, 2011

The G-20, the leaders of the 20 largest economic powers, gathered in Cannes, France this week to discuss the state of the world economy. But instead, Greece hijacked the meeting, highlighting how the Greek debt crisis threatens the entire worth economic order. For President Obama, already weakened because of the stagnant United States economy, the Greece crisis was an unwelcomed reminder that forces outside the President's control are impacting the economic environment. When a small country of barely 10 million people is the focus of worldwide economic concern, the interdependence of the world economy becomes clear. For a President who needs an improving economy to get reelected, relying on leaders in Athens to make responsible choices is hardly comforting.

The genesis of the Greek debt crisis was easy credit, much like the financial crisis that hit the United States in 2008. After joining the EU, buoyed by the EURO, Greece gained access to credit to fund public infrastructure and its welfare state. For years, Greece borrowed and borrowed, spent and spent, and reported and reported healthy finances. Eventually, it became clear that Greece was not being honest about its finances and with the world recession, Greece started running out of money to pay its lenders and to finance basic public expenditures. The IMF and the EU stepped in with various rescue packages, culminating in a package crafted this week by German Chancellor Merkel and French President Sarkozy that would have made further funds available to Greece in return for severe austerity measures, measures Greece has heretofore resisted. The plan was put in place before the G-20 meeting, to allow the host President Sarkozy to take credit and refocus the meeting on other concerns. But like many well-made plans, it quickly fell apart.

As the G-20 leaders were meeting in Cannes, the carefully crafted rescue plan for Greece fell apart when Greek Prime Minister George Papandreou unexpectedly called for a national referendum on the rescue plan. This move, likely designed to save the career of the Prime Minister, threw the entire rescue plan in doubt. Many believed that if allowed to vote, the Greeks would vote down the rescue plan because of the austerity measures it contains. That would result in a Greek default, Greece dropping the EURO, and a general increase in borrowing costs across Europe. Once the referendum plan was announced, the G-20 went into crisis mode, with world leaders pressuring Papandreou to drop the referendum plan. Faced with this mounting pressure, by week's end Papandreou dropped the referendum plan and announced efforts to form a unity government to guide the country through its economic crisis.

In the end, the G-20 leaders were able to navigate the latest stage of the Greece crisis, but if Greece can do so much to roil the world markets, what about the other troubled European economies. Ireland and Portugal have already received bailouts, and Spain and Italy are also hard pressed by their lenders. Most believe Spain is now less at risk because of actions taken by its government to control spending, but Italy is a different story. Italy has the third largest economy in Europe, and Italian Prime Minister Silvio Berlusconi was at the G-20 meeting, so the Greece crisis also put attention on him. Berlusconi's vague comments about reform garnered little support at the G-20 meeting and he was pressed by world leaders to adopt real reforms. With 2.6 trillion in public debt and rising borrowing costs, Italy may be too big to bailout, so the necessity for Italy to get its fiscal house in order cannot be overstated. Few trust Berlusconi to take the necessary steps, so the Greece crisis may just be a prelude to an even more dangerous debt issues.

The transformation of the G-20 into the Greek-20 was a reminder of the vulnerability of the world economy to bad sovereign debt. A significant national default will raise commodity prices and borrowing costs, cause a run on stock markets, and further hurt confidence. For that reason, the European debt crisis must be solved. Certainly President Obama does not relish conversations about public debt, since he has added so much of that debt in the United States, but navigating this debt crisis is critical for him because of its direct impact on the U.S. economy.

Week 147

(FEELING BLUE)

November 13, 2011

Since the 2008 election, which was a triumph for the President and the Democrats, most of the election news for the President's allies has been bad. Other than winning various special elections for the House, the Democrats have been punished at the polls. In 2009, Republicans won convincing victories in gubernatorial elections in New Jersey and Virginia, then in January 2010 Republican Scott Brown won Edward Kennedy's senate seat in Massachusetts, and then the Democrats suffered a true wipeout in the 2010 midterms. Inevitably, when one party is on the rise, eventually there is a backlash. The Democrats have been suffering from that backlash for the last two years, but now there are signs that Blue America may be on the rise again.

There were no major federal or state offices up for election in the 2011 season. Instead, the November 8 elections were a mix of referenda and state legislative races in Virginia. While the outcomes were mixed, most of the high profile votes broke for the Democrats. In biggest vote was in Ohio, where a ballot measure calling for the repeal of restrictions on collective bargaining rights for public sector unions passed with more than 60% support. Then in the evangelical heartland of Mississippi, voters rejected a referendum that would have established personhood at conception. Next, Maine rejected tougher voter registration rules that would have required registration at least two days before an election. Election night was not entirely bleak for the GOP, for example in Virginia Republicans won the State Senate, and complete control of Virginia state government for the first time since reconstruction.

No doubt these results were driven in part by local issues and local concerns, but political observers see in these results a trend line that might be helpful for President Obama. The last two years have been dominated by debates on taxes, spending, and the power of the federal government. Ideal territory for Republicans. But as Republicans won elections and began driving the agenda, a reaction has developed against the more aggressive parts of the Republican agenda. In Ohio, limits on collective bargaining rights, even for police and firefighters, were repudiated with help from national public sector unions, which spent more than $30 million to support the ballot measure. In Mississippi, opponents of defining personhood at conception pointed out that the measure would outlaw most forms of contraception, leading to defeat of that measure even in a deeply conservative state. But the question is, do these results portend a better political environment for the Democrats.

No doubt in recent weeks the public narrative has shifted from government spending to job and income inequality. The rise of the Occupy Wall Street movement may be more of the cause of this trend that the President's heated populist rhetoric, but either way this story line serves the political interests of the White House. Combined with the disarray and infighting in the Republican campaign, including the sexual harassment allegations against Herman Cain, the current environment has given some momentum to the Administration. However, it is not clear that the President can maintain this narrative through November 2012. Eventually, the Republicans will pick a standard bearer, and ironically all the problems plaguing the Republican field, like the fumbles of Congresswoman Michelle Bachmann, Perry, and Cain, are only strengthening more mainstream candidates like Mitt Romney. So a short term benefit for the President might only lead to a stronger opponent. Likewise, the Occupy Wall Street protests are interesting at the moment, but if they turn violent or more radical, they could easily backfire on the Administration. And most disturbingly, the President's poll results on the economy continue to get worse, even as economic news gets slightly better. So this Blue state resurgence might just be a brief hiatus in the President's political decline.

Week 148
(PACIFIC POWER)

November 20, 2011

It has been clear for weeks that President Obama had no intention of getting knee deep in another budget battle with Republicans. Instead, he has opted for harsh rhetoric and aggressive fundraising, rather than working for any kind of fiscal compromise. Given this approach, the President's extended trip to Asia could not have been better timed, because it got him out of Washington for the final full week of congressional super committee deliberations on reducing the federal budget deficit. The problem is, the President hoped to use his trip to the Pacific rim to project American power and leadership, but his weakness at home undermined his efforts. As a result, rather than reaffirming America's Pacific power, he returned empty handed.

The President's Pacific trip started with San Diego, where he visited a docked aircraft carrier to salute veterans and watch a college basketball game played on the flight deck. The visit was designed to be a subtle reminder of America's Pacific sea power. The President next travelled to his native Hawaii, where America was hosting for the first time in 20 years the Asia-Pacific economic forum. During the meeting, he pressed for a new Pacific free trade zone including eight Pacific powers. Several nations showed some interest, including Japan, Canada, and Mexico, but no deal was reached. The President then travelled to Australia, America's most dependable ally in the Pacific. While there, he announced a plan to permanently base 2500 US Marines in Northwestern Australia, a move designed to show America's military commitment to its ally and to warn China against any aggressive moves. The trip then took Obama to Indonesia where he presided over a major sale of Boeing aircraft and where he held a surprise meeting with the Chinese President. Also, during the trip Secretary of State Hillary Clinton made another surprise visit, this one to Myanmar to meet with leaders of the democracy movement there.

It was an ambitious and multifaceted trip, and no doubt necessary for American interests in the Pacific. The undercurrent of the entire tour was the need to counter the rising influence of China. Ever since World War II, the United States has been the unrivaled power in the Pacific. Japan, South Korean, and Australia have all flourished under the umbrella of American protection. But U.S. influence has recently waned, as we have focused more and more on the Middle East in the wake of September 11, and as economic troubles at home have weaken U.S. influence. Now, there is an increasing perception that the U.S. is being supplanted as regional hegemon by China.

The President's trip was designed to counter that perception by showing leadership on trade and making military commitments in Australia. Unfortunately, the U.S. is hampered in all these efforts by its weakness at home. With soaring deficits, high unemployment, and weak economic growth, the ability of the United States to project power in the face of a rising China is limited. In reality, if President Obama really wanted to counter China, he would have stayed at home to force a deficit reduction compromise, because it is the U.S. fiscal situation more than anything else that is hindering our ability to project power abroad. However, staying home and doing the work of budget compromise is both harder and more risky than travelling around Asia giving grand speeches. So the President toured Asia, while talks to tame the deficit collapsed back in Washington. After touting Pacific Power, he returned to a Washington weaker than the one he left only a week before.

Week 149

(SUPERBUST)

November 27, 2011

While the President was flying around Asia, the vaunted congressional super committee formed to address the federal deficit crashed on the rocky shores of partisan politics. The super committee was formed as part of the debt limit increase deal. That deal called for approximately $1 trillion in immediate spending cuts, and created the super committee to find an additional $1.2 trillion in savings. The super committee was composed of six Senators and six Representatives, with equal representation from each party. If the super committee is able to create a deficit reduction plan that can garner majority support, the bill presented by the committee would be voted on by each house of Congress without amendment or filibuster. To create an incentive for Democrats to make a deal, if no proposal passed the super committee, an automatic sequester of $1.2 trillion in across-the-board cuts to discretionary spending would ensue. To induce Republicans to compromise, 50% of the cuts would come from defense, something Republicans are eager to avoid. At the time of its formation, it sounded like a super plan, but it turned out to be a superbust.

The very formation of the super committee was an admission that Washington is broken. Whenever Congress has to resort to automatic mechanisms to force through painful legislation, it means the ordinary political process is not working. A famous example is the base closing commission, which is empowered to suggest military base closures, and its proposals must be voted up or down by each House, taking some of the heat off politicians who fear the repercussions of closing a popular local military base. The super committee took this approach to a new level by entrusting Congress's fundamental power of the purse to an automatic trigger of spending cuts.

The technique was employed because the parties and their leaders were unable to reach a compromise on taxes and spending because each party was more focused on budget politics than budget responsibilities.

This was especially true for President Obama. The White House hoped to use the debt limit debate over the summer of 2011 to break the power of congressional Republicans. By constantly condemning Republican budget priorities and repeatedly calling the congressional leadership to the White House for tongue lashings, the President hoped to portray Republicans as dangerous radicals, while showing himself as a reasonable moderate. The stalemate that ensued was the natural result of the President's tactics. The President even scuttled a deal nearly reached with Speaker Boehner when at the last minute he demanded a much larger tax increase. The President expected that all of these maneuvers would improve his public standing, but he was wrong. Markets crashed, default was briefly a possibility, and in the end a rushed deal that did not address the longer term deficit was the best our leaders could accomplish. Our government looked dysfunctional and incompetent, and while Congress was mostly blamed, the President suffered as well.

With this hard lesson learned, the Administration was not going to again risk getting mired in a budget morass. The super committee was formed and the White House made clear it was their job alone to come up with a budget plan. The President took to the road to raise campaign cash and condemn Republicans as friends of the privileged, while making no attempt to support the success of the super committee. Just before leaving for Asia, the President made brief calls to the leadership of the committee, but that was public relations, not an effort to help forge a deal. By law, the super committee had to offer its plan by November 23 or the automatics cuts would go into effect beginning January 1, 2012. The President returned from Asia only three days before the deadline, and even when back in Washington, other than some public calls for a deal, he made no effort to force a compromise. Taking their queue from the President, the Democrats held out for huge tax increases, the Republicans said no, and the committee failed.

Having once gotten burned by getting knee deep into budget negotiations, the White House decided it was better politics to not engage. If a deal was reached it could take the credit. If no deal was made, it would blame do nothing Republican radicals in Congress. A simple and understandable political strategy, but certainly not a responsible approach to governing. The President may have given himself another hammer to use against Republicans, but in so doing he set up a potentially calamitous scenario for January 1, 2012. Now, on that date all of the Bush tax cuts will expire and the automatic spending cuts from the debt limit deal will start going into effect. This will result in massive tax increases and spending cuts all at once, with no cushion to soften the blow. The shock could itself create a new recession. And this time, there is no or escape hatch as with the super committee. So the President may have gained some political advantage, but at the cost of setting up the national for a fiscal car wreck.

Week 150

(PAYROLLS)

December 4, 2011

This week the debate in Washington shifted from the debt super committee to multiple disputes circling around payrolls. In the wake of the failure of the super committee, the next move by the Administration was to paint the Republicans yet again as unconcerned about the plight of the unemployed and average Americans. The vehicle for this attack was the newest legislative proposal from the President, calling for another one-year extension of his temporary payroll tax cut and another extension of unemployment benefits for 99 weeks, with a patch on the impending 30% reduction of Medicare reimbursements thrown in as well. The President's goal with this legislation is to stimulate the economy to aide his reelection, put Republicans in the uncomfortable position of opposing a tax cut, and force the GOP to accept more unemployment benefits or risk seeming cruel to the unemployed. The entire package would add $400 billion to the deficit if not offset by spending cuts or tax increases.

Senate Democrats made the first move on the President's plan by putting up his proposal, funded by a surtax on incomes over $1 million. This was the same tactic that was used and failed with the President's most recent stimulus bill. Not surprising, the Democrat's bill got nowhere close to the 60 votes needed to proceed, but no matter, the political point was made. What was more interesting was that nearly half of the Senate Republicans voted against their leader's alternative plan, which would have extended the payroll tax cut and unemployment benefits, but paid for it with a package of spending cuts that not only offset the costs, but also reduced the federal deficit by a further $140 billion over 10 years. Many Republicans seem to have voted no because, while the temporary payroll tax cut is popular, it undermines the long term solvency of Social Security. There is also a fear the President's true goal is to make the payroll tax reduction permanent and replace it with ever higher income taxes on the affluent. Since nearly half of all Americans only pay the payroll tax (not federal income taxes), Republicans worry about reducing even further the taxes paid by so large a proportion of the population. Now that each party has made its opening move, the real negotiations will begin. Republican leaders want the payroll tax cut extended, mainly for political reasons. Democrats want it because they believe it will help the economy. If they can only figure out a compromise on paying for it, a deal could get done.

The Democrats' strategy focused on jobs was certainly helped by the November jobs report. The report was better than expected, with 120,000 jobs created and the unemployment rate falling to 8.6%. The job numbers for September and October were revised upward as well. On the surface, all the data looked very good, but the story underneath was a bit more troubling, since the job growth is still too slow to significantly impact unemployment and half of the reduction in the unemployment rate came from people taking themselves out of the workforce. The jobs outlook remains weak, although certainly better than many feared in the late summer. The President hailed the report as a sign that his policies are working. Republicans emphasized that large number of Americans are still without jobs. The critical issue will be whether the improvement in the job market will pick up pace over the next 10 months, which will greatly improve the President's chances for reelection.

The final payroll issue that was the talk of Washington was whether the President's reelection campaign is running on the public payroll. Of late, the President has spent most of his time raising money for the 2012 election and flying to battleground states and giving speeches attacking Republicans. These events are technically policy related, but everyone knows they are pure political trips. The media did an analysis and discovered the President has made more trips to key battleground states in his first three years than any other president in history. This raised the issue whether President Obama is using taxpayer money to fund his political campaign. When the President flies Air Force One to a fundraiser, his campaign must pick up a small part of the tab (a recent trip cost $6.5 million, and the Obama campaign had to reimburse the taxpayers $198,000), but for trips sold as policy speeches, the taxpayers pay for everything. The issue got so much attention that the White House went on the defensive and had to argue the trips are not about reelection. A hard case to make when almost all of the President's policy speeches are made in states he needs to carry to get another 4 years in office. But there are signs the President is getting the message, next week he is going to give a policy speech on pro-middle class measures in reliably Republican Kansas, but no worry, he will be back on the road to battleground states on the taxpayers' dime as soon as he can.

Week 151

(THE OSAWATOMIE POLICY)

December 11, 2011

Although the President has been campaigning nearly fulltime for reelection since September, this week marked the official opening of his reelection effort. Faced with the difficult task of selling himself to voters in the midst of a weak economy and public dissatisfaction with his leadership, the President has for weeks been honing his case for another 4 years. On December 6, he chose an address to a handpicked crowd in Osawatomie, Kansas to make the case for his policies. His address relied heavily on themes first offered by Theodore Roosevelt, who in 1910 gave an address in Osawatomie setting out his vision for a New Nationalism. For Obama, his Osawatomie policy was summed up as: "Investing in things like education that give everybody a chance to succeed. A tax code that makes sure everybody pays their fair share. And laws that make sure everybody follows the rules. That's what will transform our economy. That's what will grow our middle class again." Put simply, more spending, more taxes, and more regulations will restore American greatness.

The President's central premise is that "the basic bargain that made this country great has been eroded." The President then claimed this erosion was the result of policies that favor the rich, insufficient government regulation, and a failure of government to invest in infrastructure. There is no doubt that the middle class is under stress, but rather than look to causes like rising energy, health and food prices, the cost of college education, and rising tax burdens, President Obama instead focused on sins of the private sector, with nothing said of the sins of government. High energy and food prices are driven in large part by policies that limit domestic energy production and encourage grain supplies to be used for fuel. The high cost of education has been driven by government student loan programs that make cash easily available and only encourage colleges to raise tuition. Health care costs are ever increasing because of federal policies that separate the consumer from the cost of care. And as for taxes, they continue to rise at the local and state level, putting a further squeeze on the middle class.

Rather than focus on all these causes of financial stress, the President instead turned his fire on Republicans. He asserted that "their philosophy is simple: We are better off when everybody is left to fend for themselves and play by their own rules." After creating the straw man that Republicans are heartless anarchists bent on the elimination of government, he then turned his fire on the top 1% of income earners. He used Theodore Roosevelt's words to emphasize that markets must be controlled to deliver balanced prosperity. He then attacked high income earners, saying the tax cuts in 2001 and 2003 were only for the wealthy, and failed to create new jobs. And then he turned to income inequity, asserted that the top 1% has prospered, while the middle class has withered. His message was simple, what we need to restore the strength of the middle class is wealth redistribution, pure and simple.

But the President did not stop there, the next part of his speech was a tour of all the great things he would do with all the money he plans to take from the affluent. He spoke of "investments" in education, building the nation's infrastructure, and using government "to help create the conditions where both workers and businesses can succeed." And of course, all of this spending will be paid for by the rich paying "their fair share." He said "this isn't about class warfare. This is about the nation's welfare." So in the end, the President used his speech in Osawatomie to outline his vision of America, an America with more government, more entitlements, more taxes, and more regulation. The President showed with this speech that he honestly believes that the way to create jobs is not to incentivize businesses to invest and grow, but instead to control and direct business activity, and then to confiscate as much of the profits as possible.

It is hard to characterize the Osawatomie speech as anything other than a call for divisiveness and class resentment. The President placed the blame for the current burdens on the middle class squarely on private companies, the affluent, and their allies in the Republican Party. His prescription for prosperity is ever more government control. His vision for raising incomes is taking money from some Americans, and giving that money to others as government sees fit. It is a vision strikingly similar to that pursued by the welfare states of Europe, the very welfare states that are now collapsing under the burdens of the debt and unsustainable government obligations. Certainly President Obama does not want that future for America, but his Kansas speech shows he is working to create that future nonetheless.

Week 152

(END WAR)

December 18, 2011

Nothing propelled President Obama into national political prominence like the Iraq War. Starting in 2007, he used the Iraq War to distinguish himself from Hillary Clinton and cast himself as the champion of the anti-war wing of the Democratic Party. He used the war to gain the nomination and pound John McCain for his comments that American troops might be in Iraq for hundreds of years. Without the Iraq War, it is likely President Obama would never have gained the office he now holds. From the very outset of his presidential campaign, Barak Obama made clear the Iraq War was a war that should not have been fought, and that he would end the war no matter what. This week, he got to keep his promise, when on December 18, 2011, the last American combat battalion left Iraq. He ended the war, but the bigger question is what has the President left behind in the war's wake.

The Iraq War was one of the longest conflicts in American history, lasting more than 8 years. The costs of the war were high in every respect, with nearly 4500 American troops killed, nearly 33,000 injured, and more than 800 billion spent. As for the Iraqi people, it is estimated that as many as 100,000 died in the war, and many think the total is much higher than that. With so much spent in lives and treasure, it is fair to question what the war achieved. The central premise for going to war was Iraq's weapons of mass destruction and its ties with Islamic terrorism, but no such weapons were found and Saddam Hussein's ties to terrorists were always tangential at best. Given this, much of the focus of the war since 2006 has been to avoid defeat, as opposed to achieving victory. The method to avoid defeat was to create a democratic Iraqi government capable of defending itself and defeating internal threats. First, the 2007 surge was deployed to break the back of the insurgency, and then massive resources were put into training Iraqi security forces.

By the time President Obama took office, America's limited goals for success in Iraq had mostly been achieved. The insurgency was largely defeated and Iraq's security forces had greatly improved. The real challenge for the President was not the unnecessary war in Iraq, but the War in Afghanistan, which he described as a war of necessity that must be won. So the President staged a mini-surge in Afghanistan, while pursuing a careful draw-down of troops in Iraq. Challenges remained in Iraq, but they were more political than military. Despite an election more than a year ago, no new government has yet been formed, and the influence of Iran continues to grow. And while the President had pledged to end the war in Iraq, everyone expected that some residual force would remain. It was this last piece of the puzzle that President Obama had the responsibility to put in place.

The Administration tried to negotiate a final forces agreement that would have kept some U.S. troops and bases in place, but the President did not engage in the process until it was too late. The weak Iraqi government caved to internal forces wanting to eject all U.S. troops, so they demanded requirements, including the loss of immunity for U.S. troops in Iraq, that made it hard for the U.S. to agree to maintain its presence. So we came to the momentous events of December 18, when all U.S. combat troops finally left the country. The American presence is hardly gone, with thousands of contractors remaining, including nearly 5,000 security forces, but the formal U.S. military presence has now ended.

With defeat largely averted by the end of 2008, President Obama's primary task once in office was to try to end the war successfully. President Obama never talks of victory in Iraq for fear of alienating his anti-war allies, but he has spoken of objectives achieved. But the limited success we did achieve in Iraq was put at risk by the President's failure to reach a final forces agreement that would maintain a stabilizing U.S. troop presence. Now Iraq stands without direct U.S. military support. Its security forces are strong enough to defeat insurgents, but Iraq cannot control its own borders or airspace. So Iraq is easy prey for Iran and others, which would turn our tactical victory into a strategic defeat. No matter, as long as the President can brag about ending the war.

Week 153

(OUT TAXED)

December 25, 2011

For all of 2011, the White House was searching for a strategy to gain advantage over the Republicans in Congress. They tried the adult in the room mantra, marathon debt ceiling meetings, calls for ever more stimulus, the constant theme of Republican extremism, and even cautious support for the Occupy Wall Street movement. Each strategy succeeded in hurting the GOP's standing, but the President's popularity dipped as well. It seemed the President could not figure out how to get an advantage over the GOP. Then came the tax issue, and everything changed. In December 2010, the President struck a deal with the lame duck Democratic Congress to lower payroll taxes and increase unemployment benefits for 1 year. That deal was set to expire on December 31, 2011, causing a scurry to extend the tax cut and unemployment insurance benefits in the face of a still weak economy. The President was on the defensive for most of the year because the national debate had focused on federal spending, but with taxes, there was a chance to out fox (or out tax) the Republicans, and he did it.

The White House believes the President's reelection will turn on two factors: the economy and the identity of the GOP nominee. The stronger the economy, the better the chances of the President defeating even a formidable Republican opponent. The weaker the economy, the greater the chance that even a vulnerable GOP nominee could win. So clearly, the best opportunity for reelection lies with a stronger economy. As a result, the President has worked hard to try to continue to prime the pump with as much stimulus as possible. That was the objective of the December 2010 tax extension deal and his call in the Fall for another stimulus bill. But with the payroll tax extension fight, President Obama saw an opportunity to both continue stimulus efforts and caste the GOP as the party of higher taxes.

Many conservatives have been skeptical of the payroll tax cut from the outset, believing it offers little to help the economy, but does great harm to the federal budget because it decreases the revenues flowing into Social Security, thereby increasing the deficit and undermining the solvency of that program. Republicans also suspect the President wants to make the payroll tax cut permanent because it furthers his goal of wealth redistribution. Nearly half of all taxpayers only pay payroll taxes because they earn too little to pay federal income taxes. By making this tax cut permanent, and replacing the lost revenues with even higher taxes on the affluent, the Administration can portray itself as a champion of both tax cuts and tax fairness. This strategy puts the GOP in a tough spot, because it forces the GOP to oppose a tax cut. The strategy also exacerbates the tension between the Republican anti-tax mantra and their commitment to fiscal responsibility, especially because federal revenues have dropped so low that even Republicans now hesitate to support further tax cuts.

In the payroll tax cut extension debate, both parties supported the tax cut, but offered different plans to pay for it. The Democrats pushed a bill in the Senate that paid for the tax cut and unemployment benefits with a surtax on those with incomes over $1 million, while Republicans in the House passed a more modest tax cut extension and paid for it with spending cuts and reductions in entitlement benefits for the affluent. Politics were behind both proposals, creating an impasse on a tax cut both parties wanted renewed. Then Minority Leader McConnell and Majority Leader Reid struck a deal to extend the tax cut for 60 days to allow time to reach a final agreement. The compromise was paid for with spending cuts and with some GOP pet proposals (like forcing the Administration to approve or disapprove the keystone pipeline project from Canada to the Gulf of Mexico within 60 days) thrown in. This compromise passed with 86 votes in the Senate and it seemed the crisis had been averted. Then the GOP majority in the House stood on principle and rejected a two-month extension as irresponsible. It looked like the GOP was again engaging in brinkmanship to get its way. So the Republican majority rejected the compromise and called for a conference committee to craft a full year extension. The Democrats in the Senate and the White House said there was no time to forge a new deal. They called the GOP's bluff, and just before Christmas, Speaker Boehner forced his unhappy caucus to pass the compromise.

No doubt the tax cut extension debate was a win for the White House. They got to look like the tax cutters for the middle class and got to portray the Republicans as extremists who only care about decreasing taxes for the rich. With the deal, the President is going to get additional stimulus and also some additional advantage over the GOP. After a very tough year, the President was able to end on a high note, even though on substance the bill that passed focused on GOP priorities, since it was a tax cut paid for with spending cuts. The President out taxed the Republicans by beating them at their own game.

Week 154

(HOT AND COLD)

January 1, 2012

President Obama and his Republican rivals entered the 2012 election season as a study in contrasts. President Obama opened 2012 on vacation in warm Hawaii, while the Republicans were campaigning in the cold winds of the Iowa winter. President Obama faces no primary opponent, while no less than six top tier Republicans are battling it out for their party's nomination. The President ended the year on a high note, besting the Republicans on the payroll tax extension, while the GOP candidates were ripping each other apart on every issue imaginable to win the nomination. And while the Democrats continue to raise a massive cash reserve for the 2012 general election campaign, the GOP was spending its resources on internecine warfare. So the contrasts are stark, but who will be the ultimate beneficiary is yet to be seen.

This was the third year that the President and his family have taken their Christmas break in Hawaii. Since it is the state of the President's birth, it is no surprise that he travels there for his longest annual vacation. In past years, the trip to idyllic Hawaii has given fodder to his opponents, since it was a bit unseemly for the President to be frolicking in a tropical paradise while the economy cratered back on the mainland. This year, those critiques were more muted in part because recent economic indicators (new claims for unemployment, housing starts and sales, and consumer spending during the Holiday season) all seem to be pointing to a strengthening economy. There was also less focus on the President because the media's attention during the usually quiet Holiday week was on Iowa and the GOP nomination fight.

During the early stages of the 2012 election campaign, the President has had the luxury of raising money and attacking the GOP, while the Republicans have been distracted by their battle to decide who will face the President in the Fall. Conventional wisdom is that the President would benefit from a long primary battle among Republicans, a battle that Democrats hope will exhaust the GOP's resources and divide the party. The Democrats had also hoped to capitalize on a weak Republican nominee, counting on the GOP to reject moderate candidates like Romney and Huntsman in favor of conservative favorites like Perry, Paul, Bachmann, Gingrich, Cain, or Santorum. Clearly, the White House was rooting for any non-Romney to win, but only after a long drawn-out battle. Indeed, it seems the Administration had convinced itself, with all its rhetoric about extremists Republicans and Tea Partiers, that the GOP would never nominate a moderate.

So surely the White House has been disappointed in the developments over that last few months, as a series of anti-Romney candidates have self-destructed. Perry's bad debate performances, Bachmann's fact-free bomb throwing, accusations regarding Cain's extramarital conduct, and Gingrich's consulting work and three marriages, caused each to crash after meteoric rises in the polls. So in the closing days before the January 4 Iowa caucuses, it appeared that increasing numbers of Republicans were rallying around Romney as the most electable candidate, with only Congressman Ron Paul and former Senator Rick Santorum maintaining any momentum. Predicting the outcome of the Iowa caucuses is notoriously difficult because organization can drive so much of the result, but polls in the closing days seem to indicate that if he does not win in Iowa, Romney will do well enough to give him momentum into New Hampshire. Even more importantly, it looks like Bachmann, Perry, and Gingrich will do so poorly that they may be knocked out of the race altogether. This could give Romney an opportunity to win the nomination early in the primary campaign, because it looks like only Ron Paul and Rick Santorum will stand in his way. Romney bets he can quickly handle Paul because his isolationist foreign policy and support for legalized prostitution and drugs will disaffect the GOP base. As for Santorum, while a formidable campaigner, few believe he has the money and organization for a drawn-out contest with Romney.

So while it may seem the President is sitting pretty in warm Hawaii while the Republicans are savaging each other in cold Iowa, the reality might be quite different. If Romney quickly captures the nomination, the President will face a Northeast Republican with some history as a moderate, not the easiest opponent to paint as an extremist. And while the President certainly got a bump from his win in the payroll tax fight, his approval numbers quickly returned to negative territory, where they have been for months. As for the economy, how it will perform in 2012 is anyone's guess. So the President should enjoy the last few days of his Hawaiian vacation, because he is in for a rough ride in 2012.

Week 155

(FAIR SHARE)

January 8, 2012

Back from his Hawaiian vacation, President Obama wasted no time pushing his campaign themes for 2012. He travelled to Ohio on January 5 to give a speech on the economy and to announce recess appointments designed to please his liberal base and further his campaign objectives. Ignoring procedural maneuvers by Senate Republicans that have kept that body in pro forma session to prevent recess appointments, the President used his trip to Ohio to announce the appointment of 3 new commissioners to the National Labor Relations Board (NLRB) and Richard Cordray as the new Consumer Financial Protection Bureau (CFPB) director. These controversial recess appointments were designed to showcase a President fighting for the middle class. The Administration wants to frame 2012 as the fair share election, with the President as the champion of fairness.

The Administration's appointments to the NLRB were a sop to unions, giving the board a quorum to allow it to push through pro-labor changes to collective bargaining rules. The President appointed 2 Democrats and 1 Republican, including two former union lawyers. With these appointments, unions hope to stack the deck in favor of their organizing efforts. As for the CFPB, the President used that appointed to underline his commitment to a fair deal for the middle class. This new Bureau was created by the Dodd-Frank financial reform legislation and was given a broad mandate to protect consumers from abuses by financial service companies. Republicans opposed creation of the CFPB for many reasons, including a legislative mandate that grants it broad undefined powers with little oversight. A number of the powers of the CFPB could not be exercised until a director was appointed, so Republicans were stalling any confirmation to try to stop the CFPB from operating effectively. With his recess appointment, the President sought to signal that he would fight for consumers.

Then on January 6, the President travelled to the offices of the CFPB to celebrate both the Cordray appointment and the day's economic news. The Labor Department reported 212,000 jobs created in December and a decline in the unemployment rate to 8.5%. The President used this relatively strong economic news as an excuse for a victory lap at the CFPB. He used his speech to explain his economic philosophy, which he described in purely populist terms: "And what we want to do is make sure not just that we're getting back to the status quo, we want to make sure that we're dealing with those underlining problems — getting to a point where middle-class families feel like they can get ahead again. Where hard work pays off again. Where everybody gets a fair shot, and everybody does their fair share, and everybody is playing by the same set of rules." With this mantra, the President hopes to kick off a campaign reminiscent of former Senator John Edward's "People against the Powerful" crusade, allowing the President to aggressively attack monied interests in the name of helping the middle class.

Given the President's campaign theme, the Administration publicly welcomed the week's events in the Republican nomination campaign. The Iowa caucuses were held on January 3, and Mitt Romney emerged with a tight vote victory, a result that was unimaginable only a few weeks before. After unleashing his vast financial resources to destroy the Gingrich campaign, Romney blew the field wide open, allowing him to step though the gap for a very narrow win. Romney then moved on to New Hampshire, where he holds a double digit lead, and polls showed he was pulling ahead in South Carolina as well. So by week's end it appeared that Mitt Romney had the opportunity to wrap up the Republican nomination early. A few weeks ago, Democrats would have viewed this as a troubling development, but with the President's fair share campaign theme, it seemed the President almost welcomed Romney's win.

With an improving economy, the White House feels increasingly confident that the President can win reelection, despite his poor poll numbers, with his populist agenda attacking the affluent and big business. The Administration believes Mitt Romney is the perfect foil for this campaign. A wealthy Wall Street financer perfectly fits the narrative the President hopes to push. He is counting on the voters ignoring the controversial portions of his record and instead turning their ire on the successful and blaming them for the economy. Traditionally, this type of class politics has not played well in national campaigns, but the Administration is hoping things will be different this time. And anyways, it is the kind of campaign the President wants to run, because having government decide what everyone's "fair share" should be is exactly what the President wants.

Week 156
(What A Bain)

January 15, 2012

For a President who does not believe in the concept of over exposure, being eclipsed by other news must have been very frustrating. Try has he might, the focus of the media this week was on either the Republicans or unwelcome news from abroad. But all was not bad for the White House, because even though the Republican primaries dominated the news coverage, much of the focus was not on taxes or federal spending, but instead on the evils of Wall Street, private equity, and vulture capitalism. This was because Mitt Romney won the New Hampshire primary with nearly 40% of the vote, which coupled with Romney's close win in Iowa, put his opponents on life support. So they attacked Romney with the best argument they have, his tenure at Bain Capital. By so doing, Republicans made themselves sound like Democrats, delighting a White House that hopes to use Bain to inflict pain on a Romney campaign.

For most of the Republicans primary campaign, Romney has been in the lead, but he has been at best a weak frontrunner. His poll numbers rarely topped 25%, and conservatives have made clear their desire for an alternative. Fortunately for Romney, conservative contenders continued to either self-destruct or divide the Tea Party vote allowing Romney to win. Romney did exactly that in Iowa, by damaging Gingrich with negative ads on his consulting work in DC and by encouraging the Ron Paul campaign, which took crucial votes from Santorum and Perry. The strategy garnered a close win in Iowa, and yielded a blowout in New Hampshire. These wins instantly put the Perry and Gingrich campaigns in deep trouble. In response, both campaigns unleashed broad attacks on Romney's business record at Bain Capital.

Bain Capital was a private equity firm that purchased distressed companies. Romney made much of his fortune during his tenure running Bain. Some of his investments saved companies and created jobs, like his experience with Staples, but others resulted in liquidations and job losses, even while the principals of Bain made hefty profits. Hoping to capitalize on the nation's concerns about income disparities, the Gingrich and Perry campaigns aired ads decrying Bain as a corporate raider and a proponent of vulture capitalism. With these attacks, Perry and Gingrich hoped to blunt Romney's momentum and stop him from winning the next crucial primary, in South Carolina on January 21. Polls have shown that the attacks have hurt Romney and cut into his lead, but they have done just as much damage to Perry and Gingrich.

Even Republicans who do not support Romney felt uncomfortable with this attack on Bain Capital. It seemed to many that Perry and Gingrich were tarnishing the GOP free market brand. Even worse, their ads and speeches would allow the Obama campaign to recycle the attacks, claiming that even Republicans believe Romney is a vulture capitalist. The Administration could barely hide its delight. The backlash grew so strong that by week's end both Perry and Gingrich started to back off their attacks and instead focus on issues like abortion and health care, where Romney has changed his views in a way that might make conservatives nervous to support him.

In many ways, it appears Perry and Gingrich took their best and hardest shot at Romney, but failed to knock him off his perch. So for both campaign, it is looking like if Romney is not stopped in South Carolina, he will unstoppable.

All of this left President Obama out of the limelight, but very please nonetheless. The White House tried to keep in the headlines, with a trip to the Pentagon to announce a military realignment, a proposal to merge government agencies to give the impression of fiscal responsibility, and a strong condemnation of photos from Afghanistan showing marines urinating on dead Taliban. But even with these efforts, the week was about Romney and Bain, and the debate about the role and responsibility of the affluent in America. That is the exact debate the President wants to have in the Fall, so no doubt the Administration was very pleased.

Week 157

(VERY TAXING)

January 22, 2012

Taxes have been a major topic of political debate in Washington ever since the Republicans took control of the House in 2010. The White House has pushed for higher taxes on the rich to pay for deficit reduction and new spending, while the GOP has insisted on lowering taxes for job creators and cutting the deficit solely with spending cuts. This was a predictable debate between a liberal President and conservatives in Congress. However, few expected taxes to be a defining issue in the Republican primaries, since all the candidates oppose new taxes. That is why it was so surprising that Mitt Romney, who seemed to be gliding to the nomination, got tripped up this week on taxes of all issues. Not tax policy, but his own personal tax returns, which he had refused to disclose and which many expect show that he pays a lower tax rate than many middle income Americans. Romney got hammered in two consecutive debates on his tax returns, stammered when he tried to answer questions on them, and belatedly agreed to disclose them. Newt Gingrich used the issue to strip Romney of his cloak of inevitability and undermine his tenuous support among conservatives. The result was a stunning Gingrich win in the South Carolina primary and a road to the nomination for Romney that could be difficult after all.

After Romney's convincing win in New Hampshire, he leaped to a big lead in South Carolina and in Florida, which holds its primary January 31. Gingrich, Santorum, Perry, Paul and Huntsman all moved on to South Carolina after their losses in New Hampshire, but it was clear that only one or two of them could continue the fight. Huntsman quickly dropped out and tepidly endorsed Romney, then Perry withdrew a couple days later and forcefully threw his support to Gingrich. These moves did not change the dynamic in South Carolina, what flipped the result was the populist conservative attack mounted by Gingrich on the privileged rich and Romney's bad judgment to give Gingrich a weapon in the form of his tax returns.

Gingrich has performed well in the many GOP debates held thus far in the campaign, but coming into South Carolina, the debates were make or break for Gingrich. With less money, a weak organization, and a poor showing in Iowa and New Hampshire, the debates were Gingrich's last chance to stop Romney. Gingrich was aided in his last stand by a donation of $5 million from a wealthy Las Vegas casino owner, which he used to launch an ad war attacking Romney's tenure at Bain Capital. Gingrich then turned the usually pedestrian issue of tax returns into a major controversy by demanding Romney produce his, and ripping him in two debates for failing to do so. Despite knowing the questions were coming, Romney was unprepared, did not give direct answers, and seemed to dodge the issue, leaving an opening for Gingrich to claim he was hiding something. The fear that Romney had hidden weaknesses, combined with the perception of Romney as cold and inauthentic, was enough in a few short days to collapse his support. Gingrich won South Carolina with 40% of the vote, and quickly leaped ahead in polls in Florida as well. The Romney machine in South Carolina was made of glass, and it cracked on the first significant impact. Romney still has more money and a better organization, so it is unclear Gingrich can win a drawn-out primary fight, but for the moment he has the upper hand.

For President Obama, the Gingrich surge is an opportunity, but also a challenge. For weeks, the President has devoted his time almost entirely to positioning his campaign. He purposely travelled to Florida ostensibly to give a speech on tourism, but in reality to campaign and do fundraisers. His campaign had assumed Romney would be the opponent, and was prepping for a class warfare battle, with Romney as the Wall Street elitist, and Obama as the champion of the middle class. The Gingrich surge has thrown uncertainty into the mix. Gingrich is no elitist and his attacks on Romney show he is prepared to challenge the monied interests. The Gingrich crusade is a populist campaign to save America from liberal elites and a class warfare strategy does not work so well against Gingrich.

That does not mean the White House is upset with the Gingrich surge. Gingrich is a polarizing figure, with high unfavorable ratings and weak support among independents. This might lead the White House to conclude that he would be an easy opponent. But just as the Gingrich message has captured the imagination of GOP primary voters, a more restrained and dignified Gingrich with the nomination, and a chance to re-introduce himself to voters, might pose a much bigger threat to President Obama than anyone expects. Anyone who can use a few debates and tax returns to win a major primary is no one to be trifled with.

Week 158

(THE FAIR DEAL)

January 29, 2012

With the Republicans savaging each other in the run up to the Florida primary, President Obama had the opportunity to take center stage and set the terms of the debate with his State of the Union address. When the President took the podium on January 24, his mission was more to position his reelection campaign rather than to detail the challenges facing the nation. With a weak economy that is only improving slowly, the President faces the prospect of running for reelection with a majority of voters believing the nation is on the wrong track. As a result, the President's strategy is not so much to defend his record, but instead to focus on how he is different, and better than, the alternative. This strategy was on full display in the President's address, where instead of defending Obamacare, bailouts, stimulus, and the entitlement state, the President outlined his vision for a fair deal for the middle classes, where government is the guarantor of fair results and the distributor of fair income for all.

It is a steep climb for the President to convince voters that government should be trusted to be the savior of the middle class. Polls show trust in government is at an all-time low. Faced with these headwinds, in his address the President launched into a full-throated defense of the ability of government to improve lives. The President started with praise of the military and their accomplishments in Iraq, Afghanistan, and in killing Osama bin Laden. He then tried to use their example of patriotism and dedication to the national good to support his domestic agenda, stating: "Imagine what we could accomplish if we followed their example." The President's vision is for "[a]n economy built to last, where hard work pays off, and responsibility is rewarded." Then after describing his caricature of the policies of his predecessor, he argued "[o]r we can restore an economy where everyone gets a fair shot, everyone does their fair share, and everyone plays by the same set of rules." This is the Obama Fair Deal, where government does not simply set fair rules, but also determines fair results.

After setting out his concept for a Fair Deal, the President then launched into a laundry list of government programs and initiatives poll-tested to appeal to independent voters. Programs to foster manufacturing, reward job creation in the United States, improve education, expand energy production, help homeowners, grant amnesty to responsible illegal immigrants, and to spend more money on infrastructure. It was an advertisement for what government can do for you, if only you will vote for me. The President was forced to focus on modest initiatives to address middle class concerns because the massive deficit and hostility to tax increases make more ambitious efforts untenable. The President tried to convince voters that a host of small programs can improve their lives.

After working to establish the premise that government is a force for good and fairness, the President then used populist themes to draw contrasts with Republicans and attack his likely Republican opponent, Mitt Romney, without mentioning his name. The President's tactic is to claim that unemployment is high and growth is slow because the affluent are stealing the nation's wealth, leaving too little for everyone else. The President's claim is that we can solve our deficit crisis and restore the standing of the middle class by wealth redistribution; taking money from the affluent and giving it, through government programs, to the poor and middle class. It is a zero-sum philosophy that discounts growth and opportunity, and instead relies on dividing the pie. The President claimed "[w]e don't begrudge financial success in this country. We admire it," but then explained why such success is hurting the nation and why the gains of the affluent must be taken away. Every time the President praises wealth creation, you can be sure he will then explain why that wealth should be redistributed by the government. The President wants to sound like a free market supporter of small government, while he pursues expanded government and ever higher taxes.

The President's theme that the affluent are a danger to the United States is not only one of his core beliefs, but also a convenient route to attack his likely opponent, Mitt Romney. On the very day of the State of the Union, Romney was forced to produce his tax returns, showing he earned more than $20 million in both 2009 and 2010. The President wants a class warfare campaign, where he hopes to portray Romney as an out of touch Wall Street elitist. The White House is focused on a populist campaign that only government can stop oppression by the rich, so the State of the Union was devoted to a defense of the virtues of government. This is comfortable ground for President Obama, because above all else, he is a believer in the greatness of government. The question is whether the voters believe they have a better chance of getting a fair deal from government or from free enterprise.

Week 159

(REBOUNDS)

February 5, 2012

This was a week for rebounds, a rebound for Mitt Romney in Florida and Nevada, and a rebound for President Obama on the economy. For each man, the week held the prospect of a brighter political future, but also warnings on challenges ahead. For Romney, the Florida primary has always been his firewall, the barrier he would erect to repel any opponent, and with his win he reestablished his position as the clear frontrunner and presumptive nominee. For Obama, of all his vulnerabilities, the economy has been his most dangerous foe and the lack of jobs its most pointed challenge. With the January jobs report, showing 243,000 jobs created and an unemployment rate dropping to 8.3%, the President saw an opening to change the perception of the economy from weak to recovering. So for both men, a rebound was in fashion.

Mitt Romney got whipped in South Carolina. After his strong showing in Iowa and convincing win in New Hampshire, Romney believed his opponents were too weakened to effectively challenge him. He ratcheted back his attacks on Gingrich, believing the former Speaker's campaign un-revivable. But with two strong debates, an influx of cash, and riding a wave of an anti-establishment insurgency, Gingrich won. But for Gingrich to emerge as a true challenge, he had to carry Florida as well, which unlike South Carolina, is a large and diverse state, with 8 media markets and little opportunity for retail politics. Romney understood this and pounced. He unleashed his formidable financial resources to air nearly $14 million in negative advertisements to dismantle Gingrich. He succeeded. In the January 30 primary, he won 46.4% of the vote to Gingrich's 31.9%. More importantly, under the pressure of these assaults, Gingrich turned vindictive and petty, taking cheap shots and pouting at his circumstances. Romney added to his momentum by winning the Nevada caucus on February 4 with 50.1% of the vote, with Gingrich only mustering 21.1%

Most pundits believe that Romney's victories in Florida and Nevada will be followed up with strong showings in the other contests in February, including Colorado, Minnesota, Michigan, and Maine. This could allow Romney to build momentum into Super Tuesday, where his financial and organizational dominance should put him in a good position to end effective opposition. So in the course of two short weeks, Mitt Romney was able to rebound from a troubling defeat in South Carolina to reestablish his position in the GOP nomination race. But at what cost? The negative turn in the campaign, Gingrich's tough attacks on his business record, and self-inflicted wounds like his comment that he is "not concerned about the poor," all have hurt Romney's standing with voters and given President Obama an opening to establish a lead.

For President Obama, the January jobs report could not have come at a better time. With Mitt Romney victorious but bloodied, the stronger than expected jobs growth gave the President a chance to claim that his economic policies are working. The good jobs report also took some focus off some unfortunate comments by the President at the national prayer breakfast, where he seemed to claim that Jesus would support his tax increase plan. For a President who has been often criticized for his arrogance, the last thing he needed was to claim his policies are God's will. The jobs report thankfully changed the subject and allowed the President to try to reframe the debate. Clearly, a stronger U.S. economy will greatly strengthen the President's reelection campaign, but the danger for the Administration is that the White House might now take for granted a clear path to another four years.

The truth is that the unemployment rate of 8.3% is partly a product of low participation in the labor force. Indeed, if labor force participation were at 2007 levels, the unemployment rate would be closer to 11%. Also, even apart from the economy, many other policies of the President are highly controversial. We saw that this week with the backlash from the Administration's decision to require religious institutions to pay for contraceptives and abortion pills in their health plans. Catholic leaders across the political spectrum condemned the decision as an effort to force religious organizations to adopt policies contrary to their beliefs. So the White House has reason to be confident, but those who rebound usually fall back to earth, and too much arrogance from the Administration could hasten a fall.

Week 160
(MORAL MAJORITIES)

February 12, 2012

It has been the assumption of the professional political class throughout this election cycle that the economy would be the driving force in the 2012 presidential race. That may turn out to be true, but lest anyone forget, this week gave a pointed reminder that social issues are still highly relevant to the electoral landscape. Social issues propelled Rick Santorum to unexpected victories in GOP nomination contests in Colorado, Minnesota, and Missouri. The potency of the most controversial social issue of all – abortion – led the President to begin a retreat on his controversial regulation requiring religious institutions to pay for birth control and abortion pills. So in an atmosphere where it seems only money issues matter, whether they be the economy or the budget, the politicians got a reminder that moral debates can build or threaten majorities as wells.

Rick Santorum is the beneficiary of the last conservative standing phenomenon. The former two-term Republican senator from Pennsylvania who lost his seat in the 2006 Republican wipeout, is finding his support surging as other conservatives have fallen to the wayside. Just two weeks ago, it looked like Gingrich would be the conservative candidate, but his personal baggage and the Romney attack machine put the Gingrich camp on the defensive. But rather than rally to Romney, conservatives looked to Santorum as their last chance. The strength of this sentiment was on display in three contests this week. Colorado and Missouri held caucuses, while Minnesota held a primary. Few delegates were up for grabs, but Santorum's victories in all three contests nevertheless sent a strong message that many Republican voters are still looking for an alternative to Romney.

While Santorum is certainly a fiscal conservative and a foreign policy hawk, what has marked his campaign from the outset has been his strong focus on social issues and his appeal to working class Republicans and independents who feel their government and, in some ways, their country, has abandoned them. In the early months of the campaign, Santorum kept hitting these themes in consistently strong debate performances. Heading into Iowa, he was still far back in the pack, but as other conservatives self-destructed, Santorum remained steady and focused. Unlike Gingrich, Santorum has little personal baggage and a likable personality, which poses problems for the Romney camp, because a full negative assault on Santorum has the potential to backfire. In addition, two factors are fueling the Santorum surge. Conservatives who do not want to vote for Romney and social issue voters who feel a connection with the Santorum message. It is hard to see how negative attacks will easily break the bond those voters have developed with Santorum. So it seems in an election that everyone thought would be about the economy, it is a social issues candidate that is making the deepest connection in the final stretch.

The rise of social issues was not limited to Republican politics, because those same social issues rocked the Obama Administration this week. For months the White House has been working on regulations to implement Obamacare's mandate for free contraceptives for women. The health-care reform law has a religious organization exemption, but it was up to the Administration to define the scope of that exemption. The President was lobbied by the Left to make the exception as narrow as possible, and by moderates and conservatives to grant a broad exemption. In the end, the President sided with his base and issued a regulation that would have required religious hospitals, colleges, and charities to pay for contraceptives and abortion pills, even if contrary to the teachings of those religious institutions. No doubt, the President's political advisors hoped the broad popularity of contraceptives and the support he has seen from liberal Christians would mute any criticism. The Administration was wrong. Religious organizations across the political spectrum protested against the regulation as an improper interference with religious liberty.

After proclaiming for weeks that he would not back down on women's health, the issue was turning into a firestorm, with Republicans using it on the campaign trail and increasing numbers of Democrats calling for the President to moderate the policy. On February 10, the President gave a news conference offering a compromise, allowing religious institutions to exclude contraceptive coverage from their health plans, but ordering insurance companies to provide that coverage directly at no charge. The compromise satisfied some, but the Conference of Catholic Bishops condemned the new plan, saying that Catholic institutions would still be paying on contraceptives, because the free mandated coverage by insurance companies would be added to their premiums.

This whole debate was a needless one because the President could have avoided the issue by offering the compromise proposal upfront. The fact that he did not do so, and instead decided to directly attack the Catholic Church and other religious institutions, was purposeful. He wanted to send a message that private institutions must bow to the federal mandates in Obamacare or face the consequences. But it was the President who suffered the consequences when he had to retreat. The Administration thought moral issues did not matter, all that mattered was access to popular contraceptives. They were wrong, and the consequences to Obamacare could be dire, because of the Supreme Court Justices who will decide its fate, Scalia, Alito, Thomas, and Kennedy are devote and observant Catholics, who no doubt have noticed how the proponents of Obamacare hope to use it to force the federal government's will on private and religious institutions. That is not a positive backdrop for the government's arguments in favor of the constitutionality of Obamacare, which will be heard by the Supreme Court in March.

Week 161

(CAMPAIGN BUDGETING)

February 19, 2012

It is a tradition in parliamentary democracies to offer a campaign budget as a prelude to the next scheduled election. These campaign budgets are designed to improve the chances for a majority to be retuned for the governing party. This week, President Obama offered his version of a campaign budget, but with the difference that he has no hope of getting his budget passed, unlike majority parties in parliamentary systems. Instead, President Obama offered a budget of talking points, one that avoids hard decisions and panders to favored constituencies. It was a politician's budget, not one from a chief executive concerned about pressing challenges. So as the President spends nearly all his time campaigning, now even his budget is simply a campaign tool and nothing more.

The President's prior budget, offered for the 2012 fiscal year, came in the wake of the Republicans landslide and represented a cautious and wounded President, who did not dare to offer any proposal that could annoy his base or give an opening to his opponents. It was a budget that repeated old proposals, made few spending cuts, and did nothing to address the long term deficit. The Administration's 2013 budget kept the focus on pleasing the base, but differed in that instead of being born in caution, it was forged with electoral ambition. The White House's 2013 budget calls for $3.8 trillion in spending, and increase of just over 1%. As for the 10 year spending plan, the President proposed some $500 billion in additional stimulus spending, going to his usual supporters: unions, public education, and green energy supporters. The budget cuts deeply into defense, trimmed some agency budgets, but calls for increased spending for education, energy, the environment, and law and tax enforcement.

With the nation facing yet another trillion dollar deficit in 2012, the Administration's budget actually projected an increase in the 10 year deficit projection, not a reduction. What modest progress the plan proposed on the deficit was based on phony savings claimed from the end of the wars in Iraq and Afghanistan, even though everyone knows that money was never going to be spent anyways. The White House also claimed $2 trillion in spending cuts already achieved in deals with Congress as new savings, but those cuts are already law. Beyond double counting and phony savings, the plan offered more spending rather than cuts, which the White House tried to mask by proposing $1.5 trillion in new taxes, all focused on those making $250,000 and above. Included within these new tax proposals was a 30% minimum tax on incomes above $1 million. But in the end, the President's plan calls for spending most of these new revenues on new programs, with little going to deficit reduction. And when everyone agrees that entitlement spending is driving the deficit problem, the budget proposes no significant entitlement reforms, obviously because the President cares more about votes than fiscal responsibility.

The Democrats in Congress did not even want to bring the President's 2012 budget up for a vote, because they knew it was a cautious and inadequate proposal. Ironically, it was the Republican Senate minority that gave the President a vote on his 2012 budget, and it went down 97-0. The same result is almost certainly in store for this 2013 White House budget, which Republicans have already said they will bring up for a vote, knowing that the vast majority of Democrats will not support the plan. Even Democrats are uncomfortable with the President's punitive tax increases and moderate Democrats are likewise disappointed that the plan increases the long-term deficit, and avoids any tough decisions on tax reform or entitlements. Yet the President does not care whether his plan gets any support in Congress, because the purpose of his budget is reelection not policy.

In the end, the Administration has determined that nothing more can get accomplished on policy issues in 2012 and that reelection is the only thing that matters. This week, Congress passed a further extension of the payroll tax cut, along with extensions in unemployment benefits and physician Medicare payments, partly paid for with spending cuts. This is likely the last substantive bill that will pass in 2012, so the Administration's 2013 budget is for rhetoric, not enactment.

The President is currently benefiting from better economic news, and carefully avoided doing anything in his budget that would endanger his reelection strategy. So his budget contains no controversial cuts or reforms, wages class warfare on the affluent, and ignores the national debt. The Administration is betting that with a strengthening economy, few will worry about the deficit, so irresponsibility on that issue will cost the White House nothing. So the President proposed a budget not about the public policy, but rather electoral success.

Week 162
(STICKER SHOCK)

February 26, 2012

The President's political advisors have been unable to hide their glee at the brutal Republican nomination fight and the President's rising poll numbers. The conventional wisdom is that the White House is gaining from disenchantment with the Republican field and a strengthening economy, putting the President in a commanding position for reelection. Certainly, President Obama is better positioned than he was three months ago, but there are troubles on the horizon that should worry the Administration. Those challenges come in the form of rising gas prices, increasing tensions in the Middle East, and falling fundraising for the President. News came out on each of these this week, and each item underlines the unpredictability of the upcoming election.

No matter how events unfold in 2012, the election is going to be close because of decisions the President made in his first term. By forcing through Obamacare, pushing controversial bailouts and green energy programs, and racking up huge deficits, the President alienated many blocks of voters, including large numbers of voters in key swing states. The hope of the White House has been that the economy would strengthen so much that the President could overcome the unpopularity of many of his programs. To date, economic indicators have given hope to the President's supporters, making them increasingly optimistic about their prospects. But ominous reminders emerged this week that should temper their premature celebrations.

The economy is no doubt improving, but it is still weak, unemployment is high, and more than sixty percent of voters think that nation is on the wrong track. Given this, the President's positive economic narrative is uncertain at best. This instability was underlined this week as gas prices skyrocketed, with crude oil now above $105 per barrel, and gas prices are marching inexorably toward $4 per gallon or higher. The rise in oil prices is being fueled by speculation on rising demand, tensions in the Middle East over Iran's nuclear program, and its threats to interrupt shipping in the Strait of Hormuz, and a growing civil war in Syria. The last time we had an energy shock, in 2008, it was quickly followed by a financial crisis and a deep recession. Few expect anything so dire in 2012, but higher gas prices could dampen consumer spending and make voters ever more pessimistic about the economy. More importantly, higher gas prices have a disproportionate impact on families already struggling.

The President is particularly vulnerable to a backlash on gas prices because of his carbon tax proposals, his new regulations that are limiting refining capacity, his delayed review of the Keystone oil pipeline, and his Administration's restrictions on new drilling. Domestic energy production has actually risen over the last three years, but largely because of new technology and higher prices that make marginal fields profitable. No matter the increased production, the President has made himself an easy target for blame if gas prices rise to the levels reached in 2008. Prices at that level would also increase costs for many common consumer goods, putting ever more pressure on the economic recovery. So despite the current rosy scenarios being offered by the President's political operatives, there are potential storm clouds on the horizon.

This was demonstrated this week by the fundraising disclosures from the President and his political opponents. President Obama continues to outraise his rivals, but the pace of his fundraising has slowed considerably and he is now underperforming projections. That may explain why the President's campaign has encouraged its supporters to start super pacs (independent political action committees that can take unlimited donations under the cover of the Supreme Court's *Citizens United* decision), after the White House has spent months condemning them. It seems the Administration has realized that its conventional fundraising will not be able to keep pace with Republicans, and the race ahead will demand more resources. So consumers and the President's campaign both have been hit with sticker shock this week, showing that the upcoming electoral contest will be far more difficult than the President's team is currently willing to admit.

Week 163

(Loose Talk)

March 4, 2012

The White House devoted much of this week to exploiting loose talk by conservative commentator Rush Limbaugh and trying to dampen loose talk about the potential for war with Iran. In the case of Limbaugh's comments, they presented an opportunity to portray Republicans as anti-women extremists. As for Iran, the growing talk of war underlined the risks and uncertainties in 2012. Both issues helped demonstrate the unpredictability of the current political climate, where dialogue and comments from the fringes can drive the national debate. The key for the President is successfully riding these waives of uncertainty and turning them to his advantage. In the case of Limbaugh, the task may well be easy, but with Iran, the task will be much harder.

Rush Limbaugh has been a controversial figure for decades, and regularly makes comments that put him in the mainstream media's crosshairs. Liberal elites love to highlight controversial comments by personalities like Limbaugh because it furthers their favored narrative of intolerance on the right. In this instance, the controversy arose when Limbaugh waded into the stormy waters of the current debate about the Obama Administration's directive that religious institutions provide free birth control even if that coverage conflicts with their religious teachings. Republicans have framed the issue as one of religious liberty, while Democrats say it is a question of women's rights.

On February 28, the Democrats were staging a political event on the issue, when the House Democratic Steering & Policy Committee offered testimony from various women's rights personalities in support of the Administration's contraceptive policies. Among the witnesses was Sandra Fluke, a law student at Georgetown University, who criticized Georgetown's refusal to include contraceptives in her student health care coverage. She said it was improper for Georgetown to dictate "whose need is legitimate" and that the policy is contrary to the Jesuit teaching to "care for the whole person" She also said that a student should not be forced to make a choice between attending Georgetown or getting needed health care "simply because she is a woman." Limbaugh highlighted this testimony on his show, saying Fluke was asking taxpayers to pay for her sex life, making her a "slut" who wants to be "paid to have sex." He also suggested if people like Fluke wanted payments for sex, they should be forced to post videos of their sexual adventures on the internet.

These comments caused a national uproar. Limbaugh was condemned on the Left and the Right, the Republicans candidates ran from him, and many of his advertisers dropped his show. Democrats and the mainstream media used the controversy to attack Republicans, and President Obama tried to directly capitalize from the controversy by calling Fluke to offer his sympathy and support. No one could have guessed that loose talk by Limbaugh would have become such a big issue, but the comments fit perfectly into the narrative that the Republicans are anti-woman. The President rode the wave, trying to gain as much as he could from the controversy. Of course, lost in all the indignation was the irony that no such controversy arose when commentators on the Left called Sarah Palin a Bimbo or Laura Ingraham a slut.

While the loose talk by Limbaugh supplied endless fun for Democrat political operatives, the loose talk about Iran was quite a different story. For weeks, rising tension about Iran's nuclear program has been pushing that issue onto the front pages. Enhanced sanctions, Iranian threats to close the Straits of Hormuz, and skyrocketing gas prices all converged to create a sense of urgency. This helped lead to increasing talk of a military strike on Iran, talk partly fueled by Israeli Prime Minister Benjamin Netanyahu's visit to Washington this week to meet with President Obama. President Obama could not escape the intense focus on this issue even before a friendly crowd at a New York fundraiser on March 2, when he was heckled about military action against Iran, forcing him to comment that "nobody has announced a war, young Lady."

While the Limbaugh controversy was pure joy for the White House, Iran is pure terror. If Iran tests a nuclear bomb, or if Israel strikes Iran before the election, fuel prices will rise even higher, there could be a run on stocks, and the fragile recovery could be endangered. Without that recovery, there is little the White House can tout to voters, so the risks on the Iranian issue are huge. That is why the White House is trying to put a lid on the loose talk about war with Iran, but in truth the issue is beyond their control. Israel will strike Iran if necessary, and they will not worry about the President's political calendar when they do so. So for all the joy about Limbaugh's loose talk, the real story was the loose talk about Iran, which is of much more consequence to the President.

Week 164

(Super Bad)

March 11, 2012

Super Tuesday week turned out to be super bad for Republicans and a great week for President Obama. All policy making in Washington has ground to halt, replaced entirely by the upcoming presidential campaign, and every bit of news this week was disheartening to Republicans and hopeful for Democrats. The Super Tuesday primaries held on March 6 resulted in a split decision, with Mitt Romney failing to win enough states to force his opponents out of the race. Then the Republicans' chances of taking the Senate suffered two blows. Former Senator Bob Kerry announced he would run for the seat being vacated by retiring Democratic Senator Ben Nelson, and Republican Senator Olympia Snowe unexpectedly decided not to run for reelection in Democrat-leaning Maine. To top it all off, on March 9, the February unemployment report was released, showing that the economy created 221,000 jobs, the fourth straight month of job creation at that level.

For months political observers had predicted that Super Tuesday would end the Republican race, based on the assumption that Mitt Romney would perform so strongly that his rivals would give up their bids. The results from Super Tuesday were solid for Romney, but nowhere near the level needed to end the Republican nominating contest. Of the ten major contests, Romney won Idaho with 61%, Massachusetts with 72%, Alaska with 32%, Virginia with 60%, Vermont with 40%, and most importantly, Ohio with 38%. However, former Senator Rick Santorum also had a strong night, winning North Dakota with 40%, Oklahoma with 34% and Tennessee with 37%. Newt Gingrich won only his home state of Georgia with 47%. If the Republican nominating contest were only about delegates, Romney could claim a solid victory. He amassed a huge lead in delegates, with his total surpassing 400, more than double Santorum, his nearest rival. But the nominating race is not simply about delegates, it is also about unifying the party and exciting the base for the impending battle with President Obama. On those fronts, the results of Super Tuesday were disappointing. Romney continues to be the acceptable candidate, but not the favored one. He continued to get delegates, but he is not garnering much enthusiasm. And most importantly, his weakness is encouraging his rivals to stay in the race, meaning the contest will continue for many more weeks.

The White House and the Democrats are delighted with the Republicans' drawn-out primary fight. While the GOP puts its resources into internal combat, the Democrats can raise money and prepare for the Fall battle. The Democrats face a difficult task retaking the House, especially with Republicans using redistricting to fortify their majority, but things are looking brighter for the Democrats in the Senate. The Democrats hold a slim 53 to 47 majority in the Senate, and in 2012 they have twice as many seats to defend, with many of those seats in GOP states. It looked like the Republicans would have a good shot at retaking the Senate, but two seats formerly thought safe GOP wins went into the undecided column this week. The GOP thought it had a lock on retiring Senator Ben Nelson's seat in Nebraska, then former Senator Bob Kerry announced he would run for the seat. Likewise, the GOP was sure to retain the Maine Senate seat of popular incumbent Olympia Snowe, until she decided to retire because of gridlock in Washington. So now the GOP task is two seats more difficult. This cheered Democrats on the Hill and in the White House.

Democrats were further cheered by the February unemployment report. With that report, the economy has now created more than 200,000 jobs for 4 consecutive months. This adds to the growing evidence of a strengthening U.S. recovery, which is great news for the President. The stronger the economy becomes, the harder it will be for any GOP nominee to unseat the President. The President used this latest unemployment report to herald the improving economy and tout his economic policies. But all is not rosy on the economic scene. Even though the economy created more than 200,000 jobs, the unemployment rated stayed at 8.3%. This is because the improving economy has encouraged the long-term unemployed to re-enter the job market. For months, the President has benefitted from a falling unemployment rates produced by decent job growth and a smaller labor pool. But as more and more unemployed rejoin the labor force because of a stronger economy, it will get increasingly hard to move the unemployment rate lower. That combined with ever higher oil prices creates the prospect of an uneven economic rebound, where consumers remain unsatisfied because of prices at the pump and lingering high unemployment. So even with a super week, Democrats have plenty to worry about.

Week 165

(RAMPAGES)

March 18, 2012

This was a week of rampages, both foreign and domestic. The week began with a March 11 shooting rampage that left 16 civilians dead in Afghanistan. Then on March 13, Rick Santorum went on an electoral rampage in the South, winning primaries in both Alabama and Mississippi, and prolonging the Republican primary campaign. Then President Obama went on a rhetorical rampage in an energy speech on March 15, using heated words to accuse Republican of being Neanderthals on science. Each rampage was different, but each showed how events have become less restrained and more combative.

The March 16 shooting rampage in Afghanistan was by far the most worrying development. Staff Sergeant Robert Bales is a 38-year-old sniper in the U.S. Army on his fourth combat tour, with a wife and two children back in the states. It appears he put on his gear, walked off his base, went to an Afghan village and killed 16 civilians, including 6 children and 3 women. He was arrested by the U.S. military. The U.S. and Afghan political leadership are now struggling to deal with the aftermath. With the NATO presence already widely unpopular, this shooting only increased tensions, spawning new attacks and protests against U.S. and coalition forces. Talks with the Taliban were also suspended because of the attack. President Karzi of Afghanistan was quick to take advantage of the outrage, calling for U.S. forces to leave Afghan villages and requesting that Sergeant Bales be tried in Afghanistan. Clearly the Karzi government fears its internal enemies more than the United States, and now believes anti-U.S. rhetoric is the best way to ensure its survival. All these troubles, coupled with a corrupt central government, unreliable Afghan troops (some of whom have turned their fire on their U.S. allies), and falling support for the war at home, are all leading to significant instability in Afghanistan. The Obama Administration was quick to say its policy and timeline for U.S. withdrawal would not change, but no doubt the events of March 11 will make success in Afghanistan more difficult.

Rick Santorum's rampage in the South was of a very different character, but might be equally consequential. After Mitt Romney's strong but not decisive wins on Super Tuesday, the primaries on March 13 were a key test to see whether Santorum and Gingrich can muster the strength to stay in the race. Gingrich hoped to win Alabama and Mississippi, Romney called it an away game for him, while Santorum quietly and effectively continued his pitch to social issue voters. When the results came in, Santorum won both Alabama with 35% and Mississippi with 34%. Gingrich placed second in both contests, with Romney a close third. Romney was not shut out on the night, because he did win the Hawaii primary, with 45% of the vote. Santorum's romp through the South denied a knockout blow to Romney and crippled Gingrich, but from a delegate standpoint, Romney lost no ground. The math is against both Santorum and Gingrich, but it appears they do not care. Their goal is a brokered convention where Romney lacks the delegates to win the nomination outright. No one expects Gingrich will prevail in a convention floor fight, but Gingrich seems unconcerned, he is simply enjoying attacking Romney and the media with equal vigor. As for Santorum, he seems to believe if he can deny Romney the nomination and has a chance to be the alternative at the convention. Both men have an anyone but Romney agenda, which portends a long primary fight.

Despite troubles in Afghanistan and in-fighting among Republicans, the President's primary focus was on his reelection. Rising gas prices are posing a dangerous political challenge to the President, as shown by CBS and NBC polls, which both reported the President's approval rating dropping to the low 40 percent. Energy is a difficult issue for the President because he has opposed expanded oil production, instead favoring billions in taxpayer loans to clean energy companies, some of which have resulted in messy failures and bankruptcies costing taxpayers billions. Seeing the political risk, in true Chicago form, the President took the offensive during a speech on March 15 to a college crowd at Prince Georges Community College. Rather than a reasoned defense of his energy policy, the President opted instead for a heated campaign-style speech where he accused Republicans as being part of a flat-earth society that fails to recognize the wisdom of his green energy proposals. He said with only 2% of the world's proven oil reserves, we cannot drill our way to energy independence, and he went on to a sure applause line of attacking oil companies and calling for an end to subsidies he claims they receive. There was nothing surprising in the content of the President's speech, it was the tone that was disturbing. The American people want progress on energy production and gas prices, but the President opted instead to campaign and ridicule Republicans. There was no effort at reason or compromise, just attacks on his opponents and efforts to motivate his base. A sure sign he intends to do nothing about the energy crisis beyond campaigning.

Week 166
(TRAYVON MISSION)

March 25, 2012

One would have expected that the big news of the week would have been the Illinois primary, which offered the opportunity for Mitt Romney to solidify his position as the inevitable Republican nominee. Romney did get a big win in Illinois, capturing 47% of the vote and expanding his delegate lead, but that win was overshadowed by a more troubling story. On February 26, Trayvon Martin, a 17 year-old African American, was shot dead in Sanford Florida by George Zimmerman, a Hispanic community watch volunteer. The tragic death of Trayvon Martin has been in the news for weeks, but it suddenly erupted into a political controversy rattling Florida and national politics, and even prompting President Obama to wade into the controversy.

Trayvon Martin's killing was a tragedy for his family and his community. It appears he was in a gated community visiting his family when he had an altercation with George Zimmerman. The details of that altercation remain unclear, but what is certain is that at the end of it, Trayvon Martin was dead from a single gunshot from a pistol Zimmerman was carrying. Even though Zimmerman clearly shot and killed Martin, he was not arrested. After being questioned by police for some seven hours, he was released, sparking a growing controversy about gun control, racism, and electoral politics. With this combustible combination of issues, President Obama could not restrain himself from attempting to exploit it.

George Zimmerman is half Hispanic, but in the media, he has been portrayed as a white vigilante who killed a black teenager for no good reason. This storyline certainly supplied plenty of ammunition for a racism angle. Then came the gun control. One of the reasons George Zimmerman has not been arrested is Florida's Stand Your Ground law, which allows citizens to stand their ground and use force to defend themselves if they reasonably feel threatened. This law, which was supported by the NRA, has made it very difficult to press charges against Zimmerman, presumably because in his police interviews, and possibly through other evidence, Zimmerman has established at least some basis that he was acting in self-defense. The electoral issue arises because all these events took place in Florida, a huge electoral prize that President Obama can only carry if he motivates minority voters to go to the polls.

The longer Zimmerman remained a free man, the more Trayvon's parents and civil rights leader began to protest. Eventually, Al Sharpton, Jesse Jackson, and others went to Florida to demand justice for Trayvon and prosecution of Zimmerman. These marches and protests led to growing media coverage and a true national controversy. The police chief in Sanford had to step down temporarily amid the protest, and Florida's Republican governor, Rick Scott, had to appoint a special prosecutor to look into the case. The Justice Department even opened an inquiry.

The shooting of Trayvon Martin was certainly a tragedy, but no one knows the whole story. What is clear is that gun control advocates, civil rights leaders, and Democrat political operatives see an opportunity to exploit this killing for their own gain. Gun control groups are highlighting the Stand Your Ground Law as an example of gun nut policies in practice. Civil rights leaders are showcasing the Trayvon killing as an example that racial injustice persists, even though the facts are unknown and Zimmerman is Hispanic. Democrats see a chance to motivate their base and get out votes.

With all these various interests swirling, then came President Obama. The President cannot seem to restrain himself from intervening in social controversies of the day. During a press conference on March 23, after he nominated Dartmouth's President Jim Kim for President of the World Bank, the President took one question, obviously pre-planned to allow for a comment on the Trayvon Martin case. The President was careful to say he could not comment too much because the investigation was on-going, but then he went directly for personal advantage. The President showed sympathy for the family and said millions of Americans are "soul searching to figure out how does something like this happen in America." Then he said "when I think about Trayvon I think about my own kids" and that if he had a son "he would look like Trayvon." This effort to identify with the Trayvon affair without directly commenting on the investigation was an attempt to capitalize on sympathy for Trayvon's parents and signal that the President is with them and all others similarly oppressed. It was a subtle political move designed to take advantage of public outrage. The President went on a Trayvon mission to benefit himself, in the hope it will win him Florida and reelection.

Week 167

(OF BROCCOLI AND BURIALS)

April 1, 2012

Obamacare had its day in court, and it was a bloody affair. After pushing the Affordable Care Act through Congress with procedural tricks and only Democrat votes, the President has spent the last two years trying to convince voters to support the law, while his lawyers have been fighting in federal courts throughout the nation to preserve it. All along, liberals scoffed at the notion that there could be any credible constitutional challenge to Obamacare. Instead, they portrayed a lawsuit filed by 26 states and other actions challenging the law by interest groups as a last gasp by the enemies of progress. This narrative was rudely scuttled when the President's lawyers stood before nine Supreme Court Justices for three days of argument on the constitutionally of Obamacare. Far from a baseless gambit, the President's lawyers were met with questions like: if Congress can order every citizen to buy health insurance, then could the government order each of us to buy broccoli or burial insurance. The government's lawyers said "no," but not very convincingly, and now rather than a slam dunk, it looks like Obamacare might foul out.

It is not an exaggeration to say that the Obamacare hearing was likely the biggest argument to be heard before the Supreme Court in the last 50 years. That is because Obamacare poses the possibly of fundamentally changing the relationship between the federal government and its citizens, not to mention the States. The central premise of Obamacare is that the federal government has the power not only to regulate interstate commerce, but also to compel individuals to participate in commerce. Similarly, the Medicaid mandate in Obamacare would change the relationship between the States and the federal government by allowing the federal government to coerce States into participating in a federal program. Understanding the critical challenges these provisions pose to our system of delegated powers and federalism, the Supreme Court scheduled three days of argument from March 26 through March 28 to address the law's constitutionality.

The first day was dedicated to a standing issue, whether an 1867 statute prevents the Supreme Court from ruling on the constitutionality of Obamacare before it goes fully into effect in 2014. The President's lawyers pushed this argument hoping to prevent a ruling on the key questions for two years, in which time the composition of the Supreme Court might change or the program might become so imbedded or popular that a constitutional challenge would be more difficult. However, it seemed clear after the first day of argument that the Supreme Court saw no impediment to addressing the constitutional questions, so the Administration's first judicial tactic appeared to fail.

Day one did not go well for the White House, but by day two things only got worse. Day two was devoted to the most critical constitutional challenged to Obamacare, the individual mandate. That is the part of Obamacare that requires every American to buy health insurance or pay a penalty. The government's lawyers argued that this power was within the scope of the Commerce Clause because everyone at some point in their lives needs health care, so the government is not requiring people to participate in the health care market so much as regulating a participation that is by its nature inevitable. However, the conservative justices did not appear to buy that argument. Justice Kennedy questioned whether it was permissible to create commerce in order to regulate it, noting that such a power would alter the relationship between the government and the individual in a "very fundamental way." Justice Scalia said if the government can compel the purchase of health insurance, it can compel the purchase of broccoli, since everyone needs to eat. Then Justice Alito chimed in noting that the government could likewise require everyone to buy burial insurance, since we all will die. The Solicitor General Donald Verilli said that striking down Obamacare would be judicial activism in the same vein as the infamous substantive due process decision in *Lochner*. Chief Justice Roberts dismissed that argument, stating: "The key in *Lochner* [a New Deal case finding that a regulation violated substantive due process of the 14th Amendment] is that we were talking about regulation of the States, right, and the States are not limited to enumerated powers. The Federal Government is. And it seems to me it's an entirely different question when you ask yourself whether or not there are going to be limits in the Federal power, as opposed to limits on the States, which was the issue in *Lochner*." The liberal justices tried to throw a lifeline to the Administration with their questions, but when the President's lawyers could not come up with any convincing limiting principle on the federal commerce clause power, little could be done to salvage the argument.

If day two was disturbing, day three was terrifying for the White House. The morning arguments were devoted to whether the whole law should be thrown out if the individual mandate is found unconstitutional. The tenor of the discussion seemed to be what should happen when unconstitutionality was found, not if. Justice Kennedy again seemed concerned about letting the remainder of the law stand, because it would put a risk on insurers that Congress could not have intended. Justice Scalia noted that he could not recall an instance when the Supreme Court ripped out the guts of a law, and still let the rest of the law stand. The arguments concluded with the Medicaid mandate, which the government thought was its easiest hurdle, but even on that point, the conservative Justices seemed concerned about the provision.

It is hard from argument to tell how Justices will vote. Obamacare could still be upheld on some narrow ground when the final decision issues in June. But the impression from the hearing is that Obamacare is in trouble. President Obama spent the first 18 months of his Presidency pushing Obamacare through. It is his singular legislative achievement, albeit a controversial and unpopular one. For Democrats, Obamacare is a natural and necessary expansion of the entitlement state, paving the road to further social democracy. For Republicans, if Obamacare stands, the ability to resist ever more centralized control of economic activity will be deeply undermined. It is a fundamental ideological struggle, and one that might be decided by issues like broccoli and burials.

Week 168

(Unprecedented)

April 8, 2012

Just when the White House was becoming convinced that events were falling into place for its reelection campaign, the Obamacare arguments and the April 6 jobs report threatened to throw everything into confusion. The big political news of the week should have been Mitt Romney's inexorable march toward the GOP nomination. By winning the Maryland, the District of Columbia, and most importantly the Wisconsin primary (by 6 points) on April 3, the media and most Republicans proclaimed the nomination race over. But most of the national attention was not on the GOP primaries, but on the reverberating fallout from the Supreme Court arguments on Obamacare. Fearing that his biggest legislative achievement might fall to a legal challenge, the President decided to give a test run to an anti-Supreme Court campaign them, saying that any decision that might overrule Obamacare would be unprecedented. Then a different kind of unprecedented event caused concern for the White House, when the Labor Department reported only 120,000 jobs were created in March and said the unprecedented warm weather in the Spring might have made the jobs market look healthier than it really is. So unwelcome surprises were arising at every turn.

The Obama White House is always focused on political spin above all else. With no legislative agenda and no policy goal other than reelection, it was not surprising that the first reaction of the Administration to the Supreme Court argument was to test drive a war on the Court there. So at a news conference on April 2, the President took a shot at the Supreme Court, saying that "I'm confident that the Supreme Court will not take what would be an unprecedented extraordinary step of overturning a law that was passed by a strong majority of a democratically elected Congress." The President hoped his comment would be a warning shot to his opponents, but he so botched the statement that it5 was more like shooting himself in the foot. The President likes to describe himself as a former constitutional law professor, but the problem is almost everything he said was wrong. It would not be unprecedented for the Supreme Court to strike down a law passed by Congress, that has done that more than a hundred times. Also, Obamacare was not passed by a strong majority, it passed by a vote of 217 to 212 in the House, despite a huge Democrat majority. Also, the President's comments seemed to imply he doubts the Supreme Court's right to review Acts of Congress, something which is a hallmark of our jurisprudence since the 1803 decision in *Marbury vs. Madison*. Further, his reference to actions by a democratically controlled legislature seemed to imply that if the majority wants it, it must be constitutional, but we know that was the exact opposite view of the framers, which is why they created a government framework of enumerated and separated power, to check the popular will. Good thing our professor President is up for reelection rather than tenure.

After President Obama's in artful comments, the White House and the Justice Department had to spend the remainder of the week walking them back. White House Press Secretary Jay Carney got tied in verbal knots while he tried to pretend the President made no mistake in his comments. Then in a hearing before the United States Court of Appeals for the Fifth Circuit, Judge Jerry Smith was so incensed by the President's comments that he ordered a Department of Justice lawyer to provide a written statement explaining whether the Administration was now going to contest the Federal Courts' power of judicial review. Attorney General Holder was then forced to state publically that Federal Courts have the final say on whether laws are constitutional.

The lesson for the White House in this whole affair is that there is some cost in trying to make everything political. The first reaction of the Administration when it looked like Obamacare might fall was not how to fix the law and save the policy, but how to spin the issue for electoral advantage. The President is clearly leading the charge in that effort. But by attacking the Federal Courts, the President took on the one branch of government that the public actually respects. More importantly, if you are going to declare war on the courts, it is best to get your facts right, something the President did not do. So rather than setting the stage for a war on the courts campaign, the Administration got a stern warning that there could be a price to pay with that tactic.

Then the President moved from an "unprecedented" comment to an even more unwelcomed event. For the last four months, the economy has shown strong job growth, feeding into an Obama narrative that his policies are finally creating jobs. Most expected more of the same with the March jobs reports, with forecasts calling for 200,000 or more jobs created. The numbers came in at

120,000, along with reductions for the job creation figures for prior months. The unemployment rate fell to 8.2%, but only because of further shrinkage in the labor force, as more workers left the work force. Why the sudden turn in the job market? It seems the prior months of good numbers were overstated because of the unprecedented warm weather. That, combined with rising gas prices and a building recession in Europe, have led to fears the U.S. recovery will slow, certainly very bad news for the White House. So the President now has some new problems to deal with, even if they do not prove to be so unprecedented after all.

Week 169

(SANS TORUM)

April 15, 2012

What a difference one week makes. After months of improving polls, better employment data, and a divisive GOP primary campaign, the White House was feeling increasingly confident that it had the reelection of the President well in hand. Then, on April 9, 2012, former Pennsylvania Senator Rick Santorum suspended his campaign. Any hope Santorum had of winning the Republican nomination was slim anyways. He staked everything on winning his home state primary in Pennsylvania on April. But with his bank account empty, polls showing Romney gaining, and in the face of a massive advertising campaign planned by the Romney forces, Santorum called it quits. In an instant, the GOP primary fight was all but over. True Ron Paul and Gingrich are still in the campaign, but Gingrich is now running in name only, and Ron Paul is trying to make a point, not win the nomination. So the general election has now begun, and it started off very well for the Romney forces.

One of the biggest themes for the Obama campaign in the last few weeks has been the supposed war on women. Starting with the controversial regulation seeking to compel Catholic institutions to pay for contraceptives under Obamacare, Democrat forces have been working hard create a narrative that the GOP is insensitive to the concerns of women. The mainstream media quickly latched on to this theme and ran with it, and polls began to show a strong movement of independent women toward Obama. But after weeks of building this narrative, it was all threatened by some ill-considered comments from a Democrat strategist. Hillary Rosen is a Washington lobbyist and insider who also plays the role of a pundit on television. During a CNN program, she was on a panel discussing Romney's efforts to address women's concerns by pointing to his wife Ann Romney and her efforts to show empathy with women's concerns. Ann Romney is a stay at home mother of five and a pillar of the Romney campaign. To counter Ann Romney's comments on women's issues, Hillary Rosen went on the attack, claiming Ann Romney "has never worked a day in her life," the obvious implication being raising children is not real work.

The Obama campaign was quick to sense the danger and condemned Rosen's comments, but Rosen at first refused to back down, issuing several non-apology apologies before being forced to take back her statements. While the controversy raged, even the President felt the need to wade in, stating that wives should be off limits, raising kids is work, and as always, he tried to personalize the issue by noting that when Michele stayed home for period to raise his kids, she was definitely working. The reason the Obama campaign took this small flap so seriously is because it exposed a fundamental contradiction in the war on women narrative. The feminist backers of President Obama have always taken a disdainful attitude towards stay at home moms and other women who have a more traditional sentiments. While feminists are more than happy to look down their noses at such women, the White House cannot afford to, so when Rosen's comments showcased the real attitude of Obama's liberal supporters, quick action was necessary. No doubt this event will prove to be a minor one in the history of this campaign, but it certainly exposed some risks for Obama in his war on women theme.

Another theme for the President has been fairness. Increasingly, President Obama is defending his tax hike proposals and spending priorities less on fiscal discipline grounds and more in furtherance of fairness. This fairness campaign seeks to capitalize on the Occupy Wall Street movement and the effort to portray Romney as a rich and out of touch elitist. One of the President's favorite weapons for this task is his Buffett rule proposal, which would set a minimum tax rate for people earning over $1 million per year of 30%. The White House has been using this proposal, along with the President's characterization of the House's latest budget proposal as "social Darwinism," to claim that Republicans only want to help the rich, while denying benefits and programs to working Americans. The strategy has been working well, until this week, when the President seemed to admit that his Buffett rule proposal was a gimmick in terms of deficit reduction because it does not simplify the tax code and it would only raise about $5 billion per years, barely measurable when compared to our trillion dollar deficits. The Buffett rule will come up for a vote in Congress soon and is expected to fail, and no doubt the President will try to get political mileage out of it, but his admission that it is a gimmick might limit the benefit.

Bad news for the President also came on the economy. New claims for unemployment unexpectedly rose, coming off last week's poor March jobs reports. The European economy continues to slide into rescission and gas prices remain high. None of this is good news for the White House. Then a story broke that the General Services Administration (which is supposed to safeguard taxpayer money) threw a West Coast convention that wasted more the $800,000 in taxpayer money on parties and games, hardly a sign of fiscal responsibility. Then, two polls published showing Romney either tied or slightly ahead of the President for the general election campaign. The change in the polls might reflect an end to the GOP nomination contest and the emergence of a clearer choice for voters. So as the general election fight begins all that optimism at the White House is looking premature.

Week 170

(MONEY PLANE)

April 22, 2012

This week the focus of the political class quickly turned from the Republican campaign to the President's money plane. Mitt Romney all but secured the Republican nomination when Newt Gingrich suspended his campaign, so all focus was now on the general election and more importantly, the life blood of politics, money. At this early stage in the general election, the battle is all about organization, setting themes, and most of all raising money. For his part, fundraising seems to be President Obama's main occupation, and has been so for quite some time. He has done more than 140 fundraisers, many of them coupled with so-called official trips to battleground states. This week the cost to the taxpayer for his use of Air Force One for what are obviously political trips came under criticism, since it appears the Administration is using Air Force One as its personal money plane.

There is nothing new about presidents using Air Force One for trips that are more about politics than official business. Presidents are required to use Air Force One for travel, so the plane is employed for vacations, political trips, and official duties. The issue with President Obama is not that he flies Air Force One on political trips, it's the frequency of these journeys. With very few obligations on his official calendar since the debt limit deal in August 2011, the President is spending most of his time campaigning. He is flying Air Force One all over the country to give speeches to further his reelection and to raise money. As required, he reimburses the Treasury for non-official personal or political trips, but those reimbursements are not fully disclosed and cover only a small fraction of the $179,500 cost per hour of operating Air Force One. This has created an unseemly image of a President campaigning on the public dime.

There is no doubt the White House is willing to take criticism for the President's heavy fundraising schedule because money is one of his key advantages. With a still weak economy and an approval rating rarely getting above 50%, the President needs funds to wage a winning campaign. And funds he has. March 2012 fundraising numbers were released this week showing that the President's campaign raised $34.8 million and has $100 million in the bank. His super-pac, Priorities USA raised $2.5 million and has $5 million in the bank. Plus the DNC raised $17.9 million and has $24.4 million in the bank, much of that raised with the President's help. With totals like these, it is no wonder the Administration is willing to take criticism for its heavy political schedule.

The GOP is fundraising as well, they just are not using taxpayer dollars or Air Force One to do it. In March 2012, the Romney campaign raised $12.7 million, and has $10 million in the bank. This was a great fundraising month for Romney. His super-pac, Restore Our Future raised $8.7 million and has $6.7 million in the bank. As for the RNC, it raised $13.7 million and has $32.7 million in the bank. So the GOP has hardly been inactive on the fundraising circuit. These totals might leave one to think that the President and the Democrats have a huge fundraising advantage over the GOP, but looks can be deceiving. The GOP has been much more successful using super-pacs, with the Karl Rove super-pac Restoring Our Future leading the way. Restoring Our Future raised $98.8 million in 2011, has $24,4 million in the bank, and expects to raise $300 million for the Fall campaign. The President had expected to have a huge money advantage in November, but that is not going to happen.

One of the reasons the President has had to do so many political trips is that he is not doing well with affluent donors. As a result, he has had to rely on smaller donations, requiring more fundraising events. It is a matter of conjecture why big donors have closed their wallets, but the President's rhetoric against the 1% and the impression he is anti-business likely have had a negative impact on his fundraising. So we now have the spectacle of President Obama apparently spending all his time giving political speeches and going to fundraisers to get small donations using his money plane. The question is, will it hurt or help him in the end.

Week 171
(BRUTAL YOUTH)

April 29, 2012

When President Obama won his stunning victory in 2008, much of his success was fueled by the youth vote. The President energized young voters at an unprecedented level, with his message of change and his youthful and optimistic vision for America. The youth vote helped him carry states like North Carolina and Colorado, leading to his landslide victory. How things have changed in just over three years. Young voters are discouraged by high unemployment, skyrocketing college costs, crushing debt, and limited opportunities. The change they voted for in 2008 has not materialized, and they appear poised to exact a brutal cost from the President.

The White House is well aware that the youth vote is critical to reelection. With a huge majority of voters saying the country is on the wrong track, to win President Obama must use constituency politics by carrying minorities, the suburban woman vote, and the youth vote. The problem is, in many respects young voters have suffered the most from the recession. Most of the tax cuts and new entitlements have been far more favorable to seniors than the young, while unemployment for those under 25 is more than double the national average. The very youth who elected President Obama are the primary victims of the recession.

Given this, the President and his team know they have a great deal of work to do to energize and win the youth vote. One only needs to look at the itineraries for the President, Vice President, and First Lady to notice the clear focus on the youth vote. Since taking office, they have done 130 trips to college campuses, most in battleground states, ostensibly to talk about policy issues that impact the young, but in reality to campaign. This week, the President continued that effort with a trip that included the University of North Carolina, Iowa City College, and the University of Colorado. The stated purpose of these visits was to talk about federal student loan programs, which are facing a doubling of interest payments if Congress does not take action. But again, that was just the stated purpose. The real objective was reelection, made clear because Colorado, North Carolina, and Iowa are all swing states the President wants to carry.

The President's talks at each stop were not restrained or dignified policy discussions, but full throated campaign speeches laced with attacks on the GOP. The President even took a direct swipe at Mitt Romney by discussing how he and Michelle had student loans because they were not born with silver spoons in their mouths, an obvious reference to the wealth of the Romney family. Earlier in his Presidency, Obama might have been able to get away with such a clearly political trip at taxpayer expense, but not anymore. The White House press corps again went at the Administration on the issue of whether the President was campaigning on the taxpayer's dime. Some in Congress even called for an investigation into the Administration's use of Air Force One for political trips.

The criticisms thrown at the President demonstrates the difficult balancing act he is facing. He can no longer afford to give optimistic speeches about hope and change. He now has a record, and that record for youth voters is not good. So he has to try to rally the youth vote with heated rhetoric, but the more he does that, the more it looks like he is using public funds for his private benefit. In the end, the White House likely has no choice but to risk such criticism, because it has to motivate the young to vote for the President. Polls still show that the President leads among the young, but those same polls show low enthusiasm for the President, so a brutal reality might await him if his youthful supporters simply do not bother to show up on Election Day.

Week 172

(CAMPAIGN-ISTAN)

May 6, 2012

With President Obama searching for any and every positive story he can tell to support reelection, the war against Al Qaeda offers some interesting promise. The President gave the order that led to the successful raid that killed Osama bin Laden, relentless drone strikes have killed many top terrorists, and the Administration has resisted calls from the Left to close Gitmo and try high level Al-Qaeda leaders in civilian courts. All this is a credit to the President, but sometimes credit rings truer when given by someone else, rather than when it is self-proclaimed. In a White House where everything is politicized, the temptation of the one year anniversary of the bin Laden raid was too great for the President to strike a dignified pose. Instead, his campaign openly exploited this foreign policy success, even going so far as to say that Mitt Romney would not have given the order to kill bin Laden. Then, on the actual May 1 anniversary of bin Laden's death, the President made a surprise trip to Afghanistan to proclaim that success is "within reach" and to praise the performance of the troops and himself. It seems Afghanistan is just the latest prop in the President's reelection campaign.

It is understandable why the White House wants to get political mileage out of the war on Al-Qaeda, since domestic issues present a far more difficult credit-taking challenge. The President hopes to appeal to moderates by highlighting his tough attacks on terrorists, while emphasizing that he is ending the wars in Iraq and Afghanistan to please his liberal base. His most recent trip to Afghanistan (his first in 17 months) showed this exact agenda. The President claimed that he travelled to Afghanistan to sign a treaty with the Karzai government on the status of U.S. forces in Afghanistan, but the real purpose was photo ops with the troops and a dramatic address to the nation from the Bagram Air Force Base. After the usual praise of the troops, he trumpeted his role in the killing of bin Laden and then proclaimed that the Taliban were on the run, that Afghan security forces are stepping up, and that as a result success is near. He proudly announced that 23,000 more troops would leave this year, and that most U.S. forces would be out of Afghanistan by 2014. It all sounded pretty good.

The reality, however, is very different from the President's rhetoric. Most importantly, there is little evidence that the Taliban are on the run. They have staged several high profile attacks in central Kabul and continue to have safe havens in Pakistan from which to launch their attacks. Also, no one believes that Afghan security forces are anywhere near ready to handle the county's defense. American forces remain critical to any success on the battlefield. The Karzai government remains weak and corrupt. Further, various American bombing and shooting atrocities have killed many Afghan civilian, severely injuring the image and popularity of U.S. forces. Our NATO allies are quickly working to remove their troops. And despite all this, the President remains committed to his withdrawal schedule, no matter conditions on the ground.

The temptation to trumpet his successes in the war on Al-Qaeda for reelection presents considerable risks for the President. Efforts to politicize the War on Terror are not only unseemly, but also could bring a backlash. The President's claims that victory against Al-Qaeda is "within reach" are reminiscent of President George W. Bush's infamous "Mission Accomplished" claim, which haunted him for the remainder of his term. The Administration's calculation is that these excessive claims of success pose little political risk because if things go south in Afghanistan, or Iraq for that matter, that is most likely to happen after the election. So the President will make the claims now, and is willing to suffer any adverse consequences later. Keep liberals happy by ending wars, reassure independents by proclaiming victory and acting tough. It is a recipe made for political advantage, what is missing is the assurance that national security will benefit as well.

Week 173

(OUTED)

May 13, 2012

President Obama is always walking the tightrope of try to sound moderate while taking policy positions that will please his liberal base. That task is particularly tough on social issues, where the President's views are on the Left. On abortion for example, as a legislator in Illinois the President voted for nearly every pro-abortion bill put before him, even one that allowed doctors to kill babies actually born alive after botched abortions. The President tries to mask his position on abortion with silence, he basically never talks about the issue. The same was true on the issue of gay marriage, until this week. Everyone knows that President Obama favors gay marriage. He said so publicly in the late 1990's when he was running for the State Senate in Illinois. But as he emerged on the national stage, he pretended to have a different view. He voiced support for the Defense of Marriage Act and during the 2008 campaign pledged that he believed marriage should be defined as a union between one man and one woman. Then he got outed, by his own Vice President of all people.

Vice President Biden was doing the Sunday morning talk show circuit on May 6, touting the Administration's accomplishments and taking shots at the GOP, when he was asked whether he supported gay marriage. He said he had no problem with it. That, combined with increasing threats from gay donors to withhold campaign contributions, put almost unbearable pressure on the President to take a position on the issue. No doubt, the White House's plan had been to be silent on gay marriage, avoid the issue, and then publicly come out in favor of it after November. Biden's gaff made that impossible. So the President's hand was forced, and on May 9 during an interview with Robin Roberts of Good Morning America, he publicly stated his support for gay marriage. He said his change in view was born of deep reflection, conversations with family and friends, and reflection on Christ's Golden Rule: treat others how you want to be treated. It was all very smooth and polished, but no one really buys it as the real reason for his public pronouncement.

The real reason for the President's support for gay marriage, just like the real reason for pretty much everything done at the White House these days, is politics. The Administration had hoped to keep gay activists pacified by quiet support for gay marriage and secret promises to push for it after the reelection. Part of that strategy was legal attacks on the Defense of Marriage Act, which the Department of Justice has been challenging in federal court, even as the President was on record supporting it. But liberals and gay activists were losing patience and withholding money from the reelection campaign, which put mounting pressure on the President to take a stand. Always reluctant to admit his inner liberal, the President resisted as long as he could, but Biden's comments made holding out any longer impossible.

Voters will often reward a President for taking a tough stand, even if they disagree. The best recent example was President George W. Bush. In the 2004 campaign, the Iraq War and enhanced interrogation tactics were both highly unpopular, but voters supported the President because he was making difficult decisions to fight terrorism. The same might be true for gay marriage. If the President took a tough moral stand that it is simply unfair to discriminate against fellow Americans who simply want an equal right to have their committed relationships recognized, many would admire the President for it, even if they disagree. The problem is, the President had no intention of taking a principled stand, his plan was to obfuscate and distract to avoid the issue, until forced to do otherwise. This may make it much harder to get a benefit from the whole affair.

For the GOP, the President's gay marriage stand offers several opportunities, if pursued carefully. Obviously, the President's admission reaffirms that he is a true believing liberal. It also opens the President up to attacks as being a flip flopper. It also gives the Romney campaign an opening to consolidate support among conservative Christians, because whatever qualms the group might have about Mormonism, they pale in comparison to the concern about gay marriage. And even though the nation is about 50/50 on the issue, in states that matter to the Romney campaign, gay marriage is not popular. But in all of this, Romney and the GOP have to be very careful not to look prejudiced or mean spirited. Most Americans believe in fairness and compassion for all, even for those whose lifestyles they object to. The trick for the GOP will be to oppose gay marriage in a way that does not turn off moderate voters who are more concerned about the economy. But at least the GOP can plan its strategy, unlike the President who was outed from his.

Week 174

(MONEY MATTERS)

May 20, 2012

President Obama was propelled into the White House by the 2008 financial crisis, and it is starting to look like the 2012 financial mini-crisis might hinder his quest for a second term. Much of the news this week seemed like a repeat of headlines from 3 1/2 years ago. JP Morgan Chase announced a nearly $3 billion trading loss on credit default swaps. Greece appeared to lurch toward default on its sovereign debt, with no government, radical parties denouncing austerity, and new elections called by June 17. France's new President Hollande took office pledging to crack down on banks and double down on state control. The Dow Jones Industrial Average lost nearly 1000 points in two weeks. Job numbers continued to disappoint. The federal government debt continued to grow, with the parties already starting to squabble about the next debt limit increase. All these money matters are going to matter a great deal to the President's reelection hopes.

The White House's plan was simple, pump the economy with stimulus money and bailout troubled businesses, and the U.S. economy would bounce back and let the President cruise to reelection. That was the plan in 2010, but the economy did not bounce back and the President's party got pummeled. It again is the plan in 2012, but it is again not working as the Administration planned. There were some hopeful signs early in 2012, as the stock market rose and job creation started to accelerate, but by April the momentum was lost and since then it has become increasingly clear that jobs will not return in a meaningful way before the election. Since then the news has only gotten worse. While U.S. banks are far stronger than they were 4 years ago and corporate profits are strong, other forces are now retarding economic growth. The biggest drags on the economy are the continuing financial crisis in Europe and the slowing Chinese economy, each of which will have bad impacts on the United States.

For the last year, Germany has led an effort to get the economies of Greece, Spain, and Italy on a sustainable fiscal path. This austerity agenda involved spending cuts, tax increases, and strict budget controls. But the subject nations are starting to rebel, with austerity believed to be the culprit (not the cure) for continuing deflation, job losses, and economic constriction. Greek voters threw out the politicians who supported austerity. Spain's conservative government is under extreme pressure and the French elected Socialist President Hollande, an opponent of austerity. All this is a challenge to Germany's austerity agenda, leading to jitters in financial markets. JP Morgan's trading loss only added to the concern, although the scope of that loss poses no threat to that bank. None of this news is helping the U.S. economy, which is very concerning to the President.

With this as a backdrop, the G8 leaders gathered at Camp David this week for a summit on challenges to the world economy. The discussion was dominated by the troubles in Europe, with the forces for stimulus (lead by Hollande and President Obama), pressing German Chancellor Merkle to relent on her austerity program. The talks took on an extreme urgency because the current situation threatens the viability of the Euro trading block. There are already signs of a bank run in Greece, and unless more bailout money is sent to Greece, its banking system might collapse, which could lead to a Greek exit from the Euro. The fear is once Greece leaves, the same might happen to Spain and Italy. The G8 leaders pledged more stimulus and concerted action to address that threat, but the details were thin and uncertainty remains.

For the President, all these money matter are coming at a very bad time. There is not much of a window left to convince voters that the economy is improving. With these setbacks, it is looking increasingly like the President will have to run for reelection in a poor economic environment. Polls are starting to show how tough that will be, with Romney even or slightly ahead in many polls, and many battleground states getting ever more competitive. Indeed, Romney nearly matched President Obama's fundraising in April. Recognizing the threat, the Obama campaign decided to launch a large negative add campaign focused on Romney's time at Bain Capital. Many see this as an effort to define Romney before the President's position deteriorates any further. So money matters got the President elected, but it is looking like money matters are going to make it a tough fight to get 4 more years.

Week 175
(COW PIE)

May 27, 2012

With the markets still suffering jitters over the financial crisis in Europe, the reality is slowly setting in among Democrats that President Obama is facing a tough reelection campaign. Only a few weeks ago, Democrat partisans were acting like the election was already over, with talk of a Blue Wall of Democrat states and the President's strong favorability numbers. That attitude has now evaporated, and has been replaced with the White House's determination to go hard at Governor Romney to change the dynamic of the race. So the President launched an attack ad on Romney's experience at Bain Capital, continued his pleas to every favored constituency (gays, women, the young), and has begun to personally criticize Romney in his speeches. For example, after Romney spoke of a prairie fire of debt threatening the nation on a visit to Iowa, the President responded by saying that Romney was offering a cow pie of distortion. These aggressive steps so early in the campaign are sure signs of concern within the Obama campaign.

The time period between the end of presidential primaries and the nominating conventions is often called the silly season of the campaign. With little hard news to report, the campaigns and the media focus on side issues, like rumors on vice presidential picks, personal histories, and campaign gossip. Not so this year. President Obama announced his reelection campaign barely three weeks ago, but already he has determined to begin direct attacks on Mitt Romney's record. Not just through ads, but also directly in his speeches, which have increasingly taken on a harsh and divisive tone. Usually at these early stages of a general election campaign, Presidents use surrogates to launch their attacks, preferring to act presidential rather than looking purely partisan. It seems the Administration has decided it does not have that luxury.

The reason for the early direct engagement with Romney is simple: weakness. Romney has pulled nearly even in the polls, his favorability ratings have increased, while at the same time the economy continues to drag on the President's popularity. It does not help that the financial crisis in Europe has resulted in a nearly 1000 point drop in the Dow. More troubling, the President had counted on a huge money edge, but he is not going to have one. His fundraising has lagged, while Romney's has surged. In fact, Romney and his allies to date have raised $402 million, while the Obama campaign's total to date is $340 million. The President still has many advantages and is favored by many to win, but the race will be tough and tight, so the Obama campaign has decided to come out fighting.

In 1996, when Bill Clinton was running against Senator Robert Dole, the Clinton campaign used its money edge during the summer lull to define Dole and establish a lead that Clinton never lost. It seems President Obama is running the same play book. The Obama campaign has made a large ad buy, focusing on Romney's history at Bain Capital. The objective was to paint Romney has a heartless plutocrat who destroyed jobs to enrich himself. This theme fits nicely into the President's class warfare rhetoric and his pitch that the affluent are hurting the middle class. The problem is, Romney is not Dole, and attacks on Bain Capital can come off looking anti-business. The Obama campaign had hoped that the Bain Capital ads would start the process of defining Romney, but instead they ignited criticism from within the Democratic Party. First, the ads were misleading because they focused in part on activities at Bain after Romney left the firm. But more importantly, a number of prominent Democrat leaders and backers, including Newark's Mayor

Cory Booker, former Pennsylvania Governor Ed Rendell, and fundraiser Steve Rattner, all criticized the ads, saying they made Obama look anti-business. So the story became the Bain ad itself, not Romney. Plus, unlike Dole, Romney has plenty of cash, and quickly responded with a web ad emphasizing Romney's record of job creation at Bain.

One of the most appealing things about Barak Obama during the 2008 campaign was his positive rhetoric and his appeal to moderation, hope and change. With a record not so easy to defend, the President cannot afford such lofty talk in 2012, so instead his campaign is all about attacks and appeals to key Democrat constituencies. So on the stump, rather than a dignified and moderate President, we see a harsh partisan focusing on dividing Americans and attacking his opponent. In recent speeches, in addition to the cow pie comment, the President said that there may be some value to Romney's past experience in venture capital "but not in the White House" and that Romney is more worried about corporations than people. For his crowds of true supporters, all these Obama attacks draw huge cheers. But one must wonder whether they will appeal to undecided independent voters. Those are the voters Obama needs to win, but Obama also needs heated rhetoric to excite his base. So the President has to walk a very fine line. It is an uncomfortable balancing act, but for now, with things looking tough, expect more cow pie comments to come.

Week 176

(DRONED OUT)

June 3, 2012

This week, the President tried to open a new front in the campaign with a focus on his national security credentials. The White House hoped to use foreign affairs to highlight the President as a strong, decisive, and successful leader abroad. The effort started with leaked stories about a kill list of terrorists targeted by the United States. The story highlighted that the President personally reviews the list and decides which targets should be killed by drone strikes when the opportunity arises. The purpose of the story was to show Obama as forcefully defending the nation, a theme that fits nicely with the successful raid that killed Osama bin Laden. Next, a story was leaked on the intelligence agencies' use of cyber warfare to undermine the computer systems used for Iran's nuclear program. Again, the purpose was to show America on the offensive. It was all a nice political play, except that the drone kill list was drowned out by the real story of this election, the economy.

One cannot criticize the White House for trying to open a new front in the general election campaign. They have plenty of attacks to throw at Romney, but they need positive stories as well, and on the domestic front the picking are pretty slim. Obamacare is unpopular and might be struck down, so the President does not want to focus too much on that. The White House can talk about the auto bailouts, which are generally viewed as successful, but for the larger economy, not much positive can be said. Growth is slowing and unemployment is high. As for fiscal responsibility, with four straight years of trillion dollar deficits, best to stick to attacks on Republicans on that topic. So foreign policy was a natural choice for a positive campaign theme. But this election is not going to be about foreign policy, and if it is, it will almost certainly be bad news for the President.

The only way the 2012 election could turn on foreign policy is if something happens abroad that fundamentally shakes the American political system and economy. With bin Laden dead, any high profile international crisis is likely on the negative side of the ledger for President Obama. Iran could get nuclear weapons, the Euro could crumble, Egypt could fall into chaos, the Syrian civil war could spread to its neighbors, and the U.S. could suffer some horrible and deadly disaster in Afghanistan. Every one of these eventualities would be negative for the President, and if none of these events happen, the impact on the election would be neutral. For example, even if the Europeans manage to save the Euro and prevent a default by Greece, Spain, or Italy, the damage to the U.S. economy from uncertainty is already done. So there is little chance the President will find salvation abroad.

This week also taught us there will be no easy rest at home either. Just as the White House was trying to burnish the President's national security credentials, it took a body blow on the economy. The June jobs report showed only 69,000 jobs created in May, well below the modest 150,000 expectation. The unemployment rate rose to 8.2%, the underemployment rate rose to 14.8%, average worked hours dropped to 34.4 per week, and 5.4 million Americans have been without a job for 27 weeks or more. Added to all this was a reduction in the economic growth clocked for the first quarter of 2012 to 1.9%, and an expectation that growth will remain sluggish for the balance of the year. The markets did not like any of the news, with the Dow dropping 274 points on June 1, and even the White House had to admit the news was horrible, with an anonymous source commenting that there is no "sugarcoating" this news.

The events of this week act as a lesson that even the best laid political plans are subject to events. This election will be about the economy, no matter what the Obama campaign tries to do to distract the public with other issues. Governor Romney appears to understand this, so his major political event of the week was a surprise trip to the closed Solyndra headquarters to argue that Obama's agenda of government directed capitalism does not work and wastes taxpayer dollars. So the President might highlight drone attacks and toughness on foreign policy, but always lurking in the background is the economy, and there good answers are tough to come by.

Week 177

(DOING FINE)

June 10, 2012

In the wake of the troubling May unemployment report, the Obama Administration had hoped to change the debate from the poor state of the economy to the failure of the Republican House to move the President's jobs initiatives. This effort began right after the jobs report was released, and continued into this week. However, the top political news of the week and the President's own itinerary undermined the effort. While the President was trying to put the focus on the Republicans, the media turned its attention to the recall election in Wisconsin, where public employee unions failed to oust Republican Governor Scott Walker. While the White House's allies were being defeated in Wisconsin, the President was not even pushing his jobs bill, instead he was on a multi-day fundraising trip. Apparently, he will need the money, because Governor Romney outpaced the President in fundraising in May. All the while, a controversy about national security leaks (used to support positive articles about the President), is leading Attorney General Holder to appoint two U.S. Attorneys to start a criminal investigation. With all these troubling developments, the President felt the need to call a hasty press conference on June 8 to steady the ship and reframe the issues. Instead, he made a bad political week even worse by stating that "the private sector is doing fine" and what the economy needs is more public employees and more government spending. The President's campaign was anything but fine after those remarks.

This was going to be a tough political week for the President even without his press conference blunder. The bad employment report made clear the economy will not be strong on Election Day, so Democrats now understand they will have a very tough fight on their hands. However, some continued to harbor the belief that organization, union power, and demographic changes will make victory inevitable regardless of the economy. That view was dealt a blow by events in Wisconsin. Governor Walker infuriated unions by his reforms that limited collective bargaining and stopped forced dues. In retaliation, the unions and liberal groups forced a recall election, which Walker handily won on June 5. Walker captured 53% of the vote, winning by a bigger margin and by more total votes than when he was originally elected in 2010. Republicans outraised and out organized the Democrats. The White House knew defeat was coming, so they carefully avoided sending the President to Wisconsin to campaign. But no matter what, the defeat was a warning sign for Democrats.

More warning signs came from other fronts as well. Governor Romney raised $76 million in May, topping the President's $60 million total. The President's team now realizes they will not have a money advantage in the campaign. Even worse, criticism of the President's campaign schedule got even more pointed. Even the mainstream media is asking more questions about the 153 fundraisers the President has done since he announced his reelection campaign and why the President spends so much time on campaign stops and appears to do so little actual governing. Many believe the leaked stories about the terrorist kill list and cyber attacks on Iran published in the *New York Times* were designed to change this image. But if this was the plan, it backfired, because the leaks were illegal and are now under investigation.

When the President tried to get control of the debate with his press conference, he only made things worse. Everyone knows the economy is weak, yet the President said "the private sector is doing fine." Not only was this comment contrary to what the vast majority of Americans believe, but it also showed a President out of touch. The White House immediately realized the danger, and less than two hours later, the President had to march back the remarks, by saying "the economy is not doing fine." However, the damage was already done. Even more problematic was the President's prescription for fixing the economy: more government spending. The President blamed the weak economy on cuts by local and state governments, and called for more federal spending to hire more government employees and spur more government infrastructure projects.

It appears the President continues to believe bigger government, more spending, and more stimulus is what the economy needs. This will be a tough sell with Congress and the voters. It also portrays the President as someone who always thinks of government as the first solution to problems. Whether or not one believes more government is the answer, the President made a bad week even worse by implying that he does not understand or appreciate the economic challenges in America. The Obama campaign was not doing fine before this week, and now it is doing even worse.

Week 178

(Help Wanted)

June 17, 2012

One might think that with the high unemployment rate, the focus of the White House would be on encouraging more businesses to post help wanted signs. Instead, this week it was the Obama campaign that was looking for help, using both rhetorical and regulatory tools to improve its prospects. With concerns growing among Democrats and liberal activists that the President's campaign is off balance and losing ground to Romney, the President tried yet again to hit the reset button with a June 12 high profile address in Cleveland on the economy. But that was only the first tool in the President's bag of tricks, quickly followed up by his announcement on June 15 of an executive order to suspend certain deportations of illegal aliens brought to the U.S. as children. Both the speech and the executive order were more about the campaigning than about policy, which is where the President wants help most of all.

The President's address in Cleveland was billed as a major economic speech that would contrast the White House's economic strategy to that of Mitt Romney. After President Obama's disastrous comment the prior week that "the private sector is doing fine" the White House hoped to use this address to change the subject and focus fire on Romney. However, the Romney campaign showed its agility yet again, preempting the President's speech with a Romany address, also from Ohio, where the former governor took aim at the weak economy, ballooning deficit, and the President's predilection for looking more concerned about government than private citizens. By the time President Obama took the podium, he was already in rebuttal mode, rather than taking the offensive. In the address itself, the President offered nothing more than the same rhetoric he has offered many times before. He started by his usual attack on Bush Administration policies, pivoted to an argument that Romney wants to put the same policies in place again, and then drew contrasts with his proposals.

The speech was 54 minutes of the same attacks and same proposals voters have heard so often from the President. What was different this time was the critics of the speech did not come solely from the Right. MSNBC's Jonathan Alter called the speech a disappointment, and liberal Washington Post columnist Dana Milbank took the President to task for pretending that he has proposed solutions for entitlement reform and the deficit, when no such plans have been offered. With so much criticism from liberals, the speech was easy for conservatives to attack as just more populism, class warfare, and calls for bigger government. Few think the speech moved the ball for the White House on the economy. All it did was confirm that the Obama Campaign plans to push class warfare populism until the very end, no matter the consequences.

After the mixed results for this speech, the Obama campaign turned to a more potent weapon, the executive order. The recession has been very hard on young workers and minorities, the exact groups the President needs for reelection. The question has been how to motivate these people to come out and vote for the President in large numbers. The Obama campaign, at its most clever, came up with a means to appeal to both minorities and the young in one swoop. On June 15, the President by executive order suspended deportations of illegal aliens brought into the U.S. at ages of 16 years or younger who have clean criminal records, have served in the military, or can show they are working toward high school graduation or a GED. In essence, the President by executive order implemented certain key provisions of the Dream Act, which has been stalled in Congress.

This move by the President served several purposes. There is no doubt the President agrees with the policy, so certainly he is sincere in his support for these measures. But just as importantly, this executive order shows a President who is in charge and decisive, two perceptions the President wants to foster. This move also helps solidify his support among Hispanics and hopefully propel them to the polls. Lastly, the executive order's focus on young people is designed to help the President reconnect with a voting block badly hurt in the recession. Clearly good politics for the President on all fronts, as demonstrated by the muted response of the Romney campaign, which was caught unprepared and had no ready response.

While this executive order is clearly good politics, it is not so clear that it is good policy. In the first place, it rewards law breakers and will make many who have followed the rules and applied for legal status wonder why they bothered. The move will also add as many as 1.4 million young workers to the legal labor force at a time when job openings remain few. The practical impact is that these new legal workers will now compete with American citizens for a limited number of new jobs for young workers. In essence, the President has made the unemployment situation worse for young Americans by favoring young illegals. The policy also raises the question of what will now happen to the parents of eligible aliens; will they too be shielded from deportation. The ultimate response of the Romney campaign will likely be that the goal of not punishing young people brought to the United States by others is noble, but the means (executive order) was improper and the timing unfair to the estimated 50% of college graduates who are unemployed. No matter, the President wanted help for his campaign, and he got it with this executive order.

Week 179
(On Holder)

June 24, 2012

This was an active presidential week for the Obama campaign. With a G20 meeting in Mexico, whose focus would be the financial crisis in Europe, the President hoped to show international leadership and help forge a strategy to address the growing sovereign debt crisis in Greece, Spain, and Italy. While financial markets were pleased when Greek voters elected a pro-bailout government over the weekend, the relief was short-lived as borrowing costs for Spain and Italy continued to rise, a sign that investors increasingly view those economies at risk of default. As usual, the G20 meeting accomplished nothing beyond rhetoric, but it gave the President a chance to look the leader. However, what little benefit the President's campaign got from the G20 meeting was quickly eclipsed by a scandal at home involving Attorney General Eric Holder and the Fast & Furious gunrunning operation.

There are many valid criticisms that can be directed at the Obama Administration, but scandal plagued is not one of them. For the most part, the Administration has been able to avoid self-injury from internal controversies. One exception has been the Fast & Furious operation. Starting back in 2006, the Alcohol Tobacco & Firearms ("ATF") agency has been running gunwalking programs designed to track firearms. By selling firearms with tracking devices, the ATF could trace the movement of the arms, interdict them, and arrest those involved. On October 26, 2009, the Department of Justice and ATF expanded the program with a new focus on trying to get to higher level organized crime and drug figures in Mexico. The program involved letting the guns run to the highest levels of crime organizations. By 2010, more than 2000 arms were provided to crime organizations, most associated with Mexico.

Then, on December 14, 2010, ATF agent Brian Terry was killed in a firefight by a weapon sold to gangs through the Fast & Furious program. The program was soon suspended, and all recognized that the program was a mistake. However, the Administration and DOJ took the position that no high ranking DOJ officials had approved the operation. The House Oversight Committee began an investigation. To date, Attorney General Holder has testified repeatedly on the issue and claimed no knowledge. However, the Administration has been unwilling to produce certain key documents. The stakes were increased when the House Oversight Committee voted 23 to 17 along partisan lines on June 21 to hold the Attorney General in contempt for his refusal to provide the documents. The full House will vote on the contempt resolution on June 28. The White House then quickly asserted executive privilege on the contested documents to prevent their release.

Liberals are calling the Fast & Furious investigation a partisan witch hunt. Republicans in Congress believe Holder has been lying to cover up the fact that Fast & Furious was approved at high levels of the Justice Department. As a practical matter, even if the full House votes to hold the Attorney General in contempt, the only result will be a referral of the matter to the U.S. Attorney in the District of Columbia, an Obama appointee. So it is unlikely that Holder will ever be prosecuted. The true fallout will be political. Republicans focused on the anti-immigration issue see Fast & Furious as an example of wrongheaded Administration policies that have made the situation on the Mexican border only worse. The question is whether the controversy will ever rise to the level necessary to cause any real harm to the Obama campaign. With the other challenges facing the Obama campaign, the last thing the President wants is a scandal. That is likely the motivation behind the executive privilege assertion, which was surprising because of the President's heavy criticism of his predecessor's use of that privilege. But as with most politicians, consistency often gives way to political expediency, so the executive privilege has been used to keep the full story of Fast & Furious under wraps, at least until after the election.

Week 180
(ARE YOU SERIOUS?)

July 1, 2012

After Obamacare (or the Affordable Care Act), was first passed, former Speaker Nancy Pelosi was famously asked whether the legislation was constitutional, to which she responded: "Are you serious?" Democrats learned that conservatives were deadly serious about challenging the constitutionality of Obamacare when multiple lawsuits were filed, including a suit brought by 26 states challenging the law. As those suits made their way through the Federal Courts, some courts sustained the law, others found it unconstitutional. When the suits finally made it to the Supreme Court, after three days of arguments, Democrats became very nervous that Obamacare would fall. The Supreme Court ruled on June 28, finding that Obamacare exceeded Congress's power under the Commerce Clause, the Necessary & Proper Clause, and under the Spending Power. The surprise was that Chief Justice Roberts voted to uphold Obamacare, saying that Congress could not force citizens to buy health care, but did have the right under the tax power to penalize those who do not purchase insurance. After winning on all the key issues, it is now conservatives who are asking "Are you serious?"

Except for the conclusion ultimately upholding Obamacare, most of Chief Justice Robert's decision reads like a treatise on strict construction of Congressional powers. On the Commerce Clause, Roberts held: "The individual mandate cannot be upheld as an exercise of Congress's power under the Commerce Clause . . . [t]hat Clause authorizes Congress to regulate interstate commerce, not to order individuals to engage in it." On the Necessary & Proper Clause, Roberts held that: "Even if the individual mandate is 'necessary' to the Act's insurance reforms, such an expansion of federal power is not a 'proper' means for making those reforms effective." As for the Spending Power, Roberts held that the federal government could not coerce states into accepting the Medicaid expansion in Obamacare upon threat of losing all Medicaid subsidies, invalidating that part of the law and allowing States to opt out of Medicaid expansion. Despite all this, Chief Justice Roberts upheld the individual mandate in Obamacare under the tax power, holding that Congress could not compel citizens to buy insurance, but could tax them for failing to.

The inner workings of the Supreme Court are largely unknown outside the Court, so few have any real insight into why Chief Justice Roberts decided to uphold a law while agreeing with most of the arguments against it. Recent news reports have surfaced that the Chief Justice was prepared to overrule Obamacare, but changed his opinion and determined to uphold the law under the tax power. The question is why. The most likely explanation is more political than judicial. Ever since the *Bush v. Gore* decision in 2000, liberals have labeled the Supreme Court as a partisan Republican institution. After the arguments on Obamacare, both the Obama campaign and Democrat activists made clear that they would furiously attack the Supreme Court if it overruled Obamacare. Some liberal commentators even floated plans for a court packing scheme like the one attempted by Franklin Roosevelt, to address the power of conservatives on the Court.

Chief Justice Roberts is a talented lawyer as well as politically astute. He likely wanted to avoid exposing the Supreme Court to partisan attack. He also wanted to reaffirm strict construction of Congressional authority. It appears that the Chief Justice ultimately concluded he could accomplish both goals by adopting a narrow and binding strict construction of Congressional authority under the Commerce Clause, the Necessary & Proper Clause, and the Spending Power, but allow voters to decide the ultimate fate of Obamacare by upholding it under the tax power. Roberts may have even thought he was helping the GOP by giving them an issue on which to attack the President, knowing full well the unpopularity of taxes.

The repercussions of the decision will be great. Obamacare is constitutional and will be the law of the land, unless repealed. The only way to repeal it will be to vote for Romney, so it puts the issue squarely in the middle of the electoral landscape. The decision enshrined a very strict construction of Congressional powers, but also taught a safety valve through the tax power. As for the President, the decision was a clear victory. His landmark legislation will survive for now, and he has avoided looking weak and ineffective. Whether the decision will help or hurt his reelection is unclear and will depend on how strongly voters continue to oppose the law. For Republicans, the decision lets them continue their assault on Obamacare, motivate their key supporters, and focus on the tax issue. Justice Roberts seems to have given something to everyone, the mark of a skilled politician, but not necessarily a principled Justice.

Week 181

(A TAX OR NOT A TAX, THAT IS THE QUESTION)

July 8, 2012

Republicans likely were welcoming the July 4 holiday break after their disheartening defeat on Obamacare. The Supreme Court's decision finding the President's great legislative achievement constitutional continued to reverberate through the political landscape. Democrats and liberals basked in their victory, while the GOP circled their wagons, proclaiming yet again their determination to repeal Obamacare. The GOP also tried to exploit the few positive aspects of the decision, by encouraging States to refuse the Medicaid expansion and focusing on the Supreme Court's finding that the penalties in the law for not buying health insurance are taxes. But even in this, the GOP was thwarted, when Governor Romney's campaign botched the issue, stating the penalties were not a tax. So disarray on the Right continued to reign, but only until the very bad jobs report came out on July 6, giving them an opening yet again.

Republicans had hoped that June would be the beginning of the end for the Obama campaign. With the defeat of the Wisconsin recall election, an expected bad June jobs report, and the hoped-for defeat of Obamacare, they expected Obama would enter the summer bruised and bloodied. The GOP got the first two wins, but not the third and biggest on Obamacare. Scott Walker's win in Wisconsin put fear in the Democrats and placed Wisconsin squarely in play for the election. President Obama's statement that the jobs report, which showed only 80,000 jobs created and an unemployment rate of 8.2%, was a "step in the right direction" helped the GOP by again making the President look out of touch. The central theme for the Romney campaign in the election is the poor economy, and the June jobs report certainly supported that theme. This combined with weakening consumer confidence and the ever continuing problems in Europe, kept the sluggish economy as the biggest campaign issue. This was great for the GOP, because it changed the topic from the Obamacare loss and played to Romney's strength. But even with this, Obamacare still cast a pall over the GOP plans.

There was very little in the Supreme Court's decision to cheer Republicans, but they could find a few consolations. The Supreme Court's ruling that the federal government could not coerce states to opt into the Medicaid expansion by threatening to take away other Medicaid subsidies gave willing states the option to decline the expansion, hobbling part of the Obamacare scheme. Several GOP governors quickly jumped for this option. Even more potent was the Supreme Court's finding that the penalties in Obamacare are a tax. With that finding, the GOP was poised to attack President Obama for breaking his word. During the health care reform debate, the President promised not to raise taxes on the middle class to pay for Obamacare. The Supreme Court's ruling made that assurance look like a lie, offering a small silver lining in the Supreme Court's decision. Despite this clear opening, the Romney campaign seemed unwilling and unsure how to exploit it. When Governor Romney's campaign was asked about whether penalties were a tax, it said "No," fearing that the Democrats would then claim that Romney had raised taxes because his own health care reform bill in Massachusetts contained similar penalties. Then after denying penalties were a tax, the Romney campaign reversed itself and called the penalties a tax. This made the Romney campaign look unprepared for the fight to come.

With his win on health care reform, many expected a boost in the President's reelection prospects. A few polls did come out right after the decision, and they did show a modest bump for the

President. Yet those same polls showed a majority of Americans are still opposed to Obamacare and support its repeal. With this, it remains unclear whether the Obamacare ruling will help or hurt the President. The law remains unpopular, but Governor Romney will have a tough time exploiting the President's weakness on the issue because of his support for similar legislation in Massachusetts. It seems the Romney campaign is undecided on how to approach the issue, especially when it was unprepared to jump on the tax finding, which was the clearest path to go after the President on his signature legislation. All this shows why the GOP was so quick to jump on the bad employment data released on July 6. At least on that topic, they know how to attack.

Week 182
(YOU DIDN'T BUILD THAT)

July 15, 2012

One of the most remarkable things about this year's presidential election is its stability. It seems no matter the event domestically or internationally, the basic dynamics of the race have not changed. The President's approval rating has remained in the 45% to 47% range, and the polls continue to show him on average ahead of Governor Romney by less than 2 points, well within the margin of error. Many thought the President's victory on Obamacare would change that dynamic and lead to a strong bounce in the polls, but that simply has not happened. The brief boost the President received dissipated within a week, and again the race is right back where it was started. This is despite the Obama campaign's nearly $100 million ad buy to hammer Mitt Romney on his record at Bain Capital. The money has been spent, and the polls have barely moved. So this week, the President upped the ante, by picking a tax fight with the GOP on July 9, and then by giving a fiery speech in Virginia on July 13 asserting that "[i]f you've got a business, you didn't build that. Somebody else made that happen." In essence, the President words implied that anyone who has built a business and been successful owes that success to government. It appears the Obama campaign believes that class warfare and a collectivist crusade are the only things that can change the dynamics of the race.

It was clear that the Obama campaign intended to pursue an aggressive strategy when it started the week with a Monday challenge to the GOP. The President gave an address demanding that Congress increase taxes on families making over $250,000 per year as part of effort to avoid expiration of all the Bush tax cuts on December 31, 2012, often called the fiscal cliff. The President threw this challenge to the GOP even though his allies in Congress do not support his plan. The Democrat leadership in both the House and Senate have thrown their support behind a plan that would only increase taxes on those making over $1 million per year. The President clearly felt that position was not sufficiently provocative, so he decided to pursue an agenda that even Democrats in Congress do not support. The GOP leader in the Senate quickly tried to bring the President's plan up for a vote, but the Democrat majority tabled the President's plan in an effort to avoid an embarrassing vote rejecting the proposal. So in the end, we have another wholly political gambit by the President, designed solely to give him an attack line for political speeches.

The unwillingness of the President to make any real proposal to address the impending fiscal cliff is unfortunate. Without action by the White House and Congress, on December 31, taxes will rise on every American and across the broad spending cuts will be triggered that will significantly cut defense and domestic programs. Given the weak economy, most agree that the combination of tax increases and spending cuts could endanger the struggling recovery. Nevertheless, the White House refuses to work with Congress on a tax and budget reform strategy that would prevent a shock to the economy while still achieving the long term goals of deficit reduction and a tax code that encourages growth. Instead, the President is only interested in politics, attacking Republicans for favoring the rich and claiming he has offered a spending reduction program, when even liberal observers (like Dana Milbank of the *Washington Post*) admit he has not. The President wants political weapons, not solutions.

Even this tax attack was not enough for the White House, because on July 13 they went a step farther. The President has made many comments over the years that seem to indicate that he thinks government is the source of the nation's greatness and prosperity. From his "spreading the wealth around" comments, to his claim that the "private sector is doing fine," to his efforts to entitlize ever more segments of the population, it has become increasingly clear the President's vision for the future is a government directed economy whether every American is dependent on the government and where government directs economic activity on some social planning rubric. And despite the President's best efforts to obscure his true views, every once in a while, the truth comes out. That happened again this week, during an extemporaneous speech in Roanoke, Virginia. As part of his theme that individualism is a myth and that we are all dependent on each other and government, the President asserted that business owners should get no credit for taking risks, building businesses, and being successful. He asserted that" [i]f you've got a business, you didn't build that. Somebody else made that happen."

This is the President at his most candid. At bottom, he does not believe in individualism. Instead, he believes that all wealth and property in America is the product government and collective effort, and thus government, as the tool of the collectivist will, should decide who can own what, who can make how much, and who wins and who loses. So it seems a tax fight is now too tame for the Obama campaign. Instead, an attack on free enterprise itself is the new crusade.

Week 183

(AURORA)

July 22, 2012

It seemed like this week was going to be like so many others in this campaign season, a week of attack ads, political speeches, and polls. The Obama campaign continued to pound on Mitt · Romney's work for Bain Capital and his failure to release more tax returns. The Romney campaign continued to hammer President Obama for the weak economy and comments that business owners did not build their business, somebody else did. Both attacks distort the facts and further polarize the debate, but are part of a campaign that appears to be turning very negative early and will stay that way. The only thing that got the politicians off their war of nasty words was a massacre in Colorado, but the respite was short.

On July 20, James Holmes, a 24-year-old former Ph.D. student went to an opening night showing of the new Batman film, *The Dark Knight Rises*, at the Century Theater in Aurora

Colorado. However, his plan was not a night at the movies. A few minutes after the film started, he left the theater through an exit door and went to his car, put on body armor and a gasmask, and grabbed a shotgun, a rifle, and an automatic handgun. He re-entered the theater, threw a smoke bomb, and then proceeded to shoot as many of the audience members as possible. When he was done, 12 were dead, and 58 were wounded. The dead included four veterans. More would have died if Holmes' rifle had not jammed. Holmes tried to escape, but was arrested near his car. Then he told the police his apartment was booby-trapped. It took several days for the police to defuse the traps and enter the apartment. They found explosives and thousands of rounds of ammunition.

This attack shook the nation, in part because of memories of the Columbine attack, which also happened in Colorado. Both the President and Mitt Romney suspended active campaigning in response to the tragedy. The President planned a trip to Colorado to meet with the victims, while Mitt Romney gave an eloquent speech honoring the victims and condemning these senseless murders. It is a shame that it took a massacre to get the campaigns to change their tunes, if only for a few days. Yet, it did both candidates credit that they stopped campaigning in recognition of the trauma the attack caused the nation.

No one yet knows why James Holmes did what he did. Early evidence is disturbed mind. When arrested, Holmes called himself the Joker, a psychopath villain from the Batman series. It seems Holmes wanted to commit an atrocity just as the Joker did on the big screen. The difference is, the Joker's attacks were fiction, what Holmes did was real, but maybe that is a distinction Holmes was unable to recognize. There will be months of debate about why this happened and what attacks like this say about our society. For now, there appears to be no political motivation for the massacre, despite an erroneous report by ABC News that Holmes was a member of the Tea Party, a report ABC quickly corrected when the facts proved otherwise.

The ability to keep politics out of tragedies is limited. Less than two days after the attack, liberals began to argue that tighter gun control was needed to decrease the chances of future massacres. The fact that Holmes appeared to have purchased some of his weapons from Gander Mountain, a national sporting goods chain, only further fueled the gun control issue. The problem is, there is no evidence that gun control can stop massacres. The best recent example was the attack in Norway last year where 62 people were killed, despite Norway's strict gun laws. Most interesting was the response of the presidential candidates. It was predictable that Mitt Romney would not call for more gun control, but President Obama also carefully avoided the gun control issue. It seems he has already done so much to displease moderate and conservative voters, he was unwilling to add gun control to his list of betrayals. So for now Aurora has done what no one else could, stop the vicious partisan attacks, but the ceasefire will be short no doubt.

Week 184

(So Foreign)

July 29, 2012

During the summer doldrums of every recent presidential election, the candidates take a break from domestic issues to focus on foreign policy. This was not the case during the Cold War, when foreign policy was often the centerpiece of the electoral debate, but that dynamic no longer applies. Instead, domestic issues dominate all the discussion, with foreign policy at best an afterthought. Nevertheless, consistent with tradition, this week the campaigns took a brief turn to foreign policy, no doubt with the plan to quickly turn back to the economy.

Mitt Romney spent this week doing what most presidential challengers do on the foreign policy front, he went on a foreign road trip. Romney travelled to Europe, including trips to London and Poland, and then continued on to Israel. The purpose of the trip was to look presidential, get a few good photo ops with foreign leaders, and collect some cash, with fundraisers with U.S. ex-pats in Europe. Barack Obama did the same thing in the summer of 2008, but with a twist. He used his campaign-style event at Berlin's column of victory to set the tone for a new kind of American leadership and rally even foreigners to his cause. Mitt Romney had no such lofty goals. Consistent with the careful strategy of the Romney campaign, his trip to Europe was treated for what it was, a necessary but ultimately minor event in the unfolding campaign.

Even with a do-no-harm strategy for Mitt Romney's trip to Europe, he made several stumbles, which the Democrats and the press were quick to highlight. He made some mild criticisms of London's preparations for the 2012 Summer Olympics, resulting in a polite rebuke from British Prime Minister David Cameron. He then did a fundraiser with American financiers in London, despite a growing scandal about banks pricing fixing Libor interest rates. In Poland, he accused the United States of abandoning its commitment to Polish security, while in Israel, his swipes at the Palestinians drew criticism from Arab leaders. Missteps on some points to be sure, but nothing anyone will remember. In fact, the Romney campaign may have been willing to suffer some adverse consequences from some of the Governor's more aggressive comments, because they at least got the press to pay attention to the trip.

President Obama was certainly paying attention. The Democrats see foreign policy as a strong issue for them, and hope to exploit it. The Administration's aggressive anti-terrorist strategy and the killing of Osama bin Laden are strong arguments that the President has been an effective leader in foreign affairs. The White House also tried to upstage Romney, holding a signing ceremony for an aid bill to Israel just before Romney arrived there, and proclaiming that the President will visit Israel in his second term, something he failed to do in his first. The Israeli issue might be the only one of electoral import for Romney's foreign trip, since it is believed the Jewish vote is up for grabs because of the Administration's policies on Israel.

Israel and foreign policy might be an issue in the Fall campaign, but it will not be a central issue. This will be an election about domestic concerns, primarily the economy, the budget deficit, and Obamacare. Foreign policy might be mentioned, but it will not drive many votes. Governor Romney went overseas because he had to and the slow summer political season was the time to do it. Once he gets back home, little thought or strategy will be put into foreign affairs, at least not until after the election.

Week 185
(YOU CHICKEN)

August 5, 2012

While Obama and Romney continued their events, ad campaigns, and fundraisers, more and more political observers were proclaiming the campaigns uneventful and even boring. That is not a surprise, the summer presidential race is usually quiet before the party conventions. The real action has been taking place in the halls of Congress, where proxy wars are being fought daily over issues each side hopes will play to its benefit in the upcoming election. In the Senate, the GOP allowed the Democrats a vote on their tax increase bill to put moderate Democrats on record in support of repealing portions of the Bush tax cuts. For their part, Democrats continued to attack Mitt Romney for his refusal to produce more tax returns, seeing it as an opportunity to show him as a secretive plutocrat. But these were merely sideshows to the real drama, a game of chicken being played by Democrats on what is called the fiscal cliff, comprised of automatic spending cuts and the expiration of the Bush tax cuts, which will be triggered on January 1, 2013.

When Republicans and Democrats reached a compromise to allow for a debt limit increase in 2011, the plan included approximately $1 trillion in immediate spending cuts and a another $1 trillion in sequester cuts to start in January 2013. The Democrats were able allocate the sequester cuts disproportionally to the defense budget, betting Republicans would fight to avoid these cuts, and eventually agree to tax increases instead. Those cuts are now going into effect in only five months, and as predicted, the GOP is seeking to avoid the cuts. But the Democrats have refused to compromise, insisting that Republicans agree to tax increases. Patti Murray, the Democrat Senator from Washington leading the effort, has bluntly stated that she will hold the defense budget hostage to get tax increases. The Democrats are betting the GOP will blink, and appear willing to play chicken with the economic recovery in the interim.

So far, the Republicans have not caved. While seeking to avoid the defense cuts, they have steadfastly refused to agree to the tax increases. The House voted to extend all the Bush tax cuts for one year, while Senate Republicans allowed the Democrats to pass their tax increase plan solely for political ammunition, knowing the bill would die in the House. For its part, the Administration has refused to address the spending cuts, or back off on its tax increase demands. The White House will not detail how the sequester will be done, and continues to argue that only the Bush tax cuts for those making less than $250,000 will be extended. So both parties have dug in, regardless of the consequences for the economy. Democrats and the GOP did avoid a government shutdown by agreeing to spending levels for the balance of 2012, but that was fairly easy task because neither party wanted that issue in the Fall election and the spending levels were already agreed to in the budget deal done in 2011.

The Democrats' strategy on the fiscal cliff is to force the GOP to agree to a tax increase. The GOP appears to view its purity on the tax issue as more important than economic growth, at least in the short term. Both parties are taking these positions for policy and political reasons, but the big question is which party will win the presidential race, because who wins will ultimately drive the resolution of this debate. On that front, the wisdom of the Democrat strategy seems less certain. The threat of spending cuts and massive tax increases starting January 1 is no help to the economic recovery, and a faltering economy is the biggest risk for President Obama. We saw that risk highlighted this week, when the unemployment rate rose to 8.3% despite the economy producing a better than expected 163,000 jobs in July. Persistent high unemployment, combined with rising gas prices and weakening consumer demand has put the economic recovery at risk, making President Obama's task more difficult. So it is not clear the Democrats' game of chicken will achieve the desired results.

Most believe that no resolution can be reached on the fiscal cliff until after the election. Once the campaign is over, a re-elected President Obama hopes to force through a budget compromise that increases taxes and presumably cuts some spending, although the President has to date refuse to detail any new spending cuts. If Romney wins, the GOP will seek to reshape the tax code and spending along the lines of the budget plans offer by Congressman Paul Ryan. So the election will be the decisive factor on the fiscal cliff. Given the economic risks, it is not clear why the Democrats think it is wise to take positions that increase uncertainty and thereby threaten their own candidate. Maybe they just cannot resist the urge to watch the GOP squirm.

Week 186

(THE ENERGIZER)

August 12, 2012

In recent weeks, many Republicans have grown nervous about the presidential race. Despite Mitt Romney's prodigious fundraising and the still weak economy, the President appears to have gained strength, adding to his modest lead in national and battleground state polls. The Romney campaign was also starting to lose control of the political narrative because of the constant attacks on Bain Capital and Romney's tax returns. The GOP has been hitting back, including with new ads attacking the Administration's decision to make changes to welfare reform by giving states more flexibility to lessen or eliminate work and job training requirements. The Romney campaign started hitting the President on that issue, but that is far from certain to change the trajectory of the campaign. A game changer was needed, and the Romney campaign appears to understand that. So on August 11 in Norfolk, Virginia, Mitt Romney announced his vice presidential nominee, Wisconsin Representative Paul Ryan, and instantly a new energy was infused into the Republican campaign.

The announcement of the Paul Ryan pick came earlier than expected and well in advance of the GOP National Convention, which is two weeks away. The early unveiling of Paul Ryan was a recognition that the Romney campaign needed to change the campaign dynamic. Romney was very methodical in its Vice Presidential search, looking at a wide range of candidates from Senator Marco Rubio, to Senator Rob Portman, to Governor Chris Christe. But early on, Paul Ryan and Mitt Romney connected, which is key for any running mate selection. Congressman Ryan also brings many benefits for the Romney campaign. From a vetting standpoint, he presents few risks of scandal. As a 42-year-old, devout catholic, married father of 3, who still lives in the town where he was born, he has a Boy Scout reputation. He is widely recognized even by Democrats as highly intelligent, an expert on the federal budget, and a skilled speaker and debater. He is also a hero within the conservative movement. As chairman of the House Budget committee, he has championed budget proposals calling for tax and spending reform, including reforms to Medicare. Known as the Ryan Budget, his proposal has become the lightning rod of the budget debate. Also, importantly, Paul Ryan might help Romney carry Wisconsin, a key state in the GOP campaign strategy.

The huge impact of the Ryan pick was instantly evident. Conservatives were delighted and Mitt Romney seemed to have new energy and focus. The GOP raised more than $5 million the weekend of the Paul Ryan pick. Further, Ryan wasted no time calling the President out for failing to lead on the budget and other fiscal issues. The bet the Romney campaign has made is that Ryan will be a useful tool to frame the election as a referendum not only on President Obama, but also on competing visions for the size and scope of government. By picking Ryan, Romney added to his team one of the most eloquent advocates for the conservative vision of smaller government.

Yet the Ryan pick does not come without risks. Many Democrats celebrated the pick because of Ryan's controversial proposals on Medicare reform. The Democrats hope to turn the campaign into a referendum on entitlements, not President Obama. They believe Ryan offers a perfect opportunity to run a Mediscare campaign, frightening seniors into voting for Democrats. It seems Mitt Romney thought through this risk, and in his first interview with Ryan on CBS' 60 Minutes, was quick to point out the President Obama cut $715 billion from current Medicare beneficiaries, something Paul Ryan has never proposed doing. The Democrats also focused on Ryan's conservative views on social issues, including abortion. So it seems both conservatives and liberals celebrated the Ryan pick, and only the voters will be able to determine whose analysis is right.

The Romney campaign needed to get energized, excite the base, and take the battle to Obama on taxes and the national debt. Ryan was a great choice for all these objectives. The Democrats were planning on hitting Romney on Medicare anyways, so it appears the GOP was willing to take the risk the Ryan will highlight that issue. Also, from the tone of their first public events, it looks like Ryan and Romney plan to present themselves as candidates prepared to offer solutions to fix the nation's problems, in contrast to President Obama. These strategies all have risks, but at least with the Ryan pick, we can look forward to an honest debate about the proper role of government, which is by far the most important issue in the election.

Week 187

(MR. POPULARITY)

August 19, 2012

It is quite a feat for a politician to be popular with Republicans and Democrats, but Paul Ryan pulled it off. In his first full week as the presumptive GOP vice presidential nominee, he was the toast of the GOP and the favorite toad for Democrats. The Ryan pick seems to have pleased everybody, except for the voters, whose views are still unknown. What is known is that Paul Ryan has changed the campaign, in a way that Romney hopes will strengthen his bid for the White House, and for Democrats, in a way that allows them to use their favorite attack strategy: scare seniors. Each side thinks it will come out the better in this battle, but despite all the posturing, it will be Paul Ryan and his performance that will drive the outcome of the debate.

After the announcement of the Ryan pick in Virginia, the new Republican ticket started a bus tours through Virginia and North Carolina, and then Ryan headed to Wisconsin and Iowa. The crowds were huge and the enthusiasm palpable. Ryan kept his focus on budget and economic issues, and avoided major gaffes. He was aided by Vice President Biden, who took most of the fire for telling a black audience in North Carolina that the GOP planned to put them back in chains. That drew howls from the GOP and critical coverage from even the mainstream news networks. That took a great deal of pressure off Paul Ryan, and set up a nice contrast for him in his opening days on the campaign trail. So far, the Romney campaign has made careful use of Ryan, avoiding high profile hostile interviews and keeping him mostly to staged events. The idea is simple, let Ryan get his bearings before he gets deep into the fight.

Romney and Ryan plan to portray themselves as problem solvers willing to make tough decisions. Knowing that polls show that 60% of American see the country as on the wrong track, in addition to blaming Obama, the GOP has placed a bet that voters want candidates with solutions, even if those solutions are unpopular. In their 60 Minutes interview on August 12, Romney and Ryan claimed the gridlock in Washington is largely the product of a President unwilling to lead. When asked about Ryan's reform plans for Medicare, Romney was quick to point out that the only candidate in the race that has cut Medicare is President Obama, when he reduced Medicare spending by $715 billion to help pay for Obamacare. The GOP hopes this attack will blunt the Democrat's Mediscare campaign, but the Obama campaign did not appear deterred.

Ever since Ryan was picked, the Democrats celebrated, at least in public. They proclaimed the pick a disaster for the GOP and asserted that the campaign would now be referendum on the Ryan budget, not President Obama. These attacks were not left solely to the President's surrogates. President Obama began immediately to attack Ryan and the GOP, claiming their plans for Medicare reform were radical and would end Medicare as we know it. Most honest Democrats, even liberal ones like Dick Durbin, admit entitlement reform is essential for long term deficit reduction, but for the campaign Democrats want to suspend reality and pretend they will defend Medicare and Social Security from any reform. This strategy has strong precedents, because in the past Mediscare campaigns have helped Democrats. But recent history is less hopeful. In 2010, Democrats ran their usual Mediscare campaign against electing Republicans to Congress and lost 63 seats in the House and 6 in the Senate. This result may or may not be a good predictor for the upcoming election, but it certainly casts some doubt on how formidable Mediscare will be this time.

The problem for Democrats is that they want this election to be about small issues, where voters do not look at the state of the nation as a whole, but instead focus on isolated questions like Romney's tax returns, Medicare, and favored programs. They are betting that these discrete issues will drive voters from Romney, without the need for President Obama to offer any solutions for the big questions of unemployment, slow growth, and trillion dollar deficits. Democrats want voters to think small. In contrast, Romney and Ryan are asking them to think big. Ryan made this point very plain in his 60 Minutes interview. He said the American dream is fading, we are losing hope and opportunity, and that every American can feel that something is wrong. In response, he promised we could restore the American dream, but it would require leadership and hard choices, choices the GOP is prepared to make. This is an appeal of maturity and seriousness, very different from the strategy of the Obama campaign.

Week 188
(MY AKIN HEAD)

August 26, 2012

The Republicans want this election to be about the economy and President Obama's record, so any distraction from those issues could be damaging to the GOP. Mitt Romney fully expected the Democrats to use the Paul Ryan pick to distract voters from the economy by talking about Medicare, what he did not expect was a Todd Akin headache. Todd Akin is a six term Congressman from Missouri who recently won the GOP nomination to challenge incumbent Democratic Senator Claire McCaskill in November. McCaskill is widely recognized as the most vulnerable Democrat incumbent because she hails from an increasingly Republican state, but her voting record is solidly liberal and pro-Obama. Democrats understand the challenges facing Senator McCaskill and actually spent two million dollars running ads during the GOP primary portraying Todd Akin as an ultra-conservative, hoping to help him get nominated while at the same time repelling moderate voters from supporting him. It worked, Akin got the nomination. Then Akin did exactly what McCaskill wanted, he made off-the-cuff comments that made him sound like a kook.

Congressman Akin did an interview with KTVI-TV, a St. Louis television station. Akin has one of the strongest pro-life records in Congress, so not surprisingly, he was asked about his refusal to support abortion even in cases of rape. He responded: "If it's a legitimate rape, the female body has ways to try to shut that whole thing down. But let's assume that maybe that didn't work or something: I think there should be some punishment, but the punishment ought to be of the rapist, and not attacking the child." When the interview was posted on KTVI-TV's website on August 19, Senator McCaskill pounced, stating: "As a woman & former prosecutor who handled 100s of rape cases . . . I am stunned by Rep Akin's comments about victim this AM." Akin quickly tried to retract his statement, but the damage was done.

Akin's comment was not simply a stumble, it was a disaster for Republican hopes of re-taking the Senate. This was a seat the GOP was sure to win, and even with his very conservative record, in initial polling Akin was well ahead of Senator McCaskill. But that was before the "legitimate rape" comment. His comment was so offensive and ridiculous that the Republican establishment was forced to immediately abandon him. The Republican National Committee and the GOP Senatorial Campaign Committee both pulled financial support from Akin, elected GOP officials across the country called for him to drop out of the race, and even Mitt Romney called for him to step down. Under Missouri election law, Representative Akin had until August 21 to pull out of the race, in which case the state Republican Party could have chosen a new candidate. He refused to drop out, and now Senator McCaskill has gone from the most endangered Democrat in the Senate, to favored to win reelection. In fact, polls now show McCaskill with a near double digit lead.

Akin's disastrous comments were not just the downfall of his own campaign, they also hurt the Republicans nationally. For many months, the Democrats have been pushing a narrative of a GOP war on women. The hope is to portray Republicans as enemies of women's rights in an effort to expand the Democrats' already significant gender gap among unmarried women. The strategy has only been marginally successful, but the "legitimate rape" interview gave the Obama campaign a whole new opportunity to press this line of attack. Not surprisingly, President Obama jumped at this, appearing for his first press conference in months to remark that Akin's comments were "out there" and that men should respect women's choices on childbirth. The Obama campaign even attacked Paul Ryan for joining an Akin anti-abortion bill as a co-sponsor. Now, anyone associated with Akin can be painted as anti-women.

The biggest problem with Akin's self-destruction is that it again allows President Obama to focus on an issue other than the economy. The Obama campaign is built on a strategy to turn voter focus away from unemployment, slow growth, and deficits, and any GOP misstep that furthers that effort is a windfall for the Democrats. Mitt Romney and the GOP understand that divisive social issues like abortion are exactly the type of distraction the Obama team craves, and Akin handed it to them on a silver platter. Akin gave the Democrats exactly what they wanted, not just a way to keep control of the Senate, but also an avenue to keep the White House.

Week 189

(GETTING TO KNOW YOU)

September 2, 2012

The media narrative about Mitt Romney is that he is stiff, unapproachable, and has no personal touch with voters. That perception is supported by the polls, but it is hard to tell if the polls are driving the narrative, or vice versa. Nevertheless, the GOP has taken that issue to heart and in their national convention in Tampa, Florida, a major mission for Republicans was to introduce the real Mitt Romney to voters. That was not an easy task, in fact even Mother Nature threw up some obstacles, with hurricane Isaac, which forced the GOP to cancel the first day of convention events. Luckily for the Republicans, the hurricane passed Tampa, spared New Orleans, and the Republicans could proceed with their convention uninterrupted. During three days of speeches, what emerged was an effort to paint a personal picture of Mitt Romney, and a distasteful picture of President Obama. The success seems to have been modest at best, with Romney getting only a small bump in the polls, just enough to pull even with the President. Yet, that might be short-lived, because the Democrats' convention would start just four days later.

The big event of the first night of the convention was the keynote address by New Jersey Governor Chris Christe. Christe was rumored to be on the shortlist for vice president and is a hero to many in the GOP for his combative assault on big government, high taxes, and public sector unions. It does not hurt that he is a conservative elected in a fairly liberal state, something the Romney campaign would love to emulate. Christe gave a good speech about leadership and confronting bureaucrats and unions, the problem was he did not give much of a speech about Mitt Romney. It was nearly 18 minutes into Christe's speech before he even mentioned Romney by name. Many thought the speech was mostly about Christe's 2016 campaign, rather than the 2012 election. That might be a bit unfair to Christe, but it is certainly true that Christe's speech did little to help introduce Romney to the voters.

A better job on personalizing Romney was done on the second night, starting with a speech by Condoleezza Rice, the former Secretary of State in the George W. Bush Administration, and then GOP vice presidential nominee Paul Ryan. Rice's speech was about foreign policy, and the need to reaffirm U.S. leadership. It was a thoughtful and dignified critique of the Obama Administration, with an unexpected focus on education as a key to maintaining American leadership in the world. She also noted that a nation that loses control of its finances, loses control of its destiny, a reference to the threat the national debt poses to American power. Rice was followed by the most anticipated speech of the entire convention, from Paul Ryan. The Ryan pick for vice president energized the conservative base, and those folks were hoping for a speech that would reaffirm conservative's vision for limited government. Ryan delivered, but with a tone of disappointment more than outrage with Obama Administration policies. In a clear appeal to young voters, Ryan said that "college graduates should not have to live out their 20s in their childhood bedrooms, staring at fading Obama posters and wondering when they can move out and get going with life . . . None of us have to settle for the best this administration offers – a dull, adventure less journey from one entitlement to the next, a government-planned life, a country where everything is free but us." With these lines, Ryan hit the heart of the conservative criticism of President Obama: he is all promises, wants government in charge of too much, and has not delivered. Ryan made many references to Romney and tried to burnish the GOP standard bearer, but the key aspect of the speech was not Romney, but the warnings on the path President Obama has taken America.

. Thursday night was Romney's big night, the night the GOP nominee would lay out his case and connect with voters. Before the Romney address, there were touching testimonials from people Romney has helped with charity and support over the years, struggling families, dying friends, all of which put a new and much more human light on Romney, which made many wonder why these stories had not been part of the Romney campaign from the beginning. Next came Marco Rubio, the first term Senator from Florida, who offered both cutting criticism of the Obama Administration and an appeal to Hispanics and young people with his personal story. Rubio was so good, he risked outshining the nominee. When Romney took the podium, much was riding on his speech. What ensued was a strong but not great speech, where Romney gave his personal story, and again expressed disappointment in the record of President Obama stating: "This president can ask us to be patient. This president can tell us it was someone else's fault. This president can tell us the next four years he'll get it right. But this president cannot tell you we're better off today than when he took office. America has been patient. Americans have supported this president in good faith. But today, the time has come to turn the page." Romney then set out in general terms his plan for change, focused on energy independence, education reform, free trade, and pro-business policies. He then noted that "President Obama promised to slow the rise of the oceans and heal the planet. My promise is to help you and your family."

The GOP in general, and Mitt Romney in particular, put on a good show in Tampa. They highlighted women and minority Republicans, drew contrasts with President Obama, and helped better introduce Romney to voters. What they did not do is change the race. While the GOP was in Tampa, President Obama continued to campaign, mainly on college campuses. The Democrats also announced new ad buys to press their attacks on Romney and the GOP plans for Medicare. At best, the Republican convention made the tight presidential race a bit tighter, but there is still no clear momentum for either candidate. President Obama will likely retake a small lead after his convention, but it will be the economy and the debates that decide this race, not lofty convention speeches.

Week 190

(THE HARD ROAD)

September 9, 2012

The Republicans barely had time to take down their stage and banners in Tampa before the Democrats' convention started in Charlotte, North Carolina, only four days later. The Democrats chose North Carolina for its symbolism and it importance to the 2012 campaign. President Obama carried North Carolina by the thinnest of margins in 2008, which itself was amazing given that the state had been solidly Republican for years. The Obama campaign knows that if they can remain competitive in a state like North Carolina in 2012, they will win the election. Since 2008, North Carolina has trended heavily Republican, however, and Romney has a small lead in the polls there, but no matter because by choosing this state as the site for their convention, Democrats were making the point that Republicans have fewer safe havens these days.

That point was made at the podium during the convention as well. While President Obama is running for reelection in a very unfavorable environment, he has not fallen behind in the race. Even with slow economic growth, unemployment over 8%, trillion dollar federal deficits, and an unpopular health care law, President Obama is still more than holding his own in this election. That is a reflection on both his personal popularity and the tarnished GOP brand, realities that could drive the ultimate outcome at the polls. The Democrats' goal in their convention was simple, build on the already high personal popularity of the President while making the campaign not a referendum on the Administration, but a choice between two different visions for the future. The opening speaker, First Lady Michelle Obama, had the task of rekindling the excitement and admiration for Barak Obama that propelled him to the White House. She gave an outstanding speech about her husband's personal qualities and his determination to make America a better country. She was sincere, inspirational, poignant, and effective. The Obama brand was burnished, and she did her job well.

Next came Bill Clinton. On the second night of the convention, the Democrats turned to their most successful politician and advocate to lay out why President Obama must be reelected and the Republicans must be stopped. Clinton's job was to frame the election. There was a bit of irony having Bill Clinton play this role, considering the Democrats' theme of a war on women and Clinton's checkered past in that department, but such inconsistencies have never mattered much to this master politician. Clinton's speech was the best of the convention. He put President's Obama record in the best possible light and spoke about a citizenship agenda where government and the private sector are partners for the benefit of all. He then painted the Republicans as extreme individualists who would leave us all to sink or swim alone. He summed up his theme as "[w]e Democrats think the country works better with a strong middle class, real opportunities for poor people to work their way into it and a relentless focus on the future, with business and government working together to promote growth and broadly shared prosperity. We think 'we're all in this together' is a better philosophy than 'you're on your own.'" He then dismissed the GOP's criticism of the Administration: "In Tampa, the Republican's argument against the President's reelection was pretty simple: we left him a mess, he hasn't cleaned it up fast enough, so fire him and put us back in." He then made his closing pitch: "My fellow Americans, you have to decide what kind of country you want to live in. If you want a you're on your own, winner take all, society, you should support the Republican ticket. If you want a country of shared opportunities and shared responsibilities – a 'we're all in it together' society, you should vote for Barak Obama and Joe Biden." It was powerful and highly effective.

When Barak Obama took the stage the next night, there was concern that his speech would be overshadowed by Clinton's. That may have been Clinton's mischievous goal, since regardless of the kind words and the supportive speech, Bill Clinton and Obama have never been close. The President also had the carry the burden of high expectations, since his national career was propelled by his outstanding speech at the 2004 Democratic convention. But of late, the President has been a less effective orator, maybe because he has had a record to defend. He defended his record with vigor in his convention speech, which most thought was solid effort, but not equal to Clinton's address. The theme in the two speeches was the same. The Republicans are extremists who only favor the rich and want a winner take all society, while the Democrats have a vision for a society of shared interests and shared sacrifice.

The President started his speech with an attack on the GOP and its proposals for tax cuts, exporting jobs, and firing teachers. The President then said: "We have been there, we've tried that, and we're not going back. We are moving forward, America." Then recognizing that Americans are frustrated with the slow economic growth and high unemployment, President Obama pleaded "[b]ut know this, America: Our problems can be solved. Our challenges can be met. The path we offer may be harder, but it leads to a better place, and I'm asking you to choose the future." The President then talked about his successes, saving the auto industry, supposed green energy jobs, tax cuts, health care, Wall Street reform, ending wars, and killing Osama bin Laden. He also tried to strike a moderate tone, saying that government is not the enemy, but it is also not always the solution. Then he laid out a citizenship agenda, where all sacrifice for the greater good. He closed with: "If you reject the notion that this nation's promise is reserved for the few, your voice must be heard in this election. If you reject the notion that our government is forever beholden to the highest bidder, you need a stand up in this election . . . . America, I never said this journey would be easy, and I won't promise that now. Yes, our path is harder, but it leads to a better place. Yes our road is longer, but we travel it together."

With the theme laid and the job well done, the President and Vice President Biden set out on the campaign trail, confident that they had transformed the election from a referendum into a choice. But despite all the enthusiasm in Charlotte, a harsh reality struck just one day later, when the August unemployment report came out, showing only 96,000 job created and 368,000 workers leaving the job force altogether. That caused the unemployment rate to dip to 8.1%, because more people dropped out of the labor force. So once again we had a reminder that while the President is personally popular and can inspire, the economy is weak, poverty is up, household incomes and net worth are down, and jobs are scarce. In a normal election this would be enough to defeat an incumbent, but it is not clear this will be a normal election.

Week 191

(THE ARAB STING)

September 16, 2012

With a solid convention bounce and wind at his back, President Obama began the first week of his reelection campaign confident he had the advantage over his opponent. The media quickly began running articles implying the election was over and the Democrats' glee was only matched by the GOP's gloom. Clearly, the Romney campaign was hoping for a game changer that would shift the dynamics of the race, and they got one, from an unfortunate source. The assumption has always been that this election would be driven by domestic issues, but the first big event of the race came from the Middle East.

On September 11, a large crowd of Muslim protesters Cairo, supposedly enraged by a blasphemous American film about Islam and the Prophet Mohammad, stormed the American embassy, tore down the U.S. flag, and replaced it with one from Al-Qaeda. Shortly after, a similarly enraged crowd attacked the U.S. consulate in Benghazi, Libya with arms and rocket propelled grenades. In the sustained assault, three Americans, including America's Ambassador Christopher Stevens, were killed. Then further protests erupted throughout the Middle East, including in Tunisia, Yemen, Sudan, Pakistan, Morocco, Afghanistan, and elsewhere. It seemed the entire Middle East had risen up to attack America. The U.S. response was muted. Initially, the U.S. embassy in Cairo issued a statement that seemed to criticize irresponsible free speech in the U.S. more than the attacks on U.S. embassies. However, the Obama Administration quickly saw the political risks in that line of response, and pivoted to direct condemnation of the assaults. What motivated the attacks remains in dispute, with the Administration itself at odds on the issue. UN Ambassador Rice called the Libyan attack spontaneous, while others claimed it was a planned terrorist assault to mark the anniversary of the September 11 attacks.

With the Romney campaign desperate to open a new front on President Obama, it was no surprise when Romney quickly criticized the Obama State Department's initial response that seemed to blame Americans, more than the protesters, for the violence. Romney then used the rising turmoil in the Middle East as the basis for a broader critique of the President's foreign policy. President Obama began his presidency with outreach to Muslims. In 2009, he gave an address in Cairo praising the humanity and tolerance of Islam. The Administration also praised the Arab Spring protests, even though they toppled governments either friendly to the U.S., or at least not allied with radical Islam, in the case of Libya. The President supported the revolutions even though much of the protest movement was driven by Muslim fundamentalists. In contrast, the Administration has been much more cautious in support of secular rebellions against regimes clearly hostile to U.S. interests, most notably in Iran and Syria. As for Israel, President Obama has been a less than enthusiastic supporter of that key ally, this week even refusing a request from Prime Minister Netanyahu for a meeting. And on the nuclear issue, Iran continues to build a nuclear weapon, and the U.S. continues to pursue modest sanctions in response.

With this record, it is not surprising that Mitt Romney saw an opening to claim that President Obama has abandoned our friends, and supported our foes in the Middle East. The killing of Osama bin Laden and the Administration's relentless pursuit of Al-Qaeda make this a tough charge, but Romney tried it anyways. The GOP also used this line of attack to underline their theme of an America in decline, arguing that the President's policies have weakened us abroad and limited our ability to forcefully oppose challenges. While these lines of attack might offer some benefit, the real sting has come on gas prices, which have rocketed to above $4 per gallon in many places, due in large part to rising tensions in the Middle East.

Unless the protests in the Middle East spin wildly out of control, it is doubtful they themselves will have much lasting impact on the campaign. They offered a distraction this week and a reminder that all is not well in the world or in America, and to that extent they benefited Romney. However, the election will be won or lost on a more basic proposition, whether Americans are sufficiently satisfied with President Obama's performance to give him another four years despite the poor economy. That is the primary field of battle, so in many ways the recent troubles in the Middle East were just a diversion.

Week 192
(THE 47)

September 23, 2012

The opening weeks of the campaign have been discouraging for many Republicans, but the GOP started the week with some glimmers of optimism. The President's convention bump seemed to fade and polling from both Gallop and Rasmussen seemed to indicate the race was once again tied. Most importantly, the polling continued to show the President averaging under 50% in support, dangerous territory for any incumbent. Yet this modest momentum for Mitt Romney quickly faded when Democrat operatives released a video of a private Romney fundraiser with big donors, where Romney ridiculed the 47% of Americans who do not pay income taxes, said they were addicted to entitlements, and would vote for President Obama no matter what. The Democrats and their friends in the media promptly pounced, and what started as a better week for the Romney campaign, quickly became another tough slog.

President Obama himself has made more than a few comments at private fundraisers that he had to walk back. There was the famous one from the 2008 campaign where he criticized average Americans for "clinging to guns and religion" and another more recent one where he praised the virtues of wealth redistribution. Mitt Romney is now in the same mess, because of this statement: "There are 47 percent of the people who will vote for the president no matter what. All right, there are 47 percent who are with him, who are dependent upon government, who believe that they are victims, who believe the government has a responsibility to care for them, who believe that they are entitled to health care, to food, to housing, to you-name-it — that that's an entitlement. And the government should give it to them. And they will vote for this president no matter what. ... These are people who pay no income tax. ... [M]y job is not to worry about those people. I'll never convince them they should take personal responsibility and care for their lives.'"

In many ways, this statement has much greater potential to damage Romney than any of President Obama's misstatements hurt him. In the case of President Obama, his statement simply revealed his core political philosophy, which is secular, elitist, and focused on social justice. The President has been able to overcome his misstatement because of his personal popularity and the media's unwillingness to press the issue, largely because they share the same perspective. In contrast, Romney cannot rely on personal popularity or media sympathy because he has neither. He also must battle the perception fostered by the Obama campaign that he favors the wealthy and cares little for the needy. In the respect, Romney's comments were a homerun for the President.

President Obama has himself asserted that he has a 47% core base of support from minorities, union families, government workers, and committed liberals. Romney's mistake was not to focus on those groups, which everyone admits are solidly for the President, but instead claim that Obama's support comes from those who do not pay income taxes, that those people want government to pay for their lives, and that Romney does not care about them. The comment was wrong in almost every respect. Such a high percentage of people do not pay income taxes because successive rounds of tax reforms, including those by George W. Bush, have repeatedly raised the income level necessary to pay those taxes. The fact that someone does not pay income taxes does not mean they are dependent on government either, many are the working poor. It is also wrong that these people will vote for the President no matter what. Indeed, Romney is well ahead with white working class voters. Lastly, for Romney to imply that he does not care about people who do not pay income taxes makes the President's case that Romney only cares about the affluent.

When the video was released, Mitt Romney gave a 10:00 p.m. press conference to try to clarify his comments. He spent much of the rest of the week in the same exercise. Democrats highlighted the comments, and quickly started running TV ads based on them. The polls moved as well, with President Obama regaining a small but persistent lead of about 3%. So the 47 comment ended the modest Romney momentum and put the race back on comfortable ground for Democrats. Whether these comments will do lasting damage to the GOP remains to be seen, but they will certainly make the debates critical for Romney, because that might be his last chance to change perceptions and move voters in his direction.

Week 193

(WHOOPI)

September 30, 2012

There were lots of reasons for President Obama to celebrate this week. Weekly unemployment claims fell. Consumer confidence seems to be on the rise, and the stock market has been strong. With improving economic indicators, the President is having an easier time overcoming the economic headwinds that have made his reelection effort a dicey affair. The polls are now starting to bears this out, with several coming out this week showing that the President has a growing lead over his Republican challenger. Romney missteps have certainly helped, including the 47% comment that continues to dog him, but regardless, generally the political environment is improving for the President.

That does not mean the President has avoided all criticism, far from it. The biggest controversy facing the President remains the terrorist attack in Libya that killed U.S. ambassador Christopher Stevens. It appears the Administration had some warnings of plot before the attack and did little to step up security. Also, the FBI still has not gone to the scene of the attack, purportedly because of security concerns, but many think for political reasons. The President hoped to quell this criticism with his speech to the UN General Assembly on September 25, in which he sought to condemn the attack and highlight what he sees as his thoughtful approach to Middle East issues.

The President certainly gave a good speech that checked all the required boxes and included just enough phrases to try to please the all listeners. The address began with a eulogy to Ambassador Stevens, saying that "Chris Stevens embodied the best of America" and that "[t]he attacks on the civilians in Benghazi were attacks on America." The President pledged that "we will be relentless in tracking down the killers and bringing them to justice." But in offering this tough talk, the President wanted to be careful not to return to the rhetoric of the Bush Administration. So he then cautiously praised the Arab Spring and the rise of democracy in the Middle East, but warned that freedoms require tolerance. Mr. Obama described the video that supposedly sparked the violence as "crude and disgusting," but said even offensive speech must be protected. The President then made clear that "[t]here is no speech that justifies violence." This comment was an opening to his series of warnings against extremism, Assad in Syria, and Iran and its nuclear program. He praised the changes in the Middle East and his policies, which he thinks helped, and pleaded for all to try to avoid violent division.

It was a very nice speech from a President who is exceedingly good at this type of address. However, the realities are not so pretty as the rhetoric. The President loves to talk about high ideals and lecture about freedom, but he is not so good at the day to day work of fostering relationships and building alliances. He has developed no personal relationships with Middle East leaders, is openly dismissive of the Israeli Prime Minister, and took no time out during his UN visit to meet with any world leader. His aides said he was too busy for meetings on this trip, but the President did have time to go on The View and talk with Whoopi Goldberg. This gets to the root of the issue. The President is great at theatrics, gives inspiring speeches, but does he do the hard work of governing, at home or abroad. It seems like he is afraid to do that work, afraid it will somehow hurt his reelection. So everything has been put off — trade deals, the fiscal cliff solution, a budget plan — until after the election. Getting reelected appears to be the only thing that matters to the President, and people are starting to notice.

Week 194

(Romp-ney)

October 7, 2012

The depression among Republicans was palpable heading into the week of the first presidential debate. President Obama seemed to be building a strong lead nationally, was solidifying leads in key battleground states, and continued to exploit voter distrust of Romney. All this made the first presidential debate scheduled for October 3 a make or break moment for the GOP and the Romney campaign. With his fundraising and popularity starting to wane, Governor Romney needed a game changer. He got it, and now a campaign that looked all but lost might be winnable for the GOP.

The task for Mitt Romney going into the debate was daunting. After missteps, low favorability ratings, and months of negative ads from the Democrats, Romney had been effectively painted as a plutocrat indifferent to the interests of average Americans. In the debate, Romney needed to connect with middle class voters, appear in command of the issues, offer persuasive critiques of the Obama Administration, and lay out reasonable alternatives. Not an easy task, especially with President Obama's rhetorical skills. Nevertheless, Mitt Romney set about his difficult job on Wednesday night with enthusiasm and energy. What ensued was a rout, leaving Democrats and the Obama campaign bewildered and confused.

It was clear the President's game plan was to repeat all his standard attacks on Romney and the GOP, blame them for the economy, attack Romney for a $5 trillion tax cut plan, call for the rich to pay their fair share, and argue for a government that will give everyone a fair shot. However, the President set about his task reluctantly, showing no energy, spending much of the debate looking down or looking annoyed, and not bothering to engage with Romney or the viewers. When he did make points, they appeared more mechanical than heartfelt. His closing argument was halting and disjointed, and he did little more than repeat slogans voters have already heard over and over again.

The contrast with Romney's performance was striking. Despite being 14 years older, it was Romney who showed energy and interest in the issues. It was Romney who looked the President in the eye and offered his criticisms more with a tone of disappointment than disgust. When the President marched out his $5 trillion tax cut critique, Romney said that was not his plan and pledged revenue neutral tax reform. When the President asserted that Romney would raise taxes on the middle class, Romney pledged that under no circumstances would he raise middle class taxes. When the President criticized the GOP's Medicare reform proposal, Romney deftly defended it. When President Obama asserted that the GOP favors tax policies that reward companies for moving operations overseas, Romney simply responded: "I have been in business 25 years and I have no idea what you are talking about." Romney did all this with a smile, with references to the plight of average Americans, and with respect for the presidency and its current occupant.

All this left the President dazed and confused. He was not able to get past his talking points and engage Romney directly. Instead he retreated, staring down, taking notes, and looking ever more annoyed. It seemed the President felt the whole exercise beneath him and that no one should dare question his policies. In the wake of the debate, large majorities viewed Romney as the winner, and the media piled on, proclaiming Romney the clear victor. Even worse, nearly 70 million Americans watched the President's poor performance, making it the highest rated debate since 1980.

How much impact Romney's win will have on the race is yet to be seen. Early polls show Romney closing both nationally and in swing states, but much more polling is to come. The key for the Romney campaign will be to build on this victory and avoid missteps. But all was not bleak for the President. On October 5, the September unemployment report came out, showing 114,000 jobs created in September and a drop in the unemployment rate to 7.8%. This gives the President a chance to again make his economic case, but it will be hard for him to overcome the impressions created by Romney's debate romp.

Week 195

(ALL SMILES)

October 14, 2012

What a difference a week makes. Going into the first presidential debate, the Romney campaign seemed on life support. Ten days later, it was the Obama Campaign that seemed in disarray.

Right after the first debate, we heard many media commentators saying debates rarely impact the polls, claiming any Romney bounce would be short lived, and that the basic dynamics of the race (*i.e.* advantage Obama), would remain the same. This might have been wishful thinking by those who knew the President performed very badly in the first debate, but wanted to think it would not matter. However, it appears they were wrong. A slew of polling came out early in the week following the debate, showing a strong Romney surge both nationally and in swing states. The Obama campaign described it as a temporary bounce, and the media went along. By the end of the week, even liberal commentators had to agree that the race had changed, and that it had become a true dead heat. Everything was all smiles at Romney campaign headquarters.

Almost as important as the strong Romney performance at the debate itself was the impact of the debate on the media narrative of the campaign. Prior to the debate, the narrative was about a desperate GOP campaign and Romney gaffes. After, the narrative was about President Obama's weak performance and the Romney surge. A stunning turnabout, fueled in part by the media's love of a good story, even when it conflicts with their political leanings. Then leaks started to come out about the President's preparation for the first debate, how he skipped sessions to do site seeing, did not study, and took a win for granted. President Obama has always tried to avoid any signs of arrogance, but this time it was all too clear for 70 million viewers to see. A President not willing to defend his policies in a debate because he believes he is entitled to reelection.

With the Romney rout and the Romney surge, the Obama campaign needed something to change that narrative. The first opportunity was the vice presidential debate on October 11 between Joe Biden and Paul Ryan. The hope was that Biden would show the fight and enthusiasm so clearly missing in the President's performance. After 40 years in Washington and two prior presidential runs, Biden is an experienced debater. While prone to gaffes on the campaign trail, in debates Biden has usually been disciplined and focused, so the Obama campaign was hoping for Biden to stop the bleeding. As for Paul Ryan, this would be his first national debate and he would be going up against an experienced politician 25 years his senior. The Romney campaign hoped Ryan's smarts and youth would offer a helpful contrast with Biden.

The debate that ensued was spirited to say the least. Ryan calmly, yet sometime haltingly, defended the GOP ticket and program. Biden, on the other hand, took the advice of the Obama campaign to show energy and intensity to the extreme. He interrupted Ryan, made dismissive faces, smiled when Ryan was making serious points about national security and the Iranian nuclear program, and generally tried to dominate Ryan in every way. Biden's approach was dismissive, bordering on rude, and people noticed. While Biden probably got the best of many of the policy exchanges, his behavior is what got the attention. He also created controversy. On the attack on the U.S. consulate in Benghazi, Biden claimed that "we" had no knowledge that slain ambassador Stevens had requested more security. The White House had to quickly correct Biden's comment, saying when he said "we," he was only talking about himself and the President. Biden also said the U.S. would leave Afghanistan in 2014 period, with no consideration whatsoever of conditions on the ground. He also claimed that Iran was nowhere near having a nuclear weapon, a comment that might come to haunt him if President Obama is reelected.

Most polls showed a split verdict in the debate, with slight majorities saying Biden did better. But nothing in the debate moved the polls, and by week's end Romney had gained further strength, both nationally and in swing states. A host of states were moved from lean Obama to tossups, including Ohio, Wisconsin, Michigan, and Pennsylvania. The President's comfortable electoral college lead has disappeared, making clear that the nation is in for pitched battle until the very end. The next skirmish will be the second presidential debate on October 16 on Long Island. The stakes will be high for President Obama, because Romney's momentum is building and from the Democrats' perspective, something needs to stop it.

Week 196

(LONG ISLAND BRAWL)

October 21, 2012

With the Romney surge continuing and the President's supporters getting increasingly nervous, the Obama campaign was looking to the second debate to make up lost ground and gain an advantage. The President had substantial work to do as poll after poll showed not only growing support for Romney nationally, but also in swing states. Romney had pulled ahead in North Carolina and Florida, was poised to overtake the President in Virginia, and was within striking distance in both New Hampshire and Ohio. The President's problems were also not confined to the campaign. The attacks in Benghazi that killed four Americans, including the U.S. ambassador, continued to dominate the headlines, with congressional hearings exploring why the Administration for nearly two weeks after the attacks continued to make reference to an offensive video, when more and more evidence showed that the White House knew it was a planned act of terrorism. With foreign policy a seeming strength for the President, the disaster in Libya could hardly have come at a worse time.

With this daunting backdrop, the President entered the debate hall at Hofstra University on October 16 with a difficult balancing act to execute. His passive and disengaged manner at the first debate disturbed voters, but an overly aggressive performance posed dangers as well. Unlike the first debate, the President took his preparation seriously this time, secluding himself for nearly three days for preparation. Romney also took time out for preparation, but not nearly as much. Both candidates also had to adjust their strategy for a different format, a town hall where undecided voters would pose the questions and CNN's Candy Crowley would be the moderator. This format could be problematic for the President and could limit his ability to take the fight to Romney. All these factors were swirling when the candidates appeared on stage to start the debate.

There was no doubt a different President Obama came to the second debate. He was energetic, engaged, and aggressive. Taking every shot he could at Romney, including taking a page from Vice President Biden and interrupting Romney on more than a few occasions. Romney also took an aggressive approach, especially on the economy, repeating again and again that 23 million Americans cannot find a good job, that income is down over $4,000, and that 47 million people are now on food stamps. The President did not directly rebut these claims, instead he focused his attacks on the Romney tax plan, Romney's opposition to the auto bailout, and Romney's plans to cut basic programs for the needy, youth, and seniors. At times the candidates got up close and personal, pointing and accusing. Many voters of all persuasions were turned off by the tone and performance.

There were no knockout punches. Romney did well on economic issues. The President did well on social and women's issues. When asked about equal pay for equal work, the President referenced support for a bill early in his Administration on equal pay, while Romney talked about his efforts in Massachusetts to get women into leadership roles, referencing how groups sent him a "binder full of women" to review. The Obama campaign used that as a tag line to attack Romney, but in the world of gaffes, it was a minor one. When Romney criticized the President on Libya for failing to call the attack terrorism, the President said he did so in his first comments the day after. The participants then debated the point, until Candy Crowley sided with the President, a position she corrected after the debate, saying Romney was correct. Most think Romney flubbed the Libya issue, which should have been an easy target, but that was one of Romney's few clear errors.

The debate ended with neither candidate making any major mistakes. Polls showed most thought President Obama won, but only by a small margin. So the President clearly stopped his slide, but it was not so clear he stopped Romney's rise. Polls after the debate showed little impact on the race, with Romney continuing to show more and more strength both nationally and in swing states. By the end of the week, Romney had a six point lead in the Gallop tracking poll, and smaller leads in other polls. So for Obama, it was at best only a partial victory. This set the stage for the final debate, which would be the President's last chance to change the race. No doubt the election remains close and the President still has many advantages, but any notion that the Obama campaign would have an easy victory is gone.

Week 197
(THE GLARE)

October 28, 2012

Many in the Obama campaign had told themselves that Romney's bounce from the first debate would be short lived, and that a strong performance by the President would turn the tide. The President gave a strong performance in the second debate, even though his aggressiveness was a bit over the top. The Obama Campaign then waited for improved poll numbers, but they simply did not come. Romney's momentum continued, with Romney overtaking Obama in national polls and continuing to close the gap in swing states. This all made the third debate, to be held on October 22 in Boca Raton, Florida, critical for both campaigns. For Obama, it was a chance to change the dynamic of the race. For Romney, it was a chance to cement his improved image with voters.

One problem for the President's game plan is the format of the third debate. The debate would be about foreign policy and the candidates would be sitting at a table together. Not the best scenario to take the fight to Romney. However, the topic did offer opportunities for the President because, as commander in chief, he has a natural advantage in foreign affairs. The debate hit many of the expected topics, in Afghanistan, Libya, Syria, the Arab Spring, Russia, and China. Throughout, the President tried to emphasize his successes and take swipes at Romney any chance he could. To keep support on the Left, he talked a great deal about ending the wars in Iraq and Afghanistan. To please moderates, he described his decision to kill Osama bin Laden. And throughout, he tried to criticize Romney for changing positions on foreign policy, which prompted Romney to respond that attacking him was not a foreign policy strategy. The most striking thing about the President's performance was his angry glares at Romney every time his opponent was speaking. His disdain and contempt for Romney was palpable.

President Obama did his best to try to use the debate to discredit Romney, but the strategy did not work. That is because Romney came into the third debate with a strategy the President did not expect. Rather than try to continue the attacks on the Administration, Romney tried to strike a restrained and dignified tone. He criticized the Administration, but also noted agreement on issues like Egypt and the timeline for withdrawal in Afghanistan. He refused to be baited into sharp disagreements with the President. In a way, Romney seemed to almost ignore his sparring partner, instead focusing on undecided independents watching on TV. His goal was not to beat the President in the debate. Instead, his aim was to show himself to be a plausible commander in chief. In doing so, he let the President score more debating points, but to Romney the debate was not about points, it was about winning on election day.

Polls after the debate confirmed a win for the President bigger than the second debate, but by no means like the Romney win in the first debate. But surveys of undecided voters told a different story, with Romney pulling even with the President. Most believed the President did well, but not well enough to shake up the race, and those observers appear correct. The polls did not move in the President's favor, either nationally or in the swing states. Romney began to hit 50% support among likely voters in more and more polls, and Romney started to pull even in states like Ohio, and also was showing surprising strength in Michigan and Pennsylvania. The reaction of the Obama campaign, while not quite panic, was certainly vigorous. The President's rhetoric turned even more shrill, taking on the tone of ridicule and insult. The President favorite line of the week was that the GOP had a case of Romnesia, an affliction where a candidate forgets his views on issues. This seemed to be a return to the flip flopper attack on Romney. The problem is, after attacking Romney as callous, then extreme, and then simply a liar, the Romnesia attack just seemed like another gambit to catch voter attention. The Obama campaign also tried to blunt criticism that it has offered no plan for the next four years by putting out a glossy brochure on economic patriotism, which purportedly sets out the President's agenda for the future. However, even media allies of the White House criticized it as just a repackaging of the President's campaign rhetoric.

The President's entire campaign strategy was based on disqualifying Romney, but it succeeded too well. Romney was sullied so badly by negative ads, that in the first debate by simply seeming reasonable and offering ideas, he shattered the caricature so carefully created by the Obama campaign. The President also failed to disqualify Romney in the final two debates, so what was the White House to do. It had no positive plan to sell to voters, so it had to quickly manufacture an agenda and ridicule Romney. Not a strategy that is giving much comfort to Democrats.

Week 198

(Oh Sandy)

November 4, 2012

Mitt Romney entered the final full week before the election with clear momentum. For a full week he was above 50% in Gallup and Rasmussen polls, and his strength in swing states was growing. The Obama campaign had been trying for weeks to change the dynamic of the race, but neither the debates, nor new attack lines, nor ad blitz after ad blitz did anything to shake up the race. That was Mother Nature's job, and she did it with fury, in a way that changed the lives of millions of Americans and changed the race for the White House in the process. Hurricane Sandy left more than wreckage in New Jersey and New York, it also wrecked the Romney momentum, whether fatally or not will only be known on election day.

It almost seems like nature itself has been rooting for the President. The GOP convention was upended by a hurricane, and just as the Republicans were poised to cement their advantage in the presidential election, along comes another storm, far worse than the first. Hurricane Sandy was dubbed the perfect storm, a strong late season hurricane that was moving out into the Atlantic when the convergence of a strong low pressure system in the Mid-Atlantic forced it into a strong left hand turn straight into the New Jersey shore. There was plenty of early warning, and prediction of high winds, heavy rain, and a damaging storm surge. Local and state governments tried to prepare, but when Sandy came ashore late afternoon on October 29, there was no stemming her destruction. She laid waste to vast areas of New Jersey and Staten Island, with coastal communities taking it the hardest. Power was knocked out for 8 million people. New York City's subways flooded, travel was impossible, and thousands were rendered homeless.

With memories of the damage Katrina did to George W. Bush and the injury the Gulf Oil Spill response caused to his own popularity, President Obama was focused on showing his leadership during hurricane Sandy. On October 29 and 30, the President was at FEMA and gave press conferences to give assurances of a quick federal response. When the full extent of the destruction was becoming clear, he travelled to New Jersey and toured the impacted areas on foot and by helicopter with Governor Chris Christe. Obama showed himself concerned and in command. Governor Christe fawned over the President's attention, to the disgust of GOP partisans, who feared the President would get a bounce from the storm, at a very inopportune moment for the Republicans. There was little for the Romney campaign to do. Governor Romney held a charity drive on October 30 for storm victims, but returned to the campaign trail on October 31. The President started campaigning again on November 1, but the storm was a positive campaign event beyond his reckoning.

The biggest benefits the President derived from Hurricane Sandy was a change in topic and a chance to look presidential. The Obama campaign has been built on edge issues and disqualifying his opponent, and that strategy was not working. Almost made to order, Sandy gave the President a chance to look the leader, seem bipartisan and effective, and show he is in control. It started to show in the polls, with Romney losing his lead and moving into a tie in most polls, and with the GOP's momentum in swing states appearing to stall. This was a perilous turn of events for the GOP, because in a race this close, any slight change in the dynamics could spell defeat. The Romney campaign sensed that as well, and tried to open new fronts. With polls showing Romney strength in Pennsylvania and Michigan, the GOP started running ads in those states and Romney even planned a visit to Pennsylvania. The Obama campaign claimed all this was driven by desperation, while the Republicans claimed Romney was expanding the map.

As the week closed, the news was less favorable for the President. Serious gas and food shortages, slow recovery responses, and millions without heat or electricity started to take some glow off the President's disaster response. That might explain why even with this golden opportunity, the President did not take the lead, with no less than four consecutive polls showing the race tied. Most commentators claimed the President still had the advantage in the electoral college, but Republicans pointed to high enthusiasm on their side and their own effective early voting efforts. What emerged from all this spinning were two sides looking at the same polling data and coming to completely different conclusions. Democrats convinced they would win, and the GOP equally certain of victory. Hurricane Sandy shook things up, but in the aftermath there is more confusion than clarity.

Week 199

(SEEING BLUE)

November 11, 2012

Going into election day, most believed the nation was in for a long night and a very close outcome. Republicans believed they would win on momentum and enthusiasm. Democrats were sure they would win with a strong ground game and organization. Pollsters were at odds as well, some showing Romney strength, others showing a lead for the President. When the returns came in, it became clear that the Democrats were right and the Republicans were wrong. The electorate was not more Republican, Democrats showed up at the polls, urban voters went for the President even more strongly than in 2008, and the President won a close but clear victory. For the GOP, it was a bitter and discouraging defeat. For Democrats, it was a reaffirmation of the faith they had put in the President. For the nation, it was a split verdict for a divided populace.

On paper, President Obama's reelection was convincing. He won the popular vote by nearly 2 million, and only lost two of the battleground states, Indiana and North Carolina. The President racked up 332 electoral votes, against Romney's 206. A more careful review of the results showed that while the President prevailed in the vast majority of battleground states, his margins were very tight, and even a slight change in events, like, for example, if hurricane Sandy had not hit, might have altered the outcome. In Congress, with bad candidates and bad luck, the GOP lost two seats in the Senate, in a year when they were expected to make gains. In the House the news was better for the GOP. Despite President Obama's strength at the top of the ticket, Republicans lost only 7 seats, and maintained a majority of 235 seats to the Democrats 200. At the state level, the GOP also fared better, gaining governorships to grow their control of state houses to 30. So, there were aspects of the election that were positive for the Republicans, but overall it was a disturbing defeat for the GOP.

The Obama campaign did an amazing thing. They managed to reelect the President despite 7.9% unemployment, weak economic growth, a majority of voters viewing the country on the wrong track, and the unpopularity of Obamacare. They did it with 18 months of unrelenting focus from the President and the entire Administration on reelection. Nearly every speech, every trip, every policy initiative by the Administration was aimed at one goal: reelection. Every lever of federal power was used, every tool available was employed, and every attack imaginable was used. The President and his allies made everything, including policy, secondary to the goal of reelection. Clearly, the White House's view was that reelected was the imperative, and that after a victory, the Administration could turn to issues.

The President's strategy for reelection was hardnosed, aggressive, and ultimately successful. He ran a campaign without a program of his own, instead focusing on attacking his opponent. He sought to divide Americans by class, race, religion, and geography. He appealed to resentment, distrust, and envy, even telling his supporters in the final days of the campaign to vote for revenge. It worked, but at what cost. The nation is more divided now than ever. The GOP is embittered.

Nearly as many Americans voted against the President as for him, and we still have the same status quo in Washington, with Republican consent in the House needed for the President to accomplish anything legislatively. The irony is that for the President to be successful, he needs to govern in the opposite way he campaigned. He needs to work with Republicans, find common ground, and compromise. He did very little of that in his first four years, but to be successful he will have to change his ways. If he does, significant accomplishments on taxes, spending, and entitlement and immigration reform could be within reach. If he does not, four more years of gridlock awaits us, and the nation will suffer as a result.

Week 200
(THE PEACOCK)

November 18, 2012

There were many schools of thought on how the President would act upon his reelection. Many conservatives believed that after reelection, the President would lose all pretense of moderation and would openly embrace an aggressive liberal agenda. Progressives hoped this would be the case, because in their view the President's policies in his first term were too moderate. Others expected the President to recognize that compromise would be essential for success in his second term, and that his first priority would be to heal the divisions created in the election and try to build consensus for budget and immigration reform. This week, during the President's November 12 news conference, we got our first glimpse of the President's post-election strategy. Like a peacock showing its feathers to intimidate any challenger, the President's made clear he is going to try to leverage his reelection to obtain a Republican surrender on taxes, spending, and immigration. Rather than try to heal and compromise, the President threatened and attacked the GOP, warning them to submit or be run over. Not an encouraging sign for what is to come.

The likely reason for the President's aggressive tone is the very difficult task that awaits the lame duck Congress, which just returned into session. With partisan wounds still fresh and time very short, the White House and Congress have just a few weeks to avert the fiscal cliff and find a compromise on federal spending and tax policy that has to date been so elusive. Part of that process is for each side to stake out its position, which is hopefully simply a prelude to good faith bargaining. Speaker Boehner, the only Republican in Washington who had any kind of victory on election day, remains the leader of the weakened GOP cause and wasted no time asserting that the reelection of his majority was a clear signal from voters that they rejected the Democrats' spending and tax priorities. The President took the exact opposite view, asserting a mandate to increase taxes on the affluent as part of his "balanced" deficit reduction plan. From the comments this week, it looked like neither side was ready to compromise and that each had its feathers out for display.

The strong talk from each side certainly heartened partisans, but it was discouraging for those who hope for progress on the key challenges facing the nation. The simple truth remains that nothing can get accomplished legislatively until President Obama and Speaker Boehner find common ground. President Obama can strut all he wants, but few in the GOP fear him. He will never again be on a ballot, and House Republicans who kept their seats in 2012 have little to fear from the President in 2014, since midterm elections in second terms usually favor the party not in the White House. Thus, the President has little ability to steamroll the GOP. However, the Republicans likewise have no chance to further their priorities without making deals with the White House. Not only would the President veto any bill not to his liking, but it is probable nothing would ever pass the Senate in the first place without Administration support.

For all the posturing, both sides have a vested interest in compromise. On the fiscal cliff, neither Democrats nor Republicans can accept the tax increases and spending cuts that will automatically go into effect January 1, 2013, for many reasons, not the least of which because it could trigger a new recession, something no one wants. A failure to compromise would result in taxes going up on all families, indiscriminate spending cuts to domestic programs, and devastating reductions in military spending. Given this, it would seem everyone would come to the table in good faith to try to reach a deal. Indeed, Speaker Boehner gave clear signs on that, saying the election results do not support a push to raise tax rates, a subtle indication that the GOP is prepared to make changes to the tax code to increase revenues, as long as tax rates remained steady. So even in staking out their positions, the GOP gave a signal on compromise.

Not true so far for the White House. The President's press conference sounded like his campaign speeches, filled with harsh rhetoric and cutting attacks. And the White House signaled that after Thanksgiving, the President would leave Washington on a campaign-style trip to build support for his tax increase and budget plan. The President tried to strike a congenial tone in a November 16 meeting with congressional leaders, but it seems the White House believes threats are the key to success. If this strategy is just a prelude to talks aimed at a negotiated compromise, then averting the fiscal cliff is still a possibility. But if the President actually believes he won a huge mandate and that he can force the GOP to bend to his will, a fall off the fiscal cliff is likely. The President has shown that he is very good at strutting, but he needs to fold down his feathers and work in good faith with the GOP if he wants to have a successful second term.

Week 201
(RICE WARS)

November 25, 2012

Thanksgiving week is usually a slow one for politics, but not so this year. Issues both foreign and domestic kept Washington a buzz of activity. Not surprisingly, the political struggle over the fiscal cliff continued to occupy Washington, with congressional staff meetings beginning to work on a compromise, as most politicians tried to restrain partisan comments in the hope that a bipartisan deal could be struck. The White House distanced itself from these initial discussions with the President's trip to Asia, a good strategy since it was otherwise assumed to be a quiet week. Things did not turn out that way, as more controversies in and about the Middle East took center stage. Israel launched massive airstrikes against the Gaza strip and marshaled forces for a land incursion to stop incessant rocket attacks. While at home, the debate over Susan Rice, President's Obama's clear favorite to replace retiring Secretary of State Hillary Clinton, gave rise to criticism for her assertions that the Benghazi attacks were prompted by a video, not terrorism. So much for an easy glide into Thanksgiving.

The Administration hoped the President's Asia trip would highlight a Pacific focus for his second term. The President travelled to Cambodia, Thailand, and Myanmar to promote free trade and support the democracy movement in Myanmar. The trip is part of what the Administration calls the Asia pivot, an effort to increasingly turn the focus of U.S. foreign policy away from Europe and the Middle East towards what is viewed as the more critical region for the future. The President likes to call himself America's first Pacific President (based on his birth in Hawaii), and has made clear that he believes both world security and U.S. economic prospects turn heavily on good management of Asian issues, especially the relationship with China. But the events of the week showed how hard it will be to turn the focus to Asia as the Middle East continues to cause turmoil.

The Israeli conflict with Hamas in Gaza stole the show from the President's Asia trip. For months, Hamas has been supporting rocket attacks, with thousands hitting all over southern Israel. Israeli Prime Minister Netanyahu appears to have waited until after the American election to launch an assault to intimidate Hamas into ceasing the attacks. The Israeli air force pounded targets in Gaza and the Israel started to mass troops on the border. It appeared Israel might even invade Gaza, a dangerous scenario that could have risked a wider military conflict. This is especially the case given Muslim Brotherhood control of Egypt. President Obama had to step out of several meetings in Asia for calls with Egyptian President Morsi. Clearly, the Administration wanted to make sure Egypt would play a productive role in reaching a ceasefire, rather than take any steps that might lead to a wider conflict. Eventually a temporary ceasefire was achieved, but how long it will hold is anyone's guess.

While a land war in Gaza appeared to be avoided, at least temporarily, the damage to the President's trip was already done. Indeed, Middle East distractions were not limited to Gaza, there was a Middle East dispute brewing right in Washington. Secretary of State Clinton has made clear that she is going to step down, and the President has made clear that he wants UN Ambassador Susan Rice to replace her. The problem is that during the presidential campaign, the Administration sent Susan Rice out on the talk show circuit to assert that the Benghazi attacks were prompted by an American video, not terrorists. The evidence shows those statements were not consistent with the facts known at the time and many believe Rice made those statements to provide cover for the Obama campaign. Now, after using a diplomat for partisan political purposes, the President wants that same diplomat to be confirmed by the Senate as Secretary of State. Many Republicans are still angry over the Administration's handling of Benghazi, with Senator John McCain taking the lead, and have made clear that Rice will be in for a very rocky confirmation process if nominated. The President seems ready for a fight on the issue, using his November 12 press conference to warn Republicans not to oppose Rice. It seems the GOP was not listening, because more and more Republican Senators have started to signal that they will oppose Rice.

So in a week that was supposed to be quiet and was hoped to highlight Asia, the Middle East dominated again. This might foreshadow more to come in the President's second term. With the Syrian civil war, the Muslim Brotherhood running Egypt, and the Iranian nuclear program, whether he likes it or not, the President is likely to be heavily occupied with Middle East issues for much of his second term.

Week 202

(FLABBERGASTED)

December 2, 2012

Any questions about the White House's determination to try to leverage the President's reelection into a favorable budget deal were answered this week, when the Administration launched a full court press to force the GOP into raising taxes on the affluent. The President was in campaign mode, hosting events, photo ops, and a road show to further his budget plan. Until this week, no one really knew what the President's budget plan was. The only plan committed to paper thus far was the President's 2012 budget, which failed to garner even a single vote in Congress. Trying to call the Republican's bluff on the budget, the President dispatched Treasury Secretary Tim Geithner to the Capitol to present the President's plan to congressional leaders. After hearing the plan, Democrats were delighted, and Speaker Boehner was "flabbergasted."

It has become increasingly clear that the White House believes that the GOP is not willing to go over the fiscal cliff, and that if the nation does go over, the Republicans will get most of the blame. This must be the Administration calculus, because to date they have done nothing to try to find common ground with the GOP. Indeed, other than some staged events, the President has not even attempted to negotiate a deal. Instead, the White House is treating the fiscal cliff like any other political battle. This week the President hosted an event at the White House with hand-picked middle class voters to press again for "balance" in the federal budget. The President also travelled to Virginia and Pennsylvania to hold rallies for his tax increase plan. The President also staged a lunch with defeated GOP candidate Mitt Romney, mainly to create the image of bipartisanship. The President's only direct effort to reach a budget deal was a brief call to Speaker Boehner, where the President simply restated his views. All the while, the tone on the budget in Congress got more and more partisan, and progress slowed to a halt.

While all this was happening, the President dispatched Treasury Secretary Geithner to meet with Republican and Democrat leaders in Congress to present the Administration's proposal. It was a plan designed not to reach a deal, but instead up the pressure on the GOP. The White House blueprint included $1.6 trillion in new taxes on the top 2% of income earners, a plan to end congressional control of the debt ceiling, and $50 billion in additional stimulus spending. On the spending cut side, most of the reductions were based on assumed interest savings, money to be saved from ending the wars in Iraq and Afghanistan (even though that money was never going to be spent), and incorporation of the $1.2 trillion in spending cuts already implemented in 2011. A vague promise was made to reduce Medicare spending by $400 billion over ten years, with no specifics and no guarantees. All in all, it was a mostly tax and cut little plan. It is understandable why Speaker Boehner was shocked.

Republicans saw this proposal as designed to prevent a deal, not reach one. Clearly, the White House thinks it has all the leverage and can force a GOP capitulation. Before this plan was offered, there were some signs of breaks in Republican ranks, with three GOP House members supporting extending the middle class tax cuts now, without Democrat commitments on spending issues. Ironically, the White House plan presented by Geithner ended all that talk. The President's proposal was so unbalanced that it instantly unified the Republicans. It also made many Republicans more willing to go over the fiscal cliff, because in many ways that would be better than what the President proposed.

So the week ended in stalemate and impasse, making it very likely there will be no early budget deal, in fact there might not be any deal at all. With all these moves, it has become clear that the President wants a victory over the GOP, not a bipartisan compromise that could set a productive tone for his second term. He is betting the GOP will fold or take the blame. Yet in the process, the President seems willing to risk going over the fiscal cliff, potentially putting the country back into recession. The Republicans would likely take more of the blame, but a recession would hurt the President as well, and dim the prospects for getting anything done legislatively in his second term. And then we have the debt limit, which must be raised again in early 2013. Without a deal, that presents a perfect opportunity for the GOP to press for more spending cuts, so the President believes he needs to crush the Republicans now. So much for Christmas cheer.

Week 203
(VERY TAXING)

December 9, 2012

With the President throwing down a gauntlet with the budget plan he delivered to Congress, the Republicans had some very difficult decisions to make. Stick to their guns and demand private negotiations with the President, simply reject the White House plan and prepare for the fiscal cliff, or make a countermove of their own. Each course presented dangers for the GOP. The President might continue to refuse to negotiate, a trip over the fiscal cliff could be disastrous for the GOP if they get the blame, and putting their own new plan on the table raises the thorny issue of tax increases. No easy choices, but a choice had to be made because President Obama has decided to play hardball on the budget, and without an effective countermove, the Republicans risk being run over.

Ultimately, the Republicans decided to offer a counterproposal in the form of a letter from Speaker Boehner to the President. In it, the Republicans offered in increase federal revenues by $800 billion over ten years with changes to tax deductions and exemptions, not higher tax rates, called for $1 trillion in cuts to entitlements, and laid out other spending reductions that they said would result in a $4.6 trillion deficit reduction over 10 years. The letter laid out principles with very few specifics, but closely tracked the offer Speaker Boehner made during the failed deficit talks in the summer of 2011. On taxes, the GOP offered essentially the same revenue number from 2011. On spending cuts, additional details were offered, most taken from the President's Simpson Bowles deficit reduction plan, including raising the Medicare eligibility age to 67 and changing the COLA calculations for Social Security. Speaker Boehner portrayed those cuts as modeled on the Simpson Bowles proposal. The White House quickly marched Bowles out, and had him say this was not his plan and that the center of the debate had shifted since his commission issued its recommendations.

With this move, the GOP hoped to put pressure back on the White House. By making a counter to the White House plan presented the prior week, the Republicans now said it was time for the Administration to respond, especially on the issue of entitlement reform. Initially, it looked like the White House believed the pressure was still on the GOP, so no Administration counteroffer came. Instead, the GOP plan was promptly attacked for failing "the test of balance," meaning it does not raise taxes enough. The Administration then quickly sought to dismiss the plan and return to campaign mode, with more events by the President focused on tax increases. The Administration also started to release some details on how the sequester would be implemented, again designed to pressure lawmakers of both parties. The President continued to refuse any private meeting with Speaker Boehner, and in dueling press conferences Republicans and Democrats took on an increasing bitter tone.

So in the end, yet another week came and went without any substantive progress on the fiscal cliff. The parties each made proposals and gave speeches more focused on posturing than on achieving progress. The President continued to refuse to negotiate and campaigned for tax increases. The GOP offered more revenue, but stood fast on not raising tax rates and focused on spending cuts. By taking these positions, both side emboldened the extremes of their parties. Democrats increasingly opposing any significant spending cuts, while the GOP opposing any rate increases. So rather than moving the parties closer together, the proposals and rhetoric were pushing the parties further apart. It is the classic Washington dance, all posturing and putting off real negotiation until the last possible minute. But that last minute is now fast approaching, with only three weeks left to cut a deal and avoid large tax increases and the sequester. The politicians are cutting it very close, in part because of the tone set by the President, who seems determined to beat the GOP more than reach a compromise.

Week 204

(NEWTOWN)

December 16, 2012

The week in Washington started like most have since the election, with swirling debates about the fiscal cliff and political posturing on taxes and spending. But then came Newtown. On December 14, Adam Lanza, the 20-year-old son of Nancy Lanza, shot his mother, took her Bushmaster semi-automatic rifle and two pistols, and drove to the Sandy Hook Elementary School in Connecticut. The school was locked, but Adam Lanza shot his way in. The principal and the school psychologist confronted him, and he killed them. Then he opened fire on first graders and their teachers, killing 20 children ages six and seven, and four more female school employees. All of the children were shot multiple times. As the police were closing in, Adam Lanza took his own life. All told, Adam Lanza killed 27 people plus himself, and in the process shocked the nation.

It remains a mystery why Adam Lanza went on his shooting spree. In 2009, his parents divorced after a 28-year marriage, which certainly would have been painful for him. However, he was not abandoned by his father, who is an executive at General Electric and who amply provided for his ex-wife and son. Adam has a brother who lives what seems to be a normal life in New Jersey. His mother was well-liked and an attentive mother to her son. So on the exterior, while Lanza certainly went through some hardships, there was little that seemed to portend his killing spree, especially because neither he nor his family had any connection with the Sandy Hook School. Given all this, the focus quickly turned to Adam Lanza's mental state. With details still emerging, it seems like so many other recent shooters, he was a loner, detached, depressed, and mentally unstable. This alone does not explain why he killed so many so young so wantonly, but it is a familiar pattern.

The shock caused by the Newtown massacre ripped through the nation. On the day of the shooting, President Obama gave a tear-filled speech, saying it was his toughest day in the White House. Washington politicians turned their focus away from fiscal issues and instead shared in the nation's grief. It was the topic of conversation on every news channel, in every office, and in millions of homes across the nation. The horror of the crime, perpetrated on children so young, was simply incomprehensible. The fact that it occurred during the Christmas season only added to the despair.

For President Obama, there is no doubt he was genuinely shocked by the events at Newtown, and his comments sought to try to bring solace and help the nation grieve. In the coming days, his job will be to lead the nation in its grief. He may also try to lead a national dialogue on why these shootings keep happening across the nation, and what can be done to stop them. And while the nation is united in its grief, any steps that may be proposed to curb gun violence are likely to be divisive. Only a day after the shootings the mainstream media immediately turned the dialogue to gun control, a topic the President has carefully avoided since entering the White House. He will not be able to avoid it anymore.

Week 205

(STICKING TO THEIR GUNS)

December 23, 2012

There was very little Holiday cheer in Washington entering into Christmas week. The season of giving quickly turned into a time for intransigence. On the fiscal cliff, the week started with signs of progress towards a bipartisan deal, but ended in chaos and recrimination. Calls for national unity after the Newtown shooting turned partisan, with the President setting up a board to offer recommendations to reduce gun violence, with more vigorous gun control at the top of the Administration's agenda. All the while, the National Rifle Association remained quiet, waiting until December 20 to offer its first statement on the Newtown shootings. Many had hoped for some accommodation on gun control, but none was offered. Instead NRA President Wayne LaPierre called for armed guards in every school and rejected any claim that gun control could stop killings like those in Newtown. So on all fronts, the combatants were digging in for a long fight. So much for the Christmas spirit.

It had been the hope of President Obama to reach a deal on the fiscal cliff before Christmas. His plan was to put pressure on the GOP with speeches, public events, and adherence to his proposed tax and spending plan, waiting to start negotiations until the ground had softened in his favor. By December 16, the Administration had calculated the time for real negotiations had come, so the President invited Speaker Boehner to the White House for talks. It appears the Speaker was ready to deal, offering $1 trillion in new revenues from elimination of deductions and exemptions, and importantly, an increase in tax rates to 39.6% for families with incomes above $1 million. The Speaker also offered a two-year extension in the debt ceiling, something the White House wants so further debt limit fights can be avoided. These moves were welcomed by the Administration.

In response, the White House dropped its demanded revenues from tax hikes to $1.3 trillion and appeared to offer some modest additional spending cuts. By December 18, many thought a deal was at hand, and then the Speaker pulled out of the negotiations.

It is not clear what led the Speaker to walk away from the talks. One problem with the deal that was emerging was that it was going to be titled heavily towards tax increases instead of spending cuts. The Administration's last position called for $1.3 trillion in tax hikes, with only about $730 billion in actual spending reductions. The remainder of the White House's proposed cuts were mainly accounting gimmicks, including a dubious estimate of saved interest expenses and the often cited savings from ending the wars in Iraq and Afghanistan, even though that money was never going to be spent. Other problems with the emerging deal were the President's call for more stimulus spending and an extension of unemployment benefits. One can only assume that the Speaker determined that any final deal the White House was willing to support could never pass the House, so why bother with continued talks.

Instead, the Speaker announced his Plan B, which essentially focused on the House passing a tax plan and leaving the spending cut issues until 2013, when the GOP hoped the pressure from the sequester and the debt ceiling could force bigger cuts. The Speaker put a bill together that called for raising rates only on those making more than $1 million per year, while extending the Bush tax cuts for everyone else. Passage of this plan was supposed to put the pressure back on the Democrats and give the Speaker leverage, but things did not work out that way. On December 20, the Speaker had to pull his bill because he did not have the GOP votes to pass it. It seems about two dozen Republican decided they preferred the cliff to a compromise with Barack Obama. Humiliated, the Speaker put the House in recess. Now it would be up to the President and the Senate to craft a compromise.

Anyone hoping that the issue of gun control might offer a better opportunity for unity and compromise were quickly disappointed as well. On the same day the Speaker's tax bill was pulled from the House floor, the NRA ended its silence on the Newtown killings. Rather than an offer conciliation, the NRA chose confrontation, with Mr. LaPierre stating that the best "way to stop a bad guy with a gun is a good guy with a gun." Based on this theme, the NRA called for armed guards in every school. LaPierre rejected any claim that gun control could reduce gun violence, instead he said a national database of the mentally unstable and better armed law abiding citizens were the answer. LaPierre's speech was so strident that many conservatives distanced themselves from it. But even if the NRA's view is a minority one, the speech made clear that any fight for more gun control was going to be a long and bitter one. President Obama named Vice President Biden to lead that effort, which will be an unpleasant task indeed. So everyone was sticking to their guns, politicians figuratively on the fiscal cliff, and the NRA literally, and as a result there is little Christmas spirit in Washington this year.

Week 206

(MERRY CLIFFMAS)

December 30, 2012

Far from reaching a plan to address the fiscal cliff before Christmas, the nation entered into the holiday in a state of fiscal chaos. After the failure of the talks between the President and Speaker Boehner, and Boehner's failure to pass his Plan B, the House went into recess, the President issued condemnations, and all scratched their heads, wondering if any chance to cut a deal before New Year's Day remained. In fact, it seemed like Washington was almost giving up the fight. The President flew home to Hawaii for Christmas, and House members went home. As a result, the focus turned to the Senate, where Majority Leader Reid and Minority Leader McConnell were tasked with trying to salvage the situation. Sound familiar.

The events relating to the fiscal cliff have an eerie similarity to the debt limit fight the summer of 2011. Back then, the Speaker and the President tried to reach a grand bargain, they failed, the nation teetered on the brink, and then Reid and McConnell stepped in to craft a compromise. That compromise called for $1 trillion in immediate spending cuts, and another $1.2 sequester cuts over 10 years commencing January 1, 2013. So ironically, the same Senators were being called in to avert the crisis their prior plan created. However, there is a good reason to trust them again, because they found a way to avoid disaster last time. The talks between McConnell and Reid started before Christmas and continued through the holiday. It appeared their efforts were focused on a narrow deal, one that would avoid a majority of the tax increases from the expiration of the Bush tax cuts, but not address spending issues in any significant way. Given the timing, it appears even that modest goal could be hard to achieve. Most of the discussions were behind closed doors, but some leaks emerged. The GOP appeared willing to let rates rise on the highest income earners (families with income above $550,000), but would not agree to stimulus spending, or any long term extension of the debt ceiling or delay of the sequester. But by week's end, still no deal had been struck.

Through all this, the President's role has been curious. He spent the first month after his reelection giving speeches and railing against the GOP, acting as though he were still on the ballot. When he did meet with the Republicans, it was mainly for perfunctory photo ops. There were several meetings with the Speaker, but it appears the President was not willing to compromise in any meaningful way, sticking to his calls for higher taxes and offering only modest spending cuts in return. What likely torpedoed the talks with the Speaker was the White House's insistence on a long term extension of the debt ceiling, thus depriving the GOP of leverage in future spending fights. The Administration was diving such a hard bargain, that it got no bargain at all. Then the President simply denounced the GOP, said it was the Senate's problem to find a solution, and left town.

This was the President's strategy during his first term, give speeches, lecture, campaign, but let Congress craft the policy. Most thought the President took this approach for political reasons, delegating to Congress to avoid getting mired in the details of law making. So the President took a detached approach, on the 2009 stimulus, on health care, and on most other major legislation. Now, after being reelected, most thought we would see a more engaged President, but apparently that is not the Administration's plan. After failing to get a deal with the Speaker, the President appeared to fold up his tent and go home, leaving it to Congress to fix the mess. The President's reluctance to lead on the fiscal cliff has made some think he wants a crisis because he thinks it will benefit him politically.

This view was reinforced when it was announced that the President would return early from his vacation in Hawaii to work on the fiscal cliff. The President did indeed return to Washington, but not to negotiate. Instead, he waited until 3:00 p.m. on Friday, December 28 to call in congressional leaders to try to find a solution. After only a bit more than an hour of discussions, the meeting ended, and the President held a press conference to attack the GOP. Then on December 29, he taped an interview with Meet the Press, again spending most of his time blaming Republicans. So the President continued to campaign and attack, leaving the negotiations to others. Christmas week closed, with Senate leaders working furiously to craft a compromise and the nation on edge, and the President appeared to enjoy every minute of it.

Week 207

(DIVIDED AND CONQUERED)

January 6, 2013

When President Obama first ran for the White House in 2008, one of his central themes was the need for the affluent to pay higher taxes. He has continued to talk about that goal for all of his first term. Ironically, despite the rhetoric, he twice extended the Bush tax cuts because of the recession, and cut other taxes as well, including payroll taxes. With his reelection, the President was determined to finally achieve his goal of raising taxes. Throughout the fiscal cliff negotiations, the White House stuck to its position that any deal would have to include substantial tax increases. It was that demand that ultimately led Speaker Boehner to walk away from negotiations with the President. With only a few days before automatic tax hikes and spending cuts were to go into effect, it was left to the Senate to craft a compromise. Senator McConnell was making little progress in talks with the Senate Democrat leadership, so he called the White House and asked for Vice President Biden to get involved. He did, a deal was reached, taxes increased on the "rich," and the White House proclaimed victory.

Democrats declared victory because they finally were able to raise tax rates on higher earners, something they have been determined to do for years. They also took glee in watching the Republicans squirm. The President and the Democrats used the leverage of taxes potentially rising on every American to get the unthinkable, a majority of Republicans in Senate and a sizable number of Republicans in the House to vote for a tax increase. In fact, the tax increase bill passed the Senate with 89 votes, with the no votes being almost equally divided between Republicans and Democrats. The story was different in the House, where the majority of yes votes came from Democrats, but the result was the same nonetheless.

With all the cheering from Democrats, it was possible to lose sight of how little of their new tax agenda was actually achieved. Democrats wanted to raise rates on all families making $250,000 or more, but rates only went up for families making $450,000. Many Democrats wanted the estate tax to return to 55% and apply to estates in excess of $3.5 million, but the rate only went up to 40% and the $5 million exemption was kept. Liberals wanted the payroll tax cut to remain, hoping to replace it with even higher taxes on the rich, but the payroll tax cut was allowed to expire.

Progressive wanted tax rates in capital gains and dividends to match income tax rates, but the compromise raised rates only to 20%, and that only applied to those with high incomes. While the bill did include provisions to phase-out deductions for those earning more than $250,000, importantly the Bush tax rates were kept for anyone making less than $450,000, meaning 99% of taxpayers will see no rate increase. In the end, the compromise preserved most of the Bush tax cuts.

So on substance the GOP did well. The President went into the fiscal cliff fight seeking $1.6 trillion in new taxes, the deal he got included only $630 billion. The President and the Democrats wanted to delay the automatic spending cuts for a year, they got only a two-month delay paid for by $12 billion in spending cuts and $12 billion in revenues from tax changes the GOP wanted anyways. The Democrats wanted an increase in the debt limit as part of the deal, but they did not get it. So the details overwhelmingly favored the GOP. Where the Republicans were hurt was on the process and the precedent.

The chaos in the House, the last minute deal in the Senate, the Senate vote on New Year's Eve, the House's aborted effort to amend the Senate bill eventually leading to a GOP leadership capitulation, all made the GOP look very bad, very divided, and very defeated. The Democrats also saw victory in the precedent, namely getting the Republicans to finally vote for a tax increase. No matter that the President and the Democrats got very little of what they sought, on the optics, they won a victory. That victory, however, may be fleeting. Now that most of the Bush tax cuts have been preserved, the GOP will have much less incentive to compromise with the Democrats. Between mid-February and mid-March, the U.S. will reach the debt ceiling and will be unable to pay its bills, the sequester spending cuts will start, and the temporary funding bill for the government will expire. The GOP hopes to use these events to force big spending cuts, the Democrats claim they will force even more tax increases. The only thing that is certain is that we will be in for an ugly two months.

Week 208
(MY BOYS)

January 13, 2013

It is common for reelected Presidents to have substantial cabinet turnover in their second terms. This familiar pattern is certainly playing out for the Obama Administration. So far, nearly the entire foreign policy team at the cabinet level is changing, as is the crucial post of Secretary of the Treasury. While the pattern is common, President Obama's selections for replacements are surprising many. Although the President likes to pose a gregarious air, in truth he does not socialize in Washington and usually sticks with a very tight, mostly male, and deeply loyal circle of advisors. This insular style has led many to criticize the President for being aloof and disengaged. It seems the White House does not care, because this week it nominated four white males for vacant posts, three of whom are Obama insiders, while the other is a congressional ally. Anyone hoping the President would use his cabinet appointments to bring fresh ideas into his Administration or strike a bipartisan tone was quickly disabused by this week's cabinet picks. True, the President nominated Chuck Hagel, who served as a GOP Senator from Nebraska from 1997 to 2009 for Defense Secretary, but Hagel is a maverick, has few friends in the GOP, and bucked his own party on many issues. So the Hagel pick struck no true tone of bipartisanship since Democrats like him more than Republicans do. Hagel is a controversial choice not only because of his abrasive personality, but also because of his highly critical comments about Israel, comments that have led some to claim he is anti-Semitic. The President seems to have ignored those comments, likely viewing Hagel as providing a useful bipartisan veneer to his plans for steep reductions in military spending.

For CIA and Treasury, the President resisted calls to go outside his inner circle and instead nominated two of his West Wing confidants. For CIA, the President selected John Brennan, his Chief Counterterrorism Advisor and the Deputy National Security Advisor. Brennan is a former CIA agent and has been at the center of much of the Administration's counterterrorism efforts. He has drawn fire for a number of comments, including disclosing details of the raid that killed Osama bin Laden and claiming the Muslim Brotherhood is a secular organization. But for a President who values loyalty above all else, it was easy for the White House to overlook those issues. Jack Lew, the President's nominee for Treasury Secretary is yet another insider, serving as Director of the Office of Management and Budget for the last two years, a position he also held at the end of the Clinton Administration. Lew cut his teeth on Capitol Hill as an aide to former Speaker Tip O'Neil. Viewed as both a committed liberal and a budget expert, this selection signaled that the President has no plans to court the business community, instead the agenda for his second term is going to be squarely focused on a progressive agenda.

The only nomination this week that went outside the President's comfort zone was John Kerry for Secretary of State, but that was not by choice. The President wanted another of his insiders, Susan Rice, to get that job, but her nomination was doomed by comments she made about the attack on the U.S. embassy in Benghazi that seemed designed to help the President's reelection campaign. President Obama had to abandon Rice, and settled for Kerry instead, whose service in the Senate since 1985 and foreign policy credentials ensure an easy confirmation. Secretary of State is a non-political post, and Kerry is liked by both Democrats and Republicans and has mainstream foreign policy views,

Kerry's nomination is more the exception than the rule, because with all his other choices, the President signaled a plan for an aggressive and combative second term. He is building a team of liberals and loyalists, clearly preparing for battle, not compromise, with the GOP. The President seems determined to crush all Republican opposition, and for this task he needs loyalists in top posts. These selections show the President has no plans to build consensus or national unity. Instead, it looks like the nation is in for 4 long years of bitter partisan struggle, the exact turf where the President feels most comfortable.

Week 209

(DROP YOUR DEFENSES)

January 20, 2013

In the final week of his first term, President Obama squarely took aim at the GOP and gun owners, and in response, the GOP staged a tactical retreat. The President opened the week with a press conference on January 14, with the questioning focused heavily on the debt ceiling, the budget debate, and gun control. The President continued his confrontational rhetoric, openly daring Republicans on the debt ceiling, and saying America is not a deadbeat nation and must pay its bills. The liberal tone of that press conference was continued when the topic shifted to gun control. In the wake of the Newtown shootings, Vice President Biden's commission set about to craft a plan to address gun violence. The President announced that plan on January 16, and to no one's surprise, it was focused heavily on gun control. Liberals were pleased. Then the week ended with a GOP plan to extend the debt ceiling for three months without offsetting spending cuts to allow time for a budget deal with Democrats, something the Republicans had previously refused to do. The President seemed to be driving the debate and was clearly pushing the GOP around in the process.

When Presidents are reelected, they usually try to unify the nation. Not so with President Obama. Far from moderating his positions, since reelection he has become ever more emboldened to press a progressive agenda. Not only did he stand firm and force the GOP to raise tax rates, but also his attitude toward his opponents has moved from disagreement to contempt and mockery. That pattern was evident in the last press conference of his first term. The President launched an all-out assault on the Republican leadership in Congress, saying that there was no legitimate basis not to raise the debt ceiling to pay for spending Congress itself already approved. He repeated his unwillingness to negotiate over the debt ceiling, and dared the GOP to fight him on this issue. His rhetoric was harsh, a likely sign of what is to come. Without the need to face the voters, President Obama is out not simply to win on policy, but to humiliate and then destroy his opposition. Maybe his victory has gone to his head a bit, but events tend to humble politicians in time.

Yet there was no sign of humility in the President's next big event of the week, which was the unveiling of his gun violence plan. Like much else, it was staged like a campaign event, with parents of children killed in Newtown in the audience to give greater heft to his proposals. The main focus of his gun violence plan was of course gun control. The President signed 23 executive orders relating to guns and other issues, but most were symbolic and few will have any practical impact on gun control or gun violence. For that, legislation is needed. In that sphere, the President called for universal background checks for all gun purchases, re-instituting and broadening the 1995 assault weapons ban, and limiting cartridges to 10 bullets. Outside of gun control, the plan calls for $4.45 billion in new spending to improve mental health care, a recognition that most of the recent high profile shootings have been perpetrated by mentally unstable individuals. The plan and the announcement made for nice theatrics and good politics, but it is far from clear much legislation will come of it. New gun control legislation will have a hard time passing the Democrat-controlled Senate, let alone the House. And with the President openly ridiculing and attacking GOP congressional leaders at every turn, few are going to line up to support him.

After President Obama dominated the headlines for most of the week, on Friday it was the Republicans turn to take the spotlight, but they wish they could have done it in a better way. The party has been struggling to figure out the best way to deal with the impending debt ceiling, budget, and sequester cut deadlines, all of which look to converge in March. In 2011, the GOP used a debt ceiling fight to wring $2 trillion of spending cuts out of the President, and some wanted to try that again. Others worry that a debt ceiling fight might be a trap for the Republicans this time, given the President's confrontational rhetoric. The House GOP were on retreat this week, and returned on January 18 to announce their plan. They would allow a vote on a three month extension on the debt ceiling without spending cuts, but the plan called for the Senate and the House to pass a budget resolution by April 15, and if they do not, congressional pay would be withheld. In essence, the GOP wants more time to get a budget and wants to force Senate Democrats to come to the table with a plan. The Republican strategy is also a recognition of the dangers of a debt ceiling fight and a decision that it is better to let the sequester proceed or risk a shutdown than risk a default.

The media described this plan as a retreat, and it was. Whether it proves a tactical or strategic retreat will be determined when the dust settles on the budget fight. If the GOP gets real spending cuts and entitlement reform, the retreat will have been worth it. If they do not, then they will have ceded victory to the President and the Democrats. So the week ended as it began, with the President's agenda driving the debate, and the Republicans searching for a way to respond. All the momentum was with the President, but momentum is a fickle thing, and his second term is only now starting.

Week 210
(THE PROGRESSIVE COMETH)

January 27, 2013

Many predicted that if President Obama was re-elected, we would see an end to his moderate post-partisan rhetoric, and it would be replaced with the words of an unabashed progressive. When the President took the podium on the Capitol west terrace on January 21 to give his Second Inaugural Address, few doubted the progressive had come. Ever since the November election, the President has seemed a liberated man, now ready to be truly himself, since he no longer needs to fear the voters. His confrontational tone, mockery of his opponents, and determination to smash them in policy debates has been evident in his every public appearance. Despite a victory more narrow than the one in 2008 and approval ratings barely above 50% on Inauguration Day, the President more than ever believes he has a mandate for his policy agenda, an agenda that is now unmasked as purely progressive in all its details.

President Obama's Second Inaugural Address was his first chance to lay out his vision for America. Like all inaugurals, it was a speech of high rhetoric and generalities. But unlike his First Inaugural Address, it was not a speech about ending divisions and confronting crisis. No, this time, it was a speech about what kind of America we should build. The President framed his address in the immortal words of the Constitution, that "all men are created equal, that they are endowed by their Creator with certain unalienable rights, that among these are Life, Liberty, and the pursuit of Happiness." He then noted that protecting these rights means a constant struggle, and that the "patriots of 1776 did not fight to replace the tyranny of a king with the privileges of a few or the rule of a mob." Then came a catalogue of progress of the nation, from ending slavery, to building a modern economy, to the regulatory state to curb the excesses of capitalism, to the entitlement state. He acknowledged our "skepticism of central authority" but asserted that "preserving our individual freedoms requires collective action."

The President then claimed that we have overcome our recent economic adversity and that "we are made for this moment, and we will seize it – so long as we seize it together" Then the President asserted we cannot have an America where "a shrinking few do very well and a growing many barely make it." He said that America's prosperity must "rest on the broad shoulders of the middle class." He spoke about remaking government and revamping the tax code, but then committed to defending and expanding the entitlement state, saying the "commitment we make to each other – through Medicare, and Medicaid, and Social Security – these things do not sap our initiative they strengthen us. They do not make us a nation of takers; they free us to take the risks that make this country great."

The next part of the address was like a checklist of progressive causes, starting with climate change, ending the War in Afghanistan, equal pay for women, gay rights, voting rights, immigrant rights, and support for students. Each topic touched on key constituencies that propelled the President to reelection. He then stated that: "Progress does not compel us to settle the centuries-long debates about the role of government for all time – but it does require us to act in our time." Then came the critique of the Republicans, with the President stating that we "cannot mistake absolutism for principle, or substitute spectacle for politics, or treat name-calling as reasoned debate. We must act, we must act knowing that our work will be imperfect." With this, the President made his clearest call for activist government.

The President gave a fine address, but one that abandoned most of the themes from his First Inaugural. Gone were the moderate tones and the calls for unity. They were replaced by at best fleeting references to free enterprise and limited government, only to be quickly eclipsed by calls for more government, more entitlements, more constituency politics, and a more activist state. So emerged the true Obama, not a uniter, not a unifier, not post-partisan. Instead, the true Obama is a true progressive, one who is much more interested in activist government than free enterprise, one who is more inclined to central planners than free citizens, and one who believes that collectivism is the best hope for progress. His vision is not radical, but nor is it moderate. Despite his dreams of a mandate, it is a vision that will be very hard to achieve, because even with his convincing victory, the Republicans still control the House, can block any bill in the Senate, and dominate the vast majority of state governments. With that reality, one might have thought the President would have pushed for common ground, but that is not a progressive's way of doing things.

Week 211

(MIGRATING TO REFORM)

February 3, 2013

One of the biggest stories of the 2012 election was the impact of minority voters. Mitt Romney carried the white vote handily, but lost the election because minority voters came out and voted overwhelming for Democrats. All election observers expected President Obama to carry the black vote by a huge margin, but the President also took around 70% of the Hispanic vote. Not so long ago, Hispanics were up for grabs, with President George W. Bush doing very well with that constituency in 2004. But now Hispanics seem to be trending heavily Democratic, and as the fastest growing and soon to be largest minority group, that spells trouble for the GOP. So no surprise, immigration reform, which was shot down by Republicans in 2007, is back on the agenda, with bipartisan support.

President Obama has made no secret of his desire for immigration reform. He highlighted it as a major objective right after the election, and has continued to talk about it. Immigration reform serves both his policy and political objectives. Everyone agrees that the immigration system is broken and the nation cannot continue with a shadow economy supporting 11 million undocumented immigrants. Unfortunately, recent attempts at reform have failed because of heated political debates about border security, amnesty, a path to citizenship. Any effective immigration reform must address all three of those issues, which is why reform has been so hard to achieve. With his reelection and the clear clout minority votes now have, the President sees an opportunity to push through reform. On the political side, the President hopes reform will both cement his legacy with Hispanics and secure them as reliable voters for Democrats for decades. Pushing immigration reform also puts Republicans in a tough spot, because they scuttled reform last time, but doing so now might mean losing more elections.

Recognizing the political realities, on January 28, a bipartisan group of eight Senators unveiled a set of principles for immigration reform based on securing the border, giving law abiding immigrants the opportunity to get work permits to stay in the country, and then setting up a system where these immigrants could work toward citizenship, taking their place behind those already in line. These are basic principles, and ones that likely will form the center of any reform. For his part, on January 29, President Obama flew to Las Vegas to give a speech on immigration reform, where he laid out similar principles: "First, I believe we need to stay focused on enforcement. That means continuing to strengthen security at our borders. It means cracking down more forcefully on businesses that knowingly hire undocumented workers. . . . Second, we have to deal with the 11 million individuals who are here illegally. We all agree that these men and women should have to earn their way to citizenship. But for comprehensive immigration reform to work, it must be clear from the outset that there is a pathway to citizenship. . . . We've got to lay out a path — a process that includes passing a background check, paying taxes, paying a penalty, learning English, and then going to the back of the line, behind all the folks who are trying to come here legally. . . . "

Although there seems to be a growing consensus on these general principles, when it comes to tackling an issue as complex and controversial as immigration, the devil will be in the details. After the President gave his speech, the view was that his proposal called for a quicker path to citizenship than the bipartisan Senate plan. Then word leaked that the House was also working on a plan, but that blueprint would have a guest worker element but not a path to citizenship. So the debate, which has only just begun, is already swirling. In the end, however, the GOP might not be able to stop immigration reform, because the risks for them are too great. So all factions seem to be migrating to reform, but there will be many twists and turns on the way.

Week 212

(SEQUESTERED)

February 10, 2013

In averting the debt ceiling crisis in 2011, the White House congratulated itself on a clever move that they were sure would corner the GOP. That debt ceiling deal called for $1 trillion in immediate spending cuts, plus $1.2 trillion in sequestration cuts to start on January 1, 2013, conveniently after the 2012 election. The sequestration cuts would all come from discretionary spending, half from defense and half from non-defense programs. With these cuts falling so heavily on the Defense Department, the Administration was sure the GOP would never allow the cuts to take place, giving Democrats leverage on their budget priorities, namely tax increases. But a funny thing happened on the way to the sequestration, as the cuts got closer and closer, it became clear the Democrats wanted to avert them more than the Republicans. So much for those clever tacticians in the White House.

The sequestration has gotten more popular with the GOP because of the very unappealing alternatives being offered by President Obama. The President has made very clear that he is determined to pursue what the Administrations calls a "balanced" approach to deficit reduction, meaning tax increases now, and vague promises for spending cuts in the future. The Republicans got some experience with the White House's approach with spending cuts in 2011, where two spending cut deals, one for $46 billion and another for $1 trillion ultimately turned out to cut spending far less than advertised, because of accounting tricks and a White House budget staff that simply outmaneuvered the GOP. After the election, the President went on the attack, daring the GOP to let the Bush tax cuts expire and offering no compromises on spending cuts. This led the Republicans to cut a tax deal with the President, and defer the sequestration to March 1, 2013 to allow time to negotiate alternative spending cuts. However, almost as soon as the bill regarding the Bush tax cuts was signed into law, the Administration made clear it would only replace the sequester with a plan containing both spending cuts and more tax increases.

Recognizing the President's approach, the GOP beat a tactical retreat, deferring a debt ceiling fight until later in the year, and instead concentrating on the sequester and the end of the current federal government funding bill, both of which would hit in March. The media represented this as yet another White House victory. But not long after the deal was done, reality started setting in with the Democrats. Faced with a President unwilling to cut spending, meaningfully reform entitlements, or engage in negotiation, the sequester started looking pretty good to the GOP. Although the cuts would be indiscriminate and hit defense spending hard, at least they were real cuts and they were already law. No new vote would be needed to put them in place. More importantly, the sequester was the White House's idea and the President signed them into law, so try as he might, it will be difficult for him to claim someone else is responsible. So after the debt ceiling fight was postponed, the Republican leadership from Speaker Boehner, to Majority Leader Cantor, to Budget Committee Chairman Ryan all signaled that the sequester was going to happen, and that result was better than more tax increases.

When enacted, the sequester was abhorrent to Republicans. So it was quite a feat for the President to make the sequester look better than the alternatives being offered by the White House. Now, the President has a problem. He has big plans for investment spending, immigration and tax reform, and the environment, but if the economy remains weak, his work on achieving these other goals will get harder and harder. All agree the sequester will hit the economy hard, so now it is the White House and the Democrats who are desperate to avoid it. On February 5, the White House announced that the President would present a plan to replace the sequester with other spending cuts. It seemed the Administration had blinked. But when the President took the podium that day, he presented no plan, instead he vaguely promised spending cuts and tax reforms to replace the sequester, all of those reforms being tax increases. So with these comments, the White House signaled its concern about the sequester, but could not quite bring itself to offer any plan to avoid it that the GOP could support.

So it seems the Democrats have now been caught by their own trap. They succeeded in getting a tax increase passed in 2012, but one far smaller than they wanted and one that preserved most of the Bush tax cuts. That was a defeat for the GOP, now it is clear it was only a tactical one. The debate has now moved to spending cuts, the sequester is law and will happen, and from the Republicans' perspective, the President's proposals were worse that sequester. If the White House wants to avoid the sequester, which they absolutely do, they will have to win over the GOP with a reasonable program of real spending cuts. The advantage has moved to the Republicans, whether the Administration realizes it or not.

Week 213

(OUGHT TO BE)

February 17, 2013

When President Obama took the podium in the House chamber for the first State of the Union address of his second term, many expected a victory lap and a loud call for progressive policies to fix the nation's ills. That is exactly what he gave the nation. Emboldened by his election victory and current popularity, the President used his address to outline his version of America's best future. That vision is of an American where the debate is not about big government but about smart government. An America of legalized immigrants, gun control, gay marriage, higher taxes, entitlements, and activist economic policies. Gone were the moderate tones from the campaign, now replaced by unadulterated liberalism. It was a vision not of what America has been or is, but instead what America ought to be, at least according to the President.

The address began with a recitation of the accomplishments of the first term, an improving economy, falling unemployment, a rebounding housing market, and the bull market on Wall Street. The President then recognized that although progress has been made "too many people still can't find fulltime employment. Corporate profits have rocketing to all-time highs–but for more than a decade, wages and incomes have barely budged." The President's answer to this problem was clear, government policies to redistribute wealth and raise incomes. "It is our generation's task, then, to reignite the true engine of America's economic growth–a rising, thriving middle class. It is our unfinished task to restore the basic bargain that built this country – the idea that if you work hard and meet your responsibilities, you can get ahead, no matter where you come from, what you look like, or who you love." Progressive economic and social policy all rolled up into one.

Recognizing that it will be difficult to achieve this agenda given the massive federal debt, the President then turned to the issues of spending and taxes. He claimed to have reduced the deficit by $2.5 trillion already, but said more needed to be done, but in a balanced way. He then took aim at the sequester, saying it had to be averted by a combination of tax increases and spending cuts, claiming "we can't ask senior citizens and working families to shoulder the entire burden of deficit reduction while asking nothing more from the wealthiest and most powerful." The prominence given to the sequester highlights how desperately Democrats want to avoid it, even as Republicans get more and more comfortable with it. He then called for an end to brinksmanship: "The greatest nation on Earth cannot keep conducting its business by drifting from one manufactured crisis to the next." The President then tried to change the terms of the debate about government, saying: "It's not bigger government we need, but smarter government that sets priorities and invests in broad-based growth."

The President moved quickly from deficit talk to spending talk, outlining a host of initiates — industrial zones, green energy subsidies, research and development, and more stimulus spending

— all of which he claimed could be done without any increase in the deficit. As for energy policy, the President praised the domestic fossil fuel boom, but again called for comprehensive climate change legislation, threatening that "if Congress won't act soon to protect our future, I will. I will direct my Cabinet to come up with executive actions we can take . . . ." On education, the President called for universal pre-K, technical training, and efforts to make college more affordable. On immigration, he again called for reform and a path to citizenship. As for wage fairness, he spoke in favor of the Paycheck Fairness Act and an increase in the minimum wage to $9.00.

After a brief discussion on foreign affairs–progress against terrorism, ending the War in Afghanistan, and warnings to North Korea and Iran on nuclear weapons–the President closed with a return to domestic issues with an impassioned plea for reductions in gun violence. Highlighting survivors from the Newtown shootings, the President renewed his call for comprehensive gun control, noting: "Our actions will not prevent every senseless act of violence in this country. Indeed, no laws, no initiatives, no administrative acts will perfectly solve all the challenges I've outlined tonight. But we were never sent here to be perfect. We were sent here to make what difference we can, to secure this nation, expand opportunity, and uphold our ideals through the hard, often frustrating, but absolutely necessary work of self-government."

Some might say the President's speech was a reflection of a progressive dream liberated from the worry of reelection. He outlined an ambitious agenda, but one not likely to pass the Democrat controlled Senate, let alone the Republican House. Despite this, few compromises were offered to the GOP, no indications of middle ground. The speech was all progressive policy and little practical reality. It is fine to give an ambitious speech, but true progress comes from compromise and moderation. There was little of that in the State of the Union, but there will need to be more of it if the President wants to accomplish even a small portion of his agenda.

Week 214

(SCAREQUESTER)

February 24, 2013

As the sequester looms nearer and nearer, President Obama is doing everything possible to put pressure on Republicans to replace those across the board cuts in part with tax increases. As part of that effort, the Administration is rolling out is parade of horribles. Cabinet secretary after Cabinet secretary has taken the podium to outline the disasters that will ensue if the sequester is allowed to proceed. It is all part of a calculated campaign by the White House to gain a political and ideological victory. The goal is simple, to prove to the public that government spending is not only essential, but good for the country. So the time has come to scare the people about the sequester, and hopefully in the process deal another below to the advocates of limited government.

Listening to the Obama Administration, one would think that the sequester is going to mean the end of the world. Forget for the moment that the sequester was thought up by the White House and signed into law by the President, now as the cuts are about to take place, the sequester is suddenly a threat to national security. These dire warnings stand is contrast to the actual scope of the cuts. If fully implemented in 2013, the sequester will reduce currently appropriated federal discretionary spending by $85 billion. That is out of a total federal budget of $3.6 trillion, and total federal discretionary spending of $1.043 trillion. The cuts are therefore significant, but hardly devastating, especially considering that the overall U.S. economy is $16 trillion in size.

The problem with the sequester is not the size of the cuts, but where the cuts are targeted and how they are applied. The current federal budget deficit is being driven predominately by two factors: exploding entitlement spending and low federal revenues from the still weak economy. The sequester cuts do not help on either of these fronts. The cuts will be made almost entirely to federal discretionary spending, which is not where the deficit problem is centered. The cuts are also going to hit defense most heavily (about $45 billion), which will hurt private contractors, defense manufacturers, and civilian defense employees. This will damage the economic recovery and possibly raise the unemployment rate. So the sequester is the wrong solution for the right problem.

The Democrats had assumed the Republicans would do anything to avoid the sequester because of the large defense cuts. That is why the Administration came up with and supported the sequester plan. But a funny thing happened on the way to the sequester, Republican started to see it as an acceptable alternative to the President's continual calls for more taxes, and Democrats began to worry about its impact on favored non-defense programs. So now it is the Democrats who are fighting to stop the sequester, while the GOP is resigned to it.

The objective of the White House is not simply to stop the sequester, it is to win an ideological victory. The White House has to date refused to negotiate over the sequester. Instead, their plan is to demand tax increases, let the sequester take place, and hope public outrage will force the GOP to surrender. As part of that effort, the President devoted his weekly radio address to outlining the horrible effects of the sequester. He also dispatched his Cabinet officials to do the same. Retiring Defense Secretary Leon Panetta outlined a possible loss or furlough of 800,000 workers related to the defense department. The TSA warned of longer security check delays at airports. Transportation Secretary LaHood described the damage the sequester would do to infrastructure and could lead to flight delays because the FAA would have to furlough air traffic controllers. It was an ugly picture, painted on purpose by the Administration.

The big bet by President Obama is that the public will be outraged by the inconveniences the sequester will cause. Polls show the public blames the GOP more for the sequester, but for the strategy to work there have to be significant problems to apply that blame. No doubt the Administration has every incentive to make the sequester as painful as possible to further its ideological agenda, but that is risky since the Administration also has an obligation to work for the public good. For a President who stated in his State of the Union that we need to stop governing in crisis mode, it is curious that he is doing everything he can to promote a crisis on the sequester. That is because for President Obama, the sequester is an opportunity to prove the essential goodness of government, and to do that, he is willing to toy with the public good in the process.

Week 215

(No Blink)

March 3, 2013

The guiding principle of the White House's political strategy for the last two months has been that public pressure and attacks would force the GOP to back down on the sequester and accept another tax increase. All effort and focus of the Administration was on that goal, and the President seemed completely dedicated to achieving it. The President did campaign events, gave speeches and press conferences, and continually marched out his team to describe the disaster that would be the sequester. Yet this campaign to pressure the Republicans to stop the sequester failed to mask a simple reality: the President and the Democrats cared more about stopping it than the Republicans. So in the end, neither side blinked, and the sequester went into effect on March 1. No taxes were increased, spending was cut, and the Republicans held firm. Not the outcome the President wanted.

The political narrative since the election has been that President Obama has been winning the budget fight. He got the GOP to raise taxes, and extend the debt limit, and delay the sequester. All seeming victories for the White House. However, these victories were tactical at best, and created an opening for the Republicans to achieve a strategic success. The tax deal at the end of 2012 was called an Obama victory because it raised revenues, but it also made permanent most of the Bush tax cuts and included barely a third of the new taxes the Democrats wanted. The deal was a defeat for the no tax wing of the Republican Party, but it also deprived the Administration of any leverage on taxes by making all new rates permanent. Then the GOP extended the debt limit, understanding that the President would use a debt limit fight to force higher taxes. Instead, they chose to fight on the sequester ground, betting that the Democrats wanted to avoid those cuts, and concluding that between the cuts and higher taxes, they would take the cuts. That is exactly what happened. The President attacked and attacked, but it made no difference, since the President refused to negotiate and insisted on higher taxes. The GOP said no, and the sequester went into effect, with the Democrats the ones most upset about it.

Despite all the bluster, it was clear from the beginning that the President did not want the sequester to happen. It is cutting domestic and defense programs cherished by Democrats. It will force furloughs of government workers. It will require belt tightening throughout the government. Most importantly, unlike prior "cuts," the sequester was not merely a reduction in the rate of growth in government spending, it was an actual baseline reduction, something the GOP has wanted for years, and something the Democrats had always opposed. The Republican complaint about the sequester was that it cut stupidly (across the board and too much from defense), but the Democrats hated everything about it. Ironically, even though the Democrats hated it most, they did the least to stop it, since they simply assumed the GOP would cave.

By early this week, the Democrats began to realize their strategy had backfired. The White House had to start to back down from some if its most outlandish claims about the economic damage the sequester would cause. The Administration had to do damage control after it threatened Washington Post reporter Bob Woodward because he wrote a story proving the sequester was the President's idea. Then, the President called in congressional leaders for a meeting on March 1, the day the sequester was to take effect, to make it look like an effort to avoid the cuts, when everyone knew the 52 minute meeting came far too late to make any difference. After the meeting, the President took the podium, admitted the sequester would not cause immediate pain, acknowledged it would not be the apocalypse, and then conceded he would be prepared to sign a funding bill for the balance of the fiscal year at the sequester spending level. That is what a retreat looks like.

The White House is betting that the public will punish the GOP for the sequester. But if the economy continues to improve and if the cuts can be managed, the Administration's position that high government spending must be maintained for the economic recovery will be undermined. So for now, the GOP's refusal to blink looks like a risk that was worth taking.

Week 216

(MR. NICE GUY)

March 10, 2013

For a White House that is always brimming with confidence, changes in strategy can only be discerned by careful observation. After the election, it was clear the President believed the GOP was so weak, and he was so popular, that all he needed to do was pummel the Republicans, and they would cave to his will. So on taxes, spending, immigration, and gun control, the President embarked on a strategy of attack, campaign, ridicule, and no compromise. The Administration assumed victory was assured, but that turned out to be wrong. In the fiscal cliff, the strategy resulted in a tax increase of barely a third of what the White House wanted, a permanent extension of all the other Bush tax cuts, and no deal on spending. On gun control, the ambitious Administration plan ran aground on opposition, partly from Democrats. On immigration, Congress is pushing ahead with little input from the White House. And on federal spending, all the bluster and threats did not stop the sequester. It seems the Mr. Attack strategy did not work so well, so now it is time for Mr. Nice Guy.

One thing Democrats and Republicans agree on is that President Obama is not good at forging personal relationships. He does not like to meet with congressional leaders, let alone socialize with them or lobby them for support. Instead, his approach has been to lay out his legislative objectives, delegate to Congress, and then sign the bills and take the credit. When the GOP took the House and gained seats in the Senate in 2010, that strategy no longer worked, but no matter, because his focus then turned to reelection, not legislation. But now with a new term and the GOP maintaining its position on Capitol Hill, the first inclination of the White House was simply to continue the attack. Stories were leaked that the White House was willing to forgo legislative results until 2015, instead turning all its focus to taking the majority in the House. The President upped his anti-GOP rhetoric, and campaigned and campaigned. But the results have been disappointing. The GOP did not cave, in fact they seemed to have outfoxed the Democrats by getting the sequester and most of the Bush tax cuts extended, without giving the President the revenues or debt limit increase he wanted.

So surprisingly, after showing distain, if not contempt, for all things Republican, the White House has now launched a charm offensive. It started with calls to the GOP senators working with Democrats on immigration reform. Then this week, at the suggestion of Republican Senator Lindsey Graham, on March 6, the President had dinner to twelve GOP senators to discuss budget and other issues. Then on March 7, the President had lunch with House Budget Chairman and GOP Vice Presidential nominee Paul Ryan and his House Democrat counterpart to discuss spending and taxes. Next week, the President plans to meet with the Republican Senate and House caucuses. This is a departure from the Administration's prior strategy, and a subtle admission that a different approach was needed.

Second term Presidents have at best 18 months to achieve significant legislative accomplishments. After that, midterm elections and the next presidential election usually prevent much progress. The initial White House plan to focus on 2014 and try to unseat the GOP was unconventional, and overly ambitious. It would mean harsh partisanship and gridlock for nearly two years, non-stop campaigning, and more division. It would also mean continuing to govern in crisis, with budget, debt ceiling, and sequester deadlines continuing to cause uncertainty. Moreover, the chances for success were always dubious at best. The party out of power almost always gains seats in the midterm election of a second term, redistricting solidified GOP power in the House, and any Republican who survived the Obama wave and got reelected in 2012 will be tough to knock-off in 2014. Maybe this reality has started to sink in, which might be why the President seems willing to lower the rhetoric and try to work with the GOP.

The hard part for the Administration's new strategy is a lack of trust. A President who has attacked and refused to engage honestly with Republicans will have a hard time winning them over. Democrats are also worried that the President will compromise too much with the Republicans. But with legislative goals in mind, for now the President appears willing to turn on his charm and give negotiation and compromise a try.

Week 217
(NO TAX, NO CUT)

March 17, 2013

It was a week of contrasts in Washington. A President touring Capitol Hill meeting with Democrats and Republicans seeking unity and compromises on the budget, while the majorities in the Senate and the House each released starkly contrasting budget plans. The first story gave hope for true bipartisanship, while the second was a reminder that the entrenched interests of each party are driving their respective budget positions and making compromise ever more difficult. For a President who clearly wants a big budget deal to address debt issues and turn the focus to other priorities, the posturing in Congress was a reminder of how difficult his task will be. This is especially the case because the President has yet to succeed in any significant bipartisan legislative effort, in part because heretofore he seemed to have little interest in one.

It is hard to exaggerate the differences between the budget blueprints produced by the House and the Senate this week. The House plan was announced March 12 and focused achieving a balanced budget by 2023. That balanced budget goal was the price demanded by conservatives for their support for a continuing resolution taking shape to fund the federal government until September 2013. To get to balance, Paul Ryan, the author of the plan, revived some ideas from his past budgets, including repealing Obamacare and reforming Medicare into a premium support program. He kept the revenues from the recent tax increase negotiated with President Obama but included no other new taxes, and continued GOP efforts to restrain Medicaid and other mandatory spending. In the end, the plan reduced projected federal spending for the next 10 years from $45 trillion to $41 trillion and achieves a small surplus in 2023. While the plan meets Republican objectives, it is not likely to be a basis for a compromise with Democrats because of various poison pills in the measure, most notably the repeal of Obamacare.

Not to be outdone, the Senate Democrat Budget Chair Patty Murray offered her budget plan on March 13. Where the GOP focused on cuts but not taxes, the Democrat plan focused mostly on taxes, not cuts. The Democrat plan includes $1.2 trillion in new taxes in addition to the tax increase already passed on January 1. The plan included more than $100 in new stimulus spending, avoids any structural reform to entitlement programs, and replaces the sequester cuts with other spending reductions, many of them dubious. The Democrats portray the plan as a 50/50 mix of cuts and new taxes, but in reality the plan includes minimal spending restraint. Unlike the GOP plan, the Democrats did not even attempt to put together a program that would result in a balanced budget. Instead, the Democrats plan tried to get deficits down to 3% of GDP, but by 2023 the national debt would rise to 93% of the total economy under the Democrat budget blueprint.

Faced with such contrasting plans, what is a President with hopes for a grand budget compromise to do. Apparently not offer a plan of his own. Despite a legal requirement to present a budget in February, the White House has stated it will not release a plan until April. Clearly, the Administration's plan was to let the Republicans and Democrats in Congress put out their contradictory plans, and then offer one of its own that would appear to offer some reasonable middle ground. That could be good tactics, but it will only result in a deal if the President can act as an honest broker and bring the two parties together. That is new territory for President Obama, and would make him do something he has never done in his entire political career.

The President seems to realize what is needed to get the budget deal, which is why when these contrasting plans were being offered, he went to four successive meetings with each caucus in each chamber of Congress to pitch for a deal. To Republicans he promised reforms to entitlements, but said new revenues had to be part of the deal. To Democrats he reaffirmed his determination to press for higher taxes and to protect core programs, but noted more would need to be done on spending to get a deal with the GOP. The President was frank, answered questions, and in general got good reviews, but these meetings were the easy part. To get a deal, the President needs to be a dealmaker, extracting compromises from both Republicans and Democrats. Time will tell whether he can, or is willing, to do that.

Week 218
(RED LINES)

March 24, 2013

Taking a break from budget battles in Washington, the President this week took his first trip as Commander in Chief to Israel, America's most steadfast ally in the Middle East. President Obama came under criticism in his first term for not visiting Israel, which along with his criticisms of Israeli policy and public quarrels with Prime Minister Netanyahu, created the perception that he is anti-Israel. The Administrations seems determined to dispel that notion with this high profile trip at the very beginning of the second term. Unlike most trips to Israel, however, this visit was not primarily focused on the peace process. Instead, the visit was mainly about the gathering threats in Syria and Iran, areas where America needs Israel's support and capabilities. During the visit, Netanyahu and Obama acted like best friends, each knowing that in dangerous times like these, America and Israel need each other.

The biggest challenge facing America and Israel is the Iranian nuclear program. Both countries have stated that Iran is working to build a nuclear bomb, and have vowed to stop Iran. To date, the main difference between America and Israel has been the timeline. America thinks Iran is further from developing a nuclear weapon, and has preferred to rely on sanctions and diplomatic pressure to stop the program. Israel, on the other hand, has said Iran is possibly only six months from getting a nuclear weapon, and has made clear the time for military options is running out.

During this visit, President Obama and Prime Minister Netanyahu formed a united front on Iran, saying they have reached agreement on the likely timeline for Iran to develop a nuclear weapon, and both stating that containment was not acceptable. Instead, both leaders vowed that Iran's nuclear program must be stopped, and once Iran gets close to that red line, all options, including military action, are on the table.

These tough words on Iran could lead both leaders to make some very difficult decisions. Sanctions are severely hurting the Iranian economy, but to date there is no sign that Iran is willing to give up its nuclear ambitions. This week, the Iranian supreme leader seemed to open the door for direct talks with the United States, but many view that as nothing more than a delay tactic. If Iran does not change course, a military strike will be necessary to stop the program, but Iran has put so many of its nuclear facilities deep underground that it is uncertain whether a strike could now stop the program. Iran has also threatened to attack shipping in the Strait of Hormuz, which could lead to an expanded military confrontation with the United States, with broad implications for the world economy. The stakes could hardly be higher, which explains why President Obama so badly needs a friend in Israel.

Yet Iran is not the only threat gathering in the Middle East. The civil war raging in Syria is also slowly drawing America in, as an increasingly desperate President Assad has escalated the violence and atrocities he is inflicting on his people. This week, reports emerged that chemical weapons were used on the Syrian rebels. These reports have yet to be confirmed, but President Obama has made clear that the use of chemical weapons is yet another red line that Assad cannot cross without an American response. As Syria hurtles toward further chaos, more radical elements among the rebels are gaining greater influence, risking that if Assad is overthrown, a regime no more acceptable to the United States might replace him. All these factors might drive the United States to take a more active role in removing the Assad regime.

Although the President had a very successful visit to Israel, these gathering storms showed how high the stakes are for Israel and America when it comes to Iran and Syria. President Obama joked when he landed in Israel how nice it was to get away from Congress, but compared to the budget battles in DC, the threats in the Middle East are more dangerous for the White House.

Week 219

(TYING KNOTS)

March 31, 2013

After weeks of focus on fiscal battles in Washington, social issues took center stage this week with arguments before the United States Supreme Court on the issues of gay rights and gay marriage. On two successive days, the Supreme Court first heard a challenge to California's proposition barring gay marriage, and then entertained a challenge to the federal Defense of Marriage Act, or DOMA. Each case presents an opportunity for the court to decide if gays, like women and minorities, are a protected class entitled to equal treatment under the law. However, gay rights is not simply a legal issue anymore, it is a political one as well.

In less than 20 years, the nation has seen a substantial shift in attitudes on gay rights and gay marriage. In that time, gay rights has gone from a pet issue for the Left, to a mainstream

Democratic position, and an increasingly popular one. President Clinton, who signed DOMA into law, and Hillary Clinton, who only a few years ago continued to defend it, both came out in recent weeks in support of gay marriage and for repeal of DOMA. Most other national Democrat leaders have followed the same course, moving from opposition to gay marriage, to support, in just a few years' time. And the movement in support of gay marriage has not been confined to Democrats. This week, Rob Portman, the Republican senator from Ohio and a moderate conservative, announced his support for gay marriage, saying the experiences of his gay son made him think anew on this issue. Also, Ted Olsen, the most prominent GOP advocate before the Supreme Court, argued that DOMA is unconstitutional.

One might like to think that politicians are being high-minded in their new support for gay marriage, but there is much more to it than that. Most politicians are following the polls, not leading them. A host of recent surveys have shown impressive growth in support for gay marriage. One poll showed 58% nationally, with those under 30 supporting it by more than 80%. This is a huge change from just a few years ago, and certainly signals a remarkable shift in public attitudes. It is not clear why the public's position appears to the changing, but for now at least, support for gay marriage is in the ascendance.

It seems even President Obama has been taken by surprise. When he was running in 2008, he said his view was that marriage is only between a man and a woman. He stuck to that position, at least publicly, until Vice President Biden announced his support for gay marriage during the campaign, forcing the President to publicly reverse himself and come out against DOMA. Until then, the White House has been playing a purely political game, using legal tools to attack and undermine DOMA, while the President avoided public comment. When the President admitted his support for gay marriage no one was surprised, most knew he has supported it for years, and only claimed otherwise for political expediency.

For Republicans, the issue of gay marriage presents a real challenge. The Christian Right is still steadfastly opposed, which gives the GOP little room to maneuver. But for the GOP to succeed nationally, it needs to do better with young and urban voters, and those are the voters most in favor of gay marriage. Ironically, the Republicans, as the party of judicial restraint, might secretly wish that the Supreme Court would do the dirty work for them by constitutionalizing gay rights, taking the question out of the legislative process. The Supreme Court gave mixed signals on whether it is going to give that support. On California's referendum, a majority of the Justices seemed reluctant to step into the gay rights question at the state level, suggesting the issue should be allowed to percolate more. The Justices were more skeptical of DOMA, but no clear ruling could be discerned. So now the nation must await their ruling, but it increasingly looks like the public has already decided.

Week 220

(BLOW YOUR MIND)

April 7, 2013

Washington returned to budget and economic battles this week, with the President giving a preview of this budget blueprint and with some disturbing employment news that made many wonder whether the recovery is losing steam. While to date the two political parties have avoided a budget and debt crisis with their agreements to extend the debt limit to the summer and to a spending plan for the balance of 2013, in many ways the most difficult tasks remain. Those include a full spending plan for 2014, a long-term plan for deficit reduction, and a long-term extension of the debt limit. So far, each party has been staking its ground, but to date the President has not offered a plan.

There have been some good signs for the budget process. The agreement to the spending plan for the balance of 2013 was fairly painless and completed early. A rarity for Washington, but one born more of fear than goodwill. Neither party wanted a government shutdown, and with the sequester in place the Democrats essentially caved and agreed to maintain sequester level spending in 2013. Their hope is that a big budget deal will reverse those cuts, but they were not willing to risk a shutdown to stop those cuts. Also, for the first time in 4 years, the Senate has passed a budget, instead of just a continuing resolution. But that is where the good news ends.

While the House and Senate have each passed a budget, that is where the similarity ends. The House budget has no new taxes, brings the budget to balance by 2023, and reforms entitlements, while the Senate budget has more than $1 trillion in new taxes, no entitlement reform, does not balance, and has few real spending cuts. So these budgets are more position statements than plans that the other party could ever accept. With these proposals, the White House hopes the table was set for the President's budget proposal.

The Administration was supposed to submit its budget in February, but it refused to do so. The White House instead wanted Congress to go first, in the hope that the President's plan would look like a reasonable compromise between what passed the House and Senate. Certainly the plans that passed those chambers helped in that regard. This week, the White House started to give some hints on what will be in its plan, to be released next week. Jake Carney, the White House Press Secretary, said the budget to be released would be so detailed that it will "blow your mind." He gave some hints on those details. The plan will have $1.8 trillion in deficit reduction, include about $600 billion in new taxes, about $400 billion in entitlement savings, and will replace the sequester. This type of plan seems designed to appear to be a middle grounds with new taxes (but less than what the Senate has passed) and spending and entitlement cuts (but less that what the House proposed).

Once the budget is released next week, the major players will have all staked their positions. What comes next is less clear. Most Democrats have said they will oppose any entitlement cuts. Republicans say they will oppose any new taxes. The House is insisting on a balanced budget goal, one which neither the Senate nor the White House plans achieve. So where is a compromise to be made. The answer is the White House. Only the President, as a true honest broker, can bring the parties together and get a deal. But that will require President Obama to lobby, build consensus, and be bipartisan.

One thing that might spur the parties towards a deal is the economy. Most thought the recovery was getting stronger, until this week when the Labor Department announced only 88,000 jobs were created in March, far below expectations. The unemployment rate dropped to 7.6%, but that was only because nearly 600,000 people left the workforce, bringing workforce participation to its lowest point since 1979. No doubt a bipartisan budget deal would give confidence to the markets, so maybe this bad news will turn to good news. But for now, the battle lines are drawn and the outcome is unclear.

Week 221

(OUT GUNNED)

April 14, 2013

Anyone who doubted the President's commitment to gun control was reminded this week that this initiative is one the President has no plans to abandon. With other issues, including the budget, the economy, and growing saber rattling from North Korea, one might have thought that gun control would drop to the bottom of the Administration's agenda. This is especially the case because of the hurdles and political risks of pursuing gun control. It seems none of that matters to the President, because far from retreating from the issue, he is redoubling his efforts.

This was a pivotal week for gun control advocates. With a showdown looming in the Senate over gun control legislation, an all-out push would be required. The challenges for gun control advocates became clear when an all-out battle was necessary in the Senate just to start debate. More than a dozen GOP Senators signaled that they would filibuster a procedural motion just to start debate on gun control legislation. If they succeeded, the President's agenda on gun control would be stillborn. Recognizing the risk, the Administration pulled out its most potent tool in the gun control debate, the Newtown families.

On April 8, the President travelled to Connecticut to continue his pitch for gun control. He went there to highlight new legislation just passed in Connecticut and call for similar legislation at the federal level. But the purpose of the trip was not simply to give a speech. The President also met with the Newtown families and brought several of them on Air Force One back to Washington to lobby Congress. These parents of children killed in Newtown spent several days on Capitol Hill meeting with Senators in a push to defeat the GOP filibuster and start debate on gun control, and it worked.

Majority Leader Reid, trying to build on the momentum brought by the Newtown families, scheduled a vote for Thursday to start debate on gun control. In the end, the motion passed 68 to 31. A solid group of GOP Senators stood firm in opposing debate, but enough were persuaded by the political pressure from the White House and the Newtown families that the Administration was able to overcome this first crucial hurdle. But the fight necessary to simply start debate should be worrying for the White House.

The vote in the Senate was a victory for the President, but not a very significant one. The bill the Democrats plan to debate has already been stripped of several central provisions pushed by the White House, including on assault weapons ban and a ban on high capacity magazines. Senator Reid pulled those provisions, admitting that there is not even majority support in the Senate for such measures, let alone enough to overcome a filibuster. So already the bill is far weaker than the assault weapons ban passed in 1994. What remains in the bill is a plan for universal background checks based on a compromise reached between GOP Senator Pat Toomey and Democrat Senator Joe Machine, provisions address mental health issues, and several other more minor initiatives. Far less than what the President originally wanted.

So debate will start on this very modest gun control bill, but whether anything ultimately passes the Senate, and in what form, is unknown. Even if a bill does pass, then it goes to the House, where Speaker Boehner has made clear he has little interest in the measure. Further, this whole initiative poses huge risks for Red State Democrats, several of whom on the Senate side are up for reelection in 2014. So while the Republicans got out gunned in this first round, it is very likely in the end it will be the President and Democrats who will get bloodied by this debate.

Week 222

(ON THE RUN)

April 21, 2013

The Boston Marathon is the oldest sporting event in that city and the most prestigious marathon in the world. The event is so tied up with the identity of the city that the day of the race is a public holiday, known as Patriot's Day. Every year, the running of the Boston Marathon is a celebration not simply of athletic achievement, but of the city itself. That is why the events at the 2013 Boston Marathon were so horrific. About four hours into the race, as hundreds of runners were crossing the finish line, one bomb exploded, and then moments later, another. What ensued was a scene of terror, panic, and dismay. Three spectators were killed, and 170 injured, with many losing limbs. The city and the nation were shocked.

In the initial hours following the bombing, it was unclear who the culprits were, and why they launched this attack. No one was seen setting the bombs. No one claimed responsibility. Speculation ranged from Al-Qaeda, to domestic terror groups, to simply deranged killers. The whole law enforcement apparatus of both Massachusetts and the federal government went into action seeking to quickly find the culprits, who escaped the scene and were therefore on the loose. Forensics gave some initial clues. The bombs were homemade, using pressure cookers, and seemed designed to kill and maim as many in the vicinity of the blasts as possible. This pointed to bombers with some skill, but it was not clear whether they learned their trade from foreign sources or not.

While the forensics gave some hints, it would be a long road to learn the identity of the bombers by that route. That answer came much more quickly from other sources, namely cameras. The Boston Marathon finishes near Copley Square, a commercial district in the Back Bay area of Boston. The streets are lined with stores, many with security cameras, and in this age of cell phones, literally hundreds of marathon spectators were recording the end of the race at the time the bombs went off. Within two days of the bombing, the suspects were identified, and then the manhunt was on.

The suspects were two brothers named Tamerlan Tzarnaev and his younger brother Dzhokhar, from Cambridge. They are Muslims of Chechen descent, who had lived in the United States for about 10 years. Dzhokhar was a U.S. citizen who attended a well-known public school in Boston and was enrolled at UMASS Dartmouth. Tamerlan was a former boxer whose dream of making the U.S. Olympic team was dashed and appears to have been adrift. Why these two young men, who have been in the country for so long, decided to turn to terrorism will be a question that will linger for some time.

Once the bombers were identified, the next task was to catch them. A full manhunt was launched, with law enforcement searching for them with every tool available. No one was sure where they were, or how long it would take to find them. But it appears they were not content with hiding, instead, they made themselves easy to find. On the evening of Thursday, April 18, they approach an MIT police officer who was sitting in his patrol car, and shot him dead. They then carjacked an SUV, made the driver get cash for them, and then headed into the suburbs. The police located the car using the driver's cell phone, which was still in the vehicle. A high-speed chase followed, with the brothers shooting and throwing homemade bombs at the police. They were eventually cornered in Watertown, and after another firefight, Tamerlan was dead, but his brother escaped. All of Boston was put in lockdown, and a house to house search in Watertown commenced. It took until Friday evening, after the police announced that they failed to find Dzhokhar, that a homeowner noticed blood near a boat in his backyard. He reported the blood, Dzhokhar was found, and after another brief firefight, was taken alive.

So ended the first phase of the Boston bombing. Now the in depth investigation and prosecution will begin. The bombing was the first significant domestic terrorist event targeting civilians since 9/11. It is also an attack that appears to have been homegrown, not the product of infiltration by foreign fighters. When President Obama addressed the nation Friday evening, he captured the central question, why had two young men who grew up in America and had been part of law-abiding communities, turned to terrorism. That is by far the most important question in this whole episode. At least Dzhokhar survived, which might give us a better chance to answer that question. For the last decade, our war on terrorism has been focused on foreign threats, but with this attack, we are reminded that terrorism can come from home as well.

How the Boston Marathon bombing will impact public policy and political debates is unclear. It will certainly put a focus once again on domestic terrorism. The Left will likely use it to push again for more gun control. The Right will use it to call for a more muscular anti-terror policy. Despite those debates, all will agree that this bombing will distract the political class from the debates on spending, taxes, and immigration that have so consumed Washington.

Week 223
(UNDER CONTROL)

April 28, 2013

Even in the wake of the Boston Marathon bombing, Washington's attention quickly turned back to the sequester. In the weeks leading up to the sequester, President Obama and his team rolled out a narrative of disaster and calamity. One would have thought the world would end if federal spending was reduced. The scare campaign failed, the GOP did not blink, and the sequester went into effect. Not surprisingly, the world did not end, and as a result the sequester is now assumed to be the status quo. The Democrats even agreed to legislate sequester level spending for the remainder of the 2013 fiscal year. The White House claimed it did not overstate its case, and that the pain would be real and deep, it would just take time to be felt.

One of the favorite horror stories offered by the Administration was air traffic control. The White House predicted massive disruption to air travel from mandatory furloughs of air traffic controllers that would be required because of sequester cuts. The FAA and the airlines were more than happy to join the chorus of dire predictions. The Administration wanted to stop the sequester and replace it with tax increases. The airline industry wanted to stop the sequester because it feared the impact on its profits. For the first few weeks of the sequester, no disaster was evident.

The FAA started to cut, but delayed furloughs of air traffic controllers. But those delays ended on April 21, when the furloughs started to hit. The number of air traffic controllers was reduced on a daily basis by about 10%, causing modest delays on Sunday, but those delays started to build and build as the week continued. It seemed at least one of the White House's predictions was starting to come true.

One might have thought that with the air traffic delays, the Democrats might have finally found a sequester issue where they could pound Republicans and push to replace those cuts with a mix of tax increases and different spending reductions. There were a few voices among Democrats calling for exactly that, but this time it was the Democrats who blinked. The air travelers who were suffering might have been a potent weapon against the GOP, but the Democrats were not willing to use it. Instead, work began in Congress to fashion a legislative solution that would allow the FAA to shift funds and avoid air traffic controller furloughs. Republican Senator Susan Collin led the effort in the Senate, and quickly won passage of a bill that would avert further furloughs. The bill was sent to the House, which just as quickly passed it. While the President has yet to sign the bill, the White House has made it fairly clear it would not veto the bill, meaning the first national negative impact from the sequester would be averted.

Certainly, this compromise benefits air travelers and the airline industry, but another big beneficiary is the GOP. Democrats were sure the GOP would accept more tax increases rather than allow the sequester to proceed. That was wrong. Then Democrats were sure the sequester would be so horrible, the GOP would be forced to repeal it. So far, that has been wrong too. And now, when the Democrats finally had an issue to exploit against the GOP, before they could even get any benefit, they joined the Republicans in an effort to blunt the impact. Importantly, the solution that passed Congress did not restore any spending, it just allowed the FAA to use other appropriated funds to pay air traffic controllers. So the GOP got its cuts, and avoided political pain.

The White House had previously pledged to opposed any piecemeal solutions to the sequester. Now the President is sure to sign this piecemeal solution. What this means is that the Democrats to date do not have the stomach for spending fights. They accepted the GOP terms on spending levels for the balance of 2013, and now they helped the GOP fix the first big sequester fallout. Maybe the Democrats are keeping their powder dry for the big fights upcoming on the 2014 budget and the debt limit, but maybe something else is at work. Polls show Democrats and Republicans are taking nearly equal blame for the sequester, and Democrats might fear they have lost the budget high ground with their scare tactics. So despite all the claims that the GOP was losing the budget debate, the reality is the opposite. The Republicans have shown they will fight the Democrats' spending and tax plans no matter what. The Democrats have simply shown no comparable resolve.

Week 224
(Go Home)

May 5, 2013

During the 2012 campaign, the President's lackluster first debate performance changed the dynamics of the campaign and gave Mitt Romney a chance at victory. The President recovered in the second two debates and went on to win, and since has seemed determined and focused, at least until recent weeks. The President's early win on tax increases at the end of 2012 and his push for immigration and gun control energized him, but a string of defeats seems to have taken the wind out his sails. That reality came into focus during a press conference on April 30, where the President seemed ready, in his own words, to pack up and go home.

Everyone knows the President loves campaigning and giving grand speeches, while he has never been too enamored with lobbying for votes or getting into the details of lawmaking. His strengths helped get him re-elected, but his weaknesses are hurting his ability to get things done during his second term. The President was able to force through a tax increase in 2012 because the GOP was not willing to risk having all of the Bush tax cuts expire, but since then he has met resistance or outright defeat on nearly every legislative effort. He has also failed, despite meetings, lunches, and dinners with Republicans, to build any bipartisan consensus. With the GOP's control of the House and its ability to stop any bill in the Senate, that spells trouble for the remainder of his term.

The troubles facing the President were summed up the following question from a reporter:

> Mr. President, you are a hundred days into your second term. On the gun bill, you put, it seems, everything into it to try to get it passed. Obviously, it didn't. Congress has ignored your efforts to try to get them to undo these sequester cuts. There was even a bill that you threatened to veto that got 92 Democrats in the House voting yes. So my question to you is do you still have the juice to get the rest of your agenda through this Congress?

The President's response said it all:

> Well, if you put it that way, Jonathan — (laughter) — maybe I should just pack up and go home. (Laughter.) Golly. You know, the — I think it's – it's a little — (chuckles) — as Mark Twain said, you know, rumors of my demise may be a little exaggerated at this point.

This summed up a President who is increasingly frustrated, petulant, and listless.

What followed was a series of questions on failures by the FBI leading up to the Boston Marathon bombing, continuing revelations implying a cover up on the Benghazi attacks, and his failures to make progress on the budget. When asked why he does not seem to be able to work effectively with Congress, he simply placed condescending blame on the GOP:

> But, you know, Jonathan, you seem to suggest that somehow, these folks over there have no responsibilities and that my job is to somehow get them to behave. That's their job.

Then came the questions on Obamacare, which continues to be unpopular and misunderstood. Increasingly, because of GOP sabotage and Administration missteps, Democrats are worried that problems with Obamacare's implementation in 2014 will be a good election issue for Republicans. The President seemed to dismiss and belittle all those concerns:

> And — and the last point I'll make, even if we do everything perfectly, there'll still be, you know, glitches and bumps, and there'll be stories that can be written

that says, oh, look, this thing's, you know, not working the way it's supposed to, and this happened and that happened. And that's pretty much true of every government program that's ever been set up.

The overall impression from the press conference was a President who is losing his focus and losing in Congress. Maybe the reality is setting in that governing is harder than campaigning. The President is also now feeling the ramifications of his scorched earth political strategy in his first term that succeeded in getting him re-elected, but has undermined his ability to govern. The Republicans do not like the President, do not fear the President, and will only work with the President if they see it in their own policy or political interest. The President had dreams of enacting a liberal agenda, but with conservatives able to stop any bill in Congress, it is understandable why the President seems ready to just go home.

Week 225

(WHISTLES BLOWN)

May 12, 2013

In recent history, nearly all presidential second terms have been disappointments. Johnson had Vietnam, Nixon had Watergate, Reagan had Iran-Contra, Clinton had impeachment, George W. Bush had Hurricane Katrina and the financial collapse. Barak Obama had hoped to avoid the same fate by using his convincing victory, constant campaigning, and a charm offensive to attain his policy goals and avoid political missteps. The effort started with his inaugural address, where he mapped out a grand liberal vision for America, but from there it has been disappointing. Legislative effort after effort have failed, beloved Democrat social programs are being cut by the sequester, and last week the President seemed almost despondent. The only thing missing was scandal, but that came with vengeance this week, with the Benghazi whistleblowers and the IRS Tea Party scandals.

The September 11, 2012, terrorist attack on the U.S. mission in Benghazi has been a subject of controversy for months. Initially, the White House and the President said the attack that killed Ambassador Chris Steven and three others was a spontaneous demonstration caused by a video. The Administration put UN Ambassador Susan Rice on five Sunday morning shows right after the attack to sell this story. The President hesitated to call it a terrorist attack, said the U.S. had no military option to stop the attack, and that campaign politics never influenced his actions or public statements. The White House had hoped the issue would go away, but Republican partisans will not let the issue go. The Administration opted to circle the wagons, obfuscate, and belittle the investigation. Not to be deterred, the House continued to investigate. This week, the investigation brought fourth three career State Department officials, including the second in charge in Libya at the time of the attack, and released emails to expose the White House's cover up. The testimony and emails show that the response to the attack was driven by politics. Officials in Libya asked for military support during the attack and were denied, it was immediately recognized that it was a planned terrorism from the beginning, the initial White House talking points were revised and revised by the Administration until they crafted the phony story Susan Rice tried to sell, and during the post-attack investigation Hillary Clinton, who was ultimately responsible for security in Benghazi, was not even interviewed. Most disturbing of all, the State Department whistleblowers claim they have been pressured and threatened not to tell the truth.

Despite all this, the President and Democrats still say the investigation is all politics and no mistakes were made. The problem is, the defensive and ineffective White House strategy has itself given life to the controversy. By trying to crush the investigation, by changing its story over and over, and by trying to pressure people not to testify, the Administration has fueled the story more than anyone else could. In the end, it is far from clear that Benghazi will cause any serious injury to President Obama. While the White House may have been dishonest and overly political, it is not clear that any laws were broken or that anything could have been done to save the lives lost. The damage to the President comes from the distraction, which only got worse when Benghazi was compounded with the much more potent IRS scandal, that came to light this week as well.

For years, Tea Party groups have complained that the IRS was subjecting them to special scrutiny. The IRS was questioned about this multiple times in 2011 and 2012, and consistently denied the claims. However, this week word leaked out about an internal IRS investigation that discovered that the IRS has in fact targeted conservative groups applying for 501(c)(4) tax exempt status for more rigorous review. The IRS denied applications, stalled applications, and asked for inappropriate and irrelevant information about donors, members, and activities. As a result, some conservative groups have been waiting nearly three years for action on their applications.

When the story broke, the White House was caught off guard. It had no ready response, and the President made no public comment on this issue. Over on Capitol Hill, thing were very different. Democrats and Republicans condemned the IRS's actions and called for further investigation. The GOP was quick to use the controversy to highlight the dangers of the President's big government agenda and show that bureaucratic bias would be used to punish those who disagree with the with wishes of the regulatory state. So with these two scandals, which are just starting to unfold, the President faces perhaps the biggest challenge of his tenure. With his agenda stalled and scandals growing, how the Administration deals with these challenges may very well set the tone for President Obama's second term.

Week 226

(THREE FRONTS)

May 19, 2013

The last seven days for the Obama Administration will likely go down as the week of the three scandals. Never before has the White House had to deal simultaneously with so many serious threats to the President's policy agenda. The IRS scandal broke the week before and only grew in significance. The Benghazi scandal has been simmering for months and continued apace with testimony from three State Department officials calling into question the White House's story on the attack. Then news came of the Justice Department's wiretapping of AP phone lines. The combination of these three scandals rocked Washington and left the White House in crisis management.

The IRS scandal was huge news the moment it broke, and for the first five days the President made no comment, allowing story to grow ever more serious. It was not until Monday May

13 that the President commented on the scandal during a press conference with British Prime Minister David Cameron. He condemned the IRS targeting of conservative groups and called the practice outrageous. He pledged a full investigation and accountability. However, the President's comments came too late to stop the growing scandal. The White House took stronger action on Wednesday, firing interim IRS Commissioner Steven Miller and releasing further details on when the Administration found out about the targeting. Miller was scheduled to testify before a House committee on May 17, and many wondered if the firing might lead him to rely on his Fifth Amendment privilege. Ultimately, he did not, and Miller testified that the IRS used inappropriate criteria and acted stupidly, but its actions were not politically motivated. For the White House, the goal is to isolate the President from the scandal, but the investigation is only in its early stages and more information is sure to come out.

With most of Washington focused on the IRS scandal, Benghazi seemed to start to take a back seat, but not in the minds of many GOP leaders. The Republicans continue to press their investigation into the Benghazi attack, relying on the testimony of the three State Department whistleblowers, which called into question whether the White House was being candid in its initial talking points about the attack. At his May 13 press conference, the President called the investigation a side show, said nothing new has been uncovered, and that it is all just politics. However, the simple fact remains that the White House was far from forthcoming during the campaign on the attack, and may have deliberately tried to mislead the American public to prevent political damage to the President. The White House also tried to quell the controversy by releasing 100 emails showing that White House involvement in revising the talking points on the attack was reasonable, but certainly those emails do not tell the whole story because they are only the emails the Administration wants read. This might not be the most dangerous scandal for the White House, but it is not going away any time soon.

Maybe the most damaging scandal of all is the revelation that the Department of Justice wiretapped more than 30 AP phone lines in a leak investigation relating to national security issues. Despite the fact that on policy issues the mainstream media has been largely supportive of President Obama, the White House has had a difficult relationship with the press. The President promised to run the most open Administration in history. The reality has been quite the opposite, with the press is getting very limited access to the President and with the President frequently annoyed at the press whenever he gets negative coverage. So when the news came out that the Justice Department had secretly wiretapped AP telephone lines in a leak investigation, all the media was outraged. DOJ announced an investigation from which Attorney General Eric Holder recused himself. Most disturbing, the DOJ did not follow its usual procedures of notifying the media organization before seeking wiretaps. This is the one scandal that might do the most lasting damage to the President because it is likely to spawn more critical coverage and heighten the tension between the President and the press.

For a President who was already having trouble getting any of his legislative agenda through Congress, this week of the three scandals was very unwelcomed. The President tried to change the topic with a road trip on jobs, but these scandals are not going to simply fade away. What the President needs is a policy success, but that is exactly where he was floundering before these scandals broke.

Week 227

(TOPIC CHANGER)

May 26, 2013

With scandals continuing to rage around the White House, the Administration badly needed a topic change. The week started poorly for the President on many fronts. On May 22, Lois Lerner, the head of tax exempt organizations at the IRS testified before Congress. She denied any wrong-doing, but then invoked her Fifth Amendment privilege and refused to answer any questions. The image of an IRS official invoking her privilege against self-incrimination was a disturbing development for the Administration. Then when Lerner was asked to resign a few days later, she refused, forcing the IRS to put her on administrative leave. Then, the White House kept changing its story on when it knew about the IRS targeting of conservative groups. It turns out the White House Counsel knew earlier than previously represented, but the Administration stuck to the story that the President was not aware until recently.

Things also did not improve on the press wiretapping scandal. News broke that the Administration was investigating Fox News Chief Washington correspondent James Rosen as a potential criminal co-conspirator for doing basic journalism relating to national security issues. This raised the specter of a much broader DOJ effort to suppress press freedom through use of the criminal laws. These practices continued to be roundly condemned by journalists of all political stripes and led evermore comparisons to the Nixon Administration. The DOJ pledged a thorough investigation, but since these policies were pursued by DOJ itself, many questioned how DOJ can effectively investigate itself. This led to calls for an independent investigation, ensuring that this scandal will be around for some time to come.

None of this is helpful to the President's effort to govern. The White House knows that as long as the focus is on scandals, it will be very hard to accomplish anything else. So the timing of the President's address on the War on Terror was fortuitous. On May 23 the President traveled to the National Defense University to give an address on the future of the War on Terror. With nearly twelve years past since the September 11 attacks, the Administration has determined that it is time to reset the focus and objectives of anti-terror policies. The President did not claim the War on Terror is over, instead he made clear that:

> Now make no mistake: our nation is still threatened by terrorists. From Benghazi to Boston, we have been tragically reminded of that truth. We must recognize, however, that the threat has shifted and evolved from the one that came to our shores on 9/11. With a decade of experience to draw from, now is the time to ask ourselves hard questions – about the nature of today's threats, and how we should confront them.

The President then claimed that the nation's steady success against terrorists justified a change in strategy:

> Today, the core of Al-Qaeda in Afghanistan and Pakistan is on a path to defeat. Their remaining operatives spend more time thinking about their own safety than plotting against us. They did not direct the attacks in Benghazi or Boston. They

have not carried out a successful attack on our homeland since 9/11. Instead, what we've seen is the emergence of various Al-Qaeda affiliates. From Yemen to Iraq, from Somalia to North Africa, the threat today is more diffuse, with Al-Qaeda's affiliate in the Arabian Peninsula – AQAP –the most active in plotting against our homeland . . . .

With this diminished threat came a call for a more constrained and targeted War on Terror:

> Beyond Afghanistan, we must define our effort not as a boundless 'global war on terror' – but rather as a series of persistent, targeted efforts to dismantle specific networks of violent extremists that threaten America. In many cases, this will involve partnerships with other countries.

On the topic of drones, the President defended their use, but pledged to use them with caution and to protect civil liberties, stating: "But when a US citizen goes abroad to wage war against America – and is actively plotting to kill US citizens; and when neither the United States, nor our partners are in a position to capture him before he carries out a plot – his citizenship should no more serve as a shield than a sniper shooting down on an innocent crowd should be protected from a swat team." The President also called for efforts to combat terrorism beyond military engagement:

> So the next element of our strategy involves addressing the underlying grievances and conflicts that feed extremism, from North Africa to South Asia. As we've learned this past decade, this is a vast and complex undertaking. We must be humble in our expectation that we can quickly resolve deep rooted problems like poverty and sectarian hatred.

The President finished his speech with the most controversial topic of all, GITMO, pledging to close the facility by calling on Congress to lift restrictions placed on the Administration accomplish that goal. The address concluded with a call for: "Targeted action against terrorists. Effective partnerships. Diplomatic engagement and assistance. Through such a comprehensive strategy we can significantly reduce the chances of large scale attacks on the homeland and mitigate threats to Americans overseas."

The speech marked a change in policy and a signal that the era of an expensive War on Terror is over. It was also an effort to move the focus away from scandal and towards national security, much safer ground for the President. The address certainly moved the focus, at least for the moment, but no one at the White House should think the scandals have passed.

Week 228

(STILL ON HOLDER)

June 2, 2013

Any hope that the President's speech on the War on Terror was going to change the scandal focus of Washington was quickly dashed this week. For several weeks, the focus has been on the scandals themselves, but now attention has turned to a specific person, Attorney General Eric Holder, who has become the face of the Administration's scandals. Certainly Holder is not at the center of the actions that led to the IRS scandal or Benghazi, but the press wiretap was done in his shop and his DOJ has been tasked to investigate the Administration's other scandals. With the White House refusing any suggestion that a special counsel is needed, this put Holder at the center of the scandal vortex.

Attorney General Eric Holder has been a favorite target of Republicans for years. He is viewed by the GOP as a biased and partisan proponent of the Administration's policies, and someone willing to use of power of the Department of Justice to attack enemies of the Administration, and reward its friends. The list of Republican complaints about Holder is long indeed, including the Mark Rich pardon, his refusal to bring a voter intimidation prosecution against the Black Panthers, the Fast and Furious scandal, the pledge to put Al-Qaeda suspects on trial in New York City, and his vigorous attack on the Arizona Immigration law and the Defense of Marriage Act. Through it all, Holder has maintained the support of the one person who matters most, the President. President Obama's loyalty to Holder many be personal, but it is also political, because Holder can be counted on to do the Administration's bidding, making him a valuable asset.

However, the current value of that asset has been undermined not so much by Holder's substantive decisions, but by his hostile and contemptuous relationship with Congress. Ever since the GOP took control of the House in 2011, Holder has been forced again and again to testify in support of some of the Administration's most controversial policies. The hostility between him and Darrell Issa, Republican Chairman of the House Oversight Committee, is legendary. Issa led the Fast and Furious investigation, and claimed Holder lied to Congress and tried to cover up the botch federal arms sale to drug dealers that led to the death of a U.S. agent. Issa scored some political points, but was not able to use Fast and Furious to dislodge Holder, but with the press wiretap scandal, Issa has more potent ammunition.

The DOJ and Holder have been at the center of an Administration effort to clampdown on leaks of top secret information on national security. Holder claims he was walled off from the approval of the seizure of AP phone records, but there is no doubt he approved a 2010 investigation of Fox News Chief Washington Correspondent James Rosen, where Rosen was listed as a potential criminal co-conspirator. Given this, it is curious that on May 15, 2013, Holder testified to the House Judiciary Committee as follows: "With regard to the potential prosecution of the press for the disclosure of material – that is not something I've ever been involved in, heard of, [or] would think would be wise policy."

This statement has now come back to haunt Holder. He did sign an affidavit approving the potential criminal prosecution of Rosen, leading several in Congress to assert that he committed perjury by lying to Congress under Oath. Seeing the danger, Holder has quickly tried to repair his relations with the press. He offered a meeting with top press executives to discuss press policy, unfortunately, many refused to attend the meeting. Then the Administration said they would support the Media Shield Law proposed by New York Senator Chuck Schumer. The Administration even let it be known that Holder was doing some soul searching on media policy. None of this has appeased Republicans. They see in this perjury charge an opportunity to force Holder to resign, and they are not going to let go. The GOP has been aided by the usually pro-Obama media, which has roundly attacked Holder for his assaults on press freedom. Worst of all for the Administration, the focus on Holder will keep these scandals in the headlines, which is why there are now some whispers coming from the White House that Holder should go. So much for trying to change the topic from scandal.

Week 229

(BYE BYE MR. NICE GUY)

June 9, 2013

Three months ago, Washington stood in amazement as the White House launched a charm offensive with Republicans. The President sat down for lunch with Paul Ryan, hosted GOP Senators to dinner, and visited Capitol Hill to meet with Republicans. For a President who honed a sharp partisan edge to get reelected, many saw the move toward reconciliation as a recognition that to get much done legislatively in his second term, the President needed to improve relations with the GOP. However, there were many skeptics who claimed the charm offensive was just a political tactic, carried out half-heartedly and reluctantly. This week's events gave some credence to that view.

The genesis of the Administration's charm offensive came from political setbacks, not necessarily goodwill by the President. Coming into his second term, the President initially struck a strident tone, boldly calling for a leftward shift in national policy and aggressively pushing tax increases, gun control, and additional infrastructure spending. The President got his tax increase, but not much else. Gun control failed, the GOP did not back down on the sequester cuts, and none of the President's new spending proposals gained any traction on Capitol Hill. One wonders whether if things had gone differently, would there have been a charm offensive. The President helped answer that question this week, because even with his charm offensive, his agenda remained largely stalled in Congress, so Mr. Nice Guy went bye bye.

The President always seems most comfortable campaigning and attacking his opponents. With his agenda in trouble and few in the GOP trusting the President enough to work with him, the White House decided this week to just return to its old playbook. Trying to send a message that the President would use his executive powers to implement his agenda regardless of Congress, the President used a nomination event to launch his latest assault on Republicans. One of the President's most potent powers is nominations, including for federal judges. Other than the Supreme Court, the other most important federal court is the D.C. Circuit Court, where most appeals relating to the regulatory state are heard. Currently that court has eight judges (four Republican nominees and four Democrat nominees), and three vacancies. The President used his announcement of three nominees to fill those vacancies to challenge and confront Congress. With the proposed judges standing next to him, the President attacked Congress for obstructing his agenda and delaying confirmations for all manner of federal posts. He implied that the GOP was pursuing a tyranny of the minority and bolstered Democrat threats to change the filibuster rules in the Senate to make it easier to confirm nominees. Usually nominations of federal judges are nonpartisan affairs, but not this time. Instead, the nominations were just a prop for the President's political agenda.

Not surprisingly, soon after the nomination event, the President left for a series of fundraisers, which concluded in California with a meeting with the new Chinese President Xi Jinping. The First Lady has also been active on the fundraising front, and more and more fundraisers are scheduled for the coming weeks. So it appears the President has returned to the ground where he feels most comfortable. Partisan attacks on Republicans, raising political cash, and campaigning. In part, the White House may have concluded that the best defense is offense. With the controversies over the IRS' targeting of conservatives, Benghazi, and the DOJ anti-leak offensive against the media, scandal was becoming the dominate storyline. The Administration needed to change the narrative, and a return to their old ways seemed the best method to do so.

It is far from clear that the strategy will work. The President can attack Republicans all he wants, but very few on Capitol Hill fear him. The electoral landscape for 2014 is looking good for the GOP, and Republicans members who survived 2012 have little concern that the President can knock them off in 2014. So the President attacks, the GOP obstructs, and little gets done. The hope of changing the narrative also faded with new revelations of a widespread NSA data collection campaign gathering information from millions of domestic phone calls and internet searches. This raised the specter of a government indiscriminately spying on its own citizens, angering liberals possibly even more than conservatives. So taken as a whole, it looks like the President's charm offensive was just another political tactic, tried for a while, and quickly discarded in favor of the harsh partisan approach he has preferred for most of his career. So much for Mr. Nice Guy.

Week 230

(NATIONALLY DEFENSIVE)

June 16, 2013

National defense issues seemed to close in on the White House this week. The Administration was challenged by both its policies within the United States, and its policies abroad. On the domestic front, the NSA surveillance scandal became the topic of the week in Washington. The prior week's leaks about the program exploded when the leaker, Edward Snowden, revealed himself and added more details to his account. Then came Syria, where the civil war has begun to turn in President Assad's favor, and the U.S. and others have finally confirmed that the Assad regime has in fact used chemical weapons. So this week the White House was forced to make tough decisions on national security, and clearly did not like the experience.

The timing of the NSA surveillance story was particularly unwelcomed for the Administration. Following all the other scandals, it made it seem as though both the President and his Administration had lost control of their agenda and lost the public's trust. The initial leak was that the NSA has been running a surveillance program known as Prism, which involved gathering data on millions of domestic phone and internet records. The scope of the data collection was breathtaking, and shocked many. This despite the fact that the program was approved by the FISA court and was reviewed by Congress. Perhaps the reaction was so negative because the recent IRS scandal and the media leak investigation have created the perception of a federal government abusing its powers.

The NSA leak story took an even stranger turn when the leaker, Edward Snowden, revealed himself. It appears he was an employee for Booze Allen, a federal contractor that provides services in various areas, including national security. It seems Snowden got access to materials detailing Prism, and for some reason–ideological, financial, or egotistical–decided to leak them. Then he went a step further and revealed himself and gave an interview on the leaks, portraying himself as a crusader for truth and a defender of civil liberties. He gave the interviews in Hong Kong, where he is apparently hiding. He also gave further public statements defying the U.S. government and pledging to fight extradition.

The odd thing about the Prism affair is that it has enraged both the Left and the Right. The Left is dismayed that President Obama endorsed the program and expanded it. The Right sees Prism as just another sign of an Administration out of control. But rather than back away from the program, the Administration went into full gear to defend it. They noted that the NSA was not listening to any calls or reading any emails. Instead, they were only looking for patterns in communications. This was likened to looking at the outside of an envelope, but never opening it to read the contents. The Administration also claimed that several attacks had been thwarted by the program, the program was started under President George W. Bush, and Congress had been briefed on it. Regardless, the outcry continued from many fronts. Through it all, the President remained oddly passive, issuing some statements on the program, but avoiding full engagement and certainly any press conferences.

Maybe that was because the White House has other bigger problems, including Syria. The Obama Administration has made the removal of President Assad its policy goal in Syria, but has to date refused to provide any military support to the rebels. It appears the Administration believed the civil war was going so badly for the regime that it would fall without U.S. intervention. Then came the evidence that Assad's government had used chemical weapons. The President said that was a redline, but then quickly tried to back off those comments, relying on supposedly inconclusive evidence. But this week that inconclusive evidence became conclusive, and now the President is in a box. To make matters worse, the refusal by the U.S. to provide any military support to the rebels has allowed the Assad regime to turn the tide (in part because of ample military hardware supplied by Russia). So now a red line has been crossed, but it is no longer clear the rebels can win.

This situation puts President Obama in a bind. He desperately wants to avoid getting pulled into the Syrian conflict, but he also has to guard his credibility. The solution for the White House was a half-hearted response designed for nothing other than political cover. The Administration announced that in response to the Assad regime's use of chemical weapons, it would start to supply small arms to certain Syrian rebel groups. Few details were provided on who would get the arms, what would be sent, or when they would arrive. However, one thing is clear, supplying small arms to a few rebel groups will not change the conflict, meaning it is now likely the Assad regime will win and stay in power. So it appears President Obama is prepared to accept defeat in Syria, or at least he is willing to do very little to prevent it. So we have a public relations disaster from the NSA surveillance scandal, and a true foreign policy disaster in Syria. No wonder the President is looking to change the topic again, this time with a G8 conference Summit in Northern Ireland. We will see if this latest effort at a reset works this time.

Week 231
(WAY OUT THERE)

June 23, 2013

Second term presidents usually use foreign trips to burnish their legacy and avoid troubles back home, but President Obama's recent trip to Europe did little more than emphasize how weak, troubled, and disconnected he has become. The goals for the trip were modest: attend a G8 Summit, announce plans to a free trade deal with Europe, and give a grand speech at the Brandenburg Gate in Berlin. But no matter where the President went, trouble and problems followed.

The trip started with a G8 Summit in Northern Ireland. The highlight of that event was the announcement of plans to proceed with a free trade deal with Europe. Notably, the President to date has failed to complete a major trade deal with any nation and tariffs with Europe are already low, so in many ways a European trade deal is more window dressing than anything else. However, it is a popular idea with broad support, but even on that question the President encountered problems. In a meeting about international tax policy, he repeatedly called the UK Finance Minister George Osborne "Jeffrey," apparently confusing him with the famous soul singer. The President also made comments seen as critical of religious schools in Northern Ireland, further distracting from his goals.

Worst of all, the President tried to use the G8 Summit to reach an understanding with Russia on Syria, but Russian President Putin's only interest seems to be to embarrass the President. As they sat before the cameras and while President Obama talked about common goals in Syria, President Putin sat stone faced showing his utter disdain for both U.S. policy and the President who is championing it. For months as the U.S. has voiced support for the Syrian rebels, it has refused to offer any form of military assistance, and all the while Putin has been pouring in equipment to prop up his ally Assad. The tide has now turned, the rebels look to be losing. With the U.S. still unwilling to do anything significant to change the result, it is no wonder Putin did all he could to not openly laugh at President Obama's empty rhetoric on Syria. Putin added to that insult by later in the week allowing Edward Snowden, the man who leaked Prism surveillance program, to travel to Russia as he tried to obtain asylum. Yet another not so subtle show of Russia's contempt for the Obama Administration.

President Obama may have hoped things would go better in Germany, the site of his triumphant speech during the 2008 campaign. The occasion was the 60th anniversary of President Kennedy's famous Berlin speech decrying the then recently constructed Berlin Wall. Unfortunately, the President did not get as warm a reception in Germany as he had hoped. German Chancellor Merkel openly clashed with President Obama over the NSA's surveillance of international internet traffic. "There are people who have concerns about this, particularly about the possibility of data collection on a vast scale," Merkel said. "The questions that aren't clarified we will continue to discuss." President Obama responded: "This is not a situation in which we are rifling through the ordinary e-mails of German citizens or American citizens or French citizens or anybody else," Obama said. The German Chancellor was clearly not satisfied.

The President then used his Berlin speech to pursue another of his long-held goals: a world without nuclear weapons. In his address at the Brandenburg Gate on June 18, the President called for the U.S. and Russia to further reduce their deployed nuclear warheads, saying: "So long as nuclear weapons exist, we are not truly safe . . . Peace with justice means pursuing the security of a world without nuclear weapons — no matter how distant that dream may be." However, the crowd was small, the speech was not particularly inspiring, and its main theme has little support. It also appears there was no consultation with Congress or Russia before the President announced his grand vision for a nuclear free world. Russia immediately rejected the proposal, citing the U.S. anti-missile defense program with Deputy Prime Minister Rogozin stating: "Development of the shield and the sword are mutually interconnected . . . . Not to understand this is either lie, bluff or demonstration of deep unprofessionalism." Congressional leaders likewise rejected further reductions, saying they would endanger national security. So both the speech and the idea were a flop. It was an appropriate end to a disappointing trip, one that highlighted a President who has become unpopular and whose ideas seem increasingly out of touch.

Week 232

(CLIMATE CHANGING)

June 30, 2013

This week witnessed a changing climate on three issues that may define the political battles of 2013 and beyond. On three successive days, the President, the Supreme Court, and Congress each took their turn in the limelight on critical domestic issues. On June 25, the President announced a new initiative on climate change. On June 26, the Supreme Court issued its long awaited decisions invalidating the Defense of Marriage Act and California's Proposition 8 barring gay marriage. On June 27, the Senate passed an immigration reform bill, sending it to an uncertain future in the House. It was a trifecta of policy blockbusters.

The President's speech on climate change was probably the most predictable of the major political developments of the week. Since the 2008 campaign, the President has made climate change a priority. The Democrat controlled House passed a climate change bill in 2009, which helped the GOP take the House the next year. However, the White House has not been deterred. Faced with a legislative roadblock, the Administration has made clear that it would resort to executive powers to further its climate change agenda. In his speech, the President announced three steps to address climate change that do not require congressional approval. The President pledged to issue regulations to limit carbon emissions from coal power plants, authorized expanded green energy projects on public lands, and said the federal government would pursue higher mileage standards for automobiles. The President also used his speech to advise that the Keystone Pipeline would not be approved unless it is shown not to contribute to climate change, in essence further delaying any final decision.

The response to the speech was predictable: liberals and environmentalist cheered, and the GOP roared with objections. There are sure to be legal challenges and efforts at legislative repeal, but with this speech the President made clear he has given up on working with Congress on this issue, and instead will rely solely on his own executive powers. But in many way, that approach will only make these moves more controversial. With these steps, the President will certainly please allies on the Left, but it is not clear how much real impact they will have on climate issues, because despite the grand announcement, the steps that can be taken by solely executive action are limited. So this speech might benefit opponents more than the environment.

In contrast with the President's climate change speech, there was no doubt about the ultimate impact of the Supreme Court's two rulings on gay marriage. The decisions set the stage for federal recognition of legalized gay marriage in the 9 states that allow such marriages, and by its reasoning could set the stage for national gay marriage despite any contrary state laws. On DOMA, Justice Kennedy wrote the majority opinion, which found DOMA's provision overriding contrary state gay marriage laws and denying federal benefits to gay couples as unconstitutional. The decision was based on both federalism principles and passionate statements about liberty interests, statements that opponents of the decision say will be relied upon in later decisions to force all states to recognize gay marriage. The Supreme Court also let stand a lower court ruling invalidating a California Proposition 8 banning gay marriage based on a lack of standing. In combination, the two decisions constitute a historic victory for gay rights advocates and surely will open a new front in the culture wars, which will pitch traditional marriage and religious organizations against gay and liberal groups. In many ways, this fight might be more ugly than abortion, because the battle will now be about forcing states and organizations that do not support gay marriage to accept and recognize it.

The week ended with another important development, but one with a very uncertain future. After the 2012 election, momentum has grown for immigration reform. For months a bipartisan group of senators, known as the Gang of Eight, has worked to craft an immigration bill that could garner support from both sides of the aisle and have some chance of passage in the House. After months of hearings and weeks of debate and amendments on the Senate floor, on June 27, by a vote of 68 to 32, the Senate passed an immigration reform bill. The bill creates a temporary worker programs, and a path to citizenship after, and also makes significant investments in securing the border. Fourteen Republicans supported the bill, 32 voted against it. Not quite the bipartisan victory the bill's supporters hoped for, but a significant win nonetheless. Now, the truly hard part begins, because the bill now goes to the House. Speaker Boehner has said he will only move a bill that is supported by a majority of the GOP caucus. That means any bill that could possibly pass the House must be significantly different from the Senate bill, including removing a path to citizenship. With most conservative voices condemning the bill, there will surely be an ugly fight to come.

So it has been a week of momentous developments. A continuing fight on climate change, a new fight on gay rights, and a bitter struggle to try to get immigration reform. All three disputes will heighten partisan tensions and likely lead to ever more gridlock in Washington. So maybe not that much has changed after all.

Week 233

(DELAY AND DISMAY)

July 7, 2013

Despite being the first African American President, President Obama has been accused of being inattentive to African interests. The White House hoped to change that perception with a much publicized three nation trip to Africa. However, from the get go everything seemed to detract from the trip. Initially, the President was criticized for the extravagance of the trip, which appears likely to cost close to $100 million. A pretty high price tag at a time when the federal budget is being sequestered and the unemployment rate remains at 7.6%. Then, Nelson Mandela, who has been hospitalized for a respiratory infection, was reported close to death just before the President was to travel to South Africa, creating another distraction. Then, while the President was returning, a decision to delay a key part of Obamacare and a military takeover in Egypt ensured that the President's trip will become a footnote, rather than a highlight of his second term.

For months, Democrats and Republicans have been warning that the implementation of Obamacare was an impending train wreck, to use the words of Democrat Senator Max Baucus. Many states have refused to participate in the Medicaid expansion or creation of insurance exchanges, those states that are participating are having a hard time setting up the exchanges, the Administration has failed to issue clear rules or guidelines for the employer mandate, and very little has been done to educate individuals on how to enroll in the exchanges and buy insurance. For weeks, the White House was insisting that implementation was on track, but very few agreed. Then on July 3, conveniently on the eve of a national holiday, the Administration quietly announced that the employer mandate would be delayed for one year. The rationale was claimed to be business requests for a delay, but the real story is that the Administration was not ready to roll out the mandate.

Under the mandate, businesses that have more than 50 employee who work more than 30 hours per week must provide health insurance or they will be fined $2,000 per employee. However, the rules and reporting guidelines for the employer mandate have not been finalized and the draft procedures were so complicated that businesses did not know how to comply. It seems that most business have instead tried to comply by avoiding the mandate altogether, by not hiring at all or hiring part time workers. Faced with resistance from employers and a system not ready for implementation, the Administration delayed a key part of the new law. Now, employers do not have to provide health insurance for at least another year, but individuals are apparently still required to get insurance, despite the fact that the individual health insurance mandate is triggered in part by employers who do not comply with the employer mandate. Now, it is unclear how the insurance exchanges for individuals can function, since employers are not yet required to provide insurance. This situation has led critics of the new law to claim it is unraveling and sinking under its own weight.

The Administration had hoped to frame its Obamacare mandate delay and as accommodation to business and a shrewd political move designed to take the issue off the table for the 2014 election. However, that storyline only held up for about 24 hours. Instead, the talk in Washington was the problems with Obamacare and how more problems with implementation, especially with the exchanges and the individual mandate, would only mean more problems for the President and the Democrats. So this delay seems to have given ammunition to the GOP rather than disarmed them.

If the Obamacare woes were not bad enough, the President came home from his Africa trip to more challenges in the Middle East. President Obama praised the revolution that toppled President Mubarak in Egypt. He has also cautiously supported the democratically elected Muslim Brotherhood President Mohammad Morsi. However, Morsi for month has been refusing to accommodate demands from opposition parties and has been slowly trying to consolidate power. This led to street demonstrations and then this week an ultimatum from the military that the Morsi government either has to reach a compromise with opposition groups, or President Morsi would be toppled. Morsi refused any accommodation, so on July 3, the Egyptian military removed him from power.

Now Egypt appears on the brink of serious unrest or possibly a civil war. Throughout the Egyptian crisis, the Obama Administration took the posture of a dismayed bystander. The President has supported Morsi and continued military aid, and the White House has been reluctant to criticize the Muslim Brotherhood effort to consolidate power. When the military removed Morsi, initially the Administration criticized the Egyptian military, but fearful of looking like an ally of a movement that has associations with radical Islam and terrorists, the White House took a cautious tone. So after heaping praise on the revolution that removed Mubarak, now the President is faced with a destabilized Egypt. Through it all, America has been seen as a bystander letting events take their course with no clear strategic vision. So while the President tried to act the role of global leader in Africa, troubles at home and abroad reminded all of the challenges facing the President and how difficult it is for the White House to control events or purse its policy objectives.

Week 234

(Acquitted)

July 14, 2013

President Obama has always understood that racially-charged issues pose a special challenge for him as the nation's first African American President. He has tried to not be exclusively identified with his racial background, but at the same time he is fond of referring to the historic nature of his election. Despite the President's wise decision not to get too embroiled in racial controversies, from time to time incidents have arisen where he could not restrain himself. One such incident was the killing of Trayvon Martin. Martin was shot and killed in a housing complex in Sanford, Florida by George Zimmerman, a neighborhood watch volunteer. Trayvon was unarmed, Zimmerman had a handgun, a confrontation ensued the details of which will always be in dispute, but in the end Martin died. On July 13, 2013, Zimmerman was found not guilty of murder or manslaughter for the killing, a verdict that immediately caused protests.

When this confrontation occurred, minority advocacy groups were quick to pronounce Zimmerman as a racist bent on hunting down a black teenager. They emphasized that Trayvon was an honor student who was carrying nothing other than a packet of skittles, just going home, and was targeted by Zimmerman solely because he was black. The media also widely used a picture of Trayvon as a twelve year old, despite the fact that he was 17 when the incident occurred. They were also quick to paint Zimmerman as a white conservative gun nut racist. NBC News even selectively edited a 911 call Zimmerman made to make it look like his motivation was racial. There was an immediate rush to judgment, saying Zimmerman was a murderer based on the simple fact that a black teenager was dead and a white man pulled the trigger. So it was not surprising that there was outrage when the authorities initially decided not to charge Zimmerman. Even President Obama joined the chorus, remarking that if he had a son, he would look like Trayvon.

As the two week trial showed, the true story of what happened in Sanford Florida that night is much more complicated. First off, Zimmerman is not white, he is Hispanic. Second, the FBI conducted many interviews and found no evidence that he has racist tendencies, in fact he mentors black kids and is in an inter-racial marriage. Third, Trayvon Martin had marijuana in his system and called a friend just before the confrontation and described Zimmerman as a "creepy ass cracker." Fourth, there were records of a person screaming for help during the fight and may believe the person asking for help was Zimmerman. Fifth, after the fight Zimmerman had a broken nose and contusions on his head consistent with having it slammed on the sidewalk. Sixth, forensic evidence showed the shot was fired from very close range. Put simply, based on the evidence, it is just as likely that Trayvon attacked Zimmerman as the other way around.

Any watchful observer understood that the trial was going very poorly for the prosecution. In fact, many of their witnesses gave helpful testimony for the defense. No one should have been surprised when the jury of six women took only one day to acquit Zimmerman. But despite the clear weaknesses in the case against Zimmerman, the same folks who rushed to proclaim him guilty regardless of the evidence, condemned the judgment and called it evidence that the judicial system is biased against minorities and that it is now open season on black children. The outrage regarding the verdict was clearly genuine, but also seemed detached from the facts of the case.

For his part, the President has to date tried to avoid any public comment, other than stating that the jury has spoken. But few think the issue will end there. Too many liberal and minority advocacy groups are invested in this controversy to let this issue die quietly. So for a President who his struggling to make progress on his agenda, now he has the prospect of getting dragged into a major racial controversy.

Week 235

(COULD HAVE BEEN ME)

July 21, 2013

For a President who has worked hard to avoid the politics of racial controversy during his tenure, encountering a week where the national dialogue was focused almost entirely on race presented a difficult challenge. The verdict in the George Zimmerman trial continued to fuel protests and division. For the black community and liberal whites, it was a symbol of continuing discrimination and a judicial system that is viewed as stacked against minorities. For many others, the focus was on the poor case put on by the prosecution, the ambiguous evidence that seemed to point to Trayvon Martin as the attacker as much as Zimmerman, and the concept of reasonable doubt. So the nation was divided between those focusing on discrimination, and those focusing on due process.

While the President has been careful to avoid racially charged issues because of the obvious dangers such issues pose for him, he also has a penchant to lecture the nation on moral issues. Given this, he must have been truly torn about what to do in the wake of the acquittal. The White House issued a very short statement after the verdict saying the jury's decision should be respected, but since then the President took the approach of silence. But as the controversy continued to grow, it seems the President decided he could be silent no longer. So on July 19, he took the podium at the White House and gave some unannounced remarks on the case. It was not surprising that the President decided he must say something about the verdict, what was surprising is what he said and the reaction to his comments.

The President tried to use a measured tone and careful wording to avoid exciting either side in the debate, but in the end, after unpacking his comments, it is clear the President sides with those protesting the verdict and that he accepts their theory is that the system is racist. The President likes to personalize issues, because he thinks the tactic is persuasive. So he opened his comments as follows:

> You know, when Trayvon Martin was first shot, I said that this could have been my son. Another way of saying that is Trayvon Martin could have been me 35 years ago. And when you think about why, in the African-American community at least, there's a lot of pain around what happened here, I think it's important to recognize that the African-American community is looking at this issue through a set of experiences and a history that — that doesn't go away.

> There are very few African-American men in this country who haven't had the experience of being followed when they were shopping in a department store. That includes me.

> And there are very few African-American men who haven't had the experience of walking across the street and hearing the locks click on the doors of cars. That happens to me, at least before I was a senator. There are very few African-Americans who haven't had the experience of getting on an elevator and a woman clutching her purse nervously and holding her breath until she had a chance to get off. That happens often.

By these comments, the President was trying to explain the reaction of the black community to the verdict in a historical context. But then the President went beyond explaining the reaction to justifying it, siding with those who say past racism is the reason for the high violent crime rate in the African American community:

> Now, this isn't to say that the African American community is naive about the fact that African-American young men are disproportionately involved in the criminal justice system, that they are disproportionately both victims and perpetrators of violence. It's not to make excuses for that fact, although black folks do interpret the reasons for that in a historical context.

> We understand that some of the violence that takes place in poor black neighborhoods around the country is born out of a very violent past in this country, and that the poverty and dysfunction that we see in those communities can be traced to a very difficult history.

This is the point in the President's comments where he went from healer to divider. The problems in the black community are monumental, not just in terms of violence and poverty rates, but also with regard to unwed mothers and drug use. By buying into the theory that some outside historical force, namely past racism, is a predominant cause for the challenges facing the African-American community, the President is hindering a frank conversation on the problem. The very words used by the President show his own unwillingness to frankly address the problem. Rather than saying that blacks commit a disproportionate amount of crime, including violent crimes, in this country, he said "African American young men are disproportionately involved in the criminal justice system." Rather than saying that the vast majority of violent black deaths are at the hands of other blacks, he said "Trayvon Martin was probably, statistically, more likely to be shot by a peer than he was by somebody else." There is no "probably" about it.

So the President gave credence to the historical racism narrative and refused to be frank about the problems in the black community. Why? The likely reason is that he agrees with the protesters. He thinks the jury was racist, that the system is stacked against blacks, that racism is the cause of the problems in the African-American community, meaning, in the end, historical and current racism is the cause of it all. The President did not say this expressly, but the focus of his comments left little doubt about his views. The remainder of his speech was devoted to solutions, such as gun control, more legislation against racial profiling, and trying to give more opportunities to African Americans. This was a typical list of liberal solutions. No mention was made to trying to rebuild the black family, dealing with drug issues, addressing a culture that glorifies violence, and demanding that people take responsibly for the conduct of members of their community. So it seems from the President's perspective, not only Trayvon Martin, but all the protesters of the verdict "could have been me."

Week 236
(SO PHONY)

July 28, 2013

For the past several months, the President has focused on domestic issues like immigration, gun control, same sex marriage, and climate change. On none of these issues has the President found much success in Congress, and in the process the President's approval rating have gone down and down. That might be because the President has spent so little time talking about the dominant issue in his reelection, namely the economy. Faced with growing political troubles and ever more gridlock in Washington the President needed a new strategy. So came his big economic speech at Knox College in Galesburg Illinois, a speech intended to change the current trajectory of the Obama Presidency.

Having spent so little time on economic issues in the last few months, it is clear the White House believes a return to the themes that got the President reelected is needed. It is also clear the Administration wants to continue to play the outsider game, refusing to engage in negotiations with Republicans on any issue. Instead, the President has returned to his favorite activity, campaigning and attacking Republicans. His speech, which was forecasted as a major new statement on economic issues, was really little more than a rehash of his favorite economic themes. He talked about the economic crisis when he took office, the tough choices he made, the improving economy, the faults of his Republican opponents, and his vision for the middle class. All very familiar stuff.

The only thing arguably new in the speech was the increased focus on inequality. The President made clear in the speech his view that income inequality is the biggest problem facing America.

He stated that "[t]his growing inequality isn't just morally wrong; it's bad economics. When middle-class families have less to spend, businesses have fewer customers. When wealth concentrates at the very top, it can inflate unstable bubbles that threaten the economy. When the rungs on the ladder of opportunity grow farther apart, it undermines the very essence of this country." This is probably the clearest statement the President has made since taking office that income redistribution is his top objective. The President did not stop at attacking the wealthy, he then turned quickly to attacking Republicans on a host of issues, from the budget to immigration. He blamed Republicans for it all because of their "endless parade of distractions, political posturing, and phony scandals." So the speech was not only unabashedly progressive, but also partisan.

When it came to the central goal of helping the middle class, the President outlined his four cornerstones of a vibrant middle class: good jobs, education, home ownership, and opportunity. Where the speech failed was in actually offering any new ideas. Instead, it was a campaign speech, an attempt to frame the upcoming battle in Congress over the budget and the debt limit. And that is the President's problem. To achieve any of his policy goals, he needs to show leadership and engage with Congress, but he is willing to do neither. The President prefers to take pot shots at his opposition and give speeches, leaving the difficult work of legislative compromise to Democrats on Capitol Hill. The problem is, that approach is not working, and doing campaign stops is not going to change that dynamic. Neither will attacking rich people.

The central theme of the speech is that income inequality is causing our problems and Republican policies are creating income inequality. An inconvenient fact is that income inequality has grown under the Obama Administration and there is little evidence that the financial success of some is causing economic failures by others. In the President's world view, the economic pie is set, and it is for government to choose who gets what slices. With that perspective, it is not surprising that he sees the very real stresses on the middle class as the product of others doing well. But there are many other causes for the stress on the middle class, including rising taxes, higher healthcare, energy, and education costs, and most of all weak job growth and the growing prevalence of part-time employment. The President also never addresses a central cause of poverty: unwed motherhood and divorce. These very real stresses on the middle class are not caused by rich people. They are mostly caused by government policies that increase the cost of living and undermined the formation of stable families, but these are words you will never hear the President speak. So instead we have more class warfare, more calls for income redistribution, and more campaign speeches. Hardly the game changer the President touted.

Week 237

(THE COMPROMISER?)

August 4, 2013

In his continuing campaign to reignite his presidency, Mr. Obama continued his campaign style events to discuss the economy. The White House's plan is to use sharp rhetoric and a confrontational tone to energize the Left and prod Republicans to agree to higher taxes and more federal spending. The President continued that strategy this week, but with a new spin. He tried to put pressure on Republicans by offering a purported grand compromise, corporate tax reform in return for higher infrastructure spending. He claimed to be offering what everyone wants, a smarter corporate tax policy and spending on needed infrastructure improvements that will create jobs, but a closer look revealed something quite different, a pure political game.

The President unveiled his proposal in a July 30 speech in Chattanooga, Tennessee. The President proposed reducing the 35% corporate tax rate to 28%, and creating a special 25% tax rate for manufacturers. Coupled with the reduced rates would be closure of various tax loopholes and a minimum tax on corporate profits earned overseas. While the plan was touted as tax reform, it would operate as a tax increase on business, and the President proposed using the added revenue for additional government spending on infrastructure. So while the plan was spun as a middle of the road compromise, it would function as a plan for higher taxes and more government spending. No wonder the GOP immediately rejected the plan.

This proposal from the President is a good example of his governing strategy. As a lawyer, the President loves crafting clever plans that try to put his opponents in a corner. It seems the White House puts little thought into whether a policy might ever get enacted. They seem to like the political game more than getting results. The Republicans have been calling for tax reform for years, but want the reform to be revenue neutral and address both individual and corporate taxes. The Administration knows that a proposal that is focused simply on increasing taxes on business has no chance of passage. But that is of little concern, the goal was to get some headlines that the President offered a compromise and Republicans rejected it. A political point scored, but not much governance got done.

There are opportunities for compromises on taxes and spending, especially by working with the GOP dealmakers in Congress led by John McCain. But for now the White House has no interest. They seem to think the President flying around the country giving speeches attacking the GOP is the winning strategy. The problem is, no one is listening. It should be clear even to the most partisan Democrat that President Obama is getting marginalized and is being ignored more and more, even by members of his own party. His attacks and speeches are not winning greater public support, in fact his favorability rating are dipping into the low 40s. No wonder, since the economy is still week, as this month's jobs report showed. With only 162,000 jobs created in September and nearly 1 million people leaving the workforce, the job market remains bad. As for key issues like immigration, gun control, and the sequester, it looks like the Administration has simply accepted the reality that nothing will get done.

The President's real strategy is playing for time and provoking a confrontation with Republicans. These speeches and clever proposals are just the appetizers, the main course is a government shutdown. The White House has decided to force the GOP to either compromise or shutdown the government. President Obama is betting any compromise would favor him, or a shutdown would be blamed on the GOP. So the Administration is letting the budget and debt ceiling issues fester, on purpose. They want a crisis, and a fight, because they see that as the only way to get the upper hand. So we did not see a great compromiser this week, we just saw political jockeying for position.

Week 238

(30 MILLION)

August 11, 2013

Given the rough summer, the President must certainly be looking forward to his vacation. Just before leaving Washington for Martha's Vineyard, the President decided to give a press conference on August 9. This was the President's first press conference in three months, and was surely timed to be as low profile as possible, scheduled for a Friday in the midst of the sleepy August lull in Washington. After seeing the tenor of the questions, there could be little doubt why the President so rarely gives press conferences, and why his approval ratings continue to fall. The questions focused on his controversial NSA surveillance programs, the tensions with Russia, his stalled immigration reform efforts, growing terrorist threats, the problems with Obamacare implementation, and the impending budget confrontation with the GOP. Through it all, the President made sure to continue his harsh partisan rhetoric against Republicans, accusing them of being determined to deny 30 million Americans health care. But that counterattack was just brief moment of defiance in a very defensive performance. If the President was not ready for his vacation before the press conference, he was surely ready afterwards.

Recognizing the continuing problems he is having about the NSA's surveillance programs, the President's opening statement was devoted to that issue. He began by saying: "Over the past few weeks, I've been talking about what I believe should be our number-one priority as a country — building a better bargain for the middle class and for Americans who want to work their way into the middle class. At the same time, I'm focused on my number-one responsibility as Commander-in-Chief, and that's keeping the American people safe. And in recent days, we've been reminded once again about the threats to our nation." He then launched into an explanation and defense of NSA surveillance. He also outlined four reforms in the surveillance program involving reforms to Section 215 of the Patriot Act, changes in procedures at the Foreign Intelligence Surveillance Court, increasing public access to information, and forming a high-level group of outside experts to review our entire intelligence and communications technologies. This reform plan was quickly criticized by both liberals and conservatives as window dressing, not real reform.

On terrorism, the President came close to declaring victory against Al-Qaeda earlier this year, but now felt the need to walk back those comments in the face of growing terrorist threats to embassies, growing Islamist influence in the Syrian civil war, and the near civil war between the Egyptian military and the Muslim Brotherhood. On the terrorist threat, the President said: "What I said in the same National Defense University speech back in May that I referred to earlier is that core al-Qaeda is on its heels, has been decimated. But what I also said was that al-Qaeda and other extremists have metastasized into regional groups that can pose significant dangers." The President tried to declare victory in the War on Terror earlier this year to justify reforms at the Pentagon and lower military spending, but it is becoming increasingly clear that the President declared near victory just when the terrorist threat was rising. That became clear this week when the U.S. had to close 18 embassies in the Middle East because of rising terrorist threats.

On Obamacare and the impending budget battles, the President tried to turn the tide of criticism and take the offensive. Testing out his talking points for the budget battles to come, he rolled out his newest attack line, that the GOP wants to shut down the federal government in order to deny people health care: "The idea that you would shut down the government unless you prevent

30 million people from getting health care is a bad idea. What you should be thinking about is how can we advance and improve ways for middle-class families to have some security so that if they work hard, they can get ahead and their kids can get ahead." The problem is that Obamacare is getting more and more unpopular and the implementation is facing more and more problems, as shown this week when the Administration delayed the cap on out of pocket expenses insurers can place on their customers. The President hopes to tie the budget battle to Obamacare, and force the GOP to provide more money for the implementation or be blamed for a government shutdown. It is a game of chicken that the President appears determined to play to change his political fortunes, after his vacation of course.

Week 239
(NO BROTHERHOOD)

August 18, 2013

While the President was at Martha's Vineyard hoping for a quiet week of relaxation, events in Egypt exploded and intruded. On top of all the domestic challenges facing the President, and emergence of a near civil war in Egypt, American's most important Arab ally, could pose the biggest challenge to the Obama Administration to date. For a President who was so quick to abandon longtime ally President Mubarak in the midst of the Arab Spring, now the White House is faced with condemning a coup perpetrated by those who support American interests and who removed a government hostile to U.S. interests. This poses a conflict between American ideals and interests, a conflict that no one in the Administration knows how to resolve.

After Hosni Mubarak was ousted in the Arab Spring, a transitional government took power and held a democratic election for Egypt's next leader. The result brought the Muslim Brotherhood into power, with newly elected President Mohammed Morsi at its head. Once in power, the Muslim Brotherhood sought to consolidate power and slowly transition Egypt into an Islamic state. It refused to share power and sought to push through a new constitution that would consolidate control by Islamists. Morsi also tried to disable the ability of the military to oppose him by replacing top officers. But in the course of this slow and steady consolidation of power, more and more opposition arose, especially from more secular political parties. After calls for power sharing were rejected by the Morsi government, the military acted, removing him from power and essentially establishing martial law. The military government promised a quick transition to a new civilian government, but it now appears that the military is itself consolidating power.

Just as protests led to the fall of both Mubarak and Morsi, the Muslim Brotherhood has now occupied key areas and is actively protesting the military's rule. This week, the military acted, using force to evict Muslim Brotherhood supporters from their camps, killing hundreds. This resulted in violence exploding across the country and an ever more severe military crackdown. Through it all, Egypt grows ever more divided, with millions opposing the military, and millions supporting it. More and more, it looks like Egypt is in the opening stages of a civil war.

When the violence was at its worst, the President was photographed on the golf course. This was not a good image for the White House, so the next day the President offered remarks on Egypt, condemning the violence. But to date, the Administration has offered no clue on how it plans to help resolve the conflict. The United States certainly does not want an Islamic regime in Egypt, but also cannot be seen as supporting a coup that overthrew a democratically elected government. So the President seems forced to oppose those who want to be U.S. allies to support those who aspire to be U.S. foes. Through it all, the inability of the U.S. to influence the situation or lay out a plan for resolution showed a White House with no leverage and no plan. Much like Syria, it appears the Administration is playing it safe, taking no risks and offering no leadership. A very dangerous course in the volatile Middle East.

Week 240

(VERY EDUCATING)

August 25, 2013

Coming off a week on vacation at Martha's Vineyard this week, the President sought to quickly gain some momentum going into the critical fights in the Fall over the budget, the debt limit, and immigration. So the White House planned a bus tour of Western New York and central Pennsylvania to highlight his priorities and get some headlines for new proposals. The tour certainly generated some press, but the President's falling approval ratings showed that campaign events alone will not strengthen his position.

The bus tour started in Buffalo, went to Rochester, Syracuse, and Binghamton, ending in Vice President Biden's home town of Scranton. The President stuck to his usual preference for friendly audiences, with many of the events staged at colleges. This was by design, because the only new proposal offered during the bus tour was focused on college costs. Trying to build an even stronger bond with young voters, the President laid out a plan to try to control spiraling colleges costs, a plan designed to energize young voters going into the 2014 midterm election.

With college costs rising to the point where many middle class families are no longer able to afford higher education, the President's plan is to try to essentially shame colleges into lowering costs. The plan involves creating a rating system for colleges based on cost and performance and tying federal aid to those scores. While an interesting idea, it is not clear the scoring system would have any real impact on college costs. The plan also fails to address a key driver of high college costs, namely the federal subsidies themselves. The federal grant and loan programs facilitate higher college tuitions by giving easy access to cash to pay those higher costs. When it comes to federal aid itself, the President's agenda is more college aid, so that approach might counteract any benefit from the President's scoring system.

Other than his educational proposal, there was no real news from the President's bus tour. Instead, he hit his usual themes of advocating government programs and attacking Republicans. The crowds were decent and the events well planned, but how these campaign trips improve the President's political position is questionable. Continued slow growth and high unemployment, his inability to work with Congress, and tensions in the Middle East are hurting the President's standing, and until those factors change, no amount of campaign events will change the political dynamic.

A reminder on that came at the end of the week with the news from Syria, where the Assad regime appears to have again used chemical weapons. The evidence this time is so strong that the White House may be forced to take action in response to a clear violation of the redline set by the President. The emerging Syrian crisis will ensure that the President's campaign bus trip will quickly become just another political footnote.

Week 241

(OUT OF THE BOX)

September 1, 2013

As the evidence continued to mount that the Syrian government used chemical weapons, the Obama Administration's effort to build support for a strike on Syria went into high gear. Everyone in the White House seemed dedicated to that goal, everyone but the President. After stating that the use of chemical weapons would cross a redline and not be tolerated, when that redline was crossed, the President seemed frustrated that he now had to act. When the evidence of chemical weapons use became clear, the President's inclination was to wait for further confirmation, almost hoping enough doubt would arise to allow him to avoid action. When the evidence became undisputable, the President gave several speeches emphasizing that if he did act, he would act in a very limited way. The President had put himself in a box, and it was clear he was not happy about it.

In response, the White House starting looking for international cover and support, but with the President so clearly reluctant, it was not surprising that his allies did not rally. France quickly pledged support, driven in part by its emotional connection with Syria, a former French protectorate. But the trend quickly turned negative when UK refused to join the effort. Prime Minister David Cameron called for a parliamentary vote on military action and the resolution was rejected. So for the first time in 23 years, the U.S. might embark on a significant military effort without the British. But it seemed the President saw more opportunity in parliament's vote than peril. Just when the march toward an attack seemed unstoppable, the President changed his mind and stopped it.

The President met earlier in the week with Speaker Boehner, who encouraged him to take the question of an attack to Congress, but the President seemed reluctant, knowing approval in the House would be unlikely. But after the UK vote, he huddled with his inner circle of White House advisors, including Susan Rice, and on August 31 announced there would be no attack until after Congress was given a chance to vote on it. With Congress in recess, this decision, which was made without consulting either his Secretary of State or his Defense Secretary, would delay any strike until at least the week of September 9. So rather than strike quickly and decisively, the President decided that if he strikes at all, he will do so slowly and weakly.

This was not the first time we have seen President Obama buckle under the pressure of making a major military decision. In 2009, the President delayed for months before announcing his Afghanistan strategy, and in the end the strategy was more designed to facilitate a withdrawal than achieve success. Now on Syria, the same pattern was being repeated. Part of the reason might be that an anti-war theme propelled Barack Obama to the White House, so starting a new conflict gives him pause. Also the lessons of Iraq and what it did to the Bush Presidency cannot be far from the President's mind. So throughout the Syrian crisis, the President has tried to look strong while consistently refusing strong action.

That is why the President's sudden turn to Congress is classic Obama. The President as a lawyer is always looking for a clever strategy that will allow him to claim victory no matter the outcome. By asking Congress for support, the President believes he has found a no lose scenario. If Congress supports an attack, then it provides him cover and he can claim a mandate to act. If Congress withholds support, he can caste blame on them and use their rejection as an excuse not to act, which is his preference in any event. What the President does not understand is the damage that a rejection and back down will do to the power and prestige of his presidency. Congress might help him get out of the box he created, but the damage will be significant.

Week 242

(WHOSE BOMBING)

September 8, 2013

As the Obama Administration continued its reluctant and halting march toward military action in Syria, it became increasingly clear that the President, not his military, was bombing. The White House sent the Secretary of State and the Secretary of Defense to Capitol Hill, met with House leaders, offered intelligence briefings, and lobbied international leaders at the G20 Summit in St. Petersburg. The President even announced a rare prime time address to the nation on September 10. This full court press was designed to turn public opinion and rally support in Congress. The result, to date, has been the opposite.

The President stunned not only the nation, but also many of his Cabinet secretaries when he decided to take the issue of an attack on Syria to Congress for approval. Many, including Secretary of State Kerry, warned him against it. The President, based on the advice of his White House inner circle, ignored that advice and decided congressional approval was the right move. The impact was immediate. The momentum for an assault was lost, Assad was given time to maneuver, and the President put himself at the mercy of Congress. The elements of surprise and initiative were lost, to be replaced by lobbying and hesitation. Some believe the President went to Congress to give himself an excuse not to attack. Whether true or not, that has been the result.

President Obama already had a credibility problem with many of his foreign foes. While actively pursuing Al Qaeda, President Obama has been much more reluctant to confront those nations actively opposing him. From North Korea, to Iran, to Russia, to Syria, the Obama Administration has shied away from confrontation. When the President set a redline on Syrian use of chemical weapons, and that redline was crossed, even President Obama realized that there was no way to preserve credibility if he refused to act. So the President began the work to prepare for an attack, but at the critical moment, the President blinked, refused to act, and instead passed the buck to Congress. Ironically, a presidential redline and decision to preserve the credibility of the United States have actually further undermined it, because the President has projected not strength, but vacillation and indecision.

With this backdrop, it is not surprising that the campaign to build support for an attack has been a complete failure. When his Secretaries of State and Defense went to Congress, they were pummeled with skeptical questions. While Speaker Boehner and Leader Pelosi pledged support, the GOP refused to whip for votes and few thought Pelosi could garner enough support. The

Administration hosted intelligence briefings, and while the evidence was strong that chemical weapons were used, the evidence that the government (rather than the rebels), were the perpetrators was circumstantial. Few minds were changed.

The White House hoped to do better at the G20 summit, but did not. Syria dominated the agenda, as the President met with leader after leader to try to build support. He left largely empty handed. It did not help that the summit was being hosted by Russia, Assad's main ally. It was clear that President Putin was doing everything he could to undermine the American drive for military action. Russia wants to keep its Syrian client state, its naval and air bases in Syria, and is willing to do whatever it takes to protect its interests. More disturbingly, they see in President Obama a weak foe who can be manipulated. So the President was being undermined abroad and at home.

The impact on the Administration has been disastrous. Polls show opposition to the attack growing, the President's approval ratings are falling, and increasingly the White House appears isolated and besieged. All of this could have been avoided. The President could have simply launched a limited attack, declared victory, and kept his credibility. Instead, an exercise in showing American strength has turned into a farce of weakness. The wounds have been entirely self-inflicted, and no doubt the White House is scrambling to find a way out of the mess it created.

Week 243

(PUTINIZED)

September 15, 2013

After kicking the ball to Congress, President Obama started the week seemingly prepared to launch an all-out struggle to obtain congressional approval for the use of force in Syria. His aides were busy lobbying and offering intelligence briefings, while surrogates spread across Washington to make the argument for military action. The urgency of the lobbying campaign only grew more and more as lawmakers announced opposition to the use of force resolution being drafted by congressional leaders. Far from winning support, it seemed each passing day made more clear that the Administration would lose the vote in the House and possibly in the Senate as well. The President and his policy seemed in dire straits, until a lifeline was thrown from the most unlikeliest of sources, Vladimir Putin.

With support for military action quickly eroding in Washington, the President was struggling for a way to save face and avoid defeat. He put himself in a box by stating that use of chemical weapons was a redline. That redline was crossed, but rather than order an attack, the President tried to deflect the risks by asking Congress to approve military action. But this clever trick backfired on the White House as it became clear Congress would likely say no, leaving the President in a position of abandoning his call for a use of force, or acting without the congressional approval he asked for. What to do.

The answer came in an off-hand comment from Secretary of State John Kerry. When asked if there was anything that could avert a military strike, Kerry said if Syria agreed to give up all its chemicals weapons, then a military strike would not be needed. This comment was quickly seized by Russia, Syria's ally and supporter. Russia has done everything possible to save the Assad regime, including supplying weapons, obstructing any UN sanctions, and denying that the

Assad regime used chemical weapons, even when on contrary evidence is very strong. The reasons is simple. Syria is a Russia puppet state that provides bases to Russia and allows Russia to project its influence into the Middle East. So not matter the actions of the Assad regime, Russia is prepared to support its ally.

The last thing Russia wants is U.S. military action because that would threaten the Assad regime and possibly cost Russia its puppet. So when Secretary of State Kerry said an agreement by Syria to give up its chemical weapons might avert a strike, Russia wasted no time. It quickly stated it would support a plan to seize and destroy Syrian chemical weapons, and 24 hours later got the Assad regime to agree as well. By September 9, the White House, seeing a way out, ran for the door. The President embraced the plan, asked Congress to suspend the vote, used his speech to the nation on September 10' not to call for military action, but instead to call for diplomacy.

Secretary Kerry was then dispatched to Geneva to negotiate the terms of the deal with Russia. At the same time, Russia flexed its new-found muscle in the crisis by seizing the initiative away from President Obama. Vladimir Putin even published an op-ed in the *New York Times* making the case for diplomacy, defending Assad, and questioning the notion of American exceptionalism. The White House pretended not to be annoyed by the article, in part because the Administration's policy was now so dependent on Russian support that it could not chance an open rift. By September 14, the United States and Russia agreed to terms for the chemical weapons disarmament of Syria. All the while, report after report came in of frantic efforts by Syria to disburse and hide its chemical weapons.

So by week's end, America was transformed from leading a push for military action to following the diplomatic lifeline thrown by Russia. Both the President and the Administration suffered great damage in the process. The President showed himself to be uncertain, erratic, and weak, his team disorganized. The end result might be destruction of some of Syria's chemical weapons, but that will be about it. The true winners in this whole episode are Russia and Syria. Russia has saved its ally from attack and took a leading role in Mideast diplomacy. Assad, for his part, gets to survive, and has won months more to crush his opponents. So Russia and its ally win, America get a symbolic concession, and Obama avoids a defeat in Congress. This is what happens when America allows Vladimir Putin to lead our foreign policy, he wins and we get essentially nothing.

Week 244

(THE PIVOT)

September 22, 2013

After the Administration's very rough ride in the Syria crisis, its desire to change gears and focus on domestic issues was palpable. President Obama painted himself into a corner on Syria and jumped at the lifeline offered by Russia in the hope that domestic debates would offer more favorable ground. With a government shutdown looming on September 30, the need to raise the debt limit by mid-October, and the Obamacare implementation October 1, domestic issues seemed just as daunting as Syria, but at least there the President believes he has more control and fewer risks. So after a framework deal was reached with Russia on Syrian chemical disarmament on

September 14, the President scheduled a briefing for Monday, September 16 to launch his pivot to domestic issues, but maybe a bit too eagerly.

On the morning of September 16, a lone gunman entered the Washington Naval Yard, opened fire, and killed 13 and wounded many others. The city went into shutdown in fear of a more widespread terrorist event. As it turned out, the shooter, Aaron Alexis, was a disgruntled and mentally unstable veteran with no terrorist connection. That was still unclear when the President took the podium at the White House the day of the shooting. The President offered appropriate statements of sympathy with the victims and of resolve to uncover why and how the shooting happened. All standard stuff, until the President immediately, clumsily and quickly moved on to this prepared statements attacking Republicans on the budget and the debt ceiling. The image of ambulances and security forces combing the Naval Yard while the President was taking shots that the GOP was far from ideal. It seemed the President was determined to pivot to budget issues no matter the events swirling around him.

One must wonder why the White House is so eager to have a domestic fight, when those issues could be equally damaging to the Administration as Syria. The conventional wisdom in Washington is that a government shutdown in the absence of a budget deal would be most dangerous for Republicans, but that wisdom is based solely on the 1995 experience, where the Newt Gingrich GOP took the blame. This time around, with the lame duck President unpopular and the economy weak, it is not so easy to predict where the public would place the blame. But no matter, the President, after appearing so weak on Syria, was determined no matter what to be a tough guy on the GOP.

The President spent the week giving speeches and interviews taking shots at Republicans. He was not simply criticizing their budget positions, he openly ridiculed Republicans while refusing to offer any plan of his own. One reason for the President's aggressive approach was surely the infighting in the GOP. House leaders were forced a week earlier to withdraw their budget plan in the face of a conservative demand that defunding Obamacare be included in any continuing resolution to keep the government open. In the end, the leadership agreed and passed the plan on September 20. Senate Majority Leader Reid instantly proclaimed the GOP bill "dead, dead, dead." So now the action has moved to the Senate, where Democrats will now need to move their own bill to avert a shutdown.

Things were not proceeding any more smoothly on the debt limit, which will be reached by mid-October. The President accused the GOP of trying to turn America into a "deadbeat nation" that does not pay its bills, and he repeated again and again that he would not negotiate over the debt ceiling. For its part, the GOP announced a plan that would add approval of the Keystone Pipeline, tax reform, and other initiatives to the debt ceiling bill. So on the debt limit, it seemed clear another confrontation was unavoidable. The President called the GOP tactic "extortion" that had never before occurred in the nation's history, a claim even the *Washington Post* admitted was fictional.

So the only thing the President accomplished was his pivot, everything else remained the same. The is no deal on the budget or debt limit, and Obamacare remains unpopular and divisive. What happens next is anyone's guess. After Syria, the President cannot afford to look weak, but his assumption that confrontation is his best course will be put to the test.

Week 245
(Go'in Cruz'in)

September 29, 2013

The last week of September was the critical crunch time for the budget fight brewing in Washington. With Republicans in control of the House, and Democrats in the Senate, many feared that there would be an impasse and a federal government shutdown would ensue, most of all Republicans. The GOP went through a shutdown fight with President Clinton in 1995, took the worst of it, and almost lost their majority. Fearful of the same consequences, the Republican leadership in the House crafted a strategy that would allow their most conservative members to get on record with the primary conservative priority, stopping Obamacare, without risking a shutdown. Then along came the junior Republican Senator from Texas, Ted Cruz.

With current funding for the federal government set to expire on September 30, Speaker Boehner crafted a plan to allow Republicans to make their point but at the same time not risk a shutdown. His team put together a funding bill that would keep the government open through the end of 2013 at the funding level of the 2013 sequester. The bill also had a provision on de-funding Obamacare, but was structured so that the Senate Democrats could easily void the provision. The GOP leadership felt they were in a good position because the Democrats agreed to accept the 2013 sequester funding levels in the bill. Then, the conservatives revolted.

There is a group of about 30 very conservative members of the House Republican caucus who have been a thorn in the side of Speaker Boehner since the GOP took the majority. They have taken a hardline on fiscal issues and have refused to support the leadership unless their priorities were addressed. Given the size of the GOP majority, Speaker Boehner can only afford to lose 17 votes if he wants to pass bills, meaning this group can stop the Republicans from passing legislation. As the leadership was crafting its plan, Senator Cruz incited a rebellion in the House caucus, demanding that the bill to fund the government also include provisions to defund Obamacare. His lobbying paid off, Speaker Boehner was forced to withdraw his bill and write a new one that directly de-funded Obamacare. Senator Cruz promised to lead the fight in Senate on the bill, even at the risk of a shutdown. The Cruz-inspired billed passed and went to the Senate.

The prospects for the House bill in the Senate were never good. The Democrats control 54 votes, more than enough to defeat any Republican measure, and with President Obama in the White House, a veto would be a certainty in any event. After the House acted, Senator Cruz admitted as much in an interview, and House members then accused him of tricking them into a pointless exercise. The criticism seems to have inspired Cruz, so he took the floor in the Senate and began a filibuster against Senator Reid's effort to get closure on the House bill. Ironically, Cruz was filibustering a bill he championed, but he was doing so because if the Democrats achieved closure, they could immediately strip out the Obamacare de-funding provision. The Cruz filibuster lasted for 21 hours, but in the end closure was achieved and the Democrats stripped out the de-funding provision on September 27 and sent the bill back to the House.

With only three days left until a shutdown, it was now up to the House leadership to make its call. If it put the Senate funding bill up for a vote, it would pass. Likely at least 150 Republicans would support it, as would a substantial number of Democrats. In the alternative, the GOP could up the ante. That is what they decided to do. They passed another funding bill, this one delaying Obamacare for 1 year and revoking an Obamacare exemption for lawmakers and their staff. By taking this step, the GOP was playing pure brinksmanship, since the Senate would not even be back in session until 2:00 p.m. on September 30, only 10 hours before a shutdown.

In the end, the Republican leadership in the House decided it was better to opt for GOP unity and adopt the approach advocated by Senator Cruz rather than avoid a shutdown. It is a risky strategy, and maybe the exact strategy the White House welcomes. Democrats firmly believe a shutdown will be a disaster for the GOP and will set up not only a victory on the budget, but also the potential for an electoral victory in 2014. That is why President Obama has refused to make any efforts to reach a budget deal. Instead, he has adopted a campaign strategy, giving speech after speech attacking Republicans and repeating he will not negotiate with them. A shutdown is what the President wants, and the conservatives led by Senator Cruz knowingly did his bidding. The President's strategy is not without risk, because shutdown blame could quickly accrue to him, and with a debt ceiling fight in mid-October as well, his strategy of confrontation could result in some bad consequences. But for now, Democrats feel they have the upper hand, aided by their most unlikely of allies, Ted Cruz

Week 246

(SHUT'UM DOWN)

October 6, 2013

It is a rarity when President Obama and conservative Republicans share a common goal, but on the partial government shutdown they certainly did. After failing to achieve any of his legislative goals at the start of his second term, the White House did everything it could to provoke a government shutdown, seeing it as a political game changer. For their part, conservative Republicans led by Ted Cruz convinced Republican leaders to risk a government shutdown to try to force a delay or defunding of Obamacare. So each side saw a benefit to a shutdown, so not surprisingly on September 30, the current spending bill expired and we have the first government shutdown in 17 years.

GOP leaders led by Speaker Boehner did not want this fight. Their preference was to pass a short term funding bill at 2013 sequester spending level, and confront the President in the mid-October debt limit fight. But Tea Party leaders in the Senate and House would not have it. So riders were added to the funding bill to defund Obamacare, riders that were rejected by the Senate creating the current impasse. Once the GOP settled on this course, it made a shutdown almost inevitable. There were some last minute efforts to avoid a shutdown, but neither side was willing to entertain a serious compromise. After the Senate rejected the House bill defunding Obamacare, the House passed a new bill on September 28 delaying Obamacare for one year. When the Senate reconvened on the afternoon of September 30, it promptly tabled the House bill, and the partial government shutdown began.

The Democrats' reaction to the shutdown was gleeful indignation. They said the GOP had been taken over by extremists who were willing to wreck the country to get their way. Democrats taking their cue from the White House stuck firm to their no negotiation stance, demanding not only a clean funding bill, but also a clean debt ceiling increase. In essence, the Democrats want nothing less than a full Republican surrender. The bet is that the Republicans will either cave, or will become so unpopular with the voters that their resistance to the Obama agenda will be broken and their House majority endangered. So both sides have settled on hardball confrontational politics regardless of the consequences.

The White House immediately ramped up its campaign machine. First, the President went for the photo op, calling in congressional leaders to discuss the shutdown. But it was not a negotiation, it was a lecture, where the President simply explained to Republicans leaders that he would not negotiate and demanded they surrender. The event was an exercise in political theater, not governing. Then the President immediately hit the campaign trail to launch rhetorical assault after assault on Republicans. The President was surely enjoying himself, but there were some danger signs that should give the Administration pause.

The biggest concern for the White House was bad optics. At the very moment the government was being shut down over Obamacare, the mandatory enrollment process for individuals under that law went into effect. As many had predicted, the rollout was flawed. The online insurance exchanges crashed, making it almost impossible for anyone to buy the insurance they are now mandated to purchase. After a few days, the federal website had to be pulled down for repairs. Against this backdrop, the continued insistence by the President that he will not negotiate created an image of intransigence. Then on October 4, a senior White House official commented that the Administration did not care how long the shutdown lasted because they were "winning." None of this made the President or his policies look very good.

The Republicans did their best to hold their own in the face of these Democrat missteps. They started passing funding bills for specific agencies, forcing the Democrats to say no. They moved to the theme that the impasse could be ended if the President would simply sit down and talk. They tried to point to the problems with Obamacare and point to the basic unfairness that big business, Congress and many unions have been exempted, while individuals are being forced to comply with the law. While the GOP is certainly on weaker ground, there have been some encouraging signs. Polls show more people blame Republicans for the shutdown, but Democrats are a close second. The President's approval ratings are also falling. So far, the shutdown fight is not the rout Democrats had expected. So each party is seeing opportunity in this fight, meaning it is less likely to end quickly. And this is just a prelude to the debt limit fight, which is right around the corner.

Week 247

(REALITY CHECK)

October 13, 2013

As the nation entered the second week of the partial government shutdown, both Republicans and Democrats seemed determined to stick to their political talking points. The President and his allies in Congress continued to refuse to negotiate and excoriated the GOP for shutting down the government. Republicans stuck to their calls for fairness on Obamacare and for the President to agree to have a conversation on solutions. It seemed it would be yet another week of political posturing and name calling, but then both sides appeared to blink simultaneously. It appears both parties began to realize the time for political games was starting to pass and the time to find solutions had arrived.

The entire shutdown fight is a battle the GOP leadership never wanted to fight. Their plan was to pass a compromise spending plan with Democrats, and use the debt limit to fight on Obamacare and spending. Conservatives forced a confrontation and shutdown instead. The fear among the leadership is that a shutdown fight would weakened the GOP both on leverage in negotiations and in next year's election. They seem to have been right. Poll after poll began to show the Republicans taking more of the blame for the shutdown. The media also did its part, blaming them as much as possible for the shutdown at every turn. The only opening for the Republicans was the President's outright refusal to negotiate, on which they pounded him day after day. But at best that only stemmed some of the bleeding.

For Democrats, the shutdown was a golden opportunity not to be missed. They blamed Republican radicals for targeting every conceivable interest group by their determination to stop Obamacare. The President gave press conferences and interviews pushing these themes. The Democrats also upped the ante, by turning the focus to the debt limit, set to expire October 17. Using ever more cataclysmic language, the President, Treasury Secretary Lew, and a host of others predicted a near end to civilization as we know it if the debt limit is not increased. The Democrats see the debt limit as a great wedge issue because it separates the GOP from its traditional business allies. The bet was by increasing the pressure on the GOP they could induce a surrender.

However, the Republicans showed no signs of capitulation, and by mid-week the President changed his strategy. On October 9, he met with congressional Democrats and on October 10, invited the entire GOP House caucus to the White House. Much to the annoyance of the White House, Speaker Boehner instead designated 18 House representatives to attend, led by Budget committee chairman Paul Ryan. No deal was reached at the meeting, but both sides called it productive. The President said he was not negotiating. The Republicans offered plans. No deal was reached, but the signs of progress were enough to propel the Dow Jones Industrial average to a 300 point gain. More negotiations ensued Friday and Saturday, with the Senate increasingly taking the lead because the plans offered by the GOP House leadership were not acceptable to the President. This created more division among Republicans, with the House annoyed at being upstaged by Senate Republicans, whom they view as too willing to cut a deal with the Administration.

There was hope for a deal over the weekend, but a deal did not come. A framework for a compromise had been crafted by Maine Republican Susan Collins. It involved an extension of the debt limit and spending authorization until January 31, 2014, a two year delay in the medical device tax, an unpopular provision in Obamacare for both Democrats and Republicans, and a plan to create a committee to address broader budget initiatives. This seemed to offer the potential for a deal, but then feeling their increased leverage, Democrats demanded higher spending levels, so the deal died. So the week ended as it began, with no deal on the shutdown or on the debt limit, but an outline of a compromise began to appear, which might offer a chance to end the political standoff.

Week 248
(DIDN'T WIN)

October 20, 2013

With the partial government shutdown starting its third week and the debt limit set to be hit on October 17, this was a make or break week for Washington politicians. For the Democrats, having gained the upper hand in the shutdown battle, their goal was to humiliate the GOP and force an end to the shutdown and an extension of the debt limit. For Republicans, there was an increasing urgency to try to minimize the damage and end the confrontation. In the end, a compromise was crafted that was wildly hailed as a victory for the Democrats and a surrender by the Republicans. As Speaker Boehner admitted just before the House vote to end the shutdown and extend the debt limit, the GOP fought the good fight, but they "didn't win." And while the media and the Washington establishment declared an Obama triumph, what the President and his allies really won is much less clear.

It was obvious as the debt limit deadline came closer and closer, that more and more Republicans were determined to reach a compromise with the Democrats. After the GOP House leadership failed to garner support within their caucus for a plan to end the crisis, the focus turned to Minority Leader Mitch McConnell. This was a familiar role for the senior Senator from Kentucky. He was the one who crafted the compromise that ended the debt limit fight in August 2011. Now again, McConnell took center stage. The primary goal of the GOP in the negotiations was to preserve the sequester, limit the length of the debt limit extension, force negotiations on the budget, and obtain some face-saving changes to Obamacare. Ironically, despite the stories of a Democrat triumph, McConnell achieved all of these goals. The deal stuck with the Democrats funded the government until January 15 at the sequester levels, extended the debt ceiling until February 15, set up a committee to negotiate a long-term budget deal, and provided for income verification for those enrolling for Obamacare subsidiaries.

The fact that this deal was viewed as such a defeat for the GOP is a reflection of the unrealistic goals set by conservatives led by Senator Ted Cruz. Cruz and his allies forced a shutdown fight to defund Obamacare, a goal that was never achievable with Democrats in charge of the Senate and the White House. By making Obamacare and a shutdown the center of the budget battle, Cruz handed advantage to the Democrats. While unpopular, voters do not support shutting down the government over Obamacare. Likewise, government shutdowns are even more unpopular than increases in the debt limit. So by choosing this field of battle, the Republicans set themselves up for defeat. Viewed from this prism, McConnell's successes in his negotiations went unnoticed. Democrats were pressing for a 15-month debt limit increase and an end to the sequester. They got neither.

In the battle that was the shutdown fight of 2013, perception is reality. The perception was that the GOP was being unreasonable, forced a crisis unnecessarily, and lost. And in truth, the Republicans got by far the worst of the deal. Approval ratings for the President and the Democrats fell, but they fell more for Republicans. Democrats wanted a clean funding bill and a debt limit increase not tied to spending cuts, and they got both for at least a few months. Democrats had been calling for a conference to reconcile the budgets passed by the Senate and the House, and in essence the deal gave it to them. All these were Democrat victories, but hardly grand ones. The ultimate goal of the Democrats is to replace the sequester with tax increases, but the deal locked in the sequester rather than ended it, so by that measure the GOP preserved its central goal.

There is no doubt the GOP "didn't win," but they did gain something. Speaker Boehner strengthened his position with House conservatives by forcing a fight. More importantly, the Cruz faction was bloodied, which might give Boehner more control going forward. As Senator McConnell commented after the compromise deal passed on October 16, "now our newer members understand what a losing strategy looks like." It was a tough lesson to learn, but not necessarily a fatal one. And with the failures of the Obamacare implementation mounting by the day, the GOP can count on the media focus moving to more favorable ground. The key for the Republicans will be to fight better and smarter in the next funding battle, which will come in January 2014.

Week 249

(FRUSTRATED)

October 27, 2013

With the fight over the shutdown and the debt limit temporarily deferred until early 2014, the Obama Administration had hoped to capitalize on its victory by pushing the GOP to approve immigration reform. The President promptly orchestrated this pivot with a speech on immigration following the conclusion of the shutdown. The theory was that the Republicans were so damaged by the shutdown fight, and the Democrats so strengthened, victory on immigration would be at hand. But all that strategy was for naught, because as soon as the shutdown ended the full focus of the media turned to the problems with the Obamacare rollout, which have been so bad that the President had to give a speech to emphasize how frustrated he is with the state of the program. So much for that supposed momentum from the shutdown victory.

The President was fortunate that the shutdown fight took the focus off Obamacare, at least for a couple weeks. The individual mandate under Obamacare went into effect on October 1. The President had already delayed implementation of the employer mandate, but was determined to push forward with the individual mandate to buy insurance. Individuals were given until February 15, 2014 to buy plans. With a majority of states refusing to set up insurance exchanges to facilitate plan purchases, residents in some 36 States had to rely on the federal exchange, the main portal to which is the healthcare.gov website. That is where the problems started.

Although millions of Americans rushed to that website to check out coverage options, almost all went away frustrated. The website crashed, froze, prevented people from enrolling, and when people did enroll, prevented them from purchasing insurance. Three weeks into the enrollment period, the Administration was still refusing to release how many people successfully bought insurance on the federal exchange, likely because the number is embarrassingly low. Then the website crashed almost entirely, which forced the President to step in.

In his comments at the White House, the President said no one is more frustrated than him with the rollout problems, but he made every effort to discount what he saw as temporary issues. He talked about the benefits of Obamacare, and that Obamacare is more than a website. He promised the problems would be fixed with a tech surge, with Administration officials pledging a fully functional website by the end of November. The White House also extended the enrollment period to the end of March 2014. And while the Administration is resisting calls for Health and Human Services Secretary Sebelius to resign, there is no doubt the blame game has begun.

While the website has gotten the attention, other more disturbing signs have emerged. On the state exchanges that are functioning better than the federal exchange, a larger than expected proportion of applicants are Medicaid recipients or others qualifying for subsidies. For Obamacare to work, young healthy people need to enroll, so this trend endangers the whole program. Also hundreds of thousands of people are getting their policies cancelled because they do not meet the new federal minimum standards, despite the President's assurances that if you like your insurance, you can keep it. Further, many are complaining the prices for policies are too high. So while the President might very well be frustrated, he should also be worried because his signature program is showing early signs of unraveling.

Week 250

(CANCELLED)

November 3, 2013

Despite the President's declaration of a tech surge to address the problems with the healthcare.gov website, far from quelling the controversy, Obamacare continued to grow as a scandal of incompetence. With Obamacare being the signature legislative achievement of the Obama Presidency, more and more facts came to light this week about the disorganized, secretive, and incompetent effort by the Administration to implement what is arguably the most complex social welfare legislation even enacted. The utter failure of the government to do its job was starting to have dire consequences for millions of Americans, whose health insurance had been cancelled because of Obamacare mandates, but who now cannot purchase insurance because the website was down. And throughout it all, the President and the White House continued to try to salvage the situation while refusing to admit misleading the public.

For the President, the catastrophic start to Obamacare is a body blow to his image and his competence. For the first time in his presidency, he is now being satirized as incompetent and disconnected. It also appears the President has not internalized how much his image has been hurt. His response to the Obamacare crisis has been from the same old play book: give speeches, campaign, attack his enemies, and never give an inch. However, this time the strategy is ringing hollow. To get Obamacare enacted, the President promised repeatedly that if you liked your insurance you could keep it, period. Now, stories have leaked out that as early as 2010 the Administration realized that promise could not be kept. So far, more than 3 million Americans have lost their insurance because of Obamacare, and estimates are that the cancellations will eventually total close to 15 million. Everyone knows the President misled the public, but the President simply will not admit it. His whole political apparatus has been deployed to re-write, re-craft, cleverly lawyer, and dissemble what he said, trying to create accuracy out of a promise, but no one is buying it. His statements are now commonly viewed as a joke, and his efforts to justify his lie as just more dishonesty.

However, the damage to the White House is not limited to the President losing credibility, there now appears to be serious signs Obamacare itself is fatally flawed. The initial problem was the website, which crashed and continues to be taken down every night for repairs. With millions of Americans losing their insurance and with most of them reliant on the website to look for new coverage, the failure of the website is far more than an inconvenience, it is crippling Obamacare. The President promised a fully functioning website by November 30. If that deadline is missed, the political pressure to delay Obamacare will become overwhelming. Already, a dozen Democrat senators have proposed various plans to suspend aspects of the new law. The President may be able to keep his troops in line for a couple more weeks, but if the website is still not functioning sufficiently by December, the White House will have few options left.

Even more concerning are the underlying problems with Obamacare. The Administration has been fighting every effort to reveal actual enrollment numbers because they have been so low. In fact, figures released this week showed that only 6 people we able to fully register on October 1, when Obamacare went live. That number has grown since, but for the Obamacare exchanges to work, it needs 5 to 7 million new purchasers of private insurance, most of those young and healthy people. There are few signs that is going to happen by March 31. Even on the 14 state exchanges, a few of which are functioning well, most of the new enrollees for applying for Medicaid, not private insurance. There are also increasing reports that the private insurance being offered to those with cancelled policies is both more expensive and has higher deductibles. Worse coverage for more money is not a good selling point. Also, the key to Obamacare working is having young healthy people buy insurance, but because the penalties for not buying insurance are so low and the incentive to try to buy is so limited given the website issues, there is a growing fear that too few young people will participate.

There is also a sense of no accountability. Health and Human Services Secretary Sebelious was in charge of the implementation, but we now know hundreds of contracts were involved, there was little oversight or coordination, limited testing, and security on the website was inadequate. The White House was warned about these problems early and ignored them. The Administration has also claimed the President knew nothing of the problems, furthering the perception of him as disconnected. In her congressional testimony, Secretary Selelius admitted the implementation of Obamacare has been a debacle, but there has been no accountability. $600 million dollars have been spent on a website that does not work, but no one is being held responsible. Most disturbingly, because the President is viewing all this as just another political battle, he is refusing to fire anyone because that might be viewed as an admission that there were failures.

What became clear this week was the central falsehood behind Obamacare. When the President tried to sell his reform to the voters, his theme was everyone will get something better and it will cost no one anything except for the very wealthy. Everyone could keep their doctor, keep their insurance, Medicaid would be expanded, pre-existing conditions covered, insurance enhanced, and it all would be free to 99% of the people. It was all a fiction. Millions of Americans are going to be forced to buy insurance they either do not want or do not need to fund a system that will give free coverage or subsidized coverage to others. Obamacare is a massive wealth transfer from young and middle class citizens to given benefits to others, not quite the everyone wins story told by the President. This reality started to sink in as soon as those cancellation letters got delivered to people's mailboxes.

Week 251

(I AM SORRY)

November 10, 2013

For a White House that prides itself for always being on the offensive and never admitting an error, this was a sobering week. With the Obamacare rollout debacle continuing to dominate the headlines and election results sending warning signs to the Administration, the White House decided it was time for the Commander-in Chief to show some contrition. After millions were losing their insurance and millions more were unable to buy coverage because of the inoperable Obamacare website, the President could no longer get away with trying to pretend he did not make the assurance that people who liked their plans could keep them. He tried word games and blame games, but there was just no way to avoid the consequences of his false promise. So the President had to show some regret, which he did reluctantly indeed.

In an interview with Chuck Todd of NBC news on November 7, the President said: "I am sorry that they are finding themselves in this situation based on assurances they got from me. We've got to work hard to make sure that they know we hear them and we are going to do everything we can to deal with folks who find themselves in a tough position as a consequence of this." It was not quite an apology, but for this White House is was groundbreaking, and a sign of how much trouble Obamacare is in. The Democrats had tried to focus on the website, calling it a simple glitch which when fixed, would allow Obamacare to provide the affordable coverage that was promised. But the problems have compounded far beyond that. Millions losing insurance, very few able to enroll in new coverage, faulty security that puts people's personal data at risk, high rates, and few young people buying private insurance, which is essential for Obamacare to work. Literally, little about Obamacare was working, and the apology shows how concerned the President has become.

Democrats in Congress have also made sure the President understands the seriousness of the situation. The President invited Senate Democrats to the White House, and got an earful on the problems and how they must be fixed. More and more Democrats introduced bills to delay the individual mandate. Most importantly, red state Democrats demanded quick action because they fear Obamacare's problems will undermine their re-election prospects. The off year elections in New Jersey and Virginia further highlighted the risks. In New Jersey, Republican Chris Christie won a resounding victory built on his campaign to tame the size of state government. In Virginia, Democrat fundraiser Terry McAuliffe was far ahead of his Republican opponent just a couple weeks before the election, but Obamacare's problems fueled Ken Cuccinelli campaign. As McAuliffe's lead got smaller and smaller, it was clear the Obamacare issue was making a difference. McAuliffe still pulled out a narrow victory, but the warning shot was heard nonetheless.

All these political pressures, combined with his falling approval rating, pushed the President to give his semi-apology, but just showing contrition will not be enough. Obamacare is the President's signature achievement, it was passed solely with Democrat votes, and it has been forced on a populace that has never given it majority support. Given all this, Obamacare would only be accepted if it appeared to work. Instead, it has failed spectacularly. The President can try to change the topic, as he attempted this week with speeches on immigration and stimulus spending, but it will not work because Obamacare is too big a story and he is too easy a target. So all he can do is say he is sorry and try to fix the problems. The trouble is, the website is looking like only one of the problems, ensuring that Obamacare will remain a central political issue of his second term. The President better get used to apologizing.

Week 252

(FUMBLED)

November 17, 2013

With dissatisfaction growing among Democrats and popular opposition on the rise, the White House finally had to grapple with the unfolding disaster that is the Obamacare rollout. For weeks the President tried to walk back and rephrase his commitment that people who liked their insurance plans and doctors could keep them. But as millions of cancellation notices started to arrive in people's mailboxes, the Administration's hollow efforts to try to convince voters the President did not make those promises only worsened the problem. Compounding the political challenge for the White House was increasing numbers of Democrats in Congress pushing for changes in the health care law. Speaker Boehner, taking advantage of this disarray among Democrats, scheduled a vote on a GOP plan to let customers of insurance plans not compliant with Obamacare keep them, and allowing insurers to offer those plans to new customers as well. This bill could be a major embarrassment for the Administration, because absent an alternative from the White House, it was looking like large numbers of Democrats would vote for the GOP bill, which would be put up for a vote on Friday, November 15.

All week long, Democrats warned the Administration that it needed to offer a plan to fix the problem, or a wholesale revolt might ensue. The White House would only say they were working on a solution, refusing to give any details. Then, the White House announced that the President would address the issue on Thursday, November 14, clearly an effort to stop the momentum in support of the GOP bill. When the President took the podium, he offered not simply a plan, but also an admission of how badly he and his Administration had mismanaged his signature legislation. The President admitted that his team "fumbled" the health care rollout. He admitted the problems with Obamacare were "on him." He said he was not a "perfect President' but he would continue to work hard every day. He pledged that solutions would be found and that the website would be working "much better" for the "majority" of users by month's end, hedge words that made many mistrust that the website would actually get fixed. He defended the virtues of the law and his commitment to fix it, but what was most memorable was his candor on how badly his Administration had performed.

The President's strategy was not limited to apologies, he also wanted to shift the blame. All week, the White House tried to assert the cancellations were the work of insurance companies, not Obamacare, but the strategy was just not working. Everyone understood that these policies were being cancelled because they did not meet the standards set by Obamacare and that for the law to work, those policies had to be cancelled to force insureds into the federal exchange. The President hoped to deflect criticism and shift blame for the cancellations, so he announced that insurance carriers could offer these plans for one more year to current customers as long as they gave disclosures on how the plans do not meet federal requirements.

This proposal was pure politics trumping sound policy. These insurers had cancelled these plans to comply with Obamacare, and had set their pricing based on those cancellations. Now after relying on the President and following the law, the Administration changed the rules, throwing everything into confusion. Now insurers could legally offer these old plans, but could they do so practically. Many states will not allow the plans to be reinstated, and with the short time available and the need to reset pricing, it would be very hard to undo the cancellations that Obamacare itself initially demanded. Even more importantly, allowing these plans to stay in place would only starve the federal exchange of needed private insurance customers, making higher premiums ever more likely. So for anyone who understood and believed in the policy underlying Obamacare, the President's proposal made no sense. But that is not the prism through which one should assess this move, because it was not about sound policy, but rather political survival.

With this move, no matter the chaos it creates, the President can claim he tried to make amends for his earlier misstatements. The plan also gives Democrats a chance to try to place the blame on insurance companies, and try to avoid the blame going on them. The President also made these changes administratively, a clear effort to short circuit legislative efforts in Congress. The plan will hurt the viability of Obamacare in the long run, but the objective is political survival not good policy. But it is not clear the President's move went far enough. Many Democrats in Congress still called for new legislation, and 41 Democrats joined Republicans in support the GOP reform bill that passed on November 15. And all along support for the President and Obamacare continues to fall. It appears the President has now fumbled both the rollout and the fix, and if at some point you fumble too much, you lose the gamer.

Week 253

(FIAT)

November 24, 2013

With his legislative agenda stalled in Congress, President Obama has been forced to turn to his executive powers to pursue his legislative priorities. When Barak Obama was campaigning for the White House in 2008, he was a critic of President George W. Bush's use of executive powers, but has now become the most aggressive President in modern history in that realm. During his first two years in office, when Democrats controlled majorities in Congress, the President did not have to push the bounds of executive power because he was able to advance a number of his priorities legislatively. But since the GOP took control of the House in January 2011, the President has had to turn increasingly to administrative actions. The Republican minority in the Senate has filibustered many of his executive nominations. The GOP has also stalled many of his judicial appointments, trying to make it less likely that legal challenges to the President's executive actions will be heard by judges sympathetic to the President. Given this state of affairs, it was not surprising that on November 21, Senate Democrats invoked the nuclear option to stop filibusters of nearly all executive nominations. For the President to rule by fiat, he needs unencumbered control of the executive branch and the ability to pack the federal courts with as many liberal judges as possible.

Early in 2013, with the President confident of his influence after his commanding reelection, the White House focused on legislation. However, they found little success, so they quickly turned to executive power. The President could not get his carbon tax policy enacted, so he is using the EPA to regulate carbon emissions by power plants. The President could not enact gun control after the Sandy Hook shootings, so he issued some new gun regulations by executive order as possible. With immigration reform stalled, the Administration has taken executive action to limit enforcement of current immigration laws. With Democrats unable to push through union card check legislation, the President is using the NLRB to pursue union priorities. So on issue after issue, the President appears to have given up on legislation and instead is turning to regulation and executive orders.

The President's use of executive powers has been most audacious regarding Obamacare. Obamacare has never been popular and as the October 1, 2013 implementation approached, the President began delaying parts of the law to try to prevent a public backlash. First, the President delayed the employer mandate for a year until October 2014. Then when Healthcare.gov crashed, the President extended the open enrollment period until the end of March 2014. When approximately 5 million people had their insurance cancelled because of Obamacare coverage mandates, in the face of public outrage given the President's promise that people could keep their insurance if they liked it, the President used executive power to try to blunt the backlash. He issued an order allowing insurers to continue to offer their non-compliant plans for another year even though offering those plans violated Obamacare mandates. Then this week, the President delayed the start of the 2014 open enrollment from October 15 to November 15, ostensibly to give insurers more time to set their premiums. In reality, the Administration moved the deadlines because premiums are expected to sharply increase in 2014, and the President wants consumers to find out about those increases only after the 2014 midterm election. The next likely executive action on Obamacare is a delay of the individual mandate, because it appears healthcare.gov will not be fully functional by November 30 as the President promised, and enrollments in private insurance are lagging far behind schedule.

For the President's rule by fiat to be effective, he needs the executive branch fully staffed with his appointments and he needs judges who will rule for him in the inevitable legal challenges. That is what this week's vote for the nuclear option was all about. Republican Senators were filibustering three nominees for the D.C. Circuit Court of Appeals because it is the most underworked of the federal appeals courts, and it is currently even divided between conservatives and liberals. Majority Leader Reid has repeatedly threatened to use a simple majority vote to change Senate rules and limit the filibuster. On November 21 he did it, winning support for the move by a 52-48 vote. Now the President and Democrats will have nearly unchecked power to confirm executive and judicial appointments who will then hopefully implement and endorse the President's rule by executive order.

Week 254

(NOT SANCTIONED)

December 1, 2013

With Obamacare continuing to dominate the headlines, the Obama Administration was looking increasingly desperate to change the topic. Not such an easy thing to do as the Obamacare problems and delays continued to amount. This week, the Administration had to delay another key part of the law for a year, namely the insurance exchange for small businesses, because it could not adequately operate. Insurers were also raising alarms about continued problems with the pricing and information sharing functionally on healthcare.gov. All this made it ever more difficult for the White House to change the topic, but it eventually was able to do so, if only for a few days, with the help of an unlikely ally, Iran.

Ever since the United States led an effort to tighten sanctions on Iran, the pressure has been building on the Iranian regime to offer some kind of concession on their nuclear program to save their economy from further damage. In August, Iran's new President, Hassan Rouhani, took office, and immediately launched a charm offensive designed to build momentum to lift sanctions. Marathon talks ensued in November, but no deal was reached. Then on November 24, to the surprise of many observers, a six-month interim agreement was reached on Iran's nuclear program, and criticisms quickly followed.

The agreement makes the following stipulations on the Iranian nuclear program: (1) all uranium enriched beyond 5% will either be diluted or converted to uranium oxide and no new uranium at the 3.5% enrichment level will be added to Iran's current stock; (2) no new centrifuges will be installed or prepared for installation; (3) 50% of the centrifuges at the Natanz enrichment facility and 75% at the Fordow enrichment facility will be left inoperable; (4) Iran will not use its advanced IR-2 centrifuges for enrichment; (5) Iran will not develop any new uranium enrichment or nuclear reprocessing facilities; (6) no fuel will be produced, tested, or transferred to the Arak nuclear power plant and Iran will share design details of the reactor; (7) the International Atomic Energy Administration (IAEA) will be granted daily access to Natanz and Fordow, with certain sites monitored by 24-hour cameras and the IAEA will also have access to Iran's uranium mines and centrifuge production facilities; and (8) Iran will address IAEA questions related to possible military dimensions of its nuclear program. In return, Iran will receive relief from sanctions worth approximately $7 billion and no additional sanctions will be imposed.

While the Obama Administration touted this deal as a positive first step, critics pointed out that the deal gives Iran immediate relief from sanctions without requiring Iran to take any steps that would permanently stop or delay its nuclear program, like for example destroying its centrifuges. So in return for temporary controls and limitations, Iran gets immediate sanctions relief. As many pointed out, it is the sanctions that brought Iran to the table in the first place, so it is not clear how lifting them in part will lead to any permanent concessions from Iran. This criticism did not come just from Republicans or Israeli Prime Minister Netanyahu, many Democrats in Congress attacked the deal and called for more sanctions.

As for the politics, many Republicans believe the President was desperate to achieve any kind of accomplishment to change the topic from Obamacare and leaped for this bad deal. This agreement is controversial, but certainly not as controversial as Obamacare. For a White House trying to find anything else to talk about, maybe they view that as good enough.

Week 255

(MANDELA)

December 8, 2013

In the midst of the continuing Obamacare and budget battles in Washington, an event occurred that caused all factions to pause and reflect. The death of Nelson Mandela on December 5, 2013. It seemed as if his passing caused the whole world to ponder the man and his accomplishments. For a person who was so controversial for most of his life, it was amazing to see the near universal acclaim poured on him at his death. Criticized as a terrorist and Marxist during most of his life, even white South Africans and American conservatives honored him at his death. The reason is simple, despite his history of radicalism, once released from prison and elected President of South Africa, he implemented a vision of reconciliation and compassion. He rose above his past and forgave his enemies, and helped to heal his nation and the world. No wonder President Obama rushed to get in the glow of Mandela's accomplishments, because where Mandela succeeded, Obama has consistently failed.

Nelson Mandela was born on July 18, 1918. After the South African National Party came to power in 1948, he rose to prominence in the African National Congress's 1952 Defiance Campaign, and was appointed superintendent of the organization's Transvaal chapter. Working as a lawyer, he was repeatedly arrested for seditious activities and, with the ANC leadership, was unsuccessfully prosecuted in a treason trial from 1956 to 1961. Although initially committed to non-violent protest, he co-founded the militant Umkhonto we Sizwe in 1961 in association with the South African Communist Party, and led a sabotage campaign against the apartheid government. In 1962 he was arrested, convicted of conspiracy to overthrow the state, and sentenced to life imprisonment. He was released in 1990, during a time of escalating civil strife. Mandela joined negotiations with South African President F. W. de Klerk to abolish apartheid and establish multiracial elections in 1994, in which he led the ANC to victory and became South Africa's first black president. During his tenure, he invited other political parties to join his cabinet. As agreed to during the negotiations to end apartheid, he promulgated a new constitution. He also created the Truth and Reconciliation Commission to investigate past human rights violations. And although a committed Marxist in his youth, he maintained the apartheid government's liberal economic policies.

Mandela led a life of overcoming obstacles and defying expectations. From his prison cell on Robin Island, unseen for decades, he remained the leader of the anti-apartheid movement. After so many years of mistreatment at the hands of his captors, one would have expected Mandela to emerge from prison embittered and determined the settle scores. The opposite was true. Once released, his mission was to bring reconciliation, freedom, and democracy to all South Africans. Far from seeking to punish white South Africans, he sought to calm their fears and include them in the political process. He was a Marxist at the time of his imprisonment, but in 1990, he emerged into a post-communist world that did not adhere to his former philosophy. In response, he sought to bring greater prosperity through free markets. No one would have expected what Mandela did, and that is exactly why he is so revered.

Mandela's passing was a time for both sadness and joy. Sadness that a true giant of history was gone, but joy at his accomplishments and the hope he has given to millions. Mandela was not without his critics. Many said he compromised too much with white interests and failed to create true economic equality and opportunity for black South Africans, but these are criticisms at the margins. The greatness of what he accomplished cannot be denied. Given this, it is no wonder President Obama rushed to heap praise on Mandela, even commenting that it was Mandela who inspired his first active efforts in politics. Yet the great qualities Mandela showed — pragmatism, reconciliation, and compromise – are attributes President Obama has yet to display. Mandela united, too often President Obama divides. Mandela sought consensus, too often President Obama revels in partisanship. But maybe the lesson of Mandela's life will teach the President that political victory alone does not make a leader great. Greatness is made of defying expectations, and in that respect, President Obama bears no resemblance to Nelson Mandela.

Week 256

(WHAT'S THE DEAL)

December 15, 2013

Ever since the GOP took control of the House in January 2011, Washington has been in a continual cycle of budget confrontation, crisis, and last minute deals to avert disaster. The most recent episode of the budget battles was the October 2013 government shutdown. The deal reached to end the shutdown required the parties to negotiate a budget deal and report back to both houses of Congress before the end of 2013. Republican Budget Committee Chairman Paul Ryan and his Democrat counterpart Senator Patty Murray were tasked with the job of reaching a deal. Few thought they could do it, given past history. They held some meeting, but there was little evidence of progress until on December 10, they made the surprising announcement that a compromise had been reached. The deal was small, sidestepped the big issues of taxes and entitlements, but was a true bipartisan compromise. Importantly, both sides seemed equally unhappy with the outcome, a sure sign of compromises, but that did not stop the recriminations.

The total value of the deal was $85 billion, not a large amount given the size of the federal budget. About $45 billion of that is revised spending cuts and new fees to replace sequestration cuts in 2014, with another $20 billion in different cuts and new fees to replace some sequestration cuts in 2015. In addition, the deal includes about $20 billion in deficit reduction. The sequestration relief is evenly divided between defense and non-defense discretionary spending. The deal increases revenues through fees on airline travel and federal workers will have to contribute more to pensions, plus other modest spending cuts. Spending will be $45 billion higher in 2014 than under the sequestration. The deal replaces about half of the sequestration cuts in 2014 and about 25% of them in 2015. The sequestration cuts in out years were not impacted by the deal.

Democrats wanted the deal to include higher taxes. It does not. Likewise, Democrats wanted the deal to include an extension of unemployment insurance. Again it does not. Republicans wanted a bigger deal with larger deficit and entitlement reforms. They got neither. While each side was frustrated by unachieved goals, each also got some of the things they wanted. Democrats desperately wanted to end the sequester, and under this deal at least for 2014 and 2015 the sequester is mitigated. Democrats avoided a larger increase in pension contributions for federal employees and were able to obtain new spending now in return for cuts, most of which will not occur for many years. The Republicans also got some things out of the deal. Most importantly, the deal overall cuts the deficit, even if only modestly. The deal also includes no new taxes, does not include new spending like extended unemployment insurance, and does not increase the debt limit or reduce the sequester after 2016. Neither side won, and neither side lost.

Once the deal was struck, the big issue was could it pass. President Obama quickly endorsed the deal, but with plenty of shortcomings that each party could complaint about, it would take some lobbying to get it passed. Conservative Republicans protested that the deal increases spending now for cuts later. Democrats remained unhappy about the spending levels and wanted at least an extension of unemployment benefits. But the deal was good enough for Minority Leader Nancy Pelosi and Speaker Boehner to support it. The House voted on December 12, and the deal passed by a margin of 332 to 94, with the opposition coming from conservative Republicans. Now the deal moves onto the Senate.

Once the deal passed the House, the political assessments began. The biggest benefit of the deal is that it ends the risk of a government shutdown in 2014. That likely benefits the GOP the most, since it deprives Democrats of their best opportunity to gain ground on Republicans. The deal also ensures that the political battles of 2014 will remain focused on Obamacare, good ground for the GOP. For Democrats, the hope is that this deal will further fuel discord within the GOP. Speaker Boehner gave some hope to this view with his press conference after the House vote where he criticized certain outside conservative groups for attacking the bill and pushing a shutdown in October that hurt Republicans. Democrats also hoped the deal was a signal that Speaker Boehner is prepared to defy conservatives on other issues like immigration. So it was a deal that gave hope and despair to each side, the true sign of a compromise.

Week 257

(Uncowed)

December 22, 2013

With 2013 coming to a close, President Obama must be looking forward to moving beyond what has been the most difficult and frustrating year of his presidency. The failure of immigration reform and gun control legislation, the NSA spying scandal, and the disastrous Obamacare rollout have together dealt a body blow to his standing with the public. His poll ratings are at near record lows, and most importantly for the first time the public is doubting his honesty. Much of that must be attributed to Obamacare, where the President's "if you like your plan you can keep it" promise was rated the lie of the year by political observers. Given all this, some political commentators have predicted that President Obama is already a lame duck, but the White House will have none of it. In response to frustrations with inaction by Congress, it has turned to executive powers to accomplish its goals. Indeed, the President made clear in a December 20 press conference, in advance of his 17-day Christmas vacation in Hawaii, that he plans to take the offensive in the New Year.

While the President has suffered many blows this year, the Administration believes it has momentum on many fronts, and in 2014 it hopes to exploit that momentum. So for every setback, the White House hopes to point to progress. There were several good examples of that this week. Obamacare continues to be a problem, with the White House changing the program again this week by allowing more people to buy high deductible plans and delaying more penalties. Yet at the same time, the Administration points to a better working website and higher enrollment numbers. The President's opening statement for his press conference highlighted this strategy. He began by noting recent positive economic news: "In 2013, our businesses created another 2 million jobs, adding up to more than 8 million in just over the past 45 months. This morning, we learned that over the summer our economy grew at its strongest pace in nearly two years. The unemployment rate has steadily fallen to its lowest point in five years. Our tax code is fairer, and our fiscal situation is firmer, with deficits that are now less than half of what they were when I took office." He then turned to possibly the biggest driver of the economic recovery, the booming energy sector: "For the first time in nearly two decades, we now produce more oil here at home than we buy from the rest of the world." As for health care, the President asserted that the "the Affordable Care Act has helped keep health care costs growing at their slowest rate in 50 years. Combined that means bigger paychecks for middle-class families and bigger savings for businesses looking to invest and hire here in America."

After setting up this rosy picture of the state of the nation, the President said: "I firmly believe that 2014 can be a breakthrough year for America." He pointed to the bipartisan budget compromise that passed the Senate this week, avoiding the prospect of yet another government shutdown. The White House hopes this compromise will pave the way for a deal on immigration and other issues, with the President proclaiming: "I think 2014 needs to be a year of action. We've got work to do to create more good jobs, to help more Americans earn the skills and education they need to do those jobs, and to make sure that those jobs offer the wages and benefits that let families build a little bit of financial security. We still have the task of finishing the fix on our broken immigration system. We've got to build on the progress we've painstakingly made over these last five years with respect to our economy and offer the middle class and all those who are looking to join the middle class a better opportunity. And that's going to be where I focus all of my efforts in the year ahead."

Unfortunately for the Administration, there seems to be little reason for the Republican in Congress to seek compromise. In the House, recent poll numbers are making the GOP feel their majority is secure. In the Senate, partisan rancor is at a fever pitch due to Majority Leader Reid's decision to limit filibuster rights on nominees. Indeed, the Senate had to endure a string of pre-Christmas marathon sessions on nominees because the Republicans were using every procedural trick available to slow the process. A compromise delaying some votes was reached just before Christmas week, but there is no sign that the Senate will suddenly become more productive.

The challenges facing the President for 2014 became clear in the questioning at the press conference, which focused on his failures to pass major legislation, NSA spying, and Obamacare. None being good topics around which to build momentum in 2014. So the President leaves Washington for Hawaii hoping to recharge and take charge in 2014, and the economy might help him make some progress, but it seems almost everything else is working against him.

Week 258

(RESPITE)

December 29, 2013

With the President on vacation in Hawaii, Congress home for the Holidays, and the Christmas season in full swing, Washington took a short break from political battles. After a year that started with a grand progressive vision from the President's inaugural address, a vision that foundered in congressional rejection, a shutdown, and a disastrous Obamacare rollout, the nation seemed to have reached a political stalemate, with neither side able to gain the upper hand. So the Christmas Holiday gave each side a chance to recharge, reflect, and prepare for the political battles ahead in 2014. Understanding full well the difficult political landscape, the White House did not suspend its spin operation for the Holidays, far from it. Instead, it continues to try to promote the success of Obamacare, but with most of the nation focused on other things, was anyone listening.

Democrat strategists understand that 2014 will be defined by Obamacare, for good or ill. The law has never been popular, but in 2013 its popularity dropped to new lows, with the rollout making the law a joke even in liberal circles. That is why Democrat leaders issued statement after statement about how Obamacare will help them in 2014, trying to convincing everyone against all evidence that the program was working, is popular, and its champions will be rewarded by the voters. None of that is true, but for Democrats who pushed the law through without a single Republican vote, they have no other choice, they are tied to Obamacare whether they like it or not. Given that, the only option is to champion it, any other course just compounds the problem.

The Administration has done everything it can to limit the impact of Obamacare, with what seems like announcements of new exemptions and changes every week. The goal is to blunt and space out the true effects of the law, which most now recognize will limit choices of plans and doctors and increase costs. The Democrats' only goal is to prevent the system from having its full effect until after the 2014 election. At the same time, they hope to use enrollment numbers to try to portray the law as popular and successful. But in the end, for the system to work, small businesses and young people must be compelled to buy insurance on the exchanges, and ironically, every step taken by the Administration so far has undermined achievement of those goals. The Democrats are playing for time and hoping for results, nothing more.

So for President Obama, as he rests with his family in Hawaii, he is no doubt thinking about his next move. His popularity is low and his policies unpopular, but he still controls the regulatory apparatus and the bully pulpit, and he is no doubt planning on heavily using both. Yet the possibility for a political comeback is fading. Most second term presidents have at best 18 months to attain major political goals, after that midterm elections and the next presidential campaign make progress on issues very difficult. President Obama wasted his first year with failed crusades on gun control and immigration, and then self-destructed on Obamacare. His best hope lies in the improving economy, but that will not be enough, because once a politician is seen as ineffective and incompetent, it is hard to recover.

The Republicans also face challenges in 2014. Most party strategists see great opportunities in the midterm election, with control of the House appearing safe, and with the Senate increasingly in play. Yet, the GOP has had a penchant for self-destruction as well, especially those authored by a Tea Party wing that seems to favor purity over victory. The Republicans have little need or desire to cooperate with the President or the Democrats, and for that reason there is little basis for optimism for bipartisanship or progress on policy. So like the Democrats, in 2014 the GOP is focused on political maneuvers to maximize its position for the next election. No doubt the Christmas break has been welcomed by all, but no one should think anything will change when the politicians return in January, the old debates and deadlocks will continue right through November if not longer.

Week 259

(ENROLLED AND ENRAGED)

January 5, 2014

Despite the continuing Holiday season, this week it was easy to discern the early stirrings of politics in Washington. While the President continued his vacation in Hawaii, his staff was busy heralding the success of Obamacare enrollments. At the same time, Administration allies in Congress were focusing on long-term unemployment benefits, which expired at the end of 2013. Democrats see both issues as opportunities to turn the political tide, and decided not to wait until after the Holidays to begin the politicking.

Everyone seems to understand that Obamacare was the issue that hurt Democrats the most at the end of 2013 and poses the biggest dangers for the 2014 midterm elections. With this in mind, the Administration just before the New Year's Holiday was eager to announce updated Obamacare enrollment numbers. The White House announced that more than one million Americans enrolled for Obamacare on the federal website by year's end, and after adding in enrollments from the state-operated websites, that enrollment figure approached two million. Supporters of Obamacare were quick to point to these numbers as a sign that the program has turned the corner, hoping to blunt any political damage from the botched rollout.

Republicans, however, took a very different view. The Administration had projected that three million would enroll by year's end, and that target was missed by more than thirty percent. Also, the White House was counting as enrolled anyone who was able to enter the required information on the website. Thus, the GOP argued these enrollment numbers do not reflect people who actually have insurance. Also, there were continuing problems with data transfers to insurance companies. So the risk emerged that many people will think they have insurance starting January 1, 2014, but actually do not. Further, the Administration has resisted giving demographic data on those enrolling. For the program to work, young healthy people must enroll to buy private insurance. Little or no data has been provided to show that the young are enrolling in sufficient numbers. Also insurers continue to complain that the host of exemptions issued by the Administration are only going to confuse the market and cause more problems. For example, most recently the Administration exempted those with cancelled plans from penalties in 2014, creating even more disparities in treatment.

Given all this, it is clear Democrats will not be able to quickly diffuse the problems with Obamacare, so they hope for better luck with unemployment benefits. The budget deal reached at the end of 2013 did not include an extension of unemployment benefits, an important priority for Democrats both on policy and as a political wedge issue. Using the historically cold weather and the Holiday as a backdrop, the Democrats began their attacks on Republicans, calling them heartless and cruel for not extending unemployment benefits. They also made clear they plan to make unemployment benefits a key election issue. For its part, the GOP questioned the need to extend unemployment benefits given the strengthening economy, better employment data, and the view that extended unemployment benefits actually leads to more unemployment because it reduces the motivation to look for work.

Senate Democrats plan to take up an unemployment extension bill as their first priority in 2014. However, the fate of any unemployment extension does not look good in the Republican controlled House. At a minimum, the GOP will demand offsetting cuts to pay for the $6.5 billion cost for an extension in 2014, and given how important the issue is for Democrats, they may ask for even more beyond that. So despite the New Year's parties and the Holiday spirit, Washington was quickly getting ready to return to business as usual.

Week 260
(JAMMED UP)

January 12, 2014

One might have expected Washington to turn to serious business after President Obama and lawmakers returned after the Christmas break, but that was not the case. Instead, Washington was gripped by two very different political distractions, which consumed conversation in the Capitol, at least until the unemployment report came out on January 10, which brought everyone back to reality. The first distraction was a memoir by former Defense Secretary Robert Gates, and the second was trafficgate, Chris Christie's scandal of political retribution. Neither is a story likely to last, but both together captured the attention of the political class to the exclusion of all else.

The week started with a familiar episode in Washington, the tell all memoir, but this time from an unexpected source. Although a Republican, Robert Gates has served many administrations, both Democrat and Republican. He was President George W. Bush's Secretary of Defense, and was asked to stay on by President Obama. He served in that post for some three years while the United States extricated itself from Iraq, pursued the Afghanistan surge, and launched the operation that killed Osama bin Laden. By all accounts his book, entitled "Duty," is balanced, but it takes a few shots as well. It asserts that Hillary Clinton has admitted that her opposition to the Iraq surge was political. It states that Vice President Biden was wrong about nearly every major foreign policy issue for the last 40 years. And it claims that President Obama did not believe in the mission in Afghanistan, viewed it has someone else's war, and was focused on getting out, not success.

There is nothing really surprising in any of these revelations. Vice President Biden's record on foreign policy is known to be sporty, almost all positions taken by the Democrats on Iraq were political, and President Obama's lack of commitment to the War in Afghanistan is evident. So the allegations were not so much the news, as much as who was making them and what impact they would have on the Obama Administration. Gates had been viewed as a Washington wise man, serious and impartial. As a result, his decision to publically criticize the Administration naturally garnered attention. Observers were also focused on the impact on a White House that rarely accepts criticism, and a President who prides himself as a strong leader. In truth, the book is fairly complimentary of the President, so all the talk about it was more political parlor games than anything else.

Not so with the scandal in New Jersey that was the other focus of the media. Chris Christie is a rising star in the Republican Party and won a landslide reelection victory in 2013. However, since September 2013, there have been rumors that the Christie Administration closed down two access lanes to the George Washington Bridge to punish Fort Lee Mayor Mark Sokolich's refusal to endorse Christie. The governor denied this throughout the campaign. Then this week, in response to various subpoenas, emails were released that showed that Christie officials did indeed close the lanes as political punishment. In response, Christie fired his chief of staff Bridget Ann Kelly and Port Authority Board Member David Wildstein had to resign and take the Fifth Amendment under questioning. Christie also had to give a two hour press conference on January 9 to explain and apologize.

Unlike the Gates book, this was a true political scandal that could hurt a very promising politician. Christie was viewed by many as having a good shot at winning the GOP presidential nomination. He has a reputation for straight talk, but this scandal makes him look more like a bully. To date there is no evidence that he knew what his aides were doing. If that remains the case, he will likely survive the scandal, but if evidence is uncovered that he knew, then his political future is in doubt, because in his press conference and on many other occasions he asserted no knowledge whatsoever of the reasons for the lane closures.

Both the Gates story and the Christie scandal were great fun for Washington types, and distracted from the important political debates of the day, on Obamacare and extending unemployment insurance. However, reality hit home with the unemployment report on January 10, showing only 74,000 jobs created in December, and the unemployment rate that dropped to 6.7% because 347,000 people left the workforce. So while Washington was distracted, in the real world, real data showed many are still struggling.

Week 261

(I SPY)

January 19, 2014

Of the many challenges that have faced President Obama in his second term, possibly the most damaging has been the NSA spying scandal. Not only have the revelations by Edward Snowden damaged U.S. intelligence and strained U.S.-Russia relations with his flight to that country for sanctuary, but the information he published revealed the vast extent of the government's intelligence apparatus and the huge amount of data collected not overseas, but in America. The reason the NSA scandal has been so damaging to the White House is that it has shaken the faith of the liberal and progressive constituencies who have been the base of President Obama's support. The revelations of vast NSA spying on ordinary Americans, the collection of records on nearly every phone call placed in the United States, and the stories of government pressure put on technology companies to provide access to sensitive customer data matched the worst fears of privacy groups. So the President has been forced to act and atone for policies that many of his supporters would never have thought he would pursue.

President Obama won the presidency in large part based on his criticism of the intelligence and interrogation policies of the Bush Administration. However, once he took office and became more acquainted with the terrorist threats facing America, he seemed to transform from critic to advocate, supporting vast data collection programs by the NSA. On this and so many other issues, President Obama seems to have continued the policies of the Bush Administration, rather than curtailing them. Before Edward Snowden, this reality was largely obscured, but once he started to share the top secret information to which he had access, the true extent of the President's conversion became clear.

This poses a real political problem for the President. With the difficult economy, the unpopularity of Obamacare, and the normal and natural decline most second term Presidents see in their popularity, the NSA scandal threatened to push the President's support below acceptable levels, because the voters most upset about the NSA's spying are liberal groups who usually support the Administration. With this in mind, on January 17, the President gave a much anticipated address on the NSA scandal and reforms designed to balance civil liberties and security needs. What the President had to say was surely balanced, but hardly satisfied privacy advocates.

The President's address began with a history lesson on intelligence gathering, from the Revolutionary War, to the Civil War, World War II, and the Cold War. The message was that intelligence gathering is part of our history and necessary for our security. Then the President noted that September 11 created a new urgency for enhanced intelligence: "It is hard to overstate the transformation America's intelligence community had to go through after 9/11. Our agencies suddenly needed to do far more than the traditional mission of monitoring hostile powers and gathering information for policymakers." Despite the successes of our enhance intelligence capabilities, the President noted the risks: "it is a testimony to the hard work and dedication of the men and women of our intelligence community that over the past decade we've made enormous strides in fulfilling this mission. Today, new capabilities allow intelligence agencies to track who a terrorist is in contact with and follow the trail of his travel or his funding. . . . And yet, in our rush to respond to a very real and novel set of threats, the risk of government overreach, the possibility that we lose some of our core liberties in pursuit of security also became more pronounced."

Next, the President tried to cast himself as a reformer on intelligence, trying to emphasize the limitations and protections he put in place, but stating: "What I did not do is stop these programs wholesale, not only because I felt that they made us more secure, but also because nothing in that initial review and nothing that I have learned since indicated that our intelligence community has sought to violate the law or is cavalier about the civil liberties of their fellow citizens." Then the President had to deal with the real reason for his speech, namely Edward Snowden: "I'm not going to dwell on Mr. Snowden's actions or his motivations. I will say that our nation's defense depends in part on the fidelity of those entrusted with our nation's secrets. If any individual who objects to government policy can take it into their own hands to publicly disclose classified information, then we will not be able to keep our people safe, or conduct foreign policy."

The President made clear his displeasure with the Snowden revelations, and then set about announcing reforms. "First, I have approved a new presidential directive for our signals intelligence activities both at home and abroad. This guidance will strengthen executive branch oversight of our intelligence activities. . . . Second, we will reform programs and procedures in place to provide greater transparency to our surveillance activities and fortify the safeguards that protect the privacy of US persons. . . . [and] going forward, I'm directing the director of national intelligence, in consultation with the attorney general, to annually review for the purposes of declassification any future opinions of the court with broad privacy implications and to report to me and to Congress on these efforts. . . . I'm also calling on Congress to authorize the establishment of a panel of advocates from outside government to provide an independent voice in significant cases before the Foreign Intelligence Surveillance Court. . . . Third, we will provide additional protections for activities conducted under Section 702, which allows the government to intercept the communications of foreign targets overseas who have information that's important for our national security. Specifically, I'm asking the attorney general and DNI to institute reforms that place additional restrictions on government's ability to retain, search and use in criminal cases communications between Americans and foreign citizens incidentally collected under Section 702."

While all are interesting reforms, none addressed the biggest issue created by the Snowden leaks, namely the NSA's collection of data on phone calls in the United States. On that issue the President announced that: "I am therefore ordering a transition that will end the Section 215 bulk metadata program as it currently exists and establish a mechanism that preserves the capabilities we need without the government holding this bulk metadata." The President offered no definite plan, but it seems the Administration intends to continue to collect the phone data, but will have a third party hold it and the government will only get access based on a showing of need. As with the rest of the speech, the President tried to satisfy two opposing constituencies: security and privacy advocates. The result was a policy address that was balanced and thoughtful, but unlikely to satisfy either constituency, meaning the controversy will continue, much to the dismay of the White House.

Week 262

(PEACE AND WAR)

January 26, 2014

With Republicans and Democrats both preparing for the State of the Union and the inevitable political battles that will ensure after, most of Washington's attention this week was turned to issues of war and peace overseas. A Syrian peace conference, protests in Ukraine, car bombings in Egypt, and the continued security deterioration in Afghanistan all pointed to a rocky road ahead. In addition, evidence of slowing growth in China and other emerging economies led to a significant sell-off on Wall Street. So at least for this week, foreign affairs took center stage.

Syria has been a sore for the Obama Administration for years, and Secretary of State Kerry is in an all-out effort to salvage American prestige and end the killing. President Obama has been very reluctant to intervene in Syria, limiting material help for the opposition to President Assad and grasping at Russia's offer of chemical disarmament to avoid military action. Predictably, the destruction of Syria's chemical weapons has fallen behind schedule, but the civil war continues on pace, with the Assad regime steadily gaining the upper hand. Trying to broker a peace, Secretary Kerry hosted a UN sponsored peace conference in Geneva. The problem was, the key requirement for a peace deal – removal of President Assad – was also the key point of contention. The opposition and the U.S. are demanding it. The Assad regime flatly refuses to step down. So while the parties met and hurled accusations at each other, the sides got no closer to peace.

The situation in the Ukraine is little better. Ever since President Yanukovych decided to reject an trade deal with the EU in favor of a pact with Russia, protesters have taken to the streets to demand his ouster. The protests have gone on for many weeks now, and have turned ever more violent, with Ukraine security forces using brutal tactics to suppress the protests. President Yanukovych has attempted compromise, but the opposition has to date refused, setting up a confrontation that could lead to a civil war in Ukraine.

Given the problems in Syria and Ukraine, U.S. policymakers surely hoped that the remainder of the Middle East might be less restive, at least momentarily. No such luck. In Egypt, the struggle between the military government and the Muslim Brotherhood took a disturbing turn, with car bomb attacks in Cairo. These attacks, surely perpetrated by the Brotherhood or its allies, raised the specter of an Iraq style insurgency in Egypt. That is an unwelcome image, especially in view of the ongoing strife in Iraq, where this week rebels consolidated control of Fallajuh, a city for which many Americans gave their lives. Further east, Afghanistan President Karzi continued to refuse to agree to a deal to allow 10,000 U.S. troops to stay in Afghanistan to support security efforts, creating the possibility of a full U.S. pullout, one that might usher in a Taliban takeover.

None of this is welcome news for an Obama Administration that is increasingly unpopular and viewed as ineffective. The combination of foreign failures and controversial policies at home could further weaken the Administration and thwart the President's hopes for a political comeback. The stock market sell off this week made this possibility even more concerning, because at least until now the White House could point to an improving economy, but if that too falls away, it will hard for the President to find a refuge. So as the President prepared for his State of the Union, he has many more challenges on his plate than he might have expected even just a few short weeks ago.

Week 263

(MR. ACTION)

February 2, 2014

Nearly all observers on both the Right and the Left have recognized that President Obama's second term is off to a rocky start. Realizing that, the White House hoped to use the State of the Union as a reset opportunity. The goal was to show the President as a strong, successful, and moderate leader trying to get an unruly and dysfunctional Washington to work. The President's entire speech, which was very long indeed, was devoted to that task. And while the speech was long on rhetoric, but anybody really listening heard a speech that seemed just a repeat of past campaign rhetoric.

The President started his speech by listing Washington's successes, a clear attempt to convince Americans that things really are better, even if they do not feel it or believe it. He claimed: "And here are the results of your efforts: the lowest unemployment rate in over five years; a rebounding housing market — a manufacturing sector that's adding jobs for the first time since the 1990's — more oil produced — more oil produced at home than we buy from the rest of the world, the first time that's happened in nearly twenty years — our deficits cut by more than half; and for the first time in over a decade, business leaders around the world have declared that China is no longer the world's number one place to invest; America is."

Having set the premise of how good things are getting, the President moved immediately to cast himself as a man of action: "And in the coming months let's see where else we can make progress together. Let's make this a year of action. That's what most Americans want, for all of us in this chamber to focus on their lives, their hopes, their aspirations. And what I believe unites the people of this nation, regardless of race or region or party, young or old, rich or poor, is the simple, profound belief in opportunity for all, the notion that if you work hard and take responsibility, you can get ahead in America." The President listed many items for his year of action, but combating income inequality was the first item on his list: "Today, after four years of economic growth, corporate profits and stock prices have rarely been higher, and those at the top have never done better. But average wages have barely budged. Inequality has deepened. Upward mobility has stalled. The cold, hard fact is that even in the midst of recovery, too many Americans are working more than ever just to get by; let alone to get ahead. And too many still aren't working at all."

The President then laid out a vague plan for combating income inequality, involving past themes of closing tax loopholes, rewarding hard work, and education funding. Yet for a problem the President described as so dire, he offered few details on how to address it, other than asserting that he would not wait for Congress and would take as many steps by executive action as he could. Then quickly, the President moved on to a typical laundry list of objectives that makes addresses like this so hard to endure. The President called for immigration reform, knowing full well that any new law is unlikely. He tasked Vice President Biden with reforming federal job training programs, a system so wasteful, redundant, and unsuccessful that one wondered whether it was a reward or a punishment for the Vice President. The President pushed for a higher minimum wage, even though that will never come up for a vote in the House, yet alone pass. He then touted a new retirement vehicle to be implemented by the federal government: "Let's do more to help Americans save for retirement. Today most workers don't have a pension. A Social Security check often isn't enough on its own. And while the stock market has doubled over the last five years, that doesn't help folks who don't have 401(k)s. That's why tomorrow I will direct the Treasury to create a new way for working Americans to start their own retirement savings: MyRA. It's a – it's a new savings bond that encourages folks to build a nest egg."

Then the President came to Obamacare, with his message being, the law is working and Republicans should give up, because it is here to stay: "Now, I do not expect to convince my Republican friends on the merits of this law. But I know that the American people are not interested in refighting old battles. So again, if you have specific plans to cut costs, cover more people, increase choice, tell America what you'd do differently. Let's see if the numbers add up. But let's not have another 40- something votes to repeal a law that's already helping millions of Americans like Amanda." The fact that Obamacare was addressed so late in the speech spoke volumes, the Democrats are stuck with it, but want to downplay it as much as possible, at least until after the next election. The speech ended with a quick march through foreign policy, clearly the lowest item on the President's agenda, with the only notable item a veto threat of any new Iran sanctions bill.

Like many Presidents, he ended the speech with inspirational phrases: "The America we want for our kids — a rising America where honest work is plentiful and communities are strong; where prosperity is widely shared and opportunity for all lets us go as far as our dreams and toil will take us — none of it is easy. But if we work together; if we summon what is best in us . . .

with our feet planted firmly in today but our eyes cast towards tomorrow, I know it's within our reach." Some nice rhetoric, but again, was anybody listening.

Week 264

(NOT WORKING)

February 9, 2014

In his effort to show strength and decisiveness, President Obama in recent months has emphasized his ability to act unilaterally without the support of Congress. Taking that approach has allowed him to score a few rhetorical points, but on policy, the gains have been limited and the cost is starting to show. Now the Republicans are using the President's increasing reliance on executive authority as an excuse not to work with him. Worse still, the President continues to take hits on Obamacare, with more revelations this week that the law is going to reduce the nation's workforce by encouraging people not to work. So for all the muscular talk, the President seems weaker and even less capable of accomplishing his goals. Only a few weeks into the President's self-proclaimed "year of action," it is starting to look like anything but.

One disadvantage of emphasizing your ability to legislate without Congress is that it makes Congress less likely to grant a president any additional authority that he might abuse. So as President Obama has gotten more and more aggressive with use of executive orders, his Republican opponents in Congress have pointed to his actions as a reason not to work with him. Immigration is the latest and possibly the best example. In 2013, the Senate passed a bipartisan immigration reform bill. Speaker Boehner made clear his interest in pursuing immigration reform in the House, but as he was trying to craft a bill, House conservatives rebelled, in part because they feared that if a new law were passed, the White House would only enforce those portions it liked.

Despite that, the House GOP leadership tried to craft a bill that would win the support of the Republican caucus. Unfortunately, this week that effort collapsed. Speaker Boehner tried to get his Republican members to support an immigration reform bill, one less ambitious than he Senate bill, but still an effort at reform. After weeks of effort, the Speaker gave up. He hosted a press conference where he blamed the President, saying his members do not trust the White House and believe the President will abuse any new authority Congress might give him. So immigration reform is dead, in part because of the conduct of its leading proponent, the President himself.

Now the Administration was quick to say that Speaker Boehner was just making excuses for his own inability to control his majority, and that is certainly true in part. But there is a deeper reality as well. Republicans in Congress increasingly have no reason to work with the President on anything. They believe the President is abusing his authority and the White House's constant campaigning and the President's unwillingness to engage on any issue makes legislative progress increasingly less likely. Congress passed a farm bill this week, but that was a bipartisan effort where White House involvement was minimal. That might be the last major legislation for 2013. All that is left is positioning for the 2014 election, which is increasingly looking bad for the Democrats.

Maybe the President hoped that by talking tough he could build momentum, but it is simply not working. Republicans refused to extend unemployment benefits, and do not appear under any political pressure to rethink that decision. The economy remains week, as evidenced by another poor jobs report for January, with only 113,000 jobs created. Even worse, Obamacare is not getting more popular and indeed even the CBO is supplying ammunition to the GOP. This week the CBO reported that Obamacare will shrink the workforce by more than 2 million jobs because it will disincentivize work. The White House has seen CBO as its ally on Obamacare, and now its ally is helping its critics. So we have a President unable to pass any significant legislation, and what legislation he has passed is unpopular. We have GOP members in Congress seeing no reason or benefit to do anything other than focus on the midterm election. We have Democrats in Congress who can do very little without GOP support. In total, it is recipe for no one in Washington doing much real work for the remainder of 2014. The year of action appears dead, before it ever got started.

Week 265

(INDEBTED)

February 16, 2014

Ever since the Republicans took control of the House of Representatives in January 2011, the debt limit has been a political flash point. In August 2011 the struggle over the debt limit rattled markets and led to the sequester deal with the White House. There was another debt limit fight 2012 and the budget and debt limit confrontation in September 2013 led to a government shutdown. Given this track record, it seemed almost remarkable that with little fight or fanfare, Congress increased the Debt limit on February 12. Some might see this as a return to bipartisanship, but as with most things in Washington, this was just more political maneuvering by other means.

It is fair to say that the Democrats have won the political battles over the budget and the debt limit. However, while losing on the politics, the Republicans have had substantive successes. The sequester was born from a debt limit fight, and that provision led to the first real cut in federal domestic spending in decades. The fiscal cliff fight in December 2012 resulted in a tax increase, but one far smaller than Democrats wanted and rates for the vast majority of Americans remained below the levels in place in 2001. The recent 2014 budget deal restored some of the sequester cuts, but paid for them almost entirely with other spending cuts and kept overall spending levels well below 2010 levels. So while the politics have been bad for the GOP, the policy results have been respectable, especially considering that Republicans control only the House.

With this background, as we approached the debt limit battle of February 2014, many Republican leaders wanted to avoid another epic confrontation. Instead, they hoped to add a few favored measures to a debt limit increase, but not demand major policy changes. That was the goal Speaker Boehner had in mind when he met with his caucus to plot a debt limit strategy. The problem was, a group of his most conservative members would not go along with his strategy. They wanted to push for another confrontation with the White House and would not support adding only modest measures–like approval of the Keystone Pipeline or changes in veteran pension cuts – to a debt limit bill. So Speaker Boehner did not have 218 votes and knew he would get no support from Democrats.

Faced with this all too familiar situation, the Speaker had two choices. Force another confrontation, or bring up a clean debt limit increase bill and pass it with mostly Democrat votes. He chose the latter course. On February 10, GOP-controlled House passed the debt-ceiling measure on a 221-201 vote, with only 28 Republicans supporting it compared to the 199 who opposed it. Meanwhile, 193 Democrats backed the measure with only two voting "no." The Senate GOP leadership planned to adopt the same approach, and allow a vote on a clean debt limit increase where all Republicans could vote "no." Again, conservatives messed up the plan. Texas Senator Ted Cruz started a filibuster of the debt limit bill. This forced a dozen Republicans, including Senate Minority Leader Mitch McConnell, to join Democrats to overcome the filibuster on a 67-31 procedural vote. The Democratic-controlled Senate then gave final approval by a 55-43 party-line vote. Most Republicans were furious with Cruz, because his filibuster gambit forced them to support closure, making it look like they supported the debt limit increase.

Most of the media reported these events as yet another GOP defeat and a sign of the continuing civil war within the Republican Party, but in truth there is much more going on. With Obamacare still very unpopular, job growth slow, the economy weak, and the President unpopular, GOP leaders saw no benefit to forcing a confrontation with Democrats over the debt limit in advance of the 2014 midterm election. They want to keep the upcoming election about Obama, not them. Also, if they make substantial gains in 2014, they will be in a strong position for debt limit and budget battles in 2015. So this uneventful debt limit increase was mostly political tactics, and not bipartisanship.

Week 266
(BATTLE STATIONS)

February 23, 2014

More and more political analysts are coming to the conclusion that 2014 is going to be a very rough election for the President and his party. While Minority leader Pelosi and Senator Reid continue to talk optimistically, the reality is that the Democrats have no hope of taking the House and are now in real jeopardy of losing the Senate. The bad climate for Democrats stems not only from the historical pattern of the party in power losing seats in midterm elections, but also from the economy and Obamacare. Even worse, the electoral landscape is bad for Democrats. In the last redistricting, Republicans drew lines to create as many safe Republican seats as possible, making it very difficult for Democrats to achieve substantial gains. In the Senate, there are 36 seats up in 2014, 21 held by Democrats and 15 by Republicans. However, many of those Democrat seats are in States carried by Romney, while only two Republican seats are currently competitive. All this adds up to a tough year for Democrats.

Faced with this reality, President Obama had two basic choices to try to change the dynamic. Seek bipartisan compromises to address voter discontent on the economy and Obamacare or circle the wagons and go political. The President made clear this week that he is choosing the later course. The first indications came with leaks about the upcoming White House budget proposal. Last year, the Administration proposed some modest cuts to Social Security and Medicare, along with additional tax increases. Democrats opposed the entitlement cuts and Republicans would not support the tax increases, so the President's budget proposal went nowhere.

Under pressure from Democrats, the White House made known that this year's budget proposal would be very different. Calling for an end to the era of austerity, the White House leaked that the new budget plan would not include the entitlement cuts, would again call for a wide range of tax increases, and would seek additional federal discretionary spending on a host of projects. To make the plan look balanced, the Administration is forecasting a reduction in health costs to cover the new spending. How this conclusion of slowing health care costs was reached remains a mystery, but no doubt it was formulated to hide the deficit implications of the President's proposed new spending.

What this budget means is that the President is giving up on any serious budget efforts for the remainder of 2014. Instead, this is a campaign budget, designed not to pass but instead to rally the liberal base to their battle stations. This combined with the Administration's efforts to use executive authority to advance progressive policy goals is intended to create enthusiasm on the Left. The same is true with the push for extending unemployment benefits and increasing the minimum wage, neither of which has much chance of passage. In fact, the President's efforts on the minimum wage were dealt a blow this week when the CBO found that the President's increased minimum wage proposal will cost 500,000 jobs. That pretty much put the nail in the coffin for the minimum wage increase, but no doubt the President will keep talking about it.

The turn toward campaign politics was also evident from the announcement that the President would attend six more fundraisers for Democrat candidates. So with all these developments, one simple fact is clear, the Administration's primary focus for 2014 will be politics, or more specifically preventing a political debacle in the midterm. It is safe to say the year of action is officially dead.

Week 267

(RESET?)

March 2, 2014

When President Obama took office, one of his foreign policy goals was a reset in relations with Russia. For a President focused on domestic issues, the last thing the Administration wanted was a new cold war with America's former foe. So the President has tried on multiple occasions to build good relations and common strategies with Russian President Vladimir Putin. But an agenda focused on goodwill has been perceived by Putin as weakness, and rather than supporting American goals, Russia has tried to thwart them at every turn. Russia refused for years to join a strong response to Iranian nuclear ambitions, and only recently joined enhanced international sanctions, sanctions Russia is already working to soften. Despite atrocities in Syria, Russia has supported the Assad regime and called President Obama's bluff on using force in response to Syrian use of chemical weapons. Given this record, when Edward Snowden was looking for a safe haven after he leaked top secret materials on NSA surveillance, it was no surprise Russia was willing to take him in. For Putin, no affront to President Obama is too petty.

But all these provocations have been nothing compared to the Ukraine, where President Putin has revealed that he has so much contempt for President Obama that he will even invade a neighboring country with little fear of repercussions. The Ukraine was part of Russia until 1991 and has a large Russian population. Russia also has a sentimental attachment to the Ukraine and wants it firmly in its sphere of influence. Also, the Russian Black Sea fleet is stationed in Ukraine's Crimea. Given all this, when revolution started to sweep Ukraine, Putin saw his opportunity to act. Putin's strong response was also provoked by how quickly his puppet in Kiev fell from power.

On November 21, 2013, President Yanukovych's government announced it was abandoning an agreement to strengthen ties with the European Union. Protesters then took to the streets. On November 30, 2013, police attacked the protesters. On December 1, a protest attracted around 300,000 people in Kiev's Independence Square, known as the Maidan, the largest since the 2004 Orange Revolution. Activists seized Kiev City Hall. Seeing his client threatened, on December 17, Putin announces that Moscow will buy 15 billion U.S. dollars in Ukrainian government bonds and cut the price Ukrainians pay for Russian natural gas. The protests continued, and in January three protesters died during a confrontation between police and demonstrators manning barricades. The government tried to diffuse the situation, the prime minister resigned and parliament repealed the harsh anti-protest laws that set off the violence. Then on February 18, protesters attacked police lines and set fires outside parliament after it stalled on a constitutional reform to limit presidential powers. Riot police responded to the violence by trying to push protesters out of Independence Square. At least 26 people died and hundreds were injured. Then on February 21, under a European-mediated plan, protest leaders and Mr. Yanukovych agreed to form a new government and hold an early election, but parliament slashed his powers and he fled Kiev. With Ukraine in disarray, Putin saw his chance. On February 27, masked gunmen seize regional parliament and government buildings in Crimea. Mr. Yanukovych was granted refuge in Russia. By March 1, Russian troops had taken over Crimea without firing a shot.

The reaction in Europe and Washington was pure astonishment. Despite its long experience with Putin, the best the Obama Administration could muster was a critique that Putin was employing 20th century strategy in the 21st century. In essence, the White House was mad because Putin was not playing by the rules they think should apply. The truth is that the Obama Administration should have understood for years that Putin plays by his own rules, respects only strength, and will push every advantage until stopped by force or the threat of force. For years he has been playing President Obama for a fool, and the President has been willing to go along because, above all else, the President wants to avoid international conflicts. So after years of American weakness, Putin felt emboldened enough to invade Ukraine. Putin is betting the President will give speeches, condemn Russian aggression, and talk about freedom, but do essentially nothing to stop Russia's moves in Ukraine. Given recent history, the Kremlin has made a safe bet.

Week 268

(ANNEXED)

March 9, 2014

President Obama wanted this week to be about his budget proposal, a plan crafted not for enactment but rather for election politics. The nearly $4 trillion spending plan includes tax increases, ever more stimulus spending, and discards any effort at entitlement reform. It is a plan designed to buy votes and enrage Republicans. The plan was announced on March 4 and the White House had hoped to use it as a tool in the 2014 campaign. The Administration expected Republicans to try to foil his political strategy, but it was actually Vladimir Putin who ruined the White House's plans. Putin's invasion of Crimea crowded out any talk of the President's domestic priorities and highlighted a President who seems always reacting and rarely leading.

Once it became clear that Russia had invaded Crimea, the Administration seemed in disbelief. They could not comprehend that President Putin would act so rashly. What the White House misunderstood is that Putin will pursue Russian national interests as long as there is no force determined to stop him. In the face of Russian aggression, the Administration struggled to find a response. The White House's initial response was weak to say the least, revoking VISAs for Russian officials involved in the invasion. Secretary of State Kerry also reached out to European allies for a more robust sanctions regime, but found opposition. All the while, President Putin poured ever more troops into the Crimea, hoping to settle the issue with firm control on the ground.

Despite warnings from the U.S., Russia then went even further. Its puppets in Crimea announced a referendum for March 16 on whether Crimea should join Russia. This is to be a vote under the barrels of Russian guns. With this announcement, it became clear Putin did not invade Crimea just to send a message, he invaded because he plans to annex Crimea. As bold as this move might be, President Putin signaled he would go even farther, warning the any threats to the Russian populations in Eastern Ukraine could prompt further action by the Kremlin. Far from trying to diffuse the situation, President Putin made every effort to heighten his confrontation with the United States.

Now President Obama has a choice, he can take strong action against President Putin, or he can surrender to events and turn his attention back to domestic concerns. Clearly, President Putin is betting that President Obama will take the later course and that over time Russian control of Crimea will be accepted, setting a precedent for even more aggression in the future. The President continued to make tough statements about the Russian aggression, but for all the rhetoric, the Administration gave few signs of an intent to take any concerted action. Ironically, Crimea is not the only thing President Putin has annexed, because the White House is at risk of losing its agenda to Russia as well.

Week 269
(THAT SINKING FEELING)

March 16, 2014

For months Democrat political operatives have been opining on how the 2014 midterm election will not result in significant Republicans gains because an improving economy, rising popularity of Obamacare, and young and minority voters will turn the tide and blunt the GOP. This theory was so often repeated that many in Washington seemed to start to believe it, against all evidence. Since the 2012 election, the favorite themes of the media has been the civil war within the Republican party and the Democrats demographic advantage. This premise colored most of the mainstream media's coverage, preventing them from seeing what is really going on in the country, namely a significant backlash against the Administration's policies. That all came to an end on March 11, when Republican David Jolly won the special election to fill the empty congressional seat in Florida's 13th Congressional district, defeating heavily favored Democrat Alex Sink. All of a sudden, Democrats across the country started to get a sinking feeling themselves.

Democrats really should not have been surprised, the signs of big trouble in the midterms have been building for weeks. It starts with the President himself, who is deeply unpopular. Poll after poll has shown his approval rating in the low 40s, and sometimes in the 30s. An NBC News Wall Street Journal poll this week found only 41% of the electorate approved of his performance, his worst score ever in that poll. History shows an unpopular President leads to big losses in midterm elections. Even worse, public perceptions of the economy and Obamacare have not improved, in fact in most polls they have stagnated or worsened. The Democrats had hoped that a Republican misstep would change that dynamic, but when Speaker Boehner accepted a debt limit increase that took the last major political issue of 2014 off the table, that made a game changer unlikely. Despite all this, there remained many deniers, at least until the results came in Florida's 13th Congressional District.

The special election was held to fill the seat left vacant by longtime Representative Bill Young (R-Fla.), who died last year. The race has been considered an early test of Obamacare as an election issue going into the 2014 midterms. The Democrats fielded Alex Sink, former 2010 gubernatorial candidate and state treasurer, who was well financed, well known, and well supported by outside Democrat groups. Her GOP opponent was Republican David Jolly, a former Republican staffer and lobbyist in Washington, who had less money and far less name recognition. The district was carried by President Obama in 2008 and 2012 and was thought to be ripe for the picking. When the votes were counted, Jolly had 49 percent of the vote to Sink's 47 percent. More than $11 million had been spent on the race, according to the Sunlight Foundation.

The driving issue in the election was Obamacare. Jolly called for repealing it. Sink religiously followed the Democrat talking points written in Washington of "mend it don't end it." Sink's message failed and Jolly won. There are so many lessons for Democrats in this race that it should keep them up at night. First, despite their vaunted get-out-the-vote capabilities, Democrat voters simply did not show up in sufficient numbers. Second, Jolly made the race about Obamacare and Sink, who was not even in Congress and did not vote for it, still she took the blame both because she is a Democrat and she defended the law. Third, President Obama was a huge liability, with poll after poll showing that voters would vote against Democrats to send a message to the White House.

The panic among Washington Democrats was clear, even if they tried to keep it under the surface. But cracks in the Democrat coalition started to quickly emerge. Last week, the Senate rejected President Obama's nominee to lead the Justice Department's civil rights division in a stunning 47-52 vote in which seven Democrats abandoned their leadership. The reason, he previously defended a cop killer. Then this week, the Senate refused to move forward with President Obama's nominee for Surgeon General because of his statement in support of gun control. Democrats in the Senate appear desperate to distance themselves from the President, and they are looking for any way to do it. It is going to be a rough ride for Democrats, and many appear unwilling to Sink with the ship.

Week 270
(PUTINIZED)

March 23, 2014

Facing a very tough midterm election, for months the Democrats have been crafting their game plan to go on the offensive against the GOP on issues like the minimum wage, unemployment insurance, and income inequality. It was a dubious strategy from the get go because with Obamacare and the President's popularity so low, it would have taken a political transformation of epic proportions to change the political environment. Their best hope was a Republican misstep, but that did not materialize, and worse international events authored by Russia's President Putin have made the President look even weaker.

It has been a theme in Republican circles for years that America is in decline and that the policies of the Obama Administration are hastening the fall. The evidence they point to is America's economic woes, vacillation on Iran, Iraq, Afghanistan, and Syria, and a refusal to confront either Russian or Chinese aggression. Many see America abdicating leadership and creating a vacuum that is being filled by its more ruthless foes. They also see a foreign policy team in the White House they view as naïve and unwilling to take tough actions. Now this critique of a declining America seems self-evident with Russia invading Ukraine.

With the Russian invasion of Crimea, the critique of American decline took center stage, when it became increasingly clear that the United States would loudly condemn the aggression, but was unwilling to do much else. Matters only got worse this week, with the Russian parliament formally approving annexation, President Putin signing the treaty of annexation, and Russian troops aggressively ejecting Ukrainian forces from bases in Crimea. Even worse, to up the ante, Russia is massing forces on the border of Eastern Ukraine, a clear attempt to intimidate the Ukrainians, the Europeans, and America.

In the face of this Russian onslaught, President Obama has had the difficult task of trying to look tough, while not actually doing anything tough. The President has given strong speeches, but that only makes him look like a talker not a fighter. He issued some sanctions against Russian officials, but his initial sanctions package was weaker than the one supported by the Europeans. He added some limited bank sanctions later in the week, but there is little evidence that will get Putin to change course. Even worse, the President has been most forceful on what he will not do. He will not consider any military response, he will not sell arms to the Ukrainians, and he will not honor the 1994 security guaranty the U.S. gave to Ukraine. No doubt these facts have not escaped notice in the Kremlin.

It is fair to say that even a very aggressive response from the Administration likely would not have stopped Russia's grab in Crimea. However, President Obama's weak response has given ammunition to his critics who say he is weak on foreign affairs. It did not help matters that in recent weeks the White House promoted a plan to substantiality cut military spending, which only added to the perception of a President not only willing to accept decreased American influence, but one actually promoting it. And all the while, Putin continues to embarrass President Obama and get what he wants. It seems nice guys do finish last after all.

Week 271

(SPRING BREAKING)

March 30, 2014

It is Spring Break in Washington, so the First Family hit the road to separate ends of the earth to send messages to friends and foes, and at least for the First Lady, get a tour for herself, her two kids, and her mother at taxpayer expense. The White House billed Michelle Obama's trip to China as an opportunity to build good relations and send strong messages about America's dedication to freedom and free speech. For his part, President Obama was on a mission to send messages himself, to the Russian President, to Western Europeans, the Pope, and the Saudi's. The President's trip was high on rhetoric and low on accomplishments, while the First Lady's trip was little more than a public relations junket for her and her family.

Michelle Obama has gone on a number of supposedly official trips that really look a lot like vacations. Spain, Africa, Europe, and now China. She has been criticized for these trips in the past, but that did not seem to deter her from heading out for Spring Break with her family (other than the President), for sightseeing and some speech-making in China. The First Lady performed her limited official functions well, giving speeches that carefully called for more openness without openly insulting her hosts. No doubt the trip was heavily covered in China and throughout Asia and might have had some public relations benefits, but in the past the Chinese have responded mostly to pressure, not charm, and the First Lady carefully avoided confrontation.

On the other side of the world, President Obama's goal was confrontation, of the rhetorical type, with Vladimir Putin. On March 24 and 25, the President travelled to the Netherlands for a Nuclear Security Summit, bilateral meetings with President Xi Jinping of China, and a G-7 Leadership meeting. The agenda was about nuclear weapons and economic growth, but the true focus was Russia and its annexation of Crimea. President Obama gave a number of tough speeches denouncing Russia's conduct, and the G-7 announced that Russia would be suspended from the group and its meeting in June in Sochi, Russia was cancelled. President Putin laughed off these slights, and continued to tighten his grip on Crimea.

On March 26, the President continued his European tour in Belgium meeting with EU officials, again with the focus heavily on Russia. Then on March 27, the President flew to Italy for a much anticipated meeting with Pope Francis. That meeting was one of the few events in this trip not dominated by the crisis in the Crimea. Instead, President Obama hoped to enlist the help of the Pope for his crusade to reduce income inequality in the United States. By all accounts, the President and the Pope had a productive one hour meeting, with the White House claiming agreement on many issues, and the Vatican politely taking a much more measured tone. While the first part of his trip was about sending a message to Russia, this meeting was about domestic issues and an attempt get spiritual support for more income redistribution at home.

The last stop on the President's trip was probably the most difficult one. On March 28, the President flew to Saudi Arabia for a meeting with King Abdullah. The meeting was hastily arranged after Saudi officials criticized American policy on Iran and Syria and threatened to "go it alone." Saudi Arabia has traditionally been America's closest Arab ally, but the Saudi's are getting increasingly nervous that the United States will not protect them from foreign threats. Washington's endorsement of the overthrow of President Mubarak, warming relations with Shite Iran, and the failure of the Administration to follow through with airstrikes in Syria have left the Saudi's feeling vulnerable. So this visit, scheduled at the last minute and without the usual fanfare of speeches and tours, was designed to calm and reassure the Saudi's. So on both ends of the globe the Obama's worked to build friends and warn enemies, but for now it is not clear anything was really accomplished other than some interesting travel at taxpayer expense.

Week 272

(7.1 MILLION)

April 6, 2014

The White House has been desperate for good news on Obamacare for many months. Following the disastrous launch of Healthcare.gov, to the cancellations of millions of health insurance plans, to the numerous delays and changes to the law by executive order, Obamacare was becoming more of a joke than a policy achievement. That is why the March 31 open enrollment deadline was so crucial to the Administration. It was a last chance to right the ship and try to start to build momentum for the new law, and when the numbers came in, President Obama and his allies were quick to claim victory.

The Administration has known for many months that the open enrollment deadline was a critical marker for the success of Obamacare. The program is founded on the proposition that millions of American would buy private health insurance from the government run health exchanges. Without those new customers, rates would rise and the law might become untenable. So the White House continually changed the rules and extended the deadlines to give the maximum time and options to get the maximum number of new signups for health care coverage.

When the numbers finally came even, even the most ardent critics of the law had to admire the all-out effort the Administration put into getting people to sign up. The Administration had originally projected 7 million signups by March 31, lowered that benchmark to 6 million, but when the numbers came in achieved signups of 7.1 million. A huge success, at least on the surface. President Obama quickly took the podium to proclaim the debate about repealing Obamacare was over and nervous Democrats in Congress saw some hope for a 2014 election. So at first blush, things were certainly looking better for Obamacare, the President, and the Democrats.

However, underneath the story is much more complicated. The 7.1 million enrollment figure included anyone who had started the sign-up process on the federal and state exchanges, but it is not clear how many people will complete the process and enroll for a plan. For those who enroll for a plan, it is not clear how many will pay the first premium. For those who pay the first premium, it is not clear how many will pay the second premium to keep the coverage. It is also not clear how many of the new enrollees are simply people who lost their insurance months before because of Obamacare and now were just getting replacement coverage (such that they are not truly newly insured). Most importantly, it is far from clear that enough young, healthy people have signed up for insurance on the exchanges.

So the headline was great for Democrats, but it is these details that will determine if Obamacare succeeds or fails. The Administration knows this, and that is why it has been very careful about the data it will release. It rushes to release the big enrollment numbers, but refuses to give the other data, even if it has it. The reason is simple: politics. The detailed data might undermine the success story the White House is trying to paint. So far, they have gotten away with it, partly because they have delayed so many of the truly tough deadlines (like the employer mandate) to make the program look successful and to avoid the political problems of failure. But someday the law as written will have to be enforced and the true success or failure of Obamacare will come into focus. President Obama and his allies know this, which is why whenever an election is looming, they push the hard choices until after the voting. That game can be played for only so long, but at least for now they continue to play it.

Week 273

(NOT AN INCH)

April 13, 2014

After successfully hitting its enrollment target, this week the White House continued its campaign to position Obamacare in the best possible light for the upcoming midterm election. Obamacare has never been popular, but it became a subject for ridicule across the political spectrum when the healthcare.gov website failed spectacularly in October 2013. At that time, GOP opponents and a few Democrats called for Health & Human Services Secretary Kathleen Sebelius to resign. The President steadfastly refused to give in to those calls and plowed ahead with his signature law, albeit with so many modifications and delays one needs a chart to keep track of them. But once the enrollment deadline was met, at least according to White House accounting, the time came to start to clean house, and the first person to feel the broom was Secretary Sebelius.

One of President Obama's most consistent qualities is his loyalty to his team. No matter the trouble they get into, the President has stood by them. Attorney General Holder, Vice President Biden, advisor Susan Rice, and many others have drawn media or GOP scrutiny for various real or asserted missteps, but the President has remained loyal to them throughout. The same was true for Secretary Sebelius in the darkest days of the Obamacare rollout. With the website down and partisan attacks at a fever pitch, it would have been easy to throw Secretary Sebelius to the wolves. It was she who promised Congress over and over again that the website was ready, and it was she who had to take the blame for the disaster that hit during the initial rollout. But despite all the pressure, the President stood by her.

The President's allies would say that he stood by Sebelius out of loyalty, and that is certainly partly true, but there is more going on as well. This is a White House that will never give an inch to its critics. So when a policy disaster hits, as it did with Obamacare in October 2013, many in the White House, including likely the President, would have seen firing Sebelius as conceding something to the GOP. That is something the President will not do. So ironically, the more one of his aides messes up, the more the President comes to the defense, maybe out of loyalty, but largely out of partisanship. But with Obamacare hitting its enrollment target and seeming to operate at least in part, President Obamacare could remove Sebelius without any concession.

Another factor also came into play. Democrats worried that if Sebelius was fired, they would never be able to get another HHS secretary confirmed in the gridlocked Senate. That problem was solved in November 2014, when the Democrat majority changed the filibuster rules to prevent the GOP from stopping cabinet nominees. So now Sebelius could be replaced without the risk of a GOP filibuster. So the stage was set for the April 11 announcement that Sebelius would resign, to be replaced by White House budget office director Sylvia Matthews Burwell. Obama, speaking in the Rose Garden, thanked Sebelius for her "extraordinary service" and said that despite the rocky rollout, Sebelius' team "turned the corner, got it fixed, got the job done, and the final score speaks for itself." With this move the President gets to turn the page, put an experienced government manager in palace, declare a victory, and not give an inch to the GOP. A perfect example of the Obama playbook.

Week 274

(VERY TAXING)

April 20, 2014

For politicians, April 15 is either a day for a press conference or for dodging questions, usually depending on which political party he or she belongs to. Republicans have made a habit of using April 15 to frame their attacks on high federal spending and Democrat tax increases. Democrats in contrast usually just try to keep a low profile. However, this year was a bit different, because after years on high deficits and successful efforts to raise taxes on high income earners, Democrats used a recent CBO report to assert that their fiscal policies are fixing the deficit problem, while Republicans only want to make it worse with giveaways to the rich.

The April 14 update from the CBO on the surface assisted the Democrats in this argument. The CBO reported that "if the current laws that govern federal taxes and spending do not change, the budget deficit in fiscal year 2014 will be $492 billion. Relative to the size of the economy, that deficit—at 2.8 percent of gross domestic product (GDP)—will be nearly a third less than the $680 billion shortfall in fiscal year 2013, which was equal to 4.1 percent of GDP. This will be the fifth consecutive year in which the deficit has declined as a share of GDP since peaking at 9.8 percent in 2009." Great news for President Obama and the Democrats, unless you read further in the CBO report.

While the deficit is falling, the reduction will be short lived, as the CBO advised: "But if current laws do not change, the period of shrinking deficits will soon come to an end. Between 2015 and 2024, annual budget shortfalls are projected to rise substantially—from a low of $469 billion in 2015 to about $1 trillion from 2022 through 2024—mainly because of the aging population, rising health care costs, an expansion of federal subsidies for health insurance, and growing interest payments on federal debt. CBO expects that cumulative deficits during that decade will equal $7.6 trillion if current laws remain unchanged. As a share of GDP, deficits are projected to rise from 2.6 percent in 2015 to about 4 percent near the end of the 10-year period. By comparison, the deficit averaged 3.1 percent of GDP over the past 40 years and 2.3 percent in the 40 years before fiscal year 2008, when the most recent recession began."

So in true Washington fashion, the headlines might help some politicians in the next election, but the problem is far from solved. The reason is simple, despite all the grandstanding, the neither political party is willing to make tough decisions, and the President seems totally unwilling to risk any political capital to solve the problem. For Democrats, they refuse to address entitlement spending, which is driving the deficit. For Republicans, they have taken any additional revenues off the table. As a result, there seems to be no deal to be had, best evidenced by the fact that Senate Democrats decided to not even propose a budget this year.

This strategy might work for the next elections, but the decision to continually kick the can down the road will only make the deficit problem harder to solve. As the CBO noted: "In CBO's baseline projections, federal debt held by the public reaches 78 percent of GDP by 2024, up from 72 percent at the end of 2013 and twice the 39 percent average of the past four decades. . . . As recently as the end of 2007, federal debt equaled just 35 percent of GDP. Such high and rising debt would have serious negative consequences. Federal spending on interest payments would increase considerably when interest rates rose to more typical levels. Moreover, because federal borrowing would eventually raise the cost of investment by businesses and other entities, the capital stock would be smaller, and productivity and wages lower, than if federal borrowing was more limited." The good news for President Obama is that he will be out of office before the next budget crisis hits, but that hardly counts as leadership. But no matter, for this White House, all that counts is the next election, everything else is secondary.

Week 275

(EASTERN ERRORS)

April 27, 2014

One of the strategic goals of the Obama Administration has been a pivot to a more Pacific-focused foreign policy. In an effort to kick start that goal after European and Middle Eastern crises have dominated his foreign policy, this week the President left on a four nation tour of Pacific allies Japan, South Korea, and the Philippines, along with a stop in Malaysia. The objective was to strengthen relations, send a message to China and North Korea, and pursue agreements on trade and security issues. Yet while President was trying to turn the focus to the Pacific, issues in Europe and the Middle East again stole the show and made the President look adrift.

The main criticism of President Obama's foreign policy is that he has been willing to talk tough, but in the end unwilling to take tough actions. Syria might be the best example of this syndrome, where the President said use of chemical weapons would be a "red line," but after they were used, he refused to order airstrikes on Syria, instead opting for an accord written in Moscow to remove Syria's chemical weapons arsenal. That decision, combined with the Administration's Iran nuclear weapons policy, which again opts for multi-lateral diplomacy rather than threats of aggressive American action, in many ways led to the current crisis in Ukraine. Russian President Vladimir Putin has seen in both Iran and Syria that President Obama is simply unwilling to use force unless absolutely compelled to do so. As a result, Putin has been willing to press his claims in the Ukraine, starting with Crimea and now in Eastern Ukraine, because he has little fear of any forceful American response.

The White House hoped that this trip to the Pacific might change the topic and the foreign policy landscape, but those hopes were quickly dashed because in both the Pacific and in Europe, the President was hit with a string a stinging defeats. In Japan, the President had hoped to reach agreement on an international trade deal, but the talks collapsed. At the same time, the accord reached in Geneva with Russia to reduce tensions in Ukraine likewise fell apart as Russia increased its efforts to destabilize Eastern Ukraine. Adding to these woes, the newest round of Arab Israeli peace talks in Geneva also collapsed this week, removing any hope of progress on that intractable problem. Given all these failures, the President was forced to use press conferences in Asia to warn Russia rather than focus on his agenda in the Pacific.

The President's trip to Asia was not without successes. In the Philippines, the President signed a new security accord that will lead to a greater U.S. presence and more security cooperation some 20 years after America was forced to close its large bases in the Philippines. The agreement was an important strategic achievement, but borne more of necessity than opportunity. With the rising power of China, the Philippines felt forced to strengthen ties with the U.S. to ensure their security, so in some ways this accord was more a sign of weakness than strength. Beyond this agreement, the White House was not able to point to any other concrete progress in Asia. There were meetings in Tokyo, security discussions in South Korea, and efforts in Malaysia to address tensions over the anti-terrorism policies, but most of the trip was for show and offered little evidence of strengthening the U.S. position in Asia or moving the focus from the crises in Europe and the Middle East.

In the end, the trip that the White House had hoped would show foreign policy success turned into yet another globe-trotting adventure of big speeches and little progress. If the President had hoped to turn the page on his foreign policy problems, that hope was unrealized because the problems he left behind only got worse, not better. It is likely that the President is now going to be faced with the toughest foreign policy challenges of his presidency, and there appears to be little hope that he is willing to change his penchant for vacillation.

Week 276

(BOOM OR BUST)

May 4, 2014

Democrats cling to varied scenarios that will avoid a crushing electoral defeat in 2014, including Republican missteps, motivating young voters, changing public perceptions on Obamacare, and Tea Party lunacy. To date, none of the hopes has come to fruition, making the prospects for electoral salvation look pretty bleak. Yet for all the scenarios that have yet to pan out, the biggest unknown for the midterm election is the economy, and this week Democrats went from depression to elation as the economic indicators first looked bad and then much better, creating confusion but also hope for Democrats.

While the U.S. economy has been in recovery for more than four years, polls continue to show that a majority of Americans think the nation is still in recession. The reason is simple, while the economy has grown and corporate profits are strong, wages are flat, job growth is slow, food, gas, heating, and health care are more expensive, and the housing recovery has been uneven. So economists might see a recovery, but to the average middle class voter, times continue to feel very tough and household budgets remain stressed. It seems Democrat strategists have figured this out, because they are now advising Democrat candidates to avoid the word "recovery," because polling has shown that word drives voters crazy because they do not see a real recovery that is helping their lives.

Given all this, when GDP numbers for the first quarter were announced early this week, Democrats went from nervous to outright despondent. On April 30 the Commerce Department reported that economic growth in the first quarter had slowed to .1%, meaning the economy had essentially stalled. Economists pointed to many factors, including the unusually cold winter, but in the end the growth number was far below expectations and led many to believe, at least temporarily, that the recovery was at risk. Depression reigned, until two days later. On May 2, the Labor Department reported on job creation and unemployment for April 2014. The report showed job growth of 288,000, well above projection, and much of the growth was in higher paying job sectors. Very good news, especially in view of the GDP number. The Labor Department also revised upward the job creation totals for prior months. This all painted a picture of a recovering job market. The unemployment rate dropped to 6.3%, which on the surface sounded great, until one took a closer look at the numbers. Most of the unemployment rate drop was caused by more than 800,000 workers leaving the workforce, bringing the labor force participation to the lowest level in decades.

What to make of this contrasting data. It seems unclear whether we are in the midst of a boom or a bust. Likely, the reality is that some Americans are doing very well in this economy, while many, many more are doing poorly. Weak wage growth, a declining workforce, and rising cost of living is crushing the middle class, while higher earners are doing well. An ironic result for a President who says economic inequality is the defining issue of our time. In truth, the Obama economy has been great for the affluent and bad for the middle class, in part because federal policies have not been focused on economic growth or job creation but rather on regulation and redistribution. So we have an economy where wage earners suffer while owners and investors prosper. All this means the economy is not a likely savior for the Democrats. The pressure on the middle class continues and no matter what government agencies report, most average wage earners are going to continue to feel as though the recession continues. It seems Democrats are going to need to continue their search for a savior.

Week 277

(BENGAHZI'ED)

May 11, 2014

Every recent two-term President has faced a major scandal in his second term. For Nixon it was Watergate, Reagan –Iran Contra, Clinton–Monica Lewinsky, and for George W. Bush, it was Iraq and torture. No doubt Republicans have been pining for a major scandal to rock President Obama's second term and derail the Administration's agenda. There have been some opportunities, most notably the IRS's program of targeting conservative groups. While no doubt a headache for the President, no obvious evidence emerged on a connection between the program and the White House, making the issue a less than ideal scandal for the GOP. The only other scandal of significance was the effort to spin and cover-up the true story of the September 11, 2012 Benghazi attack that killed the US ambassador. However, this one seemed too complicated and too attenuated to serve Republican purposes, at least until this week when the White House itself gave the GOP a helping hand.

The Republicans' theory about Benghazi has been an Administration so obsessed with victory in the 2012 election that it ignored warnings of the attack, refused to attempt a rescue when the attack started, and then lied about the origins of the attack after Americans had been killed. Most famously, UN Ambassador Susan Rice went on the Sunday morning talk shows right after the attack and claimed it was not a terrorist incident, but instead was an impromptu protest against an anti-Muslim video. That was obvious spin, since documents obtained in various investigations show that the assault was recognized early on as a planned attack to coincide with the anniversary of September 11. The GOP theory has always been the spin was directed by the White House for political reasons. The Administration consistently denied that, and the Republicans had to date no evidence to counter that. However, this week the White House was forced to release previously withheld emails that showed that the spin was indeed directed by the Administration, and in response the House has now set up a special committee to investigate Benghazi. A scandal that once seemed dead has now returned.

The position of the Administration has been that when Susan Rice blamed the Benghazi attack on an anti-Muslim video, she was simply reflecting intelligence assessments. However, the thousands of emails released relating to the intelligence community's talking points and intelligence assessments mention the anti-Muslim video only twice, and never as the proximate cause of the attack. The White House also claimed that the talking points used by Ms. Rice were not re-written by the White House and that Administration officials only made stylistic changes to the draft. The documents released this week show that is false and that the White House removed all or part of six paragraphs from the draft, 148 out of 248 words. For example, the word "attacks" was changed to "demonstrations." This truth only came out when the White House lost a legal battle and was forced to release these emails under a FOIA request. However, just before release, the Administration on February 5, 2014 classified previously unclassified sections of the emails, making sure that content will not be released until at least 2019.

The White House has clearly been lying and stonewalling the investigation, but by doing that so aggressively, they have spurred it. Speaker Boehner has now set up a special committee to investigate the cover-up, and Democrats cannot decide whether to participate or boycott. The Administration's media strategy has been to call the entire controversy a political witch hunt. White House spokesman Jay Carney even went so far as to try to argue that certain of the newly released emails that were clearly about Benghazi actually were not. So the same Administration strategy continues. However, it is not clear what will come of all this. The mainstream media seems little interested and same is true for most of the public. Despite that, the GOP is likely to continue to pursue the issue, in part because the scandal reflects badly on the judgment and management of the Secretary of State in office when the attack occurred, one Hillary Clinton, who is also the likely Democrat presidential nominee in 2016. So there is plenty of politics on all sides of this particular scandal.

Week 278

(WAITED LISTED)

May 18, 2014

Democrats are widely viewed as the party of big government and President Obama in particular is viewed, fairly or not, as the man who brought big government to health care, so when scandal breaks out in a government health system, it poses a serious challenge for the Administration. There have been plenty of problems and embarrassments with Obamacare, but since the program is so new, no one really knows who the winners and losers will ultimately be from the program. That allows the President to talk about present benefits of Obamacare, while discounting predictions of the problems to come. Many conservatives have warned that Obamacare will lead to rationing, long wait times, and worse health care services, and this week they found support for that narrative in the Veterans Administration, which runs the biggest direct government health care system in America.

This week a brewing scandal erupted over wait times at 26 Veterans Administration facilities around the country, wait times that allegedly led to 23 patients dying in Phoenix alone. Even worse, local Veterans Administration officials are alleged to have misrepresented wait times while their patients were dying for lack of care. All of this has put an unwelcome spotlight on government's role in health care and on the Obama Administration's competence in general. Not really topics the White House wants front and center when Obamacare has finally dropped from the front pages of political coverage.

The Veteran's Administration scandal came to national attention based on events at a VA hospital in Phoenix. It is reported that in early May 2012, VA Dr. Katherine Mitchell warned Sharon Helman, incoming director of the Phoenix VA Health Care System, that the Phoenix ER is overwhelmed and dangerous. Mitchell was transferred out of the ER. Then later in 2012, the VA ordered implementation of electronic wait-time tracking. But in December 2012, the Government Accountability Office then advised the Veterans Health Administration that its reporting of outpatient medical-appointment wait times is "unreliable." Then in July 2013, Carl T. Hayden at VA Medical Center in Phoenix, questioned administrators about improperly touting their wait times. In September 2013, Mitchell then filed a confidential complaint intended for the VA Office of Inspector General. Mitchell is placed on administrative leave. Then in October 2013, Dr. Sam Foote, a doctor at the Phoenix VA, files a complaint with the VA Office of Inspector General stating that alleged successes in reducing wait times stem from manipulation of data, and that veterans are dying while awaiting appointments for medical care. On April 9, 2014, Representative Jeff Miller, chairman of the House Committee on Veterans' Affairs, noted during a committee meeting that dozens of VA hospital patients in Phoenix may have died while awaiting medical care. After that, U.S. Secretary of Veterans Affairs Eric Shinseki then placed three officials on administrative leave, and ordered audits of all VA health-care facilities around the country.

It is a story of incompetence, retribution, cover-up, and death in a system designed to serve the needs of those who were willing to sacrifice their lives in the defense of the country. Democrats and Republicans have denounced VA incompetence and more and more Republicans are calling for Shinseki to resign. For his part, President Obama has tried to distance himself from the scandal, avoiding questions on the issue and instead simply stating his continued support for his VA Secretary. But it is doubtful the President can maintain that position for long. The politics of the VA scandal are too dangerous. The President's policy premise in the realm of health care is that greater government involvement will improve the system. However, the VA is a government health care system, and it is broken and apparently corrupt. This cuts at the heart of President Obama's competence and his belief in the power of government to do good. To date the Administration has been unwilling to get ahead of this scandal, but events might soon force their hand.

Week 279
(TEA'D OFF)

May 25, 2014

Facing a daunting election campaign in 2014, Democrats had hoped that like 2010 and 2012, Republicans would select some bad candidates to help even the odds. Most political analysts believe that poor candidate selection in the two most recent national elections cost Republicans as many as five Senate seats, specifically seats in Delaware, Indiana, Missouri, Colorado, and Nevada. It is far from clear that the GOP could have won all of those races, but certainly they would have won some of them with better candidates. The conventional wisdom is that Tea Party activists are at fault, by forcing establishment Republicans into primaries and by championing inexperienced and overly conservative candidates. If that conventional wisdom is correct, then primary results so far in 2014 should worry Democrats, because the GOP establishment is striking back.

Liberal political analysts have become very fond claiming a civil war within the Republican Party, a theme that feeds nicely into the narrative of a GOP in disarray. The favorite culprit for this supposed civil war is the Tea Party, which has been portrayed as the reactionary and racist wing of the Republican Party. The mainstream media has been quick to buy into this story line, and hardly any coverage of the Tea Party lacks references to its supposed extremism and destabilizing impact on the GOP. Certainly the Tea Party has cost the Republicans some seats, but it has won plenty for them as well. The Tea Party energized opposition to the Obama agenda in 2010 and led directly to the Republican takeover of the House, which remains today the only elective portion of the federal government in Republican control. Tea Party determination also forced the sequester, which witnessed the first real reductions in discretionary federal spending in decades. These achievements of the Tea Party are largely ignored by the media in favor of the theme that the Tea Party is a disaster for the GOP.

Once again in 2014, the hope was the Tea Party would undo the Republicans again and cost them their chance to take control of the Senate. Much press coverage was devoted to Tea Party primary campaigns in Georgia, North Carolina, Kentucky, and elsewhere. But a funny thing happened on the way to the "Tea Party strikes again" headlines being prepared for print, establishment candidates have starting winning GOP primaries. First came North Carolina, where Tillis, the favored establishment candidate won and earned the right to take on Senator Karen Hagen in the Fall. Then on May 27, Senator Mitch McConnell of Kentucky decisively won against a well-financed Tea Party-backed conservative, Matt Bevin. There were also primaries in Arkansas, Georgia, Idaho, Pennsylvania and Oregon. In all, GOP establishment candidates emerged on top. In Georgia, Republicans sent David Perdue and Representative Jack Kingston, to a July runoff to fill an open Senate seat. The winner will face Democrat Michelle Nunn. In Oregon Monica Wehby, a pediatric neurosurgeon, defeated a Tea Party opponent. The Republican primary in Idaho pitted a fight between a mainstream Republican and a much more conservative opponent, and the mainstream Republican, eight-term Representative Mike Simpson beat the Tea Party challenger. The same result occurred in a Pennsylvania House primary.

Now, after proclaiming an unending civil war in the Republican Party, the mainstream media has now pronounced the Tea Party a spent force. The truth is much more complicated. The Tea Party has pushed the GOP establishment to the right, and the victories of smart establishment Republicans so far this year show that these career politicians are adapting to this new environment. Even more importantly, Republicans want to win, which has fostered a shift to support the best candidates from an electoral perspective, not simply an ideological one. This does not mean the Tea Party is dead, it just means the Tea Party is changing. In the 1970's, Ronald Reagan and his conservative allies were the equivalent of the Tea Party. By the mid-1980's, those conservatives transformed the GOP and became the establishment. In many ways, the same process is going on now, with Republicans adopting more and more Tea Party backed positions. Increasingly, it is going to be hard to tell where the Tea Party ends and where the establishment GOP begins. The Republicans hope these changes will lead to more victories in November, and Democrats, hoping to be bailed out yet again by Tea Party radicalism, should be very concerned.

Week 280

(Is Anyone Listening)

June 1, 2014

The Obama Administration had planned this week as an opportunity to tout its foreign policy vision through a speech by President Obama at West Point. No doubt the White House needs to polish its foreign policy image, after Administration weakness in Ukraine, Syria, and the announced full pullout in Afghanistan led many to assert that America is impotent. But while the President was giving his grand address at West Point, events at the VA, the economy, and turnover at his own White House were giving the impression of an Administration in disarray.

President Obama's foreign policy has been maligned by many as weak, tentative, unfocused, and overly cautious. He has been slow to defend allies, quick to unwittingly help enemies, and seemingly more determined to end conflicts than to win them. His May 29address at West Point was deigned to try to put his actions in a defendable framework and sell the narrative that his decisions have not been ad hoc improvisation, but rather part of a unified foreign policy vision. He started by arguing that America is strong, not weak:

> In fact, by most measures, America has rarely been stronger relative to the rest of the world. Those who argue otherwise — who suggest that America is in decline, or has seen its global leadership slip away — are either misreading history or engaged in partisan politics. Think about it. Our military has no peer. The odds of a direct threat against us by any nation are low and do not come close to the dangers we faced during the Cold War.

Despite all this strength, he explained that military solutions have been overused:

> But to say that we have an interest in pursuing peace and freedom beyond our borders is not to say that every problem has a military solution. Since World War II, some of our most costly mistakes came not from our restraint, but from our willingness to rush into military adventures without thinking through the consequences — without building international support and legitimacy for our action; without leveling with the American people about the sacrifices required. Tough talk often draws headlines, but war rarely conforms to slogans. As General Eisenhower, someone with hard-earned knowledge on this subject, said at this ceremony in 1947: "War is mankind's most tragic and stupid folly; to seek or advise its deliberate provocation is a black crime against all men."

Then he set out what he called his foreign policy doctrine:

> Here's my bottom line: America must always lead on the world stage. If we don't, no one else will. The military that you have joined is and always will be the backbone of that leadership. But US military action cannot be the only — or even primary — component of our leadership in every instance. Just because we have the best hammer does not mean that every problem is a nail. . . . The United States will use military force, unilaterally if necessary, when our core interests demand it — when our people are threatened, when our livelihoods are at stake, when the security of our allies is in danger. . . . On the other hand, when issues of global concern do not pose a direct threat to the United States, when such issues are at stake — when crises arise that stir our conscience or push the world in a more dangerous direction but do not directly threaten us — then the threshold for military action must be higher. In such circumstances, we should not go it alone.

The President had hoped that this explanation of his foreign policy philosophy would burnish his image, but it did just the opposite. The speech itself was panned by many as a post hoc justification for refusing to strongly confront threats across the globe. Further, few saw any discernible doctrine in the speech, just platitudes. But worst of all, most people ignored the speech because of other bad news swirling for the Administration. First bad economic news regarding a 1% drop in GDP for the first quarter called into question the strength of the economic recovery. Second, the VA scandal spun out of control, with an internal audit revealing widespread fraud on wait lists throughout the VA, leading Democrats and Republicans to call for VA Secretary Shinseki to resign, which he was forced to do on May 30. Then White House spokesman Jay Carney announced his departure, causing even more confusion at the White House. So the President's foreign policy speech was not simply a failure, it was virtually ignored.

Week 281
(NO RELEASE)

June 8, 2014

After being rocked by the Veteran's Administration wait list scandal and being forced to cave to critics and accept the resignation of VA Secretary Shinseki, the White House was quickly looking for a means to change the topic. They settled on announcing new environmental regulations and cutting a deal to free an American soldier being held by the Taliban in Afghanistan. With these moves, the President hoped to cheer his base and appeal to patriotism, and as a byproduct, take the VA scandal off the front pages. The strategy worked, but not in the way the Administration hoped. The new environmental regulations were condemned not just by Republicans, but also by Democrats running in tight races in coal producing states. As for the prisoner release of Beau Bergdahl, it was a public relations disaster when it was discovered that the United States released five dangerous Taliban leaders in exchange for Bergdahl, who appears to have deserted his unit.

For years, President Obama has been warning about the dangers of climate change and trying to build support for limitations on carbon emissions. However, his cap and trade legislation on carbon emissions failed in 2009, so the Administration's only option was regulations to be issued by the EPA. The White House put the new regulations on the slow track because it did not want them issued before the 2012 elections. But with the President approaching his final two years in office, the White House believed they could wait no longer, and on June 2 announced the new carbon regulatory scheme. The proposed regulations seek to reduce power plant carbon emission by 30% of 2005 levels by 2030. It achieves this goal by setting carbon targets by state and trying to provide some flexibility for states to meet the targets. Clearly, the President offered this proposal at this time for numerous reasons: distract from the VA scandal, appeal to his base, and achieve a long-held policy goal. The proposed regulations did change the topic, but not in a good way. Many environmentalists criticized the regulations as too weak, while coal state Democrats nearly universally condemned the proposal.

While the President's carbon emissions proposal was a political disappointment, the Bergdahl prisoner swap proved to be a disaster. On May 31, 2014, Bergdahl was released by his captors. The release was in exchange for five Taliban prisoners (Mohammad Fazl, Khairullah Khairkhwa,

Abdul Haq Wasiq, Norullah Noori, and Mohammad Nabi Omari), held at Guantanamo, who will be held in Qatar for a year before they can return home. The President triumphantly announced the deal in the Rose Garden with Bergdahl's parents, whose father sported an Afghan-style beard and who read an Islamic prayer. Clearly, the White House made the move anticipating patriotic support and, as a byproduct, the release of the Taliban prisoners furthered the goal of emptying Gitmo, one of the President yet unfulfilled promises.

However, it seems the Administration did not pay much attention to the details surrounding Bergdahl's capture. National Security Advisor Susan Rice went on the Sunday talk shows and said Bergdahl served with honor and distinction, when the evidence suggests he disserted. Soldiers in his unit quickly took to social media to make clear that Bergdahl is not a hero and claimed that many soldiers were killed looking for him. Further, under statute the Administration was obligated to consult with Congress before releasing Gitmo prisoners, but did the deal without the required notice, enraging Democrat Intelligence Committee Chair Diane Feinstein. Worst of all, many said the deal broke American policy not to negotiate with terrorists. It is hard to imagine how the White House could have botched this more.

With its moves this week, the White House had hoped to improve its position by changing the topic, but instead they further weakened the President. Maybe the Administration should have just let the VA scandal stay on the front pages.

Week 282

(OVER CORRECTED)

June 15, 2014

When Barak Obama first began campaigning for the Presidency in Iowa in 2007, his campaign was ignited by his anti-Iraq war rhetoric. He made that the early centerpiece of his campaign, and used it effectively to distinguish himself from Hillary Clinton, who voted for the Iraq War. Once in office, the President set about ending the Iraq War, eventually pulling out all U.S. troops, and recently announced that the U.S. would also pull all its troops out of Afghanistan by 2016. This determination to disentangle the U.S. from Iraq and Afghanistan has been coupled with a reluctance to intervene elsewhere in the Middle East. The Administration refused to give military aid to moderate opponents of Assad in Syria, refused to join strikes against Gaddafi in Libya, did not intervene to assist Mubarak in Egypt, and even was reticent about vocally supporting democracy protesters in Iran. Clearly, President Obama's agenda was to reverse course from the Middle East interventionist policies of the Bush Administration, but it now seems that the Administration might have over corrected.

The policy of the Bush Administration was to fight an all-out War on Terror, using ground forces, air strikes, and special operations simultaneously on many fronts. This effort was effective, but eventually led to war weariness on the home front and deterioration of support for the war efforts in Iran and Afghanistan. When President Obama took office, his stated goal was to end the Iraq war. This effort was aided by the Bush Administration's surge of troops in 2007, because by 2009 Iraq was largely stabilized. As for Afghanistan, the President was on record that the fight there was necessary, but even then he hesitated in 2009 to send additional troops to combat the resurgent Taliban. A small Afghan surge was eventually ordered, but its effectiveness has been limited. In contrast with Administration's reluctance to embark on large scale efforts, in special operations the President has been even more aggressive than his predecessor, using drone strikes and other means to kill terrorists in Yemen, Afghanistan, and Pakistan.

This policy of disengagement from large scale commitments is now showing its negative consequences. The long term plan for Iraq had always been to leave a small residual force behind after the U.S. ended active combat operations to stabilize the Iraqi army and government. However, in 2011 the Administration failed to reach a status of forces agreement with the Iraqi government, in part because the Administration was only willing to commit to leaving a small force, while at the same time demanding parliamentary approval of the agreement and protections from prosecution for U.S. forces. The result was no agreement and all U.S. forces left. Shortly thereafter, the civil war broke out in Syria, but the White refused to provide any significant military support for moderate opponents of Assad, which handed the momentum to Islamic extremists, led by ISIS, the Islamic Army in Iraq and Syria.

ISIS is so radical that it has been condemned for its brutality even by Al-Qaeda. With support from various international terrorist groups, ISIS captured much of eastern Syria, and this week launched an invasion of Iraq. ISIS quickly conquered Mosel, Iraq's second largest city and drove south toward Bagdad, eventually taking several more cities and towns within two hours of the capital. The Iraqi Army collapsed in the face of this attack, forcing Prime Minister Maliki to ask the U.S. for airstrikes to stop ISIS. So it appears that the Administration's policies have undermined the Administration's goals, by allowing ISIS to dominate in Syria and by so weakening Iraq through the full pullout of U.S. troops, that ISIS had the opportunity to destabilize that nation.

Before leaving for a golf and fundraising trip to the West Coast, a clearly beleaguered President spoke to the media, stating his team was monitoring the situation and would develop an appropriate US response. However, the White House has allowed the situation to deteriorate so badly that the choices facing the US are limited. The Administration surely will not send combat forces to Iraq, but to date it has also refused requests for airstrikes. At the same time, the President continues to refuse to provide significant support to the rebels in Syria who oppose ISIS. Now it appears large portions of Iraq and Syria are becoming new havens for terrorists that President Obama said are unacceptable and a threat to our national security. So by any measure, the situation in the Middle East is far worse than when the President took office, so much for disengagement being the answer to our Middle East challenges.

Week 283
(THE 300)

June 22, 2014

After triumphantly declaring success in Iraq in 2011 when he announced the full pullout of U.S. forces, it seems that President Obama is now having his own "Mission Accomplished" moment as Iraq appears to be crumbling. This week, the Administration struggled to formulate a response that would at least forestall an ISIS takeover in Iraq while avoiding another deep entanglement. The President took nearly a week to contemplate his next move, a clear indication of both his reluctance and his indecision. In the end, on June 19 the President announced that 300 American troops would be sent to Iraq for training and communications support. A move designed to look like the White House is doing something rather than actually accomplishing anything.

In announcing his decision to send this small force, President Obama spent more time discussing what he would not do that what he would. "American combat troops are not going to be fighting in Iraq again," President Obama said. "We do not have the ability to simply solve this problem by sending in thousands of troops and committing the kind of blood and treasure that has already been expended in Iraq." According to a report in Politico, the Administration has recognized the threat posed by ISIS: "The group ISIL operates broadly and we would not restrict our ability to take action that is necessary to protect the United States" said an Administration official. "The first job is really assessing and getting a little bit better sense of the state cohesiveness and capability the of Iraqi security services...We're going to start small and we'll see what we learn from that," another official said. The President left open the door to greater military involvement, noting that the United States is "prepared to take targeted and precise military action if and when the situation on the ground requires it." However, for now caution and military restraint is the plan at the White House. The President is hoping for a political solution, but the question is has the time run out for that.

After withdrawing all troops and largely ignoring Iraq, allowing Prime Minister Maliki to consolidate power and create a more sectarian government, it appears that the Administration wants to use the current crisis to at long last force political changes in Iraq. For that reason, the White House has resisted more vigorous military support for the Iraqi government. Instead, the ISIS takeover of northern Iraq is being used as leverage to force Maliki to form a more inclusive government. The challenge for President Obama is the clock. Having allowed the situation to deteriorate to this degree, time might have run out to force political change. This is because the Iraqi government is now desperate, so if the United States will not come their aid, they are going to have to find another savior, namely Iran.

There are already some early signs that Iraq is giving up on American support and turning to Iran. Iraq's supreme religious leader has called for Shiites to arm themselves to defend the nation. Iran is offering military supplies and equipment. Even the United States gave an indication that it would turn to Iran, noting there might be a possibility of coordinating with Iran to fight ISIS. That comment struck many analysts as ironic, since it was Iran that was supplying weapons and training to kill Americans in Iraq not so many years ago. The fact that the Administration might be willing to look to Iran to salvage its Iraq policy is even more troubling that the ISIS invasion itself.

So for now 300 lonely U.S. soldiers are being sent to Iraq by a President who clearly does not want to send them and does not want to do much to stop the march of ISIS. At best, these 300 are a face saving move for a President paralyzed by caution and who is starting to realize that too much disengagement can cause just as many problems as intervention. One thing is clear, none of this is good for the President or his domestic agenda, because chaos and weakness in Iraq only exacerbates his weakness at home.

Week 284

(9-0)

June 29, 2014

When faced with what he terms Republican obstruction and inaction, President Obama famously said "I have a pen." The strategy of circumventing Congress has become a hallmark of the Obama presidency. The President has made more than two dozen unilateral changes to Obamacare without congressional approval, issued executive orders on gun control, deportations, and the dream act for immigrants, and has relied on regulations to limit greenhouse gases when his effort to pass global warming legislation in Congress failed in his first term. All this has led to GOP accusations of presidential overreach and illegal assumption of legislative prerogatives. So Republicans have looked to the courts to stem the President's executive powers, and this week they won one fight, and pledged to start another.

One of President Obama's biggest complaints has been slow Senate confirmation of Administration nominees. The Democrats have dealt with this in two ways. In November 2013, Senate Democrats changed the filibuster rules to limit the ability of Republicans to thwart executive and judicial nominations. For his part, President Obama aggressively used his recess appointment power to fill vacancies. With regard to National Labor Relations Board (NLRB), the Republicans had refused to confirm three nominees, depriving the NLRB of a quorum, thus preventing it from issuing new labor regulations. The President relied on a brief three day recess of the Senate to recess appoint 3 new members for the NLRB. The President also used his recess appointment power to fill the director position for the new Consumer Protection Bureau. These moves cheered the President's supporters, but also led to a lawsuit challenging this use of the recess appointment power, where the Administration was repudiated by the Supreme Court 9-0.

The case was entitled *NLRB v Canning*, and it was the first time the Supreme Court had reviewed the recess appointment power. Writing for a unanimous court, liberal Court Justice Steven Breyer, after reviewing the law and history of recess appointments, held that President Obama had abused his authority in making appointments to the NLRB. Justice Breyer rejected calls from four conservative Justices for an even more restrictive reading of the recess appointment power, holding instead that such appointments can be made for vacancies during intra-session recesses, but stating a recess must be at least 10 days before a President can exercise the recess appointment power.

This was just the most recent loss for the White House in its efforts to push expansive executive powers. The striking thing was this 9-0 loss, with even the most liberal Justices (including two Obama appointees) agreeing that the President had abused his power. Almost on que, Speaker Boehner announced that the House would file a lawsuit to challenge a host of executive actions that Republicans believe are an abuse of presidential authority. It is questionable whether this lawsuit will survive efforts to dismiss it for lack of standing, but the purpose of the case is political as much as legal. Abuse of executive authority is a hot topic in GOP circles, and the lawsuit is surely designed to motivate Republicans for the Fall election.

Where does all this leave the President. With all his legislative initiatives stalled, Republicans firmly in control of the House, and making a concerted drive to take the Senate, executive powers may be the only option for the President to accomplish anything of substance in his second term. Yet in some ways aggressive executive actions are what has led to President Obama's inability to pass legislation. Rather than negotiate with Republicans, the President preferred to denigrate the GOP and issue executive orders. This creates little incentive for Republicans to try to work with President Obama. Even worse, as with Obamacare, Republicans fear if they pass new legislation, the President will only enforce the portions he likes. Many Republicans are not willing to clothe the President with any more legislative authority because of this concern. The President's aggressive use of executive powers has been repudiated in the Courts and will likely get rejected more times in the future, but courts are slow and the President has only 2 ½ more years in office. He might be willing to issue orders, even if illegal, to further his goals, knowing the court rulings will likely come when his successor is in office. So for now, even with a 9-0 loss at the Supreme Court, it is safe to expect more and more executive orders from this Administration.

Week 285
(OUT OF CONTROL)

July 6, 2014

This was a very bad week for the Obama Administration priorities of health care and immigration, with birth control and border control causing headaches for the Administration. One of the features of Obamacare touted by the White House has been the free birth control mandate, but in pursuing that goal the Administration has made only limited exceptions for religious objectors. That resulted in another loss at the Supreme Court, which held an aspect of the birth control mandate unconstitutional. At the same time, border control became a true crisis, as tens of thousands of minors from Central America have been crossing the U.S. border in Texas.

When Obamacare was first passed, the scope of the birth control mandate was left up to HHS regulations. Initially, the Obama Administration intended to exempt only churches and religious institutions. Under pressure, the Administration was forced to expand the exemption to non-profits with religious objections. However, in the case *Burwell v Hobby Lobby*, a closely held for-profit company challenged the mandate, and won. In a 5-4 vote, the Supreme Court held the HHS regulation unconstitutional because it burdened a first amendment right and it failed to use the least restrictive means to pursue the government's interest. This result infuriated liberals and blew another small hole in Obamacare, with even more challenges working their way through the Courts.

Immediately after the decision, the President and his allies pledged to use the ruling to rally their base for the midterm elections, but that effort was quickly drowned out by the crisis on the Southern border. The President has given speech after speech declaring his desire to give a path to citizenship for illegal aliens and enact immigration reform. His effort has completely failed in Congress, so increasingly he has threatened to take executive action. But at the very time the President has been pushing immigration reform, a flood of minors have made their way across the US border. Most are from Central America and are coming based on a perception, likely created by the President, that they will find sanctuary here. This has resulted in tens of thousands of minors entering the U.S., flooding the system and overwhelming the border patrol and the immigration service.

This flood of immigrates is prompting more and more protests across the country, in response to government efforts to transport these children to states across the country for housing and processing. Making matters worse, the President has set a fundraising trip to Texas for next week, but to date has refused to travel to the border to view the situation. This has prompted Texas Governor Rick Perry to demand a presidential visit to the border. All this has the makings of a major crisis for the Administration and actually makes it more risky for the President to take aggressive executive action on immigration.

These failures in the courts and on the border are doing far more than distracting the Administration from its message. It is creating an image of a White House unable to win legal battles or manage a crisis. Increasingly, the Administration is looking passive, reactive, and incompetent. No doubt the President's falling approval ratings are a reflection of these problems. A President who cannot pass legislation, cannot solve crises, and whose executive actions are getting rejected again and again in the courts, has few options left. Maybe that is why the President plays so much golf.

Week 286

(UNHINGED)

July 13, 2014

With problems mounting and criticism rising on both the foreign and domestic fronts, the White House has been working feverously to try to turn the tide. One of the President's favorite tactics is to hit the road and hit his opponents, rhetorically of course. Returning to that same playbook, the White House scheduled a bevy of trips, speeches, and fundraisers, trying to motivate the base. But this time, the strategy seems to have backfired, because the President's constant trips and increasingly undignified rhetoric have started conversations even in liberal circles that he is disengaged, disillusioned, and even unhinged.

The problems facing the Administration this summer of 2014 have deprived it of any opportunity to take command of the political landscape. The war in Ukraine, the ISIS conquest of northern Iraq, the tens of thousands of illegal immigrant children crossing the Texas border, rising tensions in Gaza, the VA scandal, the Syrian civil war, and many other events have made the White House appear incompetent and indecisive. To make matters worse, recent rebukes at the Supreme Court have inspired the House GOP to pursue a lawsuit to challenge the President's exercise of executive powers. To try to change his fortunes, the President scheduled trips to Colorado and Texas to raise money and attack the GOP. But his conduct on those trips seems to have hurt more than helped.

In Colorado, many said the President seemed completely out of touch, drinking beer and playing pool while the U.S. struggled with an influx of tens of thousands of children over the Texas border and increasing chaos overseas. Added to that bad imagery was the President's increasingly acerbic rhetoric. It seems that Speaker Boehner's planned lawsuit has gotten under his skin, because he used speeches in Colorado to play the victim, arguing that the Republicans are suing him for trying to help the American people, while they in Congress are doing nothing. There are plenty of legitimate grounds to criticize the GOP and Boehner's lawsuit, but the problem for the

President is that his tone has become so nasty and combative that it actually makes him appear less presidential and less in charge.

Things only got worse when President Obama went to Texas. The White House scheduled fundraisers in Dallas, and when the child immigrant crisis hit the Texas border initially refused to make changes to the trip. Republicans and even a few Democrats questioned how the President could travel to Texas but refuse to visit the border to see firsthand the crisis there. Eventually, the Administration began to realize the bad optics and tried to get Taxes Governor Rick Perry to join Obama for a photo op so it could appear the President was addressing the crisis. Perry initially refused to be prop for the President, but eventually agreed to a private meeting to discuss the border crisis. However, the President flatly refused to go to the border.

President Obama has no such reluctance to go to the podium, however. In speeches in Texas, the President mocked Republicans who have called for his impeachment for abuse of executive powers. "You hear some of them ... 'Sue him! Impeach him!:" Obama told supporters in Austin. "Really? Really? For what? You're going to sue me for doing my job?" From Washington, Speaker Boehner responded: "What we're talking about here are places where the President is basically rewriting law to make it fit his own needs," Boehner said. "Listen, this is a problem of the President's own making," Boehner said. "He's been President for five and a half years! When's he going to take responsibility for something?" The best the White House could do was continue the criticisms of the GOP, but the damage had been done. Increasingly, the President seems out of touch, unwilling to make decisions, and instead is searching for distraction on the road, and even loyal Democrats are starting to worry.

Week 287

(MR. BYSTANDER)

July 20, 2014

This week it seemed as though the United States and its President were ever more bystanders as events around the world and on the U.S. border got more and more chaotic. The challenges have been many, but the firm steps by the Administration have been few. It is not simply that the long pending problems in Syria, Afghanistan, and Ukraine continue getting worse, but new crises are piling up, and the White House seems unable or unwilling to grapple with them. The most troubling recent examples are the ISIS takeover of northern Iraq and the Syrian civil war, but now the Arab-Israeli conflict and the war in the Ukraine have entered a new and more dangerous phase, with the United States stuck in the position of observing and cajoling from a distance.

Many have been critical of the Administration's careful and restrained response to Russian aggression in the Ukraine. After Moscow seized Crimea, the U.S. condemned the move and imposed limited sanctions, but refused any meaningful economic or military support for the struggling Ukrainian government. Putin, sensing and seeing weakness, took aim at eastern Ukraine, supplying covert and overt support to separatist forces fighting to join Russia. Many of these separatist groups are simply proxy forces from Moscow and President Obama has condemned them as such, but has been hesitant to provide significant weaponry to the Ukrainian government.

There has been no such hesitancy in Moscow, and this week we saw the results with the shooting down of a civilian jetliner in eastern Ukraine.

Malaysia Airlines Flight 17 was schedule to fly from Amsterdam to Kuala Lumpur on July 17. The Boeing 777-200ER lost contact over Donetsk, about 50 km (31 mi) from the Ukraine–Russia border. The plane crashed 40km from Torez. All 298 people on board died. The Russian and Ukrainian governments immediately began trading accusations. Ukraine claimed that the plane was shot down at 33,000 feet by a separatist Buk surface-to-air missile supplied by the Russians. U.S. intelligence officials stated that they tracked the missile and the evidence indicated that Russian separatists fired it. Ukraine also claimed they had intercepted radio communications from separatists claiming they had shot down a plane around the time Flight 17 went down. The international reaction was immediate and highly critical of Russia. For his part, President Obama quickly took the podium to condemn both the attack and Russia's intervention in the Ukraine. Earlier in the week, the Administration had already increased sanctions and it was clear the White House hoped this latest incident would prompt the Europeans to join American calls for more aggressive sanctions to punish Russia.

If the downing of Flight 17 was not enough, the Administration also had to grapple with a mini-war breaking out in Gaza. After three Israeli teenagers were kidnapped and killed by Palestinian terrorists, in reprisal a Palestinian teenager was kidnapped and burned to death. The reaction from Hamas in Gaza was swift. They began a massive missile barrage of Israel. Efforts to bring the parties back from the brink failed, and Israel began shelling and bombing suspected missile launch sites in Gaza and threatened a land incursion. As the week ended, the fighting was only getting worse, and Israel was massing troops on the Gaza border. The Administration encouraged the parties to stop the violence, but could not change events on the ground. So yet another conflict was raging with America on the sidelines.

Closer to home, the border crisis with Mexico continued to worsen, with more and more Central American children crossing the border. In response, the White House made a $3.7 billion emergency funding request to deal with the crisis, but the proposal was met with skepticism in both houses of Congress. The President has continued to refuse to visit the border and has not even met with congressional leaders to address the crisis. Instead, he simply made a request for funding. There is little chance Congress will appropriate anything close to the President's request, and it is clear the GOP will only vote for more funding if it is tied to expedited deportations. However, the President has tried to play both sides of that issue, promising that the kids will be sent home, but assuring immigration advocates that adequate due process will be followed. While the President tries to carefully play of politics of the border crisis, the crisis rolls on.

So we see a President buffeted by crisis after crisis, and rather than confront any of them, he prefers half measures and avoidance. It would be unfair to claim that President Obama is at fault for any of these crises. True, if he had taken firmer action in Ukraine, maybe Putin would not have supplied sophisticated weapons to the separatists, but that it just speculation. What can be said is that when confronted with these challenges, the President seems unwilling or unable to act firmly in response. Instead, he seems to prefer to react to events, not control them.

Week 288
(Halbig'ed)

July 27, 2014

If the foreign policy challenges facing the Administration were not enough, the White House now has to tackle yet another challenge to the viability of one of its few legislative accomplishments, namely Obamacare. After surviving a constitutional challenge at the Supreme Court in 2012, most supporters of the law assumed the constitutionality of the law was established, and told opponents to surrender and accept the law. Instead, opposition to the law has if anything gotten more vociferous, with ever more legal challenges to the law being filed. For example, in June, the birth control mandate was struck down for closely-held private enterprises, but that ruling did not threaten the core of the law. Not so with the challenge to the law in *Halbig v. Burwell*.

On July 22, a panel of the United States Court of Appeals for the District of Columbia Circuit by a 2-1 vote held that federal insurance subsidies that help millions of Americans pay for coverage under Obamacare are illegal for those who obtain insurance through the federal insurance exchange. Only 14 States have set up their own exchanges, so this ruling if upheld by the Supreme Court would deprive citizens in 36 States of subsidies under Obamacare. This would deal a near fatal blow to the viability of the law. Ironically, on the same day another federal court, this time the United States Court of Appeals for the 4th Circuit, reached the opposite conclusion and upheld the subsidies through the federal insurance exchange. Supporters of the law pointed to this ruling to assure their allies that Obamacare would overcome this latest legal challenge, just as it overcame the Commerce Clause challenge in 2012. However, these conflicting rulings might lead the Supreme Court to take on this question sooner, which is likely bad news for Obamacare.

There is good reason to believe that if the Supreme Court addresses the subsidy issue, it will not uphold the payment of subsidies to participants in the federal exchange. The statute as written states that subsidies will be paid to participants in the State exchanges, and the five conservative justices on the Supreme Court are advocates of faithful and textual interpretation of statutes. Moreover, four of those Justices are already on record that Obamacare is unconstitutional under the Commerce Clause, so it is very likely they would find the subsidies not authorized by the law. Then there is Chief Justice Roberts. In his 2012 decision upholding the constitutionality of Obamacare, the Chief Justice said the Commerce Clause did not empower Congress to impose a penalty for not participating in commerce, namely for not buying health insurance. However, the Chief Justice then upheld the penalty under the taxing power. Conservatives have harshly criticized the Chief Justice's ruling, which seemed more political than legal. However, the *Halbig* case would not force the Court to find Obamacare unconstitutional, it would only require a finding that subsidies cannot be paid to participants in the federal exchange. This is a much more narrow ground to attack the law, and one the Chief Justice is more likely to support.

Whether these subsidies can be paid is a very serious issue for Obamacare. About 5.4 million people have applied for coverage through the federal exchange, and 87 percent of them received subsidies. Without these subsidies, many of these people will not be able to afford insurance, yet they will be subject to penalties if they do not buy insurance. Indeed, in his dissent in the *Halbig* case, Judge Harry T. Edwards said the case went to the core of the law and was a "not-so-veiled attempt to gut the Patient Protection and Affordable Care Act." Even worse, if this decision is upheld by the Supreme Court, there is little chance Republicans in Congress would fix the problem, because they want the law to fail. So just when the President may have thought the success of Obamacare was inevitable, yet another dire challenge to the viability of the law has arisen.

Week 289

(STOP THE HATING)

August 3, 2014

No matter chaos abroad and political conflicts at home, one thing President Obama seems unwilling to do is change his travel schedule. Regardless of crisis or conflict, the President is almost never willing to skip a fundraiser or political rally. Maybe that is because he is an addicted partisan, or maybe he needs loving crowds to revive his spirits. It seems the worse things get politically for the President, the more he wants to hit the road to campaign and raise money for Democrats. However, as his rhetoric gets more and more heated, the President looks ever more impotent, disconnected, and whinny. On his latest trip, the President took his ranting tone to new heights of ridicule of the GOP, simply calling them haters.

One thing American voters respect is decision making and action. Even if voters disagree on substance, they want their chief executive to accomplish things. In that respect, the last two years for the President have been a dismal failure, and his approval rating are reflecting that. The President cannot pass laws, has not been able to cajole Republicans to support his initiatives, and his executive actions have been repeatedly rejected by the Courts. To compensate for this ineffectiveness, the White House strategy seems to be to up the rhetoric to create the image of action and accomplishment. Maybe that is why the President's campaign and fundraising schedule seems to trump all other priorities. But this strategy carries risks, especially in these unstable times. So this week, as Secretary of State Kerry worked tirelessly in Europe and the Middle East to achieve a cease fire in Gaza, the war raged on in Ukraine, and the border crisis continued unabated, the President hit the campaign trail in Kansas for his favorite pastime, attacking Republicans.

It is clear that the President is irritable, so it does not take much to set him off these days. So when the House this week voted to start its lawsuit challenging President Obama's executive actions on Obamacare and refused to pass anything resembling the President's border bill, the President lost it. During a speech at Kansas City's Uptown Theater, the President complained that: "We could do so much more if Congress would just come on and help out a little bit," Obama said. "Stop being mad all the time. Stop just hating all the time. Let's get some work done together." On the GOP lawsuit specifically, the President commented: "Now everybody knows this is a political stunt . . . but it's worse than that because every vote they're taking like that means a vote they're not taking to help you. And by the way, you know who is paying for this suit they are going to file? You!" So the message is clear, Republicans are bad people and it is all their fault.

No doubt the President and his supporters love these lines, and they probably help get donations for Democrats, but it is hard to see how any of this advances the President's priorities. The political reality is that to get anything done legislatively, the President has to work with Republicans. The President is unwilling to even talk with GOP leaders, and instead seems to think ridiculing them is more productive. In the process, his attacks are getting ever more undignified and demeaning. Rather than raise the tone in Washington, which he promised to do in his

2008 campaign, he has lowered it to depths not seen in decades. It is almost like the President has given up and has decided to act out instead. Not a very inspiring example of leadership, but at least the President appears to be enjoying himself.

Week 290

(SO STRIKING)

August 10, 2014

Ever since ISIS crossed the Iraq border in strength and began conquering territory, the Obama Administration has been struggling to respond. For a President who was propelled to office on an anti-Iraq war message, the thought of re-engaging in that country's conflicts is a distasteful proposition to say the least. But as ISIS took more and more territory, including Mosel, Iraq's second largest city, pressure has been increasing for a more forceful response. This week, the pressure reached the breaking point as ISIS besieged thousands of minority Yazidi on Mount Sinjar in northern Iraq and advanced into Iraqi Kurdistan, America's best ally in Iraq. And so, as he was leaving for a two week vacation on Martha's Vineyard, the President announced airstrikes again ISIS.

It is telling that it took the Administration so long to respond to the ISIS threat. In recent months, the ISIS invasion routed the Iraqi army, captured about a third of Iraq, and ISIS garnered for itself a huge cache of money and weapons. Combined with the territory they control in Syria, ISIS is now a power in the region vying for nation state status. Indeed, ISIS's leader Ibrahim Awwad Ibrahim Ali al-Badri al-Samarrai declared a new Caliphate after his successful invasion of Iraq. The threat from ISIS is clear, creating the potential for the most dangerous terrorist haven ever in the Middle East. But in the face of this threat, the Obama Administration continued to avoid a forceful response. It promised some arms for moderate anti-Assad groups in Syria and sent a few advisers to train Iraqi troop. Otherwise, it seemed the President was more interested in using the ISIS threat to put pressure on the Iraqi government to reform, rather than trying to defeat ISIS itself.

The reasons for the White House's restraint are both philosophical and political. The Administration's policy is military disengagement in the Middle East. While the President hopes to use diplomacy to address the various policy challenges in the Middle East (including the Palestinians, Syrian Civil War, the Iranian nuclear program, and the resurgent Taliban), military options have largely been kept off the table. The President clearly believes a muscular approach to foreign policy is both dangerous and ineffective, and hopes to apply soft power to address these challenges. Politically, this approach keeps him in line with his progressive base. The problem is, his adversaries are not so hesitant to use force.

However, the soft power approach reached its limits in the face of the ISIS threat. With a humanitarian crisis growing and, Iraqi Kurdistan increasingly threatened, the Administration had to respond. So on August 8, the President announced that the U.S. would initiate airstrikes against ISIS and would work to break the siege of the Yazidi. The strikes began almost immediately, concentrating on ISIS positions threatening Kurdistan. As is his pattern, in announcing this step the President was careful to state what he would not do, namely send ground troop back into Iraq. No doubt ISIS heard that loud and clear.

Even this limited step of airstrikes immediately caused political problems for the President. Liberals in his party quickly expressed their concerns and voiced only cautious support. And then the President had bad imagery, with him going on vacation, playing golf, and going to the beach as U.S. forces go into action in Iraq. Most concerning of all is that once the U.S. begins to take action against ISIS, if those initial actions are ineffective, there will be pressure to do more. Mission creep is what the White House fears most, maybe even more than it fears ISIS. So the President has agreed to strike ISIS, but it was a very hesitant and reluctant agreement indeed.

Week 291
(RIOT GEAR)

August 17, 2014

President Obama already had more than a few issues to grapple with while attempting to get some vacation time on Martha's Vineyard, so the last thing he needed to grapple with was another controversy over race relations. The issue of race has always been difficult for the President. As the first African American President, race is an important part of his success and his appeal, but racial issues also pose perils because the President has to appeal to all racial groups and not appear partisan to any particular agenda of any particular constituency. That is likely why the President has tried to steer clear of race issues as much as possible. On those few occasions where he did wade in, he usually regretted it. When a white police officer arrested a black Harvard professor on his porch, the President was severely criticized for calling the police action "stupid," and had to host a beer summit to soothe tempers. When Trayvon Martin was shot and killed by George Zimmerman, a community watch volunteer, the President said if he had a son that son would have looked like Trayvon, but later evidence came out that Trayvon Martin likely attacked Zimmerman and Zimmerman was acquitted at trial. Recognizing the risks, the President has learned to limit his role on race relations to giving high-minded speeches. However, that has not been enough to quell the current unrest in Ferguson, Missouri.

On August 9, a black teenager named Michael Brown allegedly stole cigars from a convenience store in Ferguson, Missouri. Later that night, Darren Wilson, a white Ferguson police officer, allegedly found Brown walking in the middle of the road. What happened after that is unclear, other than the fact that Wilson eventually shot Brown six times and killed him. On August 10, vigils were held for Brown in the morning and that evening, riots and looting started. The rioting was brought under control by 2:00 a.m. the next day, but then press conferences by Al Sharpton, Benjamin Crump (the lawyer for Trayvon Martin's family), and the NAACP, were followed by more riots, eventually broken up by tear gas. On August 12, rallies and protests continued, including in front of the Ferguson Police Department, in part because the police had not yet identified Officer Wilson. That evening there were more riots and looting. Riots continued on August 13 and 14 with protesters throwing Molotov cocktails at police. On August 15, Missouri Governor Jay Nixon put the Missouri State Police in charge in Ferguson, but protests continued. President Obama offered some remarks from his vacation to try to calm the situation, and on

August 15, Ferguson was relatively quiet, but on August 16 riots again erupted, forcing Governor Nixon to declare a state of emergency and to institute a curfew. So as the week ended, the situation in Ferguson remained tense.

The media narrative on Ferguson has focused on the basic facts, an unarmed black teenager shot by a white police officer. The facts on why are still unknown, but the narrative of racial discrimination has been the focus of media coverage. The media has also been fixated on the imagery of heavily armed mostly white police officers shooting plastic bullets and tear gas at black protesters. In many instances, there has been more commentary on the military equipment being used by the police than on the riots and looting. It seems there has been a rush to judgment that the predominately white police with their heavy weapons are causing the unrest as much as the protesters and looters.

The unrest in Ferguson is also posing a difficult problem for the President. As an initial matter, the optics are horrible. While President Obama is on the beach and playing golf on Martha's Vineyard, a haven for the rich and powerful, angry protesters are rioting and looting in the heartland. Even worse, the President tried to make comments to quell the protests and if anything they got worse. Now no one can fairly say that the President is to blame for the events in Ferguson, but he is hurt by them nonetheless. In the end, a basic job of any President is law and order. Regardless of the reasons and the motivations, when there is rioting, looting and violence, voters expect the government to restore order, and when it does not, government leaders look incompetent. For the President, if the riots continue while he continues vacationing, the risk is he will seem unconcerned and detached, as well as ineffective. So the more we see scenes of hundreds of police in riot gear in Ferguson, Missouri, and more the President should worry.

Week 292

(THE FOLEY FACTOR)

August 24, 2014

For over two months, since the invasion and conquest by ISIS of much of northern Iraq, the Obama Administration has been struggling for a response. Initially, the White House seemed more interested in saying what it would not do (namely send ground forces to Iraq), than saying what steps would be taken to stop ISIS. The Administration then embarked on a dangerous game of withholding significant support from the Iraqi government until Prime Minister Maliki resigned, even if that meant further advances by ISIS. That strategy succeeded in part, because on August 15, Prime Minister Maliki finally agreed to relinquish power in favor of Haider al-Abadi, a deputy speaker of the Iraqi parliament. However, in the interim ISIS advanced unabated, eventually threatening Kirkuk, the capital of Iraqi Kurdistan. That forced the President to launch limited airstrikes, setting a precedent for U.S. military involvement. ISIS was then forced back, including losing control of the Mosul Dam, Iraq's largest hydropower facility. It seemed clear the Administration then intended to curtail the military effort, but that all changed after the execution of James Foley.

Foley is an American journalist from New Hampshire. He had covered the conflicts in Iraq, Afghanistan, and Libya. On November 22, 2012, he was captured by ISIS after leaving an internet café in Binesh, Syria. Foley's captors demanded 100 million euros in ransom (approximately $132 million) from Foley's family. In July 2014, President Obama authorized a rescue mission to find Foley. However, when Delta commandos landed in the Raqqa, Syria, Foley and other hostages had been moved. On August 19, 2014, after the U.S. government supposedly refused to pay a ransom, a video of Foley's execution by decapitation appeared on YouTube.

President Obama quickly condemned the brutal killing and Attorney General Eric Holder opened a criminal investigation and vowed that the perpetrators would be punished. However, Foley's killing has done far more than shock the nation, it has also forced the Administration to confront the growing threat posed by ISIS. Through the capture of northern Iraq, ISIS obtained hundreds of millions in cash, vast stores of weapons, and maybe most dangerously, ever more recruits. It is now the most powerful and best organized terrorist group, far exceeding Al-Qaeda at its apex. Despite the clear threat from ISIS, President Obama had continued to resist vigorous action. He only ordered airstrikes when it looked like Iraqi Kurdistan might fall to ISIS, and then even those airstrikes were limited. They were enough to push ISIS back, but not enough to defeat them. The President said these airstrikes were necessary to protect U.S. citizens in Iraq, not that they were done to defeat ISIS. With the Foley execution, that limited effort for that limited objective will no longer be enough.

Now the President is faced with what he feared most, a threat so dire that only direct and active U.S. military involvement can stem the tide. He also can no longer avoid the issue because the Foley execution made clear both the threat from and the brutality of ISIS. Even worse, the Administration let the situation deteriorate so badly that the military options are now much more limited. ISIS has substantial forces and resources, spread over a wide area in Syria and Iraq. Strikes just in Iraq will not be enough, because it will leave ISIS with its Syrian safe haven. So now the President who disengaged from Iraq, pulled out all U.S. forces, and declared near victory over terrorism has to make some tough choices to recover the initiative. James Foley's killing changed everything.

Week 293

(Don't Have A Strategy)

August 31, 2014

It was not a restful vacation for President Obama. He was beset by crises both foreign and domestic, so much so that he came back to Washington for two days in midst of his vacation apparently just to create the image of taking charge. The President returned this week to a number of pressing issues, including ISIS, further Russian escalations in Ukraine, and pressure from liberals in his party to take aggressive action on immigration reform. Added to all this is the looming midterm election, where Democrats are at risk of losing control of the Senate. A daunting task list for any President, which is why his press conference on August 28 was so damaging. The President admitted he has no strategy for ISIS, an admission that seems equally applicable to the many other crises facing him.

President Obama has great confidence in his powers of persuasion, which is likely why after taking so much criticism for his beach and golfing excursions during this crisis period, he decided to give a press conference to reset the tone and show he is in charge. Unfortunately, in the press conference it seemed more like the President was winging it. Rather than portraying an image of cool, confidence, and control, the President seemed indecisive and vacillating. After his various gaffs, his handlers were quick to swoop in and try to clarify issues, but the damage was done.

It was not a surprise that the questioning in the press conference focused on ISIS and Ukraine, by far the most serious of the long list of challenges facing the President. There seems to be a policy emerging within the Administration on what to do about ISIS. Secretary of Defense Hagel and Secretary of State Kerry have spoken publicly about the dire threat posed by ISIS and the need to combat them, including with direct military strikes at ISIS safe havens in Syria. In contrast, progressives have been pressing the Administration to take a more cautious approach, a difficult balancing act when the President has himself called ISIS a "cancer." This internal conflict was evident in the President's press comments on military strikes against ISIS, where the President said:

> In Iraq, our dedicated pilots and crews continue to carry out the targeted strikes that I authorized to protect Americans there and to address the humanitarian situation on the ground. As commander in chief, I will always do what is necessary to protect the American people and defend against evolving threats to our homeland . . . .

> Now, ISIL poses an immediate threat to the people of Iraq and to people throughout the region, and that's why our military action in Iraq has to be part of a broader comprehensive strategy to protect our people and to support our partners who are taking the fight to ISIL, and that starts with Iraq's leaders building on the progress that they've made so far and forming an inclusive government that will unite their country and strengthen their security forces to confront ISIL. . . .

> As I've said, rooting out a cancer like ISIL will not be quick or easy, but I'm confident that we can and we will, working closely with our allies and our partners. For our part, I've directed Secretary Hagel and our Joint Chiefs of Staff to prepare a range of options. I'll be meeting with my National Security Council again this evening as we continue to develop that strategy. And I've been consulting with members of Congress, and I'll continue to do so in the days ahead.

The President's comments portrayed a balanced approach to the crisis in an attempt to please his critics on the Left and the Right, but then in response to a question on whether he needs congressional approval for further military action the President said:

> You know, I have consulted with Congress throughout this process. I am confident that as commander in chief I have the authorities to engage in the acts that we are conducting currently. As our strategy develops, we will continue to consult with Congress, and I do think that it'll be important for Congress to weigh in and we're — that our consultations with Congress continue to develop so that the American people are part of the debate. . . . But I don't want to put the cart before the horse. We don't have a strategy yet. . . .

The "don't have a strategy" comment led all the headlines and confirmed the perception that the President does not have a plan. To make matters worse, Democrats plied on, with Senator Diane Feinstein commenting that the President is too "cautious." But the President's indecisive approach was not limited to ISIS, on Ukraine the President also seemed unwilling to recognize the true nature of Russia's recent escalations. This week, thousands of additional Russian troops invaded southern Ukraine. NATO quickly condemned this new attack, while the President downplayed it and rather than increasing pressure on Russia's President Putin, President Obama focused on what he would not do to stop the invasion:

QUESTION: Do you consider today's escalation in Ukraine an invasion? And when you talk about additional costs to Russia, are you ready at this point to impose broader economic sanctions? Or are you considering other responses that go beyond sanctions?

OBAMA: I consider the actions that we've seen in the last week a continuation of what's been taking place for months now. As I said in my opening statement, there is no doubt that this is not a homegrown, indigenous uprising in eastern Ukraine. The separatists are backed, trained, armed, financed by Russia.

QUESTION: Mr. President, despite all of the actions the West has taken to get Russia to pull back from Ukraine, Russia seems intent on taking one step after another — convoys, transports of arms. At what point do sanctions no longer work? Would you envisage the possibility of a necessity of military action to get Russia to pull back from Ukraine?

OBAMA: We are not taking military action to solve the Ukrainian problem. What we're doing is to mobilize the international community to apply pressure on Russia. But I think it is very important to recognize that a military solution to this problem is not going to be forthcoming.

Hardly a vigorous challenge to President Putin. Indeed, the President's unwillingness to take strong actions is not limited to international affairs. After leaking stories for weeks that the Administration would issue sweeping executive orders on immigration, halting deportations and granting temporary legal status to millions, this week the White House quickly dropped the idea, probably because endangered southern Democrats objected. So we have a President who does not seem to know what strategy to pursue either at home or abroad.

Week 294
(NATO'ED)

September 7, 2014

Ever since the end of the Cold War, NATO has seemed like an alliance in search of a mission. With the communist threat gone, defense budgets were cut and readiness deteriorated. September 11 gave NATO new impetus, and the alliance took on terrorism and joined the fight in Afghanistan. With that war coming to at least a temporary close, many wondered what would be next for NATO, but that changed when Russia began its aggression in Ukraine. So NATO's 2014 summit in Wales was far different from the symbolic gatherings of alliance leaders in recent years. Now there was real work to do, and President Obama set about doing it. Not only was Russia on President Obama's agenda for the NATO summit, ISIS (or ISIL as the President calls it) was also a major topic for discussion.

To frame the importance of the NATO summit, President Obama first travelled to Estonia. The purpose was simple: send a warning to President Putin. Russia has recently escalated its aggression in Ukraine, sending in more equipment and thousands of additional troops. This has made NATO's Eastern European members, especially the Baltic states with their significant Russian populations, very nervous. President Obama went to Estonia to send the message that Ukraine-style aggression against these NATO allies would not be tolerated. But that still left open the issue of what to do about Ukraine. There, the work of the alliance got much harder.

The Western European NATO members have been equally concerned about Russian aggression, but have been cautious in their response. Western Europe relies on Russia for energy and most NATO members have cut their defense budgets to the bone, meaning they are militarily unprepared to confront Russian aggression even symbolically. All NATO members have rejected military intervention in Ukraine and most have refused any significant military aid to the Ukrainian government. That has left sanctions as the tool of choice for the alliance, along with overdue efforts to improve military preparedness. What emerged from the NATO summit was a commitment to increase defense budgets, move more forces to Eastern Europe, create a rapid reaction force, and increase sanctions on Russia.

In his press conference at the end of the summit, President Obama summarized NATO's challenge and strategy as follows:

> We've met at a time of transition and a time of testing. After more than a decade, NATO's combat mission in Afghanistan is coming to an end. Russia's aggression against Ukraine threatens our vision of a Europe that is whole, free and at peace. In the Middle East, the terrorist threat from ISIL poses a growing danger. Here at this summit, our Alliance has summoned the will, the resources and the capabilities to meet all of these challenges.

> First and foremost, we have reaffirmed the central mission of the Alliance. Article 5 enshrines our solemn duty to each other — "an armed attack against one...shall be considered an attack against them all." This is a binding, treaty obligation. It

is non-negotiable. And here in Wales, we've left absolutely no doubt — we will defend every Ally.

Second, we agreed to be resolute in reassuring our Allies in Eastern Europe. Increased NATO air patrols over the Baltics will continue. Rotations of additional forces throughout Eastern Europe for training and exercises will continue. Naval patrols in the Black Sea will continue. And all 28 NATO nations agreed to contribute to all of these measures — for as long as necessary.

Third, to ensure that NATO remains prepared for any contingency, we agreed to a new Readiness Action Plan. The Alliance will update its defense planning. We will create a new highly ready Rapid Response Force that can be deployed on very short notice. We'll increase NATO's presence in Central and Eastern Europe with additional equipment, training, exercises and troop rotations. And the $1 billion initiative that I announced in Warsaw will be a strong and ongoing US contribution to this plan.

Fourth, all 28 NATO nations have pledged to increase their investments in defense and to move toward investing 2 percent of their GDP in our collective security. . . .

Fifth, our Alliance is fully united in support of Ukraine's sovereignty, independence and territorial integrity and its right to defend itself. To back up this commitment, all 28 NATO Allies will now provide security assistance to Ukraine. This includes non-lethal support to the Ukrainian military — like body armor, fuel and medical care for wounded Ukrainian troops — as well as assistance to help modernize Ukrainian forces, including logistics and command and control.

While President Obama did not ask NATO to take on any formal role in the fight against ISIS, the President did use the summit to lobby for an international coalition. This objective took on more urgency, because during his trip another American reporter, Steven Sotloff, was beheaded by ISIS. President Obama commented during his press conference that:

I also leave here confident that NATO Allies and partners are prepared to join in a broad, international effort to combat the threat posed by ISIL. Already, Allies have joined us in Iraq, where we have stopped ISIL's advances; we've equipped our Iraqi partners, and helped them go on offense. NATO has agreed to play a role in providing security and humanitarian assistance to those who are on the front lines. Key NATO Allies stand ready to confront this terrorist threat through military, intelligence and law enforcement, as well as diplomatic efforts. And Secretary Kerry will now travel to the region to continue building the broad-based coalition that will enable us to degrade and ultimately destroy ISIL.

However, as for the plan to defeat ISIS, that remains a mystery and a topic of debate within the White House. So despite the achievements at the NATO summit, many questions remain about both NATO's resolve and the President's ability to lead the alliance to address the challenges posed by Russia and ISIS, but at least this was a summit with a purpose.

Week 295

(THE PROGRESSIVE AT WAR)

September 14, 2014

For weeks the central question in Washington has been how will the Obama Administration address the rise of ISIS in the Middle East. A debate has been raging within the Administration on what that strategy should be, with many of the President's foreign policy advisors pushing for a more aggressive approach, while the President and his allies on the Left appearing to favor more caution. Despite the disagreements, one thing is clear, ISIS is a threat and something must be done. That is why after weeks of study, the White House announced that on September 10 President Obama would give a primetime address on ISIS and his plan to combat it. What emerged from that speech was a sort of progressive's guide to justifying war, but not any true blueprint for winning one.

There is no doubt that the fight against ISIS is one the President did not want. The driving theme of the President's foreign policy in the Middle East has been diplomatic engagement and military disengagement. Many fault that policy for helping to create the power vacuum that led to the rise of ISIS. Whether that is true or not, military disengagement is no longer an option, because with ISIS publicly beheading Americans and directly threatening our allies, the United States must respond. That was the message of the President's speech. However, the President is so sensitive to criticism from the Left that he began his speech talking about the virtues of Islam, not the evils of ISIS:

> Now let's make two things clear: ISIL is not "Islamic." No religion condones the killing of innocents, and the vast majority of ISIL's victims have been Muslim. And ISIL is certainly not a state. It was formerly al-Qaeda's affiliate in Iraq, and has taken advantage of sectarian strife and Syria's civil war to gain territory on both sides of the Iraq-Syrian border. It is recognized by no government, nor the people it subjugates. ISIL is a terrorist organization, pure and simple. And it has no vision other than the slaughter of all who stand in its way.

Next, the President framed the need to fight ISIS not in terms of our geopolitical interests in the Middle East, but instead focused solely on the threat ISIS directly poses to the United States:

> So ISIL poses a threat to the people of Iraq and Syria, and the broader Middle East — including American citizens, personnel and facilities. If left unchecked, these terrorists could pose a growing threat beyond that region — including to the United States. While we have not yet detected specific plotting against our homeland,

ISIL leaders have threatened America and our allies. Our intelligence community believes that thousands of foreigners — including Europeans and some Americans — have joined them in Syria and Iraq. Trained and battle-hardened, these fighters could try to return to their home countries and carry out deadly attacks.

Again, this was to appease the Left, which believes that military action is only appropriate to combat direct threats to America. Given this, the President focused his justification for military action on those direct threats. Then the President laid out his plan to defeat ISIS by building a broad international coalition and pursuing the following steps:

First, we will conduct a systematic campaign of airstrikes against these terrorists. Working with the Iraqi government, we will expand our efforts beyond protecting our own people and humanitarian missions, so that we're hitting ISIL targets as Iraqi forces go on offense. . . .

Second, we will increase our support to forces fighting these terrorists on the ground. In June, I deployed several hundred American service members to Iraq to assess how we can best support Iraqi Security Forces. Now that those teams have completed their work — and Iraq has formed a government — we will send an additional 475 service members to Iraq. As I have said before, these American forces will not have a combat mission — we will not get dragged into another ground war in Iraq. . . .

Across the border, in Syria, we have ramped up our military assistance to the Syrian opposition. Tonight, I again call on Congress to give us additional authorities and resources to train and equip these fighters. . . .

Third, we will continue to draw on our substantial counterterrorism capabilities to prevent ISIL attacks. Working with our partners, we will redouble our efforts to cut off its funding; improve our intelligence; strengthen our defenses; counter its warped ideology; and stem the flow of foreign fighters into — and out of — the Middle East. . . .

Fourth, we will continue providing humanitarian assistance to innocent civilians who have been displaced by this terrorist organization.

The President made clear the fight with ISIS would be long and hard, and he promised no quick victory. However, many question whether the President's plan has any chance of achieving success. While the Administration appears willing to now arm moderate Syrian rebels, retrain Iraqi forces, and launch some airstrikes in Syria, these tools alone might not be enough to defeat ISIS. Despite the fact that the President says we must defeat ISIS, he continues to promises that U.S. forces will not have a direct combat role. If the threat from ISIS is so great, why is the President unwilling to consider U.S. ground forces to meet that threat. The reasons are ideological and political. The President wants military disengagement in the Middle East, so he is unwilling to commit the full force of the U.S. military to defeat ISIS. This is clearly a political decision, not a military one. The President's approach is also ideological, because the Left will not stand for another war in the Middle East, and the President either agrees with them, or is unwilling to antagonize them. So what came out of the President's speech was the contradictory description of a dire threat and half measures to address it. Not much of a plan for success.

Week 296

(MAKING FRIENDS)

September 21, 2014

This week witnessed one of the very few bipartisan periods of the Obama second term. With strikes against ISIS and midterm elections looming, neither party was spoiling for a fight and virtually every member of the House and a third of the Senate simply wanted to get out of Washington and return home for campaigning. So with some contentious issues before Congress and little time to deal with them, one might have expected confrontation and brinksmanship. Instead, bills were passed, congratulations extended, and Congress went home.

There was a great deal to do in the last week of the current Congress. The government had to be funded and votes needed to be taken on the response to ISIS. These difficult issues were dealt with quickly and without much controversy. On the budget, the spending deal reached last year was scheduled to expire in October. Without a continuing resolution, the government would run out of money and shut down. Democrats probably secretly hoped for a shutdown, and anticipated that Speaker Boehner would have trouble getting a continuing resolution passed. Instead, it was all too easy. The House leadership proposed a continuing resolution through December 2014 at the spending levels under the prior budget deal. Conservatives did not like that deal, but they did not have the will to fight this time. So rather than opposing, they held their noses and the continuing resolution passed easily, and went to the Senate where passage was also prompt. In reality, this bill only delayed the budget debate until December, but that seemed fine to everyone, including the President.

In many ways, the President's proposal to Congress regarding ISIS was more controversial. The White House has taken the position that it does not need congressional authorization to strike ISIS. Both liberals and conservatives have taken issue with that view, but the leadership in neither party was willing to press the issue. So instead, the ISIS debate was focused on a bill authorizing $500 million to fund and train moderate Syrian rebels. This could have been a vehicle to express opposition to the President's policy, but opponents did not have enough fight in them. This was despite the fact that the President's own advisors, including the chairman of the joint chiefs, suggested ground troops would be needed, an idea the President quickly and emphatically shot down. Even this chaos in the Administration could not prompt a more determined fight.

In the end, the President's bill to fund the Syrian rebels passed 273-156, with 159 Republicans and 114 Democrats voting yes, with the opponents almost equally divided between Democrats and Republicans. It seems the wings of both parties are equally unhappy with the President. Liberals think the President must get congressional authorization and fear another quagmire in the Middle East. Conservatives also think authorization is required and they also believe the President's plan is likely to fail. So 156 members in the House expressed their dissatisfaction, but the bill passed easily, as did the Senate.

So the President got a budget and he got his money for his ISIS strategy, but these results were only tactical victories. The true budget battle will be fought in December and next year. As for ISIS, the President's policy is being questioned across the political spectrum and the White House has cornered itself by asserting U.S. ground forces will not be used no matter what. This could be a recipe for failure and stalemate, but like the other events this week, that battle will only be joined after the midterm election.

Week 297

(HOLDER GONE)

September 28, 2014

There are few members of President Obama's cabinet who have engendered more Republican anger that Attorney General Eric Holder. In the GOP's view, Holder has been an enabler and protector of the White House, using his significant powers to support aggressive executive action while thwarting Republican investigations into a host of issues. With the reputation as a political attorney general, one would have thought the GOP would be celebrating this week as Eric Holder announced his plan to resign, but like so many other things, the Republicans saw this timing as yet another political move by Holder.

The President has been under increasing criticism for his isolation. The President minimizes his dialogue with Republicans, gets very little counsel from most of his cabinet members, and does not even have close relations with Democrat leaders on Capitol Hill. Instead, the President relies on a close circle of long-time allies for advice, including White House advisor Valerie Jarrett, his wife Michelle, and his political team from Chicago. One exception to this has been the attorney general. While not part of the President's Chicago team, Holder and Obama have been friends and allies for years, and Holder was a natural choice for attorney general. As a former prosecutor and official in the Clinton Justice Department, Holder proved to be a reliable ally for the Administration. If anything, the President was a moderating influence on Holder, rather than the other way around.

On issue after issue, Attorney General Holder has pushed a liberal agenda from the Justice Department. Holder was an early advocate of both closing Gitmo and trying terrorist suspects in civilian courts, both positions where the Administration has had to backtrack. Under his leadership, DOJ has vigorously prosecuted civil rights and antitrust regulations, and pursued a number of investigations and prosecutions relating to the banking collapse in 2008. Holder has led a legal assault on state voting regulations and limitations on abortion. DOJ has also sought to shield the White House from a number of investigations, including the IRS targeting of conservative groups and Benghazi. Most infuriating to Republicans, Holder has supported the President's broad use of executive powers on health care and other regulatory issues. The attorney general has been a valuable ally to the President indeed.

Considering that, one might have thought that Holder's announced plans to step down when a successor is confirmed would have been a disappointment to the President and a cause for celebration among Republicans. However, Holder's resignation plans appear political. With the midterm elections little more than a month away, and with the GOP poised to take control of the Senate, the Administration is facing the prospect of having a hard time getting its nominees confirmed. This will especially be the case for Attorney General. This explains the timing of Holder's resignation. President Obama wants and needs a close ally at Justice and the only way to ensure that is to get a nominee through before the potential Republican Senate takeover. So Holder announced his resignation at the end of September, and Majority Leader Reid then quickly indicated that he would consider a lame duck confirmation of his replacement, presumably using the new Senate confirmation rules designed to limit the GOP's ability to obstruct. So the plan appears to be to get Holder out and get another Obama ally in before the Republicans can gum up the works.

It seems fitting that the Attorney General's last move has been as political as so many of his others. For a President who has been unable to pass any major legislation since 2010, having a close supporter and ally at DOJ has been essential, and Holder has done his job very well. It seems his resignation announcement was yet another move to help and support his friend in the White House. Whether the plan to confirm Holder's replacement in the lame duck session will succeed is unclear, because the GOP will be sure to loudly protest, but here as with so many other things, Eric Holder has been willing to do the utmost to support the President.

Week 298

(On the Ballot)

October 5, 2014

With only a month until the midterm election, President Obama finds himself in the uncomfortable position as a persona non grata on the campaign trail. With his approval ratings low, especially in Republican states where vulnerable Democrats are on the ballot, the President has been relegated largely to private fundraising events. For a man who prides himself on his political and campaign skills, it must be grating for the President to be unwanted by his own Democrat allies. To date, the White House has been able to restrain the President's natural impulse to intervene aggressively in the election, at least until this week.

In 2010, the Democrats were facing a disastrous election and President Obama was unpopular, but unmoved, the President spent months on the campaign trail, putting his personal political capital on the line for congressional Democrats. The result was a disaster for his party, with Republicans gaining 63 seats in the House and picking up 6 seats in the Senate. The Administration has at least partially learned its lesson in 2014, with the President trying to keep a low profile as Democrats fight for survival. However, a political lion can only be caged for so long, so President Obama did hit the campaign trail this week, going to possibly the only State where he might be welcome: Illinois. The event was an October 2 economic speech at Northwestern University, which had two goals, promote the Obama economy and warn that Republicans will destroy the progress made.

The President started the speech with a recitation of his accomplishments:

As Americans, we can and should be proud of the progress that our country has made over these past six years. And here are the facts — because sometimes the noise clutters and I think confuses the nature of the reality out there. Here are the facts: When I took office, businesses were laying off 800,000 Americans a month. Today, our businesses are hiring 200,000 Americans a month. The unemployment rate has come down from a high of 10 percent in 2009, to 6.1 percent today. Over the past four and a half years, our businesses have created 10 million new jobs; this is the longest uninterrupted stretch of private sector job creation in our history.

While saying the economy is better, the President then turned to his favorite issue, namely income inequality:

When the typical family isn't bringing home any more than it did in 1997, then that means it's harder for middle-class Americans to climb the ladder of success. It means that it's harder for poor Americans to grab hold of the ladder into the middle class. That's not what America is supposed to be about. It offends the very essence of who we are. Because if being an American means anything, it means we believe that even if we're born with nothing — regardless of our circumstances, a last name, whether we were wealthy, whether our parents were advantaged — no matter what our circumstances, with hard work we can change our lives, and then our kids can too. . . . This is going to be a central challenge of our times. We have to make our economy work for every working American. And every policy I pursue as President is aimed at answering that challenge.

The President then presented his agenda for helping middle class Americans, focused on more stimulus spending on energy, infrastructure, and education. The President also touted Obamacare and claimed that he had solved the Federal government's debt challenge:

And this is a game-changer for the fourth cornerstone of this new foundation — getting our fiscal house in order for the long run, so we can afford to make investments that grow the middle class. . . . Between a growing economy, some prudent spending cuts, health care reform, and asking the wealthiest Americans to pay a little bit more on their taxes, over the past five years we've cut our deficits by more than half. When I took office, the deficit was nearly 10 percent of our economy. Today, it's approaching 3 percent.

There was nothing new in any of this, it is the same thing the President has been talking about for years. Importantly, there was no mention of any tough issues, like entitlement or tax reform. Instead, this speech was focused on convincing voters that the economy is great and pushing the Administration's standard economic agenda. The President then turned political, which was the true purpose of the speech: "Now, an argument you'll hear oftentimes from critics is that the way to grow the economy is to just get rid of regulations; free folks up from the oppressive hand of the government. And you know, it turns out, truth be told, there are still some kind of dopey regulations on the books." After putting up this straw man, the President got to his real punch line:

Now, I am not on the ballot this fall. Michelle is pretty happy about that. But make no mistake: These policies are on the ballot — every single one of them. This isn't some official campaign speech, or political speech, and I'm not going to tell you who to vote for — although I suppose it is kind of implied... But what I have done is laid out my ideas to create more jobs and to grow more wages. And I've also tried to correct the record — because, as I said, there's a lot of noise out there. Every item I ticked off, those are the facts. It's not conjecture. It's not opinion. It's not partisan rhetoric. I laid out facts.

And with this, President Obama made himself the issue in the midterm election. Within hours Republicans started running ads highlighting this comment, while Democrats and the White House started running as fast as they could. The reality is that the President is currently so politically toxic that the last thing Democrats want is any focus on him in this election The timing could not have been worse, because the President's comments overshadowed the good economic news released October 3, with the economy producing 248,000 jobs in September and the unemployment rate dropping to 5.9%. Unfortunately, all this might be too late for the Democrats, because the voters perceive that the economy is not working for them, and that will not change regardless of presidential rhetoric.

Week 299

(Ebola'ed)

October 12, 2014

One of the biggest challenges facing President Obama is the perception of lack of competence. The Obamacare rollout and the VA scandal created an image of an incompetent and unresponsive government. This is dangerous for an Administration dedicated to convincing Americans that government can improve their lives. So the last thing the President needed in this political season was another example of government incompetence, but that is exactly what the White House is facing with the current Ebola scare.

Ebola is a well-known and deadly virus with its origins in West Africa. In December 2013, there was an Ebola outbreak in Guinea, which then spread to Liberia and Sierra Leone. The governments in West Africa responded slowly to the threat, and it was not until mid-2014 that a large scale international response began. Many American doctors are working to fight the disease in West Africa and there are plans to deploy U.S. troops to augment the response. Ebola is a deadly virus with no vaccine, and as the disease has spread in West Africa, so too has the fear of an outbreak in the United States. Each day, approximately 150 people travel from West Africa to the United States, and the concern is that persons infected with Ebola will cause an outbreak.

Those fears came to fruition on September 30, when the Centers for Disease Control declared its first case of Ebola in the United States. A CDC spokesperson said: "The patient is a man who became infected in Liberia and traveled to Texas, where he was hospitalized with symptoms that were confirmed to be caused by Ebola." The patient was Thomas Duncan, and he travelled from West Africa to Dallas for a wedding, arriving September 20. He became symptomatic on September 26. When he first arrived at Dallas Health Presbyterian Hospital, Ebola was not detected, and he was sent home with antibiotics, even though he told the nurse he was from West Africa. When he returned on September 28, Ebola was discovered. He was put in isolation and those with whom he had contact were put under observation. Unfortunately, Mr. Duncan died on October 8. Then on October 12, the CDC confirmed that a health worker named Nina Pham, who was treated Duncan, also contracted Ebola. The CDC said it was caused by "an inadvertent breach of protocol." This caused a great deal of concern that there could be a significant outbreak in the United States.

The reason Ebola is a political problem for the White House is that the President has to date refused to ban travel to and from West Africa. Also, the CDC has provided assurances that the federal government is fully prepared to deal with Ebola, only to find out that Dallas Health Presbyterian Hospital was not prepared, which led to others getting infected. The Administration's plan to send U.S. troops to West Africa will pose the risk of even more infections. Indeed, in July 2014 the United States had to evacuate two healthcare workers, Dr. Kent Brantly and Nancy Writebol, because both had contracted Ebola. Both recovered. So once again we are seeing a federal government that does not seem prepared or competent to deal with a threat. Given the many other recent government failures, this newest one is adding to the image of an effective President.

Week 300

(JITTERS)

October 19, 2014

In a tough election year, one of the few issues favoring Democrats has been the relatively strong economy. With unemployment falling, strong corporate profits, and lower energy prices, President Obama and his allies could point to the economy as one of the reasons not to change course by voting Republican. However, that argument started to fall apart entering into October as a bull market seemed to give way to some panic selling. Now, the Democrats have a new front to defend, at the worst possible time.

It is fair to say that the U.S. economy has shown some remarkable resilience since 2009, managing to continue slow growth and slow job market improvement for five years. Economic growth has been too slow to spur dramatic job or wage gains, but has been sufficient to build some minimal momentum. That seemed to change early this year, as growth projections for the second quarter got much stronger, as did wage growth. This made Democrats optimistic they could use the economy to blunt Republican gains. Sadly, rather than continuing to roll, the good times went on the skids, at least temporarily.

In the last four weeks, the stock market has dropped approximately 8 percent from its highs, with huge volatility. The culprits are many: international instability, falling oil prices, an emerging recession in Europe, and a general perception that the stock market is overvalued. All of this has contributed to a quick sell off, with indexes falling precipitously, especially this week. On October 14, the Dow was at one point off nearly 450 points, only to slightly recover before closing. Then on October 17, the Dow soared more than 250 points following strong earnings. With this rally, the markets cut some of their losses, but the Standard & Poor's 500 index is still 6 percent below the record high it set September 18.

No one knows if this volatility will continue or if it is nearing an end, but the timing is not good for the President. The economy was one of the few arguments he had to counter Republican attacks, but with investors and wage earners feeling increasingly nervous, touting the economy might make the Democrats seem out of touch, doing little to help their electoral prospects. So for now Republicans see another front to attack and more opportunities to fight for gains in Congress. For a President who has so often benefited from good timing and good luck, it seems like this time his luck may have run out.

Week 301

(WARRING ON WOMEN)

October 26, 2014

The Democrats have known for a long time that the 2014 midterm election would be tough for them because they would be fighting against both historical trends and an unfavorable political map. The party of the sitting President almost always loses seats in its second midterm election, a good recent example being President George W. Bush's 2006 midterm, where Republicans lost the Senate and the House. Bill Clinton was able to avoid this trend in his second midterm in 1998, but mainly because of the very strong economy and the GOP's errors in the Monica Lewinsky scandal. As for the political map, it could hardly be worse for Democrats. In the House, the Republicans dominated the redistricting process in 2010, meaning Democrats have very few good targets and many vulnerable seats. In the Senate, the Democrats big year in 2008 translates into many tough seats to defend in 2014, including GOP states like Louisiana, Arkansas, Montana, South Dakota, Alaska, and West Virginia. The Democrats answer to these daunting odds: proclaim a war on women.

One of the several demographic changes that have fueled recent Democrat successes at the polls is strength with women voters, especially unmarried college educated women. This gender gap has helped Democrats win close races and their entire 2014 strategy has been focused on trying to exploit it. So the Democrats have proclaimed that the Republicans have declared a war on women. There evidence, GOP policy positions on abortion, pay equity, contraceptives, minimum wage, and sexual assault. On these issues, Democrats argue the Republican positions are designed limit women's rights and hurt them economically. Using this theme, in races across the country Democrats have spent tens of millions of dollars on ads trying to paint Republicans as anti-woman. Sounded like a great strategy in theory, but it has not worked out so well in practice.

Despite trying to make the election about supposed women issues, the election is really about the economy and President Obama. So when Democrats in race after race spend so much time talking about women's issues, it creates the appearance that they are ignoring the voters' real concerns. Also, in several key races, Democrats overplayed the war on women issue so much, it actually ended up hurting their candidates. A good example is Colorado, when Democrat incumbent Senator Mark Udall made the war on women his central theme against Republican Cory Gardner. Gardner turned the tables by advocating free contraceptives and has taken the lead in the race. Likewise, in Iowa so committed was Democrat Bruce Braley to the war on women theme that he tried to use it against Republican Jodi Ernst, a woman, former veteran, and state legislator. The effort flopped, and a race the Democrats thought would be well in hand is now a tossup. Probably was best example of the war on women strategy is in Texas, where Democrat gubernatorial candidate Wendy David has made her campaign almost exclusively about it, and she is losing very badly to her GOP opponent.

When Democrat strategists in Washington hatched the war on women concept, it must have seemed so clever to them. They saw it as a way to motivate a core constituency and make the midterms about the Republicans, not the President and his party. It was identity politics taken to a new level, but the strategy was overdone and over used. Trying to force voters to focus on issues not at the top of their concerns, and trying to use it against opponents where it just does not fit, turned their strategy from a benefit to a hindrance. No matter, the Democrats have continued their talking points and ad buys. The strategy might be deemed a success by Democrat strategists if a sufficient number of young women show up to vote in some key races to save a few seats, but at a macro level it has been a colossal failure. That might explain why more and more desperate Democrats are returning to other favored themes, like Mary Landrieu's new focus on racism. This week Landrieu even asserted that she was behind because of Louisiana's racist past, while the national Democrats are running ads that GOP support for gun rights "caused the shooting of Trayvon Martin." When the new song does not work, best to go back to that old favorite tune.

Week 302

(SIDELINED)

November 2, 2014

President Obama loves to campaign, in fact it might be his greatest skill. The President often seems annoyed by political bargaining, not much interested in building relationships with members of Congress, and hates questions from the press, but put him on the stump and he is in his element. More than any other President, Barak Obama likes to hit the road, give political speeches, and headline fundraisers. In fact, he has done these things more than any other President in history. Given this, the current election cycle must be very frustrating for him, because he has been sidelined, with most Democrat candidates wanting him to stay as far away as possible.

President Obama has a very high opinion of his own political skills. No doubt, he ran masterful campaigns in 2008 and 2012. The President has had great success getting himself elected, but he has not done so well for members of his party. In 2010, the President promised Democrats that the GOP had no chance of taking either house of Congress, and spent weeks barnstorming the country for candidates. When the Republicans took the House with a 63 seat gain and picked up 6 seats in the Senate, it was a true shock to the President, leading to a rare moment of candors when he admitted in his post-election press conference that the Democrats took a "shellacking." No doubt, the President hoped to redeem himself in his 2014 midterm election, but his fellow party members were not willing to even give him a chance.

The true action in the 2014 midterm election is in the Senate, where the parties are battling over open seats in West Virginia, Iowa, South Dakota, and Montana. Also, Democrat incumbents are locked in tight races in New Hampshire, North Carolina, Louisiana, Arkansas, Colorado, and Alaska. The majority of these states are GOP leaning, and in every one where a Democrat incumbent is running, President Obama's voter support is very weak. As a result, endangered Democrat incumbents are doing everything they can to distance themselves from the President. Indeed, if one were to listen to Kay Hagen, Mary Landrieu and Mark Pryor, in North Carolina, Louisiana, and Arkansas, respectively, you would think they were Republicans given their constant criticisms of the President. In view of all this, President Obama has been persona non grata in these races, and none of these Democrats asked him to campaign for them, in fact they are affirmatively trying to keep him away.

So what is a campaign addict like Barak Obama to do. His main focus has been private fundraisers, because while endangered Democrats do not want to be seen with him, they still want his help financially. The President has also ventured out to do some campaigning, but only is safe Democrat states, like Illinois and Maryland. In many ways, these trips were more face saving than anything else, because it would be just too embarrassing for the President to do no campaigning whatsoever. The hope is that if the few candidates he campaigns for win, the President can make the point that he had a positive impact on the midterms.

All of this is driven by the Democrat's tactical decision to distance themselves from the White House rather than embrace the Obama agenda and record. The reason for this is obvious: the President is at the lowest ebb of his popularity in office and his major policy achievements, like Obamacare, are equally unpopular. The strategy is logical, but also a bit dishonest, because the Democrats trying to get reelected have all supported the President's policies. So their record of supporting the Administration is in direct contrast with their rhetoric on the campaign trail. Indeed, because Majority Leader Reid stopped his own members from introducing amendments that would have allowed for votes to distance themselves from the White House, most of the endangered incumbents have voting records showing support of the President exceeding 97%. This has been a major theme of GOP ads in the closing days of the campaign. So while the President has been physically sidelined, he is still the central issue in the campaign, no matter how much the Democrats try to hide him.

Week 303

(THE 2/3)

November 9, 2014

The conventional wisdom among mainstream political pundits was that in the 2014 midterm election, the Republicans would make some gains, but there would be no wave like the one that led to the GOP takeover of the House in 2010. Going into the election, it was expected that the Republicans would gain a few House seats, suffer net losses in governor races, and that the GOP would have a very hard time winning the six seats needed to take control of the Senate. Like generals who always try to re-fight the last war, political professionals assumed the factors that led to the Democrats' victory in 2012 would simply repeat again in 2014. Instead, the Republicans crushed the Democrats at every level and nearly swept the field. So much for the opinions of mainstream pundits.

The results tell the story. In the Senate, of the 10 races that were rated tossups, Republicans won eight of them (in North Carolina, West Virginia, Arkansas, Iowa, South Dakota, Montana, Colorado, and Alaska), and appear headed to another victory in a December 6 runoff in Louisiana. This was more than enough to give the GOP the majority. In the House, Republicans picked up at least 12 seats, giving them their largest majority since 1948. As strong as this was, Republicans did even better at the state level, scoring a net gain of 3 governorships (giving them a total of 31), including wins in the Democrat states of Maryland, Massachusetts, and Illinois. The GOP also did great in state legislatures, resulting in their control of 66 of the 99 state legislative chambers, their largest margin of control since the 1920's. It was a virtual wipeout, catching the Washington elites completely off guard.

Many different explanations were offered for the GOP landslide: a favorable Senate map for Republicans, bad historical trends for the party in power in midterms, low turnout, and disenchanted minority voters. However, the biggest cause, admitted by all but the most partisan Democrat operatives, was the unpopularity of President Obama, who currently has some of the worst poll numbers of his presidency. For a President widely viewed as isolated, disengaged, and ineffective, most thought the election result would be a wakeup call for the White House. Not to be, because when the President took the podium the day after the election for a press conference, he made clear would neither recognize the scope of the Republican victory nor change any aspect of how he governs.

In the press conference, the President started by talking about the strengthening economy, as though that would make people forget what happened the day before at the ballot box. When he turned to the election, unlike 2010 when he admitted his party took a "shellacking," this time, still unwilling to give an inch to his opponents, all he would say was: "Obviously, Republicans had a good night. And they deserve credit for running good campaigns. Beyond that, I'll leave it to all of you and the professional pundits to pick through yesterday's results." Refusing to take any blame, he quickly implied that the voters only want Washington to work better and the election results should be discounted because only 1/3 of registered voters came to the polls: "Still, as President, I have a unique responsibility to try and make this town work. So, to everyone who voted, I want you to know that I hear you. To the two-thirds of voters who chose not to participate in the process yesterday, I hear you, too." Then, refusing to recognize what an unpopular and divisive figure he has become, he tried to revive the excitement of his 2008 election by reusing an old phrase: "So, the fact is, I still believe in what I said when I was first elected six years ago last night. All the maps plastered across our TV screens today and for all the cynics who say otherwise, I continue to believe we are simply more than just a collection of red and blue states. We are the United States."

As for what he would do differently, other than offering some platitudes, the President made clear it would be pretty much nothing: "Well, as I said in my opening remarks, the American people overwhelmingly believe that this town doesn't work well, and that it is not attentive to their needs. And as President, they rightly hold me accountable to do more to make it work properly. . . . I'm the guy who's elected by everybody, not just from a particular state or a particular district. And they want me to push hard to close some of these divisions, break through some of the gridlock, and get stuff done. . . . So, the most important thing I can do is just get stuff done and help Congress get some things done."

What this press conference made clear is that America is in for a very turbulent and unproductive two years. The central ethic of the Obama White House is never concede anything, so even in the face of a crushing defeat, the President has remained utterly defiant and immovable.

In fact, knowing it would infuriate Republicans, the President spent most of the week emphasizing that he would soon take executive action on immigration, the move he knows will ignite a political war in Washington. In many ways, President Obama may feel more comfortable with the new Republican Congress, since he will now be free to demonize the GOP without limit. With Republicans in control of Congress, he will likely view the new landscape as an open invitation to blame Republicans for everything and pursue a purely partisan agenda. He likely believes that will help Democrats in 2016, regardless of whether it will be good for the country. So we are about to enter the era of the President as the partisan-in-chief, and it is going to get very ugly indeed.

Week 304

(GRUBERISM)

November 16, 2014

After suffering a stunning defeat in the midterm election, President Obama went overseas for an Asia tour to China, Burma, and Australia for meetings and a G20 economic summit. The President surely viewed the trip as an opportunity to both escape the political fallout of his party's defeat in the midterms and a chance to retake in initiative. Before leaving on his trip, the President repeatedly made clear in both his post-election press conference and in an interview for Face the Nation that he has no plans to either change course or conciliate Republicans. Instead, his strategy is confrontation. So while overseas, the President entered into a climate deal with China that he knew would be condemned by the GOP and during a press conference in Burma reiterated that he would issue executive orders on immigration regardless of Republican objections. It seems the President simply wanted to use the world stage to goad his opponents. He had a little unwelcomed help in that effort from an unlikely source, MIT professor Jonathan Gruber.

Dr. Gruber is an economics professor at MIT who has devoted much of his academic work to health care reform. He was an advisor to Mitt Romney when Romney reformed the health care system in Massachusetts, and he was a paid government consultant who helped design Obamacare. Gruber is a huge proponent of Obamacare, which is why it is so ironic that he has done more damage to that government program than probably any other individual. This is because this week the media finally started paying attention to Gruber's repeated public comments (now captured in no less than seven videos) that Obamacare was designed to deceive, raise taxes, end employer-provided health care, and was only pushed through because of the economic ignorance and "stupidity" of the American voter. At first it was only conservative media outlets like Fox News that covered the Gruber story, but as more and more videos emerged and more and more people became outraged by his comments, the story started to draw national attention. Even President Obama and Nancy Pelosi felt obliged to address the controversy, both claiming they barely knew Gruber and his role in Obamacare was marginal (even though both had previously publicly praised and cited Gruber).

The controversy over Gruber's comments has created a firestorm for many reasons. First, many believe his mentality — namely that average Americans are stupid and need to be told what to do by smart liberals – captures the very essence of the progressive mindset. Second, Obamacare opponents have been saying for years that the law was purposefully deceptive, designed to achieve a massive transfer of wealth, and would be used for force employees off employer-provided health care and onto the federal and state exchanges. Gruber not only admits as much, he boasts about it over and over again. That is why Democrats are scurrying to distance themselves from Gruber, while the media now terms the controversy Grubergate. So while the President was overseas trying to reset his agenda, his ally Dr. Gruber was undermining him by being a bit too candid about the progressives' agenda and attitude about average Americans.

Gruberism, another label now popular in Washington, is the philosophy that power and wealth must be transferred from ordinary Americans and put in the hands of a government run by smart liberals who can then control how ordinary Americans live their lives. President Obama would publicly deny that he practices Gruberism, but his actions this week show that he is in fact a devotee of that doctrine. Part of Gruberism is ignoring and denigrating public opinion and forcing through progressive measures by any means available. The President demonstrated on his trip that he plans to do exactly that. On climate change, he signed a deal with China to reduce carbon emissions even though it cannot be ratified by the Senate. The President thinks it must be done, so he plans to try to force it through regardless of opposition. The same is true on immigration. Despite the rebuke in the election and his prior comments that he lacked authority to grant amnesty by executive action, he taunted Republicans repeatedly that he would do exactly that. Despite the will of the voters, the President has now made clear that he will push through progressive policies whether by legal means or not. Maybe the President is trying to prove that he is more of a Gruberite and Gruber himself.

Week 305

(DEFIANCE)

November 23, 2014

In the wake of his electoral rebuke in the midterms, President Obama seems to be embarking on a novel response, pure defiance. After proclaiming that his policies were on the ballot and, after he and his party suffered a devastating defeat, rather than reevaluating his approach to policy and governance to address the voters' concerns, President Obama has instead decided to do the same things he has been doing for the last five years, just more aggressively. Unlike President Clinton, who tried to moderate and triangulate his way around a Republican Congress, President Obama's plan is total confrontation.

In many ways, the 2014 defeat in the midterms seems to be a liberating moment for President Obama. With only two years left in office and his party in taters at every level of government except the executive branch, the Administration plans no reevaluation. Quite the opposite, they are doubling down on progressive policies and partisan combat. So it is not surprising that the President waited barely two weeks to start his counteroffensive against the GOP. His goal is to start a political war with the Republicans immediately. He did exactly that with his announcement on November 20 of executive orders granting de facto amnesty to 5 million illegal immigrants.

The last thing President Obama wants is to be viewed as is a lame duck, that is simply inconsistent with his view of his own importance. So a statement had to be made that he is still a power to be reckoned with, and immigration was his vehicle. The President could have passed immigration reform when his party controlled both houses on Congress, but President Obama feared to do so before his reelection campaign. Then when immigration rights activists clamored for executive action when the Senate's immigration reform bill died in the House, the President repeatedly said he lacked the authority to grant amnesty by executive order. But being unable to pass any significant legislation, the President nevertheless threatened to use his executive powers on immigration. He held off until after the 2014 midterms, but when his party got slaughtered anyways, there was no longer any reason to wait.

The plan announced on November 20 in a prime time address to the nation has three parts, described by the President as follows:

> First, we'll build on our progress at the border with additional resources for our law enforcement personnel so that they can stem the flow of illegal crossings and speed the return of those who do cross over.

> Second, I'll make it easier and faster for high-skilled immigrants, graduates and entrepreneurs to stay and contribute to our economy, as so many business leaders proposed.

> Third, we'll take steps to deal responsibly with the millions of undocumented immigrants who already live in our country.

For the third element, through his executive orders, the President plans to shield from deportation nearly 5 million illegal immigrants, including an expansion of his dreamers program that applies to illegal immigrants brought here as children and parents of children who are citizens or legal residents, if those parents have been in the United States for five or more years. The President justified this expansive use of executive authority based on the concept of prosecutorial discretion, namely the executive can choose whom to prosecute for illegal actions. The President also asserted that his action was a common sense approach because the persons he is protecting from deportation are not likely to be deported in any event and it is better to bring them out of the shadows and get them paying taxes and fully participating in our society.

While many might agree with the result of these executive orders, how the President did this will ignite a political firestorm. Republicans practically begged him not to do it and to give them a chance to try to pass an immigration bill. The President wanted none of that, he wanted a confrontation and a political war, that is the only possible explanation why he chose not to wait. Even for many who agree with the result, the method is very troubling. Such an expansive concept of prosecutorial discretion could provide future presidents with a pretext to refuse to enforce any number of statutes passed by Congress, including tax laws, employment rules, and environmental protection. Many think the President's approach threatens our very system of separation of powers. None of this seems to matter to the White House, they wanted to make a statement and start a fight, and they certainly have done that.

Week 306

(HANDS UP)

November 30, 2014

Despite being the first African American President, President Obama continues to be reluctant to wade into issues of race. However, sometimes events of such significance arise that the President has no choice but to engage. Just such an event is occurring in Ferguson, Missouri.

On August 9, 2014, Michael Brown, an 18-year-old black teenager, was fatally shot by Darren Wilson, 28, a white Ferguson police officer. Michael Brown's body was left on the street for two hours as the shooting scene was investigated, causing fury in majority-black Ferguson. The result was riots that destroyed several local businesses and prompted a heavily armed response by local police, including use of military gear provided to local police departments. The media quickly moved to a familiar narrative of racism, focusing on claims Brown was trying to surrender, had his hands up, and was shot in the back. This image took hold, even though what actually happened the day of the shooting was very much in dispute, except for the fact that the day he was killed, Brown robbed a convenience store and pushed a store clerk, all of which was caught on a surveillance camera.

With the media narrative of racism, overly-militarized police, and black men endangered by those pledged to protect them, a grand jury decision on November 20 on whether to indict Officer Wilson struck like a thunderbolt. The grand jury refused to indict Wilson because the physical evidence and witness accounts did not support criminal charges. In fact, the evidence strongly suggested that Brown attacked Wilson, an account supported by seven eye witnesses. As for the eye witnesses who claimed Brown was shot in the back or while on the ground, they changed their stories once it became clear the physical evidence refuted those accounts.

Even though the grand jury's decision should not have been a surprise to anyone objectively reviewing the evidence, it hit with a shock in the black and liberal activist communities. Despite calls for calm and peaceful protests from Brown's family, massive riots broke out in Ferguson, with many businesses burned, resulting in Missouri Governor Nixon declaring a state of emergency. The White House was well aware of the risk of more riots, so soon after the announcement of the grand jury's decision, President Obama spoke saying:

> But I join Michael's parents in asking anyone who protests this decision to do so peacefully. . . . I also appeal to the law enforcement officials in Ferguson and the region to show care and restraint in managing peaceful protests that may occur. Understand, our police officers put their lives on the line for us every single day. They've got a tough job to do to maintain public safety and hold accountable those who break the law. . . . As they do their jobs in the coming days, they need to work with the community, not against the community, to distinguish the handful of people who may use the grand jury's decision as an excuse for violence. Distinguish them from the vast majority who just want their voices heard around legitimate issues in terms of how communities and law enforcement interact. Finally, we need to recognize that the situation in Ferguson speaks to broader challenges that we still face as a nation. The fact is in too many parts of this country a deep distrust exists between law enforcement and communities of color. Some

of this is the result of the legacy of racial discrimination in this country. And this is tragic because nobody needs good policing more than poor communities with higher crime rates.

With these words, the President tried to both quell the riots and also make the point that regardless of the basis, there is real distrust between the police and black communities. If the President had hoped the protests and riots would be limited and local, he was quickly disappointed. People took to the streets across the country, but with little rioting outside of Ferguson. The situation was getting so bad that during an immigration speech in Chicago on November 15, the President felt compelled to address Ferguson again:

> As many of you know, a verdict came down — or a grand jury made a decision yesterday that upset a lot of people. And as I said last night, the frustrations that we've seen are not just about a particular incident. They have deep roots in many communities of color who have a sense that our laws are not always being enforced uniformly or fairly. That may not be true everywhere, and it's certainly not true for the vast majority of law enforcement officials, but that's an impression that folks have and it's not just made up. It's rooted in realities that have existed in this country for a long time. Now, as I said last night, there are productive ways of responding and expressing those frustrations, and there are destructive ways of responding. Burning buildings, torching cars, destroying property, putting people at risk – that's destructive and there's no excuse for it. Those are criminal acts, and people should be prosecuted if they engage in criminal acts.

The President has taken a moderate, balanced, and restrained tone on the events in Ferguson. However, with no more elections to worry about and a clear tilt to the Left after the midterm election, it will be interesting to see how the President plans to address this emerging racial controversy. Liberals will want him to exploit it for their social and policy agenda, but will he take the bait. Even as a lame duck President who seems little concerned with election results or public views on his policies, a too aggressive tone on racial issues could further undermine any chance for a productive last two years in office. But as of late, the President seems to not be worrying about such issues, and instead is simply following his liberal instincts.

Week 307

(BLACK AND WHITE)

December 7, 2014

Events this week were driven by the politics of racial division. As tens of thousands of blacks, supported by some white progressives and professional protesters, took to the streets to demonstrate against police conduct toward black men, in Louisiana, white voters overwhelmingly threw out of office the last statewide white Democrat in the deep South. Both events have their genesis in a stunning disconnect in perceptions between black and white Americans, one that is reverberating on the streets and at the ballot box. These developments create substantial political headaches for President Obama, because there is no clear way to appeal to one side without inflaming the other.

For months, the issue of police violence has dominated the headlines, led by the shooting of Michael Brown in Ferguson, Missouri. This week, the issue gained even more momentum when a Staten Island grand jury refused to indict New York City Police Officer Daniel Pantaleo in the death of Eric Garner. Garner was illegally selling cigarettes. Several police officers approached him, and a mild confrontation captured on video ensued, where Pantaleo put Garner in the chock hold. The video clearly showed Garner repeatedly stating "I can't breathe." A few hours later, Garner died while in police custody. This event, combined with the Michael Brown shooting and other recent cases, led to more protests spreading across the country.

For black Americans, these events have cemented the view that the police are unfairly targeting black men, and using levels of force disproportionate to the threat posed. In contrast, polls show white Americans are much more inclined to look at the circumstances of each case and not draw any general conclusions on police conduct. As a result, the grand jury's decision in the Garner case was criticized almost evenly by whites and blacks, liberals and conservatives, because the video seemed to many to prove a police overreaction. This stands in stark contrast with the shooting of Michael Brown, where the evidence presented to that grand jury strongly indicated that Brown attacked office Darren Wilson before he was shot. This evidence persuaded many white Americans that Wilson did not act improperly, while it has had no perceptible impact on black perspectives, where the view still prevails that Wilson simply gunned down Michael Brown.

The similar stark racial divide was displayed at the ballot box this week. Much has been made of the Democrats' advantage with minority voters, with much less attention paid to their problems with white voters, who still make up more than 70% of the electorate. In the 2014 midterms, Republicans dominated the white vote, did better among Hispanics, resulting in huge gains even though they still lost 90% of the black vote. This trend received an exclamation point in the Louisiana runoff vote on December 6, where the GOP picked up another Senate seat and two more House seats. In the Senate contest, three-term Democrat Mary Landrieu lost to Republican congressman Bill Cassidy 56 to 44 percent. In the November primary, Landrieu got more than 90% of the black vote, but only 18% of the white vote. She likely did even worse with whites on December 6, which is why the election was not even close. Landrieu tried to win over white voters with pork barrel spending and her long Louisiana political pedigree, but that is no longer a winning formula. Instead ideology, often racially divided, is driving election results. This pattern has been seen throughout the deep South, where white Democrats are now largely extinct at the statewide and federal levels, replaced by Republicans and black Democrats representing black majority districts.

There is something very disturbing about a statewide candidate like Mary Landrieu doing so well with black voters and so horribly with white ones. The same is true for the shooting in Ferguson, where black citizens view those events from a prism so different from what many whites see. It is almost as if the two racial groups each live in and see a different reality. This difference in perception leads to the divide and the protests. For President Obama, there is no clear path to heal this divide. If anything, he has driven even more white voters into the ideological camp of the Republicans. The President is also not well positioned to deal with issues of race, because if he favors the black perspectives he might lose more white support, and minorities are his key constituency, so he cannot risk losing their support. So all that is left for the President are appeals for calm and dialogue. Given where we are on issues of race, that is not likely to be enough.

Week 308

(So Tortured)

December 14, 2014

With Republicans ready to take over control in the Senate in just a few weeks, the current Democrat majority is determined to use their last moments of control to the maximum. The most pressing item on the Senate's agenda is a budget bill to fund the government for the remainder of the fiscal year. Democrats had hoped the Republicans would overreact to the President's executive order on amnesty for illegal immigrants, forcing a government shutdown. When it became clear the GOP would not take the bait, the White House, Republicans, and the Senate Democrats were able to reach a budget compromise. But all was not bipartisanship and good cheer, because Senate Intelligence Committee Democrats used their last few days in control to issue a report finding that the CIA illegally tortured prisoners and lied about it to Congress and the White House. This parting partisan shot all but eclipsed any good feeling between Democrats and Republicans.

Under the budget compromise reached this week, all federal departments will be funded for the remainder of the fiscal year consistent with the budget caps agreed to in 2013, except for the Department of Homeland Security, which will only be funded through February 2015. This will allow Republicans the opportunity to address the President's executive orders on amnesty when funding runs out for that department early next year. The budget bill also contains items favored by Democrats (including funding for the Ebola response and operations against ISIS), along with some Republican priorities, such as changes that allow much larger contributions to political parties and an adjustment to banking regulations to allow banks more flexibility in trading derivatives.

This was a classic compromise, with items each party wanted and items each party opposes. However, the White House came to the conclusion it was the best deal it could get, and certainly better than any deal they would get next year when Republicans will be fully in control of both chambers in Congress. Even with this bipartisan deal, passage was not assured. House Minority Leader Nancy Pelosi refused to support the White House and campaigned against the bill, hoping to team up with conservative Republicans to defeat the bill and gain leverage to craft a new proposal more favorable to Democrats. The threat of a defeat got so severe that the President took to the phones to lobby for the bill, something he rarely does. In the end, the compromise passed by a vote of 219 to 206, and headed to a still uncertain fate in the Senate, where conservatives and liberals led by Senators Ted Cruz and Elizabeth Warren vowed to slow it down for different reasons, Cruz to protest against the President's executive actions, Warren to protest the changes to banking regulations.

While the leadership in Congress and the White House were struggling with this budget issue, the report from the Senate Intelligence Committee threatened to open an even wider rift between the parties. For several years, Democrats have been investigating the CIA's enhanced interrogation program, spending a reported $40 million. The committee as a whole was unable to agree to a report, so the Democrat majority issued its own report. It concluded that the CIA engaged in torture and accused the CIA of misleading Congress and not fully informing President George W. Bush of the extent of the program. The report was quickly condemned by most Republicans, nearly all former heads of the CIA, and even the White House refused to endorse it, instead simply stating mistakes has been made. The most potent criticism of the report was that the investigators refused to interview anyone at the CIA and their conclusions could put American lives at risk by enflaming foreign critics of the United States.

There is little doubt that the release of this report was a partisan exercise. Intelligence Committee Chair Diane Feinstein has been engaged in a long feud with the CIA and this was her chance to take a parting shot before she lost control of the committee. Further, the fact that the report reached such damning conclusions without even interviewing those involved in the program made it look as though it was not an objective assessment of the CIA's actions. So whatever bipartisanship was prevailing in the House, it was quickly sabotaged in the Senate.

Week 309
(VIVA CUBA)

December 21, 2014

One would have expected the big political news this week to be the federal budget compromise, which the Senate easily passed after a tight vote in the House, but instead the lead story was Cuba. It appears the White House no longer feels at all restrained by electoral politics and is now willing to simply pursue its progressive policy objectives. The President has been following that path ever sense the midterm election and took another step this week by his surprise announcement to end the United States' diplomatic isolation of Cuba, terminating a 50-year policy with little consultation with Congress and no effort to prepare the press or the public for the change. In fact, the manner in which the President pursued this initiative was designed for surprise and shock, and is all part of the Administration's strategy of showing that President Obama still commands that national stage regardless of election results.

There is no doubt that American policy on Cuba is a relic of the Cold War. The embargo and the suspension of diplomatic relations arose from Castro's Cuban revolution and the ensuing Cuban missile crisis. America has held steadfast to the policy even after the fall of the Berlin Wall and the end of the Soviet Union, in part because Castro stuck so doggedly to his communist and repressive policies. There were also strong political reasons to maintain the policy, including the influence of the Cuban exile community in South Florida. So while many Presidents have likely considered a change in Cuba policy, it was President Obama who took the fateful step, announcing the change in a December 17 surprise press conference.

The mantra that brought President Obama to the White House was "change," and in his press conference, the President used that rubric to frame both this new policy and his legacy. The President's rationale for his policy shift is simple, the embargo has not worked and has strengthened the regime rather than forced it to change:

> Proudly, the United States has supported democracy and human rights in Cuba through these five decades. We have done so primarily through policies that aimed to isolate the island, preventing the most basic travel and commerce that Americans can enjoy anyplace else. And though this policy has been rooted in the best of intentions, no other nation joins us in imposing these sanctions, and it has had little effect beyond providing the Cuban government with a rationale

for restrictions on its people. Today, Cuba is still governed by the Castros and the Communist Party that came to power half a century ago. Neither the American, nor Cuban people are well served by a rigid policy that is rooted in events that took place before most of us were born.

The President then stated that he had pledged coming into office to reexamine Cuban policy, but was thwarted by the wrongful imprisonment of a U.S. aid worker:

> While I have been prepared to take additional steps for some time, a major obstacle stood in our way – the wrongful imprisonment, in Cuba, of a US citizen and USAID sub-contractor Alan Gross for five years. Over many months, my administration has held discussions with the Cuban government about Alan's case, and other aspects of our relationship. His Holiness Pope Francis issued a personal appeal to me, and to Cuba's President Raul Castro, urging us to resolve Alan's case, and to address Cuba's interest in the release of three Cuban agents who have been jailed in the United States for over 15 years.

The White House's justification to change policy was an agreement after 18 months of negotiations to free Alan Gross and an unnamed American spy held in Cuba in return for three Cuban agents being held in the United States. With these agreements reached, the President announced that he was instructing the State Department to reestablish diplomatic relations and to ease travel and currency restrictions. The theory behind the President's move is that engagement is now more likely to change the Cuban regime than isolation, but with this change, the President was careful not to imply an endorsement of the Castro regime:

> But I'm under no illusion about the continued barriers to freedom that remain for ordinary Cubans. The United States believes that no Cubans should face harassment or arrest or beatings simply because they're exercising a universal right to have their voices heard, and we will continue to support civil society there. While Cuba has made reforms to gradually open up its economy, we continue to believe that Cuban workers should be free to form unions, just as their citizens should be free to participate in the political process.

Unsurprisingly, the Administration's move was met by both cheers and jeers. Critics asserted that the President gave Castro exactly what he wanted with no agreements to liberalize the Cuban economy or open up the political system. It seems the White House thinks that past policy did not achieve those goals, so maybe engagement might work better. But instead of using the leverage of restoration of diplomatic relations to press for changes, the Administration changed Cuban policy while asking for essentially nothing in return. Even those who might support the changes should question why the President asked for so little. It appears that the President wanted change for the sake of change, and was willing to be content with that. However, the economic embargo can only be removed by an act of Congress, so even if the White House was willing to accept so little in return for its policy change, it is doubtful Congress will be so easy on the Cuban regime.

Week 310

(ROARING BACK)

December 28, 2014

President Obama headed into his Christmas vacation in Hawaii with optimism not only because of satisfaction from exercising his executive powers on immigration and Cuba, but also because the improving U.S. economy has improved his political prospects. Despite devastating defeats in the midterm elections, the White House believes it can continue to take the political initiative and that a stronger economy will only improve the President's hand. Given this, it is not surprising the news this week made the President very happy indeed.

Ever since taking office in the midst of the 2008 financial crisis, the U.S. economy has been the dominate issue for the Administration. Slow growth and job production until 2014 gave substantial ammunition to critics of the Administration, allowing them to assert that the White House's stimulus bill and focus on Obamacare hurt both the recovery and the middle class. It has been a potent message, with poll after poll for nearly five years showing negative attitudes about the economy, attitudes that contributed to the Democrat defeats in 2010 and 2014. Now, more and more data is showing that the U.S. economy is finally starting to show stronger growth and better job creation. This news came too late to help the Democrats in 2014, but it might help the President for the last two years of his term.

While Europe is falling into recession, Russia is on the brink of an economic crisis, and Chinese growth is slowing, recent economic data is showing a very different story for the U.S. Third quarter GDP growth was 5%, the fastest growth rate since before the financial crisis. This faster economic growth has brought with it better job creation. The United States has now had job growth for 57 straight months creating nearly 11 million new jobs, according to the Council of Economic Advisers. While wage growth remains modest, falling energy prices have increased consumer buying power. Gas prices have fallen to their lowest levels since 2010 and it is expected that the average American family will save $550 on gas in 2015. And though Washington still has not reached any agreement to address the long term federal deficit, current economic growth has resulted in a $483 billion deficit for fiscal year 2014, $197 billion below the almost $680 billion deficit recorded in 2013. The 2014 deficit was 2.8 percent of GDP, the smallest since 2007.

All of this is good news for America and for President Obama, but it is not likely to make much difference to the political battles pending in Washington. While the budget deficit remains a major issue for the GOP, much of the energy of late has been focused on immigration, Obamacare, environmental policy, and terrorism. An improving economy will have little impact on those issues, and on immigration and Obamacare, the true fight is going to be in the Courts, not in Congress. Even if the improving economy makes President Obama more popular, it will not give him more leverage in Congress, because he is a lame duck and the GOP is better off opposing him rather than compromising. So the improved economy is putting a smile on the President's face, but what tangible benefits he will get from it is uncertain.

Week 311

(SO LIBERATING)

January 4, 2015

By any objective analysis, 2014 was a very bad year for President Obama. The VA scandal, the ISIS takeover of nearly half of Iraq, the failure to pass any major legislation, the GOP landslide in the midterm, and the failure to deter Russia's aggression in the Ukraine. For most of the year, the President was getting some of his worst ratings ever in the polls and more and more American's viewed him as an ineffective leader. Given all this, it is truly remarkable that as the year ended the President saw a bump in the polls and article after article talked about his resurgence. The story line is that the Democrat's losses in the midterms have liberated President Obama. So it appears from defeat there has been, at least for now, resurgence.

There is little chance that the Democrats' poor showing in the midterm elections is going to be a good thing for the White House's policy objectives. With both houses of Congress in GOP hands, the President will only be able to pass legislation with compromise and good negotiating, two things for which he has shown very little aptitude. The Republicans will be able to hold up nominations, start investigations, and force the President to use his veto pen and take tough and possibly controversial positions in the process. This combined with the fact that President Obama is in his final two years and attention is turning to the 2016 election, makes many conclude Obama is a spent force.

To his credit, rather than accepting this fate, the President has decided to counterattack in a very unorthodox manner. After election losses, our political tradition is that the parties at least talk committing to bipartisan compromise. President Obama decided to have none of this. The day after the election he was forced in his press conference to admit defeat, but at the same time he made clear he put little credence in the election result because two thirds of the voters did not come to the polls. Apparently, the President concluded that what this silent majority was demanding was more executive actions, more confrontation, and more liberalism.

So almost as soon as the election season concluded, the President began his counter attack. His executive order on immigration, new environmental regulations, the opening to Cuba, and other steps, were all designed to show that even though his party lost the election, the President can still set the agenda. This has energized the White House and his liberal base, with many saying Obama has finally decided to caste off the cloak of moderation and corporatism and finally be his progressive self. The Administration has always calibrated its policy program for election purposes, delaying the most burdensome aspects of Obamacare until after the 2012 and 2014 elections being the best example. With no more elections to fight, the President has decided he can just do what he wants without such machinations.

The result has been action. Five million illegal immigrates now have a chance to avoid deportation, Americans will soon be able to travel to Cuba, there are new environmental protections, and the President has looked determined and decisive. This has helped him politically, at least for now. Americans want their government and their President to be effective, and by being forceful, the President has changed the tone and narrative about himself. So there has been a short-term gain for the White House, but at what cost.

By deciding to launch his counterattack, the President has opened an even wider rift with Republicans. There is now little talk of working with the President and the Administration's chances of legislative accomplishment are slim. Instead, we face a prospect of Republicans passing bills addressing their priorities, and the President vetoing them. Partisanship, rancor, and confrontation will be the fruits of the President's liberation following the election. When the country is divided, presidents usually try to unite it. Instead, President Obama has decided it is better to divide even more. It is a novel approach, and a risky one. The President's entire strategy is grounded in the notion that if there is deadlock, Congress will get the blame, and that he does not need Congress to pursue his policy goals. Yet there may come a time, for example if the Supreme Court disallows Obamacare subsidies on the federal healthcare exchanges, when the White House will need Congress's help, and as soon as that happens, the real risks of the Obama strategy will emerge. But for now, the President is riding high, and enjoying it.

Week 312

(PARIS)

January 11, 2015

In the months leading up to the 2012 election, one of President Obama's key political themes on international relations was that the War on Terror was being won and Al-Qaeda was in retreat. The President touted the American pullout from Iraq, the killing of Osama bin Laden, and effective use of drones to eliminate other threats. Politically, the strategy worked, to the point where the President often mocked Mitt Romney's continued emphasis on the terrorist threat. After the election, the President continued to use the same playbook, calling ISIS the "JV team" and pushing for a faster withdrawal from Afghanistan.

What made for good politics in 2012, started to become a serious liability in 2014. The ISIS conquest of significant portions of Iraq showed that the American pullout had been too hasty, forcing the President to reengage with special forces and airstrikes to stop the ISIS advance. In Afghanistan, increasing pressure was applied to slow the U.S. withdrawal and keep a larger residual force in country. Compounding these challenges was the rise of a new threat, random attacks in various Western countries by gunman who claim affiliation with Al-Qaeda. The last two months have witnessed attacks in Ottawa, Canada and Sydney, Australia. Unfortunately, those were just a prelude to the Paris attacks.

On Wednesday, January 7, gunmen shouting "Allahu akbar!" attacked the offices of *Charlie Hebdo*, a Parisian satirical magazine that had published cartoons mocking the prophet Mohammad. They first went to the office of the magazine's editor, Stephanie Charbonnier, killing him and his body guard. They then killed seven more journals at the magazine, a maintenance worker and a visitor. During their escape, the attackers also executed a Paris police officer while he was on the ground with his hands up. The attacks were perpetrated by two brothers Cherif Kouachi, 32 and Said Kouachi, 34. A witness quoted the gunmen as saying: "You can tell the media that it's AL-Qaeda in Yemen."

The attackers escaped, causing terror in the city. On January 8, helicopters and SWAT teams scoured the Picardie region north of Paris searching for the gunman. At the same time another gunman shot a female police officer on the southern edge of Paris. In remembrance, at noon bells rang out in Paris and public transit stopped for a moment of silence. That evening the Eiffel Tower went black. On January 9, the Kouachi brothers and a hostage were cornered inside a printing house. They released the hostage and died in a gunfight with police. At the same time, another terrorist named Coulibaly took hostages at a kosher deli on the eastern edge of Paris. Police stormed the store, killed Coulibaly and four hostages, 15 other hostages were rescued.

These events in Paris captured the attention of the entire world and brought one of Europe's largest cities to a standstill. The attacks also made clear that the terrorist threat is changing from complicated large scale attacks like September 11 to low-tech assaults by small groups of gunman. These types of attacks threaten fewer lives, but are much harder to stop. The events of this week, combined with the rise of ISIS, also make clear that the terror threat, like a virus, is adapting and changing. The threat is different, but it is not gone. What certainly is gone is the talk from the Administration that terror groups are so degraded that they pose less of a threat. The threat is now different, but still terrifying.

Week 313

(ALL THAT'S LEFT)

January 18, 2015

After Ronald Reagan won his second term, his new Chief of Staff, Donald Regan, famously said his approach was going to be "let Reagan be Reagan." President Obama seems to have adopted that approach in earnest for his last two years in office. With no more campaigns to run and with only a short time left in office, the President has decided to cast caution to the wind the pursue all his desired policies with every power at his disposal. It is a bold strategy, but not a productive one, because by refusing compromise and instead following doggedly his ideological vision, the President might achieve some self-fulfillment but at the cost of actual accomplishment.

Seemingly oblivious to the fact that Republicans crushed Democrats at every level in 2014 and now control Congress, the President used his week before the State of the Union address not seeking compromise or reconciliation, but instead laying out a policy agenda designed to provoke the GOP. The President is so determined to show his relevance, that it seems to matter little to him that his policies have no chance of enactment. It is almost as though the President has decided to pretend that he won the 2014 election, hoping that by some miracle that fiction will become reality, or at the very least, he can start the kind of partisan fight with Republicans that he loves. No matter the motivation, one thing is clear, the agenda he laid out is dead on arrival at the GOP Congress.

The President started his pre-State of the Union policy campaign with a proposal to provide free community college, through a partnership between the federal government and the States, to those who maintain a sufficient grade point over. This would in essence be a new education entitlement program. Next, the President proposal a federal paid sick leave policy. Added to this was another call for a higher federal minimum wage and a request for further legislation on equal pay. These proposals are nothing new, they have been on the progressive wish list for years. Apparently deciding that these ideas were insufficiently provocative, the White House then announced that the President would call for an approximately $70 billion increase in federal discretionary spending and would seek $320 billion in tax increases to pay for his new initiatives.

All this must have been great fun for the President. He got to fly around on Air Force One, give speeches to friendly and hand-selected crowds, and offer proposal adored by his liberal base. It also afforded him the chance to look bold and engaged, and continue his narrative of resilience. The irony is, these speeches were not a victory lap or the start of a comeback, instead they are an admission that his time for significant legislative success has passed. By laying out an agenda designed to fail, the President is making clear he has no intention of working with the Republican Congress. His goal is different, and entirely self-serving. With his final months in office, he wants to burnish his image by fighting a losing battle for the progressive agenda, in the process sacrificing any opportunity genuine compromise with the GOP. The only beneficiaries of this approach might be the President himself and the next Democrat to run for the White House.

Week 314
(THE TAUNT)

January 25, 2014

State of the Union addresses are opportunities for Presidents to convey their vision to the public, outline their legislative agenda, and hopefully persuade Congress to enact some of that agenda. Most times, the speeches are long, boring, and not memorable, mainly because they usually turn into a laundry list of items designed to please key public and government constituencies. In some ways, President Obama's 2015 State of the Union fit this pattern, it was certainly very long. However, in one important respect this speech was different, because rather than an effort at compromise, it was a bragging session and a taunt to the GOP who so handily won the midterm.

When Congress has a new majority, it is customary for a President in a State of the Union to congratulate the winners and pledge bipartisanship, but President Obama would have none of that. Not only did he refuse to congratulate the GOP for winning the Senate and expanding their majority in the House, he did not even mention it. Indeed, if one just listed to the speech, one would have assumed the Democrats won in 2014 by a landslide. The entire speech was an exercise in extolling progressive policies and demanding more of them. Compromise was nowhere to be found, because the President's plan is confrontation, not compromise.

To set the stage for his policy agenda, the President began with a proclamation of victories on both foreign and domestic fronts:

> We are fifteen years into this new century. Fifteen years that dawned with terror touching our shores; that unfolded with a new generation fighting two long and costly wars; that saw a vicious recession spread across our nation and the world. It has been, and still is, a hard time for many. But tonight, we turn the page.

What then ensued was a victory lap, describing how the Administration's policies are cooling the planet, fixed the economy, reformed health care, solved the deficit, and saved the nation from foreign threats. Setting the premise that these major problems were well on their way to solutions, the President declared it time to end the era of austerity and look to government to strengthen the economy and the middle class. What followed were the policy items. A new entitlement for free community college education, federal paid sick leave, expanded federal child care, new infrastructure stimulus spending, a new gender pay equity act, and a higher federal minimum wage. To pay for all of this, higher taxes of course:

> Where we too often run onto the rocks is how to pay for these investments. As Americans, we don't mind paying our fair share of taxes, as long as everybody else does, too. But for far too long, lobbyists have rigged the tax code with loopholes that let some corporations pay nothing while others pay full freight. They've riddled it with giveaways the superrich don't need, denying a break to middle class families who do.

> This year, we have an opportunity to change that. Let's close loopholes so we stop rewarding companies that keep profits abroad, and reward those that invest in America. Let's use those savings to rebuild our infrastructure and make it more attractive for companies to bring jobs home. Let's simplify the system and let a small business owner file based on her actual bank statement, instead of the number of accountants she can afford. And let's close the loopholes that lead to inequality by allowing the top one percent to avoid paying taxes on their accumulated wealth. We can use that money to help more families pay for childcare and send their kids to college. We need a tax code that truly helps working Americans trying to get a leg up in the new economy, and we can achieve that together.

This agenda for higher federal spending paid for by higher federal taxes could hardly have had a less receptive audience than the current Congress, but no matter. This speech was not about persuasion, it was about self-actualization. President Obama wanted to prove a point: no matter the election results, he is still in charge and he will fight for his progressive agenda. The speech was a taunt, pure and simple.

The speech was also an effort to appease his liberal base, which has often accused him of compromising too much. He certainly addressed that criticism, because there was not one compromise proposal in the entire address. Indeed, much of the President's agenda would have trouble passing even a Democrat-controlled Congress. Legislative accomplishment is not the White House's goal, their goal is to fight for a progressive agenda even if that means little or nothing will in fact get accomplished in the President's last two years in office.

After paying tribute to his own accomplishments and proclaiming himself loudly and clearly as a man of the Left, the President closed by trying to reignite the passion he created with his famous address at the 2004 Democrat Convention:

> You know, just over a decade ago, I gave a speech in Boston where I said there wasn't a liberal America, or a conservative America; a black America or a white America – but a United States of America. I said this because I had seen it in my own life, in a nation that gave someone like me a chance; because I grew up in Hawaii, a melting pot of races and customs; because I made Illinois my home – a state of small towns, rich farmland, and one of the world's great cities; a microcosm of the country where Democrats and Republicans and Independents, good people of every ethnicity and every faith, share certain bedrock values.

The irony is he used this reference to his famous speech to cap an address not designed to bring us together, but in fact intended to divide us even more. No wonder, when the President said in closing "I have no more campaigns to run," some Republicans cheered, leading the President to boast: "I won both." This was an "I am smarter, wiser, and better than you" speech, and the President did not even try to be subtle about it.

Week 315

(THE SPEECH)

February 1, 2015

President Obama's State of the Union speech was designed to pick a fight with Congress. By outlining an agenda of tax increases to fund increases in federal spending and new federal entitlements, the Administration was sending a message to the GOP to expect an aggressive opponent in the White House. Given its familiarity with the tactics of confrontation, it is surprising the Administration responded with such outrage to Speaker Boehner's unilateral invitation to Israeli Prime Minister Benjamin Netanyahu to make a speech to a joint session of Congress. The Republicans did this to make clear President Obama is not the only one who can act unilaterally. The overblown reaction from the White House shows that they are certainly not used to their own medicine.

It is safe to say that there is no great love between President Obama and Netanyahu. They have clashed on settlements on the West Bank, Iran policy, and the Arab Spring. It is also clear that the two men dislike each other personally. When Netanyahu confronted President Obama during a White House photo-op to criticize the President's Mideast peace process strategy, the feud became public, but it had been raging for years. White House officials have anonymously insulted Netanyahu, while the Prime Minister has shown clear contempt for what he views as the President's weak and vacillating response to radical Islam. Given this, it is no surprise the GOP thought Netanyahu would agree to play a part in their plan to upstage the President.

One of the Administration's policies that has found criticism on both sides of the aisle in Congress is his opposition to further sanctions on Iran. There is significant bipartisan support for a new round of sanctions to pressure Iran to make a deal on its nuclear program. However, the Administration has opposed this, fearing it would undermine diplomacy underway on the issue. Netanyahu clearly sides with the Administration's critics, so Speaker Boehner invited him to address a joint session of Congress on March 3. The purpose was to both send a message to Iran and to the Administration.

The message was clearly received. The White House immediately stated that the President would not meet with Netanyahu during his visit to the United States and anonymous sources criticized Netanyahu's decision to accept the invitation. The public reason for refusing to meet with Netanyahu is the Israeli election on March 17, but the real reason was anger over the GOP's move. Given the culture of retribution at the White House, they no doubt will pull out all the stops to embarrass Netanyahu, likely involving trying to get Democrats to boycott the speech. All this anger delights Republicans, because it shows they can still get under the President's skin, just as he has surely gotten under theirs. All this is a bit petty, but petty politics is a favored art over at the White House.

Week 316
(DOUBTING)

February 8, 2015

One of the traditions for Presidents is attendance at the annual national prayer breakfast. This event gives the Chief Executive a chance to speak with religious leaders about faith and its importance to the nation. The events are largely ceremonial and rarely political, at least until the 2015 national prayer breakfast, where President Obama used his speech to showcase his perspective on religion and its influence on world affairs. Instead of talking about the value of faith, the President instead devoted his address to the dangers posed by too much religiosity. He did not focus his comments on radical Islam, he instead took aim at all religions, and in the process insulted many believers. The President began his speech by talking about those who twist religion for evil ends:

> But we also see faith being twisted and distorted, used as a wedge — or, worse, sometimes used as a weapon. From a school in Pakistan to the streets of Paris, we have seen violence and terror perpetrated by those who profess to stand up for faith, their faith, professed to stand up for Islam, but, in fact, are betraying it. We see ISIL, a brutal, vicious death cult that, in the name of religion, carries out unspeakable acts of barbarism — terrorizing religious minorities like the Yezidis, subjecting women to rape as a weapon of war, and claiming the mantle of religious authority for such actions.

President then reminded his audience that Christians too have a history of violence:

> And lest we get on our high horse and think this is unique to some other place, remember that during the Crusades and the Inquisition, people committed terrible deeds in the name of Christ. In our home country, slavery and Jim Crow all too often was justified in the name of Christ.

These comments enraged many, with critics saying they showed a basic misunderstanding of Christianity, history, and that referencing the Crusades was a propaganda victory for Islamic radicals. Then came the President's most controversial assertion, that people of faith need to have more doubt:

> And, first, we should start with some basic humility. I believe that the starting point of faith is some doubt — not being so full of yourself and so confident that you are right and that God speaks only to us, and doesn't speak to others, that God only cares about us and doesn't care about others, that somehow we alone are in possession of the truth.

The President was trying to talk about tolerance and humility, but by saying that believers need to doubt their faith, many saw his comments as an attack on religion itself. That was certainly not the President's intent, but his phraseology gave ammunition to his opponents.

What the President was trying to do is proclaim why we must fight radical Islam, but because the President is uncomfortable talking about the evil side of Islam and feels if he criticizes Islam, he must also criticize other faiths as well. So what emerges from this approach feels like a criticism of all religions, which the President certainly does not intend. The balance of the President's speech contained many admirable comments, including praise for freedom of religion and how it has made America more religious, not less:

> Our job is not to ask that God respond to our notion of truth — our job is to be true to Him, His word, and His commandments. And we should assume humbly that we're confused and don't always know what we're doing and we're staggering and stumbling towards Him, and have some humility in that process. And that means we have to speak up against those who would misuse His name to justify oppression, or violence, or hatred with that fierce certainty. No God condones terror. No grievance justifies the taking of innocent lives, or the oppression of those who are weaker or fewer in number. . . .

> And the second thing we need is to uphold the distinction between our faith and our governments. Between church and between state. The United States is one of the most religious countries in the world — far more religious than most Western developed countries. And one of the reasons is that our founders wisely embraced the separation of church and state. Our government does not sponsor a religion, nor does it pressure anyone to practice a particular faith, or any faith at all. And the result is a culture where people of all backgrounds and beliefs can freely and proudly worship, without fear, or coercion . . . .

These are words worthy of praise, but they were lost because the President first decided to assert some kind of moral equivalence between radical Islam and all other religions. So although he ostensibly tried to praise religion, in the end many felt insulted, because when you assert that an Islamic suicide bomber and the Christian missionary share a similar ailment, you cannot help but insult. At bottom, the President is unwilling to state what is obvious, that there is something about Islam that has created a kind of vicious radicalism that has no place in modern society. Until he is willing to recognize that, we will likely continue to hear about how we all should doubt our faith.

Week 317

(CEASE FIRING)

February 15, 2015

President Obama has been working very hard to project himself as an effective and decisive leader. On the domestic front, that effort has focused on expansive use of executive power. However, in foreign affair, where the President has by far the most discretion to act unilaterally, the White House when faced with nearly every foreign crisis, has taken a cautious approach focused mostly on disengagement. Many believe this approach helped lead to the current crisis in Syria and the rise of ISIS, which ironically has forced the United States to reengage in military action in both Iraq and Syria. Yet the Administration's approach has caused problems beyond the Middle East, including in Ukraine.

Despite Western sanctions, Russia has continued its support for rebels in Eastern Ukraine who are seeking to rejoin with Russia. Indeed, there is ample evidence that both Russian arms and Russian soldiers are being deployed in Eastern Ukraine. To date, there has been no indication that President Putin is prepared to end his land grab in Ukraine, and certainly no evidence he is concerned about the United States' response. This is because President Obama appears more concerned with limiting his involvement in Ukraine than helping the Ukrainians. The best evidence of this is the continuing refusal to supply arms to the Ukrainians. This fact has not been lost on Russian President Putin.

So this week, with the war getting more intense, Ukraine losing more ground, and the West continuing to refuse to provide arms to the Ukrainians, Germany, France, the United States and Russia met in Minsk to try yet again to craft a ceasefire. Germany and France had hoped to find a peaceful solution to the Ukrainian crisis, using what joint leverage they have on President Putin. With the help of Secretary of State Kerry, the parties were able to hammer out a ceasefire deal, but one that might not change much on the ground.

Under the deal, the truce is supposed to go into effect at midnight on February 14, 2015. The rival sides also have two days from the start of the truce to start pulling back heavy weapons from the frontline. In the hours leading up to the ceasefire, heavy fighting raged across Eastern Ukraine. As the ceasefire went into effect, Ukrainian President Petro Poroshenko ordered the Ukrainian military to comply with the agreement. However, heavy fighting continued around the strategic railway hub of Debaltseve, which is under siege by separatist forces. Even more troubling, separatist leaders stated that they believe continued fighting around Debaltseve is not a violation of the ceasefire.

President Obama hailed the ceasefire deal and called for all sides to adhere to the truce, but most doubt Russia will. The separatists, with Russian support, are winning, and even with sanctions and falling oil prices, there is no indication that Russia plans to abandon them. Indeed, there is every indication that Russia is playing the cynical game of sitting at the peace table while continuing to press its military advantage on the ground. Despite all this, the Administration seems determined to stand by a ceasefire that Russia will ignore. Further, the White House has refrained from any significant threats for more forceful action if Russia continues its proxy war. There could be no clearer sign that what President Obama really cares about is not getting involved in the Ukraine, even if that means Russian aggression is rewarded.

Week 318

(STAYED)

February 22, 2015

The central pillar of President Obama's strategy for his last two years in office is that through executive orders he can accomplish most of his remaining policy objectives. Relying on this assumption, the President has aggressively exercised his executive powers in a wide of range of regulatory spheres, including in environmental and immigration policy. Operating under the assumption that he has the authority to do what he wants, the President's approach to relations with the Republican Congress has been simple: pure confrontation. The President has made no effort at outreach and made no effort to work with Congress on any significant legislation. Instead, the President is purposely trying to prompt conflicts with Congress, best exemplified by his 2015 budget proposal, which included $2 trillion in new taxes and massive spending increases. It was a budget designed to infuriate the GOP. The risk in this strategy is that maybe the President misunderstands the scope of his executive powers and maybe the President might need Congress's help someday, and this week we learned that this risk is real when the President's sweeping immigration order was stayed by a federal judge in Texas.

Last year, under the guise of prosecutorial discretion, President Obama issued executive orders designed to shield more the 5 million illegal immigrates from deportation and give them rights to work and get certain federal benefits. In response, 26 States, led by Texas, challenged these executive orders and sought an injunction to stop their implementation. On February 16, just two days before the first of the orders was about to go into effect, Judge Andrew S. Hanen issued a temporary restraining order preventing the orders from going into effect. The grounds for the injunction were that the executive orders constituted new laws that failed to comply with the Administrative Procedures Act and that the states would be irreparably harmed if these executive orders were allowed to go into effect. "The DHS was not given any 'discretion by law' to give 4.3 million removable aliens what the DHS itself labels as 'legal presence,'" Judge Hanen decided. "In fact, the law mandates that these illegally-present individuals be removed. The DHS has adopted a new rule that substantially changes both the status and employability of millions. These changes go beyond mere enforcement or even non-enforcement of this nation's immigration scheme." On the issue of irreparable harm, the judge held that: "The genie would be impossible to put back into the bottle," and once the orders went into effect they would be "virtually irreversible."

The Republican reaction was immediate and cheerful. Speaker Boehner commented: "The President said 22 times he did not have the authority to take the very action on immigration he eventually did, so it is no surprise that at least one court has agreed." The reaction was very different at the White House, where Press Secretary Josh Earnest issued a statement saying: "The Supreme Court and Congress have made clear that the federal government can set priorities in enforcing our immigration laws-which is exactly what the President did when he announced commonsense policies to help fix our broken immigration system." In addition, the Administration promptly sought a stay of the injunction from the Fifth Circuit Court of Appeals.

To date, the Federal Courts have refuted President Obama more than two dozen times on various executive and regulatory actions. This is the product of the fact that President Obama is possibly the most aggressive proponent of executive power in the history of the Presidency. If the Federal Courts continue to refute the President, including in the upcoming Supreme Court case on Obamacare subsidies, the President's strategy of burning bridges with Congress while issuing executive orders might soon crumble. It might turn out President Obama needs Congress after all, and he might then regret making so many enemies there.

Week 319

(HOMELAND INSECURITY)

March 1, 2015

One of the things Republicans want to show with their control of both houses of Congress is that they can govern. Democrats and liberal media outlets have portrayed Republicans as unfit for power and unable to act responsibly, and Speaker Boehner and Majority Leader McConnell came into the new Congress on a mission to change that perception. In the Senate, the GOP tried to show they can get things done with a bill approving the Keystone Pipeline, a measure with broad bipartisan support. The GOP allowed full debate and amendments, something the Democrats never did in the last Congress. The bill overcame a filibuster, passed in the House and Senate, only to be vetoed by the President. Unfortunately, the GOP's success getting the Keystone Pipeline bill through Congress was quickly overshadowed by the need to avoid a shutdown at the Department of Homeland Security, and there, once again, the GOP hit the rocks.

When President Obama issued his executive orders seeking to legalize some 5 million illegal immigrants, Republicans vowed to oppose his actions. Some conservatives wanted to force a government showdown at the end of 2014 in connection with an omnibus bill to fund the government through September 2015. The leadership, however, did not want that fight, in part because they believed they would have more leverage when the GOP took over the Senate in January 2015. So Republicans reached a compromise with the President to fund all government agencies through September 2015 except the Department of Homeland Security, which includes the Immigration and Naturalization Service. For Homeland Security, funding was only provided through February 28, 2015, giving the GOP majorities a chance to try to include changes to the President's immigration orders in any bill to fund that agency.

This was never a smart strategy for Republicans, instead it was done of necessity. Speaker Boehner was only able to avoid a government shutdown at the end of 2014 by giving conservatives some means to protest President Obama's immigration orders, and not fully funding Homeland Security was the solution. It was also a trap, because Senate Democrats would filibuster any funding bill for Homeland Security that contained provisions limiting the President's immigration orders and the President would welcome a shutdown of Homeland Security as a means to discredit and undermine Republicans. Knowing this, the GOP leadership started 2015 looking for a way out of the trap. They thought they found a path when Federal District Judge Hanen in Texas issued a temporary restraining order against the President's immigration orders. The Republicans leadership hoped with this development, conservatives would support a clean funding bill for Homeland Security. It was not to be.

Speaker Boehner could pass a funding bill with immigration limitations, but Majority Leadership McConnell could not break a Democrat filibuster in the Senate. Majority Leader

McConnell could pass a clean funding bill, but Speaker Boehner could only get such a bill through the House with Democrat votes. All the while, the President sat back, refusing to negotiate and relishing the chaos within the GOP. This week, with funding for Homeland Security about to run out, the GOP failed to marshal the votes for a three week extension, a humiliating defeat for Boehner. So on February 27, Boehner had to retreat and offer only a seven day extension, which then passed the House on a vote of 357 to 60, and quickly moved through the Senate and was signed by the President. So some slight breathing room was achieved, but the damage was done. It is now clear that the GOP leadership must find any way to quickly escape from the trap they set for themselves.

The central challenge facing the GOP majorities is that President Obama and the Democrats have no goal other than obstructing or vetoing legislation. They are happy to force shutdowns and chaos because they think that helps them politically. The Democrats also do not seem to care if any significant legislation gets passed, so they have no incentive to work with Republicans. Only a change in this dynamic will help the GOP, and the best hope for that comes not from Congress, but from the courts, because if court decisions undermine Obamacare or the President's immigration orders, then Democrats will be forced to work with Republicans. Until then, dysfunction will continue to reign.

Week 320

(THE SPEECH, THE SURRENDER, AND THE ARGUMENT)

March 8, 2015

This week witnessed a cascade of events all stemming from the President's determination to engage in unilateral executive action to achieve his goals. The President is pursuing an executive agreement with Iran regarding its nuclear program to avoid the need to consult with or get ratification from the Senate. The President has also used broad executive powers on immigration and to implement Obamacare, including changing deadlines, requirements, and giving subsidies on both federal and state insurance exchanges. The President believes he must take these actions to make progress, and has accordingly shown little interest in working with Congress on anything. As this week showed, that has consequences, sometimes good and sometimes bad, for the President.

There is deep bipartisan concern about the deal the White House is trying to negotiate with Iran on its nuclear program. Many believe the President is too willing to lift sanctions for a deal that allows Iran to keep its nuclear program. Further, the President has made clear he will do his deal regardless of what Congress thinks and that he will not seek ratification by the Senate. In response, the House GOP used the best weapon they have, Israeli Prime Minister Netanyahu. Without consulting the White House, Speaker Boehner invited the Israeli leader to address a joint session of Congress on March 3. The President went apoplectic. He refused to meet with Netanyahu, sent his team out to condemn the speech, and urged Democrats in Congress to boycott. Yet all these things only put more attention on the speech. Netanyahu used it to full advantage, laying out a persuasive case why the White House should not make a bad deal with Iran. In the end, the opponents of the deal were strengthened, while the White House looked petty.

While the Republicans were winning a tactical victory with the Netanyahu speech, they took the opportunity to surrender on something else. Having reached a last minute deal to extend funding for the Department of Homeland Security for one week over the controversy regarding defunding the President's executive orders on immigration, the GOP used the cover of the speech to surrender. Speaker Boehner brought up a clean funding bill for Homeland Security, which passed with mostly Democrat votes, the Senate followed, and the impasse was resolved in the President's favor. It was a Republican surrender for sure, but it was a battle they could only lose, as the GOP leadership realized. So they opted to retreat, and refocus their efforts on defeating the immigration orders in court and crafting the 2016 federal budget.

Regarding the last event of the week stemming from the President's aggressive executive actions, the winner remains unclear. The statute that created Obamacare states that subsidies to buy insurance are to be paid by exchanges "established by the State." The White House interpreted this to include the federal exchange, an interpretation now challenged in federal court. On March 4, the United States Supreme Court heard argument on the issue, and from that argument it is very hard to tell who might prevail. If the Administration wins, Obamacare will be safe for now and the President can continue to resist any legislative changes to the program. If the challengers win, the survival of Obamacare will be put at risk, because without the subsidies, residents of 34 states will not get help buying insurance, which could lead to the failure of the federal exchange and the undoing of the employer health care mandate. This might be a good thing, because it might force Republicans and Democrats to reach a compromise to reform Obamacare. So here again, the President's executive actions are creating uncertainty and driving the political combat in Washington.

Week 321

(THE LETTER AND THE EMAILS)

March 15, 2015

The letter was authored by Tom Cotton, a freshman Republican Senator from Arkansas, and the emails belong to Hillary Clinton, the former first lady of Arkansas and also the former Secretary of State. For Cotton, his letter was yet another attempt to fight President Obama's unilateral actions in kind. While for Hillary Clinton, her email issues were yet another sign of her determination to control everything around her, sometimes to her own detriment.

One issue on which there has been some bipartisan accord has been Iran policy. While the White House has been feverishly trying to cut a deal with Iran, Republicans and Democrats in the Senate have been crafting a bill imposing new sanctions, based on an assumption that Iran will only respond positively if more pressure is applied. The Administration has opposed this effort and has refused to consult in any meaningful way with the Senate. Given that the President has been clear he will do his deal whether the Senate likes it or not, Republicans decided to respond in kind.

Forty-six GOP Senators decided to co-sign a letter written by Senator Cotton to the Iranian leaders. The letter warned Iran that any agreement signed by President Obama using solely his executive authority will not have the force of law and can be reversed by Congress or the next President. The letter also warned Iran that the United States would not allow it to have nuclear weapons and that it faces more sanctions if it does not abandon its nuclear ambitions. The White House's response to the letter was nearly hysterical. The Senators were accused of undermining the President, trying to torpedo the negotiations, and some even accused them of treason. Democrats in the Senate said the letter undermined bipartisan efforts on sanctions. Through it all, Senator Cotton was unapologetic, making clear Iran cannot be allowed to have a nuclear weapon and asserting that the only way combat a unilateral President is with unilateralism.

At the same time, another Democrat faced a different kind of challenge from the written word. News broke this week that while serving as Secretary of State, Hillary Clinton insisted on using her own private email account, which was run through her own private server located at her home in New York. No doubt this system was established to give Hillary Clinton complete control over these emails and who could see them. After leaving as Secretary of State in 2013, Clinton took all these records, amounting to more than 60,000 emails, with her. Only in late 2014 did Clinton provide any of these emails to the State Department, and she only did so after deleting more than 31,000 of them.

This incident once again showed how secretive and controlling Hillary Clinton has become. Her campaign in waiting limits access to the press, she only addresses friendly crowds, and she avoids interviews. Yet this time, her efforts at control spun out of control. She is now being accused of violating State Department policy, misusing classified information, and even possibly breaking the law. For days she and her campaign ignored the issue, but it would not go away, so Hillary Clinton was forced to give a press conference where she claimed she used her own email addresses solely for convenience and that every non-personal email was handed over to the State Department. However, since Clinton only handed over what she wanted to, and deleted 31,000 emails in the process, the fact is the public will never know what she was trying to hide. If anything, her heavily lawyered and rehearsed comments at her press conference only made matters worse, and ensured this issue is here to stay.

Week 322

(THE TANTRUM)

March 22, 2015

It is widely known that President Obama and Israeli Prime Minister Benjamin Netanyahu hate each other. Netanyahu has publicly rebuked the President's Middle East policies, including while sitting next to the President in the White House. Netanyahu's speech to Congress earlier this month reignited the feud between the White House and the Prime Minister. So many in the Administration were privately happy when it appeared Netanyahu was losing support heading into the March 17 election in Israel. Secretary of State Kerry has been doggedly trying to restart the Middle East peace process and get a nuclear deal with Iran, and Netanyahu has been a major obstacle to both. Unfortunately, the election did not turn out the way the President wanted, and then the tantrum ensued.

Israel's March 17 election was forced by disagreements within Netanyahu's governing coalition. The main contestants in the election were Netanyahu's Likud against the Zionist Union, which was formed by a coalition of the Labor and Hatnuah Parties. The final election turnout was

72.3% and Likud, which had been trailing in the polls, mounted a stunning comeback in the final days and won a huge victory. Likud won nearly 24% of the vote and picked up 12 seats in the Knesset, bringing its total to 30 seats. With 61 seats needed for a majority in the Knesset, Likud will still need to form a coalition government, but there appear ample opportunities to do so with the religious parties and the Kulanu Party, which was formed by former Likud member Moshe Kahlon. So the end result will be that Netanyahu will remain in power.

How did Likud manage to win so decisively when it looked to be heading to defeat. The answer is Netanyahu. The Prime Minister was determined to do anything to win. His speech to the House in early March at the invitation of the GOP was designed to build support among American Jews, a significant funding and vote source, because many can vote in Israeli elections. Netanyahu pursued the speech, even though he knew it would infuriate President Obama. Back is Israel, as the election got closer, the harsher Netanyahu's rhetoric became. When asked if there would be no Palestinian State if he won the election, he said "Indeed," a clear message to the Israeli right. On election day, he warned Jewish voters that Israeli Arabs were voting in "droves," another effort to get out his base. It worked.

In response, President Obama has decided that Netanyahu must be punished. From the American perspective, the foundation of the peace process is the establishment of a Palestinian State. By implying he would not support that goal, Netanyahu was viewed as scuttling decades of effort. The Administration also accused the Prime Minister of racism against Arab Israelis. The White House has further signaled it will not be content with simply condemning Netanyahu's statements. For decades, the United State has used its United Nation's veto power to protect Israel from resolutions on Palestinian rights and a Palestinian State. The Administration said it is reevaluating that, and now might allow such a resolution to pass. Recognizing the threat, Netanyahu has now tried to walk back his comments, but President Obama would have none of it, and continued his criticism of Netanyahu.

There is no doubt Netanyahu's election rhetoric was reckless and politically motivated, but rather than try to heal the rift, the White House has decided to instead widen it. The Administration's response to the election has gone from justifiable condemnation to unseemly retribution. It appears the White House's policy is being driven purely by the President's animosity to Netanyahu. America's alliance with Israel is the bedrock of U.S. security policy in the Middle East, but no matter, President Obama is determined to punish Netanyahu at any cost. Not very presidential or statesmanlike, but that is what happens when President Obama is scorned.

Week 323
(ON A ROLL)

March 29, 2015

The most damaging accusation that was lobbed at the GOP House before the 2014 election was that the Republican majority was dysfunctional. On key vote after key vote, Speaker Boehner was unable to muster a majority of his fractious caucus, requiring him to go to Democrat leader Pelosi for support to pass key bills. This was the result of the consistent refusal of 25 to 30 of the GOP's most conservative members to compromise and work with their leadership. These members chose ideological purity over supporting party strategy. Many Democrats hoped that pattern would continue after the 2014 election, and it looked like they might be correct. The Republican Congress needed to address funding for the Homeland Security Department, which conservatives demanded be shut down in protest against President Obama's executive orders on immigration. The GOP leadership in both the House and the Senate saw this as a trap, so Speaker Boehner turned again to Nancy Pelosi to pass a clean funding bill for Homeland Security, and the Senate quickly did the same.

Democrats celebrated this as another humiliating defeat for Republicans, but the Republican leadership simply saw it as a tactical retreat before the more important fight over the 2015 budget. With a larger majority, Speaker Boehner hoped to overcome protests from his most conservative members and pass a funding blueprint that would create a path to a balanced budget and repeal Obamacare. That is the big prize, and the Speaker was willing to suffer a defeat on Homeland Security funding to win it. On March 25, the Speaker got his prize. The House Republicans approved a $3.8 trillion budget for the 2015 fiscal year by a vote of 228 to 199, with all Democrats voting no. The budget bill passed in large part because of additional funding provided to the Department of Defense through a separate war fund. The plan calls for $5.4 trillion in deficit reduction over 10 years, including about $2 trillion from repeal of Obamacare. Close to $1 trillion would be saved from Medicaid and CHIP, a health care program for the low-income. About $500 billion would be cut from domestic discretionary programs.

While Republicans were still celebrating their success in the March 25 spending vote, the next day Speaker Boehner moved another bill, this one a bipartisan proposal. The Speaker and Nancy Pelosi have been in negotiations for several months to fix a problem with Medicare spending that has frustrated Congress for 17 years. In 1998, Congress passed limitations on reimbursements to doctors and hospitals created by a formula known as the sustainable growth rate (SGR). Although the SGR is the law, every year since then Congress has passed a patch to prevent the SGR from going into effect. This annual ritual has become an increasing problem for Congress, so Boehner and Pelosi made a deal to fix the SGR permanently. On March 26, they unveiled their deal, which passed by a vote of 392-37. The deal will cost $214 billion over 10 years, with $73 billion of that expense paid for by spending cuts or new revenue. The bill also includes provisions to transition Medicare's payment system to incentivize quality care. The bill will also make seniors earning more than $133,000 pay higher premiums.

With these twin victories, the action now moved to the Senate. The Republicans have a much smaller majority in the Senate, but on budget bills they have one big advantage, the filibuster rules can be bypassed. As the result, the GOP can muscle through their spending plan as long as they stay united. That is exactly what they did on March 27, when they passed a plan that will balance the budget in 10 years with $5.1 trillion in domestic spending cuts. The plan passed by a vote of 52-46 vote, with only Senators Ted Cruz and Rand Paul voting no, likely because both are running for president and want to appeal to conservatives. Passage was not easy, and only came after a 18-hour session with votes on dozens of amendments to the budget bill. Like the House blueprint, the Senate plan also repeals Obamacare using the very reconciliation rules President Obama employed to pass health care reform. Now that the House and Senate have passed budget bills, the differences need to be worked out in conference, and then each body will need to pass specific appropriations bills. As for the fix for the SGA Medicare payments, it is expected the Democrats will be forced to allow a vote on that measure, and it is expected to quickly pass.

So the Republican Congress, which started out very shakily indeed, seems to have finally started accomplishing something. This was exactly the leadership's plan when they surrendered on Homeland Security funding. They managed to unify their members and pass a budget based on Republican priorities. Now the real battle begins with President Obama, who has called for spending increases and new taxes. Even with these victories, the Republicans are surely facing vetoes from the White House, and then the real fight will ensue, but for now the GOP can claim it is on a roll.

Week 324

(NUKED)

April 5, 2015

President Obama was propelled to the White House on the slogan of change and his foreign policy, in many ways, he has pursued change for its own sake. He began his Presidency by eschewing long-time allies such as Britain and trying to re-set relations with foes like Russia. He then pursued a complete withdrawal from Iraq, even when experts and advisers counseled keeping a residual stability force. He claimed a pivot to the Pacific, but has been unwilling to confront China's aggression in that region. In his second term, President Obama has only quickened his pace. He pledged a full pullout from Afghanistan by 2015, opened relations with Cuba, and openly attacked Israeli Prime Minister Netanyahu. With regard to the Iranian nuclear program, the President proclaimed that he would not allow Iran to get nuclear weapons, but now we can see his goal is to befriend Iran, not ensure its disarmament.

Iran is the greatest threat to United States policy in the Middle East. It is America's most powerful foe, with huge oil resources, and significant military capability. Iran actively supported the insurgents in Iraq, causing many American deaths. It is a state supporter of terrorism, has supported Islamists in Lebanon, Hamas, the Assad regime in Syria, and insurgents in Yemen. In the wake of the United States pullout from Iraq, Iranian influence his grown, and it appears the United States may even be encouraging Iran to support the Iraqi government's effort to rollback ISIS. More and more, Iran appears to be the growing Middle East hegemon, and one that still pledges the destruction of Israel. Given all this, one would think American policy would be focused on isolating and undermining Iran. However, the President has a different agenda.

Much like his policy on Cuba, President Obama thinks the means to temper rogue states is engagement. So with the Iranian nuclear program, the President repeatedly stated that while Iran must not get nuclear weapons, the only option to achieve that is a negotiated deal. While the Administration persuaded international partners to put significant sanctions on Iran, he has stated that the only option other than a deal is war. Having unilaterally deprived himself of his best leverage, it is not surprising that Iran has resisted any deal that would ensure its nuclear disarmament. The negotiations in Switzerland have dragged on and on, with a final deadline to reach a deal now moved to March 31, 2015. No deal was reached on that date, but Secretary of State Kerry stayed on and continued his effort, and on April 3, both sides claimed that a framework deal was reached. However, as the details started to emerge, it became clear that the parties still disagree on what the deal is, and even the deal as described by the United States would not stop Iran from getting nuclear weapons.

The framework deal, which is supposed to be finalize by June, calls for lifting sanctions on Iran, but the Iranians say all sanctions must be lifted immediately, while the United States disagrees. The framework allows Iran to continue enriching uranium with some restrictions, but the United States says the restriction last for 15 years, Iran says 10. The Iranians say the framework allows them to keep and further develop advanced centrifuges at the Fordo military facility, while the United States disagrees. The United States says that Iran agreed to surprise inspections, Iran says no. As for the nuclear grade enriched uranium that Iran already has, Iran says they get to keep it in country, while the United States says the agreement requires it to be shipped out of Iran. Importantly, many key Iranian military facilities will not be dismantled, and the Iranian contest whether they will allow inspection of them. The obvious conclusion is that no deal has been reached, and even what the United States claims Iran has agreed to will not stop Iran from getting a nuclear weapon. For this reason, Israel has condemned the framework.

As President Obama has tried to defend the deal in the face of significant bipartisan opposition in the Senate, he has made clear that one of the benefits of the deal is ending the cold war with Iran and bringing them into the international fold. To achieve this, the White House appears willing to accept a bad deal and is not asking Iran to stop its support for terrorism. In essence, the Administration's policy appears founded on the notion that if we befriend Iran, they will stop trying to undermine American interests. The evidence for this is nil, but no matter. It appears the President puts no stock in the adage: those who ignore history are bound to repeat it. Far from preventing Iran from getting a nuclear weapon, the framework ensures it. The President wants to claim achieving engagement with Iran, and it will be a successor's problem when Iran gets its nuclear weapon.

Week 325

(ENEMIES CLOSER)

April 12, 2015

The debate continued to rage in Washington this week over the President's proposed nuclear deal with Iran. The White House continued to insist that the deal was the only peaceful way to stop Iran from getting a nuclear weapon, while Republicans continued to quietly build a coalition with Democrats to try to reach the 67 vote threshold to overcome a Presidential veto of any new Iran sanctions bill. All the while, Iran's supreme leader and the White House offered conflicting descriptions of the framework, with Iran insisting that the deal required immediate lifting of all sanctions. As the week progressed, it became increasingly clear that there is no real deal with Iran, instead there is simply a White House that pines for one.

The guiding principle of the Administration's Iran strategy is that a deal will bring Iran into the international community, and by doing so over the long term the threat from Iran will diminish. This is the central assumption behind the President's insistence that the United States must get a deal, and at the same time this very insistence undermined the United States' leverage in the negotiations. This approach to Iran is just the latest extension of the Administration's policy to "normalize" relations with America's sworn foes, in the hope that engagement will turn foes into friends. The President first tested this normalization doctrine with Russia, which effort was met by evermore aggressions. Not deterred, the President is now employing that same policy with Cuba, and hopes to use it with Iran.

In many ways, Cuba is a test run for the policy the President wants to pursue with Iran. The President's Cuba policy was on full display at the Summit of the America's hosted by Panama. For a long time, Cuba was excluded from this event, and for an even longer time every American President since Eisenhower has refused to be seen with, let alone meet with, any leader of Cuba. The reason is simple: Cube is a repressive communist regime that has consistently sought to undermine United States interests. But on April 11, 2015 something happened that has not occurred for more than five decades, a President of the United States met with the leader of Cuba, Raul Castro. The meeting was brief, but photos were taken and issues were discussed. The President called it a "historic meeting," but made clear "[o]ur governments will continue to have differences," but stated: "At the same time, we agreed that we can continue to take steps forward that advance our mutual interests."

This notion of "mutual interests" is at the heart of the President's policy on both Cuba and Iran, but it is not clear how "mutual" these interests are. On Cuba, the communist regime has an interest in opening up economic relations because its economy is suffering under America's embargo and its former Soviet patron is gone. America's interest is that freedom is restored to the Cuban people. However, the President's Cuba policy gives the Castros what they want, but not America. Cuba has not been required to grant political, religious, or press freedoms, or even release all political prisoners. Nevertheless, the President plans to open relations with Cuba.

It is this Cuban precedent that should be very disturbing to our allies in the Middle East. As with Cuba, the President hopes that a deal with Iran will over time modify its behavior. However, unlike Cuba, whose interests now are more economic than political, Iran has a strategic agenda that is dangerous to the United States, Israel, and our other Arab allies. Iran wants to be the premier power in the region, and even as it works on getting a deal on its nuclear program, it is actively seeking to grow its influence, most recently by its support of rebels in Yemen, who recently captured its capital and forced Saudi Arabia to launch airstrikes. Even in the face of this proxy war between America's ally and Iran in Yemen, the President has insisted that a deal with Iran will further American strategic interests. Where the President gets his faith that engagement will get nations to abandon their geopolitical objectives is a mystery, and it certainly has no precedent in history. There was plenty of engagement with Imperial Japan, Hitler's Germany, and the Soviet Union, but none of that engagement avoided conflicts for the simple reason that those nations had goals that conflicted with American interests. Only when governments changed or wars were fought did that geopolitical landscape change. In pursuing his policy, the President has decided to ignore these lessons, and pursue engagement for engagement's sake. The results will be unfortunate, but certainly predictable.

Week 326
(Scooby-Doo)

April 19, 2015

The worst kept secret in Washington for the last 18 months is that Hillary Clinton would run for President. While Mrs. Clinton has been predictably coy, saying over and over again that no decision has been made, all the while her supporters have been preparing the infrastructure for her campaign and the narrative for her inevitability. All this misdirection came to an end on April 12, when Hillary Clinton finally made it official: she is running for President. She made her announcement with a web video showcasing the lives of ordinary Americans, concluding with Clinton making it official and setting the theme for her campaign. The video was slick and the message was clear, Hillary is in. Now the fight begins.

The biggest challenge for the Clinton campaign is fatigue. The Clintons hale from two decades ago, and although the 1990's were a time of economic prosperity, it was also scandal plagued. After 8 years of a Democrat President, in 2016 Clinton will have do a careful balancing act, convince the base that she will preserve the Obama legacy, while reassuring swing voters that she is an agent for change. Not an easy task, but her announcement video gave some clues on her strategy. After showcasing average Americans from every constituency (young, old, business owners, retirees, straight, and gay), doing important things for their lives, then enters Hillary Clinton, proclaiming: "I'm getting ready to do something too," she says, standing in front of her New York home. "I'm running for president." She then offered the rationale for her campaign: "Americans have fought their way back from tough economic times, but the deck is still stacked in favor of those at the top" . . . ." Everyday Americans need a champion, and I want to be that champion" and that she wants to help Americans "get ahead, and STAY ahead." She concluded by announcing: "So I'm hitting the road to earn your vote. Because it's your time. And I hope you'll join me on this journey."

What followed from the video was a plan to reintroduce Hillary Clinton to the American people and at the same time change her image from an elitist, secretive, Washington insider. After announcing her campaign, Hillary set out on a 1,000 mile road trip from New York to Iowa to meet ordinary voters, travelling in a van named Scooby-Doo. The objective was obvious: try to portray Clinton as modest, open, and connected to the lives of ordinary Americans. During the trip she visited stores and coffees shops, and spoke to friendly faces. As for the press, they were kept at a safe distance and few questions were answered. The stated reason, the trip was about talking to voters not reporters, but there is certainly more to it than that. There are many questions that need to be answered, including ones about her decisions as Secretary of State, the deletion of her emails, and the Clinton Foundation, and Hillary Clinton has no interest in talking about any of those things. So she took a road trip on Scooby-Doo instead.

Hillary Clinton enters this campaign cycle in both the best and worst situation. It benefits from the fact that she has no credible challenger and the road to the nomination is currently hers alone. However, a coronation is dangerous, because it prevents a candidate from being tested and it can breed a complacency that could undermine a general election campaign. It is for this reason the Clinton campaign leaked a memo outlining its guiding principles, the leading one of which was humility. Clinton has to show humility and openness to connect with voters, and the campaign has to show humility to be prepared for their Republican opponent. Almost as important as humility will be the campaign's determination to avoid answering questions and to attack or deflect any criticism.

For President Obama, Hillary's formal campaign announcement was very welcome news. While Hillary is a formidable candidate, she hails from a Democrat bench of one. There is currently no other Democrat prominent enough to marshal national appeal, except for maybe Vice President Biden, but his frequent gaffs and close connection to Obama make him a weak alternative to Hillary. So President Obama needs Hillary, because at this stage of his Presidency he has one primary goal: his legacy. Other than Obamacare, most of the President's domestic policy achievements have come from regulations or executive orders, things that can be changed by his successor. So for Obama, everything depends on electing a Democrat in 2016. That is why Hillary's run is a blessing and a curse. If she runs well and overcomes voters' concerns, the Obama legacy is assured. If she runs poorly, there is no Democrat alternative, and the GOP could take the White House. That is the one thing Obama is determined to stop at all costs, and for the next 18 months we will likely see him do everything he can conjure to make Hillary his successor.

Week 327

(CASH)

April 26, 2015

There is no doubt that Hillary Clinton is an exceptionally strong contender for both the Democrat nomination and the presidency. There is also no doubt that despite all her strengths, she has significant weaknesses. Her secrecy, poor people skills, and age will all be challenges for her campaign, but her biggest challenge will be her baggage, not just from the Clinton years but also from the years after she left the White House. Her opponents have been going after her for months about the Benghazi attacks and most recently her deletion of more than 30,000 emails so that no one could ever read them. The Hillary Clinton campaign has followed its usual recipe to with these critiques: obfuscate and attack. Yet it took less than a week after she announced her run for the White House that some new baggage emerged, namely cash.

During her shadow campaign, Hillary Clinton commented how she and her husband were flat broke when they left the White House. Her campaign ran from that comment immediately, because if they were broke, they did not remain so for long. Instead, the Clintons set about enriching themselves with vigor. Million dollar speaking tours and vast fundraising for themselves and the Clinton Foundation have now made them members of the super-rich club. This crash for cash has been as aggressive as it has been unseemly, and now it has become an issue for the Clinton campaign with the publication of *Clinton Cash* by author Peter Schweizer.

The focus of *Clinton Cash* is obvious from the title. The book details lavish speaking fees and foreign donations to the Clinton Foundation, including while Hillary Clinton was Secretary of State. The book is full of details on foreign money flowing to the Clinton Foundation while Secretary of State Hillary Clinton was making decisions impacting countries from which those donations came. The book contains no hard evidence that Hillary Clinton directed foreign policy decisions based on such donations, instead the evidence is innuendo at best, but it certainly looks very bad. As an example, the second chapter of the book is entitled: "The Transfer: Bill's

Excellent Kazakh Adventure." That chapter details how Canadian mine owner Frank Giustra paid huge speaking fees to Bill Clinton and gave access to his private jet while Senator Hillary Clinton allegedly pressured Kazakh to grant mining rights to Giustra's company. The book contains many more similar episodes.

While there is no smoking gun, the book makes enough noise than even reliably liberal press outlets have decided they have to cover the issues. Indeed, the *New York Times* in the first of a series of articles examined Schweizer's claims. The first story investigated another deal involving Giustra, where Hillary Clinton approved the Russian nuclear energy agency's purchase of Uranium, which Giustra controlled. The book asserts Clinton could have vetoed the deal, but did not do so because of Giustra's influence with the Clintons. These and other stories in the book gained more momentum when the Clinton Foundation admitted it did not properly disclose a significant number of foreign donations. This and other issues have prompted the Clinton Foundation to restrict foreign donations to six reliable U.S. allies. However, this might be a step too late, because the damage may have already been done.

None of this is a knockout blow to the Clinton campaign, but these and other stories risk a death of a thousand cuts, where voters decide Hillary Clinton simply cannot be trusted. While this appears to be a problem for the Clintons, not President Obama, the impact on the President and his party could be considerable. Currently, the Democrat Party is nearly united behind Hillary Clinton, with no backup plan. If Clinton starts to appear weak, then more Democrats might join the race, fracturing the President's allies in Congress and endangering the Democrats' advantage in the presidential race. The President already faces little opportunity to make legislative gains in his last two years, and divisions within his party over the presidential nomination will only make matters worse.

Week 328
(Charm)

May 3, 2015

Baltimore is known as the Charm City. Most visitors to Baltimore only know about the Inner Harbor District, the Orioles, and Johns Hopkins University. But there is another Baltimore, one of political corruption, blight, crushing poverty, and drug abuse. That is the Baltimore showcased in the popular television series *The Wire*. Reality met fiction this week, as another case of a black man dying at the hands of the police led to yet more protests, riots, and civil unrest. For President Obama, these latest riots so close to DC present a dual challenge of trying to heal the divide while exploiting it at the same time, something he will need all his charm and skills to accomplish.

On April 12, 2015, Freddie Gray, a 25-year-old black man from Baltimore was arrested for wielding a knife. He was injured either during his arrest or while he was being transported in police custody. Gray slipped into a coma, and died on April 19, 2015. Almost immediately peaceful protests began outside Baltimore's Western district police station. Civil unrest and riots started to spread and became massive on the night of April 27, only being effectively quelled when Baltimore's mayor asked the governor to send in the national guard. At least twenty police officers have been injured, and hundreds of protesters and rioters were arrested. Many businesses and cars were destroyed and neighborhoods trashed.

On April 28, President Obama condemned the violence, stating: "There's no excuse for the kind of violence that we saw yesterday. It is counterproductive. ... When individuals get crowbars and start prying open doors to loot, they're not protesting. They're not making a statement. They're stealing. When they burn down a building, they're committing arson. And they're destroying and undermining businesses and opportunities in their own communities. That robs jobs and opportunity from people in that area."

These were strong and appropriate words, but the President was quick to pivot to his second goal, using events like those in Baltimore and Ferguson, to justify more calls for government spending and government programs. Arguing that America needs to make "massive investments," the President asserted that "there's a bunch of my agenda that would make a difference right now." However, it is always dangerous to try to take advantage of a tragedy to achieve policy objectives. The White House was brazen about doing that during the 2009 financial crisis. This time, the President is taking a more careful approach, maybe because the rationale for more government action in this instance is difficult to justify because Baltimore has been a liberal social policy experiment for more than four decades, and some say the results were seen on the streets of that city on April 27.

Baltimore has not had a Republican mayor in 40 years. It has spent billions on welfare, public housing, public schools, and other government assistance programs. The results are a city divided, with wealthy enclaves and larger districts scared by rampant blight, drugs, teenage pregnancy, and hopelessness. Now the President seems to be asserting that if government would just do even more, the result would somehow be different. The Administration certainly tried that with its 2009 stimulus bill, with its $840 billion in spending including nearly $50 billion for education spending and billions more for other so-called jobs programs. That stimulus bill produced very few jobs, and the U.S. job market is only starting to strongly recover now, six years later. Yet against all this evidence, the President asserted that what will stop riots like the ones in Baltimore is more stimulus spending.

The reality is that except for what the President can try to do by executive order, his policy agenda is dead because the GOP controls Congress. Recognizing this, the President's only hope to enact his program is to try to exploit events like those in Baltimore. He hopes the outrage and shock of those riots will galvanize support for more government spending and pressure Congress to address his agenda. There is little chance that will happen, especially since the prescription the President offers to fix Baltimore's problems are essentially the same policies Baltimore has been pursuing on the last 40 years of Democrat administrations. Yet at this stage of his Presidency, the White House has little to lose, so when more events like the Baltimore riots occur, we can be sure to expect more calls from the President for more and more government.

Week 329

(THE SOCIALIST)

May 10, 2015

President Obama often likes to make fun of his Republican critics by referencing the accusations by some conservatives that he is a socialist. The President asserts that while he believes that government policy should have a vital role in the nation's business, he also believes in free markets and free trade. Even with these pronouncements, the label of socialist has continued to dog the President, making it more than a bit ironic that one of the candidates who now plans to try to replace him is proud of his socialism. That candidate is Bernie Sanders and so far he is the only person willing to take on Hillary Clinton for the Democrat nomination. For a President and a party that has tried to pursue aggressive liberal policies while portraying themselves as moderate, Bernie Sanders might prove a very inconvenient member of the presidential candidate club.

Bernard Sanders was born in 1941 in Brooklyn, New York and moved to Vermont as a young adult after spending several years in a kibbutz. He got involved in politics in 1971 when he joined the anti-Vietnam Liberty Union Party in Vermont. He lost elections for Vermont governor in 1972 and 1976 and for the United States Senate in 1972 and 1974. In 1981 he was elected Mayor of Burlington, and served four terms. Sanders left office in 1989, briefly taking teaching positions at Harvard's Kennedy School and at Hamilton College. In 1990, Sanders was elected to the House as an independent. In 1991, Sanders co-founded the Congressional Progressive Caucus. While in the House, Sander's voting record was solidly liberal. In 2006, Sanders ran and won as open seat in the United States Senate after the retirement of Republican turned independent Jim Jeffords. Sanders won reelection in 2012.

Senator Sanders styles himself as a Democratic Socialist. In general, he favors policies similar to those of Scandinavian socialists, meaning an expansive social welfare system, strict environmental regulations, and high taxes. Senator Sanders has railed against both Democrats and Republicans as pawns of money interests. He has been especially critical of Hillary Clinton and her husband's fundraising and paid speeches. Given this, it is not surprising that Senator Sanders has decided to challenge Clinton for the Democrat nomination. On April 29, 2015, Senator Sanders told the Associated Press that he planned to run for president and would focus on income and wealth inequality: "What we have seen is that while the average person is working longer hours for lower wages, we have seen a huge increase in income and wealth inequality, which is now reaching obscene levels. This is a rigged economy, which works for the rich and the powerful, and is not working for ordinary Americans ... You know, this country just does not belong to a handful of billionaires." On April 30, 2015, Senator Sanders officially announced his presidential campaign on the Capitol Hill lawn.

Senator Sanders' goal is simple, to push the policy debate to the Left and try to build momentum for progressives and their policies. There lies the problem for the President and for Hillary Clinton. For the President to have any policy successes in his final months in office he has to work with a Republican Congress. For Hillary Clinton to win the general election, she must persuade voters she is a moderate. The Sanders campaign makes both those tasks more difficult. The President might find himself forced to oppose progressive policies advocated by Sanders, even if he privately agrees with them, because of his desire to get bills passed through Congress. For Hillary Clinton, she must appeal to the progressive base of her party, and with Sanders in the race, that will require her to take increasingly liberal positions on issues. Those positions could come back to haunt her in the general elections. Neither Clinton nor President Obama want to be labeled a socialist, but with Sanders in the race, socialism is going to be the main topic of conversation. That will not be good for either of them.

Week 330
(No Show)

May 17, 2015

The Obama Administration has kept no secret of the fact that its effort to reach a nuclear deal with Iran is part of its larger goal of accomplishing a strategic realignment in the Middle East. For decades, America's most dangerous foe in the region has been Iran. Starting with the Iranian revolution in 1979, Iran has supported terrorist groups, threatened Israel, and worked hard to thwart American interests. With a highly developed economy, vast oil resources, a highly educated population, and its position on the Straits of Hormuz, Iran projects power more than any other Middle Eastern nation. Every President since Jimmy Carter has worked to weaken Iran and counter its influence, until Barak Obama.

President Obama dreams of remaking Iran into a moderate and productive force in the Middle East, thereby changing the balance of power in the region. His plan is to bring Iran into the international community and turn its focus away from supporting terrorists and enemies of Israel. The first step in that effort has been reaching a nuclear deal. The Administration believes that reaching such a deal will not only prevent Iran from getting a nuclear weapon in the near term, but will also integrate them into the international community. It is for this reason the United States has so doggedly pursued a deal, even in the face of Iranian lies about their nuclear program and their near complete intransigence at the negotiating table. The Administration has gone even so far as to say a deal must be reached since there is no military option to stop Iran from getting nuclear weapons. Many question how the White House can get a good deal when it has preemptively deprived itself of its best leverage, but no matter, for the Administration simply getting a deal seems just as important as what the deal says.

America's longstanding allies in the region, led by Saudi Arabia and the other Gulf states, have watched the Administration's efforts to reach a deal with Iran with horror. These Sunni nations while rich, are small and weak compared to Iran, and have relied for decades on American support to blunt Iranian influence. Now their defender and ally has made clear its goal is normalized relations with Iran, creating the prospect that America plans to seek an alliance with Iran at their expense. In response, the Gulf states have decided they can no longer wait for America to act in their interests. For example, when the government of Yemen recently fell to Islamic terrorists, the Gulf states took the initiative to launch airstrikes without coordinating with the United States.

In an effort to close this growing rift with its allies, President Obama announced that he would hold a summit on May 14 at Camp David in Maryland with the Gulf Cooperation Council — Saudi Arabia, Kuwait, Bahrain, Oman, Qatar and the United Arab Emirates. The goal of the summit was both to reassure these allies and create a consensus on issues including how best to combat ISIS. Another goal was to prevent a nuclear arms race in the Middle East, in view of the recent statement by Prince Turki bin Faisal, the former Saudi intelligence chief, that "Whatever the Iranians have, we will have, too." However, the Gulf states instead decided to send their own message. Of the six heads of state invited to the summit, only two showed up. Indeed, King Salman of Saudi Arabia wanted to make a point of the snub by confirming his attendance, only to cancel at the last minute. Also, rather than persuading these allies, it appears for most of the summit the Administration was bombarded with complaints about America's refusal to counter Iran's recent aggressive moves in the region.

The Obama Administration believes that a nuclear deal with Iran will empower Iranian moderates and change Iran's foreign policy. To pursue this theory, the White House appears willing to enrage its allies and cut a nuclear deal with Iran that most observers believe will not stop Iran from getting a nuclear weapon. The President hopes to transform the politics of the Middle East, which is a noble goal, but likely a fanciful one. America and Israel are the leading powers in the region, and Iran is their major foe. Iran hopes to gain greater influence, it can only do so at the expense of America and its allies. The President seems to believe Iran will be prepared to abandon its strategic goals in return for normalized relations with the United States. There is little evidence to support this theory, and America's allies in the region decided to send this message by not showing up at the President's summit.

Week 331
(MONEY AND MESSAGES)

May 24, 2015

Ever since she launched her presidential campaign, Hillary Clinton has been dogged by controversies over her emails and the Clinton Foundation. The decision by Clinton and her advisors to delete more than 30,000 emails kept on her private server located at her home in New York was positively Nixonian. Then came the stories of the tens of millions given to the Clinton Foundation, including donations from foreign countries and businesses who had issues before Secretary of State Clinton. The Clinton campaign has dismissed the criticisms as partisan attacks, but at the same time has worked very hard to keep the press away from Clinton and to keep any emails that were not deleted away from public view. Those strategies both hit the wall this week, when a judge ordered immediate release of a first batch of State Department emails, emails that showed how Sydney Blumenthal, the head of the Clinton Foundation, was giving advice to Secretary of State Clinton. It seems there was little division between the State Department and the Clinton Foundation after all.

One of the descriptions that was applied to President Bill Clinton was shameless. Despite the Monica Lewinsky scandal, President Clinton just carried on business, pretending he did not lie under oath or seduce a White House intern. One might have thought the Clintons learned their lesson, but after leaving office they seemed just as shameless, about making money. Using paid speeches and the Clinton Foundation, the Clintons have earned hundreds of millions of dollars and built a global network to further their international influence. But not all that money was for the Clinton Foundation. Indeed, this week it was revealed that the Clintons have earned more than $30 million in the last year giving paid speeches. A pretty shocking sum, especially when a few weeks ago Hillary Clinton claimed she left the White House broke. It seems she has solved that problem.

There is nothing wrong with earning money and there is nothing new about former presidents giving paid speeches. What is new with the Clintons is both the scope of their efforts and how the Clinton money and influence machine was integrated with the Clinton Foundation, including when Hillary Clinton was Secretary of State. In view of this, it is no wonder Clinton decided to permanently delete more than 30,000 emails. Those messages might have raised questions the Clintons would rather not answer. So the emails were deleted, but at a price. Clinton's ratings for trustworthiness have tanked, and more and more Democrats have started to question how strong a candidate she would be. All the while, Hillary Clinton has tried to ignore the issue, campaign, and keep as far away from the press as possible.

However, when a federal court ordered release of Clinton's State Department emails and when the press reported the $30 million she and her husband have earned in the last year, even the Clinton campaign could not justify refusing to answer questions. So after 27 days without taking a single question from the press, this week Clinton allowed the press to ask her a handful of questions for about 5 minutes. The responses were rehearsed and unenlightening, exactly as planned, and they created more questions than were answered. With more emails to be produced over the next few months, there is little chance this controversy will go away, the question is whether it will weaken Clinton enough to coax other Democrats into the presidential race.

For President Obama, watching all this must be uncomfortable indeed. For all the criticisms the GOP has lobbed at the Administration, sleaze has not been one of them. President Obama's personal ethics are beyond reproach, which makes the contrast with the Clintons even more stark. This makes President Obama look good in comparison, but it also threatens his legacy, because the only way President Obama's policies will endure is if he is succeeded by a Democrat. The Clintons' scandals are making that more uncertain, which is bad news for the White House.

Week 332

(RETREATING)

May 31, 2015

President Obama's plan for his last two years in office is to use the improving economy and his executive authority to establish a firm foundation for his policy goals. As a result, the President has made little effort to work with the Republican Congress on any issue other than free trade. Instead, the President has focused on forceful use of his executive authority. While the benefits of this unilateralism are obvious, it brings risks as well. An executive who seeks to rule alone must capitalize on personal popularity, must show effectiveness in policy implementation, and needs his executive actions to be upheld by the courts. On all of these counts, some serious challenges have arisen to the Administration's strategy.

For a President to be effective without congressional support, he must be able to rally the people to his cause. President Obama has hoped to do this with his rising approval ratings, which have largely been fueled by the improving economy. Job growth has improved in recent months, signaling more economic strength. That combined with lower gas prices has increased voter optimism on the economy and improved the President's overall political standing. Understanding this, the Administration has sounded increasingly triumphant on the economy, at least until this week, when it was reported that the economy shrank .7 % in the first quarter of 2015. This contraction might have been caused by the severe winter, but it is a worrying sign for the White House, because with a faltering economy will come lower approval ratings.

The Administration's concerns have also been compounded by failures overseas. In June, the United States and Iran are supposed to reach final terms on a nuclear deal, but despite the claims about a framework agreement having been reached, it has become increasingly clear that the two sides are still far apart. At the same time, the White House has claimed substantial successes against ISIS, including pushing them out of Tikrit and Kobani, only to see ISIS once again take the offensive. This month, ISIS took the cities of Palmyra in Syria and Ramadi in Iraq. In Ramadi, ISIS again handily defeated Iraqi security forces. This prompted Defense Secretary Ashton Carter is assert on a visit to Iraq that the Iraqi military lacks the will to fight. At the same time, the Iraqi government has turned increasingly to the Shite militia forces loyal to Iran. So things are not going so well for the Administration on the foreign policy front.

The landscape is also looking increasingly bleak when the issue turns to the President's executive authority. After the 2014 election, the President issued his expansive executive orders seeking to give legal status to some 5 million illegal immigrants. The orders were hailed by immigration reform advocates, but they never went into effect because a federal judge issued an injunction staying the orders. The Administration asserted the injunction was baseless and would be promptly overturned on appeal. That has not happened. In fact, this week the United States Court of Appeals for the Fifth Circuit upheld the injunction, meaning the White House's executive orders will remain enjoined and if they ever go into effect, it might not be until after President Obama leaves office. At the same time, a different federal judge took a very skeptical view of an Administration request to dismiss the lawsuit filed by the House challenging the President's executive orders staying or delaying various aspects of Obamacare. It looks like that lawsuit will go forwards as well. So it appears it is far easier to issue executive orders than to have them hold up in court.

All this is pointing to a very difficult time for the Obama Administration. If the economy falters, so will the President's personal popularity. The increasing problems and chaos in the Middle East will not build any confidence in the President's effectiveness. On top of all that, the President's much touted executive orders are under assault in the courts and might not survive. This is to say nothing of the Supreme Court's ruling expected in June on whether Obamacare allows the Administration to provide health insurance subsidies on the federal exchange. If that one goes ill for the White House, its signature legislative achievement could be threatened. Given these threats and retreats on so many fronts, maybe the White House needs to start rethinking its triumphant tone.

Week 333

(PATRIOTS)

June 7, 2015

One of the most controversial laws passed during the Bush Administration was the USA Patriot Act. It was signed into law on October 26, 2001, just six weeks after the September 11 attacks and its purpose was to strengthen the federal government's ability to respond to and prevent terrorist threats. The law has been controversial since its enactment, with critics on both the Right and the Left taking issue with provisions that they believe give too much power to America's security apparatus and that provide too few privacy and civil liberty protections. As a candidate, Barak Obama was a critic of the law, but as President it has been a different story. In 2010 and again in May 2011, President Obama signed bills to extend the Patriot Act, including a four year extension of provisions relating to roving wiretaps, searches of business records, and individual surveillance. The Administration has also been very aggressive in its use of the surveillance provisions in the law. So when the June 1, 2015 expiration of key provisions of the law approached, liberals and conservatives rallied to oppose reauthorization, putting President Obama in the difficult position of looking to the GOP for support.

The Patriot Act's key provisions include enhancements to the powers of domestic security services (Title I), enhanced surveillance procedures, including roving wiretaps (Title II), anti-money-laundering provisions (Title III), improvements to border security (Title IV), removal of obstacles to investigating by expanding powers of certain law enforcement agencies (Title V), improvements to the U.S. Victims of Crime Fund (Title VI), allowing law enforcement agencies to cross jurisdictional boundaries (Title VII), expanding criminal definitions for terrorist crimes (Title VIII), and improved intelligence sharing procedures (Title IX). Many parts of the Patriot Act are not controversial, but the surveillance provisions have been the subject of heated debates, especially in the wake of the revelations by Edward Snowden that the NSA is gathering telephone data on all Americans.

Given the strong views on the Patriot Act, it was no surprise that when the law came up for reauthorization, the debate was contentious. Republicans Senator and presidential candidate Rand Paul led a filibuster against reauthorization of the surveillance provisions. His fellow Kentuckian Senator McConnell favored reauthorization without any major changes. While a majority of the Senate and the House supported renewing the Patriot Act, there was enough opposition to prevent renewal of parts of the law expiring on June 1, 2015, and some key provisions were changed. For example, Section 215 of the law was amended to stop the NSA from mass collections of phone data. Under the new provisions, phone companies will keep the data rather than the NSA and the NSA can only obtain it upon a court order.

Eventually, after all the debate, the Patriot Act was renewed, but the debate was a good example of how controversies can cross party lines. President Obama is a strong proponent of the law even though he is a liberal, while other liberals and conservatives like Rand Paul oppose the Patriot Act. The debate on renewal also offered another example of how President Obama, who so vigorously attacked the Bush anti-terrorist policies, has adopted so many of them. All the while, Hillary Clinton remained largely silent, no doubt because she supports the law but does not want to admit that for fear of offending the progressive wing of the Democrat party. For all the controversy, there is little doubt that whoever is elected President in 2016, that person will use and support the law.

Week 334

(LET'S TRADE)

June 14, 2015

After the Republicans took control of Congress, one of the few areas where the White House had hoped to work cooperatively with the GOP was trade. One of President Obama's goals has been to get fast track trade authority from Congress. That would allow him to negotiate new trade treaties, with Congress only having up or down votes on ratification. This authority is essential if the Administration hopes to get these new trade deals. Fast track trade authority went nowhere while the Democrats controlled the Senate, because unions and environmentalists oppose new trade deals. With the new Republican majority, it was hoped that fast track would finally get passed, but in this like so many of President Obama's other legislative initiatives, hopes hit the rocks of political reality.

The Administration has made little effort to work with the Republican Congress outside the sphere of fast track authority. The assumption has been that no acceptable agreements can be reached with the GOP on other issues, so the White House has essentially not even tried, and has instead looked to executive orders. The biggest exception to this approach had been free trade, where the pro-business GOP's views are aligned with the Administration. Hopes for cooperation got a big boost when the new Republican Senate passed fast track trade authority 62-37 for the President to negotiate a Pacific free-trade accord called the Trans-Pacific Partnership. When the measure passed, the President commented: "Today's bipartisan Senate vote is an important step toward ensuring the United States can negotiate and enforce strong, high-standards trade agreements . . . . I want to thank senators of both parties for sticking up for American workers by supporting smart trade and strong enforcement, and I encourage the House of Representatives to follow suit." However, the House did not.

As the bill went to the House, there were increasing signs that passage would prove difficult. The Republican majority supports the Trans-Pacific Partnership, but bitterly opposes the President and distrusts how he will seek to negotiate any deal. The Republicans also wanted to force the Democrat minority to support the measure. Fast track trade authority passed the Senate in a compromise measure that coupled it with a program called Trade Adjustment Assistance, which helps workers who lose their jobs due to trade deals. Democrats favor this program, so it was thought including it would bolster Democrat support for fast track authority. That strategy worked in the Senate, but failed in the House.

In the House, the voting was set up that two measures had to pass for fast track to be adopted. One was the fast track bill itself, which narrowly passed relying mostly on Republican votes. That other was Trade Adjustment Assistance. Even though many GOP members opposed this program because they believe it is wasteful and ineffective, the Administration hoped it could be passed with a significant number of Democrat votes. However, on the eve of the vote it looked increasingly like the bill would go down to defeat. The White House was so concerned that President

Obama went to Capitol Hill to lobby his fellow Democrats to support the bill. However, when the votes were tallied, it appeared his own party members ignored him. Even though Democrats support the Trade Adjustment Assistance program, they joined the vast majority of Republicans in voting against that part of the bill. In fact, the vote was not even close, with the bill going down by 302-126. The President was rebuffed by his own party and it appears his trade agenda is in jeopardy.

It was a stunning defeat and put emphasis on how little leverage President Obama has in Congress. The President has been aloof and has not made many friends or allies on Capitol Hill, even among Democrats. That combined with a leftward shift in his party's economic philosophy made his fellow Democrats willing to kill a program they like just to stop fast track trade authority. For their part, the Republicans had the votes to pass fast track as a standalone bill, but then it would have to go back to the Senate, where the inclusion of the Trade Adjustment Assistance program was key to passage. The Republicans in fact managed to pass the clean bill the following week, but even on the rare occasions when the President agrees with the GOP, he still has a hard time mustering the support to get his agenda through Congress.

Week 335

(Nowhere Else)

June 21, 2015

In a year that has been marked by racial confrontations, this week the nation received another horrific reminder that racial attacks are not a thing of the past. On June 17, a 21-year-old white man named Dylann Roof joined a prayer group at Emanuel African Methodist Episcopal Church in Charleston South Carolina. However, he was not there to pray. After attending the prayer group for about an hour, he took out a gun and shot and killed nine people, including reverend and state senator Clementa C. Pinckney. Roof was caught the next day in Shelby, North Carolina. He has now been charged with nine counts of murder. Research into his internet posting and interviews with acquaintances revealed that Roof was a loner filled with racial hatred, and he expressed those views by killing nine innocent people.

The nation was shocked by the horrific events in Charleston, even more so because the shooting took place at a historic black church that played a major role in the civil rights struggle. It did not take long for the national conversation to turn to race and its role in our national problems. South Carolina's legacy as a slave state and a leader in the segregation movement only added to the controversy. It did not help matters that South Carolina is one of the few states to fly the confederate battle flag on the grounds of its state capitol. The shooting created the perfect opportunity for various interest groups to call for a host of policy prescriptions that supposedly would make events like this less likely. Indeed, President Obama was quick to join the conversation. While on a trip to Europe, the President said: "Once again, innocent people were killed in part because someone who wanted to inflict harm had no trouble getting their hands on a gun. ... We as a country will have to reckon with the fact that . . . . mass violence does not happen in other advanced countries." Clearly, the Administration has decided that the events in South Carolina are an opportunity to pursue another gun control initiative. The problem is, President Obama's premise is false.

President Obama believes if we only had stricter regulations on who can have a gun, shootings like this would not happen. However, many advanced countries with far stricter gun control laws than our own have also suffered through mass shooting events. As David Harsanyi, a senior editor at The Federalist, chronicled in his article, "Actually, President Obama, Mass Killings Aren't Uncommon In Other Countries," many nations have suffered from these types of events, including: (i) the January 2015 shootings at a satirical magazine in France killing 11; (ii) the 2011 attack in Oslo by Anders Behring Breivik who killed eight people by setting off a van bomb in Oslo and who then murdered 69 more people; (iii) the February 2015 shootings in Czech Republic that killed 9; (iv) shooting in Erfurt, Germany where 16 people were killed; and (v) the killings in the Serbian village of Velika Ivanča where 14 people were killed. These are just a few examples, pages could be filled with mass shooting events all over the world in the last 10 years.

This is not to say that mass shooting are not a problem, they certainly are and they point to a violent anger driving many to acts of extreme cruelty. However, there is no evidence to support that gun rights in the United States are the cause of this violence. In fact, those states and cities in the United States with the strictest gun laws often have the highest incidents of gun violence. No matter, certain groups will try to exploit any tragedy for political gain, and President Obama wasted no time in joining the effort. Instead, maybe we should focus on why so many young men in our country feel so disconnected from our social fabric that they think it is right to murder their fellow citizens. That is where the true problem is, and no gun control law is going to solve it.

Week 336

(COURTING)

June 28, 2015

For President Obama, the Federal Courts have been both the source of some of his greatest frustrations and his sometimes savior. Many of President Obama's executive actions have been thwarted by the Federal Courts, including his recent executive orders seeking to grant legal status to some five million immigrants. Yet for his hallmark legislative achievement, Obamacare, the courts have rejected numerous attempts to undermine the law. After a month when the President publicly criticized the courts for even hearing challenges to his initiatives, he was rewarded with two decisions that reaffirmed the core of his social policy agenda.

On June 25, the Supreme Court issued its ruling in the *King vs. Burwell* case challenging an IRS regulation making tax subsidies to buy health insurance available on the federal healthcare exchanges being used in 34 states. The Obamacare statute states that those subsidies are available on exchanges "established by the State," and the challengers claimed this language prevented the IRS from allowing subsidies on the federal exchanges. In the six to three decision, the Supreme Court held that the IRS regulation did not violate the terms of the statute when the statute is read in context. Chief Justice Roberts and Justice Kennedy joined the liberal block in turning back the challenge, reasoning that the statute is ambiguous and that the disputed language should be interpreted in a manner "that is compatible with the rest of the law." The majority then found that "Congress made the guaranteed issue and community rating requirements applicable in every State in the Nation, but those requirements only work when combined with the coverage requirement and tax credits. It thus stands to reason that Congress meant for those provisions to apply in every State as well."

President Obama used the decision to try to declare final victory in the running political battle over Obamacare, stating: "Five years ago, after nearly a century of talk, decades of trying, a year of bipartisan debate, we finally declared that in America, health care is not a privilege for a few but a right for all . . . . The Affordable Care Act is here to stay." This is likely wishful thinking since Obamacare remains unpopular and every GOP presidential candidate has vowed to repeal it. To date the law has survived two challenges at the Supreme Court, but that is not going to end the debate, because the law was passed on a purely partisan basis, so Republicans have little reason or inclination to cooperate with the President on Obamacare, at least as long as the law remains unpopular.

The next day, the Supreme Court issued another decision that was hailed by the President. That was the decision in *Obergefell vs. Hidges*, which found a constitutional right to same sex marriage under the Fourteenth Amendment. With this decision, all States are now compelled to allow same sex marriage and recognize ones from other states. Before the ruling, more than thirty states recognized same sex marriage, but now all must. The ruling was a five to four vote, and with much rancor on the Supreme Court. The dissenters criticized the majority for finding a constitutional right where none exists and implying that advocates of traditional marriage as bigots. No doubt the ruling marks an amazing change in the tide for gay rights. Until 2012, nearly all leaders in the Republican and Democrat parties including President Obama supported the Defense of Marriage Act, which was passed to protect traditional marriage. However, after a comment by Vice President Biden that he supports gay marriage, President Obama was forced to state that his views had changed during an interview with Robin Roberts: "At a certain point, I've just concluded that for me personally, it is important for me to go ahead and affirm that I think same-sex couples should be able to get married."

The decision on same sex marriage was met with celebration and consternation across the country. Clear majorities, driven by changes in attitudes of the young, support gay marriage. However, by making it a Constitutional right, many traditional marriage advocates and churches worry that now they will be subject to a wave of new lawsuits trying to force them to recognize same sex marriage or risk their tax exempt status. Many believe the decision will set in motion a battle between the freedom to marry and freedom of religion, which will ultimately make the decision much more derisive than it presently appears. No matter, President Obama took the opportunity to praise the decision as a promise kept to the gay community, which has been such a key supporter of his agenda. So the President was able to head into the summer with the wind at his back, provided by the branch of government he spent much of the month criticizing, namely the Federal Courts.

Week 337

(DRACHMA'ED)

July 5, 2015

For much of the last four years, the European debt crisis and the weakness of the European monetary union have created international economic uncertainty and put a damper on economic growth. However, Europe's economic prospects have slowly improved as Spain and Italy took steps to address their debt challenges, avoiding the risk of a default by those major economies. That left Greece, one of the European Union's smallest and most indebted economy. Even though the Greek debt problem poses fewer risks of triggering a contagion that could cause a second international financial crisis, it still could undermine the monetary union. For this reason, it has been an assumption on both sides of the Atlantic that a deal would be reached to avoid a Greek default and keep Greece in the Euro zone. Those prospects dimmed this week, leading to major losses in financial markets and risks for U.S. economic growth.

The current debt crisis has its roots in the Greek elections held five months ago that brought the left-wing Syria Party into power on a platform rejecting the austerity program being forced on Greece by the EU. In the ensuing months of negotiations, the new Greek government was unable to reach an agreement for a further cash infusion to bail out its economy, primarily because it would not accept the bailout terms demanded by Germany. This week negotiations failed and Greece was unable to make a payment owed to the International Monetary Fund, putting Greece in default. Running out of cash, Greece was forced to close its banks for a week and limit cash withdrawals by its citizens to 60 Euros per day.

As a last negotiation ploy, Greek Prime Minister Alex Tsipras set a referendum for July 5 on whether to accept the EU's bailout terms. Greek voters overwhelmingly rejected the bailout. Expecting this result, Tsipras hoped the referendum would increase his leverage to get Germany to moderate its demands for tax increases and cuts to pensions and public spending as conditions for further cash infusions. Put simply, Tsipras is playing a game of chicken, betting that the EU will blink and will give Greece money on less stringent terms to avoid Greece leaving the Euro zone, which could threaten the monetary union.

All this uncertainty is now having a direct adverse impact on the U.S. economy, with U.S. equity markets giving back in just a few weeks nearly all of their gains in 2015, thereby erasing hundreds of billions of dollars of wealth. The dollar is rising because of the Euro's weakness, which could hurt U.S. exports and slow gains in employment. Recognizing this risk, President Obama has encouraged EU leaders to reach a deal with Greece, while trying to avoid getting directly involved in the negotiations. If the impasse is not overcome, Greece might soon be back on the Drachma and the Euro's future might be in question. In the end, Greece is Europe's problem to solve, not America's, but the impact will be felt on this side of the Atlantic nonetheless.

Week 338
(THAT'S LEFT)

July 12, 2015

Summer is usually the slow season for American politics, but the White House probably wants no slowdown. In recent weeks, President Obama has recorded some of his highest approval ratings of the year, and more and more, the national dialogue has been turning to issues where liberals believe they have the upper hand. Republicans like it when the nation is focused on wasteful government, deficits, foreign threats, and law breakers. However, so far this summer the dominate stories have been racism, gay rights, diplomacy, and liberal court victories. Very comfortable ground for the President, and he is benefiting as a result.

Many people call the 1980s the Reagan Era because that decade saw an ascendant Republican party capture the attitudes and aspirations of the nation. President Obama fancies himself as a liberal Reagan, if not a modern FDR. He aspires to have the nation view issues through the same prism as he does and to have his perspective capture the national mood. For his first six years in office, the Administration has spent most of its time and energy fighting the conservative backlash against the President's policies. The Democrats lost Congress, were forced to accept spending cuts, and have lost the ability to pass more liberal legislation. Not to be discouraged, the White House has focused on implementing the few laws it has been able to pass and using executive powers and the courts to further its agenda. Now is appears that the national mood has turned in the Administration's favor, giving new life to the President's progressive aspirations.

Many factors have contributed to this swing. The improving economy has made Americans more positive, and the Republicans have not been able to rally support against the President because more and more, the Administration is using regulations and the courts to push its agenda, and many initiatives have not generated national attention. At the same time, events have allowed progressives to dominate the national discussion. The shootings in Charleston, South Carolina led to a crusade against the confederate battle flag and has re-opened a discussion on race. President Obama has used that shooting to make some his most forceful comments yet on that hot button topic. Then the Supreme Court's gay marriage decision created even more momentum for progressives, while thoroughly depressing conservatives. Conservatives' latest effort to gut Obamacare failed at the Supreme Court as well, ensuring the survival of that controversial law at least until a Republican is elected President. And in foreign relations, the opening to Cuba and the Administration's all-out effort to get a nuclear deal with Iran are monuments to the President's effort to turn enemies to allies through engagement. On some fronts progressives have been thwarted, especially on government spending and immigration issues, but except for those few disappointments, liberals are definitely on a roll.

All of this has been to the President's benefit. With these victories, the President is showing ever more contempt for his critics and an increasing determination to push his executive authority to the maximum. No doubt he will seek to extend his winning streak into the Fall budget showdown that is coming with the Republican Congress. The GOP ignored the President's budget of tax increases and vast new spending and passed a program ending Obamacare and cutting entitlement spending. The White House and the Republicans are on a collision course on the budget, and far from wanting to avoid it, the President wants nothing more than a chance to confront and beat the Republicans on the budget. That would be a great way to end a strong year.

Week 339

(Getting Nuked)

July 19, 2015

For more than two years, the Obama Administration has been negotiating with Iran regarding its nuclear program. After putting in place a tough regime of sanctions, the White House said they brought Iran to the table and were determined to reach a deal. What ensued were ever continuing negotiations, missed deadlines, and a framework agreement this Spring that turned into no agreement at all because the United States and Iran disagreed about what was in it. Starting in June, marathon talks began in Vienna, which again failed to meet agreed deadlines. Not to be deterred, Secretary of State Kerry extended the talks and finally, on July 18, an agreement was reached. Almost immediately, the deal was condemned by our allies in the Middle East and by nearly all GOP members of Congress, while it was celebrated in the streets of Tehran.

The details of the deal are complicated and crucial. President Obama has consistently stated that Iran cannot be allowed to get a nuclear weapon. He has also made clear he was not willing to use military force to stop Iran. So the White House ensured that a deal had to be reached no matter what. Having given up some of its best leverage, it is not surprising that the specifics of the deal have been found wanting. The deal requires Iran to reduce its stockpiles of low-enriched uranium by 98% for 15 years and to reduce by two-thirds its number of centrifuges that enrich uranium. Its remaining centrifuges must be moved and will be monitored. The Administration claims these provisions will prevent Iran from developing a nuclear weapon for at least 10 years. UN inspections are also part of the deal, but there is a provision where Iran can object to an inspection, which will result in the request going to arbitration. If Iran violates the deal, there are "snap-back" provisions that will put sanctions back in place. What does Iran get in return. The current arms embargo will start to be lifted in 5 years and in eight years Iran can buy missile technology. Freezes on overseas assets will be lifted, giving Iran access to more than $100 billion. Other sanctions including the oil embargo and financial restrictions will be lifted over time.

Now that a deal has been reached, the U.S., U.K., Germany, France, China, and Russia will work on a resolution to implement the agreement. At the same time, in a compromise reached with Congress, there will be a 60-day window for the Senate and House to review and approve or reject the deal. However, to stop the deal any rejection would have to pass by a 2/3 majority because the President has vowed to veto any resolution disapproving the deal. So it appears likely that in 90 days the deal will go into effect and preliminary steps for implementation will start.

As soon as the details of the deal were announced, loud criticisms began and the White House immediately marshalled its forces to try to sell the deal. The biggest criticism is that the deal at best will only slow Iran's march to get a nuclear weapon, not stop it. In the process, sanctions will be lifted, which will aid the Iranian government and provide it with more resources both to oppose Western interests and pursue a nuclear weapon. The celebrations in the streets of Tehran show that far from undermining the Iranian government, the deal has strengthened it. As for Iran's pledge to destroy Israel, they did not withdraw it, instead they have reaffirmed it. It is no wonder our allies, both Arab and Israeli, are denouncing the deal. The likely result of the deal is a stronger Iran, a growing arms race, and eventually an Iran with nuclear weapons and the missiles to deliver them. This fate is likely 10 to 15 years off, but unless the dynamics change drastically in the Middle East, that is what is in store.

President Obama, despite all the criticisms, hailed the deal as a major achievement for his Administration. Like his opening to Cuba, the President is now aggressively implementing his vision for resolving international conflicts, one focused on ending old feuds and reaching out to enemies, even if that rattles allies. President Obama hopes that by engagement and by bringing rogue notions into the international order old enmities will abate and conflicts will cease. It is an ambitious agenda and one many say is naïve. It is founded on the assumption that goodwill will be returned and a willingness to compromise and negotiate will not be viewed as weakness. However, some nations still play power politics and are still willing to use force to achieve their ends. Whether it is Putin in the Ukraine, or Iran's support for terrorists, or the Syrian regime, these states do not view the world as we do and the White House has given them no reason to fear the United States. Will they respond with more aggression not less. History tells a disturbing story in that regard, but President Obama is trying to change history not learn from it.

Week 340

(TRUMPED)

July 26, 2015

While Republicans in Congress were grappling with how best to oppose President Obama's Iran nuclear deal, they were faced with an almost equally daunting challenge: how to deal with Donald Trump. For the last two presidential election cycles, Trump toyed with the idea of running for the GOP nomination, but ultimately did not. This year has been different, not only is Trump running, he is leading in both the polls and in controversial statements. This is delighting Democrats and causing consternation for Republican leaders. When faced with opposing the President on such serious issues as Iran and nuclear weapons, the Trump distraction is undermining Republican strategy, all to the benefit of the President.

When Donald Trump previously floated the idea of running for president, most people thought it was a publicity stunt to improve ratings for his various television programs. Few people took him seriously when he said he was again considering a run for president. However, it seems Trump has become so frustrated with the direction of the nation, and has become so convinced that he is the man to right the ship, that rhetoric became reality and he actually decided to jump into the race. Trump announced his campaign in June and then travelled to Iowa and New Hampshire. Then in early July he went out West, with trips to Las Vegas and Los Angeles. On July 11, he attracted 9,000 people to the Phoenix Convention Center, where Trump took aim at illegal immigrants, labelling them criminals. Trump's comments on illegal immigrants prompted Arizona Senator John McCain to criticize him for stirring up the "crazies." Trump retaliated at a campaign event in Ames, Iowa, stating that John McCain is "not a war hero." He continued: "He was a war hero because he was captured. I like people who weren't captured." This drew criticisms across the political spectrum, and prompted fellow GOP presidential candidate Lindsey Graham to call Trump as "jackass." On July 21, Trump then gave out Graham's personal cell phone number for people to call him and criticize him. Then on July 23, Trump travelled to the Mexican border to further highlight the illegal immigration problem.

If all this sounds a bit immature, it is, but it is also working. Trump is attracting a huge amount of attention to himself and his campaign, and is now leading in many polls. This has forced other candidates to sharpen their rhetoric to get noticed. It is all adding up to a very nasty fight for the GOP nomination. The appeal of the Trump campaign is an interesting phenomenon. He is an engaging speaker who exudes confidence. He also says silly and sometimes outright absurd things. However, his approach is working, in part because Republican voters are frustrated, they want a fighter, and Trump is tapping into a resentment over air dried and poll tested candidates. The Trump unplugged campaign is working so far, but is it built to last. The Democrats certainly hope so.

The rise of Trump has Democrats delighted, not simply because it makes it easier to paint all Republicans as extreme, but also because it has obscured the crisis building in the Hillary Clinton campaign. Even though she faces no significant opposition, Clinton's negatives continue to rise, her ratings on trustworthiness are horrible, and she is burning through cash at an alarming rate. Now we have learned that the Justice Department has been asked to start an investigation into her use of a private email account for classified information. These are troubling signs, but barely anyone outside the political class has noticed because of Trump. So at the moment Trump is hurting Republicans and helping Democrats, and maybe he is just obscuring the big story, that the Hillary Clinton campaign is in trouble.

Week 341
(HOME COMING)

August 2, 2015

When Barak Obama first came to national prominence, his book *Dreams of My Father* was seen as a synopsis of his world view. The book is about his father, a Kenyan, who came to the United States for an education, married a woman from Kansas, and returned home to work in the Kenyan government. President Obama had little contact with his father, but no doubt he has played a large role in both the President's identity and perspective. For those reasons, the President's trip to Kenya and Ethiopia this week garnered special attention. It was his first homecoming while in office and it was the first time that any president has visited both countries. For Barak Obama, it was a chance to connect with his past, call for progress, and herald what he sees as a coming era of progress in Africa.

The President began his five day trip in Kenya. He arrived in Nairobi on Friday July 31 for a business development summit. It was not until Sunday that he had an opportunity to interact with average Kenyans. That morning, his helicopter landed at Kenyatta University, where thousands of students were waiting. Then at the Safaricom Indoor Arena, he delivered a speech to 4,500 people, who were chanting "Obama! Obama! Obama!" as a song played "I'm coming home." The speech was a combination of praise, remembrance, and lecture.

President Obama was introduced by his half-sister, Auma Obama, who heads a foundation and hosted him when he visited Kenyan nearly 30 years ago. With President Uhuru Kenyatta of Kenya at his side, the President told Kenyans that they need to overcome ethnic divisions and end discrimination. He called for greater democracy, equal rights for women and gays, the latter request receiving less than enthusiastic applause. The President spoke of the great opportunities for progress, but also the many hurdles, stating: "Kenya is at a crossroads . . . . a moment filled with peril but also enormous promise." He also spoke personally about his frustrations with his lack of contact with ordinary people: "Part of the challenge that I've had during the course of my Presidency is that given the demands of the job and the bubble, I can't come here and just go upcountry and visit for a week and meet everybody" . . . . "I'm more restricted, ironically, as president of the United States than I will be as a private citizen." Then, when he went out to shake hands, the crowd pushed forward so hard the President's security detail had to step in.

Next, the trip took the President to Faffa, Ethiopia for an African Union meeting. President Obama is the first sitting American president to address the African Union. In his speech, he returned to several of the same themes he discussed in Kenya, including economic progress, human rights, and the fight against terrorism. He also met with Nkosazana Dlamini Zuma, chairperson of the African Union Commission, to discuss violence and religious strife in South Sudan. In all, the trip was both personal and policy driven for the President. It was an opportunity to connect with his African roots, and also a chance to push for changes that will let Africa reach its potential. The White House believes Africa's importance on the world stage will be increasing and American needs to maintain its influence there. This trip was part of that effort and also an opportune homecoming for the President.

Week 342

(BEAU)

August 9, 2015

While President Obama has been on a win streak this summer, his likely successor to the Democratic presidential nomination has had a very different experience these last few months. Hillary Clinton entered the presidential campaign with every advantage. She had huge name recognition, massive fundraising, and a nearly unified party behind her. Only second tier candidates like Bernie Sanders and Martin O'Malley, the former governor of Maryland, have stepped forward to challenge her for the nomination, making her look increasingly invulnerable. All she had to do was run a smart campaign and avoid missteps, two things she has simply not managed to do, creating a risk of a true challenge to her nomination from Vice President Joe Biden.

Some aspects of Hillary Clinton's campaign have been masterful. She has tried to be more personal, focus on issues, and connect with voters. However, all that has been overshadowed by self-inflicted wounds that have reinforced negatives perceptions regarding her honesty and trustworthiness. It all started with her emails. Just before she launched her campaign, she decided to erase some 30,000 emails she kept on a private server to ensure no one would ever see them. Then she tried to limit access to the emails she did not erase. Then we learned she was using her private smartphone and server for State Department work, some of which might have included classified materials. This has prompted an inspector general and FBI investigation. All the while, she has limited press access, avoided questions on the issue, and when she has addressed it, her answers have been both rehearsed and inconsistent. To make matters worse, the controversy has overshadowed her policy speeches and we have learned that her campaign has been spending money at an alarming rate. All of this has made many Democrats nervous.

Even with all these problems, polls show Hillary Clinton is still in a commanding position to win the Democrat nomination. That is because she has no first rate opponent. What is worrying Democrats is that polls show majorities of voters questioning her honesty, her negatives are rising, and she is behind some GOP candidates in recent polls in key battleground states. So Democrat operatives are fearful a weak candidate might be cruising to the nomination. Not surprisingly, this has resulted in attention turning to Vice President Biden. It has been assumed that Biden is not running. He has neither built a campaign infrastructure nor raised money. However, it is rumored that his son Beau Biden, who died recently at the age of 47 from a brain tumor, encouraged his father to run. This, plus Hillary Clinton's troubles, have prompted Biden to reexamine the prospects of running again for the White House.

Biden ran for the White House in 1988 and 2008. Both times has ran poor campaigns and was knocked out early. Nevertheless, many Democrat powerbrokers have made clear they are encouraging Biden to run again. Biden's team has leaked that he is having active conversations with party leaders about another campaign. It is still unclear whether Biden will run, but if he does, the calculus for Hillary Clinton and the Democrats will change dramatically. Clinton has been able to weather her missteps because she has no serious opponent for the nomination. If Biden runs, that will change immediately, accentuating Clinton's vulnerabilities. It also complicates the Democrat plan to win the national election, because they would face a long and difficult primary season and no matter who wins, they will be stuck with legacy candidates who will have a hard time separating themselves from President Obama. So while much of the media has been focusing on Donald Trump and his various outlandish statements in the GOP contest, recent events for the Democrats are much more significant.

Week 343

(NORMALIZED)

August 16, 2015

In the wake of the Iran nuclear deal, the White House wasted no time in pursuing its other experiment in engagement: Cuba. Despite significant congressional opposition, earlier this summer the Obama Administration announced its plan to normalize relations with Cuba. An important symbolic first step in that effort is opening an embassy in Havana. On August 14, the United States took that step when Secretary of State Kerry officiated at a ceremony re-opening the United States embassy. At his side were twelve members of Congress, embassy staff, and Cuban officials. Noticeably absent were any Cuban dissidents fighting for religious or democratic rights. The Obama Administration purposefully did not invite them for fear of offending their Cuban hosts, which is illustrative of the Administration's Cuba policy.

Secretary of State Kerry opened the embassy speaking in both English and Spanish, an effort to reach out directly to Cuban officials and the Cuban people. He welcomed his guests by saying "[t]hank you for joining us at this truly historic moment as we prepare to raise the flag ... symbolizing the restoration of diplomatic relations after 54 years." In his address, Kerry used very restrained language to call for greater human rights and political liberties, instead focusing most of his address on the historic nature of the event. The Administration's argument for normalized relations is that the embargo has not resulted in greater liberties for the Cuban people, so it is time to try to influence Cuba through engagement. Yet in making that determination, the White House is restoring relations and thereby aiding the Cuban government, asking very little in return. The United States did not demand the release of all political prisons, better press or religious freedoms, or more democratic rights.

Far from demanding reforms in return for normalized relations, the Administration is carefully avoiding any steps that might offend the Cuban government led by the Castro brothers. The decision not to invite Cuban dissidents is the best example of this approach. Instead of inviting them to the public opening ceremony, Secretary of State Kerry held a private event with dissidents, artists, business people, and journalists at the residence of the chief of the U.S. mission. The press was not invited to ensure the event put no pressure on the Cuban regime, which appears to be a current priority of the Administration.

One might expect with the United States so carefully avoiding any steps to offend, the Cuban government might be responding in kind. The truth appears to be the opposite. The Cuban government is more aggressively pursuing dissidents, with more arrests and beatings, and there is no indication that greater political or religious freedoms are on the horizon. Indeed, on the very day of the embassy opening, Cuban state media published an article from Fidel Castro marking his 89th birthday. The article made no mention of restored relations with the United States. Instead, the article focused on the anniversary of America's use of the atomic bomb against Japan and asserted that because of the embargo the United States owes reparations to Cuba.

The critics of the White House's policy have noticed all of this. Florida Republican Senator and Cuban American Marco Rubio stated "[a]s a symbol of just how backward this policy shift has turned out to be, no Cuban dissidents have been invited to today's official flag-raising ceremony at the US Embassy in Havana . . . . Cuba's dissidents have fought for decades for the very Democratic principles President Obama claims to be advancing through these concessions. Their exclusion from this event has ensured it will be little more than a propaganda rally for the Castro regime." Likewise, New Jersey Democrat Senator Bob Menendez said it was "shameful" and that a "flag representing freedom and liberty will rise today in a country ruled by a repressive regime that denies its people democracy and basic human rights. This is the embodiment of a wrongheaded policy that rewards the Castro regime's brutality at the expense of the Cuban people's right to freedom of expression and independence."

The Administration has largely ignored these critics and is using every executive authority available to pursue its opening to Cuba. The White House seems to sincerely believe that providing benefits to Cuba and asking for little or nothing in return will improve conditions for the Cuban people. President Obama and Secretary Kerry seem mostly focused on their legacy and want to be able to claim they have turned the page on relations with Cuba. Whether this actually helps the Cuban people is presently a secondary concern. All the while, the Cuban government gets the benefits of normalized relations and will get to strengthen their hold on power at the same time, at least in the near term. It seems that for regimes like those in Cuba and Iran, being a foe of the United States has its benefits, at least during the Obama Administration.

Week 344
(CHINA SYNDROME)

August 23, 2015

For the last six months, President Obama has trumpeted the strengthening United States economy as evidence of the wisdom of his economic policies. A steadily improving labor market, low interest rates, a strong stock market, and solid, if not stellar, economic growth all supported this theory. The strength of the economy is key, not just for President Obama but also for the Democrat party, because whoever is nominated will inevitably be viewed as an extension of the policies of the current Administration. That is why this week's stock market plunge was sobering, not just for investors but also for politicians.

There has been talk for many months that stock market prices were inflated, being fueled by continuing low interest rates that have pushed investors into equities to get returns. Many feared a correction was coming and all that was required was some triggering event. That event has now been supplied by China and commodity prices. For the last year, there have been growing signs of a slowdown in Chinese economic growth. There has also been increasing volatility in the Chinese stock market, which is dominated by small investors and heavily influenced by communist party policy. As for commodities, for months commodity prices across the spectrum have been falling, including oil and key industrial minerals like copper. These weak commodity prices are an indicator of slowing demand and weaker economic growth globally. Then the bottom fell out this week, with the Chinese stock market crashing, leading to selloffs in emerging markets, Europe, and the United States. The Dow Jones Industrial Average lost nearly 15% of its value and the S&P 500 suffered a similar decline. At the same time, oil prices tumbled below $40 a barrel, with other commodities falling as well. Investors have also become addicted to cheap money fueled by near zero interest rates. However, the Federal Reserve has made clear that after seven years of historic low rates, it is planning a rate increase this year, which is another factor that has fueled a market sell off.

It is not clear what next week will bring, except that global markets and the global economy appear to at least be heading for a period of instability if not recession. The 2016 election is still far off, but the consequences for the Administration and the Democrats could be dire. There is no doubt that the 2008 financial crisis was the undoing for the GOP's election hopes and led to President Obama's landslide victory. Hillary Clinton and whoever else might join the Democrat nomination campaign can ill afford a weak economy. For voters to elect any Democrat after 8 years of the Obama Administration, they will inevitably have to be comfortable with the continuation of the same economic policies. A weak economy undermines the ability of any Democrat to get elected. For this reason, the falling stock market and global economic instability is bad news for the Democrats. The only good news is that it is 2015, not 2016, because the economy still has time to recover before election day.

Week 345

(THE MAVERICKS)

August 30, 2015

The summer before a presidential election year is often called the silly season of American politics. Presidential campaigns have been announced, candidates are raising money and giving speeches, but the primaries are still six months away. Few voters are paying attention, but that matters little to the political class. This year, the 18 declared Republican candidates and the three Democrats challenging Hillary Clinton are all jockeying for attention, which combined with political reporters looking for things to report, results in non-stop coverage of the mundane, outrageous, and ridiculous. Usually the best course is to ignore this time in politics, remembering that the leaders and stories of 2015 probably will not matter much in 2016. However, this year might be different, because the amazing ascendance Donald Trump and Bernie Sanders may be revealing a shift in American politics that could actually impact the 2016 election.

Poll after poll show that the American people think the country is going in the wrong direction and that they are not happy with their leaders. During his presidency, President Obama has rarely polled above 50% and even though the GOP won a huge election victory in 2014, they are even more unpopular. The voters seem disgusted with politics and politicians in general, and this time might be ready to show it at the ballot box. So in this atmosphere, unconventional and anti-establishment candidates are in vogue, and even their improbable campaigns are starting to look viable. Much of the media attention has been on Donald Trump's presidential campaign, but in many ways the Bernie Sanders campaign is more amazing.

Hillary Clinton towers over the Democrat nomination contest, so much so that no major Democrats were willing to challenge her. But Bernie Sander, a socialist senator from Vermont joined the fray and started a grass roots campaign taking on the Democrat establishment. As the same time, Hillary Clinton's campaign has stumbled. Clinton continues to be dogged by her decision use a private email account for State Department business and her decision to delete more than 30,000 emails to ensure the public could never see them. A DOJ started an investigation and a federal judge has ordered those emails that remain to be produced. As more and more emails become public, it has become clear that Clinton was sending emails with information now classified, potentially breaking State Department rules and potentially federal law. Clinton has further hurt herself by first downplaying the investigation, then attacking her critics, and now mildly offering apologies. In response, her ratings for honesty and trustworthiness have crashed, and the Sanders campaign is gaining momentum, with Sanders pulling within striking distance in Iowa and New Hampshire.

On the Republican side, another maverick is also stealing the show, namely Donald Trump. When Trump first announced his campaign, most saw it as simply an exercise in ego. Trump's campaign was unscripted and seem improvised. Trump made a point of picking fights with the other GOP candidates and Fox News, and seemed to enjoy saying outlandish things, whether true or not. Most thought Trump would implode, but the opposite has happened, his popularity has swelled. Polls show him dominating the GOP field, taking double digit leads. Despite being a billionaire, Trump's support is blue collar and he is appealing to voters who want a genuine candidate, and seem willing to forgive Trump his misstatements and errors.

What we are seeing at work is fatigue in the American electorate. The Obama Administration has been the most divisive since the Nixon era and the federal government is seen as ineffective and unresponsive. Voters want a change, and are willing to support unconventional candidates to get it. Voters want to shake things up, so early on in the presidential campaign they seem willing to support these two mavericks. This poses a particular challenge to the expected frontrunners for the major party nominations, Jeb Bush and Hillary Clinton, both of whom are resume candidates, products of the political establishment, and related to former presidents. If this voter sentiment continues, they are the exact candidates voters do not want. Sanders and Trump are tapping into this sentiment to their benefit, and if the trend continues, it could pose a significant challenge to the political establishment.

Week 346
(MCKINLEY)

September 6, 2015

A major focus of President Obama's second term has been climate change. While the White House has been unable to move climate change legislation through Congress, the President has used his executive authority and his Administration's control of regulatory agencies to put in place a slew of directives and regulations designed to limit carbon emissions. These steps have been significant, but even President Obama recognizes that there are limits to what he can do without legislation. For that reason, the White House scheduled a three-day Presidential trip to Alaska, which environmentalists see as ground zero for climate change threats to the United States. The President hoped to use the trip to build public support for even more aggressive moves to combat climate change.

The President arrived in Anchorage, Alaska on August 31. Upon arrival, the President participated in a roundtable discussion with native Americans and then he spoke at a conference entitled Global Leadership in the Arctic: Cooperation, Innovation, Engagement and Resilience, with both events focused on climate change and its impacts on Alaska. Accompanied by Secretary of State John Kerry and Secretary of the Interior Sally Jewell, President Obama used his address to call attention to the threats posed by the warming climate. The President continued this theme with a visit to receding glaciers. In addition, President Obama became the first sitting President to visit the arctic region, telling native Alaskans living there that "I've been trying to make the rest of the country more aware of a changing climate, but you're already living it." The President even taped a television episode with survivalist Bear Grylls.

The President also used this trip to pay respects to native Alaskan people. In an important symbolic move, the President showed that respect by officially renaming the United States' highest peak, Mount McKinley, to Denali, the name for that mountain in the native Koyukon language. As Interior Secretary Jewell said: "With our own sense of reverence for this place, we are officially renaming the mountain Denali in recognition of the traditions of Alaska Natives and the strong support of the people of Alaska." The move was controversial, especially in President McKinley's native Ohio, where the renaming was criticized by both Republicans and Democrats. It was the type of move that could only be made by a second term President who does not need to face the voters at the ballot box. It was also a demonstration of the President's determination to honor native peoples and remove symbols of America's own colonial past. It also was not lost on observers that the President removed a Republican President's name from a major natural monument, just like the Administration is thinking about removing Republican hero, Alexander Hamilton, from the twenty dollar bill.

In many ways, this trip was a great example of the President's use of the tools remaining to him. With little chance of passing legislation on any major issue, the White House has essentially given up on working with Congress and for the most part is not even trying to propose legislation. Instead, the Administration is focused on symbolic trips, policy addresses, and executive actions. The President is willing to use every power at his disposal to push his agenda, but large and lasting changes can only be made by legislation, the exact thing he cannot pass. So instead, the President travels and makes speeches, hoping to rally the public and make a difference in policy debates. Yet increasingly, the national discussion is moving beyond President Obama and turning towards who will be his successor. This week, the President was removed from the national debate as much geographically as he has been removed politically.

Week 347

(FALLING IN LINE)

September 13, 2015

When President Obama signed his nuclear deal with Iran, it was roundly criticized across the political spectrum. Many believed the deal was a victory for Iran because it gave immediate benefits to that Islamic state through the lifting of sanctions, while in return gave the West only limited inspection rights and at best an agreement that Iran would not acquire a nuclear weapon for 10 years. Israel condemned the deal, America's gulf allies became very nervous, and the Iranians celebrated. If the deal had to face the Constitutional process for treaty ratification it would have surely died. However, the GOP cut a deal with President Obama that avoided a ratification fight, and it now appears certain that the Iran nuclear deal will go into effect.

Earlier this year, when the Administration made clear it intended to sign a nuclear deal with Iran, it also indicated that it did not intend to submit the deal for congressional approval. That enraged Republicans who had just recently taken the majority in the Senate. This standoff eventually led to negotiations on a framework for Congress to address any deal that might result from the negotiations with Iran. The GOP could have taken the position that any deal would be a treaty that needed to be ratified by the Senate as required by the Constitution. If President Obama then signed a deal and did not submit it to Congress, it could be rescinded by any successor or even challenged in the Courts. This was the confrontational approach the GOP could have taken, which surely would have led to a Constitutional fight with the White House. Instead, the GOP opted for compromise. It agreed to a framework where the Administration had to submit any deal to Congress, but a deal would go into effect unless Congress disapproved of it by a margin that could overcome both a filibuster in the Senate and a presidential veto.

Republicans agreed to this compromise because they were not sure any deal would be reached and they believed enough Democrats would vote against any deal that they could either defeat it or force the President to veto any resolution of disapproval. This deal avoided a Constitutional fight, but also gave the Democrats complete control over whether any deal would become law. Even if a deal was unpopular, the Administration would only need the support of Democrats to prevent a veto override. It may have seemed like a reasonable deal at the time, but it resulted in President Obama getting exactly what he wanted.

President Obama and Secretary of State Kerry got their deal with Iran, even though it was an imperfect one. The criticism was immediate and widespread. The White House submitted the deal to Congress for review, but withheld two side agreements with Iran, which they have refused to share with Congress. Then the lobbying began. The Administration put on a full court press to get enough Democrats to support the deal to ensure a veto could not be overridden. Despite these efforts, the House voted to disapprove of the deal by a large margin. The Republicans hoped for an equally strong vote in the Senate, where many Democrats were critics of the deal. But the White House quietly worked to persuade one Democrat senator after another to support the deal. The Administration did not simply get enough support to prevent a veto override, they obtained the votes of 41 of the 45 Senate Democrats, meaning the GOP could not get even enough votes to end a filibuster. Majority leader McConnell tried twice to get a disapproval bill to the floor, and was defeated twice, and the Iran nuclear deal thereby went into effect.

Since the Administration refused to present the two side deals to Congress, Republicans might challenge the Iran deal in court. The next president might also try to undo the deal, if that president is a critic. But for now, the Iran nuclear deal is going into effect and the GOP did not even get the pleasure of forcing President Obama to veto a disapproval resolution. So Republicans got a deal they hate and they made the President's path to get it much easier than if they had not reached any compromise with the White House. A bad bargain indeed for the GOP.

Week 348

(GET TRUMP)

September 20, 2015

With the Hillary Clinton campaign facing an ever growing crisis as her poll numbers continue to fall and with Vice President Biden looking closer to joining the race, one would think the GOP presidential candidates would be joyous. Unfortunately for the Republicans, they have not been able to enjoy the Democrats' problems because they have a big problem themselves, named Donald Trump. So this week, when the Republican candidates gathered at the Reagan Library in Simi Valley, they had a very simple goal, get Trump, and they did everything they could to try to accomplish that goal.

Donald Trump poses a difficult problem for the GOP. He has tapped into a strong current of dissatisfaction in the country, drawing new people into the political process and creating new energy for the Republicans. But at the same time, Trump poses a huge problem. Many of his policy positions are not particularly conservative, he constantly makes statements that are offensive, and he repels nearly as many voters as he attracts. He has vaulted to the top of the polls for the GOP nomination, but in a general election, many believe he would be a weak candidate. So when Republicans gathered for their second debate, it was in both their personal interests and the interests of the party to knock Trump down from his commanding position.

The September 23 Republican debate was an unwieldly affair, with 11 candidates fighting for airtime and exposure. The first GOP debate was dominated by Trump, and this one was dominated by attacks on him. The debate covered many issues, from immigration, to Iran, to abortion, but almost every topic was used as a chance to take a shot at Trump. Carly Fiorina dismissed him as "an entertainer" and Senator Rand Paul called him "sophomoric." Wisconsin Governor Scott Walker said "We don't need an apprentice in the White House — we have one right now." When called on his comment that voters would not vote for Carly Fiorina because of her face, Fiorina said simply: "I think women all over this country heard very clearly what Mr. Trump said." In a rare instance, recognizing his vulnerability, Trump responded: "I think she's got a beautiful face, and she's a beautiful woman."

Trump fought back as hard as he could, starting the debate by saying Rand Paul should not even be on the stage and he even ridiculed his appearance: "I never attacked him on his looks, and believe me, there is plenty of subject matter right there." To Jeb Bush, Trump went right at his brother President George W. Bush: "Your brother's administration gave us Barack Obama, because it was such a disaster." This forced Jeb Bush to respond, both to defend himself and his brother: "You know what? As it relates to my brother, there's one thing I know for sure: He kept us safe."

In the wake of the debate, it became clear that Trump was damaged. He did not dominate and looked defensive. There were other losers as well, including Scott Walker and Rand Paul, who failed to get a breakout moment in the debate, something their campaigns badly need. The big winner in the debate was Carly Fiorina, who stood out by her strong condemnation of Planned Parenthood's sale of body parts harvested from abortions. New Jersey Governor Chris Christie also had a strong night by trying to move the focus away from the candidates bragging about themselves. As for Dr. Ben Carson, who has been polling in second place, he was so quiet he almost disappeared from the event, but apparently that is one of the reasons he is so popular. The question is whether this debate will be a turning point in the campaign and the beginning of the end for Trump. That was the goal of the GOP field, but if this campaign has shown anything so far, it is that Trump is nothing if not resilient.

Week 349

(HOLINESS)

September 27, 2015

Pope Francis' visit to the United States has not only been anticipated by religious leaders and practicing Christians, but it has also been welcomed by progressives, even those with little or no interest in religion. This is because in his brief papacy, Pope Francis has set a tone that has given encouragement to liberals across the globe. He has been an outspoken critic of rampant capitalism and income inequality, and an advocate for immigrants and policies to limit global warming. By taking these positions, the Pope has cheered the Left, and caused consternation to conservative Catholics, many of whom are politically conservative as well. Many of the Pope's views are not in line with liberal views, including his positions on the traditional family, religious liberty, and abortion, but progressives are more than happy to look past these issues and instead focus on Pope Francis' views on more secular issues. So as Pope Francis arrived in the United States, President Obama and his allies were ready to make the most of it.

Before arriving in the United States, Pope Francis made a visit to Cuba, where he hailed the United States' decision to open diplomatic and some economic relations with that communist nation. This too was happily welcomed by liberals. While in Cuba, the Pope was gracious to his hosts by not openly embracing dissidents, but he did call on the Castro regime to respect personal and religious liberty. Next the Pope flew to Washington for his first ever visit to the United States, after which he would travel to New York City and Philadelphia for the World Meeting of Families. His first official event in the United States was a welcoming ceremony at the White House, and President Obama made sure he would not to squander that opportunity. In his opening remarks, the President tried to use the Pope as a vessel to endorse his own policies on income inequality, immigration, Cuba, and global warming:

> You call on all of us, Catholic and non-Catholic alike, to put the "least of these" at the center of our concerns. You remind us that in the eyes of God our measure as individuals, and our measure as a society, is not determined by wealth or power or station or celebrity, but by how well we hew to Scripture's call to lift up the poor and the marginalized to stand up for justice and against inequality, and to ensure that every human being is able to live in dignity – because we are all made in the image of God. . . . You remind us that "the Lord's most powerful message" is mercy. And that means welcoming the stranger with empathy and a truly open heart – from the refugee who flees war-torn lands to the immigrant who leaves home in search of a better life. . . Holy Father, we are grateful for your invaluable support of our new beginning with the Cuban people which holds out the promise of better relations between our countries, greater cooperation across our hemisphere, and a better life for the Cuban people. . . . And, Holy Father, you remind us that we have a sacred obligation to protect our planet, God's magnificent gift to us. (Applause.) We support your call to all world leaders to support the communities most vulnerable to changing climate, and to come together to preserve our precious world for future generations. (Applause.)

Far from avoiding President Obama's political message, the Pope endorsed some of it:

> Mr. President, I am deeply grateful for your welcome in the name of the all Americans. As a son of an immigrant family, I am happy to be a guest in this country, which was largely built by such families. . . Mr. President, together with their fellow citizens, American Catholics are committed to building a society which is truly tolerant and inclusive, to safeguarding the rights of individuals and communities, and to rejecting every form of unjust discrimination. . . . Mr. President, I find it encouraging that you are proposing an initiative for reducing air pollution. Accepting the urgency, it seems clear to me also that climate change is a problem which can no longer be left to our future generation. When it comes to the care of our common home, we are living at a critical moment of history. We

still have time to make the change needed to bring about a sustainable and integral development, for we know that things can change.

Next, Pope Francis traveled to Capitol Hill to give an address to a joint session of Congress. In that speech, the Pope continued with the same themes, calling on the representatives to avoid polarization, help the poor and needy, and protect immigrants and refugees. While knowing it would be unpopular with many Republicans in his audience, the Pope also called for an end to capital punishment, wealth redistribution, and policies to reduce global warming:

> The Golden Rule also reminds us of our responsibility to protect and defend human life at every stage of its development. . . . This conviction has led me, from the beginning of my ministry, to advocate at different levels for the global abolition of the death penalty. I am convinced that this way is the best, since every life is sacred, every human person is endowed with an inalienable dignity, and society can only benefit from the rehabilitation of those convicted of crimes. . . . It goes without saying that part of this great effort is the creation and distribution of wealth. The right use of natural resources, the proper application of technology and the harnessing of the spirit of enterprise are essential elements of an economy which seeks to be modern, inclusive and sustainable. . . . In Laudato Si', I call for a courageous and responsible effort to "redirect our steps" (ibid., 61), and to avert the most serious effects of the environmental deterioration caused by human activity. I am convinced that we can make a difference and I have no doubt that the United States – and this Congress – have an important role to play.

These remarks made liberals almost giddy. For Speaker Boehner, he was so moved that he visibly cried during the address, and then a day later he resigned as Speaker, saying his meeting with the Pope made him realize it was time for him to step down. While in Washington, the Pope was also willing to criticize some Administration policies, more by deed than statement. He made an impromptu visit to the Little Sisters of Mercy, who are challenging Obamacare's birth control mandate. Later in the trip, he had a meeting with Kim Davis, the Kentucky County Clerk who was jailed for her refusal to issue marriage licenses to same sex couples. However, these steps were largely overlooked by progressives, who instead used the visit to try to claim that even God is on the side of their agenda. Overall, the visit by Pope Francis was an amazing spectacle. He brought whole cities to a standstill, drew millions of admirers, and gained the admiration of even the non-religious. For a week it seemed that the United States became Pope Francis' nation, while our political leaders sat by amazed.

Week 350

(ROUTINE)

October 4, 2015

One image that has reoccurred too many times during the Obama Administration is the President standing at a podium and commenting on a mass shooting. Such events have occurred more than a dozen times during the President's tenure, usually based on a common theme of a young man, disenchanted with society, shooting innocent people in a public place. During his first term, the President condemned these shootings, but was very careful about policy responses, knowing full well he faced reelection in 2012. Now, no longer facing the prospect of an election, Mr. Obama no longer feels the need for restraint. After the Sandy Hook shootings, the President called for strengthened gun laws, but his effort failed. His frustration was evident this week when he again took the podium, this time to comment on another mass shooting, this one in Roseburg, Oregon.

On October 1, 2015, 26-year-old Christopher Harper-Mercer, a student at Umpqua Community College, went to his school with two handguns determined to kill as many people as possible. He first shot an English professor at point blank range. Then he went into classrooms and asked students about their religion. He shot anyone who admitted to being a Christian. He made people beg for their lives, and he even shot a woman trying to get back in her wheelchair. In all, nine people were killed, and nine more injured. The police arrived within six minutes, and after an exchange of gun fire, Harper-Mercer killed himself. The shooter fit a familiar profile, a loner whose history on the internet showed disturbed and potentially violent tendencies.

Soon after this most recent shooting, President Obama took to the podium and gave a palpable demonstration of his frustration. He started by stating:

> There's been another mass shooting in America — this time, in a community college in Oregon. That means there are more American families — moms, dads, children — whose lives have been changed forever. That means there's another community stunned with grief, and communities across the country forced to relieve their own anguish, and parents across the country who are scared because they know it might have been their families or their children.

Then he turned immediately to politics and gun control:

> But as I said just a few months ago, and I said a few months before that, and I said each time we see one of these mass shootings, our thoughts and prayers are not enough. It's not enough. It does not capture the heartache and grief and anger that we should feel. And it does nothing to prevent this carnage from being inflicted someplace else in America — next week, or a couple of months from now. . . . Earlier this year, I answered a question in an interview by saying, "The United States of America is the one advanced nation on Earth in which we do not have sufficient common-sense gun-safety laws — even in the face of repeated mass killings." . . . We talked about this after Columbine and Blacksburg, after Tucson,

after Newtown, after Aurora, after Charleston. It cannot be this easy for somebody who wants to inflict harm on other people to get his or her hands on a gun.

Eventually, his frustration came into full display:

> And what's become routine, of course, is the response of those who oppose any kind of common-sense gun legislation. . . . There is a gun for roughly every man, woman, and child in America. So how can you, with a straight face, make the argument that more guns will make us safer? We know that states with the most gun laws tend to have the fewest gun deaths. So the notion that gun laws don't work, or just will make it harder for law-abiding citizens and criminals will still get their guns is not borne out by the evidence. . . . And, of course, what's also routine is that somebody, somewhere will comment and say, Obama politicized this issue. Well, this is something we should politicize.

It was a moment of candor from the President. No longer worried about elections, the President made clear that he views weak gun laws as the primary cause of mass shootings. His calls for gun control have now become his reflective response to these mass shooting events. His frustration stems from the fact that he knows there is little or no chance that any gun control legislation will pass. His comments show he has given up on trying to reach a national consensus on how to address this problem. Instead, he has turned to confrontation and partisanship. Predictably, the response to his comments that shootings should be "politicize[d]," was outrage from his opponents. There is no doubt that his frustration is genuine, but there is also no doubt that the way he is expressing it will not contribute to a solution.

Week 351

(VACUUM)

October 11, 2015

When it comes to the Syrian crisis, President Obama has been a very reluctant warrior. When Syria's civil war began five years ago, many called on the Administration to arm the rebels to help topple the Assad regime, which is supported by Russia and Iran. The President refused. Then, the President set a redline regarding any use of chemical weapons. Assad used them, but the White House refused to take any military action. Instead, it cut a deal with Assad that required him to give up his chemical weapons, however, he still has some and is still using them. After ISIS took control of large parts of Syria and Iraq, the President was forced to act, but he only used limited airstrikes and made clear there would be no ground combat forces. These weak steps have led to a prolonged conflict in Syria, killing tens of thousands, and displacing millions of people, who are now streaming into Europe, which is now a crisis in itself.

For his part, Russian President Vladimir Putin has taken the exact opposite approach. Syria has been a client state of Russia for decades, and throughout the Syrian civil war, Russia has been supplying arms and support to Assad. Even with this support, the Assad regime has not been able to gain the upper hand in the conflict. So in recent weeks, Russia began deploying air force units in Syria. Once the infrastructure was in place, in the last two weeks Russia has launched a massive bombing campaign, with its main targets not ISIS, but instead regions under the control of moderate rebel forces. Russia has also launched cruise missile attacks from the Caspian Sea and has now deployed a battalion of troops in Syria to support the Assad forces. Putin wants Assad to win, and he is doing everything he can to accomplish that.

Russia has much to gain from its military campaign in Syria. It can help an ally survive, which will increase Russia's influence in the Middle East at the expense of America and its allies. Putin also wants to reassert Russia as a world superpower, and his actions in Syria aid that. Russia is heavily dependent on oil and natural gas revenues, and at least in the short term its actions in Syria have raised prices, helping the Russian economy. For Putin, Syria helps his prestige and distracts voters from the bad Russian economy. It also helps him disrespect President Obama. When Putin was in New York of the United Nations General Assembly, he met with President Obama and pledged he would put no ground forces in Syria, and that same week ground forces were deployed.

For President Obama, the Syrian crisis represents the dangers of disengagement. America refused to help moderate rebel forces early in the conflict and many believe that led to a prolonged conflict and a power vacuum, which was filled by ISIS. ISIS grew so powerful, it invaded Iraq, taking Mosel and many other areas of the country. When it looked like Iraq's Kurdish region might fall to ISIS, the Administration was forced to start airstrikes and redeploy ground troops to Iraq in a training role. The irony of Obama Administration policy in the Middle East is that the President's policy to end wars and withdraw troops has led to more conflicts and the need to redeploy American forces. Added to the mix is Russia, who is now actively fighting in Syria, and whose air forces are sharing the sky with American and allied warplanes. Syria has become a very dangerous situation for the United States and our allies, which hopefully has taught President Obama that sometimes disengaging is more dangerous than engaging.

Week 352

(COMEBACK GIRL)

October 18, 2015

For the last several months, the consistent theme of the media coverage regarding the Hillary Clinton campaign has been crisis. Clinton's ratings on honesty and trustworthiness have been damaged by the continuing controversy over her emails. Her credibility has been damaged by her decision to change positions on major issues. She has also made few friends in the media because of her reluctance to take questions and give access. All of this has resulted in Clinton looking vulnerable, to the point where many Democrats have pushed for Vice President Biden to join the race. Another beneficiary of Hillary Clinton's problems has been Vermont Senator Bernie Sanders, who has risen in the polls and built momentum among progressives. For all these reasons, the first debate for the Democrat candidates took on heightened importance. It would be a chance for Clinton to right the ship, and a chance for her opponents to try to topple her. In the end, she succeeded, and her opponents failed.

When the Democrat candidates gathered on October 13, there was no doubt that Hillary Clinton would be the focus of the attention. Her foes, Senator Sanders, former Governors Marty O'Malley and Lincoln Chafee, former Senator Jim Webb, needed to damage Hillary Clinton to have any chance to stop her march to the nomination. For Clinton, she needed to show that she has poise, command of the issues, and humanity. The topics in the debate were what everyone expected, the economy, income inequality, immigration, Syria, and health care. On each topic, Clinton showed knowledge of the issues and the ability to explain her views. Her opponents took what shots they could, but Clinton was never knocked off her game. She even got a present from Senator Sanders, who said Americans were sick and tired of hearing about her "damn emails." Sanders performed well in the debate, but there is no doubt who won: Hillary Clinton.

In the aftermath of her strong performance, Clinton basked in the glow of being yet another comeback kid. In some ways, her sputtering campaign lowered expectations to the point that her performance looked even better. She took the road to build on the momentum, while her opponents wondered what their next steps should be. The debate also will likely have an impact on Vice President Biden, because the stronger Clinton looks, the less people will press him to join the race. In many ways, Clinton's performance in the debate might open a path to the nomination that the other candidates simply cannot close.

Clinton's new found strength also carries risks. While Clinton may have solidified her position among Democrats, with the public in general it might be a different story. She is still viewed with skepticism and distrust by many. Also, her constant changes in position make her appear willing to say anything to get elected. Most recently, Clinton announced her opposition to the Keystone Pipeline and the Trans-Pacific Partnership trade deal just negotiated by President Obama. She previously supported both, but now she opposes them, no doubt to court the support of progressives. However, all her efforts to build support on the Left might undermine her in the general election, assuming the GOP can nominate an electable candidate. The prospects for that look uncertain, with Trump leading the Republican field by a healthy margin, and with congressional Republicans in disarray due to the on-going internecine struggle in the House to elect a new Speaker. So currently Clinton is rising and her Democrat opponents and the GOP are struggling. One could hardly imagine a better outcome for the Clinton campaign following the first debate.

Week 353

(11 Hours)

October 25, 2015

Many believed that this week would be make or break time for Hillary Clinton. With looming deadlines for early primary states, Vice President Biden needed to make a decision about whether to mount a run for the Democrat nomination. For Clinton, the week would be marked by her testimony to the House committee investigating the attack on the United States consulate in Benghazi that killed four Americans. The week could have been double bad news for Clinton, but it turned out to be a double win. Vice President Biden announced he would not run for the nomination and in her 11 hours of testimony, Hillary Clinton more than answered her critics and set herself on a nearly certain path to the Democrat nomination.

Ever since Hillary Clinton's campaign started to founder, there have been calls for Vice President Biden to join the race. For more than three months, Biden engaged in a very public inner struggle on whether to run. At times he sounded like a candidate, at other times he made clear he was far from a decision to join the race. Everyone understood that Biden would be forced to make a decision by late October because he needed to build his team, fundraise, and take steps to get on the ballot in the early primary states. No one was sure if he would join the race, including apparently Biden himself. However, when Biden took the podium on October 21 with President Obama at his side, it was clear his decision was not to run for President. His reasons were personal and heartfelt, and he was out.

It is hard to image better news for the Clinton campaign. After her strong performance in the first Democrat debate, Clinton gained new confidence and momentum, but Biden was still a threat and she knew it. With him the in the race, she would face a long and difficult fight. With him out, the path to the nomination looks open. Further, the timing could hardly have been better, because Biden made his announcement just a day before Clinton was heading into her testimony to the Benghazi committee, giving her another chance to defeat a threat to her campaign, namely scandal. It took 11 hours, but when the testimony was over, Clinton looked stronger, not weaker.

The focus of the Benghazi committee is the September 11, 2012 attack in Libya that killed four Americans including Ambassador Chris Stevens, which occurred during Hillary Clinton's watch as Secretary of State. There have been allegations of a cover up and a refusal by the Obama Administration to take steps to protect its diplomats in Benghazi. Wrapped into this issue are Hillary Clinton's emails and her use of a private server, because many Republicans believe Clinton destroyed Benghazi emails to protect herself from criticism. The testimony was classic political theater, with Republican committee members harshly questioning Clinton, and with Democrat members defending her. In her testimony, Clinton took responsibility for what happened in Benghazi, but also blamed the "fog of war" for confusion on the causes of the attack and the responses to it. Clinton also tried to skirt the blame for the State Department's repeated refusals of Ambassador Chris Steven's requests for added security, stating: "I did not see them. I did not approve them. I did not deny them." She also fought back against the allegation that she ignored the issue, saying: "I've lost more sleep than all of you put together." Clinton was also questioned aggressively at the end of her testimony about her emails and private server, and again she stood her ground.

The theme for the Democrats was that the investigation was a partisan affair, designed to hurt the Clinton campaign. This storyline was aided when GOP congressman and Speaker candidate Kevin McCarthy commented on how the investigation had hurt Clinton. All the Democrat members of the committee followed this theme and condemned the investigation as a witch hunt. Her loyal Democrats did their part, but Hillary Clinton more than held her own in the testimony, showing poise, mastery of the facts, and a dogged determination to stick to her talking points. The imagery of her testifying was not great, but what she said and how she said it helped her campaign more than it hurt.

Week 354

(CHAOS)

November 1, 2015

If there is one word that best describes the current state of the Republican Party, it is chaos. The battle for the GOP nomination has been dominated by outsiders Donald Trump and Ben Carson, while establishment candidates like Jeb Bush and Chris Christe have been struggling just to stay in the race. In Congress, the sudden resignation of Speaker Boehner prompted a leadership fight where the Freedom Caucus, made up of approximately 40 of the most conservative Republican members, decided to support only new speaker candidates who pledge adherence to their agenda. Without the support from the Freedom Caucus, the GOP majority could not elect a speaker, so a power vacuum ensued. Sitting aside and enjoying the show was President Obama, who used his leverage and the Republican disunity to further his agenda for higher spending.

The chaos engulfing the Republican Party came at a very inconvenient time. In addition to dealing with a leadership fight, Congress needed to reach a deal with the White House on spending and raising the debt limit, both tasks that need to be addressed by early November. For the Republicans, this spending and debt limit fight was unwelcomed, because with a presidential race in full swing, the GOP is worried it would be blamed for any government shutdown. However, with all the chaos in the party, who would negotiate a deal with the President. The answer seems to be Speaker Boehner. While the Freedom Caucus was shooting down speaker candidates, Speaker Boehner was conducting secret negotiations with the White House on a spending deal. Word only leaked out on the talks a couple days before the deal was announced, and when the details came to light, it became clear who had the upper hand in the negotiations.

One of President Obama's objectives in the spending fight was to break the domestic discretionary spending caps put in place in 2011. Unlike most spending cuts, those spending caps resulted in real reductions in discretionary spending. The Administration has tried repeatedly to raise the caps, with some limited success in 2014, but the caps have remained largely intact. In reality, these caps were one of the few concrete accomplishments of the GOP Congress since 2011. In the spending deal announced this week, the GOP agreed to a two year spending blueprint allowing for a $50 billion increase in spending this budget year and a $30 billion increase next year. In return for these immediate spending increases, the Republicans obtained agreements to reform the social security disability system and make changes to Medicare reimbursements. Overall, the spending cuts equaled the spending increases, so the deal did not increase the deficit. The problem is the new spending occurs now, while most of the cuts are phased in years from now. For this reason, most conservatives heavily criticized the deal.

Speaker Boehner had a dual motivation for reaching this deal. First, he has long wanted to cut a long term spending deal with the Administration. He had hoped for a large scale deal that would have broadly reformed entitlements and tax policy, but such a deal was unrealistic in the current political environment. So instead, he opted for a more modest two year deal. Second, as the leadership fight in the House continued, it became increasingly clear that Paul Ryan, former GOP Vice Presidential nominee and current Chairman of the Ways and Means Committee, was the only Republicans who could get sufficient support from the Freedom Caucus to be elected Speaker. Ryan is a Boehner ally who also believes in compromise with Democrats. Speaker Boehner cut his deal to clear the decks for Ryan, so that his successor would not have to deal with a budget crisis the moment he took the Speaker's gavel. So the deal was made, and Ryan was elected Speaker on October 29.

The winner in all this was President Obama. He achieved his goal of increasing discretionary spending, and in return he only had to agree to modest entitlement reforms, reforms a Democrat successor could modify or rescind with the help of a Democrat Congress. So the President got more spending now for spending cuts that might never happen. Democrats were not the only ones pleased with the deal. Many moderate Republicans wanted the spending caps loosened to allow for higher defense spending, and the deal achieved that. The real losers in the deal were the deficit hawks and those who want to roll back the entitlement state, because little was achieved on those fronts. So the GOP paid a heavy cost for its internal chaos, and President Obama was the beneficiary.

Week 355
(KEY NO'ED)

November 8, 2015

President Obama's primary policy priority for the remainder of his term is to cement his legacy on environmental policy. Unable to pass legislation in that sphere, the White House has instead focused on executive actions, including sweeping regulations on carbon emission that are currently the subject of a wave of lawsuits. The President has also committed the United States to international agreements to lower carbon emissions without seeking congressional approval, certainly another gambit that will eventually end up in the courts. The one environmental issue where the President has hesitated has been the Keystone Pipeline, the project proposed to pipe 800,000 barrels per day of Canada oil sands to the Gulf of Mexico through a 1200 mile pipeline. The Administration has been studying the project for 7 years, conveniently postponing a decision until after the 2012 election. But with no more elections to win, the President no longer needed to delay, so on November 6, he killed the Keystone Pipeline, as everyone expected him to do.

The Keystone Pipeline is a project that has garnered broad bipartisan support. Republicans, oil producing states, unions, and the business lobby all supported the deal. For a time, it also appeared both Hillary Clinton and President Obama were prepared to support it. Then politics set in. Environmental groups and progressives were determined to kill the pipeline as part of their campaign to reduce carbon emissions. The Administration was caught in the middle, being heavily lobbied by unions to support the project, and environmentalist to kill it. As a delaying tactic, the White House initiated study after study on the project, most of which concluded that it would have a negligible environmental impact. But the pressure from the Left was too strong, to the point where Hillary Clinton reversed her position on the project, while the President increasingly criticized it. Indeed, after the GOP took control of the Senate, Congress pass a bill approving Keystone, which the President then promptly vetoed.

Considering all this, it was no surprise when the President took the podium at the White House on November 6 to finally kill the Keystone Pipeline. With Secretary of State Kerry at his side, the President stated that, based on the advice of Mr. Kerry, he had concluded that the pipeline was not in the national interest of the United States. The President stated: "America is now a global leader when it comes to taking serious action to fight climate change, and frankly, approving this project would have undercut that leadership . . . ." No doubt this announcement was designed to set the stage for the President's attendance at the United Nations summit on climate change in Paris in December. The President also used his announcement to attack the critics of his climate agenda: "We know that human activity is changing the climate . . . . We know that human ingenuity can do something about it. We're even starting to see that we might actually have the political will to succeed. So the time to heed the critics and cynics is past. The time to plead ignorance is surely past. The deniers are increasingly alone, on their own shrinking island." In the end, the decision to kill the Keystone Pipeline seems to be mostly about politics, not the merits of the project itself. Indeed, the President admitted that the project was not an environmental risk: "All of this obscured the fact that this pipeline would neither be the silver bullet to the US economy proclaimed by some, or the death knell to climate proclaimed by others."

Several factors made this an easy decision for the White House. Falling oil prices made the political cost of the decision minimal. With no more elections to face, the President did not have to worry about a backlash from unions and business interests. Most importantly, killing the pipeline gave the President another chance to make a political statement about climate change. He made that statement forcefully indeed, but whether he made a good decision is a very different question.

Week 356

(CONTAINED)

November 15, 2015

On November 12, 2015, in an interview with George Stephanopoulos of ABC News, President Obama was asked about ISIS, or ISIL as the President calls it, and he stated as follows:

> I don't think they're gaining strength . . . . What is true, from the start our goal has been first to contain and we have contained them. They have not gained ground in Iraq and in Syria they'll come in, they'll leave. But you don't see this systemic march by ISIL across the terrain. . . . What we have not yet been able to do is to completely decapitate their command and control structures. We've made some progress in trying to reduce the flow of foreign fighters and part of our goal has to be to recruit more effective Sunni partners in Iraq to really go on offense rather than simply engage in defense.

Comforting words from a President who has been criticized for setting the stage for the rise of ISIS, discounting them when the threat became clear, and hesitating to take strong action against them. The approach of the Administration has been to take just enough steps to confront ISIS to appear aggressive, but not to commit too deeply to any fight. However, the opportunity for such extemporizing is likely over, because just one day after President Obama's comments, ISIS struck savagely in the heart of Europe.

On the evening of November 13, 2015, ISIS launched a series of simultaneous attacks in Paris, involving mass shootings, hostage taking, and suicide bombings. The attacks began around 9:00

p.m., in Saint-Denis, when three suicide bombers struck the Stade De France, where a soccer match was in progress. At the same time, terrorists attacked at four other locations, including a concert venue and cafes. The attackers killed 130 people, with 89 dying at the Bataclan Theater, where the attackers took hostages and engaged in a three hour fight with police. In addition to the fatalities, 368 people were injured, more than 80 critically. Seven terrorists died in the attacks. ISIS immediately claimed responsibility.

In response to the attacks, French President Francois Hollande declared a state of emergency and called the attacks "an act of war" and that they were "planned in Syria, organized in Belgium, perpetrated on our soil with French complicity." With intelligence support from the United States, two days later, France launched new airstrikes against ISIS targets in Syria and launched hundreds of raids across France to kill or capture suspects or accomplices. Across Europe, other nations also raised their states of alert, especially Belgium, where many of the attackers lived. The attacks also put in sharp focus on the Syrian refugee crisis, because it appears at least one of the attackers got into Europe posing as a refugee.

The Paris attacks have shattered the West's complacency in the face of the ISIS threat. President Obama epitomizes that complacency. When ISIS began its rise, he called them the "JV team." After the Administration pulled all United States forces out of Iraq, the President was caught completely off guard when ISIS captured much of northern Iraq. In response, the President authorized airstrikes and limited on the ground training support, but under rules of engagement so restrictive that the military was unable to aggressively take on the ISIS threat. With the help of Kurdish troop, ISIS has been pushed back in portions of northern Iraq, but they still hold Mosel, many other keys towns, and their base of operations in Syria has not been disrupted. President Obama clearly fears getting entangled to deeply in the ISIS fight, so he wants to do just enough to look strong but without committing to do what is necessary to actually defeat the threat. The problem with this approach is that it presupposes that ISIS cannot strike back, we now know they can. For a President who so harshly criticized President Bush's proclamation of "Mission Accomplished" in Iraq in 2003, he might have just done the same thing, much to his detriment.

Week 357

(THE COALITION)

November 22, 2015

In the wake of the Paris attacks, a near panic has set in on Europe. France remains in a state of emergency, with security forces staging raid after raid to try to capture terrorist suspects. On November 17, Paris police followed suspected terrorist ringleader Abdelhamid Abaaoud to some apartments in the Paris suburb of Saint-Denis. The next day, security forces launched a raid that left Abaaoud and another dead, and eight others arrested. In Belgium, where the terrorists who staged the Paris attacks were based, intelligence pointing to a potential Paris style attack led authorities to issue public warnings and increase security. At the same time, Belgian law enforcement authorities were franticly searching for Mohamed Abrini, who was believed to be one of the terrorists in Paris for the attacks, and Salah Abdeslam, who had been seen with him. Elsewhere in Europe, security forces have taken increasingly aggressive measures to track and stop other potential terrorists.

The response to the Paris attacks has also extended to the Middle East. On November 15, France began a series of expanded airstrikes in Syria targeting ISIS. French President Holland also began calls for an international coalition to take on ISIS, asking world leaders, including Presidents Obama and Putin, to put aside their differences and unite in the fight against ISIS. Other European leaders, including Britain's David Cameron, likewise issued calls for more aggressive measures against ISIS. Strangely sidelined in all these discussions was the purported leader of the world's democracies, namely President Obama. After the Paris attacks, the President's restrained comments and refusal to commit to any new measures against ISIS led many world leaders to conclude that the American President remains unwilling to take more aggressive action against the Islamic State.

So when world leaders gathered for the G20 Summit in Antalya, Turkey on November 15, many hoped President Obama would rally world leaders. With French President Holland leading the response to the attacks, the G20 leaders gave strong rhetorical support for enhanced efforts against ISIS. For example, Turkish President Tayyip Erdogan, who currently chairs the G20, said: "We will redouble our efforts, working with other members of the coalition, to bring about a peaceful transition in Syria and to eliminate Daesh [ISIS] as a force that can create so much pain and suffering for people in Paris, in Ankara, and in other parts of the globe." President Obama also held an unscheduled meeting with President Putin to discuss the ISIS threat. However, those who hoped the President would be the one to rally a world coalition were disappointed.

Instead, the focus was on President Putin, who called for an international coalition against ISIS and who thereby made himself the center of attention of international lobbying efforts. Increasingly, President Obama appeared sidelined in the discussion, in part because of his refusal to support increased military measures against ISIS. All this made stark the United States' abdication of leadership in the fight against ISIS. Even in the face of an attack that the United States could have leveraged into a full commitment from world leaders to fight ISIS, President Obama refused to rally his allies. This is most likely because it is the President of the United States who does not want to fully join the fight. Unlike President Obama, President Putin will not ignore such an opportunity to further his interests in the Middle East, to the detriment of America's agenda.

Week 358
(WAR GAMES)

November 29, 2015

If tensions in Europe were not high enough after the Paris attacks, the escalating confrontation between Turkey and Russia this week only added to the sense of crisis. Turkey and Russia are historical enemies, having fought for centuries over control over the Balkans, the Caucuses, and access to the Mediterranean. During the Cold War, Turkey joined NATO and firmly aligned itself with the West. Most recently, Turkey and Russia have clashed over Syria, where Russia is supporting the Assad regime with ever more aggressive military action, while Turkey is supporting the rebels, including ethnic Turk fighters in northwestern Turkey. Given all this, it was not surprising that as Russia continued to bomb Assad's opponents, including Turkish rebels, Turkey would look for an opportunity to send a message to Russia. It did so on November 24, when Turkey shot down a Russian military jet.

On November 24, Russian military aircraft were conducting missions over northwestern Syria, very close to the Turkish border. Turkey asserts that a Russian Su-24 attack aircraft and one other aircraft crossed repeatedly into Turkish airspace. Turkey claims it warned the Russian jet through an emergency channel 10 times over five minutes to move away from Turkish airspace. The planes did not respond, and instead flew into Turkish airspace for 17 seconds. Turkey scrambled F-16 fighters, which then launched an air-to-air missile that shot down the Su-24 at 19,685 feet, with the plane crashing in the Jabal Turkman area of the Turkish province of Latakia. Russia disputed the claim that it had violated Turkish airspace and that it had received no warnings. Of the two crew members on the plane, navigator Oleg Peshkov survived and was rescued, and claimed he received no warning. Pilot Konstantin Murakhtin was killed, and another Russian died in the mission to rescue the pilot. Russian President Putin claimed that the United States military "which leads the coalition that Turkey belongs to, knew about the location and time of our planes' flights, and we were hit exactly there and at that time." The United States denied this assertion.

After this incident, the Russian government went on military alert and threatened Turkey with retaliation. Since Turkey is a NATO member, any confrontation between Russia and Turkey has implications for all of Europe, so other European leaders quickly stepped in to try to calm the situation. However, President Putin continued his bellicose rhetoric, condemning Turkey and the West both for shooting down the Russian fighter and for their policies in Syria. Russian also proceeded to put in place sanctions to punish Turkey. It is doubtful that this incident will lead to any direct military confrontation between Turkey and Russia, but it highlights the growing and ever more dangerous implications of the Syrian civil war.

All of Europe is on edge after the Paris attacks, the confrontation between Turkey and Russia, and the continuing refugee crisis. All of these events have their genesis in the Middle East crisis, and more specifically the Syrian civil war and the rise of ISIS. Russia also has suffered from ISIS sponsored terrorism in the form of the bombing of a Russian civilian aircraft over the Sinai in November. However, as long as the West and Russian are at odds over Syrian policy, it is uncertain how the current crisis can be resolved. Russia is supporting Assad and bombing Assad opponents, including allies of the United States and Turkey. The United States and her allies are in the same airspace bombing ISIS targets. The risk of accidents and confrontations between the West and Russia is only going to increase until there is a coordinated strategy of the outside powers. All this makes for a dangerous situation, and one that might prompt Western European leaders and President Obama to finally focus on taking decisive steps in Syria.

Week 359

(IT'S TERRORISM)

December 6, 2015

Americans watched the news coverage of the terrorist attacks in Paris with horror, wondering if we would soon be attacked as well. The President sought in public appearances to reassure the nation, while the Republican candidates called for stronger action against ISIS and caution on accepting more refugees from Syria. All the while, as our attention was focused on Paris and the Middle East, a Muslim couple in California with a six-year-old child plotted to bring Paris-style terror to America. On December 2, 2015 they succeeded, horrifying the nation and it appears finally galvanizing the Obama Administration into taking more vigorous steps to fight Islamic terrorism.

On December 2, 2015 at the Inland Regional Center in San Bernardino, California, the County Department of Public Health was holding a training event and Holiday Party with about 80 employees in attendance. One of those employees was Syed Rizwan Farook, and American-born United States citizen of Pakistani descent, who was a health inspector. Farook lived in Redland with his wife Tashfeen Malik, a legal resident from Pakistan. Farook attended the party, but then left only to return with his wife. When they returned they were wearing black ski masks and tactical gear, and both carried assault rifles and automatic pistols. They enter the banquet room and began shooting, killing 14 people and injuring 22 more. They then left the scene in their rented SVU, only to be caught by the police four hours later, who then killed them in a shootout. They left behind three pipe bombs, which were detonated by a bomb squad. The next day the FBI opened a counter-terrorism investigation, and it soon became clear that Farook and his wife had been radicalized and had pledged allegiance to ISIS. This left no doubt that the attack in San Bernardino was terrorism, and the White House recognized it as such. The 14 who died in the attack ranged from 26 to 60 years old, with 9 from San Bernardino County, and the others from nearby counties.

The impact this assault had on the nation was stunning. Americans across the country were horrified that this type of attack could happen in the United States, and many wondered when the next attack might come. Not surprisingly, the President and his allies immediately called for more gun control measures, but most observers recognized that even the stringent gun control laws in France did not stop the terrorist attacks there. Once political leaders started to come to grips with the fact that this was a true terrorist event, the tenor of the debate changed from the usual fight over gun control to how best to confront the terrorist threat. In the past, President Obama has resisted calling domestic attacks by Muslims terrorism, the best example being the Fort Hood attack, which the Administration continues to treat as a criminal matter only. However, the evidence in the San Bernardino shootings was too stark for even the White House to pretend that it was anything other than a terrorist attack on our own soil.

How the San Bernardino attack will impact the debate on the response to terrorism is unclear. Republican presidential candidate Donald Trump quickly called for suspending all Muslim immigration into the United States. He was roundly criticized by the press, Republicans, and Democrats, but his call was popular and actually helped him in the polls. As for Hillary Clinton, she was forced to explain why she refuses to use the term Islamic terrorism, when it is obvious that is exactly what the San Bernardino attacks were. As for the President, he scheduled a rare Oval Office address for December 6 to reassure the nation. However, the last thing this Administration wants is to commit itself to a bigger fight with Islamic radicals, so it is unlikely the President will do much other than admit what we all know: the San Bernardino attacks were domestic terrorism.

Week 360
(PRIORITIES)

December 13, 2015

With the nation still shaken after the San Bernardino attacks, President Obama decided the time had come to give on Oval Office address on terrorism. Recognizing the trauma San Bernardino has caused to the country, the President's goal was to reassure and refocus the nation on his priorities, namely gun control. Yet the address seemed halfhearted and was widely criticized, because the White House offered nothing new beyond self-justification, repeats of calls for restrictions on guns, and calming phrases. This was in sharp contrast to the Administration's genuine excitement and jubilation with the agreement reached at the international climate change summit. The President sees fighting terrorism as an obligation, whereas combating climate change is his passion.

President Obama has only given a few Oval Office addresses, and his last was many years ago. However, the events in San Bernardino were so horrific that the White House decided an Oval Office speech was required. With the Administration under criticism for its slow response to ISIS, it was hoped the President would unveil some new strategy to fight terrorism. It was not to be. Instead, the speech was simply a rerun of old arguments designed to further the President's gun control agenda. The President began his address by paying homage to the victims, and then he turned quickly to defend his Administration's actions:

> Our nation has been at war with terrorists since al-Qaeda killed nearly 3,000 Americans on 9/11. In the process, we've hardened our defenses — from airports to financial centers, to other critical infrastructure. Intelligence and law enforcement agencies have disrupted countless plots here and overseas, and worked around the clock to keep us safe. Our military and counterterrorism professionals have relentlessly pursued terrorist networks overseas — disrupting safe havens in several different countries, killing Osama bin Laden, and decimating al-Qaeda's leadership.

After recognizing that the terrorist threat has evolved from complex operations like 9/11 to attacks by independent cells of a few radicals, the President laid out his agenda to defeat the threat by: hunting down terrorists, training local forces to fight ISIS, coordinating with allies, and reaching an international agreement to end the Syrian civil war. These are all things the public has heard before. Then the President turned to his domestic priority:

> To begin with, Congress should act to make sure no one on a no-fly list is able to buy a gun. What could possibly be the argument for allowing a terrorist suspect to buy a semi-automatic weapon? This is a matter of national security.

> We also need to make it harder for people to buy powerful assault weapons like the ones that were used in San Bernardino. I know there are some who reject any gun safety measures. But the fact is that our intelligence and law enforcement agencies — no matter how effective they are — cannot identify every would-be

mass shooter, whether that individual is motivated by ISIL or some other hateful ideology. What we can do — and must do — is make it harder for them to kill.

The purpose of the President's address was not to announce some new or more vigorous strategy, but instead to use the San Bernardino attacks to call again for gun control. It was a political exercise that the President pursued without excitement or enthusiasm.

Fighting terrorism is a job, but in contrast, fighting climate change is where the President's heart is. That is why at the end of the week the White House was positively ecstatic about the outcome of the United Nations Climate Change Conference in Paris. For years, the Administration has pursued a strong international accord to fight climate change, while pushing at home for legislation and regulations on carbon emissions. Knowing that climate change legislation will not pass Congress, the President's negotiators worked to craft an international deal that would not need congressional authorization. What emerged from the climate change conference was the December 12, 2015 Paris Agreement, a commitment from 196 countries and international organizations that will become binding when formally joined by at least 55 countries that together account for at least 55 percent of global greenhouse emissions. These countries must join the agreement by April 2017 and also adopt domestic measures to enforce the agreement. The goal of the accord is to limit global warming to less than two degrees celsius compared to pre-industrial levels and to achieve zero greenhouse emissions by the end of the 21st century, paid for in part by billions of dollars in aid to developing countries. The current Congress will never approve those funds, so whether this agreement will ever be adopted by the United States is uncertain.

The agreement was hailed by its proponents as a groundbreaking deal to address climate change by major emitters, including China and India. However, upon closer inspection the accord appears to be less than it appears. The agreement is not legally binding on any country until adopted by each. The agreement also includes a mechanism to update it every five years, a convenient tool to move the goalposts as needed, with no specific goals for any particular country. Indeed, the 12-page document is little more than aspirational, with each signatory agreeing to address climate change "as soon as possible." Never mind, the President proclaimed that the agreement would change the world. So the week saw the President deal with the unwelcomed toil of fighting terrorism, but he was later rewarded with the joy of supposedly saving the planet.

Week 361

(MONEY MATTERS)

December 20, 2015

Money was the topic of conversation in Washington, as it usually is, but this time a bit more than normal. The week saw the Federal Reserve finally implemented its liftoff program for higher interest rates, while Congress passed a compromise budget increasing discretionary spending and extending certain tax cuts. The Federal Reserve's move could slow the economy by increasing the costs of borrowing, but the budget passed by the Republican Congress might modestly prime the pump by putting more money into the economy through spending and tax breaks. Many conservatives cheered the Federal Reserve's decision, seeing its prior near zero interest rate policy as unsustainable, but at the same time they condemned the budget deal as more deficit spending. Not surprisingly, many liberals had the opposite reaction.

The Federal Reserve has been following a low interest rate policy to stimulate the United States economy, and interest rates have not been raised since June 2006. The 2008 financial crisis put such a strain on the banking sector that the Federal Reserve has had to spend years pumping money into the economy, through low interest rates and bond buying, first to stabilize the financial system, and then to prompt growth. The economy has slowly recovered, buy only now seven years after the crisis, has the economy approached near full employment. For more than a year, observers have been predicting a rate increase, but on December 16, the Federal Reserve finally made its move and adjusted the target range for the Fed Funds Rate (the rate banks charge each other for overnight loans) from 0% to 0.25% to a range of 0.25% to 0.5%. While the move is small in percentage, its statement about the health of the economy is huge. The rate increase will ripple through the economy, increasing the costs of borrowing in every sector. It also reflects the view that the economy is now strong enough that the Federal Reserve can move away from its unprecedented zero interest rate policy. Federal Reserve Chair Janet Yellen defended the move saying: "I feel confident about the fundamentals driving the US economy, the health of US households, and domestic spending . . . . There are pressures on some sectors of the economy, particularly manufacturing, and the energy sector...but the underlying health of the US economy I consider to be quite sound."

For months, the stock market has been jittery about a rate increase, causing wild swings, but the Dow rose 224 points after the announcement, likely because the increase was only a quarter of a percent. This positive reaction might also reflect the fundamental strength of the United States economy. While the energy and commodities sectors have been hit hard by falling prices, unemployment is half of the 10% it hit in 2009, 12 million jobs have been created in that time, and the Federal Reserve raised its 2016 economic growth forecast to 2.4%. Given all this, the Federal Reserve believes that the economy can withstand higher interest rates, and those higher rates could prevent inflation. Those worrying about a negative impact on the economy could also take solace from the spending bill passed by Congress, which if anything adds stimulus to the economy.

The budget deal that passed Congress on December 18 was the first one crafted by House Speaker Paul Ryan. The deal had its genesis in a compromise reached between the White House and out-going Speaker John Boehner. That deal was based on increases in discretionary spending paid for by future budget cuts that conservatives says are unlikely to ever happen. Boehner left it to Paul Ryan to work out the details, and the $1.1 trillion 2,000 page budget bill passed this week did just that. However, even though Ryan is popular with conservatives, this budget deal is not.

Deficit hawks see this budget bill as an unholy alliance between big business and liberal advocacy groups. Big business received a host of extended tax breaks, while liberals received increased domestic spending. The deal will increase the deficit even including the future spending cuts, if they ever happen. Indeed, the more Republicans delved into the details of the bill, the less they liked it. Among other things, the budget bill: allows President Obama to shift up to $500 billion to fund the UN climate change agreement; does not stop the EPA expansion of the definition of wet lands; allows for a 1.3 percent pay raise for federal workers; and provides $27 billion for public housing. GOP business allies got tax cuts they wanted, but on almost everything else, the White House and Democrats furthered their priorities. So while the Federal Reserve was taking money out of the economy, the politicians in Washington were putting it back in, with the help of a Republican Congress.

Week 362

(DISGUSTING)

December 27, 2015

Christmas week is usually very quiet on the political front. President Obama is usually in Hawaii for the Christmas Holiday and Congress is not in session. The same is true this year, but one thing is different: Donald Trump. While most of the political class was taking a break and preparing for the ensuing presidential election contest in 2016, Trump was taking advantage of the vacuum and doing what he loves best, making headlines. In recent weeks, much of his fire has been turned on fellow Republicans, especially those like Marco Rubio who are emerging as real threats to his campaign. Yet recently, Trump has been focusing his assaults on Hillary Clinton, possibly reflecting his view that the GOP nomination campaign is well in hand, so he can turn his attention on the presumptive Democrat nominee. To date, Trump's formula for success has been to be as provocative, sometimes even insulting, as possible, which usually has only increased his support in the polls. He took that tactic even farther this week when it came to Hillary Clinton and her December 19 debate with her Democrat opponents.

Hillary Clinton's opponents in the December 19 debate were Vermont Senator Bernie Sanders and former Maryland Governor Martin O'Malley. Both were taking as many shots at Clinton as possible, in the hope of knocking her off her leads in Iowa and nationally. In commenting on the debate, Trump focused very little on the substance or the issues, instead he turned his attention to Ms. Clinton's brief absence from the debate stage. During a commercial break, Ms. Clinton left the stage, and as David Muir from ABC News was asking a question of Senator Sanders, she walked back on the stage, saying "sorry." It is obvious that Ms. Clinton took a bathroom break, and in that Trump saw an opportunity to criticize:

> What happened to her? . . . I'm watching the debate and she disappeared . . . . Where did she go? Where did Hillary go? I thought she quit. I thought she gave up. They had to start the debate without her, phase two. I haven't started with Hillary yet, Hillary's going to get beaten. . . . I know where she went, it's disgusting, I don't want to talk about it. . . No, it's too disgusting. Don't say it, it's disgusting, let's not talk.

Why Donald Trump thinks a bathroom break is so disgusting is unclear, presumably he goes to the bathroom as well. As he has done with his GOP rivals, it seems Trump gravitates to base insults to ridicule his opposition. In fact, Trump did not stop with his "disgusting" comments, he went on to use a crude Yiddish term to describe Clinton's loss to President Obama in the 2008 Democrat nomination fight: "She was favored to win, and she got schlonged, she lost, I mean she lost."

The amazing thing about the Trump campaign is that regardless of the criticism by the media, Democrats, and Republicans, and regardless of how rude and classless he behaves, he gets stronger. It seems his supporters are so disenchanted with the establishment that his every improper comment makes him only more attractive to them. So Trump, no matter how rude his statements, remains in a strong position to win the GOP nomination. This is very disconcerting to the Republican establishment, but it is a great gift to the media, because even in the slow Christmas news cycle, they can rely on Trump to supply tantalizing headlines.

Week 363

(THE SLOWING)

January 3, 2016

When the Federal Reserve finally decided to raise interest rates in December 2015, it marked the end of an unprecedented 8 year period of near zero interest rates and aggressive monetary stimulus. The Federal Reserve took these steps first to stabilize and then to stimulate the United States economy in the wake of the 2008 financial crisis. The Federal Reserve concluded that the United States economy had sufficiently stabilized to warrant a return to a more normal approach to monetary policy. Unfortunately, almost as soon as the rates were raised, signs emerged that the economy might not be that strong after all.

The American economy has been in the midst of one of the longest peacetime recoveries in history. Since late 2009, the economy has been expanding, but at such a sluggish pace that the reality for many American has been a longstanding recession, not a recovery. Yet, in the last year the economy has moved towards full employment, creating confidence and fears of inflation. That is why the Federal Reserve acted. Unfortunately, within days of the rate increase, a torrent of economic data started to show a slowing economy. The Dallas Federal Reserve's Manufacturing index fell to its lowest level since May. There was a .4 percent decreases in capital orders in November 2015. Economists projected fourth quarter growth of just two percent. The National Association of Realtors reported a 10.5 percent drop in sales of existing homes. Industrial production dropped .6 percent in November. Then Christmas week, seasonally adjusted jobless claims increased 20,000 to 287,000. So that strong United States economy started looking not so strong.

It did not take long for financial markets to react. The combination of bad economic news in the United States and increasing signs of a slowdown in China and turmoil in the stock markets there, led to a general sell off on Wall Street. Stock market indices were sharply lower the last week of 2015, leaving the Dow and S&P 500 down for the year. On the last trading day of the year, the Dow was down 1.03 percent, the S&P 500 lost 10.95 percent; and the NASDAQ declined 1.15 percent. With increasing signs of market instability in China, traders worried about a continuing rough ride in January.

The impact a slowing economy could have on the Obama Administration and the 2016 election might be significant. In recent years, the President has all but ignored economic issues, instead turning his focus to gun control, immigration, and global warming. A strong economy allowed him to make this pivot, but a weak one will quickly open him up to criticism. For Hillary Clinton, no matter her rhetoric, she is in essence running for the third Obama term, and a weak economy will immediately weaken her, and maybe even make a businessman like Donald Trump more palatable to voters. So the slowing economy does not simply have Wall Street worried, plenty of people in Washington are worried as well.

Week 364

(BACKGROUND)

January 10, 2016

President Obama began his last year in office making clear that he is determined to pursue his policy goals regardless of Congress and regardless of events gripping the nation. He has been the most aggressive proponent of executive authority since Abraham Lincoln, and after taking aim at immigration and environmental policy, his new target is gun owners. So as the stock market was falling and world focus was on the battles with ISIS in the Middle East, the President took the podium not to calm the nation on those issues, but instead to pursue one of his favorite pet projects: gun control. His plans was simple, issue executive orders to re-write legislation to make a political point, even when his supporters admit his orders would not have stopped attacks like the one in San Bernardino.

For years the President has called for expanded background checks as part of his gun control agenda. He has gone to Congress several times seeking legislation on the issue, with no success. Now, he seems to have determined that he has the power to alone enact the very measures he had unsuccessfully asked Congress to support. He ordered the Bureau of Alcohol, Tobacco, and Firearms (ATF) to require anyone who is engaged in the business of selling firearms to obtain a license to sell and to conduct background checks, which would apply to sales at gun shows and sales over the internet. A violation could result in five years in prison and a $250,000 fine. The President also ordered ATF to issue a rule requiring background checks for the sales of certain specific firearms. The President also instructed the FBI to overhaul the background check system. He also called for more funding for ATF and for mental health checks, and instructed federal officials to cooperate with the states more on enforcement issues.

Gun control proponents have been asking for legislation to close what is called the gun show loophole, which allows certain private sales of firearms without a license or background checks. The thinking for many years is that only Congress could close that loophole, since the loophole was created by legislation. Indeed, President Obama had this view as well, evidenced by the fact that he has repeatedly asked Congress to close the loophole. However, it appears that the President has now determined that he never needed Congress to act after all. Instead, the White House believes it had the authority all along to change the gun show loophole by executive order, which is what the President just did

Many on the Left cheered the President's actions, seeing them as yet another effective end run around a Republican Congress. Never mind the fact that the Federal Courts have repeatedly rejected the Administration's executive overreaches, most famously by rejecting his executive order seeking to legalize five million immigrants. No doubt these recent executive orders will again be taken to the courts, and gun rights advocates think the Administration will yet again be rebuked. That does not seem to concern the President. His goal is to pursue his policy objectives by whatever means possible, whether legal or not. The Administration knows some of its actions will be overturned by the courts, while others might survive. What matters most to the White House is that the President forcefully advocates for his views and seeks to implement them, on his own if necessary.

It is not clear how many of the President's executive orders will stand the test of time. Many have already fallen at the courts, others could be reversed by his successors. Ironically, the most lasting aspect of the President's rampant use of executive power might not be the orders themselves, but the precedent he is setting. President Obama has created a new approach to the presidency, one that circumvents Congress and pursues rule by fiat. In the short term, that approach will cheer those who agree with a President, but in the long term the aggressive use of executive power undermines the separation of powers and threatens the legitimacy of our democracy. No matter, President Obama wants to imprint his agenda on America, and if Congress will not support him, he has decided to just do it himself regardless of the consequences.

Week 365
(SWAN SONG)

January 17, 2016

When President Obama took the podium in the House chamber on January 12 to give his last State of the Union address, he had a dual agenda, promote his own accomplishments and refute Donald Trump. It was an address crafted to make the President appear the rational pragmatist, in contrast to the intolerant voices of his critics. The President used his speech to not only herald his achievements, but to declare that his vision is the future and those who disagree are the past. It was in the end a purely political exercise designed to set the stage for his hoped for Democrat successor.

The President started his address trying to dispel what every President in his final year resists: the notion that he is a lame duck. He made clear he plans to continue to push his agenda in his final year:

> And I will keep pushing for progress on the work that I believe still needs to be done. Fixing a broken immigration system. Protecting our kids from gun violence. Equal pay for equal work. Paid leave. Raising the minimum wage. All these things still matter to hardworking families. They're still the right thing to do. And I won't let up until they get done.

Then the President made clear that those who oppose his agenda of change are simply the intolerant voices of the past:

> America has been through big changes before — wars and depression, the influx of new immigrants, workers fighting for a fair deal, movements to expand civil rights. Each time, there have been those who told us to fear the future; who claimed we could slam the brakes on change; who promised to restore past glory if we just got some group or idea that was threatening America under control. And each time, we overcame those fears. We did not, in the words of Lincoln, adhere to the "dogmas of the quiet past." Instead we thought anew, and acted anew. We made change work for us, always extending America's promise outward, to the next frontier, to more people. And because we did — because we saw opportunity where others saw only peril — we emerged stronger and better than before.

As for his agenda to make America stronger, the President focused on four main themes:

First, how do we give everyone a fair shot at opportunity and security in this new economy? Second, how do we make technology work for us, and not against us — especially when it comes to solving urgent challenges like climate change? Third, how do we keep America safe and lead the world without becoming its policeman? And finally, how can we make our politics reflect what's best in us, and not what's worst?

On the economy, the President took credit for the economic recovery and then took aim at his favorite culprits to justify more wealth redistribution and more government programs:

I believe a thriving private sector is the lifeblood of our economy. I think there are outdated regulations that need to be changed. There is red tape that needs to be cut. There you go! Yes! But after years now of record corporate profits, working families won't get more opportunity or bigger paychecks just by letting big banks or big oil or hedge funds make their own rules at everybody else's expense. Middle-class families are not going to feel more secure because we allowed attacks on collective bargaining to go unanswered. Food Stamp recipients did not cause the financial crisis; recklessness on Wall Street did. Immigrants aren't the principal reason wages haven't gone up; those decisions are made in the boardrooms that all too often put quarterly earnings over long-term returns. It's sure not the average family watching tonight that avoids paying taxes through offshore accounts.

On making technology work for us, the President's talked about new government programs to enhance technological developments, but his real focus was climate change, which the President tied to national security:

Climate change is just one of many issues where our security is linked to the rest of the world. And that's why the third big question that we have to answer together is how to keep America safe and strong without either isolating ourselves or trying to nation-build everywhere there's a problem.

Then after praising America's strength, he tried to make the case that America has been leading and winning around the world and it is America's opponents who are losing:

In today's world, we're threatened less by evil empires and more by failing states. The Middle East is going through a transformation that will play out for a generation, rooted in conflicts that date back millennia. Economic headwinds are blowing in from a Chinese economy that is in significant transition. Even as their economy severely contracts, Russia is pouring resources in to prop up Ukraine and Syria — client states that they saw slipping away from their orbit. And the international system we built after World War II is now struggling to keep pace with this new reality.

Lastly, the President called for less division, where he most clearly took aim at the GOP as embodied by Donald Trump and his call to temporarily ban Muslim immigration into the United States:

> And that's why we need to reject any politics — any politics — that targets people because of race or religion. Let me just say this. This is not a matter of political correctness. This is a matter of understanding just what it is that makes us strong. The world respects us not just for our arsenal; it respects us for our diversity, and our openness, and the way we respect every faith. His Holiness, Pope Francis, told this body from the very spot that I'm standing on tonight that "to imitate the hatred and violence of tyrants and murderers is the best way to take their place." When politicians insult Muslims, whether abroad or our fellow citizens, when a mosque is vandalized, or a kid is called names, that doesn't make us safer. That's not telling it like it is. It's just wrong. It diminishes us in the eyes of the world. It makes it harder to achieve our goals. It betrays who we are as a country.

The President did take some blame for the rancor in our politics, but he made clear he sees himself as an honest broker and his opponents as the ones with base motives:

> Too many Americans feel that way right now. It's one of the few regrets of my presidency — that the rancor and suspicion between the parties has gotten worse instead of better. I have no doubt a president with the gifts of Lincoln or Roosevelt might have better bridged the divide, and I guarantee I'll keep trying to be better so long as I hold this office.

> But, my fellow Americans, this cannot be my task — or any President's — alone. There are a whole lot of folks in this chamber, good people who would like to see more cooperation, would like to see a more elevated debate in Washington, but feel trapped by the imperatives of getting elected, by the noise coming out of your base. I know; you've told me. It's the worst-kept secret in Washington. And a lot of you aren't enjoying being trapped in that kind of rancor.

In the end, the President's last State of the Union will not be a speech long remembered and it will not change the political debate in Washington, largely because that was not its purpose. The President offered no olive branches to the GOP and made few new proposals other than calling for a "moon shot" to end cancer. Instead, its goal was to burnish the President's legacy while attacking the voices of the past, namely the GOP. Surely, it was well written and the President tried to portray himself as a voice of moderation, but the speech was a political manifesto and little more, and one designed to try to ensure that the next occupant of the White House is a Democrat. Given this purely partisan goal, it is not surprising that the speech was widely viewed as a failure.

Week 366

(DIS-ESTABLISHMENT)

January 24, 2016

For months, the media's political coverage has been focused on Donald Trump and the fight for the Republican nomination. Trump constantly supplies theatrics and controversial comments, so he has dominated the headlines, drowning out not only the other GOP candidates, but also to a degree the focus on the Democrat nomination fight. The fascination with Trump has partially obscured the most interesting development in the 2016 campaign, the emergence of Bernie Sanders as a credible challenger to Hillary Clinton. In many ways, the emergence of Sanders and Trump are the product of the same phenomenon: disenchantment with the establishment. Millions of Americans on the Left and the Right are so frustrated with the direction of the nation and the current power structure in Washington that they have flocked to two fringe candidates who in any other electoral environment would have been dismissed early on. It is a dangerous development for both the Republicans and the Democrats, and should seriously concern President Obama.

Trump is a fringe candidate mostly because of his rhetoric, as opposed to his resume or policy goals. Trump has made clear he plans to tax Wall Street more, address unfair trade policies, and strengthen American foreign policy. These are not fringe positions. His calls for temporarily banning Muslin immigration is more radical, but seems mostly a politically motivated effort to appeal to public fears. In many ways, Trump's overall agenda is more populist than conservative, and more moderate than one might expect. Trump's campaign at its base is mostly sophistry, where Trump has figured out the more he attacks the establishment, the more popular he becomes.

What is happening in the Democrat campaign has the same source, disillusionment, but is possibly more problematic. There, a leftwing Vermont Senator and avowed socialist is seriously challenging the most popular, best funded, and most widely supported Democrat presidential candidate in decades. The contest between Sanders and Clinton should not even be close. Clinton has the full support of the Democrat establishment, while Sander's policy proposals are so far left that most elected Democrats would never dare to support them. He has proposed free collage education for all, huge reductions to defense spending, massive new regulations on a wide array of industries, and unprecedented tax increases. In short, he has proposed turning America into a Scandinavian-style social democracy. It is an agenda on the very fringe of the American Left, but what is amazing is that the country is so frustrated that his agenda is being embraced. This week, polls show Sanders tied or maybe a bit ahead in the Iowa caucuses and leading by a huge margin in New Hampshire. So while Trump's outrageous rhetoric has masked a fairly mainstream populist agenda, on the Democrat side, Sander's truly radical policy platform is both understood and embraced.

Sanders fully understands what is happening, and has decided to get even more aggressive in his assaults on Hillary Clinton. His strategy is simple, paint her as part of the establishment and use her experience against her. For example, on the topic of the Iraq War Sanders recently said:

> I think on the crucial foreign policy issue of our time, it turns out that Secretary Clinton, with all of her experience, was wrong and I was right. Experience is important. Dick Cheney had a lot of experience. A whole lot of people have

experience but do not necessarily have the right judgment. I think I have the right judgment to conduct sensible foreign policy.

For Sanders, painting Hillary Clinton as a past ally of Vice President Cheney is a double indictment, implying that she is both too moderate and too tied to the establishment to be trusted. In response, the Clinton campaign has moved their candidate's rhetoric ever more Left, in an attempt to appeal to the excitement being created by the Sander's campaign.

So on the GOP side, we have a bombastic and often offensive candidate with a populist agenda in the lead, while on the Democrat side, Sander's radical agenda is capturing nearly all the enthusiasm. In a traditional political year, neither Trump nor Sanders would be acceptable candidates, but this is not a traditional year. Voters are frustrated and want change, and are willing to support fringe candidates to get it. This is a problem for both political parties, but likely a bigger one for the Democrats, because if Hillary wins the nomination, she will be seen as a continuation of the status quo, while if Sanders wins, his agenda will likely make him unelectable. None of this is good news for President Obama, because for his legacy to endure, he needs to be succeeded by a Democrat.

Week 367

(FINICUM)

January 31, 2016

Of all the areas where President Obama has aggressively used his executive authority, federal lands have been a special focus. The President has protected millions of acres from development, limited grazing, heavily regulated oil and gas exploration, and most recently issued executive orders to restrict coal development. The President has used federal lands, where his executive authority is broad, to showcase both his environmental and energy policies. While these executive orders are not especially controversial in the Eastern United States, in the West and Alaska, his policies have been strongly opposed by farming, mining, and natural resources interests, who have seen their ability to use federal lands restricted. This has caused a backlash, and contributed to the President's unpopularity in the rural West. Indeed, that unpopularity has grown so great that it has now led to armed conflict.

On January 2, 2016, a group of armed men led by LaVoy Finicum and Ammon Bundy occupied buildings at the Malheur National Wildlife Refuge in Western Oregon, in protest of what they view as the ever increasing restrictions the federal government is placing on the use of federal lands. The protesters declared that they occupied to refuge to protect the constitutional rights of all Americans to use federal lands, rights they believe are being trampled upon. After taking over the refuge, they made a point of taking down some fences to symbolize their demand to lift federal restrictions on use of public lands. Initially, authorities tried not to escalate the situation, instead focusing on efforts to negotiate an end to the protest. However, as the occupation dragged on for weeks, political and law enforcement authorities became increasingly impatient, and started planning to end the protest by force. They implemented that plan on January 26, when they arrested some of the protesters, including their leader Ammon Bundy, when they left the refuge to participate in a community meeting. In that operation, LaVoy Finicum was shot and killed by police when Finicum appeared to be reaching for a handgun in his vest. In all, eight of the protesters were arrested in three separate police raids.

Finicum's decision to confront the police was consistent with his prior statement that: "I'm just not going to prison . . . . Look at the stars. There's no way I'm going to sit in a concrete cell where I can't see the stars and roll out my bedroll on the ground. That's just not going to happen. I want to be able to get up in the morning and throw my saddle on my horse and go check on my cows. It's OK. I've lived a good life. God's been gracious to me." The other protesters pointed to Finicum's death as more evidence that the federal government has become despotic, stating: "It appears that America was fired upon by our government . . . . One of liberty's finest patriots is fallen. He will not go silent into eternity." As for the authorities, they defended the use of force. However, even the death of Finicum has not ended the protest because those remaining at the refuge are still refusing to leave.

President Obama has been careful not to inject himself directly into the response to the protest, instead he has allowed the FBI and local authorities to take the lead. The careful response of the White House shows their understanding of the depth of anger in the rural West over federal land policy. Many in the West believe their traditional way of life is under siege and that the Administration is only concerned with winning points with liberal environmental and clean energy groups. The White House knows that if they directly respond to protests like the one in Oregon, that might only lead to more confrontations. At its base, this protest was the product of the President's determination to use his executive authority to pursue his ideological goals despite the divisions that might cause.

Week 368

(FLIPPED OUT)

February 7, 2016

While President Obama is not on the ballot this year, there is no doubt he is watching the results as though he were, because his legacy hinges on who wins. If a Democrat takes the White House, most of his policies and executive orders will be preserved, while if the GOP wins, the next president will devote most of his or her term to undoing what President Obama has done. That is why President Obama was paying close attention to the first electoral battle of 2016, the February 1 Iowa caucuses. Although Iowa has a poor record of predicting the eventual nominee of either party, the results could help show whether Hillary Clinton is still the likely nominee, and whether the Republicans are inclined to pick an electable candidate or a fringe one. When the votes came in, there was both good news and bad news for President Obama, ensuring a long and suspenseful nomination fight to come.

Democrat strategists have been truly surprised by both the rise of Bernie Sanders and the weakness of Hillary Clinton. The elderly Sanders is handily winning the youthful liberal vote, and the more radical his policy proposals, the more popular he becomes. That is why Iowa is such a critical test for Clinton. In 2008 she lost Iowa to Barack Obama, which led to her eventual nomination defeat. The Clinton campaign wanted to make sure history did not repeat, so they pulled out every stop to win the Iowa caucuses. They did it, but just barely. In raw votes, Clinton and Sanders each got 50%. By individual precincts, Clinton won 701, and Sanders 697, but Clinton's winning margin came from coin tosses in precincts where the candidates were tied. No matter, the Clinton campaign declared victory, the Sanders forces complained, and then both campaigns moved on to New Hampshire for the next battle.

While the fight in Iowa was a draw, most political observers and certainly the White House viewed it as a win for Clinton. Iowa's Democrat caucus base is very liberal, perfect territory for Sanders. The fact that he did not win outright there indicates weakness in his campaign, weakness that Clinton will exploit when the campaign moves on to big Democrat states like New York, Illinois, and California, and southern states where the black Democrat vote dominates. So even though it looks like Sanders will win easily in new Hampshire, the tie in Iowa was enough to stabilize the Clinton campaign, and put it in a position to ultimately win. This surely cheered the White House, since Clinton is viewed as the more electable Democrat. In fact, President Obama went out of his way to praise Clinton just before the caucuses, making his preference known.

While Clinton's performance in Iowa certainly made the President happy, the results on the GOP side were less cheerful for the White House. Democrat strategists have been delighted by the rise of Donald Trump, whom they view as unelectable. Based on polls, it had looked like Trump would win Iowa and New Hampshire, which might make his drive for the GOP nomination unstoppable. Yet in recent weeks, two other Republican Senators, Ted Cruz and Marco Rubio, seemed to be gaining strength in Iowa, and that was borne out when the results came in. Ted Cruz won the caucuses with 28% of the vote, and Trump barely came in second with 24%, trailed very closely by Rubio with 23%. After Trump boldly and repeatedly proclaimed that those who come in second are losers, it was a bitter pill for his campaign, which promptly asserted voter fraud and called for a re-vote. Cruz won with superior voter outreach and a strong appeal to the conservative base. As for Rubio, he seems to have peaked in support just before the caucus, especially with those concerned with supporting the most electable Republican.

The fall of Trump and the rise of Rubio is what made the Iowa results concerning for the White House. There is genuine concern that Clinton is a weaker general election candidate than it might appear, so the Administration hoped the GOP would nominate a fringe candidate who would be easier to defeat. Trump is a flawed general election nominee, as may be Cruz, whose personality and hard edged conservativism might turn off moderate voters, but Rubio is a different matter. He is young, from Florida, Hispanic, and has the potential to appeal to both moderates and conservatives. He is the candidate the Democrats least want to face, and his strong showing in Iowa certainly put a damper on an otherwise happy night for President Obama.

Week 369

(COURTING)

February 14, 2016

Most observers believed this week's big political story was going to be the New Hampshire primary, and the week certainly started that way. The results were stunning for both Republicans and Democrats. On the GOP side, Donald Trump won the primary with nearly 36% of the vote, followed by Kasich, Cruz, and Bush, with 16%, 12% and 11% respectively. For the Democrats, Bernie Sanders garnered 60% of the vote, with Clinton winning only 38%. The night was a triumph for outsiders and the disenchanted, on both the Right and Left. The focus of Washington immediately turned to whether Trump could be stopped and how badly Clinton had been damaged, at least until February 13 when an entirely different event stole the headlines: the death of Supreme Court Justice Antonin Scalia.

Justice Scalia was nominated to the Supreme Court by President Reagan in 1986, and received wide bipartisan support in the Senate during his confirmation hearing. Upon joining the Supreme Court, he became the intellectual leader for originalist constitutional interpretation and textual interpretation of statutes. That constitutional jurisprudence is focused on the text and the intent of the framers, as opposed to interpreting the Constitution in view of current cultural and political perspectives. For three decades, as the Court grew progressively more conservative, at least until President Obama's nominees joined the court, Justice Scalia led the charge to reinterpret the Constitution to be more in line with the intent of the framers. This resulted in decisions restricting commerce clause powers, expanding free speech and religious liberty rights, limits on racial preferences, and greater executive branch powers. Justice Scalia was also known for scathing dissents and a jocular personality.

The death of Justice Scalia was unexpected. He was found dead at a private resort in Texas, having died in his sleep. He appears to have had a history of heart problems, but the cause of his death has not been made public. While the cause of death is currently unknown, the impact of his passing was immediately realized by all in Washington. For more than two decades, the Supreme Court has had a tenuous conservative majority, with Justices Scalia, Thomas, and Alito currently anchoring the conservatives, and Chief Justice Roberts and Justice Kennedy providing less reliable conservative votes. President Obama has made two appointments to the Court, Justices Sotomayor and Kagan, but those justices replaced other liberal justices, thus not impacting the Supreme Court's conservative majority. With Scalia's death, President Obama has the opportunity to create a liberal majority on the court.

Almost as soon as reports of Justice Scalia's death became known, Republicans called for the Senate to refuse to confirm any nominee until after the election, while Democrats asserted that President Obama should nominate a replacement and the Senate must hold hearings and a vote on confirmation. The reason for such quick and forceful responses to Justice Scalia's death is explained by what is at stake. The Supreme Court has been the final arbitrator of many of the Administration's policies, from Obamacare to various executive orders. Indeed, just a few days before Justice Scalia's death, the Supreme Court stayed the EPA's new regulations limiting carbon emissions by power plants and the President's executive order legalizing millions of illegal immigrants is also going before the Court. With issues such as these at stake, it is no surprise that both Republicans and Democrats are ready for a fight over Scalia's replacement. Indeed, there was a Republican presidential debate the day of his death, and the first questions were all about the fight over replacing Justice Scalia. No doubt, President Obama will nominate someone who will pressure Republicans to hold a vote, while conservatives will threaten a filibuster. The fight will be on, and the goal will be to influence both the Supreme Court and the presidential election.

Week 370

(JUST SAY NO)

February 21, 2016

The unexpected death of Justice Scalia has added a new dimension to the already heated political atmosphere in Washington. With the 2016 presidential election already in full swing, it took little time for the fault lines to appear and for each party to start its maneuvers for advantage. It started just a day after his death at a GOP debate, where the question was whether President Obama should nominate a replacement in an election year. Not surprisingly, the Republicans said he should not, while Democrats pressed for a quick confirmation hearing in the hope of achieving a liberal majority on the Supreme Court. Indeed, even the memorial services for Justice Scalia became politicized, when President Obama decided not to attend the funeral mass, and instead visiting during calling hours at the Supreme Court. When all the politics are overlaid with the presidential campaign, it made for a very divisive week in Washington.

There is no dispute that President Obama has the authority under the Constitution to nominate a replacement for Justice Scalia. The reason that nomination is critical is because Justice Scalia was the key fifth vote for the tenuous conservative majority on the Court. With a nomination, the President could put a third Justice on the Court, and thereby put liberals in the majority. With issues such as affirmative action, abortion restrictions, and executive power before the Court, a liberal majority would hugely impact many pressing domestic issues. While the President has the power to nominate a Justice, only the Senate can confirm any nominee to a permanent seat on the Court. In recent decades, when Justices have died during a presidential election year, the Senate has not confirmed a replacement until after the election, but will that be the case this year.

So the issue became would the President nominate a replacement for Scalia, and would the GOP even hold a confirmation hearing. President Obama wasted no time wading into the debate, making clear just days after Justice Scalia's death that he intended to fulfill his constitutional duty. On the GOP side, conservatives immediately put pressure on Senate Majority Leader McConnell and Senate Judiciary Committee Chairman Grassley not to hold any confirmation hearings. However, there was no united front in the Republican caucus on the issue. Moderate and endangered Republican Senators like Susan Collins of Maine and Mark Kirk of Illinois both seemed open to the Senate at least holding a hearing on a nominee. For the White House, the focus quickly turned to finding a nominee who would put the maximum pressure on the Republicans to hold a vote.

Hillary Clinton also joined the debate, as it became increasingly clear that she would be the Democrat nominee. After losing badly to Senator Sanders in New Hampshire, the Clinton campaign was focused on stopping Sander's momentum in Nevada, where a caucus would be held on February 20. If Sanders could be beaten there, Clinton would be in a commanding position, because upcoming contests in South Carolina and Super Tuesday on March 1 would include many southern states where Clinton's support among black voters might be decisive. Clinton got the victory she needed, winning the Nevada caucus by 53% to Sander's 47%, and she quickly added to her stump speech calls for the GOP to confirm President Obama's nominee.

The fight over Justice Scalia's replacement will rage for months. The President will likely nominate someone in March, and then the Republicans will have to determine how to respond. To up the pressure on the GOP, the White House even threatened to make a recess appointment to the Supreme Court if the Republicans refuse to confirm his nominee. No doubt the President will pick a nominee the Republicans will find hard to block, likely using a woman, minority, or a supposedly moderate nominee. The key issue will be the unity of the Republican caucus and whether the GOP will stick together to refuse to hold hearings. Even if the Republicans are pressured to hold hearings, Democrats would need 14 Republican votes to break the almost certain filibuster of any attempt to hold a confirmation vote.

Week 371
(GIT NO)

February 28, 2016

One of President Obama's first acts upon entering office was an executive order closing the prison camp at Guantanamo Bay (Gitmo), where some of the most dangerous terrorist captured by United States forces are imprisoned. During his 2008 campaign, Mr. Obama said Gitmo was hurting American security and helping terrorist recruiting efforts because it had become a symbol of harsh American treatment of Muslims. However, the White House soon realized that closing Gitmo was far more complicated than they expected. There was the issue of where to house its very dangerous inhabitants, and how to fund closing Gitmo with Congress firmly opposed to the move. As a result, while the number of prisoners at Gitmo has been declining, after seven years the President still has not been able to close the facility. Seeing this as unfinished business, on February 23, the President released an eight page plan to close Gitmo and gave a press conference to promote his plan. Not surprisingly, this announcement has met just as much criticism as his executive order issued seven years ago.

There are many legal impediments to any effort by the Administration to close Gitmo. Congress has written into law that the prisoners there cannot be brought into the United States. There is little chance Congress would fund closing the facility and representatives from any states where prisoners might be moved are sure to oppose. Despite this, it is clear the President views closing Gitmo as an imperative, to the point that he even threatened to close the facility and move the prisoners into the United States under his authority as commander in chief, thereby ignoring enacted legislation and Congress' power of the purse. Regardless of this bravado, the President admitted how challenging this move will be:

> I am very clear eyed about the hurdles to finally closing Guantánamo: The politics of this are tough . . . . I don't want to pass this problem on to the next president, whoever it is. And if, as a nation, we don't deal with this now, when will we deal with it? . . . . The plan we're putting forward today isn't just about closing the facility at Guantanamo. It's not just about dealing with the current group of detainees, which is a complex piece of business because of the manner in which they were originally apprehended and what happened. This is about closing a chapter in our history. . . . Keeping this facility open is contrary to our values . . . . It undermines our standing in the world. It is viewed as a stain on our broader record of upholding the highest standards of rule of law.

Currently, about 2000 personnel work at Gitmo, which houses 91 prisoners, and the facility costs about $450 million to operate annually. The President's plan calls for moving most of the remaining prisoners to other countries, but the most dangerous inmates would be moved to facilities in the United States. The White House's plan was very general in all other respects, but even so it took little time for the plan to be condemned. House Speaker Paul Ryan said the proposal "fails to provide critical details required by law." Speaker Ryan continued: "It is against the law — and it will stay against the law — to transfer terrorist detainees to American soil." Senator McCain, Chairman of the Armed Services Committee, said it was "not a credible plan for closing Guantanamo, let alone a coherent policy to deal with future terrorist detainees."

The President's determination to wade into this controversy shows how focused he is on his legacy. Gitmo is likely the President's most longstanding unfinished business. He pledged to close the facility and has not done so. In his last year, he wants to finish that task to show he has kept his promise. The question will be how far he is willing to go to fulfill his legacy. If he truly wants to close Gitmo, he will have to do so by executive order and contrary to legal prohibitions, and thereby will be accused of acting unlawfully. Any such move will be challenged in court, but if in the interim the facility to closed and the inmates moved, the President might believe he can achieve his goal whether is legal or not. So how the President ultimately deals with this issue will tell us much about how willing he is to stretch executive power to enhance his legacy.

Week 372
(SMALL HANDS)

March 6, 2016

Super Tuesday is often the watershed moment in presidential primary campaigns. It can resuscitate a campaign, end one, or put a candidate firmly in control of the nomination fight. For Hillary Clinton and Donald Trump, Super Tuesday offers the opportunity to crush the remaining opposition and put themselves in commanding positions to win their parties' nominations. For the Democrats and President Obama, Hillary's new found strength is encouraging, because it creates the prospect of having their preferred candidate face an opponent that most liberals think will be easy to beat, namely Donald Trump. For Republicans, Super Tuesday offered a last chance to try to stop the Trump juggernaut, and his GOP revivals appeared increasingly desperate to try to do that.

Trump's campaign is based on generalizations, and petty insults pointed at his opponents. He has insulted his Republican rivals for their looks, weight, intelligence, judgment, and integrity, often in comments laced with profanity. Trump has used very harsh rhetoric, which Republicans over and over again assumed would ultimately hurt his campaign. To their surprise, with each insult Trump has gotten more popular. So with Super Tuesday approaching, in their desperation, his rivals started playing from the Trump handbook. It even got to the point where Senator Marco Rubio made fun of his small hands, saying "you know what they say about somebody with small hands." This was a new low, and something Hillary Clinton enjoyed immensely, as she watched the Republicans rip themselves apart using the crudest possible language.

Despite going deep into the mud, the Republicans only slightly slowed Donald Trump's march to the nomination. As the election results came in on March 1, Trump garnered the vast majority of Super Tuesday victories, with wins in Vermont, Massachusetts, Virginia, Alabama, Georgia, and Tennessee. Rubio only won Minnesota, but Trump seems to have fallen short of a knockout blow, because Senator Ted Cruz won Texas, Oklahoma, and Alaska. The results from Super Tuesday solidified Trump commanding position, and will likely force both Rubio and Ohio Governor Kasich to drop out if they do not win their home states, which vote in mid-March. The only warning sign for Trump is the emergence of Ted Cruz, who now seems well-positioned for a one-on-one fight with Trump.

On the Democrat side, Super Tuesday was a super day for Hillary Clinton. With an election map of southern states with large black populations, it was expected that Clinton would do very well, and she did. Hillary Clinton won Massachusetts, Virginia, Alabama, Georgia, Texas, Oklahoma, and Tennessee. These victories added to Clinton's substantial lead in delegates. However, the race is not over yet, because Bernie Sanders won just enough contests to keep his campaign alive, notching victories in Vermont, Minnesota, and Colorado. After election night, Sanders made clear he plans to take his campaign to the convention. This point was emphasized when Sanders won the Kansas and Nebraska caucuses on March 5, even though Clinton won the Louisiana primary that same day.

Most of the media coverage has focused on the crude nature of the GOP nomination battle and the efforts of the Republican establishment to stop Trump, creating the prospect of a civil war within the GOP. This has made for a great deal of delighted coverage from the mainstream media, and certainly is being thoroughly enjoyed by President Obama. However, a closer look reveals some trends that Democrats should find disturbing. While GOP turnout in nomination contests is breaking records, Democrat turnout is down substantially from 2012 and 2008. This usually implies an unmotivated base, a troubling sign for any candidate. Also, the FBI investigation into Hillary Clinton emails is pushing forward, with investigators this week granting immunity to a Department of State staffer who has key knowledge of how Clinton handled her emails. So while all might seem like celebration and champagne in the Democrat ranks, very troubling signs remain.

Week 373

(GET THEM OUT)

March 13, 2016

There is no denying that Donald Trump has tapped into a strong feeling of resentment and fear in the American electorate. Throughout his campaign, he has masterfully appealed to these sentiments, and in the process galvanized millions of American who had given up on the political process. Trump's rallies are larger and more energetic than anything most observers can recall, and his supporters seem prepared to forgive nearly anything Trump says, no matter how vulgar, sexist, inconsistent, or idiotic. This has left his opponents stunned, because it appears nothing can put a dent in Trump's popularity. Now, however, it appears the very enthusiasm and energy that Trump has harnessed might be his undoing, because he has so excited his supporters that their commitment is turning to violence.

For many months, Trump rallies have attracted both supporters and protesters. For his part, Trump has turned these protesters to his advantage, using them as a foil for his rhetoric and energizing crowds with his calls that they be thrown out. Trump even leads chats of "get them out." On occasion, he has even referred to violence with less than disapproval. Given the excitement he creates with his supporters, it is not surprising that they have taken out some of that energy on protesters, to the point that fights started to break out at Trump rallies. This did not go unnoticed by liberal groups, like moveon.org, which started to organize protests designed to interrupt Trump rallies and prompt violence. They achieved their goal, with fights breaking out. On cue, the media took notice of the emerging violence, focusing on whether Trump was purposefully creating it. The theme was obvious and played into liberal preconceptions of conservatives as tending toward fascism and violence.

Starting this week, this growing violence at Trump rallies became the focus of media coverage of the Trump campaign. In typical fashion, rather than condemning violence, Trump simply denied that he had promoted anything and refused to call on his supporters to pull back. However, even the Trump campaign started to recognize the risk, forcing them to cancel a rally in Illinois for fear that large numbers of liberal protesters would try yet again to spark violence. The other Republican candidates, desperate to try to stop Trump's momentum, quickly pounced as well, condemning Trump for promoting violence. Unsurprisingly, Hillary Clinton, Bernie Sanders, and President Obama all jumped in as well. All of this has created the specter that Trump is giving rise to disturbing and possibly dangerous behavior in the electorate, and something that could spin out of control. Whether that is true of not, it is beyond dispute that this rising violence will not endear Trump to undecided voters, which is bad news of the GOP if he becomes the nominee.

Week 374

(On the Merricks)

March 20, 2016

When Supreme Court Justice Antonin Scalia died on February 13, an immediate political battle ensued. Republicans who control the Senate stated they would confirm no Obama nominee, while the President made clear his constitutional duty to nominate a replacement and that he expected the Senate to hold a hearing and a vote on his choice. Since those immediate reactions, a political trench has started. Democrats probed for any GOP Senator who might be a crack in the wall of opposition to considering a nominee, while Democrat interest groups lobbied the White House on who the President should nominate. Liberals called for a bold progressive choice, while others pushed for a more moderate nominee who might pressure the Republicans to hold a vote. On March 16, the President announced that Judge Merrick Garland was his choice, a pick designed to both cement a liberal majority on the Supreme Court and pressure the Senate to hold a vote. The President asserted that the Senate is obligated to hold a vote. Republicans quickly pointed out that Vice President Biden, when he was a Senator, took the position that Supreme Court nominees should not be voted on in an election year.

Judge Merrick Garland was born in 1952 in Chicago, went to Harvard Law School, and has worked as a United States attorney and in private practice. In 1995 he was nominated to the Court of Appeals for the District of Columbia Circuit by President Clinton, eventually winning confirmation in 1997 without a dissenting vote. His record is that of a moderate liberal who is tough on criminal defendants, deferential to regulatory agencies, and potentially supportive of a restrictive view of gun rights. Even though he has been a judge for nearly 20 years, his judicial record on issues like abortion and affirmative action is scant. This is because the court from which he hales rarely gets those types of cases, and instead has a docket heavy with regulatory and administrative cases. That is why judges from that court are so often favorites for the Supreme Court, because it is often hard to tell their true ideology.

In choosing Garland, the President picked someone from his hometown with a stellar reputation with both Republicans and Democrats. The White House hopes that Judge Garland's reputation as a moderate and highly qualified judge will pressure the Republicans to hold hearing and a vote. For Republicans, Judge Garland poses a risky choice. The GOP has the votes to block any confirmation, but Garland might prove a better option as compared the type of judge Hillary Clinton might nominate if she is elected president, especially if the Republicans lose their majority in the 2016 election. However, even though a number of GOP senators reaffirmed their respect for Garland, no obvious cracks appeared in the Republican caucus. Indeed, at least 15 Republicans would be needed to join Democrats to force a vote, because there is no doubt that GOP members would filibuster any attempt to hold a confirmation vote. For his part, the President demanded a vote for Judge Garland, but it is looking like he will not get one.

President Obama understands very well that replacing Justice Scalia with a liberal might be the most important achievement of his presidency after the passage of Obamacare. A liberal Justice in that seat will give liberals a clear majority for the first time since the early 1980's. Achieving a liberal majority on the Supreme Court would help cement the Obama legacy, because many of the President's policies and executive orders have been attacked and overturned by the Federal Courts. A liberal majority would allow the President's vision on the power of the regulatory state and executive authority to prevail. Further, on abortion and affirmative action, a liberal majority would cut back on the marginal progress conservatives have made on those issues. On the death penalty, many believe the Supreme Court was already heading toward banning capital punishment, and a liberal majority might finally achieve that goal.

Given all this, it is obvious that President Obama would have nominated Judge Garland only if he was convinced that as a Justice he would be a dependable liberal. While he has a reputation as a consensus builder and a moderate, he has not had to rule on many of the key issues that would appear before him on the Supreme Court. One area where his record is clear is on deference to regulatory agencies, and in that arena, it is clear his views fit very well with the President. So in the end, Garland is a classic stealth candidate, qualified and apparently moderate, but a judge who would be a dependable liberal. Given all this the Republicans have little choice but to stop a vote, even if the Justice they ultimately get if the election is lost might be much worse.

Week 375

(BRUSSELS)

March 27, 2016

The White House had hoped that the major story of the week would be President Obama's historic trip to Cuba. After boldly reestablishing diplomatic relations with Cuba despite the opposition of Congress, the President travelled to Cuba to both highlight the change in policy and to confront the Castro regime on its human rights record. The Administration believes that open relations and travel to Cuba will do more to undermine the Castro government decades-long embargo, and the President's trip was designed to underline this point. Yet while the President was trying to highlight his new opening to Cuba, he was rudely reminded of the old challenge that has dogged him from the start of his presidency, namely terrorism.

Ever since the Paris bombings in 2015, European authorities have been tracking the only known perpetrator believed to still be alive, Sala Abdeslam. Several of the Paris bombers came from Brussels, so that city has been the focus of anti-terrorist activities the last several months. On March 18, Belgian authorities finally captured Abdeslam after two raids in the Molenbeck neighborhood of Brussels. The police immediately began to interrogate him, which prompted his comrades to accelerate the timeline for their next planned attack, which took place on March 22nd, just four days after Abdeslam's arrest.

Brussels is the headquarters of both NATO and the EU, and is also the home a large and restive Muslim population. This has made Brussel a fertile terrorist recruiting ground and a prime target for attacks. So the entire city was gripped with terror on March 22nd by twin suicide bombings at the airport and at a train station. The first bombing occurred outside security at the Brussels airport at 7:58 a.m. near the British Airways check-in desk, when three suspected attackers set off two bombs, killing a dozen people. Belgian authorities closed all rail transport to the airport at 8:20 a.m. and began closing roads, but it was too late to stop the second attack. At 9:11 a.m. a bomb exploded at the Maalbeek metro station in central Brussels in the middle carriage of a three car train, killing at least 20 people. All public transport was shutdown at 9:27 a.m. A third bomb was found at the airport, which police detonated. Authorities confirmed that the terrorists used nail bombs to maximize casualties. Overall, 35 people were killed in the bombings, including three bombers, and more than 300 people were injured. It was the worst terrorist attack in Belgian history.

The suspected bombers include two brothers, Ibrahim and Khalid El Bakraoui, Belgians of Moroccan descent. The other suspected bomber was Najim Laachraoul. There is also a fourth suspect, who is believed to have left the unexploded bomb at the airport, who has not yet been identified or captured. Some 90 minutes after the attacks, authorities located an apartment in a northern suburb of Brussels where they discovered explosives, a nail bomb, and an ISIS flag. The apartment also contained pictures of the home of Belgian Prime Minister Charles Michel, potentially indicating plans for further attacks. This has only heightened fears in Europe of further attacks, which ISIS tried to increase by quickly taking credit for the Brussels bombings.

All this happened while President Obama was in Cuba, hoping to turn attention to his new foreign policy initiatives, rather than focusing again on past challenges that have only grown more problematic. The President quickly condemned the attacks, but refused to change his itinerary. So as European authorities were scrambling to track down the missing bomber and ensure no other attacks were imminent, the President attended a baseball game with Raul Castro, laughing and smiling with the crowds. This can be partly explained by the White House's determination not to be held hostage by events, but more importantly the President does not want to focus on terrorism, where the rise of ISIS has been a headache for the Administration. Instead, the President prefers to talk about climate change, Cuba, and other issues. So no wonder he preferred to watch a baseball game with an unrepentant communist dictator rather than show solidarity with our European allies who are under assault. One event helps his legacy, while the other undermines it.

Week 376

(Crimes and Punishments)

April 3, 2016

The success of the Donald Trump's presidential campaign has been built on being provocative and unscripted. Donald Trump has continually strengthened his grip on the Republican nomination by insulting and belittling his opponents, making bold policy pronouncements with few specifics, and by refusing to ever apologize. It is a strategy that has served him well for months, and no matter how outrageous or crude his comments, he rose in the polls. In response, it seems Donald Trump has come to believe that he can say anything and his supporters will still love him, so he has continued to run a campaign on the fly with little organization, focus, or preparation. Given this, it is not surprising that he appeared for an exclusive television interview on March 30 with MSNBC's Chris Matthews using the same formula. However, this time his lack of preparation and bluster might have gone a step too far.

During the wide-ranging interview, Chris Matthews pressed Trump on his position on abortion. Before starting his presidential campaign, Trump had repeatedly stated that he was pro-choice. Now, Trump says he is pro-life, which has prompted many in the media to question whether he changed his position to endear himself to Christian conservatives. Matthews was determined to press Trump on this issue, and did so repeatedly. This culminated in a series of questions on who should be punished for illegal abortions. It was evident from the interview that Trump has put very little thought into the abortion issue and had no prepared response. When pressed by Matthews for a yes or no answer on whether performing abortions should be punished, Trump said: "There has to be some form of punishment." "For the woman?" Matthews asked, and Trump responded: "Yes." Trump also agreed that banning abortions would force some women to pursue the procedure illegally, to which he responded: "Well, you go back to a position like they had where they would perhaps go to illegal places, but we have to ban it."

Even the Trump campaign quickly realized that this time their candidate might have gone too far. Trump's comments were not only condemned by pro-choice groups, but also pro-life organizations also criticized him, since it has been a long-standing position of the pro-life movement that women are victims of abortions, not the culprits . Likewise, President Obama and Hillary Clinton wasted no time condemning Trump. In a rare move for the Trump campaign, his team had to go into immediate damage control, issuing the following clarifying statement:

If Congress were to pass legislation making abortion illegal and the federal courts upheld this legislation, or any state were permitted to ban abortion under state and federal law, the doctor or any other person performing this illegal act upon a woman would be held legally responsible, not the woman. . . . The woman is a victim in this case as is the life in her womb. My position has not changed — like Ronald Reagan, I am pro-life with exceptions.

Even with this statement, the damage was done.

Many times before, Trump's Republican opponents had believed that one or another of Trump's offensive comments would finally deflate the Trump balloon. It has not happened, but many think this comment will be different. Trump's statement about punishing women for abortion reveals so many of the weaknesses in the Trump candidacy. First is the misogyny of the Trump world view. His first instinct when asked a question about any particular woman, friend or foe, is to either praise or ridicule her physical appearance. It seems Mr. Trump cannot get beyond how women look to consider their views, concerns, or values. Next is his lack of discipline, where he appears to believe he can say anything and people will believe him, whether there is any basis for his statements or not. Most importantly is his ego, which is so outsized that he seems to think anything he believes is automatically correct.

Trump's comments to Chris Matthews may or may not be the undoing of his campaign, only time will tell on that. However, they should weaken him, and now that he is facing only two opponents, Senator Cruz and Governor Kasich, his path to get enough delegates to take the nomination outright could get harder and harder. For example, in Cruz, Trump is facing a determined and highly organized foe, who is winning the ground game in small states and in the delegate selection process, and who is slowly chipping away at Trump's lead. It will still be hard for Cruz or anyone else to stop Trump, but Trump certainly helped his opponents this week with his comments on abortion.

Week 377

(WISCONSIN)

April 10, 2016

One of the most amazing things about the presidential nomination fight in 2016 is that both political parties are in the throes of an anti-establishment backlash, and one that is upending all prior expectations. On the Democrat side, it was assumed that once Vice President Biden decided not to run that Hillary Clinton would have an open path to the nomination. On the Republican side, it was assumed that well-known and well-funded establishment candidates like Jeb Bush would outlast all opponents and march to the nomination. Both assumptions and the conventional wisdom that underlies them have been proven not simply wrong, but utterly misguided. The results in this week's Wisconsin primary emphasized that point.

Wisconsin is a swing state, but one that Democrats have consistently won for nearly three decades. Democrat primary voters tend to be white, liberal, and young, while the GOP electorate is equally white, but older, evangelical, and conservative. Given these demographics and the anti-establishment wave sweeping the country, Hillary Clinton had a great deal to worry about when it came to Wisconsin. Bernie Sanders has proven to be a tenacious opponent, consistently winning liberal and small states by appealing to the leftmost elements of the Democrat party. Just when the Clinton campaign hoped to put down his insurgency after her strong victories in the South and Ohio, Sanders assembled a string of small state wins and then devoted all his energy to Wisconsin, which he then won over Clinton 56 percent to 43 percent. Sanders swept in almost all categories, most convincingly with young and progressive voters. Indeed, Clinton left Wisconsin before the voting even started, understanding full well that she was headed to defeat, and hoping to move on promptly to her home state of New York, which will be more friendly territory.

The story on the Republican side was different, but equally anti-establishment. Donald Trump has dominated the large primary contests, and in doing so forced out of the nomination contest of all the GOP candidates except for John Kasich and Ted Cruz. Now his primary opponent is Senator Ted Cruz, a candidate almost as anti-establishment as Trump. Trump, with political views that are unorthodox, non-ideological, and often inconsistent, has appealed to the patriotism of disenchanted working class Americans, and in doing so has created a political revolution much like what Sanders is creating on the Left. Senator Cruz in contrast is a hardcore conservative and almost as disliked by the GOP establishment as he is by liberals. So he is the anti-establishment candidate of the right. For Cruz, Wisconsin offered a chance to deal a body blow to Trump's chances of accumulating enough delegates to win the nomination outright. Ironically, Cruz is using the Barak Obama playbook, winning small state contests and winning the ground game of delegate recruitment. In Wisconsin, Cruz had a primary electorate too conservative and religious to flock to Trump, and he did not waste his opportunity, winning the state by a margin of 48 percent to 35 percent.

After Wisconsin, everything is going to be different as the parties move into the last few months of the nomination process. Sander's win means he will no doubt stay in the fight all the way to the convention, forcing Clinton to spend money and time on the nomination contest and preventing her from moving to the middle for the general election. For Trump, his loss in Wisconsin and Cruz's continuing ability to outmaneuver him in the fight for delegates means Trump's chances of winning the nomination outright are in question, setting up a potential contested convention, where Cruz believes he will emerge as the nominee. So it appears likely Wisconsin is going to ensure the GOP gets an anti-establishment candidate, but maybe not the one everyone expected. For Democrats, the odds are still long for anti-establishment maverick Sanders, but even if Clinton wins the nomination, she has been forced to adopt much of the Sanders agenda in the process.

Week 378

(RIGGED)

April 17, 2016

A funny thing is happening to Donald Trump on his march to the Republican nomination. Even though he has won big in most of the major primaries to date (except for Texas and Wisconsin where Ted Cruz prevailed), Trump is not garnering delegate totals to match his popular vote tally. That is because winning primaries is only part of the game to obtain delegates. The other part involves knowing the rules of delegate selection, and participating and actively lobbying in the state by state delegate selection process. The Cruz campaign knows the rules thoroughly, is working the system, and is winning caucus states and outmaneuvering the Trump campaign at every turn. In response, rather than trying to match the sophistication and skill of the Cruz team, Donald Trump has instead launched an attack on the Republican Party, calling its nomination process rigged. It is not clear how attacking the party he hopes to lead is going to aid getting the GOP nomination, but that does not seem to matter much to Donald Trump.

The early signs that the Cruz campaign was beating Trump in delegate selection have come from small caucus states, where Cruz's organization has successfully gotten out its voters, leading to Cruz sweeping nearly all of the delegates in those states. Cruz has also mounted a sophisticated effort to win over delegates in larger states. For example in Colorado, Cruz managed to get his supporters named to the vast majority of delegate spots, even though Trump did well in that State's primary. That pattern continued this week, when Cruz captured 14 of 14 delegates up for grabs in the Wyoming state convention on Saturday, April 16, in addition to the 10 delegates he took in the caucus voting. Cruz left nothing to chance, travelling to Wyoming to ensure winning the delegate slate. Speaking to supporters, Cruz proclaimed: "If you don't want to see Donald Trump as the nominee, if you don't want to hand the general (election) to Hillary Clinton, which is what a Trump nomination does, then I ask you to please support the men and women on this slate."

Trump refused to go to Wyoming, and instead on April 16, he spoke to the press during stops in New York asserting that: "The system is rigged." Later, Trump went even so far as to say he knows the rules for getting delegates, but he refuses to follow them in protest over a corrupt system: "I don't want to waste millions of dollars going out to Wyoming many months before to wine and dine and to essentially pay off all these people because a lot of it's a pay-off . . . . You understand that, they treat 'em, they take 'em to dinner, they get 'em hotels. I mean the whole thing's a big pay-off, has nothing to do with democracy." Not surprisingly, Trump's team made little effort to win delegates at the Wyoming convention, sending only two out-of-town staffers. In contrast, the Cruz campaign had a full team present, a hospitality room, and stayed in touch with delegates by phone, email, and otherwise. The same story has played out in Georgia, where Cruz beat Trump in several congressional district conventions, even though Trump won the Georgia primary on Super Tuesday.

Donald Trump's decision to attack the Republican Party rather than fight Cruz for delegates seems to be the product of Trump's lack of discipline, bombast, and instinct to simply attack rather than strategize. Trump has threatened riots if he is not nominated and seems to believe he can bully and threaten his way to victory. That strategy might work in the New York real estate world, but it is far from clear it will work for nomination politics. At this stage in the nomination campaign, a frontrunner is usually trying to unify and rally the party whose support he hopes to win. As with so many other things, Trump again sees the world differently, and seems to believe that building consensus is akin to compromising and apologizing, things he simply will not do. So instead, he has declared war on the party he hopes to lead, and how that is going to help him beat Hillary Clinton and reverse the Obama legacy is anyone's guess.

Week 379

(NEW YORK...NEW YORK)

April 24, 2016

After the results in the Wisconsin primary, many started to wonder if the frontrunners in the nomination campaigns had finally been knocked off their roads to victory. Both Trump and Clinton suffered humiliating defeats in Wisconsin, but all along they had one thing working in their favor, New York. After Wisconsin, the next major primary that could make or break the campaigns for Trump and Clinton would be conveniently held in their mutual home state of New York. This offered both an opportunity and a challenge. A victory in New York would for each steady the ship and reassert their dominance. However, a loss might be fatal, because if they cannot win their home state, then each would be vulnerable in the primaries to come. So in many ways, the New York primary might decide the nomination fight in each party.

Both Trump and Clinton had huge advantages over their opponents in New York. Trump has been a celebrity in New York business, entertainment, and politics for more than two decades. His name recognition is unrivaled, as is his reputation, both good and bad. For Clinton, her roots are not nearly as deep, but her ties to the New York Democrat party are strong. She chose New York as her home state after leaving the White House, and she was elected senator in New York in her first political campaign. Likewise, Bill Clinton chose to headquarter the Clinton Foundation in Harlem, New York, creating further ties to the Empire State. Both Clintons actively fundraised for the New York Democrat Party, and both have campaigned aggressively for New York Democrats. So even though their association with New York has been brief, the Clintons' ties to the political establishment are very deep.

In view of all this, it is not surprising that as the nomination contest moved to New York, it was moving to favorable territory for both Trump and Clinton. For Trump, his advantage was not only his prominence in New York, but also the weakness of his opponents. Fighting Trump in New York was Ted Cruz, whose hard edged conservatism and his prior comments about "New York values," made New York very unfriendly territory. For John Kasich, while his politics might fit well with the New York GOP, few New Yorkers know him, making catching Trump very difficult. Surprisingly, it was Clinton was faced the harder challenge in New York. The Sanders campaign has connected with young voters and Sanders' liberal politics easily found a home in the New York Democrat party. Sanders devoted huge resources to New York, and his rallies drew massive crowds, large enough to make many Clinton operatives nervous.

Going into primary night, few doubted that Trump would win big, but for Clinton it was a far closer question. Once the votes were counted, it became clear that both Trump and Clinton won easily. Trump carried a massive 60% of the vote, with Kasich coming in second with only 25%. Despite his massive crowds, Sanders unperformed in New York, with Clinton winning 58% of the vote. So in the end, both Clinton and Trump dominated. Clinton's victory was a body blow to the Sanders campaign, and makes his ability to stop Clinton doubtful. Trump's victory likewise showed his strength, and the weakness of his opponents. So as election night closed, the Democrats appeared poised to nominate their preferred candidate, while the GOP was faced with the prospect of an unsavory yet unstoppable Trump juggernaut. No doubt President Obama looked at the results and smiled, because the potential matchup of Trump versus Clinton presents the prospect of a Democrat victory that will cement his legacy.

Week 380

(Stomping Grounds)

May 1, 2016

It is amazing to observe how the raucous nomination fights among both Democrats and Republicans have captured the complete attention of the media, almost to the exclusion of everything else. Last week, President Obama made an important trip to Saudi Arabia to try to rebuild ties with a key ally who believes the United States is now less committed to its security. The President landed to a low key reception Riyadh, where King Salman did not receive him, a not so subtle hint at his displeasure, and the tension continued throughout the visit. The trip was covered by the media, but only fleetingly, because Donald Trump and Bernie Sanders make much better copy. So the President's trip seemed forgotten almost as soon as it was over, and once again the media turned its focus to the campaign.

One of the reasons the New York primary was so important to those challenging the frontrunners is that the next series of contests favored them heavily, because they would take place in New England and the Mid-Atlantic. The April 26 primaries in Rhode Island, Connecticut, Pennsylvania, Maryland, and Delaware could give both Trump and Clinton the chance to cement their leads, making any effort to stop them almost impossible. As a result, after losing in New York, Bernie Sanders, Ted Cruz, and John Kasich were each desperate to find votes. In the end, on the GOP side, the effort was futile. Trump won Rhode Island, Connecticut, Pennsylvania, Maryland, and Delaware by massive margins of 63%, 57%, 56%, 54%, 61%, respectively. Kasich managed to finish second in most of the contests, but that made little difference, because Trump piled up so many delegates that the ability of his opponents to stop him before the convention now seems nil.

The story was much the same on the Democrat side. In the April 26 primaries, Sanders only managed a victory a Rhode Island, where he received 55% of the vote. Clinton prevailed in the other contests in Connecticut, Pennsylvania, Maryland, and Delaware, winning with 51%, 56%, 63%, and 60%, respectively. These victories helped Clinton build on her already massive delegate lead. However, Sanders gave no indication of any intention to drop out of the race. He proclaimed his determination to take the fight all the way to the convention, and still has the ability to force Clinton to rely on super delegates (Democrat party leaders and elected officials) to win the nomination. Now the campaign's focus starts to return to the West, possibly better terrain for Sanders, but, at best, he now has the ability only to annoy Clinton, not stop her.

With all this drama, it is not surprising that the media's attention has been consumed by the campaign. Congress appears to be unwilling or unable to accomplish much of anything, and while the President gives speeches, does foreign trips, and raises money, he no longer seems focused on trying to accomplish anything legislatively in his last few months in office. He continues to issue regulations and wade into the campaign from time to time, but he is now mostly a bystander. Instead, figures like Donald Trump and Bernie Sanders, with their outsider campaigns fueled by the same underlying anger and discontent at America's direction, dominate the conversation. President Obama seems resigned to this, likely because there is nothing he can do about it.

Week 381

(THE ALLIANCE)

May 8, 2016

After Donald Trump's romp through the Northeast and Mid-Atlantic primaries last week, anti-Trump forces are now desperate to try to stop the billionaire businessman from getting the Republican nomination. So desperate in fact that Senator Cruz and Governor John Kasich entered into a strange alliance, with Kasich agreeing not to campaign in the Indiana primary, a must-win for Cruz, and in return Cruz will support Kasich in later events. The deal is a sign of panic, and a sure indication that absent extraordinary measures, the Trump machine cannot be stopped. It was an interesting idea, but one that totally failed, because Trump proved as unstoppable in Indiana as he has been nearly everywhere else, and not long after the polls closed in Indiana, Trump was the last man standing.

One of the surprising twists in the GOP nomination fight is that it appears the Republicans will settle on their nominee before the Democrats will. It was assumed that Hillary Clinton would easily defeat her opponents and quickly wrap up the Democrat nomination. She has not, both because of her weakness and the tenacity of the Sanders campaign. While Clinton has a commanding lead in delegates and the support of nearly all of the super delegates, the Sanders side has all the energy and keeps winning primaries, most recently Indiana on May 3. Sanders took 53% of the vote against Clinton's 47%, giving new life to the Sanders forces and ensuring that the fight would continue. In fact, the Sanders campaign has been clear it intends to take its crusade all the way to the Democrat convention, in order to ensure that its priorities become part of the party's platform. So the fight goes on.

On the Republican side, it was assumed a bloody primary battle would continue all the way through the July convention in Cleveland, in view of the number of candidates and the divisions in the party. Those predictions did not anticipate the Trump phenomenon. Trump quickly dispatched most of the top-tier Republicans candidates, and as the campaign moved to Indiana, only Ted Cruz and John Kasich remained. Cruz and Kasich made their alliance, which started to fall apart almost as soon as it was announced. However, Trump won the Indiana primary with 53% of the vote, against Cruz's 37%. That same night after voting ended, Cruz suspended his campaign, and Kasich did the same the next day. So against all predictions the Republican nomination fight ended on May 4, and Donald Trump will be the Republican nominee. So the GOP fight has ended, while surprisingly the Democrats continue to battle on.

Although the primary campaign has ended on the GOP side, many Republican leaders remain very concerned about Trump. Conservatives dislike his policy positions, while GOP leaders fear his lack of discipline and unpredictability. In a press conference after the Indiana primary, Speaker Paul Ryan refused to immediately endorse Trump, prompting Trump to indicate that maybe Ryan should not chair the Republican convention. The media made the most of all of this. All the while, Hillary Clinton, President Obama, and the Democrat establishment could not hide their delight. Even though the primary fight continues on the Democrat side, the assumption is both that Hillary Clinton will get the nomination and that she can easily beat Trump. One must wonder if the Democrats are making the same mistake the Republicans did, namely underestimating Donald Trump. So all those smiles at the White House might be a bit premature.

Week 382

(Orders and Courts)

May 15, 2016

For an Administration that has all but given up on the idea of passing legislation, it is not surprising that so much of the key policy news in Obama's second term has come not from new laws, but instead from executive orders and court opinions. The President has had little success passing any important legislation in his second term, so has instead relied on the various powers of his office to advance his agenda. This has led to court fights and uncertainty, as more and more of his actions are challenged for their constitutionality, and often reversed. This trend was on full display this week, when yet another executive action by the President on Obamacare was overturned by a Federal Court, while the Administration simultaneously issued edicts and filed lawsuits to try to advance its gay and transgender rights policies, much to the consternation of thousands of school districts across the country.

Since the passage of the Obamacare legislation, many aspects of the law became unworkable. Typically, that would require the passage of additional legislation to fix the issues and provide clarity. When the GOP took control of the House in 2011, that became a practical impossibility. That, combined with the unpopularity of the law, has forced the Administration to rewrite many of the legislation's provisions by regulation or executive order. The most famous example being the delayed implementation of the individual and business mandates to provide insurance coverage, and the application of penalties to individuals for not doing so. However, the Administration has become so aggressive in rewriting the law that the House took the extraordinary step of filing a lawsuit to try to stop certain of the more egregious executive overreaches.

Most legal commentators said that the House did not have standing to sue the Administration and that the lawsuit was simply a political stunt. However, to date those predictions have proved inaccurate. The House's lawsuit is captioned the *United States House of Representatives vs. Burwell*, Burwell being the Secretary of Health and Human Services, and the case was assigned to Judge Rosemary Collyer, who was appointed by George W. Bush. The case is focused on subsidies provided under Obamacare, subsidies that the House asserts it never appropriated. On September 9, 2015, Judge Collyer ruled that the House did have standing to sue. Then on May 12, 2016, the court held that since Congress did not specifically appropriate money for the subsidies, public money cannot be used to fund the subsidies. The White House's response to the decision has been nothing short of apoplectic. It called the decision unprecedented, incorrect, and proclaimed it would be reversed on appeal. Nevertheless, the case again shows the ongoing risks of relying on aggressive use of executive power to pursue policy goals traditionally addressed by legislation.

However, while condemning the House lawsuit, the Administration continued to issue edicts and file lawsuits of its own, this time on the issue of transgender rights. North Carolina recently passed a now famous bathroom law providing that people need to use bathroom that matched the gender on their birth certificates. This has enraged gay rights advocates and prompted protests and boycotts. The White House has asserted that the North Carolina law is unconstitutional and threatened to file suit. North Carolina has not rescinded the law, so the Administration has now filed a lawsuit against North Carolina seeking to overturn the law. No doubt this legal battle will last for months before its outcome is decided.

However, the Administration was not willing to stop there. This week the Department of Education and the Department of Justice sent a letter to every school district in the nation threatening them with loss of federal funds if they failed to adopt policies that allow persons to use bathroom and locker room corresponding to their gender identity, regardless of the gender on their birth certificates. The legal grounds for this mandate is a particularly aggressive interpretation of Title IX that has never been endorsed by the courts. Regardless, the Administration issued its edicts both to make a political point and to force local school boards to address transgender rights or face the risk of lawsuits and loss of funds. This step represents a new phase in the President's use of his executive powers, one where he directly threatens local school boards to either agree with his agenda or face dire consequences. So increasingly we have government by litigation, with all the uncertainty and inconsistency that entails.

Week 383

(Egypt Air)

May 22, 2016

One thing political campaigns cannot account for are unforeseen world events that can change the trajectory of a race. That was clear in both 2008 with the financial collapse and in 2012 with Hurricane Sandy, both of which had a profound impact in the presidential campaigns those years, to the benefit of President Obama. Amid all the silly attacks and rhetoric of the current campaign, we were reminded that world events can change a race and expose the strength of certain candidates, and the weaknesses of others. We saw a first trace of this on May 19, when an Egypt Air flight went down in the Mediterranean. And while this event will not fundamentally change the 2016 presidential campaign, it provided clues on how events like this, if they occur in the Fall, could determine who takes the White House.

Egypt has had an infamous record when it comes to terrorist events. On October 31, 1999, Egypt Air co-pilot Gameel Al-Batouti proclaimed "I rely on God" eleven times in Arabic before he crashed his plane off the coast of Massachusetts. Then in October 2015, a bomb brought down a Russian Metrojet airliner over the Sinai Peninsula, killing 224 people and calling into question Egypt's security screening at its airports. These incidents made many question the Egyptian safety procedures. Then came the May 19Egypt Air Flight 804 from Paris to Cairo with 66 people on board. The plane went down south of Greece, with no distress call. Evidence found to date on the cause of the crash is unclear, but some fragments uncovered to date point to a bomb. Interestingly, no major terrorist group has to date claimed responsibility. The plane's black box and voice recorder will be the key to the investigation. However, Egyptian President Abel Fattah el-Sisi said: "This could take a long time but no one can hide these things. As soon as the results are out people will be informed."

It did not take long for the downing of Egypt Air Flight 804 to enter into the political debate in the United States. For her part, Hillary Clinton cautiously addressed the incident, emphasizing that the investigation into the cause was still underway. President Obama took a similar approach. However, Donald Trump's reaction was completely different. At a campaign event he proclaimed that "it was a bomb" and then proceeded to discuss the tough measures he would take against terrorists. In these reactions, we see the essence of each candidate's political instincts. Hillary Clinton is cautious and analytical, and is very careful about taking positions that could injure her later. Trump is the total opposite, and has elevated provocation and bold proclamations to an art form.

It is hard to tell which politician's approach will be the better one, and which would benefit most from incidents like this if they occur closer to the election. Clinton is betting that in a national or international crisis, Americans will gravitate to her as more experienced and thoughtful. Trump's instincts are very different. He plans to play on the fear Americans have of terrorists and show how strong he would be in dealing with them. He also plans to paint Clinton as weak and unwilling to adequately confront the threat. That is why he was so quick to assert that a bomb brought down Egypt Air Flight 804, when the evidence to support that assertion was clearly insufficient. In these responses, each candidate was playing to her or his strength, and each gave hints on how each might exploit the next crisis for political gain.

Week 384
(REPORTING)

May 29, 2016

It is very hard for President Obama to capture any headlines these days. The White House hoped that the President would make a powerful statement about nuclear disarmament with his May 27 trip to Hiroshima, where he gave an apology and wrote in the guest book: "We have known the agony of war. Let us now find the courage, together, to spread peace, and pursue a world without nuclear weapons." The trip was supposed to build on his commitment to reduce the nuclear threat. However, all of Washington was focused on a different nuclear event, namely Hillary Clinton's emails. While many Democrat strategists are positively giddy about the prospects of a presidential contest against Donald Trump in the Fall, in the background there has lurked a nagging concern, Hillary Clinton's emails. As is now well known, Hillary Clinton used a private email system run out of a private server set up in her home in New York. When this came to light, Clinton first tried to ignore the issue and then obfuscated, but the FBI has since mounted a major investigation into whether this email use compromised national security. Hillary Clinton has repeatedly claimed that her use of private email was allowed by the rules and that she was only doing what other former Secretaries of State had done. Well, those claims have now been thoroughly refuted, not by her political opponents, but by the Department of State Inspector General.

The Department of State Office of Inspector General headed by Steve Linick issued its report on May 26, 2016. The report noted that since 2005, the State Department has required that day-to-day operations by email should be conducted on government servers. The report also said that Clinton was required to clear her use of a private server, but there is "no evidence" she ever did so. The report also said that Clinton should have turned over all her emails before she left office, not 21 months later, as she did. The report further said that the only other Secretary of State who used private email was Colin Powell, at a time when government rules on email use were less strict, despite Clinton's claims that many of her predecessors had done so. Interestingly, Clinton and most her close aides declined to be interviewed for the inspector general's investigation.

It is not surprising that Clinton declined to be interviewed for the investigation, because the report refutes nearly all her claims about her email use. Clinton has repeatedly asserted that her use of private email was allowed by the State Department. For example, on September 7, 2015, Clinton said: "What I did was allowed by the State Department. It was fully above board." However, the report found that since 2007 State Department employees have been required to use government servers. The report also found that Clinton "had an obligation" to get clearance to use a private server, that there is no evidence that she did that, and that if she had sought permission, it would have been denied. Clinton has also asserted that she fully complied with her obligation to preserve her emails by copying other state department employees on those emails. For example, on March 10, Clinton said: "I fully complied with every rule I was governed by." However, the report found that Clinton's method of preserving emails did not comply with the Federal Records Act. Lastly, the report noted that hackers attempted to access Clinton's private server on January 9, 2011 and May 13, 2011, and found that Clinton should have reported those incidents, which she did not.

In almost every respect, the report gave support to critics who have taken aim at Hillary Clinton's email use. What the report did not address in detail is whether Clinton also broke federal law regarding classified materials through her use of a private email system. That is the issue currently being investigated by the FBI, which has deployed hundreds of employees and agents as part of the investigation. The combination of the report and the FBI investigation creates the prospect that Clinton could have broken not only State Department rules, but also federal law. As for the timing, it could hardly be worse for Clinton, because these revelations are being made public dangerously close to the election.

Given all this, Democrats might have started laughing a bit early about the candidate the GOP has nominated. Donald Trump has some deep flaws as a presidential nominee, but he has the advantage that most of those flaws are already known and none appear to be potentially criminal. In contrast, Hillary Clinton is currently at the mercy of the FBI investigation, and there remains at least a chance that she may have broken the law. Clinton is already disliked and distrusted, and the email controversy only reinforces the view that she is secretive and untrustworthy. Maybe that is why Bernie Sanders continues to refuse to drop out of the race for the Democrat nomination, and why so many Democrats remain nervous about their nominee.

Week 385

(THE ENDORSEMENT)

June 5, 2016

Both the Democrats and the Republicans have a unity problem these days. For the Democrats, the persistent strength of Bernie Sanders and his unwillingness to end his fight for the nomination, along with Clinton's continuing weakness in the polls, is causing consternation. With Sanders determined to take his fight to the nomination, the Democrats face the prospect of a contested convention, exactly what they thought only the Republicans would face. The upcoming June 6 California primary might change things if Clinton wins convincingly, or if President Obama intervenes and convinces Sanders to drop out, but otherwise it appears unity is some way off for the Democrats.

The story is different on the Republican side, but the same unity issues prevail. The GOP has picked its nominee, Donald Trump, who won the nomination fight easily. However, the Republican establishment and conservatives seem unwilling to accept this reality, and even though it is clear Trump will be the party's nominee, many are still talking about supporting a third party candidate or refusing to endorse Trump until he convinces them that he will be disciplined, less divisive, and would govern as a conservative.

This concern came into full light when Speaker Paul Ryan withheld an endorsement soon after Trump won the nomination. Speaker Ryan said he needed to talk with Trump first, which the press did its utmost to portray as a major split within the Republican Party. Since then, Trump has taken some modest steps to reassure the GOP establishment and conservatives, including leadership meetings in Washington and creating a better campaign organization. While some Republican leaders are still refusing to endorse Trump, many are now reconciled to him, as Speaker Ryan showed this week.

Paul Ryan is undoubtedly the most senior and most respected Republican leader, and a person who has effectively bridged the gap between the establishment and the Tea Party. So when he finally endorsed Trump on June 2, he was telling the party to move to acceptance and join forces to defeat the Democrats. The endorsement came by way of a guest column in Wisconsin's *Janesville Gazette* newspaper where Ryan praised Trump as someone who could further the conservative agenda. Ryan wrote: "It's a question of how to move ahead on the ideas that I—and my House colleagues—have invested so much in through the years. It's not just a choice of two people, but of two visions for America." Ryan then detailed Trump policy agenda calling it both bold and conservative, and saying that for the conservative agenda "Donald Trump can help us make it a reality."

This endorsement came a few weeks after an in-person meeting between Ryan and Trump in Washington in May and many subsequent phone conversations. It was also no doubt inspired by polls showing Trump running surprisingly close to Clinton both nationally and in battleground state polls. Many GOP strategists are starting to see an avenue for Trump to be competitive in the Fall, which is prompting many Republicans to consider rallying to Trump. Trump has also taken steps to normalize his campaign, including bringing in respected GOP operatives and setting up a fundraising apparatus. It appears many in the Republican Party are now reconciled to Trump, and see at least a chance of victory, provided that he curbs some of his more outrageous conduct.

That is why the Paul Ryan endorsement is so important for Trump and the GOP. It is a clear sign from the party's leader that the time has come to move on, respect the voters' choice, and unify in an effort to stop Hillary Clinton. Nearly all Republicans see Trump as an imperfect vehicle for that effort, but he is the voters' choice, so they have to live and work with him. That was clearly Speaker Ryan's conclusion, and likely many other Republican leaders will follow suit. As for Trump, the question is, after winning the nomination in an unconventional way, can he change his approach and broaden his appeal for the general election. To win he needs to, but is it far from clear that he will, which might make some Republicans regret any endorsement, but truly what other choice do they have.

Week 386

(HISPANIC)

June 12, 2016

For months the media has been focused on the accusation that there is some underlying racism fueling the Trump campaign. Trump's calls for building a wall along the Mexican border and for a ban on Muslim immigration have given some credence to these claims, as has the fact that Trump draws most of his strength from the less educated and older white population. This has led many to see the Trump campaign as a last gasp of the angry white voters who are facing demographic changes that will soon end their ability to dominate American politics. For Trump to have any chance of victory, he needs to build support beyond this voter base, and many Republicans had hoped that once the nominee, he would start outreach efforts and try to build a more disciplined and conventional campaign. Trump had a window to do that after he captured the nomination, and many Republicans hoped he would. But true to form, Trump does as he wishes regardless of consequences, so just when he should have been broadening his support, he narrowed it, with what many see as a racist attack on a federal judge.

Trump is currently facing a lawsuit over Trump University, a for profit business education school he sponsored and which many have claimed was a scam. Trump University has been the focus of numerous campaign attacks against Trump, and will surely figure into the Clinton campaign's strategy. Despite this, rather than try to defuse the issue, Donald Trump decided to throw fire on it by launching an attack on the ethnicity of the federal judge who is presiding over the lawsuit. That judge is Gonzalo Curiel, who sits on the United States District Court for the Southern District of California. Judge Curiel is of Mexican descent and in an interview with the Wall Street Journal Trump he said that Curiel could not be a fair judge in his case because of his heritage, which gave him an inherent conflict of interest. Immediately after this comment, Trump was accused of racism. When questioned about the comment on CNN, Trump refused to back down, stating that the judge has made "rulings that people can't even believe. . . .He's proud of his heritage. I respect him for that. . . . He's a Mexican. We're building a wall between here and Mexico." Then CNN's Jake Tapper asked Trump if he is saying he cannot do his job because of his race, is that not racism. Trump responded: "No, I don't think so at all." Trump's attack on Judge Curiel came shortly after the judge ordered the release of documents relating to Trump University in response to a request from the Washington Post.

Trump's comments presented an opportunity that the Clinton campaign quickly pounced upon, accusing Trump of lacking the temperament needed for the high office he seeks. Clinton also asserted that Trump has "thin skin." In response, Trump proclaimed: "I don't have thin skin. I have very strong and very thick skin . . . . I have a strong temperament. It's a very good temperament and it's a very in-control temperament, or I wouldn't have built this unbelievable company. I wouldn't have built all of the things I've been able to do in life." True to form, with this controversy as with so many prior ones, Trump has refused to back down, even when many Republicans were as disturbed by the comments as Democrats.

This most recent episode has made one thing clear, Trump has no intention of changing his style, taking advice, or moderating his tone or attacks. Trump has achieved his business success by being aggressive and combative. So far, he has won the GOP nomination by being the same way. He believes he can win the White House with the same approach. So expect to see more of the same until election day. Ironically, what Trump wants to do is exactly what President Obama and the Democrats want as well. They want a combative, offensive, undisciplined Trump campaign, and he is going to give them exactly that.

Week 387
(ORLANDO)

June 19, 2016

This week was an example of how unexpected events can change the tenor of a political campaign. Just as the political class was fixated on Donald Trump's comments about whether a Mexican judge could be fair to him in the lawsuit over Trump University, a serious and truly shocking terrorist attack struck again within the United States. At 2:00 a.m. at an Orlando gay night club, Omar Mateen, claiming loyalty to ISIS, launched a deadly lone shooter attack that killed 49 people. The attack shocked the entire country, from average citizens to the President and those vying for his job. Not only was the attack vicious, but so was the political rhetoric that followed, making a scared nation appear even more divided.

The details of the attack are disturbing because they show how easily a lone gunman can cause massive carnage. Pulse is a gay nightclub in Orlando and on June 12, it was hosting a latin night. There were about 320 people in the club at 2:00 a.m. just before last call. Omar Mateen was a 29-year-old American born in New Hyde Park, New York. His parents are Afghan and he was raised as a Muslim. Mateen had been at the club before, either for surveillance or because he was a patron. When he arrived during last call, he was armed with a Glock 17 handgun and a SIG Sauer MCX semi-automatic. As he entered the club, he was seen by a police officer and gunfire was exchanged, but Mateen managed to enter the club. Once inside the club, Mateen immediately began shooting. The club was very dark and the music was loud, so many patrons did not immediately realize that there was a shooter. Once that reality set in, there was panic, and all the while Mateen kept firing. Mateen entered a bathroom where people were hiding and opened fire. It appears that Mateen's rifle then jammed, so he took hostages. Mateen reportedly said: "I don't have a problem with black people" and that he "wouldn't stop his assault until America stopped bombing his country." During the attack. Mateen made a 911 call and associated himself with the Boston Marathon bombers and claimed allegiance to ISIS. Then at 2:45, he called New 13 of Orlando and said "I am the shooter" and then claimed the attack for ISIS. By this time, a large number of police had arrived at the club, but Mateen claimed to have hostages, and it was believed he might have an explosive device, so a standoff ensued. Just before 5:00 a.m., the police used an armored vehicle to drive through a wall and enter the club, and after a gunfight, Mateen was killed. Thirty hostages were freed, while one officer received minor injuries. Forty-nine people were killed, and some 53 injured, making it the deadliest mass shooting in United States history.

In the days after the shooting, it was revealed that Mateen had been on the FBI's watch list and that he had posted statements on social media supportive of ISIS on the day of the attack. Since 2007, Mateen had worked as a security guard, and supposedly passed psychological exams in 2007 and 2013 to purchase and possess firearms. Co-workers stated that he often made threats to shoot people. At the time of the shooting, he was married to his second wife, Noor Zahi Salman, and had a young son.

It did not take long for political leaders to respond to the attack. President Obama gave an address on the afternoon of June 12, calling the attack "an act or hate" and an "act of terror." The President also renewed his call for more gun control, leading to a filibuster in the Senate later in the week on that issue. For his part, Donald Trump used the attack to accuse the Obama Administration of being soft on terror and claiming that the President was more interested in attacking him than terrorists: "We've tried it President Obama's way — doesn't work. He gave the world his apology tour, we got ISIS, and many other problems, in return." So as the nation mourned, our political leaders quickly started their internecine warfare. Trump hopes this attack will help him because of his tough stance on terrorism, but it has already helped him in one respect, no one is currently talking about Trump University.

Week 388

(BREXIT)

June 26, 2016

With the nation still reeling from the attack in Orlando and the growing realization of the threat of Islamic terrorism within the United States, the country quickly had to grapple with another foreign threat, this one of the economic and geopolitical variety. Since the end World War II, America's ties with Western Europe, both military and economic, have been the cornerstone of our international strategy. Even with the rise of China and America's increasing focus on the Pacific, the European powers and the European Union remain the United States' most steadfast allies. So when Europe faces instability, like the recent Greek debt crisis and the Russian invasion of Ukraine, the impact is felt in America. This week's referendum in the United Kingdom on whether to stay in the European Union was another opportunity for events in Europe to shake confidence here in the United States. That is exactly what happened this week, when the United Kingdom voted to leave the European Union, posing a threat to the very foundation of post-war European stability.

The European Union is one of the primary reasons Europe is living through its longest period of peace and prosperity in history. What started as a basic economic treaty between Germany, France, and the low countries has over 60 years grown into a common currency, a European central bank, open borders, and a single economic zone. The European Union has become the vessel for the dream of one United Europe. For all the successes of the European Union, there have also been many shortcomings. The effort to integrate less developed economies like Greece into the European Union led to a debt crisis that has almost destroyed the union. Also, the increasing power and mandates of the unelected bureaucrats in Brussels have spawned a backlash across Europe, with movements rising in many nations to leave the union. Many believe one major defection could destabilize all of Europe, which is why the referendum in the United Kingdom was so critical.

The United Kingdom has always been an uncomfortable member of the European Union. Its traditional policy has been to avoid permanent alliances on the continent, which is why the

United Kingdom did not originally join the union. When the nation faced a severe economic crisis in the late 1960's, it decided to apply for membership, only to be vetoed by France. The United Kingdom was only admitted in 1973, and once in, it still hesitated to fully commit to the European project. For example, the United Kingdom opted not to join the common currency. Within the British Conservative Party, there has always been an anti-European Union faction, and when David Cameron ran his last election campaign, he had to promise a referendum on leaving the European Union to win their support. That referendum took place on June 23, and its outcome cost David Cameron his premiership.

Under Article 50 of the Treaty on European Union adopted in 2007, any member nation has a right to leave the union. That very question was put to the voters in the United Kingdom in the recent referendum, which became known as Brexit, short for British Exit. The vote was a repeat of a referendum held in 1975, when voters by a margin of 67% to 33% opted to stay in what was then called the European Economic Community. The outcome was different this time. The leave campaign was led by Conservative politician Boris Johnson, the former mayor of London. The leaders of the Conservative, Labor, and Liberal Democrats all campaigned to stay. When the votes came in, 52% voted to leave, and 48% to stay. The impact was immediate. Stock markets across the world crashed, Prime Minister Cameron resigned, Scotland said it would again vote for independence, and other foes of the European Union called for referenda in many other member states. The whole European project was called into question.

In the United States, the reaction was restrained, except for the response of Donald Trump. President Obama made clear his preference that the United Kingdom stay in the European Union, and showed great but measured disappointment in the result. Hillary Clinton likewise struck a cautious tone on the result. In sharp contrast, Donald Trump made clear from the beginning that he thought the United Kingdom should leave the European Union, and he celebrated the outcome as though he was a direct beneficiary. It is possible Trump thinks the same waive of nativism and discontent the carried the leave campaign to victory will fuel his success in winning the White House. Many other entrenched politicians now have the same fear, and now all of Europe is now wondering what its future will be.

Week 389

(MEET AND GREET)

July 3, 2016

There is no longer any mystery on the match up for the 2016 presidential contest. Even though many in each party are far from happy about their respective nominees, Hillary Clinton and Donald Trump will face each other in the Fall. Now most of the suspense in the campaign is coming not from the nomination fight, but from the almost daily gaffs from Trump and the daily leaks from the investigation into Hillary Clinton's use of a private email server while serving as Secretary of State. Trump's gaffs have to date been the primary focus, but this week that changed because of a suspicious meeting on an airport tarmac in Phoenix between Bill Clinton and Attorney General Loretta Lynch.

On June 27, Bill Clinton and Loretta Lynch were both in Phoenix for unrelated events. As Bill Clinton was getting ready to depart from Phoenix, Lynch was arriving for a community policing event. As the husband of the Democrat nominee for President, Bill Clinton has every interest in getting his wife elected, and part of that calculus is avoiding an indictment relating to Hillary Clinton's use of email while Secretary of State. For her part, Loretta Lynch is President Obama's Attorney General, and as such she oversees the FBI's investigation of Hillary Clinton and she would make the ultimate decision whether to pursue an indictment. Bill Clinton would have an interest in trying to positively influence the Attorney General, and the Attorney General would have every reason to try to avoid any appearance of bias. Given this, it is no surprise that a political firestorm broke out when the press reported that Bill Clinton met privately with Attorney General Lynch on her private jet as it was parked at Sky Harbor Airport.

Republicans immediately jumped to the conclusion that Bill Clinton was trying to influence Lynch's decisions relating to the Hillary Clinton investigation. Since no media was present for the visit, no one will ever know what was discussed, but theories abound. Lynch was immediately subject to withering criticism, with some even calling for her resignation. When pressed for comment, Lynch acknowledged the meeting, but claimed there was no discussion of the investigation into Hillary Clinton or the congressional report that examined the Benghazi attack. Instead Lynch stated: "I did see President Clinton at the Phoenix airport as I was leaving, and he spoke to myself and my husband on the plane . . . . Our conversation was a great deal about his grandchildren. It was primarily social and about our travels . . . . There was no discussion of Benghazi, no discussion of the State Department emails, by way of example." On the issue of whether the meeting created an appearance of impropriety, Lynch said the investigation is "being handled by career investigators and career agents who always follow facts and the law and do the same thorough and independent examination in this matter that they've done.'"

Donald Trump's response to the meeting was immediate and critical. On the Michael Gallagher radio show Trump said: "It is an amazing thing . . . . They actually went on to the plane as I understand it. That's terrible. And it was really a sneak. It was really something that they didn't want publicized as I understand it ... I think it's so horrible." Due to the uproar, Lynch was forced to later state that she would take herself out of the decision making process for the investigation and that she would rely solely on the FBI's recommendation. However, the damage had been done and if no charges are brought the meeting will give fodder to those who assert that the Justice Department would never pursue charges against Hillary Clinton because of her status as leader of the Democrats. In one respect the meeting should be worrisome for Hillary Clinton, because one part of her campaign is clearly outside of her control, namely her husband, and Bill Clinton should have known better than have a private meeting with the Attorney General, which is exactly why so many people are suspicious about it.

Week 390
(THE SHOOTER)

July 10, 2016

The Black Lives Matter movement and the issue of police treatment of African Americans has remained a point of deep discord in American society. Each time the police shoot a black person under questionable circumstances, it fuels a reaction. Until now, those reactions have been confined to protests, and occasional riots and looting. All that changed on July 7, when apparently in reaction to shootings of black men in Minneapolis and Baton Rouge, Micah Xavier Johnson used the occasion of a Black Lives Matters protest in Dallas to attack police. When the killing finally ended, five police officers were dead and eight injured, along with two bystanders. The attack left the nation in shock and confronted President Obama and other leaders with the challenge of how to respond.

Dallas was an odd location for this mass shooting event, in that the Dallas police department has a good record of working with the black community and none of the controversial shootings to date have happened in Dallas. That did not seem to matter to the shooter, who appears to have been motivated to strike back at police, even if his victims themselves had done no wrong. The occasion for the attack was a Black Lives Matter protest organized by a group called Next Generation Action, one of several held across the nation on July 7. Approximately 800 protesters participated peacefully. At 8:58 p.m., as the protest was ending, Johnson, a veteran who served in Afghanistan, starting shooting from elevated positions with a semi-automatic rifle with a high capacity magazine. The police had trouble finding Johnson and scrambled to block intersections. It appears Johnson may have fired indiscriminately to draw officers to certain locations so he could take aim at them. It was reported that Johnson also got behind one officer and shot him multiple times from point blank range. As officers closed in on Johnson, he was hit and fled to a parking garage. Then there was a standoff between Johnson and officers. During negotiations Johnson said he had acted alone and said he would only speak with black police officers. When negotiations failed, at 2:30 a.m. the police sent in a remote control vehicle carrying explosives, which killed Johnson. In the end, five officers died and eight were wounded.

From his history, there was little indication that Johnson would launch this type of attack. He was 25 years old and from Mesquite, Texas, was one of four siblings of divorced parents, and he served in the U.S. Army Reserves, and was deployed to Afghanistan from September 2013 to April 2015. Dallas Police Chief Brown said that during negotiations, Brown "stated he wanted to kill white people, especially white officers." Former co-workers said he was distrustful of police. The fact that there was so little prior indication that Johnson would launch such an attack made the attack even more disturbing. Politicians from across the spectrum tried to calm the nation. Texas Governor Greg Abbott commented: "In times like this we must remember—and emphasize—the importance of uniting as Americans." For his part, President Obama said the attack was a "vicious, calculated, despicable attack" and a 'tremendous tragedy." The President also immediately called again for gun control. Leaders of the Black Lives Matter also condemned the attack.

For President Obama, the attack in Dallas was a reminder that the threat of mass shootings is not coming just from radicalized Muslims, like that ones who pursued the attacks in San Bernardino and Orlando. In many ways, the Dallas attack is even more problematic for the President than the other recent shootings because the motive of the shooter was intertwined with the complex issue of race relations in America. There is a great disconnect between blacks and whites when it comes to the police, and each side has trouble understanding the other's perspective. For the President, this disconnect is dangerous, because any statement he might make in support of one side, could quickly enrage the other. So the President is forced to condemn aggressive police and mass killers like Johnson, but that is hardly a satisfactory response to this type of event. Maybe that is why President Obama always returns to gun control, but doing so is a mere rhetorical exercise, since he has no ability to persuade Congress to lend support. So we have a President largely paralyzed in the face of this violence, with no easy solution to be found.

Week 391

(LAW AND ORDER)

July 17, 2016

With the nation still reeling from the attack in Dallas, political leaders were scrambling to try to find a way to calm the public and prevent further violence. For his part, President Obama travelled to Dallas to praise the fallen officers and speak for peace and reconciliation. At a memorial service on July 12, he was joined by former President George W. Bush in an effort to show unity. However, not all political leaders were focused on restoring calm. The Trump campaign saw in the shootings in Dallas something more, namely a chance to change the focus of the upcoming campaign and to play on the fear and concern growing among the public. With Dallas as the backdrop, the Trump campaign's new theme is law and order.

Throughout his campaign, Trump has railed against growing violence in the inner cities. He has done this in part to play upon the fears of voters. He has also focused on crime to support his immigration positions, implying that illegal immigrants are behind a crime wave. Crime statistics do not support that assertion, but Trump has espoused it nevertheless, and used it as further grounds for his call for a wall between the United States and Mexico. The growing violence against the police fits easily with this narrative, and if anything strengthens it. The Trump campaign has realized this, and now hopes to capitalize on it.

Their first target unsurprisingly was Hillary Clinton, whom they ridicule as weak and a lawbreaker herself. Many Democrats were concerned about this line of attack, especially in view of the FBI's investigation of Clinton's use of a private server for classified emails. When FBI Director James Comey announced on July 5 that Clinton had been "extremely careless" in her use of emails but that "no reasonable prosecutor" would bring charges against her, Democrats were relieved. However, the public reaction to the decision has been very different, with a majority of voters criticizing the decision and Clinton's marks for honesty and integrity are now falling even further. This has even translated into a rise in the polls for Trump, who is now within striking distance of Clinton in many surveys. So far from being strengthened by the FBI's decision, in many ways Clinton now seems weaker.

Trump's law and order themes were further aided by the Nice attacks. On July 14, a Muslim drove a truck through a crowd during a Bastille Day celebration in France, killing more than 80 people. This newest high profile terrorist attack provided a perfect opportunity from Trump to again claim the mantle as the law and order candidate. He used the attack to criticize the policies of President Obama and Hillary Clinton, and he delayed his vice presidential announcement to show concern. On July 16, he then announced in a Manhattan ballroom that Indiana Governor Mike Pence was his choice, and in a 28-minute introduction of Pence, which was really more of a replay of his campaign stump speech, he proclaimed that his was the "law and order" ticket. Pence, a well-respected, conservative Christian with ample Washington experience, was chosen to try to unify the party and win over conservatives. In making this choice, Trump was protecting his flank. His true focus is not winning over conservatives, but instead a frontal attack on Hillary Clinton, using the public's fear and unease to convince voters that only he can restore order and ensure safety. So now we are going to have a law and order campaign pursued by someone who is likely the most unpredictable, undisciplined, and aggressive candidate we have ever seen. No doubt, this is going to get ugly.

Week 392
(THE NOMINEE)

July 24, 2016

It was the event most feared by the Republican establishment and most welcomed by the Democrat party: the Republican Convention in Cleveland where Donald J. Trump would be nominated by the GOP for President of the United States. Both view him as a fatally flawed candidate who will lose is Hillary Clinton. This view was reinforced as the convention started, with the stop Trump forces trying to change convention rules to prevent his nomination and Melania Trump plagiarizing from Michele Obama's 2008 convention speech. This discord and confusion reinforced the view that Trump is too undisciplined to run a successful presidential campaign. With all this as prelude, Trump's acceptance speech on July 21 became ever more important.

A nominee's acceptance speech is a critical opportunity to introduce himself to the voters. Trump had the option to use this speech to soften his image. However, Trump instead even more aggressively trumpeted his agenda, and in doing so, positioned himself as the defender of ordinary Americans being hurt by a rigged system that Hillary Clinton seeks to maintain. Trump started his speech by promising: "Together, we will lead our party back to the White House, and we will lead our country back to safety, prosperity, and peace. We will be a country of generosity and warmth. But we will also be a country of law and order." He then described the current state of America:

> Our convention occurs at a moment of crisis for our nation. The attacks on our police, and the terrorism our cities, threaten our very way of life. Any politician who does not grasp this danger is not fit to lead our country. . . . It is finally time for a straightforward assessment of the state of our nation. I will present the facts plainly and honestly. . . .We cannot afford to be so politically correct anymore. So if you want to hear the corporate spin, the carefully-crafted lies, and the media myths, the Democrats are holding their convention next week, go there. . . . But here, at our convention, there will be no lies. We will honor the American people with the truth, and nothing else.

Trump then detailed the problems facing the United States:

> These are the facts: Decades of progress made in bringing down crime are now being reversed by this Administration's rollback of criminal enforcement. Homicides last year increased by 17 percent in America's fifty largest cities. That's the largest increase in 25 years. . . . What about our economy? Again, I will tell you the plain facts that have been edited out of your nightly news and your morning newspaper: Nearly four in 10 African-American children are living in poverty, while 58 percent of African-American youth are not employed. Two million more Latinos are in poverty today than when the President Obama took his oath of office less than eight years ago. Another 14 million people have left the workforce entirely. Household incomes are down more than $4,000 since the year 2000, that's 16 years ago. . . . The budget is no better. President Obama has almost doubled our national debt to more than $19 trillion, and growing. And yet, what do we have to show for it? Our roads and bridges are falling apart, our airports are Third World condition, and forty-three million Americans are on food stamps . . . . Not only have our citizens endured domestic disaster, but they have lived through one international humiliation after another.

Then Trump squarely assessed the blame: "This is the legacy of Hillary Clinton: death, destruction, terrorism and weakness." Trump then outlined his plan for America:

> Tonight, I will share with you my plan of action for America. The most important difference between our plan and that of our opponent, is that our plan will put America first. Americanism, not globalism, will be our credo. As long as we are led by politicians who will not put America first, then we can be assured that other nations will not treat America with respect the respect that we deserve. . . . The American people will come first once again. My plan will begin with safety at home – which means safe neighborhoods, secure borders, and protection from terrorism. There can be no prosperity without law and order. On the economy, I will outline reforms to add millions of new jobs and trillions in new wealth that can be used to rebuild America.

Trump then cast Clinton as the defender of the status quo and made a direct play for Bernie Sanders' supporters:

> Big business, elite media and major donors are lining up behind the campaign of my opponent because they know she will keep our rigged system in place. They are throwing money at her because they have total control over everything she does. She is their puppet, and they pull the strings. . . . And when a Secretary of State illegally stores her emails on a private server, deletes 33,000 of them so the authorities can't see her crime, puts our country at risk, lies about it in every different form and faces no consequence – I know that corruption has reached a level like never ever before in our country. . . . I have seen firsthand how the system is rigged against our citizens, just like it was rigged against Bernie Sanders – he never had a chance.

Although Trump clearly wanted to use his speech to win over Bernie Sanders supporters and portray himself as an agent for change, he refused to back off his more controversial positions. He maintained his call to suspend immigration from any nation "compromised by terrorism." He promised again to build a wall on the Mexican border. He further stated that he would scrap and renegotiate the nation's current trade deals, most of which were supported by the GOP. Trump did make a play for conservatives by promising to cut taxes, reduce regulations, and nominate conservatives to the Supreme Court, but his speech was focused more on appealing to the disaffected than the party faithful. Then he gave his final pledge:

> I have had a truly great life in business, but now my sole and exclusive mission is to go to work for our country, to go to work for you. It's time to deliver a victory for the American people. We don't win anymore, but we are going to start winning again. But to do that, we must break free from the petty politics of the past. . . . To all Americans tonight in all of our cities and in all of our towns, I make this promise — we will make America strong again. We will make America proud again. We will make America safe again. And we will make America great again.

The effectiveness of the speech will be measured in the days and weeks to come, but one thing is clear, Trump does not plan to back off his positions or his style. Many pundits think that will be fatal, but those are the same pundits who said he would not win the nomination in the first place.

Week 393

(HILLARY)

July 31, 2016

When the Democrats gathered in Philadelphia for their national convention, they were more than a little nervous. Despite the chaos and conflict at the Republican convention in Cleveland, Donald Trump gave a forceful acceptance speech and appeared to emerge as a strong foe for the general election. For Democrats, the goal was to unite the party, reintroduce Hillary Clinton to the American people, and take the fight to Trump. That process began with Bernie Sanders endorsement of Hillary Clinton on Monday, Bill Clinton's masterful speech in support of his wife on Tuesday. Then came the main events, President Obama's speech on Wednesday night and Hillary Clinton's acceptance speech on Thursday to cap the convention. For Obama, the goal was to protect his legacy. For Clinton, the objective was to win the trust of her party and the voters.

As the incumbent, President Obama had to walk the tightrope of proclaiming his successes while portraying Clinton as an agent for change. The President started by outlining his achievements and his disagreements with Trump's vision of America:

> A lot's happened over the years. And while this nation has been tested by war and recession and all manner of challenge–I stand before you again tonight, after almost two terms as your President, to tell you I am even more optimistic about the future of America.

After the worst recession in 80 years, we've fought our way back. We've seen deficits come down, 401(k)s recover, an auto industry set new records, unemployment reach eight-year lows, and our businesses create 15 million new jobs.

After a century of trying, we declared that health care in America is not a privilege for a few, but a right for everybody. After decades of talk, we finally began to wean ourselves off foreign oil, and doubled our production of clean energy.

We brought more of our troops home to their families, and delivered justice to Osama bin Laden. Through diplomacy, we shut down Iran's nuclear weapons program, opened up a new chapter with the people of Cuba, and brought nearly 200 nations together around a climate agreement that could save this planet for our kids.

We put policies in place to help students with loans; protect consumers from fraud; and cut veteran homelessness almost in half. And through countless acts of quiet courage, America learned that love has no limits, and marriage equality is now a reality across the land.

After outlining his successes, he laid out his vision for what still needs to be done:

So tonight, I'm here to tell you that yes, we still have more work to do. More work to do for every American still in need of a good job or a raise, paid leave or a decent retirement; for every child who needs a sturdier ladder out of poverty or a world-class education; for everyone who hasn't yet felt the progress of these past seven and a half years. We need to keep making our streets safer and our criminal justice system fairer; our homeland more secure, and our world more peaceful and sustainable for the next generation. We're not done perfecting our union, or living up to our founding creed–that all of us are created equal and free in the eyes of God.

Then came the time to attack Donald Trump, which President Obama did directly and brutally:

But what we heard in Cleveland last week wasn't particularly Republican–and it sure wasn't conservative. What we heard was a deeply pessimistic vision of a country where we turn against each other, and turn away from the rest of the world. There were no serious solutions to pressing problems–just the fanning of resentment, and blame, and anger, and hate. And that is not the America I know.

Then the President made a plea for unity and rejection of the Trump agenda:

Most of all, I see Americans of every party, every background, every faith who believe that we are stronger together–black, white, Latino, Asian, Native American; young and old; gay, straight, men, women, folks with disabilities, all pledging allegiance, under the same proud flag, to this big, bold country that we love.

Andrew P. Zappia

That's the America I know. And there is only one candidate in this race who believes in that future, and has devoted her life to it; a mother and grandmother who'd do anything to help our children thrive; a leader with real plans to break down barriers, blast through glass ceilings, and widen the circle of opportunity to every single American–the next President of the United States, Hillary Clinton.

As for Trump and his view of America, the President did not hesitate to show his utter contempt for the man and his agenda:

And then there's Donald Trump. He's not really a plans guy. Not really a facts guy, either. He calls himself a business guy, which is true, but I have to say, I know plenty of businessmen and women who've achieved success without leaving a trail of lawsuits, and unpaid workers, and people feeling like they got cheated.

America is already great. America is already strong. And I promise you, our strength, our greatness, does not depend on Donald Trump.

In fact, it doesn't depend on any one person. And that, in the end, may be the biggest difference in this election–the meaning of our democracy.

Ronald Reagan called America "a shining city on a hill." Donald Trump calls it "a divided crime scene" that only he can fix. It doesn't matter to him that illegal immigration and the crime rate are as low as they've been in decades, because he's not offering any real solutions to those issues. He's just offering slogans, and he's offering fear. He's betting that if he scares enough people, he might score just enough votes to win this election.

Finally, the President closed with a strong endorsement of Hillary Clinton and a call to reject the politics of Trump:

So if you agree that there's too much inequality in our economy, and too much money in our politics, we all need to be as vocal and as organized and as persistent as Bernie Sanders' supporters have been. We all need to get out and vote for Democrats up and down the ticket, and then hold them accountable until they get the job done.

That's America. Those bonds of affection; that common creed. We don't fear the future; we shape it, embrace it, as one people, stronger together than we are on our own. That's what Hillary Clinton understands–this fighter, this stateswoman, this mother and grandmother, this public servant, this patriot – that's the America she's fighting for.

President Obama set the bar high for Hillary Clinton, but he also nicely set the table for her. In her acceptance speech, Clinton tried to both humanize herself and lay out why Donald Trump is not an acceptable option for President. Clinton started her address with a call for unity, to try to contrast herself with the divisive rhetoric of Donald Trump:

> We have to decide whether we all will work together so we all can rise together. Our country's motto is e pluribus unum: out of many, we are one. Will we stay true to that motto? Well, we heard Donald Trump's answer last week at his convention. He wants to divide us–from the rest of the world, and from each other. He's betting that the perils of today's world will blind us to its unlimited promise. He's taken the Republican Party a long way ... from "Morning in America" to "Midnight in America." He wants us to fear the future and fear each other.

She then called for Americans to be optimistic in the face of today's perils:

> Well, a great Democratic President, Franklin Delano Roosevelt, came up with the perfect rebuke to Trump more than eighty years ago, during a much more perilous time: "The only thing we have to fear is fear itself." Now we are clear-eyed about what our country is up against. But we are not afraid. We will rise to the challenge, just as we always have.

Hillary Clinton then laid out her agenda as a direct contrast to the policy positions of Donald Trump:

> We will not build a wall. Instead, we will build an economy where everyone who wants a good paying job can get one. And we'll build a path to citizenship for millions of immigrants who are already contributing to our economy! We will not ban a religion. We will work with all Americans and our allies to fight terrorism.

As for Trump's assertion that America has become weak and lost her greatness, and that only Trump can restore America, Clinton responded:

> So don't let anyone tell you that our country is weak. We're not. Don't let anyone tell you we don't have what it takes. We do. And most of all, don't believe anyone who says: "I alone can fix it." Those were actually Donald Trump's words in Cleveland. And they should set off alarm bells for all of us. Really? I alone can fix it? Isn't he forgetting? Troops on the front lines. Police officers and firefighters who run toward danger. Doctors and nurses who care for us. Teachers who change lives. Entrepreneurs who see possibilities in every problem. Mothers who lost children to violence and are building a movement to keep other kids safe. He's forgetting every last one of us. Americans don't say, "I alone can fix it." We say, "We'll fix it together."

Clinton then painted a specter of a Donald Trump who seeks to rule America by the force of his own will: "Remember: Our Founders fought a revolution and wrote a Constitution so America would never be a nation where one person had all the power." Then she set forth her vision of America in contrast to the vision of Donald Trump:

> That's why "Stronger Together" is not just a lesson from our history. It's not just a slogan for our campaign. It's a guiding principle for the country we've always been and the future we're going to build. A country where the economy works for everyone, not just those at the top. Where you can get a good job and send your kids to a good school, no matter what zip code you live in. A country where all our children can dream, and those dreams are within reach. Where families are strong. communities are safe. And yes, love trumps hate. That's the country we're fighting for. That's the future we're working toward. And so it is with humility ... determination ... and boundless confidence in America's promise, that I accept your nomination for President of the United States!

Clinton also tried to address the lack of trust that has dogged her campaign from the outset: "The truth is, through all these years of public service, the "service" part has always come easier to me than the "public" part. I get it that some people just don't know what to make of me. So let me tell you." She then gave her family history and tried to caste herself as someone of humble origin who has lived the America dream. She then proclaimed herself as a champion for everyone:

> In this campaign, I've met so many people who motivate me to keep fighting for change. And, with your help, I will carry all of your voices and stories with me to the White House. I will be a President for Democrats, Republicans, and Independents. For the struggling, the striving and the successful. For those who vote for me and those who don't. For all Americans. Tonight, we've reached a milestone in our nation's march toward a more perfect union: the first time that a major party has nominated a woman for President. Standing here as my mother's daughter, and my daughter's mother, I'm so happy this day has come. Happy for grandmothers and little girls and everyone in between. Happy for boys and men, too–because when any barrier falls in America, for anyone, it clears the way for everyone. When there are no ceilings, the sky's the limit.

.

Clinton also did not forget the Bernie Sanders supporters, and made a direct appeal for their support:

> We're still facing deep-seated problems that developed long before the reces- sion and have stayed with us through the recovery. I've gone around our country talking to working families. And I've heard from so many of you who feel like the economy just isn't working. Some of you are frustrated–even furious. And you know what, you're right. It's not yet working the way it should. Americans are willing to work–and work hard. But right now, an awful lot of people feel there is less and less respect for the work they do. And less respect for them, period. Democrats are the party of working people. But we haven't done a good enough

job showing that we get what you're going through, and that we're going to do something about it. So I want to tell you tonight how we will empower Americans to live better lives. My primary mission as President will be to create more opportunity and more good jobs with rising wages right here in the United States ... from my first day in office to my last! Especially in places that for too long have been left out and left behind.

To blunt the claims that she is owned by Wall Street, accusations made by both Sanders and Trump, Clinton then took direct aim at corporate America:

I believe American corporations that have gotten so much from our country should be just as patriotic in return. Many of them are. But too many aren't. It's wrong to take tax breaks with one hand and give out pink slips with the other. And I believe Wall Street can never, ever be allowed to wreck Main Street again.

She then outlined her liberal credentials for all to hear:

I believe in science. I believe that climate change is real and that we can save our planet while creating millions of good-paying clean energy jobs. I believe that when we have millions of hardworking immigrants contributing to our economy, it would be self-defeating and inhumane to kick them out. Comprehensive immigration reform will grow our economy and keep families together–and it's the right thing to do.

As for Donald's Trump's agenda, Clinton offered nothing but contempt:

Now, you didn't hear any of this from Donald Trump at his convention. He spoke for 70-odd minutes–and I do mean odd. And he offered zero solutions. But we already know he doesn't believe these things. No wonder he doesn't like talking about his plans. You might have noticed, I love talking about mine.

Clinton then laid out her policy agenda and who would pay for it in simple terms:

In my first 100 days, we will work with both parties to pass the biggest investment in new, good paying jobs since World War II. Jobs in manufacturing, clean energy, technology and innovation, small business, and infrastructure. If we invest in infrastructure now, we'll not only create jobs today, but lay the foundation for the jobs of the future. And we will transform the way we prepare our young people for those jobs. Bernie Sanders and I will work together to make college tuition-free for the middle class and debt-free for all! We will also liberate millions of people who already have student debt. Now, here's the thing, we're not only going to make all these investments, we're going to pay for every single one of them. And here's how: Wall Street, corporations, and the super-rich are going to start paying their fair share of taxes. Not because we resent success. Because when more than 90% of the gains have gone to the top 1%, that's where the money is. And if companies take tax breaks and then ship jobs overseas, we'll make them pay us back. And we'll put that money to work where it belongs . creating jobs here at home!

Then she turned to probably her best attack on Trump, focusing on whether he has the temperament to serve as commander in chief:

> Ask yourself: Does Donald Trump have the temperament to be Commander-in-Chief? Donald Trump can't even handle the rough-and-tumble of a presidential campaign. He loses his cool at the slightest provocation. When he's gotten a tough question from a reporter. When he's challenged in a debate. When he sees a protestor at a rally. Imagine him in the Oval Office facing a real crisis. A man you can bait with a tweet is not a man we can trust with nuclear weapons.

It was an impressive speech with well-crafted attack lines and well delivered. Clinton likely achieved her goals in the speech and positioned herself well for the Fall campaign. Whether it will be enough to blunt Trump's momentum will depend largely on whether Trump makes mistakes and whether Clinton effectively takes advantage of them.

Week 394

(KHANED)

August 7, 2015

Donald Trump came out of the Republican nomination with some significant momentum. He gave a strong acceptance speech, he rose in the polls, and many Republican leaders appeared willing to rally to him in the hopes of a victory in November. Trump had a chance to consolidate his position and take the fight to Clinton. All it would have taken is some discipline and determination. But having won the nomination being provocative and confrontational, it seems Donald Trump was determined to follow that same script. A hallmark of the Trump campaign has been to attack anyone who criticizes him. So when the Khizr Khan and his wife took the podium at the Democrat convention to talk about their son who died serving his country in Iraq and to criticize Donald Trump, Trump responded in kind, and in so doing forfeited all the momentum he had gained.

The feud between the Khan family and Donald Trump has it genesis in Trump's December 2015 call for a ban on Muslim immigration. Trump made this proposal in response to the influx of Muslim refugees into Europe, rising terrorist attacks both in Europe and the United States, and the White House's plan to accept more refugees into the United States. Trump said this policy was a threat to national security, so he proposed his ban. The proposal was controversial from the start, and many Republicans tried to use the ban against Trump during the primary campaign. Trump moderated his plan, calling for only a temporary ban, but would not back down. This proposal, combined with Trump's many remarks critical of Muslims, surely factored into the Democrats' decision to put the Khans on the podium at their convention.

Humayun Khan was killed in Iraq in 2004. Given the sacrifice his family made for America, his Pakistani-born father, Khizr Khan, was outraged by Trump's call for a ban on Muslim immigration. He gave an interview to Vocativ stating: "We are proud American citizens. It's the values [of this country] that brought us here, not our religion. Trump's position on these issues do not represent those values." On July 28, Khan spoke to the Democrats' national convention, and his words were provocative to say the least: "If it was up to Donald Trump, he never would have even been in America . . . . He vows to build walls and ban us from this country. Donald Trump, you're asking Americans to trust you with their future. Let me ask you, have you even read the United States Constitution . . . . You have sacrificed nothing, and no one." The next day Khan appeared on MSNBC's The Last Word and called on Republican leaders in Congress to repudiate Trump.

Not a man to accept criticism, Trump fired back during an interview with ABC News. He refused to back down from his proposal and ridiculed Khan's speech: "Who wrote that? Did Hillary's script writers write it . . . . I think I've made a lot of sacrifices. I work very, very hard." Trump also said that Khan's wife, Ghazala, did not say anything because of her religion and that the Khans' had "viciously attacked" him. Trump also sent a number of tweets critical of Khan's remarks. On July 31, Khan responded, telling CNN that Trump is a "black soul." Khan then went on NBC's Today show and said: "This candidate amazes me . . . . His ignorance — he can get up and malign the entire nation, the religions, the communities, the minorities, the judges and yet a private citizen in this political process. ... I cannot say what I feel?"

The result of all this controversy was that the media coverage for the entire first week after the Democrat convention was about the Trump/Khan feud, Trump's view of immigrants, and his refusal to back down. Republicans and veterans groups condemned Trump's criticisms of the Khans, and some even called for him to relinquish the nomination to let another Republican run. Trump would have none of it, and continued to give provocative speeches. All the while, poll after poll showed Hillary Clinton gaining a sizable advantage over Trump. Having positioned himself for a potential victory, Trump's penchant for attacking anyone and everyone finally hurt him when it came to the Khans, much to the delight of Trump's opponents.

Week 395

(ECONOMICS)

August 14, 2016

President Obama and Hillary Clinton could not have been more happy with the opening weeks of the presidential campaign. Donald Trump left the GOP convention with momentum and a lead, and in two short weeks squandered it all by picking unnecessary fights and making questionable statements. The Trump campaign seems to understand the problems its candidate is creating for himself, because it started this week with an effort to hit the reset button. Trump's extemporaneous rally style was put aside, and instead on August 8, Trump took the stage to give an address on his economic policies to the Detroit Economic Club, with a teleprompter. It was an effort to change the tone and show himself as a thoughtful policy advocate. The speech drew mixed reviews, but at least the discussion was about policy and not outlandish statements, which is what the Trump campaign wanted.

In many ways, Trump's economic policy is closer to that of Bernie Sanders than the GOP establishment. He favors higher taxes on Wall Street, wants to protect entitlements, is a critic of trade deals, and advocates for large scale infrastructure projects, not a traditional Republican agenda. In his address, he tried to frame his policy views as consistent with and but also challenging to traditional GOP priorities. The speech was set in Detroit, a good background for Trump's America First economic agenda, and Trump used that as his theme:

> When we were governed by an America First policy, Detroit was booming. Engineers, builders, laborers, shippers and countless others went to work each day, provided for their families, and lived out the American Dream. But for many living in this city, that dream has long ago vanished. When we abandoned the policy of America First, we started rebuilding other countries instead of our own. The skyscrapers went up in Beijing, and in many other cities around the world, while the factories and neighborhoods crumbled in Detroit. Our roads and bridges fell into disrepair, yet we found the money to resettle millions of refugees at taxpayer expense.

Trump then blamed Hillary Clinton for Detroit's economic woes: "In short, the city of Detroit is the living, breathing example of my opponent's failed economic agenda. Every policy that has failed this city, and so many others, is a policy supported by Hillary Clinton." He then caste himself as the candidate of the future:

> She is the candidate of the past. Ours is the campaign of the future. . . . Our opposition, on the other hand, has long ago run out of ideas. All Hillary Clinton has to offer is more of the same: more taxes, more regulations, more bureaucrats, more restrictions on American energy and American production. If you were a foreign power looking to weaken America, you couldn't do better than Hillary Clinton's economic agenda. Nothing would make our foreign adversaries happier than for our country to tax and regulate our companies and our jobs out of existence. The one common feature of every Hillary Clinton idea is that it punishes you for working and doing business in the United States. Every policy she has tilts the playing field towards other countries at our expense. That's why she tries to distract us with tired political rhetoric that seeks to label us, divide us, and pull us apart.

Trump then outlined his policy agenda. He accused Clinton of planning a $1.3 trillion tax increase, while he seeks tax cuts and tax simplification. Trump then outlined the failures of what he termed the Obama-Clinton economic policies:

> Their policies produced 1.2% growth, the weakest so-called recovery since the Great Depression, and a doubling of the national debt. There are now 94.3 million Americans outside the labor force. It was 80.5 million when President Obama took office, an increase of nearly 14 million people. The Obama-Clinton agenda of tax, spend and regulate has created a silent nation of jobless Americans. Home ownership is at its lowest rate in 51 years. Nearly 12 million have been added to the food stamp rolls since President Obama took office. Another nearly 7 million Americans were added to the ranks of those in poverty. We have the lowest labor

force participation rates in four decades. 58 percent of African-American youth are either outside the labor force or not employed. 1 in 5 American households do not have a single member in the labor force. The average worker today pays 31.5 percent of their wages to income and payroll taxes. On top of that, state and local taxes consume another 10 percent. The United States also has the highest business tax rate among the major industrialized nations of the world, at 35 percent. It's almost 40 percent when you add in taxes at the state level.

Trump blamed much of this economic record on over regulation and promised to dramatically reduce regulations and free the economy for better growth, proclaiming: "It is time to remove the anchor dragging us down." Trump also pointed to bad trade deals as a source of America's economic problems and promised to renegotiate them, and he pledged to kill the Trans Pacific Partnership trade deal. Trump also asserted that the Obama-Clinton energy policies are costing America jobs: "As a result of recent Obama EPA actions coal-fired power plants across Michigan have either shut down entirely or undergone expensive conversions. The Obama-Clinton war on coal has cost Michigan over 50,000 jobs. Hillary Clinton says her plan will put a lot of coal companies and coal miners out of business."

Trump closed his address with a promise that his economic agenda will bring back jobs and opportunity. "Detroit – the Motor City – will come roaring back. We will offer a new future, not the same old failed policies of the past. Our party has chosen to make new history by selecting a nominee from outside the rigged and corrupt system. The other party has reached backwards into the past to choose a nominee from yesterday – who offers only the rhetoric of yesterday, and the policies of yesterday. There will be no change under Hillary Clinton – only four more years of Obama. But we are going to look boldly into the future." With this address, Trump has tried to reset his campaign and his own prospects. Many will disagree with the agenda he outlined, but simply having that discussion is good for Trump, because it means the voters will not be talking about his gaffs. That was the purpose of the speech, but it will take more than one speech to undo the damage Trump has done to himself.

Week 396
(THE SHAKE UP)

August 21, 2016

While President Obama and his family enjoyed their annual vacation in Martha's Vineyard, things were anything but restful at the Trump campaign. Poll after poll has shown Trump falling farther behind Hillary Clinton, and Trump's lack of discipline on the campaign trail has prevented him creating any kind of persuasive narrative against Hillary Clinton. Instead, the campaign has been in almost continual damage control mode, dealing with a series of off-the-cuff comments from Trump that cover the spectrum from wildly inaccurate to offensive. Many in the GOP have been wondering when someone in Trump's inner circle will stand up to him and make Trump realize that he is sabotaging his own campaign. Apparently that someone is not going to be campaign chairman Paul Manafort, who resigned on August 19.

Manafort is a veteran GOP operative and when he joined the Trump campaign in March many believed it signaled that Trump would be moving toward a more conventional and disciplined campaign. That did not happen. Instead Trump continued to run his campaign as he has from the beginning, based on free form stump speeches, vicious attacks on his opponents, and few detailed policy plans. Manafort made some progress on campaign organization and fundraising, but it quickly became clear that he would not be able to control Trump's public behavior. Then came the issue of Manafort's lobbying and consulting work for the now overthrown Ukrainian President Viktor Yanukovch. This has created controversy because of Trump's apparent admiration for Russian President Putin, Yanukovch's sponsor. As the press began to focus more and more on this issue, it started to become clear that Manafort would be a problem for the Trump campaign, not a savior. So Manafort resigned.

However, Trump's choice of a replacement did not build confidence in Republican circles. Rather than go to any number of veteran GOP political operatives, Trump named as his new campaign chairman Stephen Bannon, the executive chairman of Breitbart News. Breitbart is an anti-establishment conservative media outlet that is just as likely to attack the Republican establishment as it is Democrats. Bannon has no significant prior campaign experience and many believe he will encourage Trump to continue his current style of campaigning, rather than try to get him to change course. All this is making the GOP nervous that Trump is setting himself up for a historic loss to Hillary Clinton. The one silver lining for Republicans is that at the same time Trump also brought in Kellyanne Conway as campaign manager. She is a well-respected pollster and political consultant with good relations with the GOP establishment. She may be the last hope to try to organize the Trump campaign into an operation that might have a chance of winning.

So while President Obama vacationed and Hillary Clinton quietly campaigned, both likely enjoyed observing a Trump campaign in disarray. The only good news for Trump is that it is still only August and that Hillary Clinton, even though ahead, is still not very popular. Trump has already squandered his post-convention momentum, and now he has to right his campaign and appeal to the voters he has lost in the last 3 weeks. Maybe this shake-up will help that effort, or maybe it will be just another sharp turn in Trump's erratic run for the White House. Either way, we are sure to be in for some interesting months ahead.

Week 397

(JUDICIAL WATCHING)

August 28, 2016

It is hard to imagine how much fun the Hillary Clinton team must be having over the last few weeks as Donald Trump lurched from controversy to controversy, and as her lead in the polls grew and grew. Last week's shake-up in the Trump campaign only added to the perception that his campaign was slowly disintegrating. President Obama was surely enjoying the show from his vacation and Democrats around the country were rejoicing. For her part, Hillary Clinton has kept a low profile, doing few campaign events and avoiding the press. Clearly, the Clinton campaign's plan is coast and let Trump self-destruct. This might appear a good strategy, assuming Clinton can avoid her own self-inflicted wounds, especially over her emails. However, that became increasingly difficult this week, when court papers revealed that Hillary Clinton was not truthful about her email deletions, casting doubt again on the trustworthiness of the Democrat nominee.

Most Democrats assumed that Hillary Clinton was in the clear when the FBI announced that it would not pursue charges against her for her use of emails. The Clinton campaign declared victory and tried to move on. However, the FBI's announcement was not the end of the story. It quickly became clear that the FBI was also investigating ties between the Clinton Foundation and the State Department under Hillary Clinton, including the issue of whether donors to the foundation were given access and favors. Also, despite the FBI's decision, there are several private lawsuits seeking more details on Clinton's emails, including one by Judicial Watch, a conservative public interest law firm. In public court papers filed this week in Judicial Watch's suit, it was revealed that the FBI had recovered some 14,900 deleted Clinton emails that Clinton never provided to the State Department. In early August, those emails were provided to the State Department. Even worse, some of those emails relate to the Benghazi attacks that killed the American ambassador. A federal judge has now ordered that those emails be produced by September 13.

Hillary Clinton has been far from consistent in her public statements about her email deletions. Her story has changed as needed to suit the political pressures of the day. She has gone from denial, to explanation, to apology, and then back to denial. One of her primary responses has been that she only deleted personal emails. For example, in March 2015 Hillary Clinton described the types of emails she deleted as follows:

> E-mails about planning Chelsea's wedding or my mother's funeral arrangements, condolence notes to friends, as well as yoga routines, family vacations, the other things you typically find in inboxes. No one wants their personal e-mails made public, and I think most people understand that and respect that privacy.

A very convenient response designed to quell the controversy. The problem is, the court documents released this week show that this statement is simply untrue. We now know that emails Clinton deleted from her private server included materials relating to the Benghazi attacks, which were the subject of a congressional investigation. So Hillary Clinton again appears to be lying. What is worse for the Clinton campaign, the court ordered the State Department to produce deleted Benghazi related emails by September 13, which will keep the issue alive and potentially lead to more embarrassments for Clinton.

If Hillary Clinton were a popular and trusted leader, she might be able to get by this latest controversy with little impact. However, even though she is ahead in the polls, surveys show she remains untrusted and unpopular. While she still leads, this week her ratings for trustworthiness took hits with the latest revelations. The only thing favoring Clinton is her opponent. Trump is even more unpopular than she is. Maybe this will be enough for Clinton to prevail in November, but it is now clear the fight is going to be tougher than she thought, and her plan to skate into the White House might need some reevaluation.

Week 398

(Immigrating)

September 4, 2016

One of President Obama's most controversial legacies will be his immigration policies. For liberals, the dramatic rise in deportations under this Administration has caused frustration because of the contrast with the President's rhetoric and calls for immigration reform. For Republicans, immigration has been even more controversial, with the Senate's passage of a bipartisan reform bill, which was killed by the House. Then the President made the issue thoroughly partisan when he attempted to use his executive powers to legalize millions of immigrants, only to be defeated in the courts. Given all this, it is no surprise that immigration is a major issue in the presidential campaign. Hillary Clinton has taken an even more liberal position on immigration, in an effort to win Hispanic votes. Donald Trump built his campaign on attacking the Obama Administration's immigration policies and calling for the construction of a wall on the Mexican border, to be paid for by Mexico.

As Trump has tried to steady his campaign, in recent weeks there have been signs that Trump might take a softer stand on immigration. When his campaign scheduled a major address on the issue on August 30 in Phoenix, many expected Mr. Trump to roll out a modified policy, but he did not such thing. Then Trump announced he would be making a trip to Mexico to meet the Mexican President just before the address. The table seemed to be set for a major move on the issue, but instead Trump used his address to restate and reinforce his determination to secure the border and deport illegal aliens. Trump began his address by stating:

> I have just landed having returned from a very important and special meeting with the President of Mexico – a man I like and respect very much, and a man who truly loves his country. Just like I am a man who loves the United States. . . . We agreed on the importance of ending the illegal flow of drugs, cash, guns and people across our border, and to put the cartels out of business. . . . We also discussed the great contributions of Mexican-American citizens to our two countries, my love for the people of Mexico, and the close friendship between our two nations. It was a thoughtful and substantive conversation. This is the first of what I expect will be many conversations in a Trump Administration about creating a new relationship between our two countries.

After these diplomatic comments about his visit to Mexico, Trump laid out his fix for the problem, proclaiming "to fix our immigration system, we must change our leadership in Washington. There is no other way." The then caste the problem as one created by the elites:

> The fundamental problem with the immigration system in our country is that it serves the needs of wealthy donors, political activists and powerful politicians. Let me tell you who it doesn't serve: it doesn't serve you, the American people. . . . When politicians talk about immigration reform, they usually mean the fol-lowing: amnesty, open borders, and lower wages. Immigration reform should mean

something else entirely: it should mean improvements to our laws and policies to make life better for American citizens.

Trump then explained his perspective on the problem and said it was time for the county to have an honest conversation and put the interests of American citizens first:

> But if we are going to make our immigration system work, then we have to be pre-pared to talk honestly and without fear about these important and sensitive issues. . . . We also have to be honest about the fact that not everyone who seeks to join our country will be able to successfully assimilate. It is our right as a sovereign nation to choose immigrants that we think are the likeliest to thrive and flourish here. . . . Countless Americans who have died in recent years would be alive today if not for the open border policies of this Administration. This includes incred-ible Americans like 21-year-old Sarah Root. The man who killed her arrived at the border, entered federal custody, and then was released into a U.S. community under the policies of this White House. He was released again after the crime, and is now at large. . . . On top of that, illegal immigration costs our country more than $113 billion dollars a year. For the money we are going to spend on illegal immigration over the next ten years, we could provide one million at-risk students with a school voucher. . . . While there are many illegal immigrants in our country who are good people, this doesn't change the fact that most illegal immigrants are lower-skilled workers with less education who compete directly against vulnerable American workers, and that these illegal workers draw much more out from the system than they will ever pay in. . . . We will treat everyone living or residing in our country with dignity. We will be fair, just and compassionate to all. But our greatest compassion must be for American citizens.

Then Trump explained his plan:

> Number One: We will build a wall along the Southern Border. . . . Number Two: End Catch-And-Release. . . . Number Three: Zero tolerance for criminal aliens. . . . Number Four: Block Funding For Sanctuary Cities. . . . Number Five: Cancel Unconstitutional Executive Orders & Enforce All Immigration Laws. . . . Number Six: We Are Going To Suspend The Issuance Of Visas To Any Place Where Adequate Screening Cannot Occur. . . . Number Seven: We will ensure that other countries take their people back when we order them deported. . . . Number Eight: We will finally complete the biometric entry-exit visa tracking system. . . .Number Nine: We will turn off the jobs and benefits magnet. . . . Number 10: We will reform legal immigration to serve the best interests of America and its workers.

This was more specificity than Trump has offered previously on the immigration issue, but there was no compromise in the agenda he outlined. Then to those illegal immigrants currently in the country, he was very clear: "For those here today illegally who are seeking legal status, they will have one route and only one route: to return home and apply for re-entry under the rules of the new legal immigration system that I have outlined above. Those who have left to seek entry under this new system will not be awarded surplus visas, but will have to enter under the immigration caps or limits that will be established. . . . Our message to the world will be this: you cannot obtain legal status, or become a citizen of the United States, by illegally entering our country." The speech was quickly attacked by Democrats and criticized by the mainstream media. However, Trump supporters cheered the address. Clearly, the Trump campaign has calculated that it has more to gain on the immigration issue than it has to lose. The Clinton campaign thinks the same thing, from the exact opposite perspective. Which one is right will be determined in November.

Week 399

(IRREDEEMABLY DEPLORABLE)

September 11, 2016

As the 2016 election moves into full swing, President Obama has been very careful about the role he will play. To date the President has avoided stealing the limelight from Hillary Clinton, and although he has done a few campaign events, he has in general kept a low profile. That is not to say that he has been silent. When it comes to Donald Trump, the President has stated repeatedly that he thinks Mr. Trump is not qualified either in skills or in temperament to be president. Mr. Obama's distain for Donald Trump is palpable, and deep. Yet the President has been very careful to indict the man, not his supporters. The President has understood that Trump's campaign has been fueled by deep discontent in a large segment of the American population. He also learned from the 2008 campaign, we he criticized rural voters for clinging to guns and religion, that insulting the voters is never a good campaign strategy. However, for all her sophistication, it appears Hillary Clinton missed that lesson.

After the Democrat convention and a host of missteps by Trump, Hillary Clinton built a huge lead in the polls and it looked like she might be heading to a landslide. However, in recent weeks her lead has diminished, and indeed disappeared in some key states. Trump's new campaign team has given him more discipline, and Clinton's email troubles and general unpopularity has made the race very competitive. In this new environment, it was more important than ever for Clinton to avoid doing anything that might make her appear elitist or untrustworthy. Instead, she did exactly the wrong thing when she decided to insult Trump's voters at a fundraiser. The event was the LGBT for Hillary Gala in New York City on September 9. Speaking before a friendly and liberal crowd, Clinton said:

> You know, to just be grossly generalistic, you could put half of Trump's supporters into what I call the basket of deplorables. Right? The racist, sexist, homophobic, xenophobic, Islamaphobic — you name it. And unfortunately there are people like that. And he has lifted them up. He has given voice to their websites that used to only have 11,000 people — now 11 million. He tweets and retweets their offensive hateful mean-spirited rhetoric. Now, some of those folks — they are irredeemable, but thankfully they are not America.

The reaction to this comment was furious, and not just from Republicans. The Clinton campaign immediately tried to recast the comment, some Democrats asked her to clarify, and a host of

Republicans, including Trump, demanded an apology. Even the friendly mainstream media was critical of the comment, saying it showed Clinton's elitism and distain for ordinary Americans. Democrat operatives tried to blunt the damage say saying that the quote was taken out of context. That is partly true, because Clinton next said in the speech:

> But the other basket — and I know this because I see friends from all over America here — I see friends from Florida and Georgia and South Carolina and Texas — as well as, you know, New York and California — but that other basket of people are people who feel that the government has let them down, the economy has let them down, nobody cares about them, nobody worries about what happens to their lives and their futures, and they're just desperate for change. It doesn't really even matter where it comes from. They don't buy everything he says, but he seems to hold out some hope that their lives will be different. They won't wake up and see their jobs disappear, lose a kid to heroin, feel like they're in a dead-end. Those are people we have to understand and empathize with as well.

However, even looking at Clinton's entire speech in context, it is clear that she asserted that half of Trump's supporters, perhaps 20 to 30 million people, are irredeemably deplorable.

With Trump himself so easy to attack, one must wonder why Hillary Clinton decided to take aim at his supporters, ordinary Americans. In doing so, she did not criticize simply their judgment, she attacked them as racist, sexist bigots. The clear implication being, if you are supporting Trump rather than me, you must be a bad person. The comment played perfectly into the Trump campaign's strategy to portray Clinton has an untrustworthy elitist who looks down on ordinary Americans. It made Clinton look less likeable, not more, and will likely lead to further erosion in her very small advantage. So Clinton, despite all the praise of her intelligence, seems to have forgotten a central rule of politics, never insult the voters.

Week 400

(UNSTEADY)

September 18, 2016

There is no doubt that this week the White House was getting increasingly nervous about the trajectory of the presidential campaign. After building a huge lead in late August and early September, Hillary Clinton has now given back all that ground. While Donald Trump was relentlessly campaigning, Clinton spent most of August and early September raising money. This gave Trump time to reignite his campaign. Trump has also been aided by Clinton, including her comment last week that half of Trump's supporters were "the deplorables." With all this, the last thing the Clinton campaign needed was another misstep, but on September 11,they got that, literally.

For years certain conservative groups have promoted the idea that Hillary Clinton is in bad health and is hiding that fact from the voters. It all started with a concussion and blood clot in 2012, with conspiracy theorists using that as a basis for stories of Clinton's dire health, including that she had suffered a stroke that has impaired her mental capacity. There are very few hard facts to support those claims, but Clinton's own penchant for secrecy has if anything perpetuated them. For example, Clinton has been unwilling to release her health records, but for that matter, so has Donald Trump. Even with all this, Clinton's health has not been a major issue in the campaign, until this week.

On September 11, 2016, Hillary Clinton was in New York City for a ceremony marking the 15 years since the September 11 attacks. About 90 minutes into the program, Clinton disappeared, having been shuttled away by the Secret Service. Her campaign gave no details to the media, and only when pressed did campaign spokesman Nick Merrill describe Clinton as feeling "overheated" at the commemoration ceremony. Clinton was driven to her daughter's Manhattan apartment, where she stayed for 90 minutes. When she emerged from her daughter's apartment, Clinton said: "I'm feeling great. It's a beautiful day in New York." Then she was taken to her home in Chappaqua, New York, without the press corps that travels with her. Mrs. Clinton was not seen publicly for the rest of the day. Later was it revealed that on September 9 Clinton was diagnosed with pneumonia and dehydration. This fact was not revealed to the press until late in the day after she left the ceremony. Still worse, the press obtained a spectator's video showing Clinton collapsing while trying to get into a van, needing to be carried into the vehicle. Clinton then left the campaign for four days, not returning to any public events until Thursday, September 15.

Showing uncharacteristic restraint, Donald Trump avoided comment on the issue other than wishing Clinton a speedy recovery. Apparently finally taking some advice from his campaign team, Trump realized that the video itself would be the story, so he would not need to add to it. For the Clinton campaign, the timing was horrible. Having lost her lead in the polls, now Clinton had to deal with questions about her health on top of all the other issues she is facing. By the end of the week, Trump had pulled nearly even in the polls and was gaining ground in a host of key battleground states. So the week ended with the Clinton campaign looking unsteady in more ways than one.

Week 401

(FOREIGN AND DOMESTIC)

September 25, 2016

One of the things a president is obligated to do is protect the nation from threats, both foreign and domestic. For Donald Trump, this has been a strength in his campaign, because he has called for a more vigorous fight against ISIS abroad and for law and order at home. On these issues, he has rated far above Hillary Clinton and President Obama. After her very tough week last week, the developments this week only caused more angst for the Clinton campaign, because as their candidate was working to recover from her health scare, the nation was hit by violence and turmoil connected to ISIS abroad and civil unrest from a police shooting at home. These events captured the nation's attention, and drove the political debate on the campaign trail.

The foreign attack came from yet another homegrown terrorist inspired by ISIS. From September 17 to 19, there were four bombings or bombing attempts, two in New York City, one in Seaside Park, and one in Elizabeth New Jersey. On September 17 in the morning, a pipe bomb exploded during a charity run at Seaside Park. Around 8:30 that same evening, a pressure cooker bomb exploded in Chelsea in Manhattan. No one was killed in either explosion. Another pressure cooker bomb was found on West 23rd Street. Then on September 18, several unexploded bombs were found at the Elizabeth, New Jersey train station. It did not take long for the FBI to find the bomber. On September 18, he was identified as Ahmad Khan Rahami, an American citizen from Afghanistan. He was located by police shortly thereafter, and after a shootout where three officers were injured, he was captured. While no evidence has been found to date that he is associated with a terrorist cell, ample evidence has been found that his actions were inspired by radical Islam and ISIS.

Obviously, these terrorist attacks put the nation on edge, which only grew worse when massive violence erupted in Charlotte, North Carolina after another controversial police shooting. On September 20, 43-year-old Keith Scott, an African-American, was fatally shot by Charlotte police officer Brently Vinson, also an African-American. The police had gone to an apartment complex to look for a different man wanted on a warrant. The police saw Scott exit his vehicle with what looked like a gun in his hand. Whether Scott had a gun is a matter of controversy, and the available videos of the incident are inconclusive. However, when Scott failed to drop whatever item he was carrying, he was fatally shot by Vinson. According to Charlotte-Mecklenburg Police Chief Kerr Putney, Scott did not follow instructions to "drop the weapon." His family claims Scott did not have a gun and protests quickly broke out. Then, during the evenings of September 20 and 21, massive and violent protests erupted, with protesters throwing objects at police and the police using tear gas. Protesters also shut down freeways. There was also extensive looting and dozens were arrested. Most of the looting took place in the EpiCentre entertainment district. North Carolina Governor Pat McCrory declared a state of emergency and deployed the National Guard.

The images from both New York and Charlotte were disturbing and changed the focus for both the Trump and Clinton campaigns. For Trump, he used the events to call for hitting ISIS hard and for law and order at home. Clinton took a more balance approach, pledging to wage a smart and aggressive fight against ISIS, while on Charlotte, Clinton called for calm but took no further position for fear of endangering her support in the African American community. No doubt these scenes of violence and chaos helped the Trump campaign, which has been accused of stoking fear. This week, there were legitimate reasons to be fearful, which is helpful to Trump. As for President Obama, he made public statements on both incidents, but otherwise kept largely in the background, reflecting the fact that the political dialogue is fast moving past the President and focusing on his potential successors.

Week 402

(WINGING IT)

October 2, 2016

Going into the first presidential debate on September 26, Donald Trump found himself in an enviable position. After having squandered the lead he built in July, his campaign had fought back to a position nearly even with Hillary Clinton. Clinton still maintained many advantages in the race, but most experts saw Trump's chances of winning improving. Given this, the first debate was a substantial opportunity for Trump. It would be the highest profile event since his nomination acceptance speech and would give him a chance to show that he could be knowledgeable, thoughtful, and presidential. If he could show those things, he had a better than even chance to win over undecided voters who dislike Clinton and who are looking for alternatives. However, that would mean departing from the debate strategy Trump used so successfully in the Republican nomination fight. The question was, would he change his tactics, or would he debate Hillary Clinton the same way he debated his GOP rivals, with bombast, cutting lines, and very few details or facts. Not surprisingly, in the debate he used his old strategy, and not very successfully.

Hillary Clinton is not well-liked or lovable, but she is determined, focused, and smart. Her strategy going into the debate was to show a human side, bury Trump in detail, and show from many different angles why Trump is not fit to be president. Clinton's agenda also included appealing to Bernie Sanders supporters, who have so far not embraced her. She tried very hard to do this, by attacking the rich and corporations in Sanders-like style:

> We also have to make the economy fairer. That starts with raising the national minimum wage and also guarantee, finally, equal pay for women's work. I also want to see more companies do profit sharing. If you help create the profits, you should be able to share in them, not just the executives at the top. And I want us to do more to support people who are struggling to balance family and work. I've heard from so many of you about the difficult choices you face and the stresses that you're under. So let's have paid family leave, earned sick days.

For his part, Trump focused on bad trade deals that he claims are destroying American jobs, with a special emphasis on Mexico: "When you look at what's happening in Mexico, a friend of mine who builds plants said it's the eighth wonder of the world. They're building some of the biggest plants anywhere in the world, some of the most sophisticated, some of the best plants." Trump also called for lower taxes and reducing regulations to spur job growth, to which Clinton responded: "The kind of plan that Donald has put forth would be trickle-down economics all over again. In fact, it would be the most extreme version, the biggest tax cuts for the top percent of the people in this country than we've ever had. I call it *Trumped-up* trickle-down, because that's exactly what it would be."

If not illuminating, at least these exchanges were about policy. However, much of the debate focused on personal attacks. For example, Clinton said Trump benefitted from the housing collapse, to which Trump responded: "That's called business, by the way." Then Clinton and moderator Lester Holt said Trump supported the Iraq War, to which Trump responded repeatedly "call Sean Hannity," a reference to a Fox News host who has frequently interviewed Trump. As Trump made more and more claims that Clinton found absurd, she commented: "Donald, I know you live in your own reality, but those are not the facts."

Then came the accusation and innuendo phase of the debate. Trump attacking Clinton for deleting 33,000 emails, and Clinton attacking Trump for refusing to release his tax returns, by saying: "I have no reason to believe that he's ever going to release his tax returns, because there's something he's hiding. And we'll guess. We'll keep guessing at what it might be that he's hiding, but I think the question is, were he ever to get near the White House, what would be those conflicts? Who does he owe money to?" This prompted Trump to proclaim: "I will release my tax returns against my lawyers' wishes when she releases her 33,000 emails that have been deleted. As soon as she releases them, I will release." When Clinton accused Trump of hiding his tax returns because he does not want to show that he pays very little in taxes, Trump responded: "That makes me smart" and later he said: "Now, if you want to change the laws, you've been there a long time, change the laws. But I take advantage of the laws of the nation. Because I'm running a company. My obligation right now is to do well for myself, my family, my employees, for my companies. And that's what I do."

Then Clinton attacked Trump for a supposed record of failed projects, stiffed vendors, and litigation, saying: "I can only say that I'm certainly relieved that my late father never did business with you." Clinton was also ready for Trump's attacks on her for taking so many days to prepare for the debate: "I think Donald just criticized me for preparing for this debate. And yes, I did. And you know what else I prepared for? I prepared to be president. And I think that's a good thing." Not pulling any punches, Clinton also implied that Trump is a racist:

> Donald started his career back in 1973 being sued by the justice department for racial discrimination. Because he would not rent apartments in one of his developments to African-Americans and he made sure that the people who worked for him, understood that was the policy. He actually was sued twice by the justice department. So he has a long record of engaging in racist behavior. And the birther lie was a very hurtful one.

Likewise, Clinton took aim at Trump for being a sexist:

> And one of the worst things he said was about a woman in a beauty contest. He loves beauty contests, supporting them and hanging around them. And he called this woman Miss Piggy. Then he called her Miss Housekeeping, because she was Latina. Donald, she has a name.

Throughout the debate, Clinton showed poise and focus, command of detail, and thorough preparation. Far from fearing an aggressive Trump, Clinton turned the tables by being the attacker herself. As for Trump, he punched back as much as he could, but his lack of preparation showed, because he missed many opportunities to rebut Clinton. As is his pattern, Trump also engaged in his usual bevy of self-praise, discussing what a great business person he is and that he had a winning "temperament." Trump is so used to living in a world where he is constantly praised and never challenged, he does not seem to understand that when running for president, the process is about the country, not him. Trump made no fatal errors, but Clinton's performance was better and stronger, and Trump gave few reasons for an undecided person to vote for him. That is what happens when someone wings it in a debate, and when someone does that, he loses.

Week 403

(LEAKED)

October 9, 2016

Throughout this presidential campaign, President Obama has continued to keep a low profile, probably because when your political opponents are in the process of self-destructing, often the best strategy is to just sit back and watch. That must have been his attitude this week as any effort by Donald Trump to recover from his weak debate performance was undermined by two news stories, partly stemming from leaks, that reinforced two key avenues the Clinton campaign has been using to attack Trump. First came a *New York Times* story on October 2 featuring a leak of Donald Trump's 1995 income tax return showing that he recorded a loss of $916 million, big enough to help avoid taxes for a decade. Then came an October leak of an *Entertainment Tonight* video and tape showing Trump apparently laughing and bragging about what could be termed sexual assault. For a campaign already starting to buckle, these two stories seemed enough to possibly rip the Trump machine apart.

It is not clear who gave the *New York Times* a copy of Trump's 1995 tax return, it could have been the Clinton campaign or even someone on the GOP side. It mattered little, because once the story was published it fed nicely into Hillary Clinton's narrative that Trump has refused to produce his tax returns because they would show he pays very little in taxes. The *New York Times* story showed that in 1995, Trump recorded a nearly $916 million loss from his real estate empire. There was no indication that recording this loss was improper, indeed Trump has been audited many times since this return was filed. The issue is not so much impropriety as fairness. The size of this loss would have allowed Trump to offset income for more than a decade, enabling him to avoid paying income tax. Hillary Clinton quickly took up this attack line, stating that Trump is a great example of a system that allows the super wealthy to avoid paying taxes. Clinton also used it to undermine Trump's claims of being a great businessman. The story put the Trump team off message and forced Trump to go into damage control mode, or at least Trump's brand of damage control, namely asserting that he was smart to take this loss exactly because it helped him avoid paying taxes.

While still struggling to deal with this story, at the end of the week the Trump campaign was hit by an even more devastating press report. On October 7, *The Washington Post* released a September 2005 video made at NBC Studios of Trump and Access Hollywood host Billy Bush having a lewd conversation about women. In the video, Trump brags to host Billy Bush about his attempt to seduce *Entertainment Tonight* host Nancy O'Dell:

> I moved on her, and I failed. I'll admit it. I did try and fuck her. She was married. And I moved on her very heavily. In fact, I took her out furniture shopping. She wanted to get some furniture. I said, "I'll show you where they have some nice furniture." I moved on her like a bitch, but I couldn't get there. And she was married. Then all of a sudden I see her, she's now got the big phony tits and everything. She's totally changed her look.

Then Trump comments about Arianne Zucker, whom Bush and Trump were going to meet, saying:

> I've got to use some Tic Tacs, just in case I start kissing her. You know I'm automatically attracted to beautiful—I just start kissing them. It's like a magnet. Just kiss. I don't even wait. And when you're a star, they let you do it, you can do anything... Grab them by the pussy. You can do anything.

The video caused a firestorm. Trump was accused of laughing and bragging about sexual assault. This time, recognizing the threat, Trump released a video apologizing for his comments.

The GOP leadership and vice presidential nominee Mike Pence all publicly disapproved of the comments, while Senator John McCain said he could no longer support Trump as the Republican nominee. House Speaker Paul Ryan said he would no longer defend or support the Trump campaign. Many called for Trump to drop out of the race, which he steadfastly refused to do. Instead, Trump went on the offensive, doing a press conference with four women who have accused Bill Clinton of raping them. With the second presidential debate on October 9, the whole nation was fixated on what Trump would do to address the issue.

With the Trump campaign now looking like it is heading into free fall, no doubt President Obama had an ever widening smile on his face. For months Obama had criticized Trump for being unfit for the presidency, and now these recent press reports bolstered this view. Most Republicans now openly worried that Trump might even cost them Congress, giving a President Hillary Clinton the power to enact her legislative agenda. It is now beyond doubt that the GOP has chosen a flawed nominee, something that most of the Republican leaders have known for a long time.

Week 404

(UNSHACKLED)

October 16, 2016

The release of the NBC Studios video showing Trump apparently joking about sexual assault has led to a panic among many Republican leaders. Trump's running mate Mike Pence refused to defend the comments, while many other GOP leaders, including former presidential nominee John McCain, withdrew their support from Trump. Even House Speaker Paul Ryan was forced to state that he would no longer campaign for Trump. All the while, President Obama and Democrat leaders sat back to watch the carnage and revel in the prospect of not only holding the White House, but potentially even taking back Congress. One might have thought that Donald Trump would have taken the message and tried to calm his party and build unity going into the last four weeks of campaigning. Instead, Trump joyously declared war on his own party, stating that the GOP leadership's criticism of him has "unshackled" him, allowing him to say and do what he wants in his run for the White House.

From the beginning of his campaign, Trump has had an acrimonious relationship with the Republican leadership. Initially, the GOP establishment tried to avoid confrontation with Trump, hoping his campaign would flame out. When it started to become clear that Trump might win the nomination, the Republican leadership tried to stop him, but could not. Then once Trump secured the nomination, they tried to bring him into the fold, but Trump never really sought to either align with the GOP or find common cause with its leadership. He had more of a takeover mentality, seeing himself the leader of a revolution centered on his agenda of protectionism, nativism, and isolationism. None of these positions found much support among the GOP establishment, but they accepted the reality of Trump's leadership of the party and hoped for the best. The amazing thing was, despite all his missteps, Trump was running well against Clinton, and nothing brings a party together like the prospect of victory. Then came the NBC video.

Trump has a history of making sexist and racist comments, but the NBC video made it impossible for the Republican leadership to continue to support Trump. Bragging about grabbing women by their private parts was just too reprehensible for GOP leaders to tolerate. Then this week reports were release of nearly a dozen women claiming that Trump had groped or kissed them inappropriately. The timing was horrible for the Republicans and for Trump, forcing GOP leaders to disavow Trump. In response, Trump launched an all-out attack on his own party, saying their disloyal reaction now allowed him to "unshackle" his campaign and do and say what he wants to. In usual form, Trump also took to Twitter, saying: "NOW: @RealDonaldTrump: "Disloyal Rs' are far more difficult than Crooked Hillary. They come at you from all sides. They don't know how to win – I will teach them!"

The media and Democrats loved it, proclaiming disarray and civil war within the Republican Party. Poll after poll have shown falling support for Trump, and panic within the GOP has set in. For her part, Hillary Clinton largely sat back and enjoyed the show, trying to avoid mistakes and let Trump undo himself. It seems that for Trump, every error and misstep he makes convinces him more that he should do exactly what he wants regardless of consequence or advice. It is almost as though Trump has manufactured his own reality, and anyone who contradicts him will be on the receiving end of his wrath. That goes for the GOP and Hillary Clinton.

Week 405

(UNACCEPTING)

October 23, 2016

Falling behind in the polls, the final presidential debate offered possibly a last opportunity for Donald Trump to resurrect his campaign and gain some ground on Hillary Clinton. Going into the debate, Trump recognized its importance and appears to have put some effort into preparing. While most of the debate was about substance and policy, that was lost by the big headline of the night, namely Donald Trump's refusal to say that he would respect the results of the election. For weeks, as the polls began to look worse and worse for Trump, more and more of his campaign speeches have been devoted to claims that the election was rigged. These comments echo similar claims he made during the GOP primary whenever he seemed to be losing a key contest. Given these assertions, it was obvious that Trump would be asked a question about it at the debate. He was, and he gave the answer Democrats were hoping, and thereby did further damage to his campaign.

Hillary Clinton has shown herself to be a disciplined and skillful debater. She has been well prepared, delivered her well-practiced lines, and has taken every opportunity to bate Donald Trump. In contrast, Trump has been bombastic and unrehearsed, and very thin on detail. This approach worked for Trump during the GOP primary debates, but has been far less successful in his debates against Clinton. Going into the debate, after suffering badly from his controversial comments about women and accusations of sexual assaults, Trump knew that he has to change the conversation. So for most of the debate, he talked policy, and did it fairly well. But when moderator Chris Wallace asked him if he would accept the verdict of the voters, Trump prevaricated, and in the end simply said he planned to keep us "in suspense."

Clinton, the mainstream media, and even some Republicans quickly condemned Trump. During the debate, Clinton said she was "horrified" that Trump refused to say if he would respect the verdict of the voters. President Obama also chimed in, saying it was yet another comment proving that Trump is unfit for the White House. Even worse, Trump's statement feeds into the concern of undecided voters that Trump is a risky choice, a candidate who cannot be trusted to respect our constitution, our laws, or our institutions. For his part, Trump saw no issue with the comment. During a rally shortly after the debate, he said to a cheering crowd that he would respect the results of the election "if I win." This was red meat for his supporters, and a clear effort to provoke and belittle his critics.

By refusing to commit to respect the results of the election, Trump hurt himself more than he appears to understand. His comments likely pushed many undecided independents and Republicans into the "Never Trump" camp. It also showed once again that for Trump, his campaign is all about him: his agenda, his preconceived notions, and his ambition. Trump has shown again and again that anyone who does not support whatever he says will be deemed an enemy, whether a fellow Republican or not. Now it appears that even the American voters fall into the camp, if they are unwise enough to not vote for him. It is possible that Trump might lose by so much that even he cannot claim the election was rigged, but even so he might refuse to accept the result regardless.

Week 406

(TRIPLE THREAT)

October 30, 2016

With the polls continuing to point to a dominant win by Hillary Clinton, the week started on a somber note for the Trump campaign. Trump continued to be dogged by his insensitive comments about women, to the point where his campaign has been unable to turn the focus back on his opponent. At the same time, an increasing sense of panic gripped the Republican Party, as fears started to grow that Trump would not only sink himself, but all sink the GOP majorities in Congress. Then, as circumstances appeared their darkest, events amazingly turned in the Republican's favor. On October 24 it was announced that insurances premiums for the Obamacare exchanges would increase more than 20% in 2017, fueling Republican rhetoric against the health care law. Then on October 26, new emails leaked by WikiLeaks showed some unsavory interplay between the State Department and the Clinton Foundation, giving credence to the claims of corruption and influence pedaling. Both of these stories were then completely eclipsed by the announcement on October 28 by FBI Director James Comey that he was reopening the investigation into Hillary Clinton's use of emails after some 650,000 emails were found on the laptop of Anthony Weiner, the estranged husband of Clinton confident Huma Abedin. It seemed like in one week the entire landscape of the campaign shifted to ground more favorable to Donald Trump.

Even through Obamacare was enacted seven years ago, the law has never built much popular support. Millions have been added to insurance rolls, but most of the gain has come from expanding Medicaid. The private insurance exchanges on the other hand have had many challenges. The problems initially started with computer breakdowns. When those were fixed enrollment rose, but each successive year more and more insurers left the exchanges, more exchanges failed, and prices continued to rise. By mid-2016, many of the state exchanges were in crisis, being able to only offer much reduced options and much increased premiums. Far from strengthening the individual private insurance market, Obamacare seemed to be destroying it. The GOP and Trump have continued to rail against the law, to great applause, but this week's news put Obamacare's problems back in the headlines, opening up a new and more effective attack on Hillary Clinton.

The news on Obamacare was quickly followed by the leaks relating to the Clinton Foundation, leaks that seemed to show yet again a very close relationship between the Secretary of State and the foundation. The emails showed efforts to use the State Department to set up meetings where foreign leaders would make large gifts to the foundation and hire Bill Clinton to give paid speeches, creating at least the appearance that Hillary Clinton was using her influence for private gain. Trump seized on this story as well, saying it showed yet again the corruption at the heart of everything the Clintons do. These leaks gave Trump plenty of new ammunition, and he quickly used it.

Hillary Clinton was already having a bad week when the new came out on Friday that the FBI was reopening its investigation of her emails. This came to pass because of unrelated investigations of former Congressman Anthony Weiner's alleged solicitations of underage girls. In connection with those investigations, law enforcement obtained Weiner's laptop, and found on it some 650,000 emails, some of which were from Hillary Clinton. FBI Director Comey had previously promised to advise Congress of any investigations, and against the advice of Attorney General Lynch, sent a letter to Congress to advise of the reopened investigation. This news exploded in Washington and around the country. It gave new relevance and strength to Trump's claims that Hillary Clinton should be indicted and that she was escaping justice because of a rigged political system. Trump immediately jumped on the story and continued his attacks on Clinton, and more people seem to have started to listen.

Just when the election seemed well in hand for Clinton, these three events have changed the dynamic of the campaign. They gave new hope to the Trump campaign, and gave new worries to Democrats. It is too early to say whether the stories will significantly change the polls or improve Trump's prospects, but at the very least they will give him a chance to try to change the dynamic and maybe close some of the gap. These controversies also make clear that if Clinton still wins, the nation will be in for an ugly period of accusation and investigation, because in defeat the GOP is sure to grab for Clinton scandals to try to weaken a President Hillary Clinton. Either way, these stories are going to have a huge and lasting impact on the political dialogue no matter who wins.

Week 407

(GAINING GROUND)

November 6, 2016

After spending weeks in freefall, FBI Director James Comey's October 28 announcement that he was reopening the investigation into Hillary Clinton's emails has breathed new life into the Trump campaign. The timing, less than two week before the presidential election, left little time for the Clinton campaign to react and less time for Trump to make any misstep that might squander the opportunity given. Considering Clinton's commanding position in the polls, many analysts doubted that Comey's announcement would be enough to deny Clinton victory. Then polling started to come in, and the landscape started to look very different, and Democrats began to get very nervous.

For more than a month, after Trump's weak debate performances and the NBC Studio tape where Trump appeared to joke about sexual assault, the Clinton campaign steadily built a significant lead in national polls. While most every survey showed Clinton under 50%, she consistently polled on average 3% to 4% ahead of Trump. At the state by state level, Trump was doing better, but Clinton seemed well positioned to win Democrat strongholds in the Midwest, and appeared poised to take at least one of the key swing states (Florida, North Carolina, or Ohio), without which Trump could not win. The picture was bleak, making many Republicans start to fear that they would lose the Senate and that even their large House majority was at risk. It is fair to say GOP panic was setting in.

Despite all this, Trump seemed confident. He continued his harsh rhetoric, his focus on a large rallies, his disdain for mounting a ground game, and his commitment to campaign hard in Midwestern states Republicans have not carried since 1988. Many GOP leaders were starting to see Trump as operating in his own reality, where he saw victory where everyone else saw defeat. Many started calling him delusional, and President Obama and his Democrat allies started early celebrations of a victory that would cement the Obama legacy. Throughout it all, Trump and his devoted supporters continued their march toward what seemed like forlorn hopes of victory. But them came James Comey.

Ever since the email controversy broke in 2015, Hillary Clinton treated it with disdain. Her story kept changing, and excuses kept mounting, and her calculated apologies seemed well crafted but deeply insincere. However, when the FBI announced in July that it would not seek to pursue charges against Clinton, her campaign closed the book on the issue. However, Donald Trump did not. He used the controversy as an example of why the system is rigged, and he attacked Clinton on the issue at every opportunity, calling her "Crooked Hillary" to massive applause. When Comey notified Congress on October 28 that he had reopened the investigation, it added fuel to a fire that Trump had kept going for months. The question was, could it make a difference with him so far behind.

As the week continued, an answer started to appear. Clinton's lead in national polls began to disappear, and several polls showed Trump now ahead. Trump started to pull away in states like Ohio, and quickly appeared to close the gap in places like Florida and North Carolina. Through it all, the Clinton team held fast, claiming that their Midwestern "Blue Wall" would hold, ending any chance of a Trump victory. While Trump devoted more and more time and money to places like Wisconsin and Michigan, the Clinton campaign scoffed, considering those states already won. But despite it all, a pattern started to appear that the election was going to be closer than first thought. Maybe call it the Comey effect, but by week's end, it appeared very real indeed.

Week 408
(BLUE FALL)

November 13, 2016

Donald Trump was an unconventional GOP nominee, with an unconventional style, who ran an unconventional campaign, and on November 8, he won an unconventional and stunning victory. Public polls and prominent analysts all agreed that Hillary Clinton was heading to victory in the general election. She was ahead in national polls and in the key battleground states of Pennsylvania, Michigan, Wisconsin, and Minnesota. The Democrat ground game was also cited as a reason why Clinton had the advantage. Then there was the vaunted Midwestern Democrat Blue Wall, states that Republicans had not carried since the 1980's and the key to Clinton's advantage in the electoral college map. With all this, it seemed to most impossible that Trump might win, but he did, by doing two amazing things. He took white working class voters away from the Democrats by massive margins and he obliterated the Blue Wall.

It is said that generals often make the mistake of fighting the last war, and the same assessment can be made of the Hillary Clinton campaign strategy. Barak Obama won two presidential elections with what has been called micro politics, which focuses on voter identity and get out the vote efforts. President Obama's winning coalitions were comprised of minority voters, gays, young voters, and urban elites. He took positions to appeal to these voters and got them to the polls in huge numbers in key states, and thereby managed to win two elections while losing the white vote and in 2012 losing independents. It was a strategy that worked great for President Obama, but it also required Democrats to largely ignore white working class voters, the former base of the party. The strategy was also based on the assumption that certain battleground states were actually Democrat locks, so all a Democrat presidential candidate needed to do was carry one of the GOP must-win states, and the election would be won. Barak Obama pulled off this strategy twice, and the Clinton campaign assumed it could not fail. It did, in a profound manner.

It is hard to tell if Donald Trump is a political genius, or just lucky, but it cannot be disputed that he destroyed the Democrats' vaunted micro politics. Rather than focus on voter identity, the Trump campaign was based on an America First theme of restoring jobs, border security, and the rule of law. He took this message to the parts of America ignored and ridiculed by the Democrats' micro politics, decaying industrial cities, rural areas, and coal producing regions. He ignored the ground game, which he outsourced to the RNC, and instead used mass rallies and free mass media coverage to drive his campaign. He appealed to raw patriotism, frustration, and even the anger of voters who felt America had left them behind. His business background, forceful rhetoric, and unrelenting focus on the American worker motivated millions of new voters to engage in the process and head to the polls. They were the key to his victory.

Watching the election coverage as the results came in was an amazing display of how out of touch the elites were with what was really happening in America. Reporters, with access to exit poll data, saw results indicating a big night for Hillary Clinton. Early coverage focused almost entirely on what a difficult task lay before Trump. But as the actual results started to come in, a very different picture emerged. Trump was not only winning solid Republican states by huge margins, but he was showing surprising strength in states like Virginia, Pennsylvania, and Michigan. The mainstream media news anchors could not hide their disbelief. Quickly, Florida, North Carolina, and Ohio fell to Trump, meaning Clinton failed to carry any of the must-win GOP states.

By midnight, the election hang on Pennsylvania, Michigan, and Wisconsin, with Trump ahead in all three and the Clinton team hoping for a miracle. By 2:30 a.m. it was over, Trump carried Pennsylvania and Wisconsin, with Michigan still too close to call, but with those victories he held at least 290 electoral votes and the presidency. It was not just a win for Trump, the Democrats failed at all levels. Despite the GOP having twice as many seats to defend, the Democrats gained only two seats in the Senate, leaving the GOP with a 52 to 48 majority. In the House, GOP losses were in the single digits, preserving a more than 40 seat majority. Republicans gained at the state level, ending the night with 33 governorships and more power in state legislatures. It was a not simply a Trump victory, it was a Republican blowout.

After his victory was clear, around 3:30 a.m. Trump gave a conciliatory victory speech, congratulated Hillary Clinton for running a good campaign, and called for unity. Clinton did not appear that night, but instead gave her concession speech the next day, clearly overwhelmed and distraught. Almost immediately, protests started in cities across the country, with activists chanting the slogan "not my president." The fact that Hillary Clinton appears to have carried the popular vote did not help matters, fueling claims the results were illegitimate. President Obama, recognizing the tension in the country, quickly invited President Elect Trump to the White House. The two met privately for 90 minutes on November 10, and after met with the press. President Obama said all the right things about respecting the voters' choice and working for a smooth transition. Trump was largely silent before the press, beyond saying a few words praising President Obama. Some say he looked stunned himself that he had won, and in that respect he shared something with the protesters.

For President Obama, the Trump victory was a disaster for his legacy. Trump has called for the repeal of his two main legislative achievements, Obamacare and the Dodd-Frank Wall Street reform legislation. Even worse, for the last 6 years President Obama has ruled largely by executive order and regulations, measures Trump has vowed to rescind. Democrats believe they are on the right side of history, meaning their policies are the future and Republicans are just fighting a rear guard action to defend the past. Indeed, President Obama is fond of using that phrase. Maybe that is why in all their confidence they not only lost touch with much of America, but also openly ridiculed and demeaned it. Hillary Clinton and the Democrats thought they could not lose, but all it took was an often profane, sometimes uninformed, and always bombastic real estate mogul who was listening to the forgotten Americans to hand them their biggest defeat since Ronald Reagan.

Week 409

(OFF BALANCE)

November 20, 2016

In the wake of Donald Trump's election victory, the race was on to define Trump and to figure out what kind of President he would be. For Democrats, Trump's victory was so devastating that they grasped simultaneously to many varied explanations for their defeat. Their first impulse was to blame Clinton and cry racism. Clinton was criticized for the stupidity of setting up a private email account and for political malpractice for ignoring states like Wisconsin when there were faint signs of Trump strength. However, Democrats were not content to blame their own, they also quickly took aim at the victors. It started with former Obama administration official Van Jones on election night calling Trump's victory "whitelash," and continued with a rising chorus of assertions that Trump won based on racist voters and a racist campaign. Democrats, having lost the election in part because of their obsession with identity politics, could not help themselves from seeing their defeat through the same lens. As for the Left, they took to the streets in urban areas around the country calling for civil unrest in protest of the result. All the while, President-Elect Trump remained largely silent as he started to put his administration together. His first steps in that effort gave his foes ammunition, while giving conservatives reasons to hope.

When President Obama met with Donald Trump on November 10, many thought it would be a tense and uncomfortable meeting. The President called Trump "uniquely unqualified" to be President, while Trump attacked the President as well. However, the meeting turned out differently. President Obama cares most about his legacy, and rather than wallowing in defeat, he used his first meeting with Trump to try to lobby him to preserve aspects of the Obama legacy. Put simply, Obama was trying to work Trump, and he used every ounce of praise and flattery he could muster to do it. Soon after that meeting, President Obama went on his last foreign trip, visiting Greece, Germany, and Peru, strong symbolism of him vacating center stage to Mr. Trump.

Republicans understood why President Obama was offering so many kind words for Mr. Trump, and it made them nervous. What Trump did next was surely a disappointment to the President, not the GOP. The GOP establishment has long believed that Trump was neither a Republican nor a conservative. Many secretly feared that Trump would promptly show his liberal stripes if elected. Trump's first appointments demonstrated something very different. Trump quickly tapped RNC Chair Reince Priebus as Chief of Staff, Alabama Senator Jeff Sessions for Attorney General, General Michael Flynn for National Security Advisor, and Representative Mike Pompeo for the CIA. All solid conservatives, signaling a hardline on both foreign policy and law enforcement. In addition, Trump held public meetings with both loyalists and rivals, including Mitt Romney who met with Trump on November 19 in New Jersey. All signs were that Trump would put in place a conservative administration.

Most of Trump's initial moves kept his liberal critics off balance, but one appointment offered an easy target. In July 2016, Trump made Steve Bannon his campaign chief strategist. Bannon, a former naval officer and investment banker, had been executive chair of Breitbart News, a right-wing media outlet associated with the alt right movement. On November 13, Trump announced that Bannon would be appointed a Senior Counsellor to the President. The Bannon appointment was a boon for the Left. They immediately indicted him as a racist and used his appointment as evidence that Donald Trump's administration would target minorities. The mainstream media happily repeated every accusation against Bannon and Democrats seized on the issue, calling for Bannon's resignation. In response, Trump has simply ignored them all, and continued putting his administration together, with Bannon at his side. As during the campaign, Trump is ignoring his critics and doing what he wants, and by doing so, he continued to keep his critics off balance.

Week 410

(A COUNTING)

November 27, 2016

Although the media gave some attention to President Obama's last foreign trip, almost all of their focus was on the second week of the Trump transition. Trump's initial appointments after the election were solid conservatives and loyalists, what came next was a parade of meetings with Republican friends and foes alike, a kind of beauty contest for politicians. The unconventional candidate was also running an unconventional transition, making public the meetings and discussions that most incoming presidents try to keep private. Trump was not just interviewing, he was also keeping score and demanding accountability from his foes, including the media. However, rather than resign themselves to the Trump victory or seek some common ground, the reaction on the Left was instead to continue their attacks on Trump and to seek a senseless recount of the results in Wisconsin, Michigan, and Pennsylvania.

Trump made much during his campaign of the fact that he would bring in the "best people" to run his administration. To try to keep that promise, this week Mr. Trump continued his public interview process. Last week he had a meeting with Mitt Romney, and this week dozens of potential appointees made their way to Trump Tower in New York City to audition for positions. Rather than try to keep the process confidential, Trump did the opposite, he let the public into the process. Near the end of the week, he filled a few key spots. He tapped wealthy GOP activist and school choice proponent Betsy DeVos for Education Secretary and South Carolina's Nikki Haley for UN Ambassador. Both are favorites of conservatives and add some diversity to the Trump cabinet. The key positions of Defense Secretary and Secretary of State remained undecided, with the former position being hotly contested between Mitt Romney, Rudy Giuliani, and General David Petraeus.

However, Donald Trump was not spending all his time interviewing, he also spent some quality time with the media, but not in the way they usually expect. One of Trump's keys to success was his ability to get free media coverage and to circumvent the media through twitter and other social media. Despite the consistently negative coverage, Trump was able to effectively get his message through by these means. It is fair to say that the mainstream media was not simply critical of his campaign, many outlets like the *New York Times* and NBC openly sided with Clinton. Maybe the media elites thought that after the Trump victory he would try to ingratiate himself with them, hardly. On November 21, Trump invited leading representatives of all the major networks to Trump Tower, where he gave them a tongue lashing. He told them their coverage was biased, unfair, and unprofessional. He singled out several of his guests, especially those from NBC, for particular criticism. In essence, he threw down a marker that if they go after him, he will go after them. The next day, Trump met with the *New York Times* editorial board, but only after sending several tweets implying he might cancel the meeting. He did show up, and did the same thing, but also answered substantive questions, showing more flexibility on certain policy questions than he did on the campaign trail. For example, he said he would keep an "open mind" on President Obama's Paris Climate Accord and that he would keep in place some parts of Obamacare. Trump keeps running circles around the media, thoroughly befuddling them.

As for the Democrats, President Obama is quickly vanishing from the scene, but continues to have frequent private conversations with Trump on the transition. As for the rest of the Democrat Party, they continue in denial and in search of excuses for their defeats in things like racism, the electoral college, and the meaningless fact that Clinton seems to have won the popular vote by more than 2 million. But for some on the Left, their mourning is not limited to excuses and self-denial, they have also veered to self-delusion. Green Party candidate Jill Stein has used the Trump victory to raise more than $3 million dollars to conduct recounts in three key states Trump won by narrow margins: Wisconsin, Michigan, and Pennsylvania. Stein filed her recount paperwork this week in Wisconsin, and plans to do the same next week in the other states. Election experts say there is no chance these recounts will change the result. Despite that, the Clinton campaign has joined the recounts. It seems the Left will do anything other than reconcile themselves to a Trump victory. So while Trump has been keeping score, scolding, and interviewing, the Democrats are doing anything rather than accept the reality that they were defeated and Donald Trump is President-Elect.

Week 411

(DE-STABLISHMENT)

December 4, 2016

One of the rally cries of the Trump campaign was fight the "establishment." When Trump used this term, he was referring to the political and business leaders who, in his view, have been making a mess of the country. By campaigning against the establishment, Trump drew to his cause millions of voters who had previously checked out of the political process. It was the key to his success. However, Trump's victory was not an anti-establishment victory, it was a Republican victory. Trump prevailed at the top of the ticket, but Republicans did very well down the ballot in Congress and in the States, putting the GOP its most dominant position since the 1920's. This has made many wonder if Trump was really going to be a different kind of president, or if he would be quickly coopted into the very "establishment" he condemned. Early in his transition, as with so many things Trump, the answer is elusive.

Trump ran for president from a hard right position, but since winning the election he has promised not to prosecute Hillary Clinton, praised President Obama, and said he would keep parts of Obamacare and the Paris Climate Accords. That has made many people think his campaign was all a ruse, and once in office he would be a moderate. President Obama clearly hopes so, and has been frequently speaking with Trump on transition issues. But just when you think you have him figured out, Trump fakes you out. The best example is his cabinet. While making moderate comments on certain issues, Trump is busily putting together a cabinet more conservative than Reagan's first administration. This week he announced Elaine Chao, Majority Leader Mitch McConnell's wife, as Secretary of Transportation. He picked harsh Obamacare critic Congressman Tom Price as HHS Secretary. He selected Steve Mnuchin, a former Goldman Sachs partner, for Secretary of the Treasury, and former Marine Corps general James Mattis as Secretary of Defense. For Obama, despite Trump's kind words and hints at moderation, these picks made clear that Trump plans to thoroughly dismantle the Obama legacy.

Some could see Trump's cabinet picks as a sign that he is actually going to be a conventional Republican after all. Indeed, Trump had a second meeting this week with Mitt Romney about potentially tapping him for Secretary of State, the clearest sign yet of Trump being folded into the Republican establishment. But just when Trump is starting to look conventional, he starts sending even more tweets, on every issue imaginable. This is not typical presidential behavior. Trump emphasized he would not act like a typical president with his deal with Carrier Corporation. Carrier is known for air conditioning products, and recently announced it was moving 2,000 Indiana jobs to Mexico. Trump campaigned against companies moving jobs overseas, blaming the trend on bad trade deals, high taxes, and over regulation. Before even taking office, Trump decided to send a message to companies thinking of exporting jobs. Trump called Greg Hayes, the CEO of Carrier's parent company United Technologies, and negotiated a deal to keep 1,000 jobs in Indiana based on threats to put tariffs on Carrier if they moved the jobs. Trump flew to Indiana to announce the deal, which he and Vice President-Elect Mike Pence negotiated, offering Carrier some $700,000 in annual tax benefits to keep jobs in Indiana.

With his confusing public statements, his cabinet picks, his tweets, and his Carrier deal, Trump is keeping his critics off balance and sending a message to his political opponents, corporate America, and the media. The message is that he will communicate directly with the public, will pressure business, will push his agenda, and in doing all this he will not be categorized or controlled. Sounds pretty anti-establishment after all.

Week 412
(GASP)

December 11, 2016

It is fair to say that President Obama is a hero to the environmental movement. Starting with the 2009 stimulus bill, which devoted tens of billions of dollars to clean energy projects, President Obama has consistently pushed an agenda favored by the environmental movement. The one area where the Obama administration fell short was on legislation to support its environmental initiatives. Early in his firm term, the President hoped to pass a cap and trade bill the create a marketplace to limit carbon emissions. However, the focus on the Obamacare legislation, plus opposition from the GOP, prevented the White House from pushing the cap and trade bill through during the brief period when Democrats had a filibuster-proof majority in the Senate. Following the Republican congressional victories in 2010, the President largely gave up on passing environmental legislation, and instead turned to regulations and executive orders to further his environmental policies. This was culminated by the decision in 2016 to enter into the Paris Climate Accords without Senate ratification. This strategy seemed successful, and then came Donald Trump.

The great benefit of pursuing policy goals by legislation is that once enshrined in law, the policy can only be changed by a further act of Congress. Early on after the GOP took control of Congress, President Obama largely gave up on working with Republicans on environmental issues and declared "I have a pen," which was the President's way of saying he would pursue his agenda without Congress. What followed was a series of regulations and executive orders on clean water, carbon emissions, wetlands, and fossil fuel production. Many of these executive actions were successfully challenged in the courts, but many others remain in place. In the end, President Obama's legacy on the environment rests almost entirely on these executive actions.

That is likely why the President has been working so hard to lobby President-Elect Trump. He hoped by these efforts to save parts of his legacy, including his environmental initiatives. Initial signs were hopeful for the President. For example, Mr. Trump said he would take a look at the Paris Climate Accords rather than simply pulling the United States out of the agreement. This must have seemed potentially positive to President Obama and environmental activists. But then came the Scott Pruitt nomination to head the EPA.

On December 8, President-Elect Donald Trump nominated Oklahoma Attorney General Scott Pruitt to lead the EPA. It was not surprising that Trump nominated a Republican for that post, what surprised was that he picked a leading and vocal critic of nearly all of President Obama's environmental policies. As a state attorney general, Pruitt led the charge in challenges to the Administration's executive actions on the environment. Pruitt made clear in a statement after he was nominated that he would be taking the same approach at the helm of the EPA: "The American people are tired of seeing billions of dollars drained from our economy due to unnecessary EPA regulations, and I intend to run this agency in a way that fosters both responsible protection of the environment and freedom for American businesses."

The reaction by environmental activists was expectedly harsh. The Sierra Club said that Pruitt running the EPA was like "putting an arsonist in charge of fighting fires." Energy production interests were as happy about the nomination as environmentalists were upset. Not only is Pruitt a critic of the President's executive actions on the environment, he is also a climate change skeptic. Since the Left sees human contribution to climate change as an undeniable and undebatable truth, the nomination of a EPA chief prepared to challenge those assumptions has made the global warming community apoplectic. It is also clear that Senate Democrats intend to put up a fight over the Pruitt nomination. Minority Leader Schumer said soon after the nomination that "Attorney General Pruitt's reluctance to accept the facts or science on climate change couldn't make him any more out of touch with the American people — and with reality . . . . President Elect Trump promised to break the special interests' grip on Washington, but his nomination of Mr. Pruitt — who has a troubling history of advocating on behalf of big oil at the expense of public health — only tightens it." Despite these tough words, there is little Democrats can do to stop Pruitt confirmation, since Democrats changed the filibuster rules to exempt all executive nominations other than the Supreme Court.

The reality is now setting in that President Obama's legacy on environmental and other issues, while impressive at the moment, is not durable since on most issues other than Obamacare, he failed to pass legislation to cement his policies in place. Further, despite Donald Trump's initial hints at moderation, the Pruitt nomination continues a trend where Trump is putting together what will likely be the most conservative GOP cabinet since the 1920s.

Week 413

(THE RUSSIANS ARE HACKING)

December 18, 2016

In the wake of their election defeat, President Obama and the Democrats have been grasping for excuses and explanations. Culprits have included disaffected rural voters, the electoral college, the FBI's investigation into Hillary Clinton's emails, fake news promoted on Facebook, and a bad campaign strategy by Hillary Clinton. This search for excuses has in part been fueled by the popular vote result, which now shows that Clinton out polled Trump by some 3 million votes. This has led many Democrats to try to delegitimize Trump's victory. Indeed, many on the Left have mounted a campaign to try to get electors to switch their votes to someone other than Trump, based on assertions that the election results were illegitimate. This perspective fueled the recount effort by Green Party Candidate Jill Stein, a recount that failed to change any results. However, one rumor about the 2016 election that caused concerns across the political spectrum is that the Russian tried to influence the election results through hacking. This rumor erupted into controversy this week.

It is well known that President Obama has a very poor relationship with Russia's President Putin. The two have clashed over a broad scope of issues including Syria and the Crimea. In this confrontation, Putin has used old-style power politics, while President Obama has relied mostly on indignation and the values of the "international community." The result has been that Russian has gotten its way in most respects, while the United States has looked weak and ineffective. In the 2016 campaign, Hillary Clinton adopted President Obama's critical attitude about Russia, while Donald Trump steadfastly refused to attack President Putin, and in fact went out of his way to defend the Russian leader. In view of this, it is not surprising that Putin's government favored Trump in the campaign, and worked to help him get elected. Russian hackers are widely believed to have obtained and released confidential records of the DNC in an effort to harm Clinton and sow discord among Democrats. However, the bigger question has been whether Russian hackers tried to alter the actual election results.

There have been concerns for years that growing reliance on electronic voting machines could make them vulnerable to hacking. After Trump's victory, driven by small-margin wins in Wisconsin, Michigan, and Pennsylvania, many wondered if the Russian might have been able to alter results to tip the election in Trump's favor in those states. It was this very suspicion that fueled the millions of dollars that flowed to Jill Stein to fund her recount efforts. Those recounts failed to alter the results or find evidence of any wide-spread fraud, but the controversy did not end there. This week, President Obama announced an official review of whether Russian tried to influence the election. The review was based on conclusions reached by the CIA. It was also revealed that the FBI had drawn no such conclusion. The focus of the investigation is whether Russian "tied" to influence the results, without implying that it actual did impact who won.

There are very good national security reasons to investigate whether a foreign power tried to impact a U.S. election. Many might view that as an unfriendly act at a minimum, or at worst, potentially an act of war. The story has been a convenient one for Democrats looking for any excuse other than their own positions and strategy as a reason for their defeat. For Donald Trump, President Obama's announcement of the investigation was viewed as a political game to try to undermine the legitimacy of his victory. Trump took to Twitter to criticize the investigation and cast doubt on whether the Russians did anything wrong. His reflective defense of Russia is giving many, including some in the GOP, concerns. It has also created the first direct conflict since the election between President Obama and President-Elect Trump. However, if the investigation proves Russian meddling, the question will be whether Trump will take action, or will instead continue to defend Putin no matter what.

Week 414

(Nuke'Em)

December 25, 2016

With President Obama in Hawaii and President Elect Trump at his Mara Lago resort for Christmas, most would have expected a very quiet period in political news. Trump has to date filled most of his cabinet position and the only expected news of the week was the formal state meetings of the electoral college on December 19 for votes to be cast for President. Despite persistent efforts by progressive and major media outlets like the *New York Times* to get electors to vote for someone other than Trump, in the end only two of Trump's 306 electors changed their votes. Ironically, more Clinton electors refused to vote for her than did electors for Trump. So Trump was formally elected President, and most then assumed that we would be in for a couple weeks of quiet in the political world. What most forgot is that we now live in the era of the Twitter presidency, where there is never a day off, and one Tweet form Trump on nuclear weapons made what should have been a quiet week into a busy one.

When Trump first started his run for President, he was derided for his use of Twitter. His opponents tried to use his often unrestrained and inconsistent Tweets against him, and they universally failed. Once elected, many thought Trump would reduce his use of Tweets, and they were wrong. Trump has in many ways run a transition by Tweet, speaking directly to his supporters and controlling his new cycle through his use of Tweets. This week, Trump expanded the practice into foreign relations by a Tweet on nuclear weapons. On December 22, Russian President Putin gave a speech calling for expanding and modernizing Russia's nuclear arsenal. This is part of a pattern of Russia trying to help Trump and testing the resolve of the United States. On nuclear weapons, maybe Putin was seeing how far he could now push Trump, who has previously made every effort to defend the Russian leader. So after Putin made his speech on nuclear weapons, Trump Tweeted this: "The United States must greatly strengthen and expand its nuclear capability until such time as the world comes to its senses regarding nukes."

With both the American and Russian leaders calling for expanding nuclear arsenals, many saw a specter of a new nuclear arms race. Trump's Tweet also emboldened Trump's many critics to again assert he is unfit for the presidency. Nuclear weapons are a very important and sensitive issue, so by Tweeting on nuclear weapons, many asserted Trump demonstrated yet again that he is not ready to be President. For his part, President Obama tried to stay out of the controversy, allowing his aides to simply comment that nuclear weapons are a delicate issue that need deliberative analysis. It is also far from clear what Trump meant by his Tweet, was he proposing modernizing the existing arsenal, developing new nuclear weapons, increasing the size of the United States' arsenal, or some or all of the above. This remains a mystery.

Soon after the Tweet, the media began its critiques, calling the statement dangerous and irresponsible. However, what the media missed in the Tweet was its message to Russia. With this Tweet, Trump made clear to Putin that America would match threat by threat. Trump also communicated to China, North Korea, and other foes that his would be a muscular administration. Putting a little fear in America's foes might be exactly what Trump intended by his Tweet. Also, one thing Trump values is unpredictability, and this Tweet was part of that. By Tweeting, Trump is not simply bypassing the media and communicating directly with his supporters, he is also keeping both the media and his opponents off balance. The strategy is as new as it is effective.

In many ways, Trump is modernizing the presidential bully pulpit to the social media age, and in a way no one else ever contemplated. At the same time, Trump is not so quietly telling Putin he has met his match. Amazing what can be done with only 140 characters.

Week 415
(SETTLING SCORES)

January 1, 2017

President Obama has garnered much praise for how he has handled the election of Donald Trump. Despite his biting criticism of his successor during the campaign, when the nation was on edge and protesters were taking the streets across the country, two days after the election the President invited Mr. Trump to the White House in a sign of unity and stability. Since then, the President and Mr. Trump have spoken frequently about policy and transition issues, even leading some liberals to think that Trump might be turned into an ally. However, those hopes quickly dissipated when Trump starting picking his cabinet. But we now know that President Obama never had any intention to go quietly, and this week he started settling some scores.

After eight years as President, it is not surprising that President Obama has kept score against his foes. President Putin, Israeli Prime Minister Netanyahu, the energy lobby, and House Republicans surely top his list. Some of these foes have even mocked the President in is final weeks, with Russia even going so far as to call him "a political corpse." Well, the President showed that he is a corpse that can still throw a few punches. On Russia, after intelligence reports showing efforts by Putin to influence the presidential election, the President expelled more than 30 Russian diplomats. This step, just short of cutting off diplomatic relations, was meant to show his final disdain for Putin, a man who has outmaneuvered President Obama at every turn.

Then came Israel. For eight years, the Administration has tried to make progress on the peace process, only to be opposed by Prime Minister Netanyahu. The Prime Minister even went so far as to criticize the President before the press at the White House. Obama clearly has a long memory, because this week he got his revenge. The United States has almost always vetoed UN security council resolutions critical of Israel. This week a resolution was presented criticizing Israeli settlement activity in the occupied territories. Instead of issuing its usual veto, the Administration abstained, and there is evidence that behind the scenes the White House actually supported the resolution. Then the Secretary of State gave a speech harshly critical of Israel, saying that Israel is "leading toward one state, or perpetual occupation . . . . If the choice is one state, Israel can either be Jewish or democratic. It cannot be both." Some on the Left praised these moves, but many Republicans and Democrats were critical, thinking the Administration went too far. Indeed, the moves were so controversial that Britain and Australia publicly distanced themselves from the Administration. President Obama might have gotten some pleasure from thrusting a stick in the eye of Israel, but it likely only helps Donald Trump, who immediately came to Israel's defense.

As for the energy industry and the House GOP, President Obama has not forgotten how they fought him in Congress and in the courts over his various environmental policies. To get some final revenge, this week the President made some 1.5 million acres in Utah and surrounding States, which contain many key mineral resources, national monuments, thus preventing any development. He has also recently taken executive actions to bar offshore drilling in many areas. Understanding that his environmental legacy is vulnerable because of his failure to get Congress to support his initiatives, by these moves the White House hopes to salvage some of his legacy. The problem is, these steps have infuriated many, motivating them to even more aggressively seek to overturn Obama's environmental legacy.

It was a week of settling scores, regardless of the controversies created. It surely felt good, but that joy might be fleeting, because the Trump Administration has made clear that on day one the rollback of the Obama legacy is the top priority.

Week 416

(Last Lobby)

January 8, 2017

Departing presidents usually try to avoid overtly partisan acts in their final days in the White House. Lame duck administrations will commonly issue some pardons, promulgate some regulations, declare national monuments, and even make a few moves on the international scene, but openly campaigning against the policies of the next president is unusual. Since the election, President Obama has taken all the usual steps of a departing president, at least until this week. In the face of Donald Trump's pledge to repeal Obamacare and the newly sworn in GOP congressional majorities, President Obama seems unwilling to accept his soon to be status as a political observer. Instead, in his final days in office he made one last trip to Congress to lobby to save his health care law.

The scene on January 5, 2017 may have been unprecedented in American history. While Vice President-Elect Mike Pence was meeting with the Republican leadership in Congress on the Trump Administration's agenda, Barak Obama was also on Capitol Hill, meeting with Democrat leaders on strategies to try to save Obamacare. The two men neither spoke nor crossed paths, but they were very publicly working at cross-purposes, one as the representative of a new administration, the other as the leader of the old one. It was all very symbolic, and many thought unseemly. It is also far from clear what President Obama's trip could accomplish. The Republicans are in the majority, have pledged to repeal Obamacare, and through the reconciliation process can do it with no Democrat votes. No matter if a losing effort, President Obama made the trip.

It was reported that during meeting, President Obama said "Don't rescue" the Republicans on Obamacare. After passing the controversial legislation with no GOP votes, President Obama clearly wants the Republicans to take any blame for problems or disruptions that will surely happen during the repeal. This seems even more certain because the Republicans have settled on a strategy to repeal now, and replace later, letting Democrats claim that the GOP has no plan to replace a program that has allegedly provided insurance coverage to 20 million people. Clearly bitter about the Republicans' ability to undermine public support for his signature legislation, he urged Democrats to call whatever replaced his signature legislation "Trumpcare" and work to undermine it. When asked by reporter why he went to Capitol Hill, Obama said he was simply trying to "Look out for the American people." In truth, he was counselling Democrats on how to stick it to the GOP. They seem to be following his advice, because Democrats promptly unveiled their new slogan for President-Elect Trump's health care agenda: "Make America sick again."

For his part, Vice President Elect Pence refused to that President Obama's bait, simply stating that "Make no mistake about it: We're going to keep our promise to the American people — we're going to repeal Obamacare and replace it with solutions that lower the cost of health insurance without growing the size of government." The Republicans have given themselves six months to complete this task, which many see as unrealistic. However, the GOP is wasting no time. On the very first day of the new session, the Senate passed a procedural resolution allowing them to repeal Obamacare with 51 votes. In view of all this, why would President Obama want to risk his reputation and his final political clout on a losing effort? The reason is simple, he hopes not only for a GOP disaster on health care, but also to take credit when the disaster happens. A fairly petty motive for a president in his final days.

Week 417

(YES HE COULDN'T)

January 15, 2017

On January 10, 2017, President Obama stepped on a stage in Grant Park, where he spoke on election night in November 2008 to give his farewell address after 8 years as President. In many ways the speech took the form of a State of the Union address, where President Obama not only described the accomplishments of his Administration, but also set forth his vision on where the nation should go next. He gave the address with the backdrop of the impending Trump Administration, which has committed itself to reversing the Obama legacy. So the speech was not only an effort to describe progress made, but also a call to defend that progress.

Conservatives have often accused President Obama of lacking patriotism, somehow having more of an internationalist perspective on American exceptionalism. Early in his speech, President Obama tackled this issue head on, asserting that:

> So that's what we mean when we say America is exceptional — not that our nation has been flawless from the start, but that we have shown the capacity to change and make life better for those who follow. Yes, our progress has been uneven. The work of democracy has always been hard. It's always been contentious. Sometimes it's been bloody. For every two steps forward, it often feels we take one step back. But the long sweep of America has been defined by forward motion, a constant widening of our founding creed to embrace all and not just some.

It was a true progressive's view of American exceptionalism. Then Obama outlined what his administration has done to further these progressive goals:

> If I had told you eight years ago that America would reverse a great recession, reboot our auto industry, and unleash the longest stretch of job creation in our history, if I had told you that we would open up a new chapter with the Cuban

Andrew P. Zappia

people, shut down Iran's nuclear weapons program without firing a shot, take out
the mastermind of 9/11, if I had told you that we would win marriage equality, and
secure the right to health insurance for another 20 million of our fellow citizens
if I had told you all that, you might have said our sights were set a little too high.
But that's what we did. That's what you did.

However, the President did not limit his speech to self-praise. Like George Washington and
Dwight Eisenhower, he used his farewell address to warn the nation of risks ahead. His focus
was protecting our democracy, a focus clearly inspired by Trump's election win and fears on the
Left that the nation is now dabbling with fascism:

That's what I want to focus on tonight: The state of our democracy. Understand,
democracy does not require uniformity. Our founders argued. They quarreled.
Eventually they compromised. They expected us to do the same. But they knew
that democracy does require a basic sense of solidarity — the idea that for all our
outward differences, we're all in this together; that we rise or fall as one.

There have been moments throughout our history that threatens that solidarity.
And the beginning of this century has been one of those times. A shrinking world,
growing inequality; demographic change and the specter of terrorism — these
forces haven't just tested our security and our prosperity, but are testing our democracy, as well.

Then the President turned to what he sees as the threats to our democracy, namely faction and
division driven by lack of economic opportunity and wealth:

To begin with, our democracy won't work without a sense that everyone has economic opportunity. . . . But for all the real progress that we've made, we know it's
not enough. Our economy doesn't work as well or grow as fast when a few prosper
at the expense of a growing middle class and ladders for folks who want to get
into the middle class. That's the economic argument. But stark inequality is also
corrosive to our democratic ideal. While the top one percent has amassed a bigger
share of wealth and income, too many families, in inner cities and in rural counties,
have been left behind — the laid-off factory worker; the waitress or health care
worker who's just barely getting by and struggling to pay the bills — convinced
that the game is fixed against them, that their government only serves the interests
of the powerful — that's a recipe for more cynicism and polarization in our politics.

President Obama's cure to this economic insecurity that is driving division is a continuation
and expansion of his progressive agenda:

And so we're going to have to forge a new social compact to guarantee all our
kids the education they need, to give workers the power to unionize for better
wages; to update the social safety net to reflect the way we live now, and make
more reforms to the tax code so corporations and individuals who reap the most

from this new economy don't avoid their obligations to the country that's made their very success possible.

President Obama also focused on racial division as a threat to our democracy:

> There's a second threat to our democracy — and this one is as old as our nation itself. After my election, there was talk of a post-racial America. And such a vision, however well-intended, was never realistic. Race remains a potent and often divisive force in our society. . . . But we're not where we need to be. And all of us have more work to do. . . . For blacks and other minority groups, it means tying our own very real struggles for justice to the challenges that a lot of people in this country face — not only the refugee, or the immigrant, or the rural poor, or the transgender American, but also the middle-aged, white guy who, from the outside, may seem like he's got advantages, but has seen his world upended by economic and cultural and technological change. . . . For white Americans, it means acknowledging that the effects of slavery and Jim Crow didn't suddenly vanish in the '60s — (applause) — that when minority groups voice discontent, they're not just engaging in reverse racism or practicing political correctness.

President Obama then said that the next biggest threat to our democracy is partisanship fueled by ignorance, a clear reference to his successor, Donald Trump:

> And this trend represents a third threat to our democracy. But politics is a battle of ideas. That's how our democracy was designed. In the course of a healthy debate, we prioritize different goals, and the different means of reaching them. But without some common baseline of facts, without a willingness to admit new information, and concede that your opponent might be making a fair point, and that science and reason matter then we're going to keep talking past each other, and we'll make common ground and compromise impossible.

Lastly, President Obama warned that the final threat to democracy is the weakening of democratic institutions: "Our democracy is threatened whenever we take it for granted. All of us, regardless of party, should be throwing ourselves into the task of rebuilding our democratic institutions. When voting rates in America are some of the lowest among advanced democracies, we should be making it easier, not harder, to vote."

President Obama ended his address by praising the Constitution, thanking his wife and his supporters, and honoring the military, then closing with his praise of the next generation, which he hopes will continue his progressive agenda:

> Let me tell you, this generation coming up — unselfish, altruistic, creative, patriotic — I've seen you in every corner of the country. You believe in a fair, and just, and inclusive America . . . . I am asking you to hold fast to that faith written into our founding documents; that idea whispered by slaves and abolitionists; that spirit sung by immigrants and homesteaders and those who marched for justice; that creed reaffirmed by those who planted flags from foreign battlefields to the

surface of the moon; a creed at the core of every American whose story is not yet written: Yes, we can.

It was a long address that seemed a bit out of touch given the state of the nation and the verdict of the voters. However, the purpose of the address was clear: it was a call to the Obama coalition to fight to preserve the Obama legacy. That legacy is imperiled, and President Obama knows it. But it will take far more than a speech to save it.

Week 418
(THE END)

January 22, 2017

When President Obama took the podium on January 20, 2009, he could gaze at a nation that had elected its first black president, had embraced his call for a progressive agenda, and had genuine excitement for the prospect of change. The nation was in an economic crisis that many feared could lead to another depression and had turned to a young and untested leader. In rising to the occasion, President Obama saw himself as a transformational figure who would remake American politics, end division, and create a new social contract with the people. It was a grand vision, maybe so grand as to be arrogant, but President Obama had a chance to fundamentally change the country, and he was prepared seize it.

Yet early on, President Obama's desire to end division came in conflict with his determination to pursue a progressive agenda. His first major action was a massive stimulus bill. He initially sought bipartisanship, but when Republicans asked for changes to the bill, his response was "elections have consequences" and he pushed his stimulus bill through Congress without a single GOP vote. He then did the same with Obamacare. In taking this approach, he cemented the very divisions he said he sought to close. These decisions in the first year of his presidency reverberated through his remaining seven years in office. Republican opposition hardened, President Obama got more partisan, and gridlock took hold.

It is possible that President Obama believed too much in his own rhetoric, his own view of himself as a transformation leader, and his conviction that his views were the future, while conservative philosophy was part of the outmoded and irrelevant past. His 2008 victory gave credence to that view because in its aftermath the Republicans were thoroughly decimated. However, in abandoning bipartisanship and pushing unpopular progressive legislation, President Obama proved to be a great benefactor of the GOP. The Republicans took the House in 2010, held it in 2012 even with President Obama's reelection, took all of Congress in 2014, and captured the White House in 2016. All of this was a reaction to the decisions President Obama made in his first year in office.

President Obama created and reinforced the very gridlock he wanted to end. After 2010, his Administration failed to pass any significant legislation. He initially tried to reach compromises with the GOP on the budget, immigration, and other issues, but he failed. This pushed the nation into repeated budget confrontations, and in the end resulted in what Republicans wanted, namely spending restraint. President Obama used this gridlock to his advantage in the 2012 campaign, and won a great victory for himself, but for not his party. By the time of the Republican victories in 2014 and 2016, the GOP held its most dominate position in national politics since 1928. Far from the end of conservatism, the Obama Presidency gave new life to it.

President Obama's answer to Republican opposition was to essentially give up on legislation, and instead use regulations and executive orders to rule by fiat. This cheered the Left, but many of his regulations and executive orders were defeated in the courts, and even more will be reversed by his successor. The same will be true of Obamacare and his budget priorities, which will be the first victims of the Trump Administration.

For all these failures, one cannot ignore that under President Obama's watch the nation did not fall into a new depression, the economy did recover, many more Americans obtained health care, and we avoided any major new wars. Obama may have been fairly criticized for being a weak and ineffective leader, especially in foreign affairs where foes like Putin and Assad seemed to outmaneuver him repeatedly, but America as a whole is not weaker in 2017 as compared to 2009. Our debt is higher, and our world prestige may be lower, but the nation remained stable, largely prosperous, and powerful.

Where America has not done better is in its sense of unity. The nation is more divided racially, geographically, economically, and culturally. President Obama's policies and his politics were focused on winning support of urban elites, minorities, and suburban women, and that strategy succeeded for him. At the same time, millions of Christian, rural, and working class voters felt their President had forgotten them and their nation had not only left them behind, but had disowned them. It was these voters who flocked to the GOP in the midterms and who had elected Donald Trump. President Obama had a grand vision for how he wanted to change America, but his vision was not grand enough to encompass them.

As he left office on January 20, 2017, escorted to his helicopter by President Trump, Barack Obama must have realized that he would not be the transformational figure he had foreseen. He would be no new Lincoln, or FDR, or Reagan. Instead, he left office a president of accomplishment, but much of it fleeting. A president of high intellect and great integrity who was never able to bring people of different views together. A president of promise, who ended up disappointing many. A president who could win victories for himself, but not for party or his philosophy. History may end up being very kind to President Obama, but as the helicopter flew away, one can only think of the hope that might have been and what change had actually come to pass.

About The Author and Acknowledgements

Andrew Zappia is an attorney who lives in Rochester, New York with his wife and two children. He has authored articles on various legal, historical, and current event topics, including pieces published in Legal Times, Crisis Magazine, the Rochester Democrat & Chronicle, Legal Times, Diversity & Division Magazine, the New Jersey Law Journal, and other publications. He is also the author of the Franchise Law Chapter in the treatise Commercial Litigation in New York State Courts.

This book would not have been possible without the support of Mr. Zappia's family and the assistance of Susan Foster, who helped revise and proof numerous drafts and provided many valuable insights.

This book was written in Mr. Zappia's individual and personal capacity. The opinions expressed in this book are the author's own. They do not represent the opinions of any employer or any entity whatsoever with whom he has been, is presently, or will be affiliated.

CPSIA information can be obtained
at www.ICGtesting.com
Printed in the USA
LVHW101135111120
671376LV00002B/17